GUMBO
YA-YA

Compiled by
LYLE SAXON, *State Director*,
EDWARD DREYER, *Asst. State
Director*, ROBERT TALLANT,
Special Writer

*Material Gathered by Workers of
the Works Progress Administration,
Louisiana Writers' Project, and
Sponsored by The Louisiana State
Library Commission.*
Drawings by CAROLINE DURIEUX
Jacket and Decorations by
ROLAND DUVERNET
*Illustrated with
Photographs*

*A Collection
of Louisiana Folk Tales*

GUMBO
YA-YA

PELICAN PUBLISHING COMPANY ⬧ GRETNA 1988

BOOKS BY LYLE SAXON

Father Mississippi
Fabulous New Orleans
Old Louisiana
Lafitte the Pirate
Children of Strangers

BOOKS BY ROBERT TALLANT

Mardi Gras (Pelican) 1976
Voodoo in New Orleans (Pelican) 1983
The Voodoo Queen (Pelican) 1983

Copyright © 1945 by the Louisiana Library Commission
Essie M. Culver, Executive Secretary

Copyright © 1987 by Pelican Publishing Company, Inc.
First Paperback Edition, June 1987
Second printing, May 1988

Library of Congress Cataloging-in-Publication Data

Gumbo ya-ya.

Includes index.
1. Tales—Louisiana. 2. Folklore—Louisiana.
3. Louisiana—Social life and customs.
GR110.L5G84   1987   398.2'09763   86-30584
ISBN: 0-88289-645-8

Manufactured in the United States of America
Published by Pelican Publishing Company, Inc.
1101 Monroe Street, Gretna, Louisiana 70053

Preface

GUMBO YA-YA — 'EVERYBODY TALKS AT ONCE' — IS a phrase often heard in the Bayou Country of Louisiana.

This *Gumbo Ya-Ya* is a book of the living folklore of Louisiana. As such it is primarily the work of those characters, real or imaginary, living or dead, who created this folklore. We wish to express our indebtedness, therefore, to Madame Slocomb, who was so polite that she invited even the dead to her parties; and to Valcour Aimé and the golden plates at the bottom of the Mississippi; to Monsieur Dufau and his *ciel-de-lits*, and to Tante Naomie, bold in her 'bare feets' at the blessing of the shrimp fleet; to the ghost of Myrtle Grove and the *loup-garous* of Bayou Goula; to Mike Noud and 'The Bucket of Blood,' and to Jennie Green McDonald, left alone in the original Irish Channel; to Mrs. Messina, who had everything, including half an orphan, and to Mr. Plitnick, who had the timidity; to Miss Julie, who rouged her roses, and to Mrs. Zito, who made everybody cry to beat the band; to Chief Brother Tillman, for whom Mardi Gras was life, and to Creola Clark, 'who kept her mind on Mama'; to John Simms, Junior, the chimney sweep on a holiday, and to all the vendors of pralines and *calas tout chauds;* to Evangeline and to Lafitte the Pirate; to Annie Christmas and Marie Laveau; to Père Antoine and Pépé Lulla; to Mamzelle Zizi and Josie Arlington and the hop head's love, 'Alberta'; to Long Nose and Perfume Peggy; to Mother Catherine and the Reverend Maude Shannon; to Coco Robichaux and Zozo la Brique; to Crazah and Lala and Banjo Annie; and to the Baby Doll who had been a Baby Doll for twenty years.

The material for this book was gathered by members of the Louisiana Writers' Program of the Work Projects Administration. The idea was suggested by Henry G. Alsberg in 1936; he was then the National Director of the Federal Writers' Program. We in Louisiana were pleased with the idea, and at every possible opportunity assigned workers to the task of collecting the folklore of the State.

The Louisiana Library Commission, of which Essae M. Culver is Executive Secretary, has sponsored this book, as well as the earlier publication, the *Louisiana State Guide*. The city of New Orleans sponsored our first publication, *The New Orleans City Guide*.

It may be well to remember that Louisiana was first a French colony, then Spanish, and that the territory was nearly a century old before becoming a part of the United States. It was an agricultural territory and many thousands of Negro slaves were imported. In the plantation sections the Negroes outnumbered the Whites five to one; consequently their contribution to the folklore of the State has been large.

The Creoles, those founders of the French colony, contributed their elegance, their customs, and cuisine. They influenced their slaves and, in a sense, their slaves influenced them.

In Southwest Louisiana lived the Acadians — or Cajuns, as they are affectionately called — those sturdy farming folk who, driven from their homes in Nova Scotia at the end of the eighteenth century, populated that area.

It would seem that the whole of Louisiana was a peculiarly fecund part of the Americas; the forests were filled with birds and animals, the bayous and lakes were teeming with fish, and the Creole mansions and the Cajun cottages were full of children.

In a leisurely collection of the folklore of the various racial groups, we have attempted to have the collecting of material done either by members of the groups themselves or by those long familiar with such groups. For example, in the stories pertaining to the Creoles much of the work was done by Madame Jeanne Arguedas, Madame Henriette Michinard, Monsieur Pierre Lelong, Caroline Durieux, and especially by Hazel Breaux, who worked untiringly collecting Creole and other lore. Many old families were consulted and their stories, their rhymes and jokes, have been written down here for the first time. We are grateful, too, to Archbishop Rummel and to Roger Baudier of 'Catholic Action of the South' for advice and help.

The Cajuns have produced many State leaders, from Governor Alexandre Mouton to Jimmy Domengeaux, the present representative of the Bayou Country in Congress. In this book, however, we have attempted to treat only of those humbler dwellers of their part of the State. Harry Huguenot, Velma McElroy Juneau, Mary Jane Sweeney, Margaret Ellis, and Blanche Oliver worked in those outlying districts.

Much of the information pertaining to the Negro was collected by Negro workers. Robert McKinney gathered most of the material in the chapter entitled 'Kings, Baby Dolls, Zulus, and Queens.' Marcus B. Christian, who was Supervisor of the all-Negro Writers' Project, also contributed to the book, as did Edmund Burke. Many Negroes who were not connected with the Project offered information and suggestions. Among these were Joseph Louis Gilmore, Charles Barthelemy Rousseve, author of *The Negro in Louisiana*, President A. W. Dent of Dillard University, and Sister Anastasia of the Convent of the Holy Family.

In so far as we know, certain aspects of life in New Orleans have not been recorded before, such as the chapters dealing with Saint Joseph's and Saint Rosalia's Day, the Irish Channel, the Sockserhause Gang, Pailet Lane, and the 'scares' in the chapter entitled 'Axeman's Jazz,' in which are told the stories of such folk characters as the Axeman, the Needle Man, the Hugging Molly, and the Devil Man. We have attempted also to explain the mercurial and characteristic reactions to these horrors. Maud Wallace, Cecil A. Wright, Catherine Dillon, Rhoda Jewell, Zoe Posey, Joseph Treadaway, and Catherine Cassibry Perkins contributed to these sections as well as to others.

The plates in this volume are from drawings by Caroline Durieux; the ghost map, the headpieces, and the tailpieces are by Roland Duvernet. Photographs, except for those where credit is specifically given, were made by Victor Harlow.

We are grateful to those earlier writers who recorded some of the phases of Louisiana folklore — Alcée Fortier, Lafcadio Hearn, Grace King, and George W. Cable — as well as to such contemporary writers as Doctor William A. Read, Edward Laroque Tinker, Roark Bradford, and Doctor Thad St. Martin.

LYLE SAXON
EDWARD DREYER
ROBERT TALLANT

Contents

List of Illustrations

Chapter 1

Kings, Baby Dolls, Zulus, and Queens

EVERY NIGHT IS LIKE SATURDAY NIGHT IN PER-
dido Street, wild and fast and hot with sin. But the night before
Mardi Gras blazed to a new height.

The darkness outside the bars was broken only by yellow
rectangles of light, spreading over the *banquette*, then quickly
vanishing, each time saloon doors opened and closed. Music
boxes blasted from every lighted doorway. Black men swaggered or staggered past, hats and caps pulled low over their eyes,
which meant they were tough, or set rakishly over one ear,
which meant they were sports. There were the smells: stale
wine and beer, whiskey, urine, perfume, sweating armpits.

In one dimly lighted place couples milled about the floor, hugging each other tightly, going through sensuous motions to the
music. Drug addicts, prostitutes, beggars and workingmen, they
were having themselves a time. A fat girl danced alone, snapping her fingers.

Young black women tried to interest men, who sagged over
the bars, their eyelids heavy from liquor and 'reefers.' One
woman screamed above the din: 'I'll do it for twenty cents, Hot
Papa. I can't dance with no dry throat. I wants twenty cents

to buy me some wine.' She did a little trucking step, raised her dress, 'showed her linen.'

Harry entered. Somebody shouted: 'Shut off that damn music box. Come on, Harry. Put it on, son!'

Harry, a lean brown boy in a red silk shirt and green trousers, held a tambourine high, beat out an infectious tom-tom tempo with one fist, huskily sang words that had no meaning, but in a rhythm that was a drug. His greasy cap low over one ear, thick lips drawn back from large white teeth, he performed a wild dance, shoulders hunched, scrawny hips undulating.

> Hock-a-lee-hock-a-lee-weeooo!
> Hock-a-lee-hock-a-lee-weeooo!
> Wa-le-he-hela-wa-le-he-weeoo-oo!

There were comments. 'Man, those Indians gonna step high tomorrow.' Harry's chant was one of the Indians' songs.

A small girl shoved her way through the crowd around the singer. 'Wait'll you see us Baby Dolls tomorrow,' she promised. 'Is we gonna wiggle our tails!' A man threw an arm around her neck, drew her away, over to where they could do some 'corner loving.'

In the back room was the real man of the night. His face a trifle blank from whiskey, his eyes sleepy, King Zulu held court. This was his royal reception. Just now the King was pretty tired. The Queen rose suddenly and moved away from the table, her hips shaking angrily. If the old fool wants to go to sleep, let him. She'll find herself somebody who can keep his eyes open and likes some fun. She's a queen, and a queen has to have her fun.

Nobody ever goes to bed on this night. Ain't tomorrow the big day? Not until morning do they ever go home, and then only to array themselves in costumed splendor.

But there is never any weariness about King Zulu on Carnival Day. With his royal raiment, he magically dons fresh energy. A few shots of whiskey and the trick is done. His head is up, his posture majestic — at least in the beginning of the day. Later he may droop a bit.

Strongarmed bodyguards and shiny black limousines, rented

from the Geddes and Moss Undertakers, always accompany him to the *Royal Barge* at the New Basin Canal and South Carrollton Avenue. Cannons are fired, automobile horns blast, throats grow hoarse acclaiming him. Many a white face laughs upward from the sea of black ones, strayed far from the celebration just coming to life down on Canal Street.

There was suspense this morning. Impatient waiting. At last, about nine o'clock, a tugboat pushed the *Royal Barge* away from its resting place. Whistles shrieked. The horns and the applause of the admiring throng increased. The King took a swig from a bottle, yelled to one of his assistants, 'Listen, you black bastard, you can help me all you want, but don't mess 'round with my whiskey.' Then he turned and bowed graciously toward the shore.

The other Zulus helped His Majesty greet the crowds.

'Hello, Pete. We is in our glory today.'

'What you say, black gal.'

'Ain't it fine?'

Never have any of the Zulus been highhat. Ed Hill, one of the organization's overlords, said: 'See Zulu people? There is the friendliest people you can find. They ain't no stuffed shirts.'

The Zulus emerged as a Mardi Gras organization in 1910, marching on foot, a jubilee-singing quartet in front, another quartet in the rear. Birth had come the year before, when fifty Negroes gathered in a woodshed. William Story was the first king, wearing a lard-can crown and carrying a banana-stalk scepter. By 1913 progress had reached the point where King Peter Williams wore a starched white suit, an onion stickpin, and carried a loaf of Italian bread as a scepter. In 1914 King Henry rode in a buggy and from that year they grew increasingly ambitious, boasting three floats in 1940, entitled respectively, 'The Pink Elephant,' on which rode the king and his escort, 'Hunting the Pink Elephant,' and 'Capturing the Pink Elephant.'

It was in 1922 that the first yacht — the *Royal Barge* — was rented, and since then the ruler of the darker side of the Carnival has always ridden in high style down the New Basin Canal.

Clouds hung low this Mardi Gras Day of 1940. King Zulu and

his dukes sniffed heavenward. Let it rain. Little old water never hurt a mighty Zulu. White-painted lips never lost their grins.

At Hagan Avenue the floats and supply of coconuts awaited them. With all the dignity he could summon, King Zulu mounted his 'Pink Elephant,' and the others clambered aboard theirs. Carefully, His Majesty arranged his red-velvet-and-ermine costume. Then a signal, and the parade was on.

Out Poydras Street to Carondelet they rolled, the thirteen-piece band swinging out with 'I'll Be Glad When You're Dead, You Rascal, You,' in torrid style, sixteen black 'policemen' leading behind the long-legged Grand Marshal, who slung his body about and around like a drum major. The music was so hot the King started doing his number.

Onlookers leaped into the street, shouting, 'Do it, boy, King Zulu is got his day.'

Once specially appointed black 'Mayor' Fisher, president of the club, shouted: 'Doesn't you all know we is on our way to see the white mayor? Let's make time.'

And time was made. Hot feet hit the street. More viewers joined the parade and danced up a breeze. The maskers on the floats slung coconuts like baseballs, right into the midst of their admirers.

Once the perspiring monarch uncrowned himself. Prince Alonzo Butler was shocked. 'King, is you a fool or not? Don't you know a king must stay crowned?'

This particular king wasn't really supposed to be king at all, and he felt mighty lucky about it. Johnny Metoyer was to have been the 1940 ruler, but Johnny had died months before. An 'evil stroke' had hit Johnny suddenly the November before and within a few days Johnny was gone. This parade was partly in celebration of his memory.

'Them niggers is going to put it on rough for ole John,' Charlie Fisher had vowed. 'There ain't going to be no hurting feet and things like that, either, 'cause them niggers don't get no hurting feet on Mardi Gras Day. No, indeed. Them feet stays hot and, boy, when they hits the pavement serenading to that swing music, you can hear 'em pop. It's hot feet beating on the blocks.'

Manuel Bernard was the 1940 King Zulu and he was a born New Orleans boy. Other days he drives a truck.

Gloom was in the air before Johnny Metoyer went to glory. He had been president and dictator of the organization for twenty-nine years, but had never chosen to be king until now. And this year he had announced his intention of being king, and then resigning from the Zulu Aid and Pleasure Club. This, everyone had agreed, probably meant disbanding. It just wouldn't be the same without ole John. Even the city officials were worrying. It seemed like the upper class of Negroes had been working on Johnny, and had at last succeeded.

The Zulus had no use for 'stuck-up niggers.' Their membership is derived from the humblest strata, porters, laborers, and a few who live by their wits. Professional Negroes disapprove of them, claiming they 'carry on' too much, and 'do not represent any inherent trait of Negro life and character, serving only to make the Negro appear grotesque and ridiculous, since they are neither allegoric nor historical.'

When, in November, 1939, word came that Johnny Metoyer was dead, people wouldn't believe it. The night the news came, the Perdido Street barroom was packed. Representatives of the Associated Press, the United Press and the local newspapers rubbed shoulders with Zulus, Baby Dolls and Indians. The atmosphere was deep, dark and blue. Everybody talked at once.

'Ain't it a shame?'

'Poor John! He's gotta have a helluva big funeral.'

'Put him up right so his body can stay in peace for a long time to come.'

Somebody started playing 'When the Saints Come Marching In,' written by Louis 'Satchmo' Armstrong, Metoyer's bosom friend. Then it is suggested that a telegram be sent to Armstrong. He's tooting his horn at the Cotton Club on Broadway, but it is felt he'll board a plane and fly down for the funeral.

A doubt was voiced that any Christian church would accept the body for last rites. 'John was a man of the streets, who ain't never said how he stood on religion.' Probably, others said confidently, if there were enough insurance money left, one of the churches could be persuaded to see things differently. Of course, he would be buried in style befitting a Zulu monarch. Members must attend in full regalia, Johnny's body must be carried through headquarters, there must be plenty of music, coconuts on his grave. Maybe Mayor Maestri could be persuaded to proclaim the day a holiday in Zululand.

But Johnny had a sister; Victoria Russell appeared on the scene and put down a heavy and firm foot. All attempts to make the wake colorful were foiled. 'Ain't nobody gonna make a clown's house out of my house,' said Sister Victoria Russell.

Even the funeral — held on a Sunday afternoon, amid flowers and fanfare and a crowd of six thousand — was filled with disappointments. Louie Armstrong had not been able to make the trip down from New York. Sister Russell banned the coconuts and the Zulu costumes.

At the Mount Zion Baptist Church Reverend Duncan mumbled his prayers in a whisper, peeping into the gray plush casket every now and then. He opened with a reprimand. 'Does you all know this is a funeral, not a fun-making feast?'

A drunken woman in the church yelled: 'I knows. It brings a pitiful home.'

Reverend Duncan went on, while pallbearers raised Zulu banners. 'In the midst of life we is in death.'

The congregation sang, 'How Sweet Is Jesus!'

Reverend Horace Nash knelt and prayed: 'Lawd, look at us. Keep the spirit alive that makes us bow down before you. Keep our hearts beating and our souls ever trustful today and tomorrow.'

Somebody shouted, 'Don't break down, brother.'

Outside waited a fourteen-piece brass band and eighteen automobiles. Thousands marched on foot. The band struck up 'Flee as a Bird,' and the cortège was on its way toward Mount Olivet Cemetery. Everyone was very solemn, and there was not a smile visible. All Zulus wore black banners draped across their chests and their shoulders.

Then, after the hearse had vanished into the cemetery, the entire aspect of the marchers changed. The band went into 'Beer Barrel Polka,' and dancing hit the streets. Promenading in Mardi Gras fashion lasted two hours, ending in Metoyer's own place of business, where the last liquor was purchased and consumed. Sister Russell, returning to the scene, then ordered all Zulus out.

Later a meeting was called in Johnny Metoyer's bedroom. His belongings had been removed, but his razor strop still dangled on one wall. A member, gazing at this sadly, remarked, 'John was the shavingest man you wanted to see.'

At eight-thirty Reverend Foster Sair opened with a prayer.

'Lawd, we is back within the fold of the man who caused us to be. We is sittin' here in his domicile. Help us never to forget John L. Metoyer. Let us carry on the spirit of our founder. O Lawd, preserve our club. Make it bigger and better. Let no evil creep into it. Amen.'

Inspired by this, it was immediately decided that the Zulus would 'carry on,' that there would be a parade this year, anyway. Then Vice-President Charlie Fisher announced he was stepping into the presidency, and that all other officers would advance in office in proper order.

Definite insults followed from those who disapproved.

'Shut up!' someone admonished them. 'You is talkin' about the President now.'

There was more argument and bickering in the meetings that followed. Manuel Bernard, friend of Fisher, was at last chosen to be the 1940 king. At this meeting the music box in the front bar wailed forth with 'The Good Morning Blues,' and dancers were kicking and stomping, twisting their supple bodies the way they felt. It disturbed the meeting a little, but someone said: 'Let the music play, 'cause the mournin' is over. We is all gotta do some flippin' around now.'

So the Zulus didn't fade out after all, but marched in high style in 1940, and Manuel Bernard, rocking back and forth on the high throne of his float, was a proud and happy man.

Finally the parade reached the City Hall and paused before the crowded stand. The white mayor wasn't present, but a representative received coconuts and a bow from His Majesty. The band played 'Every Man a King,' Huey P. Long's song, and the dancing was wild. It was King Zulu's day.

The next long stop was at Dryades and Poydras Streets. A proprietor of a beer parlor at that intersection presented the King with a silver loving cup containing champagne.

'Damn, that's good,' said His Majesty, and smacked his lips.

A bevy of short-skirted black girls invited him down just then, but no dice. 'Ain't no funny crap today. Remember last year?' Last year King Zulu left his float to follow a woman and held up the parade for two hours. So these girls, whom the boys call the 'zig-a-boos,' disappointedly went their way.

Strange things happen even to a king. It suddenly went down the line, 'The King has done wet himself.' Didn't make much difference, though. He had spilled so much whiskey on his costume, nobody could tell what was what.

Everybody was a little drunk now. The grass hula skirts all Zulus wear over long white drawers swished faster and faster as the maskers on the floats 'put it on,' and the nappy black skull caps adorning their heads were set at dashing angles. The parade moved swifter now toward the Geddes and Moss Undertaking Parlors, where the Queen and her court awaited them on a balcony over the street.

A thunderous ovation greeted King Zulu at South Rampart and Erato Streets. A high yellow gal fanned her hips by him and he temporarily deserted his float. 'Mayor' Fisher hauled him back to the dignity and comparative safety of his high perch atop the float. 'I never thought this could happen to a king,' His Majesty sighed. Pretty girls like that wouldn't want the King when he was 'jest a man.'

'It's damn funny,' Fisher sniffed, 'how womens is. Now that woman knows the King is busy, still she wants him. Every time I think how much trouble Zulus give me I get mad.'

All over South Rampart Street women were jumping up and down and feeling hot for the King. The musicians were wet with perspiration and from the showers that had fallen during the morning, but they kept beating out the music and getting hotter all the time.

After knocking out several numbers, the entire band filed into a saloon for drinks, and when they came out everybody started 'kicking 'em up.' The dances grew more violent. Women lowered their posteriors to the ground, shaking them wildly as they rose and fell, rolled their stomachs, vibrated their breasts. A crowd of Baby Dolls came along, all dressed up in tight, scanty trunks, silk blouses and poke bonnets with ribbons tied under

dusky chins. False curls framed faces that were heavily powdered and rouged over black and chocolate skins. The costumes
were of every color in the rainbow and some that are not. They
joined the crowd, dancing and shaking themselves.

'Sure, they call me Baby Doll,' said one of them, who was over
six feet tall and weighed more than two hundred pounds. 'That's
my name.

'I'm a Baby Doll today and every day. I bin a Baby Doll for
twenty years. Since I always dressed like a Baby Doll on Mardi
Gras the other girls said they would dress like me; they would
wear tight skirts and bloomers and a rimmed hat. They always
say you get more business on Mardi Gras than any other day,
so I had a hard time making them gals close up and hit the
streets. See, mens have fun on Carnival. They come into the
houses masked and want everything and will do anything. They
say, "I'm a masker, fix me up." Well, them gals had a time on
Mardi Gras, havin' their kicks.

'The way we used to kick 'em up that day was a damn shame.
Some of the gals didn't wear much clothes and used to show
themselves out loud. Fellows used to run 'em down with dollar
bills in their hands, and you didn't catch none of them gals
refusing dollar bills. That's why all the women back Perdido
Street wanted to be Baby Dolls.

'We sure did shine. We used to sing, clap our hands, and you
know what "raddy" is? Well, that's the way we used to walk
down the street. People used to say, "Here comes the babies,
but where's the dolls?"

'I'm the oldest livin' Baby Doll, and I'm one bitch who is glad
she knows right from wrong. But I do a lot of wrong, because I
figures wrong makes you as happy as right. Don't it?

'Sure, I tried religion, but religion don't give you no kicks.
Just trouble and worry.

'Say what you like, it's my business. I'll tell anybody I sells
myself enough on Mardi Gras to do myself some good the whole
year around. There ain't no sense in being a Baby Doll for one
day only. Me, I'm a Baby Doll all the time.

'Just follow a Baby Doll on Mardi Gras and see where you

land. You know, if you follow her once, you'll be following her all the time. That's the truth.

'I ain't no trouble-seeker, but I got plenty trouble. The other day a man come into my house with fifty cents, but a dime short. I just picked up a chair and busted it over his head. That nigger is always comin' in short. He punched me in the nose, and we went to jail. The judge turned me loose, but he says, "Gal, don't you come back here no more." And I says, "No, sir, Judge." When I stabbed Uncle Dick the next day they give me three months. But Dago Tony got me out.

'I didn't want to cut Uncle Dick, but he kept messin' around. I sure don't like nobody to mess around with me. I just can't stand it.'

Baby Doll has been living with Uncle Dick for five years now. She beats him up regularly. She has stabbed him and hit him over the head with rocking chairs, bricks, and sticks. Uncle Dick is a retired burglar and 'switch-blade wielder'; that is, he used a knife that opened when he pressed a button and he could 'kill a man dead' in a split second. But things got too hot. Now it is whispered he is a stool pigeon for the police in the crime-infested neighborhood where he lives.

He depends on Baby Doll, but she's a tough number. Besides her profession, she curses a blue streak, uses dope, is a stickup artist, smokes cigars and packs a Joe Louis wallop.

'Dago Tony has been around himself,' Baby Doll went on. 'He is all right. Me and him done pulled plenty lemons together. He got the peelin' and I got the juice.'

A 'lemon' is a method of extracting a man's bankroll when he is busy with a woman.

'Dago Tony got me into a business once that was too hot to keep up, but, man, was it solid! He'd give the drunks a big hooker with knockout drops in their glass, and when they passed out I was on 'em. The trouble was I had to hit too many of them niggers over their heads. They'd wake up too quick. I seen so much blood drippin' from people's heads I got scared and cut that stuff out. I'll tell you, a Baby Doll's life ain't no bed of roses.'

Baby Doll began to think she had talked too much. Other

things began to creep into her mind, too. Some young black men edging the crowd were giving her the once-over, and business is business.

'You're holdin' me up. I got to hit the streets. There's more money for me in the streets than there is here. Maybe I'm missin' a few tricks.' And she was off through the crowd around the floats, walking 'raddy' to attract attention.

'*I* was the first Baby Doll,' Beatrice Hill asserted firmly, when questioned about the history of the organization. 'Liberty and Perdido Streets were red hot back in 1912, when that idea started. Women danced on bars with green money in their stockings, and sometimes they danced naked. They used to lie on the floor and shake their bellies while the mens fed them candy. You didn't need no system to work uptown. It wasn't like the downtown red-light district, where they made more money, but paid more graft. You had to put on the ritz downtown, which some of the gals didn't like. You did what you wanted uptown.'

Uptown prostitutes got high on marijuana and 'snow.' They still do. Beatrice is fifty-two and is about beat out now. Her arms and legs are thickly spotted with black needle holes. She still uses drugs, and admits it. Also, she goes to Charity Hospital and takes treatment for syphilis. Back in 1912 she made fifty to seventy-five dollars a day hustling and stealing. Her man, Jelly Beans, got most of it, and they blew the rest 'gettin' their kicks.' Beatrice is all bad and proud of it. She's been to jail for murder, shooting, stealing, and prostitution. She boasts of her hectic past with gusto and vanity.

'Them downtown bitches thought their behinds was solid silver,' she recalls contemptuously, 'but they didn't never have any more money than we did. We was just as good lookers and had just as much money. Me, I was workin' right there on Gravier and Franklin Streets.

'We gals around my house got along fine. Them downtown gals tried to get the police to go up on our graft, but they wouldn't do it. Does you remember Clara Clay, who had all them houses downtown? Well, we was makin' good money and used to buy up some fun. All of us uptown had nothin' but good-lookin' men. We used to send them downtown 'round

them whores and make 'em get all their money until they found
out and had 'em beat up. Then we stopped. I'm tellin' you that
was a war worse'n the Civil War. All the time we was tryin' to
outdo them downtown gals.

'I knew a lady, name was Peggy Bry; she used to live at
231 Basin Street. Well, anyhow, Miss Bry gave a ball for the
nigger bitches in the downtown district at the Entertainers'
Café, and she said she didn't want no uptown whore there. All
them gals was dressed to kill in silks and satins and they had all
their mens dressed up, too. That was goin' to be some ball. We
heared about it long before. So, we figures and figures how we
could go and show them whores up with our frocks. I told all
my friends to get their clothes ready and to dress up their mens,
'cause we was goin' to that ball.

'Everybody got to gettin' ready, buyin' up some clothes. Sam
Bonart was askin' the mens what was the matter and Canal
Street was lookin' up at us niggers like we was the moon. We
was ready, I'm tellin' you. I figures and figures. So, I figures
what we would do. I got hold of a captain, the baddest dick on
the force, and I tells him what was what. I tells him a white
whore is givin' a ball for niggers and didn't want us to come.
He says, "Is it a public hall?" And I says it is. He tells us to get
ready to do our stuff and go to that ball. You see, the Captain
knows we is in a war with them downtown bitches. Me, I
figures he was kiddin', so I went to him and told him if he'd come
downtown with us I'd give him a hundred dollars. He says, sure
he would.

'Child, we got the news around for the gals to get ready. And
was they ready! Is the sun shinin'? It was a Monday night and
Louie Armstrong and his Hot Five and Buddy Petit was gonna
be playin' at that ball. We called up Geddes and Moss and hired
black limousines. You know them whores was livin' their
lives! All the houses was shut down, and the Captain was out
there in front. I'm tellin' you when that uptown brigade rode
up to the Entertainers' Café, all the bitches came runnin' out.
Then they saw the Captain and they all started runnin' back
inside. We just strutted up and filed in and filled the joint. I'm
tellin' you, that was somethin'!

'The first thing I did was to order one hundred and four dollars' worth of champagne, and the house couldn't fill the order. The bartender said, "You got me." I took all the place had, and the band starts playin' "Shake That Thing," and dedicates it to me. This white bitch, Miss Bry, comes runnin' up to me and says, "Look here, this is my party for my friends." I says: "Miss Bry, I'm the one showed you how to put silk teddies on your tail. Who is you? What's your racket?" Then the Captain walks up, lookin' hard, and he says: "Miss Bry, you ain't got no right in this public dance. If you don't shut your trap, I'll pull you in." Man, would you keep quiet? Well, that's what she did.

'One of my gals — I think it was Julia Ford — got up on a table and started shakin' it on down. We took off all her clothes, and the owner of the place started chargin' admission to come in to the dance. Miss Bry raised particular hell about this, then went on home. We broke up that joint for true. The Entertainers ain't never seen a party like that one.

'Let me tell you, and this ain't no lie: Every girl with me had no less than one hundred dollars on her. We called that the hundred-dollar party. Say, niggers was under the tables tryin' to find the money we was wastin' on the floor. I remembers one nigger trying to tear my stockings open to get at my money till my man hit him over his head with a chair, and that nigger went to the hospital. 'Course it all ended in a big fight and we all went to jail.

'It wasn't long after that when a downtown gal named Susie Brown come to see me. She says she wants to work uptown, so we give her a chance. She got to makin' money, and soon she was called the best-dressed gal in Gravier Street. I didn't mind, me. She was workin' in my house, and her bed percentage was fine. I done seen time when I made fifty dollars in a day just waitin' for Susie to get done turnin' tricks.

'Shux, that wasn't nothing. When them ships come in, that's when I made money. All them sailors wanted a brownie. High yellows fared poorly then, unless they got in them freakish shows. When I took in fifty dollars in them days it was a bad day. I was rentin' rooms, payin' me a dollar every time a gal turned a trick. Then I had two gals stealin' for me, and I was turnin' tricks myself.

'Lights was low around my house and some awful things was done right in the streets. The police? Shux, does you know what we 'was payin' the law? Every gal paid three bucks a day and the landlady paid three and a half, but we didn't mind at all, 'cause we made that with a smile.

'Everywhere we went like the Silver Platter, the Élite, the Black and Tan and so on, people used to say, ''Look at them whores!'' We was always dressed down and carried our money in our stockings. See like around Mardi Gras Day? We used to break up the Zulu Ball with money, used to buy the King champagne by the case. That's another thing, we had the Zulus with us. Shux, we took Mardi Gras by storm. No, we wasn't the Baby Dolls then; I'm talkin' about before that.

'In 1912, Ida Jackson, Millie Barnes and Sallie Gail and a few other gals downtown was makin' up to mask on Mardi Gras Day. No, I don't know how they was goin' to mask, but they was goin' to mask. We was all sittin' around about three o'clock in the morning in my house. A gal named Althea Brown jumps up and she says, ''Let's be ourselves. Let's be Baby Dolls. That's what the pimps always calls us.'' We started comin' up with the money, but Leola says: ''Hold your horses. Let every tub stand on its own bottom.'' That suited everybody fine and the tubs stood.

'Everybody agreed to have fifty dollars in her stocking, and that we could see who had the most money. Somebody says, ''What's the name of this here organization?'' And we decided to call ourselves the Million-Dollar Baby Dolls, and be red hot. Johnny Metoyer wanted us to come along with the Zulus, but we said nothin' doin'. We told Johnny we was out to get some fun in our own way and we was not stoppin' at nothin'.

'Some of us made our dresses and some had 'em made. We was all lookin' sharp. There was thirty of us — the best whores in town. We was all good-lookin' and had our stuff with us. Man, I'm tellin' you, we had money all over us, even in our bloomers, and they didn't have no zippers.

'And that Mardi Gras Day came and we hit the streets. I'm

tellin' you, we hit the streets lookin' forty, fine and mellow. We got out 'bout ten o'clock. We had stacks of dollars in our stockings and in our hands. We went to the Sam Bonart playground on Rampart and Poydras and bucked against each other to see who had the most money. Leola had the most — she had one hundred and two dollars. I had ninety-six dollars and I was second, but I had more home in case I ran out. There wasn't a woman in the bunch who had less than fifty dollars. We had all the niggers from everywhere followin' us. They liked the way we shook our behinds and we shook 'em like we wanted to.

'Know what? We went on downtown, and talk about puttin' on the ritz! We showed them whores how to put it on. Boy, we was smokin' cigars and flingin' ten- and twenty-dollar bills through the air. Sho, we used to sing, and boy, did we shake it on down. We sang "When the Sun Goes Down" and "When the Saints Come Marchin' Through I Want to Be in That Number." We wore them wide hats, but they was seldom worn, 'cause when we got to heatin' we pulled 'em off. When them Baby Dolls strutted, they strutted. We showed our linen that day, I'm tellin' you.

'When we hit downtown all them gals had to admit we was stuff. Man, when we started pitchin' dollars around, we had their mens fallin' on their faces tryin' to get that money. And there you have the startin' of the Baby Dolls. Yeah, peace was made. All them gals got together.'

The parade was about ready to get started again now. The King heaved a slow curve at the proprietor of the saloon and the coconut fell right smack on his head. Everybody laughed except 'Mayor' Fisher. It was an indication that His Majesty was drunk.

'When the time comes,' moaned Fisher, rolling white eyeballs around in a fat, black face, 'that I can stop worryin' about that King and everybody else, I'm goin' to feel heaps better. It's time to cut out this foolishment, anyway. We is on our way to meet the Queen.'

The band began swinging it faster, and the Zulus' hot feet beat faster, too. Everybody was feeling fine. King Manuel stretched out his arms congenially, and kept laughing out loud, though his head was low, and the pavement looked about to jump right up and slap him in the face.

It was about one-thirty when they reached the small building, where thousands waited to see the Queen greet her lord.

The King posed for cameramen, and bowed to everybody graciously. He leaned over and accepted flowers and a ribbon key of welcome from Doctor W. A. Willis, whose wife sponsors this use of the funeral parlors every year.

Gertrude Geddes Willis made an address: 'My powerful monarch, it is a pleasure to welcome you to Geddes and Moss Undertakers. May your every wish be granted for your subjects and yourself, and may you live forever in the splendor that fits a king.' She handed His Majesty a bottle of champagne, ordered the waiters to bring more for the rest of the Zulus.

Then there was an awed hush as a maid led the Queen out upon the platform, and sighs passed through the dusky crowd that were a tribute to her beauty. There were gasps when it could be clearly seen that she wore an expensive-looking white satin gown, lavishly trimmed in lace, a multi-colored train of metallic cloth, a rhinestone crown, and carried accessories to match. 'The white lady I used to work for gave me all my accessories.' Queen Zulu revealed later. 'She took me downtown, and she said: "Ceola, I want to fix you up right. I want you to be a damn good queen." Those were her exact words.'

King Manuel toasted his Queen in champagne, as his float remained beneath the balcony, and she sipped some, too, smiling down on her admiring subjects in the street below.

The ceremonies over, the court went inside for more refreshments. No one was permitted to follow them upstairs to their private quarters, where liquor of all kinds was consumed and a thousand fancy sandwiches enjoyed.

The Queen was left to have her fun, too, and she usually does very well. In fact, there's always a certain amount of worry about letting a queen wander about during the hours between the reception and the ball to come later in the evening. It has been suggested that she be locked up during that time, but the queens have always objected strongly to that proposed measure.

The Zulus' parade was over now, but there was always plenty

going on around town. Things were really just getting warmed up.

Suddenly; this Mardi Gras afternoon, there appeared on a street corner a lone figure of an elaborately garbed Indian. He stood there, a lighted lantern in one hand, the other shading his eyes, as he peered into the street ahead, first right, then left. This Indian's face was very black under his war paint, but his costume and feathered headdress were startlingly colorful. He studied the distance a moment, then turned and swung the lantern. Other Indians appeared, all attired in costumes at least as magnificent as the first, and in every conceivable color.

A second Indian joined the first, then a third. These three all carried lanterns like good spy boys must. Then a runner joined them, a flag boy, a trio of chiefs, a savage-looking medicine man. Beside the first or head chief was a stout woman, wearing a costume of gold and scarlet. She was the tribe's queen, and wife of the first chief.

A consultation was held there on the corner. The chiefs got together, passed around a bottle, and argued with the medicine man until that wild creature, dressed in animal skins and a grass skirt, wearing a headdress of horns and a huge ring in his nose, jumped up and down on the pavement with rage. When, at last, it was decided that since there was no enemy tribe in sight, they might as well have a war dance, Chief 'Happy Peanut,' head of this tribe of the Golden Blades, emitted a bloodcurdling yell that resounded for blocks, 'Oowa-a-awa! Ooa-a-a-awa!'

Tambourines were raised and a steady tattoo of rhythm beat out. Knees went down and up, heads swayed back and forth, feet shuffled on the pavement, as they circled round and round.

The Queen chanted this song:

> The Indians are comin'.
> Tu-way-pa-ka-way.
> The Indians are comin'.
> Tu-way-pa-ka-way.
> The Chief is comin'.
> Tu-way-pa-ka-way.
> The Chief is comin'.
> Tu-way-pa-ka-way.

The Queen is comin'.
Tu-way-pa-ka-way.
The Queen is comin'.
Tu-way-pa-ka-way.
The Golden Blades are comin'.
Tu-way-pa-ka-way.
The Golden Blades are comin'.
Tu-way-pa-ka-way. . . .

The songs the Mardi Gras Indians sing are written in choppy four-fourths time, with a tom-tom rhythm. The music is far removed from the type usually associated with Negroes. The Indians never sing a blues song, but chant with primitive and savage simplicity to this strange beat, which has an almost hypnotic effect. The beating on the tambourine and rhythmic hand-clapping are the only accompaniments to the singing. Most of the words have little meaning, though some display special interests of the tribe, such as

Tu-way-pa-ka-way.
Tu-way-pa-ka-way.
Get out the dishes.
Tu-way-pa-ka-way.
Get out the pan.
Tu-way-pa-ka-way.
Here comes the Indian man.
Tu-way-pa-ka-way,
Tu-way-pa-ka-way.

Sometimes the chief of the tribe sings alone a boastful solo of his strength and prowess.

Oowa-aa!
Tu-way-pa-ka-way.
Oowa-a-a!
Tu-way-pa-ka-way.
I'm the Big Chief!
Tu-way-pa-ka-way.
Of the strong Golden Blades.
Tu-way-pa-ka-way.

The dances are wild and abandoned. Unlike the songs, there may be detected traces of modernity, trucking and bucking and 'messing-around' combined with pseudo-Indian touches, much leaping into the air, accompanied by virile whooping. All this is considerably aided by the whiskey consumed while on the march, and the frequent smoking of marijuana.

The tribes include such names as the Little Red, White and Blues, the Yellow Pocahontas, the Wild Squa-tou-las, the Golden Eagles, the Creole Wild Wests, the Red Frontier Hunters, and the Golden Blades. The last numbers twenty-two members, and is the largest and oldest of those still extant.

The Golden Blades were started twenty-five years ago in a saloon. Ben Clark was the first chief and ruled until two years ago, when a younger man took over. Leon Robinson — Chief 'Happy Peanut' — deposed Clark in actual combat, as is the custom, ripping open Clark's arm and gashing his forehead with a knife. That's the way a chief is created, and that is the way his position is lost.

Contrary to the casual observer's belief, these strangest of Mardi Gras maskers are extremely well-organized groups, whose operations are intricate and complicated.

Monthly meetings are held, dues paid and the next year's procedure carefully planned. All members are individually responsible for their costumes. They may make them — most of them do — or have them made to order.

The regalia consists of a large and resplendent crown of feathers, a wig, an apron, a jacket, a shirt, tights, trousers and moccasins. They vie with each other and with other tribes as to richness and elaborateness. Materials used include satins, velvet, silver and gold lamé and various furs. The trimmings are sequins, crystal, colored and pearl beads, sparkling imitation jewels, rhinestones, spangles and gold clips put to extravagant use. Color is used without restraint. (Flame, scarlet and orange are possibly the preferred shades.)

Amazingly intricate designs are often worked out in beads and brilliants against the rich materials. A huge serpent of pearls may writhe on a gold lamé breast, an immense spider of silver beads appears to be crawling on a back of flame satin. Sometimes a chief will choose to appear in pure white. A regal crown of snowy feathers, rising from a base of crystal beads, will adorn his head, and all other parts of his costume will be of white velvet heavily encrusted with rhinestones and crystals. All costumes are worn with the arrogance expressed in such songs as

> Oh, the Little Red, White and Blues,
> Tu-way-pa-ka-way,
> Bravest Indians in the land.
> Tu-way-pa-ka-way.
> They are on the march today.
> Tu-way-pa-ka-way.
> If you should get in their way,
> Tu-way-pa-ka-way,
> Be prepared to die.
> Tu-way-pa-ka-way.
> Oowa-a-a!
> Oowa-a-a!

Ten years ago the various tribes actually fought when they met. Sometimes combatants were seriously injured. When two tribes sighted each other, they would immediately go into battle formation, headed by the first, second and third spy boys of each side. Then the two head chiefs would cast their spears — iron rods — into the ground, the first to do so crying, 'Umba?', which was an inquiry if the other were willing to surrender. The second chief replied, 'Me no umba!' There was never a surrender, never a retreat. There would follow a series of dances by the two chiefs, each around his spear, with pauses now and then to fling back and forth the exclamations, 'Umba?' 'Me no umba!' While this continued, sometimes for four or five minutes, the tribes stood expectantly poised, waiting for the inevitable break that would be an invitation for a free-for-all mêlée. Once a police officer was badly injured by an Indian's spear. After that occurrence a law was passed forbidding the tribes of maskers to carry weapons.

Today the tribes are all friendly. The following song is a warning against the tactics of other days.

> Shootin' don't make it, no no no no.
> Shootin' don't make it, no no no no.

> Shootin' don't make it, no no no no.
> If you see your man sittin' in the bush,
> Knock him in the head and give him a push,
> 'Cause shootin' don't make it, no no.
> Shootin' don't make it, no no no no.

The Golden Blades marched all day through main thorough-fares and narrow side streets. At the train tracks and Broadway came the news the spy boys had sighted the Little Red, White and Blues.

The tribes met on either side of a vacant space of ground, and with a whoop and loud cries.

'Me, Chief "Happy Peanut." My tribe Golden Blades.'

The other replied: 'Me, Chief Battle Brown. My tribe Little Red, White and Blues.'

Palms still extended, they spoke as one, 'Peace.'

Then they met, put arms around each other's necks. Together they proceeded toward the nearest saloon, the two tribes behind them mingling and talking, the medicine men chanting a weird duet:

> Shh-bam-hang the ham.
> Follow me, follow me, follow me.
> Wha-wha-wha-follow me.
> Wha-wha-wha-follow me.
> Shh-bam-hang the ham.
> Wha-wha-wha-follow me.
> Wha-wha-wha-follow me. . . .

At the bar, the chiefs gulped jiggers of whiskey, then small beers as chasers. Members of both tribes crowded about and imbibed freely.

When decision was made to depart, each tribe filed out a different door, tambourines beating.

In the street Chief 'Happy Peanut's' wife revealed to her husband that she didn't think Chief Battle Brown's mate was anything to brag about. 'Shux!' she sneered disgustedly. 'She didn't look so hot to me. She don't have no life in her. Man, she's gotta

Have it like I like it!
Tu-way-pa-ka-way.
Use it like I use it!
Tu-way-pa-ka-way.
Do it like I do it!
Tu-way-pa-ka-way.
Like a good queen should.
Ee-e-e-e!'

The Queen, finishing her song, went into her dance. With hands lifted above her head, her fingers snapping to keep time, with tongue darting in a serpentlike movement in and out of her mouth and hips and stomach undulating, Queen 'Happy Peanut' executed an extremely unorthodox Indian dance. There was to be no doubt left in the minds of onlookers that she was red hot and full of life.

Suddenly the medicine man began hopping around and moaning over a figure lying prostrate on the ground. Utter astonishment caused the Queen to interrupt her dance when the identity of the form was announced. It was her spy girl, who had wandered slightly ahead of the others.

'What's the matter, she can't take it?' taunted a bystander.

Upon him the medicine man turned the full venom of his wrath, 'Umm-m-m-n! A-a-a-a-ah!' He made a sign, as if casting a spell over the tormentor, to the amusement of the gathering crowd.

The Queen briefly glanced at the girl.

'She didn't eat no breakfast this morning,' she explained. 'She'll be all right. We is gonna eat at the next stop.'

Upon reaching South Claiborne Avenue, the spy boy ran back to the flag boy, the flag boy whispered to the wild man, who sent a runner scampering back to the chief. The Creole Wild West Indians were coming!

The Creole Wild Wests were already in a place, eating and drinking, when the Golden Blades caught up with them. The two tribes greeted each other in high spirits, with much shouting and laughter, all but Chief Brother Tillman.

He leaned against the bar, his eyes, from which the power of vision was fast fading, troubled and brooding, his mind sad with

The "Baby Doll" appears on Mardi Gras and again on St. Joseph's night

A group of "Baby Dolls"

Queen (second from right) and Maids of Honor at the Zulu Ball

King Zulu, the Negro monarch of Mardi Gras

On Mardi Gras it is traditional for Negroes to dress as Indians; they have done
so for nearly a century

the realization that this was probably the last time he would be able to take part in this Mardi Gras tradition. As far back as any Indian can remember there has always been a Brother Tillman.

'They didn't want me to go out this year,' he said. 'They thought I couldn't see well enough. Well, we'll see who can see. This is my only pleasure. Oh, yes, I drink, but I don't drink for fun. I drink to hide the truth. Can you understand that? How about a drink? And let's have some music! Come on, Peanut. What's this, anyway? A funeral?'

But as soon as the dancing started, he was talking again. 'It's just that I've seen so much of this. It's been my life. And to think I might not see it again. My sight isn't good now, you know, but I wouldn't let them know it because I might make another year. But let's cheer up! Have another drink?'

When the time came to leave, Brother Tillman rose and led his band of Wild Creoles from the saloon, walking with erect dignity, his chin high. Though his costume was simple for a chief — plain buckskin trimmed with a black fringe, a crown of jet feathers on his head — he bore himself with unaffected but proud nobility.

Onward traveled the Golden Blades, chanting their strange songs, pausing to dance wildly, their tambourines relentlessly throbbing the monotonous rhythm. Drinking, eating, fighting, loving, forgetting yesterday and tomorrow.

Laughing and singing one moment, imbued with genuine savagery the next, the Indians are still feared by many Orleanians, who will go to great lengths to avoid a tribe coming in their direction. It is almost as if those dock laborers and office-building porters have reverted for a day to the jungles of their ancestors.

Here and there the Golden Blades met other tribes, the Golden Eagles, the Yellow Pocahontas, the Red Frontier Hunters. They forced their way into packed bars and out again, laughing, cursing.

There were few mishaps, but a member or two strayed and vanished for the day. One daring 'brave' leaped aboard a truck filled with white maskers, who threw confetti on his crown and taunted him by derisively singing the famous old Creole cry,

Mardi Gras,	Mardi Gras,
Chou-a-la-paille,	Chew the straw,
Run away,	Run away
Taille la l'sill	And tell a lie!

The day's marching ended just after nightfall outside of the Japanese Tea Garden on St. Philip and North Liberty Streets.

Tired but still happy maskers gathered here. This is the Mecca of all Negroes on Mardi Gras Night, for here the Zulu Ball, the grand climax of the day, takes place. The Indians' eyes are weary now, and their feet tired, but they never allow themselves to relax. They keep imbibing all the liquor they can get their hands on, keep their songs and dances going. A Baby Doll or two straggles past, mingling with the crowd. A Baby Doll has to keep busy all the time. At last, from within the Tea Gardens, come the strains of the Grand March as the Zulu Ball begins.

Inside the ceiling is decorated with colored paper, bright new lanterns shed vari-colored lights, palm leaves and coconuts contribute a tropical atmosphere, fresh sawdust is sprinkled on the floor and the six-piece orchestra is feeling extra hot.

The King and Queen lead the Grand March, and the band swings out with a torrid selection. No staid monarch is King Zulu. He leaves that for the white balls, where the kings must remain on their thrones most of the evening. King Zulu is out there trucking on down and giving the women a break. He's really head man, and before the night is over he's likely to feel like a super-Casanova, so many are the invitations whispered into his ear. Sometimes he makes a premature exit, one particularly fascinating damsel having proved too much for his will power. Two years ago, when King Zulu departed, so did most of the champagne and cake. After two hours Johnny Metoyer, then ruling Zululand with an iron hand, phoned his house.

'He ain't here,' his wife informed Johnny, with vengeance. 'I'm looking for him, too.'

Then Johnny did some thinking and he did some swearing. He and Charlie Fisher telephoned every saloon in town and visited a lot of them. At last His Majesty was located. He was in a beer parlor with four high yellow women, nine quarts of champagne and having the time of his life. The King was having a ball all by himself.

'Niggers like you,' was Royalty's retort to the bawling out administered by Metoyer and Fisher, 'ain't supposed to get nothing.'

The Queen does all right at the Zulu Ball, too. If a girl can't establish herself solid after this day and night, there is something radically wrong. She can sort out her propositions and pick one or a dozen of the best.

This Zulu Ball is the end of it. But it has been swell, all the maskers tell each other. The best year yet, they always agree. Zulus, Indians and Baby Dolls creep home in the small hours of the morning, fall into bed and sleep most of the next day. There are few New Orleans Negroes at work or on the streets the day after the Carnival.

But that night they begin to straggle into the various bars along Gravier and Poydras Streets. There is the usual blare of music boxes, hot dancing, arguments and 'corner loving.' Liquor again pours down parched throats. It isn't quite as exciting as Mardi Gras, but it isn't dull. There is never a dull night in the streets where the Zulus and the Indians and the Baby Dolls live and play, in the streets where every night is Saturday night.

Most of the discussion is of the day before, but the subject always shifts to the Saint Joseph's Night to come, as everyone looks eagerly forward to the next time they can really cut loose.

March 19, always an important date in the New Orleans calendar, has been a second Mardi Gras to Negroes for the past two decades. It is tradition that Zulus, Indians and Baby Dolls don their costumes that night and revive the spirit of Fat Tuesday for a few hours.

There are no parades, of course, but they wander about on foot, visiting the bars, having dances and parties at various places, strutting their stuff.

On Saint Joseph's Night, 1941, the music box roared as usual, and in the arms of criminals, hopheads and hoboes the Baby Dolls danced and carried on. A huge woman, dressed as a gypsy queen in garish colors and her black face reddened with rouge, did a solo number, popped her fingers and messed around. Harry, that genius with the tambourine, beat it vigorously, and executed his inimitable dance on the crowded floor.

The Indians were there too. So were the 'Gold Diggers,' an organization that gave the Baby Dolls some competition. They wore similar costumes, and, as if to assist them along the way, were accompanied by a 'policeman' — a male friend dressed in a burlesque uniform and cap, and carrying a club. They boasted escorts, too, each Gold Digger having a boy friend, who wore a 'dress suit' of pale blue satin, a top hat, and flourished a cane. The Gold Diggers wore blue satin costumes trimmed with white fur, false curls, and also carried canes. The liveliest of the crowd was also the largest, a Gold Digger weighing well over two hundred pounds, who, nevertheless, strutted her stuff with the grace and vigor of a bawdy sprite.

But the Western Girls, so called because one year they all came as Annie Oakley (these are a group of Negro female impersonators headed by 'Corinne the Queen'), are perhaps the gayest of all. In evening gowns and wigs they try to outdo the real girls. The ones who top their extremely dark faces with golden-blonde and flaming red wigs are the funniest. As for Corinne, she always maintains her regal bearing, explaining, 'I'm a real queen, and don't nobody never forget it!' The other 'girls' aren't the least bit jealous, either, but love Corinne dearly because 'she's such a gay cat.' And Corinne has genuine claims to majesty. In 1931 'she' was Queen of the Zulus! That year the King said he was disgusted with women, so he selected Corinne to reign as his mate over all of the Negro Mardi Gras!

Chapter 2

Street Criers

THE MULE–DRAWN WAGON PULLS UP AT A corner in one of the residential sections of New Orleans. The Negro vendor cups his hands before his mouth and bellows:

> Watermelon! Watermelon! Red to the rind,
> If you don't believe me jest pull down your blind!
>
> I sell to the rich,
> I sell to the po';
> I'm gonna sell the lady
> Standin' in that do'.
>
> Watermelon, Lady!
> Come and git your nice red watermelon, Lady!
> Red to the rind, Lady!
> Come on, Lady, and get 'em!
> Gotta make the picnic fo' two o'clock,
> No flat tires today.
> Come on, Lady!

Behind the hawker in the wagon is a tumbling pile of green serpent-striped melons; beside him on the seat is one halved to show that it is 'red to the rind.' Despite this, the melon you purchase will be 'plugged' as proof that yours is ripe. The peddler opens his mouth again to inform you that

> I got water with the melon, red to the rind!
> If you don't believe it jest pull down your blind.
> You eat the watermelon and preee — serve the rind!

The vendor selling cantaloupe is an Italian. He sings out,

> Cantal — ope — ah!
> Fresh and fine,
> Just offa de vine,
> Only a dime!

The operator of a wagon selling a variety of vegetables offers this one:

> Nice little snapbeans,
> Pretty little corn,
> Butter beans, carrots,
> Apples for the ladies!
> Jui-ceee lemons!

Another, with curious humor, yells, 'I got artichokes by the neck!'

The streets reverberate with their cries: 'Come and gettum, Lady! I got green peppers, snapbeans, tur-nips! I got oranges! I got celery! I got fine ripe yellow banana! Tur-nips, Lady! Ba-na-na, Lady!'

These peddlers use every means imaginable to cart their wares — trucks, mules and wagons, pushcarts and baskets. A Negress will balance one basket on her head, carry two others, one in each hand, hawking any vegetables and fruit in season. Particularly discordant screams rend the mornings when it is blackberry season.

> Blackber — reeees! Fresh and fine.
> I got blackber — reeeees, Lady!
> Fresh from th' vine!
> I got blackberries, Lady!
> Three glass fo' a dime.
> I got blackberries!

> I got blackberries!
> BLACK — BERRIEEEEEEEEES!

Negro youths often work in pairs, one on each side of a street, each carrying baskets and crying alternately or in unison: 'I got mustard greens 'n Creole cabbage! Come on, Lady. Look what I got!' Or, 'Irish pota-tahs! Dime a bucket! Lady, you oughta see my nice Irish po-ta-tahs!'

Many housewives purchase their food supplies from these itinerant vendors, the prices often being a bit below those of the shops and markets. Many have regular peddlers or basket-'totin' ' Negresses who come daily to the kitchen door. They will often, even to this day, present favorite customers with a bit of parsley or a small bunch of shallots as *lagniappe*.

A truck at a curb in the business section of New Orleans is operated by an Italian who offers 'Mandareeeens — nickel a dozen!' A Negro in a spring wagon in the next block outdoes him with 'Mandareens — twenty-five fo' a dime!'

When strawberries appear, preceding the blackberry season, peddlers, both white and colored, both male and female, appear all over the city. Even Sunday mornings resound with cries of

> I got strawberries, Lady!
> Strawberries, Lady!
> Fifteen cents a basket —
> Two baskets for a quarter.

The housewives emerge, peer into the small boxes of berries, inspecting carefully, always raising the top layer of fruit to see the ones beneath. There is a little trade trick of putting the reddest and biggest berries on top, green, dry or small ones — the culls — underneath to which all Louisiana housekeepers are wise.

Between the strawberry and blackberry seasons cries of 'Jewberry, Lady! Nice jewberries!' may be heard. This is the dewberry season.

In Abbeville, an elderly French woman drives a mule before an ancient, creaky wagon, and peddles fruit and vegetables each morning, calling her wares in a weird mixture of French and Cajun English. Known as Madame Mais-Là, she pulls up before

a house and announces: 'Hello, dere! *Voulez-vous légumes aujourd'hui? Des bonnes carrots. Des bonnes papates douces. Des
pommes de terre. Des choux-fleurs. Non? Pas ça aujourd'hui. Bien.*
Geedy up, dere!'

The vending of food in New Orleans streets is a custom as old
as the city itself. In earlier days the peddlers were even more
numerous. Buying from these wandering *marchandes* was extremely convenient. Prices were low, the produce of good quality; often it was possible, after a bit of wrangling, to strike off a
bargain.

Earlier counterparts of present-day hawkers were the Green
Sass Men, no longer in existence. The *Daily Picayune* of July 24,
1846, describes them thus:

> Their stocks were very small, consisting generally of vegeta-
> bles, a small amount of fruit such as figs, peaches and melons
> and — by way of variety, although not strictly a vegetable
> product — cream cheeses. These commodities were generally
> carried in old champagne baskets balanced on the heads of the
> Green Sass Men, and their cry, as near as it can be translated, is
> ''Ears yerfineniceartaties, artichokes, cantelopes, feegs and
> arnicerkereama — cheeses! 'Ear! 'Ear!'

Most of the French and American slave-owners of long ago
were a thrifty lot, and those slaves too old to be of other use were
often put out into the city streets to peddle the surplus products
of the plantations. Throughout the year, day in, day out, their
cries resounded through the streets of New Orleans. All masters
were required to purchase licenses for their slaves, but often
added thousands of dollars per year to their incomes by so doing.
De Boré, of sugar fame, who owned a huge plantation in New
Orleans where Audubon Park now spreads, 'produced at least
six thousand dollars per annum' in this fashion, according to one
authority. Newspapers of the period criticized slave street-
vending as a 'very picayunish business,' but it lifted many of the
Negroes' owners into affluence.

Each season had its special commodities. Early spring saw the
arrival of strawberries, of Japanese plums. Later, watermelons,
dewberries, blackberries and figs appeared. Wild ducks, rice

birds and other game were sold on the streets during winter. At the French Market Choctaw Indian squaws sat stoically at the curbs, offering gumbo filé — powdered sassafras, frequently used instead of okra to thicken gumbo — other herbs and roots, baskets and pottery. Fat Negresses in starched white aprons and garish *tignons* sold cakes, molasses and coffee dripped while you waited. Other peddlers offered everything from cheap jewelry to live canaries in cages. Chickens, alive but limply resigned to fate, trussed up in bunches like carrots, were carried up and down the city streets by men who poked their heads into the windows of homes and yelled, 'Cheeec-ken, Madame? Nice fat spring cheee-ken?'

The peddlers of fish probably were the most insistent. The *Daily Picayune* of April 4, 1889, reports:

> During the Lenten season, when fish were in great demand, the basket peddlers of the finny product do an excellent business, especially in selling the inferior kinds of fish. Their wares are not always of the freshest and in many cases on the verge of decomposition, yet they succeed in imposing upon the careful housewife or servant by stout protestations that their fish are perfectly fresh.... They ring at doorbells and if not promptly answered jerk the wire as though they would pull the bell from its fastenings. A simple refusal to purchase incenses them, and they thrust their offensive-smelling fish in the faces of persons, and if they are still refused frequently give vent to curses and abuse of those whom they seek to impose on.

A salesman of oysters, carrying his merchandise in tin pails, was also common at one time, crying,

> Oyta! Sally! Oy — ta! Sally!

Or sometimes,

> Oyster Man! Oyster Man!
> Get your fresh oysters from the Oyster Man!
> Bring out your pitcher, bring out your can,
> Get your nice fresh oysters from the Oyster Man!

There was the Icecream Man, humorously depicted by Léon Fremeaux, in a volume of sketches titled *New Orleans Characters*, as a barefooted Negro wearing patched trousers, holding in one hand a white cloth, carrying in his other a basket, and on his head, at a perilous balance, an icecream freezer! His cry was

> *Crême à la glace;*
> *Crême à la vanille!*

Or, facetiously,

> Icecream, lemonade,
> Brown sugar and rotten aig!

Fresh milk and buttermilk were sold on the streets, the fresh milk from horse-drawn wagons described by the *Daily Picayune* as ' ... a tall green box, set between high wheels and almost always driven by Gascons. The two large bright brassbound cans that ornamented the front of the wagon, compelled the driver to stand up much of the time in order to see clearly before him.' The Buttermilk Man carried his large can of buttermilk through the streets several times a week, crying, 'Butter-milk! Butter-milk, Lady?'

Very early in the life of the Creole city, even water was sold in this fashion, being dispensed from carts loaded with huge hogsheads. Wine, too, was often vended.

THE BREAD AND CAKE VENDORS

The most famous of these were the *cala* vendors. A *cala* is a pastry which originated among Creole Negroes — a thin fritter made with rice and yeast sponge. Creoles did not have the prepared yeast cakes sold today, so yeast was concocted the night before, of boiled potatoes, corn meal, flour and cooking soda, left in the night air to ferment, then mixed with the boiled rice and made into a sponge. The next morning flour, eggs, butter and milk were added, a stiff batter mixed, and the *calas* formed by dropping spoonfuls into a skillet.

'*Belles calas, Madam! Tout chauds*, Madame, Two cents!' thus called the cala vendors for years. A long cry was,

Belles calas,	Beautiful rice fritters,
Madame, mo gaignin calas,	Madame, I have rice fritters,

Madame, mo gaignin calas,	Madame, I have rice fritters,
Madame, mo gaignin calas;	Madame, I have rice fritters;
Mo guaranti vous ye bons	I guarantee you they are good
Beeelles calas . . . Beeelles calas.	Fine rice fritters . . . Fine rice fritters.
Madame, mo gaignin calas,	Madame, I have rice fritters,
Madame, mo gaignin calas,	Madame, I have rice fritters,
Si vous pas gaignin l'argent,	If you have no money,
Goutez c'est la mêm' chose,	Taste, it's all the same,
Madame, mo gaignin calas tou, tou cho.	Madame, I have rice fritters, quite, quite hot.
Beeles calas . . . Beeelles calas,	Fiiiine rice fritters . . . Fiiiine rice fritters,
Tou cho, tou cho, tou cho.	All hot, all hot, quite hot.
Madame, mo gaignin calas,	Madame, I have rice fritters,
Madame, mo gaignin calas,	Madame, I have rice fritters,
Tou cho, tou cho, tou cho.	Quite hot, quite hot, quite hot.

Clementine, a Negress, well-dressed in a bright *tignon*, fichu of white lawn, tied with a large breast pin, a starched blue gingham skirt and stiff snowy apron, would sing,

> *Beeeeeelles calas — Beeeeeelles calas — Aaaaaa!*
> *Madame, mo gaignin calas,*
> *Madame, mo gaignin calas,*
> *Tou cho, tou cho, tou cho.*
> *Beeeeeelles calas — Belles calas*
> *À madame mo gaignin calas,*
> *Mo guaranti vous ye bons!*

Another Negress sold her *calas* in front of the old Saint Louis Cathedral, cooking them in a pan over a small furnace, while the customer waited. Without raising her voice she would mutter hoarsely and incessantly, '*Mo gaignin calas . . . Madame, mo gaignin calas . . . Calas, calas, calas, calas, tou cho, calas, calas, calas; Mo gaignin calas, Madame . . . calas, calas, calas, calas. . . .*'

Some vendors sold not only *calas* of rice, but also *calas* of cowpeas, crying,

> *Calas tout chauds, Madame,*
> *Calas au riz calas aux fèves!*

Another cry was

> *Too shoo-o-o-o-oh*
> *Tout chauds — all hot!*
> *Calas — calas — tout chauds,*
> *Belles — calas — tout chauds,*
> *Madame, mo gaignin calas,*
> *Madame, mo gaignin calas, tou*
> *Chauds tou chauds!*

One of the last professional *cala* vendors on New Orleans streets was Richard Gabriel, a colored descendant of these Creole Negroes. He improved the system somewhat, pushing a cart similar to the sort used by the peanut vendors, and chanting in more modern fashion,

> We sell it to the rich, we sell it to the poor,
> We give it to the sweet brownskin, peepin' out the door.
> *Tout chaud, Madame, tout chaud!*
> Git 'em while they're hot! Hot *calas!*
>
> One cup of coffee, fifteen cents *calas,*
> Make you smile the livelong day.
> *Calas, tout chauds, Madame, Tout chauds!*
> Git 'em while they're hot! Hot *calas!*

Other songs are

> The little Jamaica boy he say,
> More you eatta, more you wanta eatta.
> Get 'em while they're hotta. Hot *calas!*
> *Tout chauds, Madame, tout chauds.*

And

> Tell 'em what they do you, take off that Saturday frown,
> Put on that Sunday morning smile, to last the whole day 'round.
> *Tout chauds, Madame, tout chauds!*
> That's how two cups of *café,* fifteen cents *calas* can make
> You smile the livelong day.
> *Tout chauds, Madame, tout chauds!*
> Get 'em while they're hot! Hot *calas!*

There used to be two *cala* women who would sing alternately:

1st: *Calas, Calas,* — all nice and hot
    Calas, Calas, — all nice and hot
2d: Lady, me I have *calas!* Laaa-dy, me I have *calas!*
    All nice 'n hot — all nice 'n hot — all nice 'n hot. . . .

Well known was the Cymbal Man, who, according to the *Daily Picayune* of July 24, 1846, confined his rambles to the French section of New Orleans, offering also 'doughnuts and crullers,' which were favorites with the Creoles. His musical 'toooo-shoooo-oooo' never failed to bring most of them out.

The Corn Meal Man, noted for his wit and humor, would prowl the streets, blowing on a small brass trumpet worn on a cord about his neck. His greeting was usually, '*Bon jour, Madame, Mam - zelle!* Fresh corn meal, right from the mill. *Oui, Mam - zelle!*' accompanied by a hearty laugh. The *Daily Delta* of June 3, 1850, reports him doing business on horseback, saying, ' . . . his fat, glossy horse looks as if he partook of no scant portion of the corn meal!' A very early corn meal peddler was known as Signor Cornmeali.

Among the most famous of the cake vendors were the Gaufre Men or Shaving Cake Men, who sold not shaving soap, but pastries that had the appearance of timber shavings. These were kept in a tin box strapped to the back, while the Gaufre Man announced his approach by beating on a metal triangle as he strode the city streets. The last Gaufre Man, bewhiskered but always clean and neatly attired, never revealed the secret of his thin, crisp, cone-shaped pastries. When he died, the recipe died with him, and *gaufres* are now unknown in New Orleans.

Hot potato cakes, made usually of sweet potatoes, were sold by Negro women. These vendors, Emmet Kennedy says, were heard mostly in the French Quarter around nightfall. In his *Mellows* he describes their cry as follows:

Bel pam pa-tat,
Bal pam pa-tat, Madame,
Ou-lay-ou Le Bel Pam Patat,
Pam patat!

Everything the old Creole Negresses sold was either 'bel' — beautiful — or 'bon' — good.

A bread made of Irish potatoes was also sold, to the following song:

Pain patatte,	Potato bread,
Pain patatte, Madame,	Potato bread, Madam,
Achetez pain patatte,	Buy potato bread,
Madame, mo gaignin pain patatte.	Madam, I have potato bread.

Hot pies were another favorite commodity, the vendor carrying his wares in a cloth-covered basket, crying, 'Ho' pies — *chauds!* Ho' pies — *chauds!'*

There are modern versions of these last. Each day pie peddlers appear on the docks of New Orleans, moving among the longshoremen, carrying their pies — and often sandwiches and candy — in a basket. Occasionally a pie man will appear in one of the residential sections, with a monotonous cry of ' Hot pies — — hot pies — hot pies — hot pies!' A Negro woman, always dressed in snowy white, hawks pies and sandwiches through the business district of the city, rolling her merchandise along in a baby carriage.

At least one man still sells bread on the streets. Pushing a cart he calls out, ' Bread Man! Bread Man! I got French bread, Lady. I got sliced bread. I got raisin bread: Lady! I got rolls, Lady! Bread Man, Lady!'

> The Waffle Man is a fine old man.
> He washes his face in a frying-pan,
> He makes his waffles with his hand,
> Everybody loves the Waffle Man.

For years those who believed this little ditty ran out at the shrill blast of the Waffle Man's bugle. Children eagerly thrust their nickels forward to purchase one of his delicious hot waffles sprinkled liberally with powdered sugar. His wagon, horse-drawn, was usually white and yellow and set on high wheels. One Waffle Man still appears daily in New Orleans, vending waffles from a brilliant red-and-yellow wagon. But now he caters mostly to fully grown males of the stock-exchange neighborhood.

THE CANDY AND FLOWER VENDORS

The Candy Man, according to the *Daily Picayune* of July 15, 1846, 'carried his caraway comfits and other sweets in a large green tin chest upon which was emblazoned, in the brightest yellow, two razors affectionately crossed over each other.' Unlike the other vendors, this Candy Man had no cry, but attracted attention by beating on a metal triangle. Until a few years ago, later Candy Men, driving squarish, high wagons, paused at corners, blew piercing blasts on trumpets and sold taffy in long, wax-paper-wrapped sticks.

Pralines have been sold on New Orleans streets through all the city's history, and always the delicious Creole confections of brown sugar and pecans have been vended by Negresses of the 'Mammy' type. Today they appear, garbed in gingham and starched white aprons and *tignons*, usually in the Vieux Carré, though now they represent modern candy shops. '*Belles pralines!*' they cry. '*Belles pralines!*' Day by day they sit in the shadows of the ancient buildings, fat black faces smiling at the passers-by, fanning their candies with palmetto fans or strips of brown wrapping paper. Usually, besides the pralines, Mammy dolls and other souvenirs are sold.

Flowers are not sold on the streets as frequently as they are in some other cities, but in the Vieux Carré elderly flower women and young girls and boys peddle corsages of rosebuds and camellias in the small bars and cafés, chanting at your table, 'Flowers? Pretty flowers for the lady?'

THE CHARCOAL MAN

Char-coal, Lady! Char-coal! Chah-ah-coal, Lady!

Until recently practically everyone employed Negro washwomen, who boiled clothes and other washing over small furnaces in the backyards, and charcoal was always in demand. Almost every day this familiar cry rang through the streets. Lafcadio Hearn described one cry of the Charcoal Man's as

Black — coalee — coalee!
Coaly — coaly; coaly — coaly — coal — coal — coal.
Coaly — coaly!
Coal — eee! Nice!
Chah — coal!
Twenty-five! Whew!
O Charco-oh-oh-oh-h-oh-lee!
Oh — lee — eee!
(You get some coal in your mout', young fellow, if you
     don't keep it shut!)
Pretty coalee — oh — lee!
Charcoal!
Cha — ah — ahr — coal!
Charbon! Du charbon, Madame! Bon charbon? Point! Ai-ai!
Tonnèrre de dieu!
Cha-r-r-r-r-r-rbon!
A-a-a-a-a-a-aw!
Vingt-cinq! Nice coalee! Coalee!
Coaly-coal-coal!
Pretty coaly!
Charbon de Paris!
De Paris, Madame; de Paris!

Leonard Parker, a Negro, remembered the following one:

Char-coal! Charcoal!
My horse is white, my face is black.
I sell my charcoal, two-bits a sack —
Char-coal! Char-coal!

Though modern use of laundry facilities has made the Charcoal
Man a rarity now, he may be seen occasionally — and heard —
seated on a broken-down wagon, drawn by an equally broken-
down horse, often adorned with a straw bonnet, singing out
his repetitious chant of 'Char-coal, Lady! Char-coal!' Today his
merchandise is neatly packed in paper sacks.

Then there is his brother, once just as evident in the city, now
just as rare, who cries, 'Stone-coal, Lady! Stone-coal!' and who
is being gradually forced out of existence by present use of steam
and gas heat, instead of the old-fashioned grate fires.

THE CLOTHES POLE MAN

'Daily he goeth forth out beyond the limits of the city, into lonesome and swampy places where copperheads and rattlesnakes abound. And, there he cutteth him clothespoles, wherewith he marcheth through the city, in the burning glare of the sun, singing a refrain simple in words but weird in music.' So wrote Hearn of the Clothes Pole Man.

This queer merchant, always colored, wanders through the streets, usually wearing an ancient derby, ragged coat and trousers. Fremeaux's sketch shows him in the derby, a light lavender shirt, dark frock coat and patched pants. On one shoulder is a folded cloth on which rest his poles.

'Cl's po-u-u-les!' he cries. 'Cl's po-u-ules!'

Housewives buy the poles at prices which range from ten to twenty-five cents. A favorite cry is

> Clothes poles! Clothes poles!
> Hear the man comin' with the clothes poles!
>
> Only a nickel, only a dime!
> Clothes poles — Clothes pole man!
> Clothes pole man sellin' clothes poles!
>
> Clothes poles, Lady!
> Nice clean clothes poles!

The poles are cleaned and 'skinned' after being cut, and must be forked at one end. There is evidence that the same pole may be sold several times, if the merchant is smart enough. One housewife, after her poles had been disappearing in a peculiar fashion, watched the yard one moonlight night and captured a small Negro making off with several of them. He confessed he sold them back to the same Clothes Pole Man who had been selling them to her.

THE CHIMNEY SWEEP

Wherever he has appeared, the Chimney Sweep has been a fascinating and picturesque character. It is still possible to see the New Orleans variety, and he has changed very little in appearance despite the many years his cries have echoed through the city's streets. Unlike the sweep of London, he wears a tall, battered silk hat, a swallowtail coat, and he is always a Negro, usually as black as the soot in which he works. There is always the coil of rope on one shoulder, several bunches of palmetto and a sheaf of broom straw. As he wanders through the neighborhood he shouts:

> *Ra-mi-neau! Ra-mi-neau! Ra-mi-neau!*
> Lady, I know why your chimney won't draw,
> Oven won't bake and you can't make no cake,
> An' I know why your chimney won't draw!

Hired, he scurries agilely up to the roof, sometimes assisted by a smaller, younger, but equally black edition of himself, and as he works he sings. One odd song common to the New Orleans Chimney Sweep is:

Val-sez, Val-seur,	Waltz, Waltzer,
Val-sez pour cé-lé-brer	Waltz to celebrate
La S'te Marie.	St. Mary's Day.
Dieu sait si l'annee prochaine	God knows if next year
Nous célébrerons la S'te Marie!	We will celebrate St. Mary's Day!

Others cry: 'R-R-R-R-Raminay! *R-r-r-r-r-ramonez la chiminée du haut en bas!*' 'Ramonez,' 'Raminay,' 'Ramineaux' and 'Ramineau' seem all to be corruptions of the French 'Ramoneur' or Chimney Sweeper.

Some travel in pairs and alternate their call thus:

1st Sweep: *Ramonez la cheminée . . . Rrrrrrramonez la cheminée!*
2d Sweep: *Valsez; valseur, valsez pour célébrer la S'te Marie. . . .*

A contemporary team of sweeps, Willie Hall and Albert Hutchins, sing:

> Get over, get over slick,
> Save dat chimney, save it quick.

Willie and Albert chant the 'Chimney Sweeper's Blacks,' apparently their own composition.

Here's yo' chimney sweeps,
We goes up to the roofs,
Sweep the smokestacks down right now,
Don't care for soot, anyhow.
Rami — neau! Rami — neau! Rami — neau!

Sweep 'em clean! Sweep 'em clean!
Save the firemen lots of work,
We hate soot, we never shirk,
Sweep 'em clean! Sweep 'em clean!

Willie cheerfully waxed biographical.

'I been a chimney sweeper for forty-five years now. I'm most eighty years old, and I've made me a good livin'. There was a season to it, but I've always had my regular customers. I done swept some of the best chimneys in town.'

One reason the Chimney Sweep keeps singing as he works is to let anyone who might be below know the chimney is being cleaned and to protect him from being showered with soot. All during his work the songs go on and the cry comes,

'RO — MI — NAY!'

THE BOTTLE MAN

The Bottle Man is still seen now and then. Either Italian or Negro, driving a horse and wagon, he cries, as the horse bobs sleepily along, 'Any old bot'? Any old bot' today?'

Now he pays — rather reluctantly — in cash. But in other days his approach was a signal for the children to run forth at the blast of his horn in as an enthusiastic response as ever answered the Pied Piper of Hamlin. The Bottle Man of a past era pushed a cart along the *banquette*, and his payment for 'old bot's' was much more interesting than mere money. For while his cart had an upper section devoted to a huge bin which held his collected bottles, the lower section was a drawer filled with the most amazing collection of trinkets ever possessed by anyone except Santa Claus. For their bottles the youngsters received tops, whistles, horns, rattles or pink-and-white peppermints! Bargaining was spirited and educational. The children's aim was to get as many toys as possible for their bottles; the Bottle Man's, to give as little.

During the nineties a fleet of thirty or forty luggers visited the plantations above and below the city, collecting bottles. The *Daily Picayune*, July 12, 1891, described how nearly every week three or four of the boats discharged their cargo of old bottles at the wharves in New Orleans. Many dealers employed twenty or more collectors and there was always a good market for beer bottles, whiskey and champagne bottles, condiment and relish bottles of all sorts. Medicine bottles were never resold, the lone exception to what the Bottle Man would buy.

Most of the Bottle Men of today have added other merchandise to their business — generally rags and bones. Usually the cry is

> Any bottles, any bones, any rags today?
> Any old bottles
> Any old bones today?

There are men, too, who specialize in rags, chanting:

> Old Rag Man! Get your rags ready!
> For the old Rag Man!
> Money to be made!
> Get your rags ready for the old Rag Man!

A kindred soul is the itinerant Junk Man, who may purchase any scrap iron, discarded pieces of furniture and such valuables.

THE TIN-A-FEEX MAN

> In a feex — tin-a-feex!
> Tin-a-Feex Man!

So he sang through the neighborhoods, usually Italian, carrying a small furnace, a few tools and some solder. The cry of 'Tin-a-Feex! Tin-a-Feex Man!' used to bring forth all the pots and pans in the neighborhoods through which he passed.

THE BROOM MAN

The Broom Man is blind, tall and growing old. Bent under the weight of the brooms and mops he carries on his back, he rambles along, thumping loudly on the pavements with a cane, as much to attract attention as to feel his way. Often he appears wearing a baseball catcher's mask over his chalky, sightless face, across the top of which runs a strap which helps to hold his wares in place. His cry is monotonous, a mere gibberish, punctuated with sharp explosions.

> Mopanbroom! Mopanbroom! MopanbroOM!
> Herecomes themopanbroom!
> GetyourmopanbrOOM!
> MopanbroOMmopanbroOMmopanbrOOOOM!

THE COFFEE WOMEN

Negro women owned most of the coffee stands that were scattered through old New Orleans. These women dispensed cups of freshly made coffee from little street stands to the melodious chant of '*Café noir!*' and '*Café au lait!*' In her *The Story of the French Market* Catherine Cole writes: '... Old Rose, whose memory is embalmed in the amber of many a song and picture and story, kept the most famous coffee stall of the old French Market. She was a little Negress who had earned money to buy her freedom from slavery. Her coffee was like the benediction that follows after prayer; or if you prefer it, the Benedictine after dinner.'

Zabette and Rose Gla were two other well-known coffee women. Zabette had her stand in front of the Cathedral. In the curious journalese of the day, the *Daily Picayune* describes Rose Gla as '... one of the comeliest of her race, black as Erebus, but smiling always and amicable as dawn. Her coffee was the essence of the fragrant bean, and since her death the lovers of that divine beverage wander listlessly around the stalls on Sunday mornings with a pining at the bosom which cannot be satisfied.'

Zabette is described as dispensing 'choice black coffee in tiny cups to her clients' and a notable sale is recorded when 'an old song was composed extempore by a representative Creole on a certain morning succeeding a sleepless night, which she took as the price of a cup of coffee and which began in this wise:

Piti fille, piti fille, piti fille,	Little girl, little girl, little girl,
Piti fille qui couri dan dolo....'	Little girl who ran in the water....

Zabette also sold homemade pastries and *bière du pays* — beer brewed from pineapples.

During the eighteen-forties a quadroon woman had a stand on Canal Street, a block from where Henry Clay's statue once stood. A woman named Manette operated a coffee stall in the French Market. Children sent to market would always keep a *picayune* from the market money given them for a sip of her delicious and fragrant brew before starting homeward under the weight of their well-filled baskets.

THE KINDLING MEN

Before the coming of the factories that sawed wood into stove lengths, wood sawyers made the rounds, ringing bells in the gates and calling loudly: 'Any wood today, Mam? C'n saw two cords for a dollar an' one cord for fifty cents. Yes'm. Thank yo', mam! I'll just pitch right in.'

Carrying in his saw and buck, sticking an old pipe in his mouth he would start right in, singing all the while:

> Oh-o-oh, Mah Lady,
> Oh-o-oh, Mah Lady,
> Oh-o-oh, Mah Lady Jo-o-oe!

Dinner was usually part of his price. 'Yes, 'm, I shore could use a bite. This sure is good ham. Yes, 'm. Thank yo', mam!'

THE KNIFE SHARPENER

For years a man with a grindstone mounted on a wheelbarrow-like frame went about the streets, blowing a three- or four-note whistle which signified to housewives that the knife grinder was in the neighborhood. Another knife sharpener of early days carried only two small pieces of steel fastened together in a sort of Saint Andrew's cross. Into this cross he would thrust the knife, leaving it thin and keen.

Occasionally a knife grinder is still heard rambling through the city, usually crying: 'Any knifes to sharp'? Any knifes to sharp' today?'

THE UMBRELLA MAN

The Umbrella Man is usually a somewhat seedy gentleman, inquiring in loud and nasal tones: 'Ombrellas to maynde? Any old ombrellas to maynde?' On his stooped back is his load of umbrellas and parasols, for unless the work required is very minor, he must take them home or to his shop.

ZOZO LA BRIQUE

Zozo la Brique (Zozo the Brick) was a well-known character among the Creoles some years ago. She peddled the red brick dust so popularly used to scrub stoops and walks in certain sections of New Orleans. Zozo insisted upon being paid in nickels, which it is said she hoarded. There is even a story that Zozo's miserliness increased until she eventually starved herself to death, and that a considerable sum — at least several hundred dollars — was found hidden in her mattress, all in nickels. Zozo carried a pail of brick dust in each hand and another balanced on her head. Generally considered to be slightly demented, children were always teasing her because of her nickname of 'Zozo' — which of course meant 'bird.' Anita Fanvergne recalled that youngsters would run behind her in the street, yelling, 'Zozo, look at that bird up there!' Zozo would only reply, 'Tsh! Tsh!' She is said to have loved children, and never to have become angry with them. As much as she prized them, she would often spend her precious nickels for sticks of peppermint candy to give to the youngsters who taunted her.

There were many other street merchants, some itinerant, others stationary, with stands or stalls or simply 'squatters' rights' along the curbs of the city. *Marchands* carrying their stocks on their backs and heads, in pushcarts and horse-drawn wagons, satisfied most of the needs of the Creole households.

Practically everything was sold in this way in earlier days. There were the Bird Men, who affected a Spanish costume — sombrero, blue nankeen frocks, and pantaloons tucked into rough boots. Trapping their merchandise in the swamps and countryside just out of the city limits, the Bird Men carried them through the streets in small cages suspended from poles across their shoulders. The *Daily Picayune* of July 15, 1846, mentions a hawker who 'offered everything from dry goods to gold watches,' carried on a circular portable bench or table, in the center of which he walked as he rambled through the neighborhoods, crying loudly, '*Au rabais! Au rabais!*' (The *rabais* man always claimed to undersell his competitors. The cry '*Au rabais!*' might best be translated as 'Off price!' Today, Orleanians are likely to refer to any small notions or drygoods store as a '*rabais* shop.')

Bayou peddlers came down the waterways, singing their songs. Others journeyed down the Mississippi in boats: the Jew with his hundred-blade penknife and scores of other articles; the Yankee with his curious knick-knacks. French, Spaniards, Americans, Negroes, Mexicans, Indians — all offered their wares. Along the streets Italians sold gaudily painted plaster saints. On hot summer evenings wandering *marchands* hawked palmetto fans, calling, '*Latanier! Latanier!*'

Candle vendors crying, '*Belle chandelles! Belle chandelles!*' (Beautiful candles! Beautiful candles!) offered candles of myrtle wax, guaranteed to make even the 'darkness visible.' Negresses sold bowls of hot *gumbo* on the streets, delicious pastries and *estomac mulâtre*, a gingerbread humorously known by that name (mulatto belly). And the crayfish vendors brought housewives out to purchase the principal ingredient for their delicious crayfish *bisque* with cries of '*Crébiche, Madame! Belle 'crébiche!*' (Crayfish vendors are still seen and heard, hawking the delicacy — already boiled — from tin buckets, crying: 'Red hot! Red hot!' People hearing them say: 'Here comes Red Hot!')

Rich basses and shrill trebles, whining, pleading, cajoling, screaming, the cries blended and mingled into a symphony of the city:

> *Au Rabais! Au Rabais!*
> *Latanier! Latanier!*
> *Ramonez! Ramonez!*
> *Belles des Figues! Belles des Figues!*
> *Bons petits calas!*

> *Tout chauds! Tout chauds!*
> *Comfitures coco!*
> *Pralines, Pistaches!*
> *Pralines, Pacanes!*

And from these first sellers of fans and figs, of pastries and pralines, of candles and *calas*, descended the vendors of today.

On hot summer nights children — and adults, too — wait for the Snowball Man, who peddles scoops of crushed ice over which your choice of sweet syrup is poured. The price is usually from three to five cents, and for an extra penny you may have two kinds of syrup. Most Snowball Men use pushcarts, gaily decorated with colored crêpe paper or oilcloth. The syrups — strawberry, raspberry, spearmint, chocolate, vanilla, pineapple, orange, lemon and nectar — are sometimes given other names, occasionally after movie stars, such as 'Mae West Syrup.' In the Carrollton section 'Charlie' has been king of the Snowball Men for years. He sells his wares from a small truck, stopping at corners, and ringing a bell. Children say: 'Here comes Charlie!' when they hear his bell a block or two away and run inside to beg pennies from their parents; many gather on street corners to wait for Charlie when it is time for him. No railroad ever had a better time schedule. At the intersection of Carrollton and Claiborne Avenues, people say: 'It must be about eight o'clock. There's Charlie!'

Icecream vendors are, of course, popular, too. They usually ride bicycles to which a box containing their cream is attached, though many use a pushcart arrangement or drive a wagon. Most ring a bell instead of calling out. However, Arthur Hayward cries: 'Ha! Ha! Here comes Arthur! Mamma, that's the man!' Arthur has even advertised in the Personal Columns of New Orleans newspapers as follows:

> A well known man by the name of Arthur Hayward, better known as the Ha Ha man. He has his new Aeroplane. He will be out Sunday. Mother, look for him. That's the man they call Ha Ha, all the school children's friend. Mother, that's him going up Magazine Ave. Mother, that's him. Now he's on Laurel St., Mother, sitting in his new aeroplane.

Mexicans sell hot tamales from white pushcarts at many inter-
sections in the residential neighborhoods. All Orleanians know
the vendor of chewing gum who extends five packages on five
wire prongs, crying incessantly, 'GUMGUMGUMGUMGUMGUM-
GUMGUMGUMGUM...' and who consequently has earned the
name of Gumgumgum. On the *banquette* before auction sales
there is always a colored man or boy who beats a drum to attract
attention — Boom! Boom! Boom! Boom! — *ad infinitum*.
This custom, old as the city, continues unchanged. One of Fremeaux' sketches published in 1876 — an aged Negro beating a
drum just outside such a sale — might almost have been drawn
today.

Spasm bands, composed of small Negro boys using makeshift
instruments, who tap-dance and 'put it on' for pedestrians, are
often seen in the streets of the Vieux Carré. They run behind
strollers and, catching up, immediately go into violent twistings
and contortions, accompanied by pleas of 'Gimme a penny,
Mister! Gimme a nickel, Mister!' Some do their dances without any musical accompaniment at all, and some of the dances
are definitely individual.

In the French Quarter cafés and bars peddlers offer hardboiled
eggs and stuffed crabs. There is an ancient Chinaman who sometimes appears with stuffed crabs, at other times with pralines,
and who is said to play poker with every nickel he earns. On
the *banquettes* the 'one-man band' attracts attention with his
ability to keep drum, cymbals, banjo and harmonica all going at
the same time. And late at night in one club or another, Madame
St. Martin, the Creole flower vendor, will sell you an old-
fashioned nosegay of sword fern, cashmere bouquet and Louis
Philippe roses.

But the best known of all French Quarter characters today is
Banjo Annie, who, dirty and ragged and drunken, in a costume
that often includes two torn dresses and a man's cap, trails her
way from bar to bar muttering to herself or shouting invectives
at the bartenders who will have none of her playing and singing.

The vendors of Lottery tickets always do a thriving business,
and so do the gentlemen who linger in shadowy doorways or in
front of barrooms to inform you that there is 'a little game goin'

on in the back.' If you stand at one of the cheaper bars other men will approach and whisper invitations in your ears to purchase such merchandise as razor blades or shoestrings, combs or contraceptives.

Thus the street vendors can satisfy practically every need. As the barroom peddlers supply the equipment for certain entertainment, so do taxicab drivers in the Vieux Carré supply the means, calling out — and in no whispers — 'Wanta see some girls tonight, buddy? How about some pretty girls tonight?'

The Irish Channel

'THE CHANNEL WAS SORT OF EXCITING AT TIMES, but we never had no killings,' says Jennie Green McDonald, rather indignantly. 'It was just a real cosmopolitan neighborhood, except for a few Italians. And I ought to know! My grandfather, Patrick Green, come from Ireland in 1840 and he settled right in the Irish Channel. Sure, and what in the name of Heaven would he be doing settling any place else? To think I am the last Irisher left in the Irish Channel!'

And that is Mrs. McDonald's distinction. She and her family are actually the last of the Irish in that famous (or infamous; it is definitely a matter of opinion) neighborhood. This, of course, is splitting hairs a bit, and the statement will be denied with heat such as probably only the Irish are capable of generating. The fine point will certainly be argued and temperaments flare, if you make the statement in that section of New Orleans bounded by Magazine Street, the river, Jackson Avenue and Felicity Street. There will be those who agree and those who will not, and, even at this late date, Irish confetti may fly. Nevertheless, she speaks the truth, does Jennie Green McDonald.

The trouble is all in the difference of opinion as to where the

Irish Channel is — or was. The average Orleanian will probably testify to some such borders as those given above. He may even go farther and extend it uptown as far as Louisiana Avenue, some fifteen blocks. But even if conservative he will certainly include more than a hundred city squares. Actually the Irish Channel was only one smàll street, properly named Adele Street, that ran but two blocks, from St. Thomas to Tchoupitoulas Streets, and lay between Josephine and St. Andrew Streets. Today this Adele Street is inhabited almost entirely by Negroes, so that the Irish Channel no longer exists at all.

But not so long ago it was one of the most interesting parts of the city, with a way of life and a character contrasting violently with Creole New Orleans. As a matter of fact in its beginning it was not in New Orleans at all, but in what James Renshaw, in the *Louisiana Historical Review*, January, 1919, called 'the lost city of Lafayette.'

There are at least two beliefs as to how the Irish Channel earned its name. One story is that at Adele Street and the river, in front of Noud's Ocean Home, a saloon of some reputation, was a light, and that Irish seamen coming up the river and seeing the light exclaimed, 'There's the Irish Channel!' Another is that Adele Street was often flooded with water. Probably the truth is that it was simply because of the large proportion of Irish inhabitants.

The earliest records of Irish in New Orleans are in the archives at Seville, where the names of hundreds of Irish living in the city during the Spanish Domination were recorded. Even Don Alexander O'Reilly — 'The Bloody O'Reilly' — second Spanish governor of Louisiana — was an Irishman, though the Irish do not admit him, but blame him on his Spanish rearing and environment. An accurate estimate of how many Irish settled in the Colony prior to 1820 is impossible, since New World ports usually lumped Irish, Scotch and English immigrants together under the term 'English,' a habit the Irish must have resented! We do know that during the great migrations of 1846 and 1856, after the Irish famines left Erin with scarcely half of her population, one-third of the total number of persons entering America was from that country. Accurate records show that between 1850 and 1860 the Irish ranked first among Europeans entering the port of New Orleans.

Some of these departed the city quickly for such towns as Natchez and Bayou Sara, where Irish colonies grew in size and in importance. But many remained, often intermarrying with the Latin Orleanians; there is little doubt that much Irish blood flows in Creole veins. Yet, between 1840 and 1847 great social prejudice arose against the Irish in New Orleans, and a tendency was born among them to segregate themselves and settle in a group. Some measure of this prejudice existed all over the country during that era; they were accused of being radical, of sowing moral contagion, of bringing death plagues to the various communities, of abusing and ruining civil liberties, even of being unclean.

In the forties, just outside the closely packed city of New Orleans, there were a number of towns and villages, among them DeLord, Annunciation, Foucher and Lafayette. The last, by far the most important, was actually offering competition to New Orleans, and boasted of wharves lined with boats and a thriving commerce. Many of the Irish deserted the Creole town and found work in Lafayette. On the riverfront they wrested employment from the Negroes, and slave labor being unable to compete with the more skilled labor, the slaves were sold to plantations. For themselves, the Irish seem never to have had any use for slavery. They lived simply in small cottages and like the Germans made their own hard-working way. There was great dislike for the black man. As late as the period of the first World War it was dangerous for a Negro to walk anywhere near the Irish Channel, though this was partially because of the competition between them for work on the river. (In the end the black man won this fight; today nearly all wharf workers are Negroes.)

After the Irish settled there the city of Lafayette continued to grow and prosper. Cotton presses, slaughterhouses, brick kilns and other businesses arose. The adjoining towns of Annunciation and Livaudais were incorporated, later the Faubourg Dellassize was added. In 1844 the boundaries already stretched from Phillip Street to Felicity Road, from the river to Nyades Street (now St. Charles Avenue). The corporate life of Lafayette was but nineteen years. At last there was nothing to distinguish it from New Orleans but an imaginary line on Felicity Road. In 1852 the town was formally annexed.

But the city was less Creole now, was becoming increasingly Anglo-Saxon. The prejudice against the Irish had simmered down. Still the Irish kept to their own section. Adele Street and its vicinity were scrupulously avoided by all who did not live there. A stranger in the neighborhood was usually greeted with a shower of bricks. This inhospitable custom became so general that anyone displaying a black eye or a bandaged skull was asked if he 'had passed through the Channel lately.'

Even today practically every local prizefighter claims to have been reared in the Irish Channel. Oldtimers protest angrily: 'If they were born on Constance and Fourth Street, twenty blocks from Adele Street, and are half Dago and half Swedish, they still claim to be Irishmen from the Irish Channel. That's because Irish Channel and fight has always meant the same thing.'

Yet not all the residents of Adele Street were Irish, even in its heyday. There was a generous mixture of German families with such names as Weber and Mertzweiler and Sonnemeir. But they lived in peace with their neighbors and seem to have been Irish in sympathy and spirit, to have mingled with them as one race, and to have fought in Irish fights. And, of course, the Irish spread from Adele Street all throughout the section, partially explaining the confusion as to where and what was the Irish Channel.

Richard A. Braniff, interviewed just before his recent death, recalled there being 44 buildings in the Channel, consisting of 24 double and 9 single cottages of low structure; there were only 2 two-storied houses. There were also 5 grocery stores, 1 barroom, a rice mill, 2 cooper shops and an empty lot. Mike Noud, 'a tall and handsome Irishman,' and his wife, Mollie, ran the saloon, Ocean Home. St. Thomas Street, at one end of Adele Street, gradually became settled with Irish, too. Tchoupitoulas Street, at the other end, became the principal business thoroughfare during the 1870's, and was lined with establishments of all sorts: barrooms, oyster saloons, furniture stores, barber shops, lottery shops, tailors' establishments, pharmacies and wholesale houses, and shoe, dress, cigar, candy and confectionery shops.

Anthony Cullen still lives in the section and would reside nowhere else. 'This was the real business district of the city,' he said, speaking of the vicinity of Tchoupitoulas and North Diamond Streets. He pointed to the building of the Bartlett Chemical Company. 'That was the Diamond Hotel. You don't have to believe me, but it was the first hotel in the city. Next door (now the Dixie Mill) used to be the Jennie Lind Oyster Bar, and it was named for Jennie Lind because she used to come out here and eat oysters every day she spent in New Orleans. Feibleman's (New Orleans' Sears Roebuck's now) was right on Tchoupitoulas and St. Joseph. That's where they started out in business. Everything is changed completely now. It wasn't anything like this! You wouldn't recognize it as the same neighborhood. There were lots of fine homes, they're almost all gone and forgotten now.'

The *Daily Delta*, July 10, 1861, published a completely unvarnished opinion of the Irish Channel, stating: 'The inhabitants appear for the most part to be an intemperate and bloodthirsty set, who are never contented unless engaged in brawls, foreign or domestic — such as the breaking of a stranger's pate or the blacking of a loving spouse's eye. These are the ordinary amusements.'

This was naturally denied with his usual vigor by Channel champion Richard Braniff. 'The Irish Channel always bore a wonderful reputation because of the splendid class of people who lived there,' he said. 'There was only one Irish Channel and there will never be another.'

Jennie Green McDonald adds her bit with: 'Everything was very peaceable. A ship would come in loaded with German, Russian or English sailors, and the boys would come into the saloons and of course get into a fight. But our boys would bring 'em right home for a clean shirt and patch up where they'd been cut or hit too hard, and wash all the blood off and all. Everything was done real nice and quiet. Never no killings, just like I told you.'

'People get all mixed up when they talk about the Irish Channel,' said oldtimer Gus Laurer. 'It never did cover all the streets

The Rex Parade passing the St. Charles Hotel on Mardi Gras
Courtesy of New Orleans Item

Adele Street is the heart of the Irish Channel

"I'm Irish and proud of it," says Mrs. Louise Allen of St. Thomas Street. "We've always lived here."

"Many a good fight have I seen," declares Irish Michael Horn

Cover of a piece of sheet music of the Axeman's Jazz period

they say. A Channel links two bodies of water, doesn't it? Well, the Irish Channel is right here — that little Adele Street, running from Tchoupitoulas to St. Thomas. I remember when there wasn't nothing but Irish on it.

'Sure, and they had a reputation as fighters. Did you ever know as when an Irishman would not rather fight than eat? The gangs were the worst, especially the St. Mary's Market Gang, the Shot Tower Gang, and the Crowbar Gang. But it wasn't all fights and gangs. People in the Channel made good money then. Stevedores and longshoremen were well paid and they lived on the fat of the land. Now it's different. When they get a dollar they go run to start buying something on time. Every Monday morning the woodpeckers are out here. Knock-knock-knock! Knock-knock-knock! Everybody out here calls the collectors the woodpeckers. My God, but this neighborhood has changed! Especially with the new government housing slums. What in the name of the saints is going to happen when all those Irishers get cooped up together in those apartments? You talk about an Irish fight! Wait until they get started one day.'

Sitting on the stoop before his modest home, seventy-one-year-old Gus Laurer folded his hands over his cane and rested his chin on them, his eyes twinkling in the hot sun. 'We had more fun in the old days than the young people do now,' he contended. 'Then we had horse-cars — that was back in '78 or '88 — I don't recall which. We would ride down St. Charles Avenue to Canal and Baronne Streets — there was a turntable there — and then ride back up, all the way to Carrollton. There was one line out Magazine Street we called the "Snake Trail" because it turned so much. We had no moving pictures, but we went to the opera and the theatre. We danced at Delachies' Picnic Grounds, Hopper's Garden, and the Washington Artillery Hall. There were benches on the levees and we'd go walking out there with our girls, and on Sunday afternoons we'd sit and watch the boats passing up and down the river. We used to have big times at old Spanish Fort. We took a train to get there; the fare was fifteen cents. Sometimes we'd go out to Milneburg, too. Then we had to ride the old "Smoky Mary." Don't take my word for it, but some people say that was the second train in the United States.'

A Negress passed with two big market baskets, one on each arm, crying, 'Blackberries! BlackBERRIEEES!'

'Go on with you!' said Mr. Laurer. 'I don't want any nigger in a blanket today. That's what I call blackberries and cream. That looks just like niggers in a blanket, doesn't it?'

Asked about the Channel in other days, Mrs. Placement replied calmly that as far as she could recall all the inhabitants were 'lovely people.' She admitted that there 'were some fights, but nothing real serious, or if there was, we women didn't know it. We raised big families then, stayed home and did all our work and minded our own business. We hardly went nowhere except to wakes.'

Mrs. Placement mentioned that like the Creoles when an Irish Channel colleen was wed she remained unseen for several weeks. 'And when they was pregnant,' she said, 'they had some decency and did not boldly show their condition. They would wait until after dark to walk around. Now as soon as they find it out they holler loud enough to be heard two blocks: "Oh, Mrs. O'Brien, what do you think? I'm going to have a baby!" And the brazen things flounce downtown to shows and everywhere. Sometimes when I see 'em on the street I say to myself: "I will be surprised if they get home in time!"'

Michael Myers and Honnes Hahn are old cronies who spend their days in rocking chairs on the *banquette* before their homes on Rousseau Street near Adele. They sit and rock and talk of the 'auld times,' and when the sun reaches their spot they quietly shift to the shade of a house or a tree. They admit the neighborhood was tough.

The Crowbar Gang and the Pine Knot Gang operated right here in Rousseau Street, and they well remember both collections of brawling Irishmen. 'However,' said Michael, 'there was seldom a murder. But if strangers come around here, they would be asked: "What in the hell do you want?" If they did not answer quickly, they would have to be carried back to the other side of Magazine Street. The toughest spot was the corner of St. Mary and Religious Streets. There was three murders on that corner.'

Michael and Honnes both knew the Dallio boys well. They

were notorious petty criminals, who later went big time, robbed a bank and shot a guard to death. 'They lived right here at St. Thomas and St. Mary,' Honnes divulged. 'Their mother ran a saloon and people said she sold dope to school children.' One of the Dallio boys was killed by the police while trying to escape from a patrol wagon. The other was hanged.

The Bucket of Blood Saloon, on the corner of Rousseau and St. Mary, was a popular rendezvous for the more virile males of the Channel. Rat Tooth Flynn was one of the most violent customers, but Rat Tooth met his destiny swiftly. It seems that one of his pals, a certain Foley, robbed a store, and that the unscrupulous Rat Tooth nonchalantly broke the law of their particular jungle and 'stooled' on him. Thereupon Foley met Rat Tooth and chased him from the environs of the Bucket of Blood to Magazine Street, forced him to do a maypole dance around a telephone post, and 'blasted him to hell.' Shortly afterward Foley followed him from the gallows.

There are many little folk-tales regarding the gangs who gave the Channel a generous portion of its notoriety. One of the liveliest of these groups was the St. Mary's Market Gang. It is easily remembered when it was foolhardy to pass the St. Mary Market after dusk. Even the police dared not enter that vicinity at night. Some will assert there were no killings, but others disagree. One gray morning, from a hook where a beef carcass was usually suspended, hung a bulky canvas bag. Inside was the corpse of a sailor.

Jim Dolehan remembers that incident and others. 'The St. Mary's Market crowd was the only gang out here that ever got into serious trouble,' he said. 'There was the time they shot and killed Sergeant Fitzpatrick, the Negro policeman, who had his beat in that section. Of course the Irish resented having a Negro policing their neighborhood, but the Sergeant was a fine fellow and lots of people liked him. That was in August, 1892. You know, there was only one shot fired, and the man who fired it is still walking around free, though lots of innocent men were arrested. That was one mystery that was never solved.'

On August 9, 1892, the *Times Democrat* carried an article about the St. Mary Market and about another colored policeman assigned to the beat:

Officer Moore, a colored officer, during his term of duty on the St. Mary's Market beat has made things decidedly warm for the unruly hoodlums who hang around the market. One of the policemen remarked last night, 'This is a good place to put a man if he is wanted killed.' In order to give a proper conception of the locality of the shooting and the means of assassinating an officer it is but necessary to say that St. Mary's Market, in the western wing of which the shooting took place, is one of the most notorious hard beats in the city. The market is the rendezvous of crooks of the most daring characters who hang around the darkened recesses of the place and waylay pedestrians who have the temerity to pass that way. The market proper is without a light of any kind, save at the lower end where the rays of a couple of incandescent lights at the coffee stand afford poor illumination. The gang which infests the market has long been the cause of uneasiness to the people and has succeeded in giving the officers no end of trouble.

'The other gangs used to beat hell out of people walking in the Channel. They just resented outsiders. Sometimes they'd steal a little bit, but most of the time it was to give to the poor. There was the Ripsaw Gang operating on Erato and Constance, the Danites around the Magazine Market, the Mackerels at Calliope and Magazine, the Crowbar and the Shot Tower Gangs. Oh, plenty of 'em! The boys would jump on a train loaded with coal and throw pieces of it off; then they'd bring all that coal to the poor. Of course, they'd beat hell out of anybody walking in their territory, and sometimes the gangs would war on each other or with them downtown Sockserhausers.' This from Harry Nelson.

Gus Laurer believes that, despite all the gangs, conditions were better than now. 'You didn't have the real serious crime like now,' he said. 'It was all good clean fighting. We kept the niggers and other people who didn't belong out of the Channel and we made the bastards on the riverfront pay us good money.'

Even the women of the Channel seem to have indulged in a little roughhouse occasionally. 'A furious female named Mary O'Brien,' states a writeup in the *Daily Delta*, July 3, 1861 — 'one of the wild women of St. Thomas Street — was last night arrested for attacking and seriously wounding her neighbor, Ellen McGuire, with a hatchet, with a view to terminating her existence.' The *Delta* goes on to explain how it was all over a stalwart Channel youth, and that Mary went to jail for quite a spell.

Mrs. Curry, a quiet, middle-aged woman, has charge of the Public Bath on St. Mary Street. Not a native of the vicinity, but from a more placid neighborhood, she sees it all quite objectively. 'This has always been a rough section,' she said. 'It always will be. Even today there is plenty of drinking and fighting. I tried to rent a room upstairs over the baths, as I live here alone and would prefer to have someone in the house with me, but no one I would have will ever rent it. They're all afraid of the neighborhood.'

Richard Braniff explained how some of the gangs earned their names. The Shot Tower Gang was so-called, according to Braniff, because they always gathered near a 'shot tower' in the Channel — a place where lead shot was manufactured. The Crowbar Gang used crowbars to pry open windows and doors when necessary to do so. Most of the others possessed appellations that referred to the sections in which they lived.

But life was not all gangs and fightings.

By the time of incorporation with New Orleans, Lafayette had become a city of striking contrasts. The rear section around Chestnut, Prytania and Nyades Streets was filled with the residences of prosperous merchants and cotton speculators. There were brick sidewalks and formal gardens. This neighborhood is still known as the 'Garden District' throughout New Orleans. Even in the vicinity of Annunciation Square, close to the Channel, there were many fine homes, though the Square was a hangout for the gangs, who regularly smashed benches and committed other vandalism. Yet the owners of these mansions remained in the environment for years, driving forth in their carriages to the awe of the poorer Irish, submitting to the surreptitious peeping of Irish boys, who climbed fences and sneaked looks through windows, staring at the butlers and other servants — at a family like the Ryans, themselves of Erin, who maintained a staff of eight household servants and lived, in the eyes of the Channel inhabitants, an existence of absolute elegance — at the Bresslins, whose eighty-five-thousand-dollar home was furnished in all the magnificence of the era, including gilt and crystal chandeliers, huge family portraits in oils and antique furniture resplendent with gilt, in the tradition of the day.

Conditions were different immediately around the Channel. Few of the streets were anything but mud. Filthy water flowed through the gutters and there was little street lighting, practically no sewerage or drainage. All drinking water was obtained from cisterns. Butchers then slaughtered their own meat, and along the riverfront were numerous slaughterhouses — the cattle pens were at the foot of St. Mary Street — and the whole neighborhood reeked with a fearful stench. Every once in a while the cattle would escape the pens and stampede, invading yards and even the houses of the residents. James Renshaw in his article in the *Louisiana Historical Review*, already mentioned, tells how bulldogs were trained to take a grip on the head of stubborn cattle, forcing them into obedience. A Mrs. Hogan made pin money by always keeping a mule which she would rent to the city from time to time, to be used for the purpose of pulling dump carts. Occasionally, as it must to all, death came to the mule, and on these tragic instances neighborhood children would gather in Mrs. Hogan's backyard to 'ride' the dead mule and play at other games in which the cadaver might take part. Irish Channel children found much diversion, too, 'swimming' in the gutters after a heavy rain — or in riding street posts through the water-filled gutters — often such posts lay about awaiting erection.

Yet, despite all this, Henry C. Castellanous in his *New Orleans, As It Was*, speaks of the section as being 'pretty.' According to him, orange trees and gardens grew in many of the yards, and a low levee planted with willow trees ran along Tchoupitoulas Street. All cross streets in those days ran to the river's edge.

Money was plentiful. Irish longshoremen and stevedores were well paid. Screwmen — who 'screwed' or packed the cotton into the ship's hold — sometimes received as much as twenty-five dollars a day. The section abounded with saloons and gambling halls where the rivermen spent the money as quickly as they made it. Noud's Ocean Home, the Bucket of Blood and Bull's Head Saloon thrived and prospered. There was an entire group of gambling places near the St. Mary's Market. Every Sunday afternoon cockfights attracted crowds and the owners of the prize roosters could be seen strutting through the streets, as proudly as would the fowls they carried.

Quoits were played in open lots, the binders used to strengthen timbers being used as rings. Night watchmen paraded the streets at night with 'rattles' in an ineffectual effort to suppress crime. A major diversion was when the Sockserhausers journeyed uptown to some place like the Bull's Head Saloon to meet one of the Irish Channel gangs in a free-for-all. The fame of the Irish grew, particularly as fighters and drinkers, and it is said that the average Irishman washed down each of his five daily meals with whiskey.

But there were sturdy family men on Adele and the near-by streets. On Saturday nights and on Sunday afternoons groups and families would picnic at the Orange Grove Picnic Grounds located at Upperline and Laurel Streets, or at Shey's Backyard at Carrollton and St. Charles.

Families were large and housewives cooked plenty of wholesome — if coarse — food. Stews, cornbeef and cabbage, potato pancakes, red beans and rice were eaten during most of the week. On Sundays there would be a huge spread, usually including roast turkey or chicken. In those days the Irishwoman returning from market would be certain that the feet or the tail feathers of her fowl protruded from the bag she carried, so the neighbors would know she could afford turkey or chicken. Others displayed the corpse of the deceased bird in the window for the same reason. The very poor, not to be outdone, would frequently steal some feathers from a market or a neighbor's garbage pail and march down their street with the feathers showing from their package of groceries. In holiday seasons peddlers drove turkeys and geese through the streets, offering them for sale, with riotous noise and effect.

Harry Nelson remembered many of the Channel oddities. 'The real Channel — Adele Street — was inhabited by all respectable families,' he said. 'It was the riverfront saloons that gave it the bad name. There were so many of those places — Mike Noud's Ocean Home, the Bull's Head Tavern, the Isle of Man, Tom Barlow's place at Tchoupitoulas and St. Andrew. Then there was that social hall — the Hammerling — my father kept a store right next to it back in 1876. Kids had lots of good games and clean fun then. We swam in the gutters and in the river. Sometimes the cops chased us and I'd run all the way to Adele Street naked as the day I was born.

'Some people called Adele Street "Goat's Alley" and it was always filled with goats. Every family in the Channel had four or five goats.

'Talk about parades! The screwmen paraded every 25th of November and we really had a turnout. There'd be flags and banners strung all over the streets. The marchers wore long black coats like preachers, doeskin pants, high silk hats and blue aprons with silver fringe. And they always had on big "regalias" — them was sashes about a foot wide that went over the left shoulder and tied around the body, hanging almost to the ground on the right side. Every year the screwmen gave a big ball. Tickets were one dollar for gents, ladies by invitation. And you had to be somebody to get in! No hard characters allowed. The Irish gals were a week getting their hair "tilted up" and their clothes fixed. A man in full dress always met you at the door and he'd give the lady a hand-painted program with a silk tassel holding a little pencil. And they would stand for no fighting at them affairs. They'd throw you out on your behind.'

The Sunnyside Saloon on Tchoupitoulas Street was a favorite hangout for Irish Channel athletes. Amateurs would always be glad to fight for the benefit of any group who would collect a hundred dollars or more. Besides boxing and cockfights, the Irish loved dog fights, and champions were developed, some of which had names oldtimers can still remember. Richard Braniff told of a battle between two dogs. '"Tiger" was the champ,' he said. 'The challenger was called "Napoleon Jack." When the fight started Tiger was so slow it looked like Napoleon Jack was going to clean him up for a while. Then Tiger went over in the corner and got rid of some big chunks of meat, came back and whipped hell out of that other hound. Someone had fed the champion a big meal so he wouldn't be able to fight.'

Mr. Braniff also remembered that 'John L. Sullivan trained at the Carrollton Gardens and he used a bag of river sand for a punching bag. He could hit that thing to the ceiling and they didn't use gloves in those days. No women were allowed in prizefights, but I remember one time one dressed like a man and sneaked in. However, they caught her and threw her out.'

All Channel bars — as did most others — had free-lunch counters, and the Channel bars offered free smoking. There would be a huge jar of tobacco at each end of the bar, and when a customer wanted to smoke, the bartender would reach down and extract a clay pipe with a long stem and give it to him, inviting him to help himself to tobacco.

'Of course there was plenty of lottery,' said Mr. Braniff. 'There was Charles Howard's big drawing every month at the old Academy of Music, with a capital prize of seventy-five thousand dollars. When the women went marketing they always stopped and bought their lottery tickets. That ain't changed much!'

Girls, he said, were raised very strictly. 'If a girl ever got fooled by a boy it was too bad. She'd just have to go right down in the red-light district then and there. Nobody ever forgave her and as far as her family was concerned she was dead. But if a boy just got a little rakish with a girl and she'd go home and tell her old man, he or her brothers would beat hell out of him. Boys couldn't date girls at all like they do now. When I took a girl out once she was my girl, and if another boy asked to take her out he'd have to fight me and lick me first.'

Perhaps Irish wakes belong in the front row as far as entertainment was concerned. Corpses were often waked two or three nights, and practically the entire Channel attended each wake. There would always be food, whiskey and clay pipes for all.

All pictures and mirrors were covered as soon as a person died, and clocks were stopped. Mrs. Placement added that 'a pan of water with a loaf of bread in it was always put under the corpse to keep down the smell and camphor was kept freshened around.'

'Everything they say about Irish wakes is true,' vowed Harry

Nelson. 'There was plenty of drinking and smoking out of those long clay pipes with shag tobacco; and the only singing was when they got to crying, and it was almost like a tune, that famous Irish Cry! The widow would say: "Oh, Michael, why did you lave me? Oh-o-eee-oh!" That's the way it sounded. You see, it's easy for the Irish to cry. Their bladders is right in their throats. They'd put money on the corpse's eyes and some people would steal it when they knelt to pray by the coffin. If the dead person belonged to an organization they'd turn out and march.'

'They'd have a feast that night,' James McGooey remembered, not without nostalgia. 'People would come from all over the city, especially them German Sockserhausers from "way downtown." Everybody'd go on into the parlor and look at the corpse and say fine things, though some of 'em had never seen the man when he was alive. Then they'd go out in the backyard, get drunk and fill their bellies with food. One night we got wise to one gang from downtown what was always coming up to our wakes and we followed them down and beat hell out of 'em. It was a downright satisfaction, I tell you. Their leader was an Irishman in this case, you see, and they got by because he'd come in and cry and talk to the widow and pat her hand just like an old friend. That fight was a wonder! We was all beat to a whisper, but they was worse. They stopped pulling that wake racket from then on. Later when the Channel got soft I came to be friends with some of them. You'd be surprised if I told you who they was. One is the president of a big wholesale house, another is a big shot in a bank, several others are politicians, and one runs one of the best saloons in the business district. And there they was! I guess they was all fine lads, just after the free food and liquor. We always served the best whiskey in town at wakes in the Irish Channel, you see.'

Mrs. P. J. Donegan, who operates a funeral parlor on Jackson Avenue, remembers hearing the Irish Cry only twice. 'There was a death in the house next to us,' she said. 'I heard "Oh-o-eee-oh!" I thought it was a dog howling at first, then I realized it was the widow next door *keening* — giving the Irish Cry. The other time my husband was sitting out on the front steps and a woman who had just lost her husband came and sat next to him, and began her *keening*. Every once in a while she'd holler: "Oh, Georgie, why did you lave me? My Georgie! My Georgie! Why did you lave me?" Then she'd go: "Oh-o-ee-oh! Oh-o-ee-oh!" The only thing was her *keening* wasn't so good, because she was sort of drunk.

'I remember one time a man died and he was so swollen they had to put a big rock on his stomach as he lay in his coffin. They had quarters on his eyes, too. A friend came in, knelt by the coffin, weeping and howling, and when nobody was looking swiped the quarters off the dead man's eyes. Then he began to pray, and as he prayed that rock slid off the corpse's stomach and hit the side of the coffin. Bang! That praying Irishman let out a scream and ran out of the house. But he still had the quarters.'

One resident of the section said: 'When my father died it was a real Irish wake. We had tobacco and drinks and food for everybody. The neighbors stayed all night and the more they'd drink the louder they'd cry and yell, until it seemed like they was trying to see who could yell the loudest. Lots of strangers came just for the food and drinks. I recall my mother telling about one old woman who walked in. She came up to my mother and asked her, "Who's the bastard that's dead?" Mother was indignant, of course, and she said, "He isn't any bastard. He's my husband!" The old woman looked at her for a minute, then she said, quiet-like, "Well, I'm a sonofabitch!" '

As in other parts of the city, death notices were pinned or tacked to trees and fences in the Channel neighborhood. Hundreds of twigs of orange leaves were gathered and carefully sewed to a clean white sheet. This was spread over what was known as a 'cooling board' and the board was placed on two chairs or sawhorses, and here the body lay until it was placed in the coffin. Often it lay there until almost time for the funeral. The women of the family, assisted by friends and neighbors, gathered and prepared sandwiches and potato salad, baked cakes and cookies. The men dug deep and went out to buy quarts and quarts of good whiskey. Sometimes a bit of shamrock or a carefully hoarded piece of Irish earth was placed in the hands of the corpse.

If the house were very small — and they usually were — tables were set out in the backyard, these often being simply boards on sawhorses. Here the feast awaited the mourners when night came, with whiskey and sometimes kegs of beer open to all. The wake was no mournful affair. Jokes were told and songs of the old country sung. The males got into all sorts of mischief. If one fell asleep the others were likely to take off his pants and hide them, or to paint his face black with a burnt cork. Sometimes more extreme, or perhaps only more intoxicated, jokers would take the corpse off the 'cooling board,' stand it up in a corner and pour whiskey down its throat — to 'help the auld boy on his long journey.'

But at last, after the long wake, the hour of the funeral would approach. Word was spread from mouth to mouth and everyone gathered in the room with the deceased. Someone near the body would say, 'Jim was a good man!' At this, the widow always started to cry softly. Another would say something similar. Another. Soon the words became a kind of chant, passing from lips to lips, accompanied by the cries of the women, which grew in intensity and volume until some were almost screaming. Worked up to a frenzy, men and women would howl, until the house was filled with the eerie sounds. The wailing and weeping would continue until the priest arrived for the services.

There might or might not be a band in the cortège, depending on whether or not the deceased had belonged to certain organizations. If he had, the music played en route to the cemetery would be low and mournful. Returning from the cemetery, livelier numbers were in order — spritely Irish tunes or popular music of the day — 'Good-bye, My Honey, I'm Gone' and 'Won't You Come Home, Bill Bailey?' No one dared to return to his home immediately; to do so was to bring the 'dust of the grave into the house' — a certain harbinger of death.

The Channel Irish were, of course, very superstitious, though not a single individual among them would ever have admitted it. Sometimes the nails in the coffin lids were removed so 'the soul could rise without trouble on Judgment Day.' Often the feet of the corpse were left free and uncovered, probably for the same reason. It was an omen of death to dream of a letter edged in black. A sneeze at the table meant someone present would soon die. A bird flying into the house through an open window foretold the same tragedy, as did a white spot on the mirror; clothes that were burned were never patched, for that, too, would mean death. Watchers at wakes frequently carried a pinch of salt in their pockets, tasting it from time to time to ward off 'evil.' The candles of the dead were never blown out, but pinched out with the fingers.

Yet some of the best-known Irish superstitions seem to have been left in Erin. Evidently the *banshee* couldn't cross water. New Orleans Irish made no claims to hearing its cries.

There were many other superstitions. It was bad luck to leave a house by any exit but the one by which you entered, a belief still prevalent in New Orleans, people usually apologizing with 'Of course, I'm not superstitious, but...' The salt superstitions were numerous. Salt was never borrowed. To accept salt was to accept evil. Packages of salt were always left behind, as was the broom. (This, too, has survived; many educated Orleanians will not move a broom.) Salt thrown on the front steps the first Friday of each month brought good luck to the household. It was even bad luck to run out of salt.

Breaking a clothesline was very, very unfortunate; there was no telling what might happen. It was good luck to keep a goat — it is probably true, though, that the Channel folk kept theirs for practical, rather than superstitious, reasons. To have your hair cut on Friday invited tragedy. All you had to do always to have at least one piece of silver was to burn onion peelings. A sprig of verbena in your wallet or purse kept money there. The ninth bone from the tail of a black cat was highly valued and kept in the pocket for gambling luck. Sometimes butterfly wings were tied to the right leg for the same effect.

It was extremely unfortunate if you thoughtlessly held your shoes above your head. You would lose everything you possessed. The belief that to wash your feet and leave the water under the bed was bad luck may be traced back to Ireland, where it is thought the 'little people' will leave a house where there is such a flagrant display of laziness.

There were several wise women in the Channel, who seem to

have been combination seers and midwives in most cases. Then
there was a 'witch man' known as Buddy Lolliger who possessed the disagreeable ability to cause an automobile wreck
merely by wishing it would happen. There is evidence that the
women practiced a rather commonplace type of voodoo occasionally, with love charms, pins stuck in images, etc.

Like the Creoles, the Channel Irish tormented newlyweds with
charivaris, but here it was of a rowdy character surpassing anything of which the gentler Creoles had ever dreamed. Often it
degenerated into out-and-out blackmail. In 1849 the Mardi Gras
almost lost its existence. It had long been a custom to throw
flour at passers-by. Channel youths threw quick lime instead,
and bricks. One respectable lady was hit in the head and
knocked unconscious. Then the better elements of the city peti-
tioned the City Council to abolish the Carnival, though, of
course, this was not done.

Richard Braniff told of the wonderful fighters the Channel
produced. 'There were a great many men along the riverfront
and around the Irish Channel who were great fighters because of
their strength and splendid build,' he said. 'Joseph Powers,
Shorty McLaughlin, Bob Bitters, Bryan Connors, are only a few
of the names I recall at the present. Tom Daugherty, Tom Casey,
Paddy Erie and Freddie Krummel were all good men who earned
their reputations by actually fighting in the prize rings of our
city. Charley Cole, James Hill, James Noud (son of Mike Noud,
proprietor of the Ocean Home), Tom Harrison, Black Walsh and
Harry Nelson were all clever men. The Sunny South Athletic
Club, located on Tchoupitoulas near Josephine, was owned by
Billy Armshaw, better known as "Big" Armshaw. He was another fine and handsome young man, who conducted sparring
exhibitions every Saturday night. There was always a pair of
boxing gloves with a horseshoe in each glove, very handy to
accommodate any and all rowdy customers, who after getting a
few drinks under the belt could finally declare that they wanted
to fight anyone in the house. Of course such an individual would
be accommodated at once. Many a good white hope must have
been amongst the splendid set of men who worked along the
riverfront, because of the remarkable strength and beautiful

build of these young men, who were the pick of the nation.'

Mr. Braniff recalled other characters of the Channel's past. There was Skinner Norton, for instance, whose feet were always so swollen he never could wear shoes. He would walk through the neighborhood carrying a wharf plank twenty-four feet long, twelve inches wide and three inches thick on his shoulder, which he would sell for twenty-five cents to buy something to eat — or drink. There was 'Anti' O'Rourke, who, though a hard drinker, made his living diving into the river from the tops of the large steamboats plying the Mississippi. During the summer 'Anti' O'Rourke would attract thousands of persons, who would congregate along the riverfront to watch his 'sensational' dives from the *Natchez* or the *Robert E. Lee*. Of course, before performing, 'Anti' always took up a collection from the passengers on the boat. Mr. Braniff added, 'He learned many of the younger generation his famous Anti Dive, now known all over the country as the Jackknife Dive.'

Billy McCue is remembered because of his steadfast belief in the superstition that if you added a room to a house some member of the family would die. When Billy married his girl, Katie, he built her a four-room house. Billy and Katie had eight children, the neat little cottage became overcrowded, and Katie begged Billy, who had prospered with the years, to add a room or two. This Billy firmly refused to do, though he did not then explain his refusal. After many years, when five of the children were married, and the other three had entered the priesthood, Billy gave up his grocery business and he and Katie moved to the country. Only then did he tell her: 'My old Irish mother had a superstition about adding rooms to houses. I knew if I had done so we might have lost some of our fine lads and lassies.' It is reported that the new tenant of the house, possessing numerous offspring, added two rooms, and that five years later every member of the family except his wife and the youngest child was dead.

Sir Henry Morton Stanley, world famous explorer and finder of Doctor Livingston, spent some of his boyhood in the Channel neighborhood. Born John Rowlands, a British subject, he came to New Orleans at eighteen and was taken into the home of

Henry Hope Stanley. Later, in gratitude, he changed his name to that of his benefactor. It is thought he remained in the Stanley home — still standing at 904 Orange Street — for about two years, until joining the Confederate Army at the outbreak of the War Between the States.

John Culligan recalled Perfume Peggy, who died about 1938. Peggy gained fame early in life as the cause of much olfactory commotion. 'She couldn't fool a blind man when she walked into a room,' said Mr. Culligan. 'She even stunk on picnics. It was Hoyt's German Cologne she used. That was the most popular perfume in the Channel — just like all the girls used Tetlow's Face Powder.'

Peggy overdid her perfuming; it was generally agreed that she probably bathed in it. 'Whew!' breathed Mr. Culligan. 'What a smell!' Probably because of this, though one of the prettiest girls in the Channel, she didn't marry until she was fifty years of age. It is said her husband drank heavily and that this was the only reason he could tolerate his wife's fragrance. Then Peggy made him stop drinking, and soon thereafter he left her. But Peggy wouldn't give him up so easily. Everywhere he went she followed. Once when he had gone in a house to get another woman, she hid in the rear of his car, a monkey wrench in her fist. That time her perfume saved him a fractured skull. When he emerged, he smelled Peggy and he and his new girl friend made a hasty departure. Perfume Peggy had to be contented with smashing up the car as thoroughly as possible with the monkey-wrench.

In her latter years Peggy changed her brand. Given to attending lotto parties (occasionally she was thrown out at the insistence of patrons with sensitive nostrils), she came to believe it was Hoyt's that caused her to lose constantly. She found a brand she preferred — Jockey Club — and her luck changed immediately. For the balance of her life she used this Jockey Club, which, incidentally, was even stronger, according to Mr. Culligan.

When Peggy died her husband took charge of the body, had her buried from home instead of from a funeral parlor. Complying with her last request, he sprinkled the corpse with so much

Jockey Club that the scent filled the house and nobody could stay in the room very long the night of the wake. 'When Peggy was put into her tomb,' Mr. Culligan concluded — 'and I'm not lying — there was so much perfume on her that I could smell it after the vault was sealed. You couldn't smell the flowers at all for it.'

Simon Leopold, a Jew, is well remembered around the Irish Channel. Every day he stalked through the neighborhood, selling notions from the pack on his back. He extended credit generously, but each Saturday evening, when the men were home with their pay, Simon was there to collect. Then there was Rebentisch, who had a sign reading, 'Barber Shop. Cutting and Bleeding Shop. Leeches' before his establishment. A specialty was using leeches to cure black eyes, a not unusual disfigurement in the Channel. George Morrell remembered how Rebentisch extracted teeth. He would use a pair of pliers big enough to 'open a water plug, and once he caught hold of a tooth it meant certain dispossession.'

Mr. Morrell also recalled Braselman's Store, at the intersection of Magazine and St. Andrew Streets. 'That was the big shopping place for Irish Channel people. The women would go there to buy bolts of red flannel with which to make underwear with long sleeves and legs. Of course we always wore our shirt sleeves rolled up to show the red flannel underwear beneath. Everybody wore them then, especially the longshoremen and screwmen, who did such hard work they were always sweating and catching cold.'

Doctor John L. Jones was one of the most beloved persons in the Channel of some thirty or forty years ago. Doctor Jones drove through the section every day and almost every night, caring for sick Irish. Actually he was the physician employed by the Longshoremen and Screwmen Association, but the whole neighborhood idolized him. For Doctor Jones treated anyone who was sick, whether they had money or not, and when he prescribed medicine and the family had no money, he dug into his pockets and contributed that, too. Michael Myers and Honnes Hahn told this story concerning the big smallpox epidemic which struck the Channel:

'Tom Moran was the first to die,' they said. 'He lived on Rousseau and Josephine Streets, just a block from the Channel. The Board of Health wouldn't let people what had died of small-pox have a funeral, but buried them right away. Doctor Jones was across the street and he watched men carrying out Tom's coffin, coming down that narrow alley, liquid dripping out of the thing all the way — they soaked the body in some sort of disinfectant before they buried it, you see — and Doctor Jones saw 'em dump the coffin on a wagon, watched it creak away out of sight. He got to thinking and he knew there was five other Morans down with the disease, and that nobody would go near 'em. Without thinking anything of it at all, he crossed the street and walked right into that plague-ridden house and began nursing them people. And three out of the five got well!

'You see Doctor Jones was always experimenting. Some say that's what killed him. He was experimenting on himself up at Touro Infirmary, working with goats, trying to find a cure for tuberculosis. He kept snakes and he used their poisons for medi-cines. He had a salve called "Dr. Jones' Black Salve." People told a story about a fellow with a wooden leg who rubbed some on that leg and grew a new meat one.'

Many of the stories of Doctor Jones revolve about his forget-fulness. He would enter a house, leaving his horse and buggy outside, and boys in the neighborhood would steal the horse and buggy and go riding. Doctor Jones would come out, com-pletely forget the horse and buggy and walk home. But he was so beloved that the boys always returned his property as soon as the ride was over. He was always leaving his hat, his coat or his medicine bag some place and forgetting them. He never remem-bered to carry paper on which to write down his prescriptions. Once he wrote one on a door and the Irishman, whose wife he was treating, ripped the door off the hinges and carried it to the drugstore on his shoulder. Often he wrote them on his own cuff, tore off the cuff and presented it to the people of the house.

The Irish Channel remembers Mrs. Hickey, too. Like most of its inhabitants, Mrs. Hickey kept goats. She had four or five and they were such pets that they ate their meals at the table with Mrs. Hickey. One day the goat wagon — a vehicle designed for

the same purpose in regard to goats as the dog wagon for dogs —
picked up Mrs. Hickey's goats, whereupon the lady burst from
the house and gave chase. Catching up with the wagon, she
unlatched the door in the back, freeing not only her own goats,
but all the others. The next day Mrs. Hickey received a court
summons. Mrs. Hickey's devotion to her goats was paralleled
by another New Orleans woman. This one had a horse, which
she would ride through the streets from time to time. Her small
house possessed only a narrow alley and a tiny backyard, so the
horse was kept in the kitchen, where it slept before the wood
stove on cold winter nights.

Professor Clark used to delight the Channel Irish by donning
eight suits of clothes and diving into the river in the neighborhood of Adele Street. He would strip off one suit after another
and come up attired in a bathing suit. Sometimes he would have
himself tied in a bag, weighted with stones, and thrown into the
water. He would be down so long that all the women would
squeal with terror, but of course Professor Clark always emerged
unharmed.

Father Fagan is one of the best-known characters in the section
today. Almost all New Orleans Irish are Roman Catholic and
hold great esteem for their priests, but when the priest is as typical an Irishman as Father Fagan, himself born and reared near
the Channel, their reverence approaches adoration.

One of the Redemptorist Fathers at 2030 Constance Street,
Father Fagan takes great pleasure in 'bawling out' his parishioners from the pulpit. He'll boom at the late comers to Mass:
'What's the matter with you? Were you out too late last night
to get to church on time this morning?' A small, highstrung
Irishman, he never tires of singing the Channel's praises. His
bright eyes snapping behind his glasses, he said: 'I've lived all
my life in the Channel and it's the finest place in the country to
live! I was reared right here at St. Mary and Annunciation. We
had cows and pigs and goats. Oh, the Irish Channel people were
a pretty tough lot, but they were fine people. The screwmen and
the longshoremen used to make good money, but they never
saved any of it — God bless 'em. They drank, of course, and
there was a saying that they ate turkey on Sunday and pig tails
the rest of the week.'

Perhaps it is only on Saint Patrick's Day that Orleanians now realize how many Irish there are in a city supposed to be overwhelmingly Latin. There are still many Irish organizations and clubs, and the day is widely celebrated with parades, banquets, dances and Masses at Saint Patrick's Church. Each year a pretty Irish colleen heads the parade, and all the marchers wear derbies and as much green as possible.

On this day oldtimers who had lived their lives in the Channel neighborhood mourn the changes that have come about. The real Channel — Adele Street — is inhabited entirely by Negroes, except for Jennie Green McDonald and her family. Muddy and disreputable, the little street gives no hint of its past. At St. Thomas it comes to an end at the brand-new brick buildings of the recently constructed Federal Housing Project. The oldtimers hate these modern apartments, though the young people delight in the bathrooms and electric refrigerators, and despite prejudice against the invasion, among the tenants are such names as Kelly, O'Brien, Burke and O'Donnell.

But Jennie Green McDonald says she will remain in Adele Street. 'We own this property,' says she, 'and we'll stay here. We own the house next door, too, and real refined colored people rent it. I wouldn't want to live in them government slums. They look like a jail. But the young people like that newfangled stuff. I'll stay in the Irish Channel, even if it has become the Black Sea.'

Chapter 4

Axeman's Jazz

'NO, SIR!' DECLARED MAMIE SMITH EMPHATI-cally, her eyes huge and white in her fat black face. 'I sure don't go out much at this time of year. You takes a chance just walkin' on the streets. Them Needle Mens is everywhere. They always comes 'round in the fall, and they's 'round to about March. You see, them Needle Mens is medical students from the Charity Hospital tryin' to git your body to work on. That's 'cause stiffs is very scarce at this time of the year. But them mens ain't workin' on my body. No, sir! If they ever sticks their needles in your arm you is jest a plain goner. All they gotta do is jest brush by you, and there you is; you is been stuck. 'Course I believes it!'

Hundreds of New Orleans Negroes believe it. Fear of the Needle Men, which dates back to early days, could possibly be traced to voodooism. Then epileptics were thought to have had a spell cast upon them. Sometimes such an individual would die in the streets during an attack, and when this occurred Negroes were certain the Needle Men had been at work. Mamie believes in protecting herself from these corpse-hunting 'students.'

'Sure, I carries my gun,' she said. 'I always got it with me.

I don't fool around! Any of them Needle Mens come after me
they gonna be makin' stiffs of theirselves. Oh, yes, I goes to
church. I been on the board 'leven years now. I jest been
'pointed head of the toilet committee. My duties is to show the
new members where the toilet is at.'

Apparently Needle Men have actually appeared on several
occasions, though this is debatable. In 1924 there was a Needle
Men scare in the Carrollton section of the city. It was reported
that these 'fiends' slunk about the darkest streets, sprang from
behind trees or from vacant lots overgrown with weeds, jabbed
women with their needles and fled. Cruel skeptics insinuated
the 'victims' were suffering from a combination of imagination
and Prohibition gin, but indignant females, of all colors, swore
to the existence of these particular Needle Men.

On a Sunday night in February, when good citizens were returning from church, the police managed to arrest a pair of
Negroes, one armed with a twenty-six-inch bayonet. The man
with the bayonet protested he packed the weapon to protect
himself against the Needle Men, but the police were certain they
had their man. Both prowlers were tried in night court, sentenced to thirty days, and the Needle Men vanished from Carrollton.

Only a few years ago Needle Men appeared, according to
reports, and began stabbing young women while they were
seated in moving-picture theatres, rendering them partially unconscious and carrying them off into white slavery and a fate
'worse than death.' For months in New Orleans downtown
cinemas, women were screaming and fainting and crying out they
had been jabbed with a needle. But so far as can be ascertained,
the period offered no more disappearances than usual, nor is it
known that any New Orleans women strayed down the prim-
rose path via this particular route.

Similar to the Needle Men, at least in intent, are the Black
Bottle Men. The Black Bottle is reputed to be a potent dose
administered to the innocent and unknowing on entry to the
Charity Hospital. Instant death is certain to follow, the body
then to be rendered up to the students for carving.

The explanation for this is simple. Every person entering

Charity Hospital is given a dose of cascara upon admission. Pure cascara is nearly black and when magnesia is added, as is the custom, it becomes a deep brown, the change in color causing Negroes to fear it is a death-dealing drug.

Still another terror among the colored folk of New Orleans is the Gown Man.

'The Gown Man is tall and slim and wears a black cap and long black gown that reaches to the ground. He goes after the womens when they is alone, but he won't touch 'em if a mans is around. He has a long black automobile, I done seen it, parked down at the bottom of the levee. I really doesn't know what he's tryin' to do, but I does think he is after doin' us girls some harm. I'd be willin' to bet my haid that he wants somethin' from us girls and if he is a white mans I really doesn't think so much of him 'cause he ought to go chasin' his own kind.' So spoke Olivia Collins who lives at Camp Street near the levee of the Mississippi River. 'I knows one thing,' Olivia concluded firmly. 'He's a real mans, and not no ghost!'

Not all the women agree to that last assertion, however. There are many who are certain he is a 'ghost.' Around the neighborhood of the levee he usually appears driving his long and shiny car, but when he shows up in other sections he drops out of trees and sends the women fleeing and screaming for their lives and virtues.

A similar character haunted the city of Baton Rouge for several years during the early nineties. 'Hugging Molly' was a white-robed individual who would hide among the bushes along North Boulevard until some girl came along; then he would rush out and crush the terrified female in a passionate embrace. Disguised in a sheet, his intention was evidently to appear as a woman to the casual observer.

Soon the whole town was trembling for fear of meeting the dreadful creature, Negroes being particularly alarmed at the resemblance of his drapery to that worn by the — at that time — still well remembered **Ku Klux Klan**. In later years, when 'Hugging Molly' died, in a dingy room in a loft, there was found the paraphernalia he used for a disguise. Apparently a mentally unbalanced, but relatively harmless creature, he had committed no crimes other than his amorous squeezings.

The Mother Hubbard Man haunted the streets of Alexandria for several weeks during August, 1919. Clothed in a loose black robe, he was seen nightly by a number of people in the Negro section of the town known as the Sonio Oil Mill quarters. The Negroes were greatly frightened, but he committed no crimes, and vanished as abruptly as he had appeared.

About fifteen years ago the Domino Man appeared in the Gentilly section of New Orleans. In those days the suburb was sparsely inhabited and there were many empty lots with high weeds and trees. School children passing through thickly wooded lanes on the way to school began to be frightened by a creature wearing a white robe and hood, who had the agility of a monkey. He would drop from trees, chase little girls, gesticulating wildly, then vanish. He could leap from the ground into a tree and disappear. Men were known to have fired directly at him and feel confident they had hit him, only to have him reappear the next day, unharmed. Apparently his only desire was to frighten the children. All witnesses swore he never made an attempt to attack the children nor even to follow them very far. As soon as they screamed or ran, he vanished. As the children were always too frightened to be certain of his size, it was suggested he was not a man at all, but a monkey someone had dressed up as a practical joke. Others concluded that since most of the children were Catholics he was undoubtedly a member of the Ku Klux Klan.

Louisiana has had whole towns placed under 'spells.' For several decades the town of Columbia existed under a curse placed upon it by a hanged murderer. It began about 1890 when a white man killed a colored woman during an argument. The woman, a midwife and cook, was well liked in the town. Soon after his arrest an irate mob broke into the parish jail and lynched her slayer. It is said that before his death the murderer stated that each ten years thereafter Columbia would be burned to the ground. Another version has it that certain friends of the man made the threat.

Whichever it was, shortly afterward the entire town was reduced to ashes by flames. A decade later, in 1900, there was another fire which did considerable damage. In 1909 the entire business district burned. In 1919 fire razed four office buildings.

The *New Orleans States* of Saturday, March 7, 1914, carried the following headlines in large black type:

FIEND CLIPS SCHOOL GIRL'S HAIR

Two Other Young Women Meet Like Fate

Jack-the-Clipper had appeared on the scene to inspire horror among these proud possessors of what was known then as 'a wealth of woman's crowning glory.' The newspaper reported:

> Three New Orleans girls have fallen victim to Jack-the-Clipper, who was abroad Friday, snipping the plaited locks of young schoolgirls. Many other girls were said to have lost their hair, but are suppressing it because of the resultant unpleasant notoriety. Superintendent Reynolds has detailed special officers to watch for the miscreant, who has been operating mostly on street cars and in moving-picture theatres.
>
> It is not thought that any hair dealers are guilty, for the tresses were slashed but a few inches from the end, while the guilty parties had an opportunity of cutting off two or three feet of hair.

During the next few weeks there were a number more cases reported to the police, and the opinion grew that most young ladies suffered in silence rather than endure the 'resultant unpleasant notoriety.'

On March 13, 1914, the *New Orleans States* reported:

> Since stories have begun to appear in the papers regarding the unmentionable thief who has been cutting off hair, New Orleans girls have come to realize that they wear wealth on their heads. Not only that, but they are taking great pains to guard it.
>
> A chattering group of school girls boarded a car Thursday at the corner of the Sophie B. Wright High School. Thick braids of black, brown and golden hair hung down their backs. As soon as they had found seats, giggling stopped long enough for them to reach round with the trained precision of a comic opera chorus and bring their braids to the front and tuck them carefully in the front of their coats.

One whose hair wasn't long enough to reach worked with her refractory curls until she had them all safely tucked from sight in the crown of her hat.

Jack-the-Clipper vanished as abruptly as he had appeared, apparently having satisfied his fetichism.

During the period from 1921 to 1923 there were recurrent epidemics. These were the years when bobbed hair was coming into fashion, when the value of the crowning glory was rapidly diminishing, and to bob or not to bob was the profoundest of questions. This new 'fiend' invaded the sanctity of feminine boudoirs and hacked the tresses into rough-edged bobs. Perhaps it is significant that these 'victims' were all young women imbued with a passion to adopt the mode, but who had been forbidden to do so by old-fashioned parents or husbands.

But it was in May, 1918, when the greatest reign of terror New Orleans had ever known began. This time a very genuine fear settled over the city. For the next year and a half Orleanians were to awaken nights at the slightest noise and strain their ears for any sound that might resemble that of a chisel scraping against a door panel, and to open their morning papers with trembling hands. The Axeman had appeared in the city, ruthlessly hacking and slaughtering his victims while they slept peacefully in their beds. He provided little humor.

There were many who contended that the Axeman was not a man at all, but a supernatural being, a diabolical fiend and agent of the Devil. There are some who still contend that he was. There is little chance now that anyone will ever know.

On a Thursday morning, May 23, 1918, Joseph Maggio, an Italian grocer, and his wife were butchered with an axe while they slept in their apartment behind the Maggio grocery. Police discovered a panel in a rear door had been chiseled out, providing entrance for the murderer. The axe, smeared thickly with the Maggios' blood, was discovered under the house. Nothing in the rooms had been stolen. Valuable jewelry reposed atop a dresser; money was found under blood-soaked pillows on which the Maggios had slept, in drawers, even on the floor beside the bed.

Detectives went to work frantically. Several suspects were arrested, but had to be released for lack of evidence. One curious clue, its meaning as much a mystery today as then, was the following chalk mark on the *banquette* near the victims' home:

Mrs. Joseph Maggio will sit up tonight. Just write Mrs. Toney.

Police, digging into records, discovered several cases in the past bearing amazing similarities to the Maggio tragedy. In 1911 there had been three actual murders and a number of attacks on Italian grocers and their families. In all the cases an axe had been used and entry to the homes had been achieved through removal of a door panel. None of the crimes had ever been solved.

The Maggio crime aroused Little Italy and terror spread that another outbreak of Mafia or Black Hand crimes, such as the first series of axe murders was believed to have been, might follow.

Almost exactly a month after the Maggio case came the second crime. Louis Bessumer, a grocer residing behind his store, and his common-law wife, Mrs. Annie Harriet Lowe, were discovered by neighbors one morning lying in their own blood in one of the rooms. Beside them, like a macabre signature, reposed an axe. A panel of the kitchen door was gone. A chisel lay on the rear steps. Nothing had been stolen.

Regaining consciousness in Charity Hospital, Mrs. Lowe first described the intruder as large, young and very dark. Weeks later, dying, she accused Bessumer of the attack, and the grocer, recovered, was tried for Mrs. Lowe's murder. This was a war year, Bessumer was a German. Rumor spread that he was an enemy agent and, as is common at such times, prejudice against his nationality caused much bitter feeling. However, it could never be ascertained how he could have butchered Mrs. Lowe, then fractured his own skull, so he was released. Neither was there any real evidence of subversive activities.

Early in August Mrs. Edward Schneider, alone in her home in Elmira Street, awakened to see a dark, phantom-like form towering over her bed. She shrieked as the axe fell. Neighbors discovered her unconscious, her head cut and bloody, several teeth knocked out. She recovered.

A few nights later, Joseph Romano, Italian grocer at Tonti and Gravier Streets, fell under the axe. His niece, Pauline Bruno, occupying the next room, gave an account of the attack.

'I've been nervous about the Axeman for weeks,' she told a reporter of the *Item*, August 10, 1918, 'and haven't been sleeping much. I was dozing when I heard the blows and the scuffle in Uncle Joe's room. I sat up in bed. There, at the foot of my bed, was this big heavy set man. I think he was white, but I couldn't swear to it. It was just a quick impression. I screamed. My little sister, asleep beside me, sat up and screamed, too. We were horribly scared. Then he ran. He was awfully light on his feet. It was almost as if he wore wings.

'We rushed into my uncle's room. He was stretched out on the bed with two big cuts in the back of his head. We got him up and propped him in a chair in the front room. "I've been hit," he groaned. "I don't know who did it. Call the Charity Hospital." Then he fainted. Later he was able to walk to the ambulance with some help. I don't know that he had any enemies.'

Romano died a few hours later, without being able to give any clue as to the identity of his assailant.

Now literal hysteria swept through many quarters of New Orleans. In Italian families, members divided into regular watches and stood guard over their sleeping kin, armed with loaded shotguns. Little Italy, believing itself in most danger of attack, waited nervously. Who would be next?

Opening his saloon the morning of August 11, Al Durand found an axe and a chisel outside the door, which, evidently, had been too thick for the intruder.

The Axeman was, according to witnesses, actually seen in the neighborhood of Tulane and Broad, masquerading as a woman. Citizens organized into bands and launched a man hunt, without success.

On August 21 a man was seen leaping a back fence at Rocheblave and Cleveland Streets. The locality was in an uproar for hours.

On August 12, the *States* reported:

Armed men are keeping watch over their sleeping families while the police are seeking to solve the mystery of the axe attacks. Five victims have fallen under the dreadful blows of this weapon within the last few months. Extra police are being put to work daily.

At least four persons saw the Axeman this morning in the neighborhood of Iberville and Rendon. He was in front of an Italian grocery. Twice he fled when citizens armed themselves and gave chase. There was something, agreed all, in the prowler's hand. Was it an axe? Superintendent Mooney is asking for the cooperation of all Orleanians in every effort to capture this fiend.

Little Italy divided its time between guarding the kitchen doors and kneeling at the family altars. Saint Joseph was receiving more than his usual share of donations. The police whirled like dervishes.

Joseph Dantonio, retired Italian detective, gave the following interview:

'The Axeman,' Detective Dantonio pontificated, according to the *States*, August 18, 'is a modern "Dr. Jekyll and Mr. Hyde." A criminal of this type may be a respectable, law-abiding citizen when his normal self. Compelled by an impulse to kill, he must obey this urge. Some years ago there were a number of similar cases, all bearing such strong resemblance to the present outbreak that the same fiend may be responsible. Like Jack-the-Ripper, this sadist may go on with his periodic outbreaks until his death. For months, even for years, he may be perfectly normal, then go on another rampage. It is a mistake to blame the Mafia. Several of the victims have been other than Italians, and the Mafia never attacks women.'

In the last part of August the rear door of Paul Lobella's grocery and residence at 7420 Zimple Street, was chiseled through. No one was home at the time. The same day another grocer, Joseph Le Boeuf, whose store was only a few blocks from the Romano home, reported an attempt to chisel through a panel in one of his rear doors. Aroused, he had frightened the intruder away. An axe, apparently hastily dropped, lay on his back steps. The next day an axe was found in the yard of A. Recknagle, grocer, at 2428 Cleveland Street. There were the scars of a chisel on a back door. All this had its compensations, however. The grocers were receiving free advertisements in the newspapers.

On September 15, Paul Durel, grocer at 2239 North Robertson Street, discovered an attempt had been made to chisel through his door. A case of tomatoes resting against the panel had foiled the Axeman. During this period a number of burglaries were committed also, the robbers sometimes entering through a door panel, thus aping the methods of the Axeman.

Then, as suddenly as he had appeared, the Axeman vanished. Orleanians, citizens and police, gradually learned the art of breathing freely again, as week followed week, month followed month, and door panels remained intact.

But on March 10, 1919, at three o'clock in the morning, Mrs. Charles Cortimiglia, wife of a grocer in Gretna, just across the Mississippi River from New Orleans, awakened to see her husband struggling with a large man in dark clothes, who was armed with an axe. As Cortimiglia fell to the floor, his head a gory mass of blood, his wife clasped her two-year-old daughter Mary in her arms and begged the intruder for mercy, at least for the child. But the axe fell relentlessly. Mary was killed, her mother received a fractured skull.

Regaining consciousness in Charity Hospital several days later, Mrs. Cortimiglia accused a seventeen-year-old neighbor, and his father, of the attack. It was several weeks before Cortimiglia was able to give a statement. Then he contradicted his wife's assertion, saying it was not the accused persons, but a 'dark, unknown man.'

Police, discovering the Cortimiglias and their neighbors had been on bad terms, arrested the young man and his father and charged them formally with the murder of little Mary Cortimiglia. Despite his youth, the son was over six feet tall and weighed more than two hundred pounds. Detectives on the case admitted it was impossible that such a large person could have entered through the small opening made by removing a panel. One odd theory advanced at this time was that the axe murderer might be a woman — or a midget! Despite the fact that all recovered victims had described their assailant as large, how could a big man crawl through such little space? All doors had been locked, the keys removed; it would have thus been impossible for the intruder to have unlocked a door by inserting his hand. And the doors were still locked when the attacks were discovered.

Following the Cortimiglia murder, New Orleans and vicinity was again aroused. The *States*, March 11, summed it up as follows:

Who is the Axeman; and what are his motives?

Is the fiend who butchered the Cortimiglias in Gretna Sunday the same man who committed the Maggio, Bessumer and Romano crimes? Is he the same who has made all the attempts on other families?

If so, is he madman, robber, vendetta agent, sadist or some supernatural spirit of evil?

If a madman, why so cunning and careful in the execution of his crimes? If a robber, why the wanton shedding of blood and the fact that money and valuables have often been left in full view? If a vendetta agent of the Mafia, why include among victims persons of nationalities other than Italian?

The possibilities in searching for the motives in this extraordinary series of axe butcheries are unlimited. The records show no details of importance which vary. There is always the door panel as a means of entrance, always the axe, always the frightful effusion of blood. In these three essentials the work of the Axeman is practically identical.

In the same article Superintendent Mooney said: 'I am sure that all the crimes were committed by the same man, probably a bloodthirsty maniac, filled with a passion for human slaughter.'

Then, on Friday, March 14, 1919, another newspaper received a letter from a person who declared he was the Axeman. The letter read as follows:

Hell, March 13, 1919

Editor of the Times-Picayune
New Orleans, La.

Esteemed Mortal:
They have never caught me and they never will. They have

never seen me, for I am invisible, even as the ether that surrounds your earth. I am not a human being, but a spirit and a fell demon from the hottest hell. I am what you Orleanians and your foolish police call the Axeman.

When I see fit, I shall come again and claim other victims. I alone know whom they shall be. I shall leave no clue except my bloody axe, besmeared with the blood and brains of he whom I have sent below to keep me company.

If you wish you may tell the police to be careful not to rile me. Of course, I am a reasonable spirit. I take no offense at the way they have conducted their investigations in the past. In fact, they have been so utterly stupid as to amuse not only me, but His Satanic Majesty, Francis Josef, etc. But tell them to beware. Let them not try to discover what I am, for it were better that they were never born than to incur the wrath of the Axeman. I don't think there is any need of such a warning, for I feel sure the police will always dodge me, as they have in the past. They are wise and know how to keep away from all harm.

Undoubtedly, you Orleanians think of me as a most horrible murderer, which I am, but I could be much worse if I wanted to. If I wished, I could pay a visit to your city every night. At will I could slay thousands of your best citizens, for I am in close relationship with the Angel of Death.

Now, to be exact, at 12:15 (earthly time) on next Tuesday night, I am going to pass over New Orleans. In my infinite mercy, I am going to make a little proposition to you people. Here it is:

I am very fond of jazz music, and I swear by all the devils in the nether regions that every person shall be spared in whose home a jazz band is in full swing at the time I have just mentioned. If everyone has a jazz band going, well, then, so much the better for you people. One thing is certain and that is that some of those people who do not jazz it on Tuesday night (if there be any) will get the axe.

Well, as I am cold and crave the warmth of my native Tartarus, and as it is about time that I leave your earthly home, I will cease my discourse. Hoping that thou wilt publish this, that it may go well with thee, I have been, am and will be the worst spirit that ever existed either in fact or realm of fancy.

THE AXEMAN

Orleanians did their best that Tuesday night — a Saint Joseph's Night — to satisfy the Axeman's passion for jazz and to purchase immunity with music.

In fact, the Axeman was invited to be a guest at one party. Oscar Williams, William Schulze, Russell Simpson and A. M. La Fleur inserted an advertisement in the newspapers Tuesday morning, inviting the murderer to a stag affair at 552 Lowerline Street that evening. Minute instructions were given as to his means of entry. He was requested not to mar any doors, but to utilize a bathroom window, and was assured no doors would be locked in the house. His hosts deplored the fact that there would be no jazz music at the party, but only a suitable rendering of 'Nearer, My God, to Thee.' He was promised every consideration as a guest and at least four scalps. 'There is a sincere cordiality about this invitation,' stated the hosts, in the *Times-Picayune*, March 19, 1919, 'that not even an Axeman can fail to recognize.'

Cafés all over town were jammed. Friends and neighbors gathered in homes to 'jazz it up.' Midnight found the city alive with the 'canned music' of the period — inner-player pianos and phonographs. In the levee and Negro districts banjos, guitars and mandolins strummed the jazziest kind of jazz. Joseph Davilla, well-known New Orleans composer of popular music, wrote the theme song for the night. Mr. Davilla titled his composition 'The Mysterious Axeman's Jazz' or 'Don't Scare Me, Papa.' Not a single attack occurred that night. Evidently the Axeman failed in his promise to 'pass' over the city, or else he was well satisfied with the celebration in his honor.

The night of August 3, 1919, Miss Sarah Laumann, a girl of nineteen, was attacked with an axe while she slept in her home. Though she received a brain concussion she recovered. But this raised the terror to new heights. Miss Laumann was not the proprietor of a grocery; she was not Italian; her assailant had not entered by a door panel, but had used a window. The Axeman was no longer confining his victims to one type, nor using one means of entry. This seemed to enlarge the list of prospective victims.

Then he vanished, apparently taking another vacation. During the following few months, though police relaxed their vigilance not an iota, there were no indications of his operations anywhere in the city.

It was October when he reappeared for his final slaughter. Mike Pepitone, a grocer, was butchered in his bed on the twenty-seventh of that month. His wife and six children, asleep in an adjoining room, were unmolested. A picture of the Virgin Mary, hanging above Pepitone's bed, was splattered with his blood.

Then, at last, after eighteen months of his dreaded visitations, the Axeman vanished from New Orleans forever. Though families still kept watch and the police continued feverish and frantic endeavors to locate some clue to the identity of the murderer, nothing else happened. The nights passed as peacefully as if he had never stalked the dark streets, seeking a back door for his chisel, a sacrifice for his axe.

There were aftermaths. The Gretna youth, already sentenced to be hanged for the murder of the Cortimiglia child, and his father, sentenced to life imprisonment as an accessory, were freed on December 6, 1920, a full pardon being granted. Mrs. Cortimiglia had suddenly and mysteriously refuted all her testimony against the two men, confessing at this late date that she had never seen her assailant clearly. She told Jefferson Parish authorities that Saint Joseph, patron saint of all Italians, had appeared to her in a dream and instructed her to tell the truth and to beg her neighbors' forgiveness. So that Monday morning the two Gretna men walked out of the little town jail into a driving rain, free citizens.

But, far away on the Pacific Coast, more than a year after the Axeman's exit, a former Orleanian, Joseph Mumfre, fell dead in a street of the bullets fired from a revolver in the hands of a woman. The woman, identified as Mrs. Esther Albano, was later discovered to be the widow of Mike Pepitone, last of the Axeman's victims.

Immediately police tried once more to untangle the web that probably linked all the cases. Some decided that Mumfre had been the long sought Axeman. He was known to have been at one time the leader of a band of blackmailers who had preyed relentlessly on Italians in New Orleans. Curious coincidences were revealed. Mumfre had been sent to prison just after the first axe murder in 1911. In the summer of 1918 he was paroled, just at the time the Axeman had reappeared. Immediately after the Pepitone killing Mumfre had left for the Coast, and the Axeman had again vanished. However, there was no evidence of his connection with the ghastly crimes.

Some people still contend that the Axeman was not a man at all, but, as the letter in the newspaper stated, 'a fell demon from the hottest hell . . . the worst spirit that ever existed either in fact or in the realm of fancy.'

Twenty years after the Axeman's visit, another demon arrived in Louisiana. This was a far less harmful spirit, however, though many believed he was the Devil himself. In September of 1938 there appeared in Algiers, on the other side of the Mississippi from New Orleans, a mysterious stranger who rode on the air, wrecked bars and homes and insulted women. He is described as having had long black horns, bright pink ears shaped like sunflowers and eyes like a chicken. He could make himself disappear or change into a baboon right before your eyes. And he announced he was the 'Devil Man.'

The Devil Man never killed anybody permanently, but he caused a lot of temporary deaths from fright. One night a man and his wife were coming home from a dance in their automobile and were stopped by a man who asked for a ride. The woman did not like his looks, so he was refused. Ten miles later they met the same man again, and the couple became nervous and threw their liquor out of the car. Ten miles later the same man stopped them once more. But this time he didn't bother to ask for a ride. He performed in a much more picturesque fashion. He just changed himself into a devil, right before their eyes, casually. Of course, the woman fainted. Somehow the man managed to keep the car going down the road. A few miles farther the Devil Man made a fourth appearance, this time riding a brown horse. The Ford won the race.

The couple told the neighbors about their experience and the neighbors told the police, causing the latter to begin an extensive search for this remarkable individual. There are stories of the police meeting him, firing their pistols, and having the bullets returned to them by way of hairy hands.

Soon the Devil Man was insulting Negro women in the streets, and some of them didn't like it very much. There were so many different stories of meeting the Devil Man that Sergeant Holm of the Algiers police ordered everyone arrested who so much as said they had seen him. But the only actual arrest made was of a wild-eyed, dark brown fellow who said his name was Clark Carleton, that he came from the hills of Arkansas and had been sent to this 'latitude' by the great spiritual monarch, King Zulu. This monarch, said Clark, was not to be confused with the King Zulu of New Orleans' Mardi Gras, being the 'great benefactor and advisor to Neptune, who comes only to those who speak his language.' And Clark said he spoke his language very fluently. However, he said he wasn't really the Devil. He was greater than the Devil!

George Horil, white proprietor of the Paradise Inn, tried to prevent the police from arresting Clark and substantiated some of the stranger's statements. But his influence failed. What could the police of any civilized country do with a man who claimed to be greater than the Devil?

Horil told another version as to how the Devil Man story began.

'That Negro came into my place about a month ago,' Horil said. 'He told me he was hungry, and said, "I'm from the hills of Arkansas. My ears look like they are waiting for to hear the up yonder spirits and my eyes look like they are looking for the moon. Even the Devil would feed me." I could see the man was hungry, so I gave him a piece of pie, some milk and a sandwich. I'll admit he did look funny. Well, long about that time some school children came along and started laughing at the man, who was standing in front of my place, now. They kidded him so much that he became angry, and he said, "If y'all don't let me alone, I'm goin' to put the Devil on you." Then the kids started yelling. "Devil Man! Devil Man!" They drew such a crowd that the man got scared and ran off.

'Then the story got around that he disappeared into the graveyard opposite my place. Some of the beer parlors began saying the Devil Man had been to their joints, bought whiskey and disappeared. They said he would come back, and crowds of people would hang around these places in hopes of seeing him, some of them carrying guns and rifles. Of course most of them would buy drinks and plenty of them. One fellow said, "If the Devil Man takes me to Hell I want to be good and drunk."

'One of the places put a sign outside, saying the Devil Man was doing all his drinking in his bar. And the people went for it. They packed the place.'

Louis Kohlman, proprietor of Kohlman's Bar, said his business had doubled itself. The owner of Karper's beer parlor stated: 'The Devil Man nearly ruined my business. The people wouldn't come out at night, especially when they heard this Devil Man had poured whiskey down a woman's back in my place.' The desk sergeant at the Algiers police station said cynically, 'There isn't any Devil Man, not even the man we have arrested. He's just trying to make some money.'

But while the body of the captured Devil Man languished behind prison bars, his spirit apparently stalked the streets of New Orleans. On the night of September 13, 1938, there were more than two hundred calls at police headquarters regarding peculiarly Satanic activities. It was reported that the Devil Man was entering bars and frightening bartenders into giving him free drinks simply by removing his hat and letting them view his horns. One call offered the information that the Devil Man was in the Big Apple, a popular Negro rendezvous in South Rampart Street, doing the Big Apple. There were evidently several Devil Men at work.

However, the one in the prison cell announced, with no little pride:

'My name is Clark Carleton, and I am the Devil Man — but greater than the Devil. I came from the hills of Arkansas on September 6, 1938. I walked under the stars and Neptune guided me through the darkness of the night. I reached Port Allen, Louisiana, and from there I rode the ferry into Baton Rouge; then I came to New Orleans, still under the guidance of Neptune and possibly one of his assistant stars. I stopped at the Page Hotel. I came to New Orleans as the sun came down in the skies.

'Yes, they got me in jail, but it's my spirit that is haunting the people, because I have not been treated right by the police.

That's why I'm going to keep on troubling them. If I wanted to, I could get out of sight right now — I could disappear away from all of you.' At this point a policeman offered the information that Clark had 'disappeared' one day, breaking jail, and had been recaptured.

'You want to know how I got my powers? Well, Neptune came to me in the form of a fishhook in June and May of 1937. I was reading my Bible at the time. Oh, yes, I'm a Baptist man, but I believe in the Divine, too. Neptune told me to walk straight ahead, that I would find a two-headed man stranded on a rock. I found him but he disappeared. Then I knew I had the power.

'I went to fourth grade in school. I ain't no amnesia victim, but I don't remember anything about my people or anything else about myself. Tonight I'm going to divide myself with Neptune and maybe when you come back I will be able to tell you more. But, please tell everybody that I'm not going to hurt anyone, my spirit is just passing around New Orleans and Algiers like a bird because I have been mistreated by the police.'

On September 24 somebody shouted 'Devil Man' in the basement of the Craig Negro Public School. A near riot was the result. Little colored boys and girls ran screaming for homes and mothers. Teachers barred all doors to lock themselves in. Anxious parents ran to the school for reassurance.

Opinions regarding the Devil Man varied greatly. In one respect, however, most colored citizens agreed. As staunchly religious Sister Susie Mack phrased it, 'Ain't nobody got no business messin' around with no man what professes to be the Devil!'

Evidently this Devil Man did at last go too far. The last heard of him was when a 'devil baby' with 'horns 'n all' was reported born in one of the Negro sections of New Orleans. 'The Devil sure got us now!' was the mournful conclusion whispered from door to door.

But Louisiana can take it. As Brother Peter Williams, ebon pillar of Mother Keller's church, said with immortal wisdom and magnificent tolerance:

'It is our policy to give every man a hearing, be he devil or baboon.'

Chapter 5

Saint Joseph's Day

'I HAVE THREE ORPHANS AT MY ALTAR' — MRS.
Messina sat heavily in a chair, her knees spread wide apart, and
mopped at her flushed face with a damp ball of a handkerchief.
From her perspiring state and the tantalizing aroma drifting
from the rear of the house it was simple to deduce she had just
finished preparing the food for the altar at the opposite end of
the room. Steam still curled upward from a white bowl of dark
green artichokes. 'One of my kids is only half of an orphan,' she
explained. 'His pa's still living, but he don't have no steady
work, so he's worse off than a whole orphan!'

Mrs. Messina waved a thick red hand in the air, slapped a fat
knee resoundingly. 'You like my altar, eh? I have five hundred
different kinds of food. Besides the three sorts of Saint Joseph's
bread, I have stuffed artichokes, stuffed crabs, stuffed peppers,
stuffed celery, stuffed eggs and stuffed tomatoes. I have lobsters,
red snapper fish, shrimps, crayfish, spaghettis, macaronis, spin-
ach, peanuts, layer cakes, pies, pineapples...' Mrs. Messina
took a breath. 'My God! I have everything! This is the fifth
year I make an altar. Five years ago my little girl she get sick
and when she get well she can't talk. My baby is deaf and dumb.

I almost go crazy. She is my life! My God, I lose my mind!'

Mrs. Messina blew her nose. 'We had a little market then, and one day an old lady come in begging for her Saint Joseph's altar. I give her a dollar and I told her if she's come back I'd give her a basket of fruit. I tell you the truth. I will always be glad that old woman come to see me — I was so crazy. My baby was too little to understand why she can't talk. When I take her out she tear off my hat and pull at my clothes to show me something. She stomp her feet and her face get so red she almost bust. All the time I come home a wreck.

'Well, like two, three days before Saint Joseph's Day that old lady come running into my place all excited like, and she say: "Mrs. Messina, I had a vision. I seen Saint Joseph with my own two eyes. He say I must go get that little girl who can't talk and make her the Virgin at my altar."

'I tell you my kid looked beautiful! I dressed her up all in white with a wreath in her hair. And right after that year I started my altars, because next day Saint Joseph come to me. He say, "Mrs. Messina, why don't you have an altar for me, yourself?" I say, "Saint Joseph, please give my kid back her speech, or you take her yourself." See how crazy I was? But right away then she starts to get better. But, my God, what I go through for that kid! Without Saint Joseph I couldn't stand it. This might be my last altar. I got to think about it. If I make another vow, then I'll have to keep on making 'em.'

Mrs. Messina's altar was a large one. A big statue of Saint Joseph dominated a central group of plaster saints who wore gaudily painted robes of red, blue and gold. There were paper flowers of pink and blue, scarlet and orange, and vases and bowls filled with real Easter lilies, carnations and roses. Trailing bridal wreath wound about the top, from which were suspended silver bells and ornaments obviously borrowed from last year's Christmas Tree. Three tiers and a long table held platters of food of every kind and description. Tall lighted candles flickered toward the ceiling, for it was nearly time for the noon hour 'Feast of the Saints.'

When the priest arrived, five people took seats at a small table. In the place of honor facing the altar was an elderly man in a loose brown robe, wearing a pasteboard crown and carrying a long stick with a snowy lily attached to the end of it. He, it was whispered, was the good Saint Joseph himself. And the girl opposite him, wearing the light blue veil over her dark hair, was the Virgin Mary. Three children grouped about them: a boy wearing a halo fashioned of pasteboard and a raincoat and a girl in a white cambric dress and veil, and another in ordinary clothes. These three were Mrs. Messina's two and one half orphans.

The priest took a position behind 'Saint Joseph,' chanted some prayers in Latin and sprinkled water over the altar. Then he turned and said: 'Now you are all blessed! Go ahead and eat.' And he left the room.

Then 'Saint Joseph' knelt before the altar and in a moment every person in the room was on his knees. The prayers over, a woman stepped forward, gathered a bouquet of red carnations from the altar and placed it in the arms of the 'Virgin Mary.'

Now the news spread that a procession would take place to a near-by church, where a petition would be made that Mrs. Messina's eldest daughter, who was pregnant, might have an easy delivery.

'Saint Joseph' in the lead, everybody marched three blocks to the church and returned, carefully retracing the same route on the way back to the house that they had used upon leaving. To have varied this in even a small degree would certainly have brought bad luck. Perhaps Mrs. Messina's eldest daughter might not receive the full benefits of the petition just made.

Again seated at the table, in precisely the same order as before, the five were served from the altar, each receiving a tiny portion of everything. Only after they had finished eating could the family and neighbors eat, and the lucky beans, bits of Saint Joseph's bread and bay leaves be distributed. Outside the house people were gathering, most of them lean and poorly clad. Whatever was left would be given these poor. Such is the custom on Saint Joseph's Day.

Originating in Sicily, and long a day for feasting and dancing among Italians, Saint Joseph's Day is widely celebrated among the Italians in New Orleans and near-by towns. The date,

March 19, is considered a day's respite from the fasting and spiritual sackcloth and ashes of the Lenten season, and is sometimes known as Mi-Carême (Mid-Lent).

Legend holds that in the Middle Ages a group of Italians were exiled from their country and set adrift on the sea in a small boat. In despair they prayed to Saint Joseph for guidance and protection, promising to honor him each year if their lives were spared. Cast upon the shore of an uninhabited island, they immediately erected an altar of branches and palmetto leaves and decorated it with wisteria, wild red lilies and other flowers.

But even before that Saint Joseph had received some measure of recognition. In the fourth century, Helena, mother of the Emperor Constantine, erected a basilica at Bethlehem in honor of Saint Joseph. The Coptic Church included the feast of Saint Joseph, the Carpenter, in its church calendar, the date being set at July 20, and in most of the early churches Joseph was honored along with Saint Simeon, Saint Anna and other saints associated with the birth and infancy of Jesus.

The first church dedicated to Joseph was erected in Bologna in 1129, his feast day being celebrated shortly before Easter at that period. However, church leaders of the fourteenth century, including Saint Gertrude, Saint Thomas Aquinas and Saint Bridget of Sweden, declared he had never received his rightful place and insisted that he be accorded more fitting honors. It was only then that this festival was officially inserted in the Franciscan calendar, and under the papal rule of Sixtus IV, the date was set at March 19. In 1726 Pope Benedict XIII placed Joseph's name in the Litany of Saints, and in 1870 Pius IX solemnly declared him the patron saint of the Roman Catholic Church.

But New Orleans Italians have never required any urging to honor Saint Joseph. The morning of March 19 finds Catholic churches filled to overflowing, at noon the ceremonies at the home altars are held with ever-increasing enthusiasm, and the night is celebrated with dances and parties all over the city.

Interesting is the companion tradition of the swallows of San Juan Capistrano at the California mission. The *New Orleans Item* reported the annual return of the swallows on March 19, 1940, as follows:

The swallows of San Juan kept their age-old rendezvous beneath the eaves of historic San Juan Capistrano Mission today. They began arriving out of a murky sky from the south around 6:30 A.M., and within a few minutes were waging their annual warfare with the swifts which had moved into their quarters since their departure last Saint John's Day, October 23. As usual, the swallows were victorious, and soon they were settling themselves for their summer's stay.

For a century, tradition has held that the swallows have left the adobe walls of the mission, founded in 1776 by the Order of Saint Francis, annually on the feast day of its patron saint, and have returned on Saint Joseph's Day.

The popular song of 1940, 'When the Swallows Come Back to Capistrano,' was composed by a New Orleans Negro — Leon René, formerly a student of Xavier University.

The larger Saint Joseph altars in New Orleans are built in tiers, upon which is arranged the food, which usually includes everything that can be bought in markets or delicatessens and many homemade Italian delicacies unknown in other American homes. Always occupying the place of honor in the center is a large statue of Saint Joseph, and grouped about this, statues of other saints. There are huge candles, some weighing as much as ten pounds, gilded and embellished with representations of angels and flowers. Electric lights, Christmas-tree ornaments, vases and bowls of fresh and artificial flowers are placed here and there among dishes and platters of food. The *Times-Picayune* described the edibles on one altar thus:

> There were three types of Italian bread, made in the shapes of wreaths, as offerings to the Holy Family. A stuffed lobster, a baked redfish and quantities of shrimp occupied places of prominence. There were alligator pears, prickly pears, nuts, Japanese persimmons, fried cauliflower, fig cakes, snap beans, stuffed crabs, doughnuts, peanuts, crayfish, pineapples, grapefruit, mulberries, onions, celery, nectarines, oranges, almonds, tomatoes, grapes, plums, artichokes, dates and frosted layer cakes by the dozen.
>
> In and out between the squash, spinach, fruit cake and ripe peaches were bowls of antipasto relish and bottles of wine. Neat cones of pigulasto, a pastry of dough and molasses, lent

an ornamental touch with the many vases of roses, lilies, carnations and sweet peas. Sweet-scented pittosporum twined
about the structure. Most of the food was to be given away.. ...

Everyone is invited to come and pay homage to Saint Joseph.
In the New Orleans newspaper columns known as the Personal
Columns — always filled with curious notices peculiar to the
city — public invitations are extended annually to anyone wishing to visit the altars.

> Mr. and Mrs. V. Gennusa, Sr., 5230 Laurel Street, invite you
> to visit their St. Joseph's Altar, March 18 and 19.

> Mr. and Mrs. P. Farrugia, 1301 Prytania Street, invite you to
> visit their St. Joseph's Altar.

> We cordially invite the public to visit a St. Joseph's Altar at
> 2046 Magazine Street.

> Mrs. J. Mosena, 3605 Banks Street, invites the public to visit
> her St. Joseph's Altar, March 18, at night, March 19, in day.

> St. Joseph's Altar, on March 19th, in St. Expedit Temple, 3933
> Hollywood Street.

> You can visit 100 St. Joseph's Altars from list of names at
> shrine of E. A. Zatarain, 925 Valmont Street.

> Mr. and Mrs. Natale Schiambra request their many friends to
> visit their St. Joseph's Altar at their residence, 406 S. Genois
> Street, on March 18 and 19.

> The public is invited to visit the St. Joseph's Altar of Mr. and
> Mrs. Sebastian Ambrosia, 1662 Annunciation Street. Monday
> and Tuesday, March 18 and 19.

> There will be a St. Joseph's Altar at St. Raymond's Chapel,
> 3108 Melpomene.

> Public is invited to visit St. Joseph's Altar, 925 Governor
> Nicholls Street. Mrs. John Quagline.

> Everybody cordially invited to St. Joseph's Altar, 1839 Touro
> Street. Mrs. S. Lombardo.

The Saint Joseph's bread and the lucky beans are the most important items on the altars, and a small piece of bread, a lucky
bean and sometimes a bay leaf or two are given every visitor.

The beans will bring good luck, and the bit of bread kept in the house all year will protect the occupants from ever starving. Most visitors leave a coin at the altar.

Some Italians, having made a special vow, beg for the food for their altars, going from door to door, store to store and friend to friend, asking for money or a donation of food.

Statues of Saint Joseph holding the Christ Child have long been popular for private altars in the homes of New Orleans Creoles; and many New Orleanians carry miniature representations of the saint in small capsules in their pockets or pocket-books. If a favor is asked of Saint Joseph and not granted, the figure is sometimes stood on its head as punishment until the wish is fulfilled.

The night of Saint Joseph's Day has always been a time for parties and dances in New Orleans. These celebrations, of course, always end promptly at the stroke of twelve, for at midnight Lent is resumed, and fasting and penance again become a part of daily lives. For a century Saint Joseph's Night has been an important date on the social calendar of New Orleans. As early as March 16, 1858, the *New Orleans Daily Picayune* reported:

'GRAND BAL PARÉ ET MASQUE'
(Saint Joseph's Day)

At the Orleans Theatre, on the evening of St. Joseph's Day, Friday, the 19th inst., a grand fancy dress and masquerade ball is to be given, on the plan of those of the Grand Opera in Paris. From the preparations made and making for this affair we are induced to anticipate a magnificent result. Tickets may be procured at the box office of the theatre.

Masquerades and dances still take place in New Orleans and its vicinity that night. Many clubs give parties, and most of the Saint Joseph altar-donors terminate the night in dancing. Everyone considers it a joyous intermission in the Lenten season, which is so strictly observed here. Even night-clubs and cafés have more than usual crowds. And these parties are by no means confined to the Italian element, or even to those people of Roman Catholic faith, but are enjoyed by all types and national-ities of Orleanians. Negroes celebrate Saint Joseph's Night by donning their Mardi Gras costumes, a peculiar custom dating back many years. On South Rampart Street, blacks, browns and high yellows step high, wide and fancy, and there are numerous balls and dances.

In 1940, March 19 fell in Holy Week, and Archbishop Joseph Francis Rummel of New Orleans asked that there be no altars and no celebrations on this date, that April 2 be substituted. There was much consternation. Orleanians were faced with a crisis only to be compared with the two Thanksgivings of recent memory. Some Italians dutifully obeyed, but others refused, asserting Saint Joseph wouldn't like his day changed. So New Orleans had two opportunities and two excuses to give parties, and no Orleanian, Italian or otherwise, ever quibbled over an extra celebration.

Mrs. Coniglio had her altar March 19.

'Ain't it a shame to change Saint Joseph's Day?' she demanded. 'It's not right to do a thing like that. The whole world, she's gone crazy!' She sighed disgustedly. 'How'd you like somebody to change your birthday?'

Mr. Coniglio volunteered his opinion.

'We have a fine altar for thirty-four years. Saint Joseph he never say change no date. Saint Joseph Day is March 19th and March 19th she stay!

'My wife and me come from Corleone — that's in Italy — like immigrants, and when we come, Caterina — that's my wife — she is very seeck. She go to the hospitals and all the doctors stand around and look at her like they don't know nothing, and they don't do nothing. So Caterina, my wife, she makes a promise to Saint Joseph to make him a altar every year if he makes her well. Sure, the doctors come see her every day, but they do no good. It's Saint Joseph make Caterina well.

'She promise to beg for her altar, so she ask everybody for money. Some people say no, some give a nickel, some people gets mad. So Caterina she says she's stop asking people. She pay for everything herself. Then Saint Joseph he get mad. You would not believe it, but Saint Joseph come to Caterina in a dream like and he say: "You promise to beg for my altar. You must ask at least three people to keep your vow." So Caterina ask three people every year now. Her Uncle Pete he gives a dollar, my daughter Lena gives fifty cents and Caterina's friend — she's the lady lives next door here — she gives a quarter. Like that Caterina keep her vow and Saint Joseph don't get mad.

'Some people make a speculation with Saint Joseph. They beg from everybody — a nickel here, a quarter there. Pretty damn soon they make for themselves a lot of money and keep it all for them. My family is not like that. But we have our altar this year as always. What we promise Saint Joseph we do. I don't care what anybody say. I call the priest to bless it and he say, "Okay. Goo'bye!" '

But Mrs. Caparo disagreed. 'Most of the priests wouldn't bless their altars,' she insisted. 'And what good is an altar if it ain't blessed? The Father told me I did right having mine on April 2d.'

Mrs. Caparo's altar was huge and extremely elaborate. Exact copies of sacred objects found on the Roman Catholic altars had been constructed of cake and coated with various icings. There were crosses, decorated with stylized plants, hearts, roosters and stars, all of cake and pastry. Everyone in the neighborhood had contributed. Even friends in the country had sent little lambs of cake, stuffed with figs and covered with a fleece of grated coconut. These last were Mrs. Caparo's special pride, and rested in a place of honor near Saint Joseph's feet.

The Caparo family did not consider the altar in an entirely religious light. Every now and then one of the children would make a running dash, snatch a cake or doughnut from a dish and vanish as quickly as he had appeared. The only admonishment given would be a half-humorous warning that Saint Joseph would make his teeth rot if he ate his food now.

'When they send my boy to war,' Mrs. Caparo explained, 'I promise Saint Joseph if he send my boy back and he not have to fight and not get himself hurt, I make him an altar every year. So, my boy, he's in the camp, see? And I was all the time cry and all the time pray and pray. The next day my boy was to leave to go fight, the lady from downstairs she comes upstairs and tells me she has a telegram for me. It is from my boy, and he says he's gonna come home tomorrow, is not have to fight on account of there's something wrong with his neck. I get so happy I cry and laugh all together at one time! Right away I go see the sisters on Rampart and Conti Streets. They send away for me and I get a statue of Saint Joseph for fifty dollars, and I make an altar every year and put the statue on top.'

Among the saints on the altar was a picture of Huey P. Long.

'No, I don't consider him a saint or nothing,' Mrs. Caparo explained. 'I just feel sorry for him. He looks like my other boy who was drowned. My boy is drowned in the river.'

A heavy-set, gray-haired man entered the room. 'I am Plitnick,' said he — 'Mrs. Caparo's hoosband. You wouldn't believe it, but I am a Jew. All the time I study and write. I am vorking on some short stories, but I have the timidity and I am afraid they are no good. Joost now I am studying the conscious. You see, there is the subconscious, the conscious and the superconscious. We Russians understand the finer things of life. That is why we are all the time so sad.'

Mrs. Caparo explained. 'Mr. Plitnick is my second husband. I keep my first husband's name because everybody know me by that. He was kicked in the heart by a mule and was killed. It was terrible.'

Mr. Plitnick frowned. 'Go get some Saint Joseph's bread and cake.'

'Keep the bread until it storms,' instructed Mr. Plitnick's wife, Mrs. Caparo. 'If it storms and you take a piece and throw it outside and say, "Saint Joseph, make the storm go away!" you see it go away and not touch you. He's a great man, Saint Joseph!'

One of the most elaborate and most famed altars in New Orleans is the annual one at the delicatessen of Biaccio Montalbano at 724 St. Philip Street. His place of business is a shrine all year.

Entering a screen door from the *banquette*, you find yourself in a narrow room, furnished with a long counter, shelves and a glass showcase, and on the shelves, among jars of antipasto and anchovies, cheeses and sausages imported from Italy, are numerous statues of saints, crucifixes and holy pictures. Statues, too, occupy half of the counter, and at the far end is an altar in which burn crimson vigil lights and on which repose statues of the Holy Family. Another third of the counter is colorfully occupied by an array of at least fifty gaily decorated highball glasses, filled with oil and floating tapers, some always burning, having been lighted by those who come here to make a wish. All the walls and the ceiling above are covered with portraits of the Christ, of saints, of various popes. A bowl on the counter offers Saint Joseph's beans, and another bowl receives offerings from anyone wishing to drop a few coins.

Behind this is the 'Roma Room' — really the dining-room of the establishment. Over the two doors leading into it, in letters of gold, are inscribed the words:

HIS HOLINESS POPE PIUS XI HAS BESTOWED ON BIACCIO
MONTALBANO, DIRECTOR OF THE ROMA ROOM, APOS-
TOLIC BENEDICTION FOR PRAYING IN CHURCH 2000
HOURS FOR 2000 DAYS.

All the walls and the ceiling are here, too, colorfully decorated with holy pictures. Toward the top of the walls, completely encircling the room, is the 'Way of the Cross,' a series of pictures depicting Jesus' journey to Calvary and the Crucifixion. Beneath this is a varied array of saints' pictures, photographs of several popes and high dignitaries of the Roman Catholic Church. Framing the pictures on the ceiling and dangling downward are Christmas-tree ornaments of every shape and color. And at every door leading from the Roma Room is a font containing holy water.

A large radio and phonograph combination at one end of the room is converted into an altar, its top holding statues of the Holy Family, its front and sides plastered with pictures. Mr. Montalbano owns a collection of recorded sacred and classic music. At the other end of the room is a portrait of George Washington, flanked on each side by three pairs of pictures: the first, identical representations of 'Peace'; the second, identical colored chromos of the Pope; and the third, identical portraits of Franklin D. Roosevelt. On one wall is a vivid picture in brilliant red and green colors of a pretty and voluptuous Italian maid, daintily holding a bunch of yellow bananas in one plump hand.

'We sure had us a time!' said Mrs. Rose Datri. 'I cooked

thirty-two pounds of spaghetti. You should have seen the ceremony at my altar. It was grand! We had saints — three poor children from the neighborhood — to knock on two different doors in the yard, coming to our door last. Mamma asked who they were. They answered, "Jesus, Mary and Joseph," and Mamma threw the door wide. Then everybody kissed the hand of "Jesus" and made a wish. When they sat down we fed them orange slices to break their fast, and after that they ate some of everything on the altar. One of the little boys ate so much he got sick. No, I can't remember if it was "Jesus" or "Joseph." '

The ceremony at the home of Mrs. Vita Alphonse differed slightly. At noon a knock came on the door.

'No, there is no shelter here,' someone called through the door, in soft Italian. (This is an enactment of the Holy Family seeking shelter in wayside inns.)

Again the knock came, and the answer was the same, 'No, there is no shelter here.'

The third knock was answered: 'Who is it?'

'I am Saint Joseph,' came the reply. 'I seek shelter for Mary, Jesus and Saint Albert.'

Then, amidst cries of welcome, 'Enter! Enter! We are deeply honored!' the quartet was admitted.

The mother of the household knelt and prayed, her eyes fixed on the statue in the center of the altar.

'Oh, Saint Joseph, help us! Saint Joseph, protect us! Saint Joseph, we love you! Saint Joseph, we give thanks for all our blessings!

'Our Father, who art in Heaven. Hallowed be thy name...

'Hail, Mary, Mother of God...'

The 'saints' ate. Then the family and friends.

The Sacred Heart Orphanage has an altar, the entire auditorium being utilized for this purpose. At one side of the room is a life-sized statue of Saint Joseph, surrounded by large and small tapers, candelabra and vases filled with white Easter lilies. Besides the usual delectable foods on the altar, there were long tables holding piles of Italian bread, fashioned in all sorts of figures, including twists, braid, crosses, circles and crescents, and bundles of spaghetti, macaroni and cavatuni tied together with blue satin bows. Stacked on the floor near the tables were sacks of sugar, rice, beans and flour. This altar is donated each year by Mr. and Mrs. Lawrence Orlando. Some of the food, however, is contributed by other people. Everything is retained for the children of the orphanage.

One of the Italian nuns here was much impressed at having her picture taken near the altar.

'If I look fat in my face,' she confided, 'I'll send it to my mamma in Italy. If I look skinny in my face, I won't. She worries for me.'

Similar is the altar at the Cabrini Day Nursery. For years this altar has been given by Mr. Peter Orlando, brother of the donor of the one at the Sacred Heart Orphanage. Here, too, the food is kept for the children.

Curious is the adoption of this Italian custom by New Orleans Negroes. The *Item Tribune*, March 17, 1940, announced: 'Elaborate preparations have been made in the Negro spiritualist churches for Saint Joseph's Day. Among the churches taking part are the Saint Joseph Helping Hand Spiritualist, Algiers; the Eternal Love Christian Spiritualist, Clio Street; Saint James Temple No. 7, Felicity near Freret; Star of the East, Constantinople and Saratoga Streets; and Saint Paul No. 7, Saratoga near Thalia Street.'

Reverend Maude Shannon says it was a divine call that made her build the first Saint Joseph's altar for Negroes fourteen years ago.

'I come out of my door that mornin',' says Reverend Maude, 'and I heared a voice talkin' to me just as plain as if there'd been someone walkin' by my side. The voice says I must get together the sisters of the church, and we must gather candles and cakes and make an altar for Saint Joseph's Day. So I threw out my hands to show the voice I done heared its words, and I called the sisters together and we went out with baskets to gather the food for our flock.'

Reverend Shannon is head of an independent Negro church, the Daniel Helping Hand Mission, but her altars exhibit no radical departures from the ones of the Roman Catholic Italians, even including among the altar foods antipasto, Italian salads and pineapple cakes. Reverend Shannon indicated can after can of food, candy, fruit, bowls of potato salad and hard-boiled eggs split in half and stuffed with pickle and yellow egg yolks.

'Sometimes when I had my first altars,' she said, 'I'd get scared they ain't got enough food on 'em for all the peoples what's comin'. One time when I was givin' it out to the poor, there is so many peoples, I don't know what to do. I started prayin' to the Lord the whole time I was passin' out the stuff. And the good Lord must've heared me, 'cause the faster I gived it away, the more food there is, and after all them peoples is fed, there is still more, so we just puts that in baskets and sends it to the orphans. Then I thanked the Lord for his timely aid, and went to bed.'

Though she won't discuss it, there is a rumor that the money to pay for the Reverend Shannon's altars is contributed by the gamblers in her section of the city. They come to get the lucky beans and leave money behind.

But Saint Joseph's Day, with its altars, celebrations and religious ceremonies, belongs to the Italians. And the altars are by no means confined to New Orleans, though they are perhaps more numerous and more elaborate there, but may be found in all sections of Louisiana where Italians reside.

Proof of their devotion to this saint is the fact that a recent tabulation of names given to boys in New Orleans showed that 'Joseph' was far in the lead of all others and had been for a number of years. Perhaps Saint Joseph's appeal to them lies largely in their knowledge that he was one of the common, hard-working people of the world like the vast majority of mankind. Someone in the *Times-Picayune* of March 13, 1937, framed it in these words:

> Saint Joseph is loved by his followers as a man among men, a carpenter who worked as men must work, who grew hot and tired as ordinary people do, who smashed his thumb with his hammer and got splinters in his hands — and yet was deemed worthy to live as the husband of the Mother of God.

Chapter 6

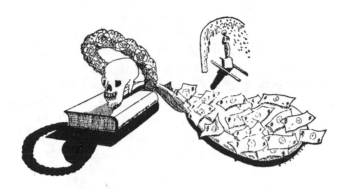

Saint Rosalia's Day

Saint Rosalia was daughter of a noble family descended from Charle-magne. She was born at Palermo in Sicily, and despising in her youth earthly vanities, made herself an abode in a cave on Monte Pelegrino, three miles from Palermo, where she completed the sacrifice of her heart to God by austere penance and manual labor, sanctified by assidu-ous prayer and the constant union of her soul with God. She died in 1160. Her body was found buried in a grot under the mountain, in the year of the jubilee, 1625, under Pope Urban VIII, and was translated into the metropolitical church of Palermo, of which she was chosen a patroness. To her patronage that island ascribes the ceasing of a griev-ous pestilence at the same time.

From *Lives of the Saints*
By John Gilmary Shea, LL.D.

'YOU SEE,' EXPLAINED MRS. ALES, WITH TEARS IN her eyes and a nervous tug at her sunbonnet, 'was like this. Saint Rosalia is a beautiful young girl. Her papa is afraid she's gonna be a old maid, and he want her to get married. Me, I can't remember her mamma's name, but her papa's name is Ricaldo, and he is a king. But she don't want to get married. She wants to be pure and stay a virgin. All the time they is fight. He want to and she don't want to. One day she is combin' her hair in her room, and her crucifix start talkin' to her. They make plans, and that night an angel come and take her up on top a mountain. No one, not even her papa, knows where she's at!

'She die, and still nobody don't know where she's at. Long time after there is like a plague in Palermo. Then a young man see Saint Rosalia in a dream, and he tell the people they find her poor bones everybody what ain't dead yet gonna get well. They go up on the mountain and bring her bones down. Then everybody happy.' Mrs. Ales blew her nose vigorously.

About fifty years old, but with white hair and eyes startlingly blue for an Italian, Mrs. Anna Ales is a resident of Harvey, Louisiana, where one of the state's two Saint Rosalia processions is held annually. Wearing a starched sunbonnet and a dress almost to her ankles, she proudly exhibited some of the exquisitely embroidered linens she had just laundered for the Saint Rosalia Church in Harvey, explaining that she intended to work for the Church all her life. She made a vow to do that in 1918, when the influenza epidemic swept through Harvey. That was the beginning of the celebration of the saint in that town.

'Everybody was sick,' said Mrs. Ales. 'We asked Saint Rosalia to stop the plague, and the plague stopped, so we promise to hold a procession just like in Palermo and in Kenner. Me, I had my mother and sister sick, and I was like crazy. All the time I cry and cry. Like that, soon as I make my promise, they get well. Was same thing when I was dyin'. I had three operations, nine doctors; nothing do me no good. I ask Saint Rosalia for help, and, like that, I was well.

'We do all the work here ourselfs. Cook the food for the festival, make crowns for the angels, everything. Me, I make all the angels' crowns.' She showed a small wreath of silver-paper leaves. 'I tell you the truth, sometimes I get so tired making crowns for angels, I almost scream my head off! They got two hundred of 'em, and, me, I started that idea! They got about a hundred little boys, too, they call acolytes, but *they* ain't no angels.'

The Harvey celebration takes place either the first or the second Sunday in the month of September; on the other Sunday another procession is held at Kenner, Louisiana. The events occur on different dates because of the proximity of the villages to each other, Harvey being just across the Mississippi from New Orleans, Kenner about ten miles above the city. One year one town has its celebration first, the following year the other. This not only keeps the peace, but allows each to attend the other. Anyway, Saint Rosalia's Day is actually established as September 4.

Harvey begins the celebration with a festival and bazaar in the churchyard the Saturday night before. Sunday morning there is High Mass, and that afternoon all who make the pilgrimage meet at Saint Joseph's Church in Gretna at one-thirty. From here they walk the two miles to Harvey, carrying a life-sized statue of the saint, who in this representation wears blue and white robes, a wreath of flowers about her flowing brown hair, carries a skull and prayer book in one hand and a crucifix and lily in the other, and is set on a wooden base with long trestles, requiring the services of a dozen bearers.

The day of the 1941 celebration she wore an additional wreath of real flowers and her ankles were banked with bouquets brought by the worshipers; from her shoulders dripped streamers of red, green and golden satin to which was pinned paper money, this being another custom of the occasion. As she was borne from the church, Frank De Salvo, president of the Victor Emmanuel III Society, stepped forward, unpinned the bills, and made notations in a book. While he was engaged in this, women crowded forward, many with tears striping their cheeks, mumbled prayers, and laid gnarled, workworn fingers on the hem of the image's plaster robes, and on her feet. 'We have to park the statue outside the churches at both the beginning and the end of the pilgrimage,' explained Mr. De Salvo, 'so the people can touch it and ask favors.'

But this was quickly over, and the procession took formation out in the street: first, Boy Scout Troop 200, with a large American flag at the head; then Father Wester, pastor of Saint Joseph's Church, flanked by a half-dozen altar boys; next the banners of the organizations taking part — 'Victor Emmanuel III Society, Harvey, La.,' read one; 'Organization Italiana San Guiseppe di Amesville, La.,' another; finally 'Fratellanza Italiana di Santa Rosalia, Kenner, La.,' revealing the presence of members of the organization which would hold its celebration on the Sunday to come. Behind these came the thirteen-piece Roma Band, with Saint Rosalia and her bearers following.

After this marched two hundred little girls, all less than five years of age, all dressed alike in white dresses with stiff little wings attached to their shoulders and Mrs. Ales's crowns on their heads. All were very angelic, keeping their hands clasped before them, and praying loudly. The acolytes marched next, half as many small boys of the same ages, dressed in white robes, blue capes and white skull caps. Not so pious, these were inclined to push and shove and giggle. Finally one in the rear released a particularly audible howl, and a red-faced stout woman rushed forward, gave his shoulders a shake, scolded in Italian, then vanished to the rear, making the sign of the cross.

Next came the Children of Mary, an order of girls of adolescent years, all in snowy white with flowing veils of ethereal blue. These recited 'Hail Marys' over and over, one tall, thin, very dark girl serving as leader. Her voice high above the rest, it was always she who began each new line of the prayer, and in the same sing-song tempo. Each of the Children of Mary carried a paper fan advertising the 'Rotollo Motor Company.'

The men followed, most of them in white linen. After them were the women, who, though they walked behind their men, did not trail humbly, but marched proudly, most of them well fed and of comfortable ages, nearly all carrying umbrellas as sunshades. Many of them were barefooted or in their stockings. Two State motorcycle policemen took the lead, and immediately there was a buzz of conversation and verbal expression of last-minute thoughts.

'Anthony, you carry my shoes!'

'Carry 'em yourself. I ain't no mule.'

The ringing voice of a long dark girl: '*Blessed art thou among women . . .!*'

'Gladys, where'd you leave the car?'

'My Gawd! I don't know, me!'

The Child of Mary: '*Fruit of thy womb . . . !*'

An irreligious youth perched on a bread box before a grocery called out, 'Look at de Mardi Gras parade!'

'Here comes de second float!' announced a pal lounging against a post.

'*Blessed art thou among women . . . !*' The long dark girl.

The angels burst into song. The acolytes giggled. The men talked. The women, rosaries entwined in their fingers, prayed, or gossiped, or sang; a few wept steadily. Many cars trailed the pilgrims, moving at a snail's pace. There was, literally, much color. The president, the grand marshal and the marshals all wore red, white and green ribbons across their chests; the bearers of the statue, white duck trousers and green tunics trimmed with gold braid. Two others, not carrying, but walking, one on each side, wore white trousers and deep purple tunics. A stout little marshal with fierce mustaches wore an immense round badge that resembled an old-fashioned bouquet, of red, pink and yellow paper roses finished off with wide streamers of red, green and white satin.

Two men argued loudly over the fact for the first time the flag of Italy was not carried. Each had an excellent, though sophistic argument, one stating that 'the Catholic Church is really Italian, since Rome is in Italy, and the Pope is Italian, and he is in Rome, and most everybody in Harvey is Italian, so Harvey is Italian, and Saint Rosalia is Italian, etc., etc.' What, he demanded, did Mussolini have to do with it? 'Saint Peter was Italian, too,' he concluded, a bit triumphantly.

'You alla time wanta be a damn dago!' said the other. 'Harvey is American, and you are American, and now Saint Rosalia is American, and Saint Peter was never no Italian. He was a Jew!'

The first man said he wished he had a beer.

There were stops for icewater from pitchers and glasses set out before the picket fences along the way. ·The bus came along, got 'stuck' in the middle of the marchers, and there was a noisy exchange of wisecracks between the passengers and the pilgrims. But at last — the bus still in the middle — the procession reached Harvey, and here the street leading to the church, and the church itself, were elaborately decorated with flags and banners. The *banquettes* were lined with people crying greetings. As the procession reached the church, the bells clanged and

banged, a cannon went off with a great roar; there was a crack-
ling, explosive din of firecrackers. Puffs of black smoke drifted
over the heads of the marchers.

'*Blessed art thou among women....!*' screamed the long dark girl,
with renewed vigor.

Boy Scout Troop 200 lined the walk leading to the church, and
here Saint Rosalia was 'parked' for another few minutes, and
the women came forward to touch the statue, and pray, and weep.
The fireworks grew louder and louder. The Roma Band climbed
to a platform in the churchyard and began to play. Already the
grounds were filled with people buying and gambling at the
bazaars. In a room which was a wing of the church proper, a
juke box was going full blast, and several young people were
dancing. Here tables and chairs were set up, where later meat-
balls and spaghetti and steaming bowls of gumbo would be sold.

Saint Rosalia was unscrewed from her base and carried into the
church, the fat little man with the mustaches and the old-
fashioned bouquet badge running excitedly up and down the
aisle, supervising operations, as the statue was carefully replaced
in the niche it occupies all year. The church was jammed with
the devotees, all incongruously mingling the festive spirit of the
day with much genuflecting and holy-water sprinkling, as Father
Wester stepped before the altar and began the Benediction.

This over, the bazaars did a rushing business, selling drinks,
sandwiches and candy; cakes and baskets of groceries were raffled. Everyone had a fine time. The celebration lasted until midnight, closing with a great display of fireworks, during which
a huge representation of the saint whose day was being honored
was sent flashing against the night sky.

Mrs. Zito, one of Saint Rosalia's most enthusiastic admirers in
Kenner, was unusually excited a few days before the celebration
in that village. In fact, Mr. Zito was outside their grocery, taking some fresh air, possibly because the atmosphere within was
too electric. 'Mamma knows all about Saint Rosalia's Day,' he
admitted. 'Mamma!'

There was the slap-slap sound of loose slippers, and Mrs. Zito
appeared, a short and stout woman with a great pile of graying

hair and a kindly face. This morning she wore a house dress as loose as the slippers on her naked feet, and twin rivers of perspiration streamed from her temples. 'It depends on what you gotta know,' said Mrs. Zito modestly. 'That is the whole thing. First, I gotta know what you gotta know.'

Mrs. Zito's grocery is unusual — one tremendous room, with walls and floor of broad unpainted boards. At one end are the counter and shelves, at the other long benches, a sewing machine and a juke box. Between is enough space to hold a Carnival ball. Even now the music box was offering 'Fan It!' with Woody Herman and His Orchestra giving their all. Mr. Zito executed a few dance steps.

'Looka my jellybean!' roared Mrs. Zito. 'I tell you, Papa is a kick! We got us fourteen children — two dead — and look how little Papa is. You would not believe it, huh, to look at him?' Unlike his spouse, Mr. Zito is the size and weight of a twelve-year-old boy. Now he grinned with embarrassment, ceased dancing, and vanished behind the case containing meats.

Mrs. Zito leaned back comfortably in the room's one rocker. 'Every year when the parade passes here, I make my spich,' she said. 'I been makin' it for four years. I say four years, but maybe is more. Papa, is it four years I been makin' my spich?'

Papa's eyes, nearly bald skull and wispy white mustache appeared around the edge of the meat case. 'Is more than four years!' he yelled across the big room.

'Papa says is more than four years,' asserted Mrs. Zito.

'Is much more than four years,' Mr. Zito reiterated.

'Is much more than four years,' Mrs. Zito echoed. 'Maybe is five-six years. I cannot tell you. What I say in my spich? That is also a thing I cannot tell you. You cannot say it in American, see? Is got to be word for word. It is too beautiful. My God, it is beautiful!' Mrs. Zito wiped her streaming brow with a handkerchief. 'Maybe sometime my daughter is transpose it to American for you.'

'No can be done!' Mr. Zito crossed the room. 'They is not got the American words for the Italian words. It is too beautiful.'

'Papa says it is too beautiful,' said Mrs. Zito. 'You see, I say two pieces. No! No! Not one. *Two* pieces. I tell you the truth, they is so beautiful everybody cry to beat the band.'

She was weeping now, and had to touch her handkerchief to her eyes. 'All I can say is this,' she sighed. 'Santa Rosalia go up on the mountain all by herself. You see, she is so young and innocent, and she suffer and suffer. I tell the peoples that in my spich, see? She isa up on this mountain, and the Devil he come and tackle her. Everywhere she go, the Devil he keep tacklin' her. At last she run away, but he catch her, and tackle her again. And then she fall on her knees, and the Devil he look at her, and he say he could not tackle her to save his life. She is look so pure and innocent he could not do nothing, see? My mamma tell me all about it. Sure. And her mamma tell her. That's a way we believe, see? And that's like I say in my two pieces, only is so beautiful in Italian nobody can stand it, they all cry to beat the band!'

Mrs. Zito was weeping profusely now, but she stopped, sniffed, turned toward the screen door leading to the living-quarters behind the store. 'Francis!' she cried loudly, 'did you watch the pot on the stove? Put a glass of water in it. It's the beans, Francis?' There was no answer, but evidently all was as it should be, for she murmured: 'Excuse me, pliz! What was I saying?

'You know when I'm makin' my spich I don't hardly know what I doin', I tell you the truth. All I got on my mind is my two pieces. Every year we ask for the grace. That is our belief. You see, Santa Rosalia cannot do nothing herself. No. You ask her for the grace, see? Then she go ask God. She tella God what you want. God shake His head "yes!" you get it! But God shake His head "no!" you outa luck. That's a way we believe, see?

'I'ma be the stuff Sunday, too,' concluded Mrs. Zito, blowing her nose exuberantly. 'I'ma be dressed up like a jellybean. Hot dog!' She gazed upon the diminutive Mr. Zito. 'Papa better be careful. Maybe I get me a new jellybean.' At this both she and Papa Zito roared with laughter.

Kenner's Saint Rosalia procession began in 1899, after a promise made to the saint for her proficiency in stopping a plague of charbon, which was destroying the cattle and mules so essential to the livelihood of the Italian farmers of the vicinity. August Christina, president of the 'Fratellanza Italiana Society,' which has charge of the event, was happy to give a brief history of the affair.

'You see,' he explained, 'it started back in Palermo years and years ago. I don't know how many years ago. It was in the olden times. Rosalia hid in a cave on a mountain, and maybe three, four hundred years after, they found her. I believe she was dead, but her bones was intact. She had always cured pestilences. That's why people here walk barefooted and all every year. She stopped the charbon in 1899. We have a real big crowd now; there were over seven thousand last year.'

Walking barefooted or in stockings, carrying lighted candles — which are placed in the church at the end of the procession — and donating money are the principal ways of repaying Saint Rosalia for favors granted. But Mr. Christina said: 'They promise all sorts of things, and whatever they promise they do. You have to give 'em that. Sometimes they're hard to do, too.'

Mrs. Genovese is one of Kenner's oldest residents. She took part in the first procession and in every one since. Mrs. Genovese was 'in the city, but she be back Sunday,' according to her daughter, a stout middle-aged woman, who swayed back and forth in her rocking chair as she talked.

'You better talk to me,' she advised. 'My poor mamma could not do you no good. You no understand nothing she say. She is Italian.

'Sure. I been in the prossession lots of times. My mamma never miss one since it start. See, we believe like that. American peoples is superstitious. They don't think like us, see? But this year, me, I don't even want to see the prossession. I justa lost my husband, and I can't stand nothin' like festival — or nothin'. They ask for all sorts of things — like jobs, cure illness. Looka Mrs. Verde. You know she is Joseph Santopadre's daughter. He live here, but she live in New Orleans. She was dying. Sure. The doctor chop her open, look inside, send her home to die. Other doctors come look at her, say she ought to be dead, but she ain't dead. Her papa promise Saint Rosalia a pair of diamond earrings she get well. This year she walk in the procession. Sure. Is all wonderful to us, but I know American people is superstitious.'

And Mrs. Verde was happy to talk about herself, her operation and her miraculous cure, though she revealed an unexpected angle to the last occurrence.

'My father made the promise to Saint Rosalia,' she explained. 'He has great faith in her, but' — and here Mrs. Verde leaned forward and spoke almost in a whisper — 'personally, just between you and me, I think it was Mother Cabrini who cured me. I've always had much better results from her. In any case, it was wonderful, a real miracle. I was literally eaten away with cancer. Practically no insides left at all. Of course, I shall walk in the procession Sunday, and I shall give thanks to Saint Rosalia for my cure — through Mother Cabrini, my favorite, beautiful saint.'

Despite torrential rains the morning and early afternoon of the 1941 celebration, people filled the church in Kenner as the starting hour of 3 P.M. neared. Practically all of Kenner and neighboring settlements seemed to be present. Many people from New Orleans journey to the village to take part or to view the event. All day the highway is lined with cars, and many ride the 'Kenner Shakedown,' the name given the little sky-blue bus running between the two places each half-hour.

At the entrance to the elaborately decorated church, men sold white silk badges for an offering and large pictures depicting Saint Rosalia appearing in a vision to the young man who first saw her. These last were marked definitely at ten cents each. Many women entered carrying large candles; soon the church aisles were crowded with them, waiting a turn to kneel before the statue, already on its base and trestle before the altar.

Kenner's Saint Rosalia, slightly smaller than Harvey's, wears a green garment partly covered with a golden robe, a short lavender mantle, and a wreath of flowers. She carries the skull and the crucifix, and for this occasion her head was adorned with a bejeweled crown, and streamers hung from throat and wrists, to which much paper money had already been pinned. Concealed in flowers banked about the feet was a receptacle for coins.

Upon reaching her the women made their offerings — pinned

bills to the streamers or dropped coins — then knelt in prayer. Each, before moving on, would lay a hand tenderly upon the statue's feet or robes. Then they stepped to the side where a nun, assisted by two young girls, was busy collecting more money and making notations in a book each time she received a contribution. In return, the young ladies were busy handing out small candles, which were lighted and placed on a stand at one side. Each of these, however, was allowed to burn only for two or three minutes, then extinguished and tossed into a box beneath the stand, to make room for a new one. They are supposed to be relighted and burned on other days. The church resounded with the clinking of coins as the nun dropped the money into another box.

As time passed the crowd became almost a milling mob, nearly all of them women. They lined every aisle, packed into the rear of the church, knelt two deep at the altar railing. They struggled to get close to the statue, to purchase candles from the nun. In the rear a baby bawled ceaselessly. There were the smells of garlic and cosmetics. Women reassured each other — and themselves — regarding the weather. One said loudly: 'It won't rain on her when she gets out there. She'd stop a storm.'

Women wept — an old, old woman, in trailing black skirts, a black sunbonnet, with only one eye, from which tears flowed constantly — a fat woman, holding a huge candle in one fist, an umbrella in the other.

At three-twenty-five fireworks began to go off outside the church, and amidst the intonations the 'Fratellanza Italiana' came up the aisle, one committeeman carrying the society's large green banner. All wore badges and emblems of some sort, mostly wide ribbons of red, green and white across their chests. A great heart made of red velvet and covered thickly with jewelry, including rings, bracelets, watches, chains, stickpins and earrings, was carried in. Standing on a chair, one of the committeemen unpinned the money from the streamers and fixed the latter behind the statue, then tied the heart about the image's neck so that it hung in front of the statue.

All the lights in the church flared on and Father Higginbotham appeared with his altar boys, led the way down the aisle, Saint Rosalia close behind, on the sturdy shoulders of her bearers. Outside, Clancy's Band burst into a spirited version of 'The Courier.' Anthony Ochello, Grand Marshal, stepped to the front.

And the rain *had* stopped. The skies were clearing, with even a patch of blue showing here and there. However, the streets and roads were still sloppy, and soon everyone was muddied to the knees. The crowd rapidly lengthened and thickened, until it stretched six country blocks. Biaccio Montalbano, well-known delicatessen man of New Orleans and, by his own admission, the holiest man in the city (see 'Saint Joseph's Day,' page 102), was right up in front, walking close to the statue. He wore what was easily the most remarkable regalia in the procession. He had three large holy pictures, depicting Saint Rosalia, strung one beneath the other on a red cord which was tied around his neck. The pictures hung from his chest almost to his knees, making his walking somewhat difficult. In each outspread arm he carried a large picture of the saint. From the pockets of his seersucker coat protruded crucifixes, one on each side, one having a chain of bright red beads so long it nearly dragged in the mud. Frequently Mr. Montalbano would induce one of the marchers to kiss one of the pictures of the saint, and then he was all grin and obviously in ecstasy.

There was excitement at the first stop across the street from the church, after the pilgrims had turned. While Mr. Ochello was busy collecting money from those who came forward to pay off favors granted, a Mr. Viterella went into action, taking first place as star of the event. Arms up and gesturing wildly, he began to scream volubly in Italian. 'Viva Santa Rosalia!' he yelled. 'Viva Santa Rosalia!' There were answering cries from the crowd: 'Viva Santa Rosalia!'

'Santa Rosalia Day is Santa Rosalia Day!' cried Mr. Viterella. 'I'ma preach the whole way.'

The crowd became indignant, cried, 'Is a disgrace!'

'Viva Santa Rosalia!' yelled Mr. Viterella. 'I'ma preach the whole way!'

'He's drunk!' they shouted. 'Is a disgrace. Shut up!'

'Cuta off my head!' invited Mr. Viterella. 'Come on, cuta off

Mrs. Caparo has a fine altar to St. Joseph

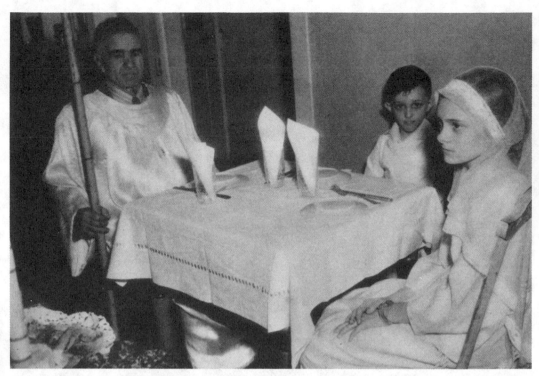

"Saints" eating by the St. Joseph's shrine of Mrs. Spann and Mrs. Schnaupper on St. Mary's Street

An elaborate cake baked in honor of St. Joseph

Montalbano's altar to St. Joseph
Courtesy of F. A. McDaniels, New Orleans

St. Rosalia is carried in honor from church to church

Mrs. Zito makes 'a beautiful speech' in honor of St. Rosalia

my head! I will not shut up. Is only one Santa Rosalia Day.
Let them what want go to Harvey, them what want come here.
Am I right or am I wrong?'

It was evident Mr. Viterella objected to the custom of holding
the two processions on different Sundays. 'Hold up your hands!'
he cried. 'Am I right or am I wrong?'

A few hands went up, but most of them obviously were not on
his side. They booed. They jeered. They laughed at him. A
large woman carrying a candle in a paper bag, its flame flickering
just over the edges, wept audibly.

'Cuta off my head!' screamed Mr. Viterella again.

But now the procession was starting again, and he was comparatively quiet for the rest of the way. The next stop was at
Grand Marshal Ochello's house, where icewater in big galvanized tubs was served in shiny cups. The Ochellos had promised
this to Saint Rosalia. At last Hanson City was reached, and the
next pause was at Mrs. Zito's grocery store.

A wooden table was brought out and upon this was set the
statue. Another table appeared and upon this was set Mrs. Zito
— with some difficulty. She was excited, and she clutched a post
while she delivered her 'beautiful spich,' contenting herself with
only one hand for gestures. She spoke very loudly, accompanied
by rigid salutes, and by wide and graceful sweeps of her arm.
Sometimes she pounded her fist into the air. At other moments
she clutched her bosom. She became more and more emotional,
her voice cracking, and tears streaming from her eyes and down
her plump cheeks. She cried 'to beat the band,' though no one
else seemed to do so. Once a passing freight train drowned her
'spich' entirely, but she paused not an instant. She was really
dressed like a 'jellybean,' too, wearing tight patent-leather
shoes, silk stockings, a starched dress of light blue cotton and
two deep water waves in her coiffure.

There were other stops — at Cavallino's bar for pink lemonade, at Franzone's Grocery for root beer. At last they were back
at Williamson Boulevard, and nearing the church, where a final
stop was made before J. Christina's Grocery and Bar.

Suddenly, a stout, white-haired man appeared, dragging a
kitchen chair. He spread a sheet of newspaper on the chair, then

he stood upon it. Word passed through the crowd that he was Mr. D'Amico, that he was from New Orleans and that he was about to make a speech. He did. It was very long, very loud, and in Italian. The crowd bore it patiently for a quarter-hour, then became restless, though some used the time to come forward, lay hands upon the statue and mumble prayers. Mr. D'Amico talked on. His face dripped perspiration, his voice hoarsened, but nothing diminished his implicit faith in his own oratorical powers.

At last President Christina made some remarks, implying that Mr. D'Amico might shorten his address. Then he told him to shut up. Finally he signaled the band, who immediately drowned Mr. D'Amico in music. President Christina gave another signal, and the men lifted Saint Rosalia and proceeded around the speaker; soon the procession was on its way. His face purple with rage, Mr. D'Amico dropped to the ground, dragged himself and his chair in the general direction of J. Christina's Grocery and Bar.

Cannon and firecrackers went off again as Saint Rosalia was carried into the church, as many of the crowd who could following. As Father Higginbotham began the Benediction, Clancy's Band played loudly in the yard outside.

Afterward, there was a bazaar in the school basement next door. A large keno game was the favorite amusement, offering prizes in money and groceries. There were games for children — grab bags, 'fish ponds.' Beer, soft drinks and sandwiches were sold. Later there would be a big dance at Clancy's Gymnasium, and at midnight, outside the gymnasium, there would be a great fireworks display, when, as in Harvey, a brilliant Santa Rosalia would be sent up in flaming firework magic. Then the Saint Rosalia celebration is over for another year.

Chapter 7

Nickel Gig, Nickel Saddle

SARAH LAWSON, COLLECTOR OF RAGS AND PAPER, washwoman, owner of six cats and seven dogs, withdrew her fat, very black arms from the tub and shook off the snowy suds. Some of the little bubbles floated for a second, then puffed out in tiny explosions. Sarah began to sing:

> Four, 'leven and forty-four,
> Four, 'leven and forty-four.
> Goin' down this mornin'
> 'Cause I got to go.
> But if I hit this gig,
> Ain't gonna bust these suds no more!

''Course that song is about the Washwoman's Gig,' Sarah said. 'I know you done heard of that one. Ain't hardly no company taking it now. When them numbers hits, they hits. The Bag of Silver was cleaned out with that gig two years ago. Man, listen:

> Four, 'leven and forty-four,
> Four, 'leven and forty-four,
> Soapy water and dirty clo'es.

I'm bustin' these suds
Up to my elbows!

'Boy, all I'd have to do would be to hit that ole Washwoman's Gig, and I'd be sittin' on top of the world. Man! Man! Does I know more of that Lottery Song? Sure, I does. They got all kinds of words. Some is like this:

Four, 'leven and forty-four,
Four, 'leven and forty-four,
My man, he's lazy.
He ain't no good,
But if I hit this gig,
He's gonna dress up like he should!

Four, 'leven and forty-four,
Four, 'leven and forty-four,
'Fore I lose my haid,
'Cause my man's in that
Yaller woman's bed!

Four, 'leven and forty-four,
Four, 'leven and forty-four,
He walked out my door.
Last night he said, Honey,
I'm comin' back
When you git your big black money!

Four, 'leven and forty-four,
Four, 'leven and forty-four,
Let me hit that gig.
I'm needin' my man so bad
I'm feelin' freakish;
It's makin' me mean, lowdown and sad!'

The *Louisiana Weekly*, Negro newspaper, reported on January 9, 1937, regarding the famous Washwoman's Gig:

Lightning might not strike twice in the same place, but the Washwoman's Gig, 4–11–44, has been going the rounds again this week. Its appearance in a downtown company two weeks ago financially embarrassed their stockholders. This week the gig made its appearance at the Pelican and many gloomy faces became happier looking and many a heart commenced to beat faster. The gig, it is said by followers of the pastime, makes its appearance about once a year and brings sudden deficit to bankrolls. Lottery vendors say there is so much money played on 4-11-44 that it would break the Bank of Monte Carlo to pay off when the gig makes its appearance. . . .

'Lottery is my fate!' Martha White rolled her big eyes around in her dusky face, heaved her huge bosom in a mighty sigh. 'You is lookin' straight at a woman what has been tryin' to hit them numbers steady for a long time. I hit 'em for a nickel every once in a while, but them quarter licks sure does come in slow, I'm tellin' you. Trouble is I ain't never had enough money to play a system I knows.'

Her rocking chair creaked and wheezed. 'I likes to rock my weary soul,' she said, 'and Gawd knows it's weary. Sure I goes to church sometimes. Whenever the spirit moves me. But the spirit don't move me so much no more. Lottery gits in the way of my spirit.'

On the wall above Martha's bed three numbers were scrawled in heavy black pencil, four, eleven and forty-four — the famous Washwoman's Gig!

'No, I don't play that no more,' she said. 'No vendor'll take it. But I done tried everything else. Even hoodoo. But no hoodoo's ever gonna work with Lottery. It's dreams what counts. Hoodoo's all right when you wants somethin' or you wants to git rid of somebody, but you git rid of your Lottery vendor and where is you at? No, sir. All I needs to do is follow my dreams.

'You know I didn't used to believe in dreams? But once I dreamed I fell off a barn, and that means you gonna get married. I sure laughed at that — old woman like me what's done changed life two times and 'spectin' to change again pretty soon. But you know next day a crazy old preacher comes around askin' for my hand! I says, "Man, is you a damn fool?" and he leaves. Ever since then I believes in dreams and I plays in Lottery. See, when you dream 'bout a cabbage, play nine and thirty in a capital. One night I dreams I'm fallin' down a chimney. I

just ups and plays me that Chimney Gig, five, fifty-six and three.
Sure, I won. If you dreams of your husband, always play six,
forty-one and fifty; if it is your sister, play five, fifteen and forty-
five. That Blood Gig is really fine; any time you dreams of blood
be sure to put your money on five, ten and forty. And if you
dreams of Chinamans, you can't lose on the Chinaman's Gig,
one, two and three.

'When you dreams you sees an angel, there's the Angel Gig,
fourteen, sixty-five and nineteen. You can't miss. When you
dreams your nose is leakin', you get a gig on fourteen, one and
six. They done got a war on, ain't they? Play that War Gig,
ten, three and twenty-one. If I had me five dollars a week to play
my system, I believes I could get rich playin' my dreams, but
them Welfare peoples takes care of me, and they don't know I
plays Lottery. That ain't in my budget.' She giggled.

'I'll tell you somethin' bad. Don't never dream you is on the
gallows. That's the worstest dream there is. But if you does,
you play forty bottom. You can't lose. Watch out for mole
dreams. Them is really somethin'! If a girl dreams she's got a
mole on her belly, it's a plain fact she's gonna have trouble all
her life: 'Course she can always win Lottery on a nine, eighteen
and sixty-nine gig. If you dreams you got a mole on your
cheek, your numbers is sixteen, fifty-two and fifty-six. Names
is good things to dream about. For Joseph play eighteen,
thirty-five and sixty-two; for Francis, eleven, sixteen and twenty-
four; Albert means you ought to play seventeen, two and six.
I guess they got gigs for every name in the world.

'The best dream of all is to dream about a woman's petticoat.
That means you is really gonna win Lottery.'

Walk up Rampart Street in New Orleans any time, morning,
noon or night. Stop in any restaurant, any bar, and you'll find a
little corner devoted to policy writing. These remain open until
drawing time, then close, to reopen immediately afterward.
Go over to the vendor and place a gig. A gig is three numbers.
Play a nickel, a dime, a dollar, five dollars. To win, all three of
your three numbers must come out in the next drawing. Want
to insure your money? Put a saddle on it. Play a nickel gig and
a nickel saddle. That saddle means if only two of your numbers

come out on the list, you win something — forty cents for a nickel.

Stop and get a shoeshine. In one corner of the shop will be a vendor sitting behind an unpainted wooden table. The boy who pops his polishing cloth over your toes talks readily, volubly.

'Lottery shops? Yes, sir. There's three in this block. The Bag of Gold, the Clover Bloom and the Horseshoe Blue.

'Sure, I'd rather play Lottery than gamble at a dice table. You can't use no system with dice, but you sure can with Lottery. Like on Monday you play a nickel gig and a nickel saddle. Then you don't play no more until the list comes out. Then you play again. Hell, you can't lose no more than seventy cents in a week. But you gotta stick to your numbers. They bound to come out sometimes. It's just like feedin' up a little ole shoat. You gotta fatten that pig up first. Then you kills him.

'And you gotta play your hunches. You gotta play what comes to you. Dreams is a good way. Everybody plays their dreams. Sure I got me a dream book.'

There are numbers for every dream, for every hunch. Everyone has his own personal superstition about how to win at Lottery. Ideas like these prevail:

'I burns things, me. I burns candles, lamps and all kinds of powders. It sure do work too.'

'I knows a woman who mixes up black pepper and cinnamon and sprinkles it all around her house. She won lots of money that way. She lives off Lottery.'

'I always plays my numbers by what I thinks and dreams. I don't play on nothin' I can see, that's livin', or nothin' I can touch with my hand. My numbers is all from the spirit.'

'The other night I dreams a tall and handsome brown man was makin' love to me. I played sixteen for his color, seven for his height and forty-two for the age he looked about to be. All three of them numbers come out.'

'I plays Lottery like you goes to your office. It's my whole life, man. I wouldn't give it up for nothin'. If I had to choose between work and Lottery, I sure would take Lottery, 'cause I feels I can make money and still have all my time to myself.'

'Lottery ain't no sin. I feels I is justified in playin' it, 'cause then I gits what I wants without havin' to steal. So, you see, it ain't no sin.'

'I can only git my numbers when I is in my port.'

And by no means do the Lottery vendors confine themselves to Rampart Street, though they may be thickest there. They are literally everywhere, uptown, downtown, in every neighborhood.

New Orleans has always been a gambling town. Rooms for gaming were opened in the very first taverns and grog houses. With the Louisiana Purchase in 1803 and the subsequent opening of the Mississippi River to commerce, came swarms of professional gamblers and adventurers of all kinds. During the Creole era, six houses of chance were licensed by the Legislature at five thousand dollars a year each, four-fifths of the money to go to the Charity Hospital, one-fifth to the College of Orleans. These houses were small and only one roulette wheel or faro game was allowed to each.

The first gaming 'palace' was opened by John Davis, known as the father of gambling throughout the United States and one of the most colorful figures in New Orleans's early history. Owner of the Orleans Ballroom, he operated a magnificent establishment next door, containing the most elegant furnishings, the most costly and luxurious appointments, offering the finest service of foods and liquors and every game of chance imaginable.

Others followed rapidly, each vying with the others in elegance, in inducements for patronage. Many served tempting buffet suppers; one even offered an elaborate dinner of many courses each Sunday evening, served on plates of solid silver, all the food without charge. Evening clothes were compulsory in places so pretentious.

It is doubtful that any American city ever offered more reckless gambling than that which took place in New Orleans during this period; twenty-five thousand dollars would change hands at a single roll of the dice. Many wealthy men squandered hundreds of thousands of dollars a year in these establishments. Policy, Faro, Roulette, Craps, Poker and other card games were all popular. Davis's house boasted special rooms for Brag, Écarté and Boston. Professional gamblers from the steamboats plowing the dark waters of the Mississippi met here nightly, to win and lose, to fleece the naïve, to quarrel and duel, occasionally to kill.

Craps, having appeared early in the city's history, is believed to have been brought to the city by Louis Philippe and his brothers, the Duke de Montpensier and the Count de Beaujolais, when they were guests of Bernard de Marigny, head of a wealthy and distinguished Louisiana family, in 1798. De Marigny, whose personal passion was gambling of any sort, introduced the game to the fashionables of the city. And in later years, when he divided his princely estate, in what was then the outskirts of the city, into blocks and squares, he named one street the *Rue de Craps*, perhaps with irony, for it is reported that he was extremely unlucky at the game. But after a decade, when a Methodist Church was built on the *Rue de Craps* and became known as the Craps Methodist Church, it was thought best that the street become Burgundy Street, which it remains until today.

Louis Philippe maintained his interest in de Marigny and the game of Craps for years. One year when a certain Doctor Cenas and his gay, attractive wife were visiting in Paris, they were presented at Court. As the Cenases entered the ballroom and the announcer called out, '*Doctor et Madame Auguste Cenas de la Nouvelle Orléans*,' the royal countenance beamed and His Majesty demanded to know at once if, since they were from *Nouvelle Orléans*, they might be acquainted with the well-known de Marigny. And upon reassurance that they were, Louis Philippe gave them an audience which lasted for hours and reportedly consisted almost entirely of a discussion of the New Orleans gambler and the game known as Craps.

Today in the colored sections of the city there are always circles of men 'rollin' the bones,' playing *Indian* dice, which is any game of Craps unsupervised by a syndicate and without a player for the 'house.' Any Negro game of Craps will echo with such comments as these:

'I'm shootin' a dime, Lightie. I got a man!'

Lightie replies with a song:

> Look down, rider, spot me in the dark,
> When I calls these dice, break these niggers' hearts.

Roll out, seven, stand back, craps,
If I make this pass, I'll be standin' pat.

Fingers pop. 'When I get home let the story be told. Come
on, baby. Do it like Sally did it in Memphis. When the train
came she wasn't there. Let me roll a long time, 'cause I'm fresh
out of air.'

'Hit an eight. Flat on your back and do a flip-flap. Eight,
where is you?'

'Jump a rump and hop till I tell you to stop.'

Lightie's nasal tenor is loose again:

> Don't have to ride no boxcar,
> 'Cause I ain't goin' that far,
> Don't have to shed no tears,
> 'Cause I ain't got no years,
> Don't have to fuss and fight,
> 'Cause I got all night,
> To win this mo-neeeeeeey!

'You better get on that train, boy!'
'Boxcars don't pull that freight.'
'Craps two. They're comin' up again.'
'Can't you see them dice is cuttin'?'

Lightie:

> Last night I went to a game of Craps,
> Thinkin' I'd win some money perhaps,
> I thought them coons would have the fits,
> So I proudly said, 'I'll shoot six bits!'

> 'Come seven,' I said. The dice rolled three.
> I said, 'Gentlemen, youse has done cleaned me.'
> 'Clean already!' cried Liver-Lip Jim,
> 'Hell, you wasn't so smart when you first come in.'

The dice crack against the pavement again.
'My nutmeg done lost its charm, damn it.'
'Six and eight, while you wait.'
'Callin' five, shine your line.'
'Damn them snake eyes!'

'Shoot all. I got to get it while it's hot.'
'Come on, Red, swing out this lick.'
'Dime on any crap.'
'Little Joe, everywhere I go.'
'Roll out, seven!'
Another song:

> My baby needs a new pair of shoes; come along, you seven,
> She can't get 'em if I lose; come along, you seven.
> Roll them bones, roll 'em on a square, roll 'em on a sidewalk,
> Street and everywhere; we'll roll 'em in the mornin', Joe.
>
> Roll them in the night,
> We'll roll them bones the whole day long,
> When the cops are out of sight,
> We will roll them bones.

'Shake, baby, shake! You don't shake you don't get no jelly-cake.'
'Roll, baby, roll. You don't get my gold.'
'Come, seven!'
And the dice roll. Uptown, downtown, in the great gambling-houses flourishing in the parishes just above and below the city, the ivory cubes leave tense fists to go flying and tumbling, winning and losing nickels, dimes, dollars, thousands, for the addicts of this game of Craps.

Every number on the dice has at least one name. The best known are: 2 — Snake Eyes, 3 — Craps, 4 — Little Joe, 5 — Fever, 6 — Big Six, 7 — Natural, 8 — Ada from Decatur, 9 — Nina, 10 — Big Dick, 11 — Natural, 12 — Boxcars.

All over New Orleans are opportunities for every sort of gambling. Behind barrooms and beer parlors, restaurants and pool-rooms, races are 'booked.' This is almost as commonplace as Lottery. Numerous card games are always in progress in upper rooms. Yet all this is at least semi-surreptitious. But in the miniature Monte Carlos in Jefferson and St. Bernard Parishes there is little or no attempt at concealment. In these places, some of them almost modern counterparts of the luxurious establishments of John Davis's era in size and magnificence, the lights burn brightly every night, from six in the evening until late.

Recently one of them began opening for afternoon 'matinées' for housewives.

Laborers and bankers, scrubwomen and society women, clerks, doctors, professional gamblers — all strata of society are represented, people with nickels and people with dollars and people with fortunes to risk. Until long past midnight it is almost impossible to squeeze in at one of the tables where the roulette wheels are spinning or the dice rolling. All sorts of games are popular at those clubs, from nickel slot machines and pinball machines to dice games where thousands of dollars change hands at a throw of the little ivory cubes. From time to time a 're-form' State Government closes these places; but they always reopen.

At least in the sheer number of persons who play it, Keno is the most popular game of all. A form of Lotto, seven hundred persons can play at a time. Cards cost five cents each and it is usual to play several cards at one time. Players thrill as the caller shouts the numbers and they flash in red on immense tabulating boards. Several times each night there are 'gold rolls,' at which time the winner usually receives about seventy dollars, occasionally more. An entire evening may be spent playing Keno at a very small cost.

Bingo parties are popular in New Orleans and its vicinity. Everyone gives them, from churches and political organizations to people raising their rent. And Bingo is another form of Keno.

But Lottery boasts even more addicts than does Keno. For years Lottery has been an integral part of New Orleans and Louisiana life.

The Louisiana Lottery Company was authorized to operate by Legislature in 1868 when it promised to pay $40,000 a year toward the upkeep of the Charity Hospital in New Orleans. The first drawing offered a Grand Prize of $3700 on a twenty-five-cent ticket. This was increased the following year to a fifty-cent ticket and a $7500 Grand Prize. At last it rose to such heights that a capital Grand Prize of $600,000 was being offered twice a year with a forty-dollar ticket. No one person ever won this huge prize in its entirety, but a New Orleans barber once held a ticket for twenty dollars and was paid his $300,000 without question.

The original charter of the Louisiana Lottery Company was for twenty-five years. This was canceled in 1879, but a new one, including even greater privileges, was granted the following year.

The accompanying advertisement from *The Mascot* of December 2, 1882, is typical:

LA. S. L.

TAKE NOTICE

This is the only lottery in any State ever voted on and Endorsed by the People

SPLENDID CHANCE FOR A FORTUNE!

THE LOUISIANA STATE
LOTTERY COMPANY

Will Give, at New Orleans, La., on
Tuesday, December 19, 1882,

A Promenade Concert,

During which will take place, the

EXTRAORDINARY DRAWING
Class M.

Under the immediate supervision and management of
Gen. G. T. Beauregard of Louisiana and
Gen. Jubal A. Early, of Virginia

NO SCALING!   NO POSTPONEMENT!

OVER A HALF A MILLION DOLLARS DISTRIBUTED.

ALL PRIZES PAID IN FULL!

One Capital Prize................$100,000
One Capital Prize............... 50,000
One Capital Prize............... 20,000

11,279 Prizes, all Amounting to
$522,500

The Drawing will Positively commence at Eleven
o'clock a.m., on the morning of
TUESDAY, DECEMBER 19, 1882

LOOK AT THE SCHEME!

EXTRAORDINARY SCHEME!

100,000 TICKETS AT $10 EACH.

In 1898 the company was able to offer the State $1,250,000 for a renewal. But by now Lottery was highly unpopular as having a pernicious effect on the poor and as possessing tremendous political power, which was being misused. Lottery became almost the sole issue of the gubernatorial campaign that year.

In 1895 the federal statute prohibiting interstate transport of the tickets was passed. The company promptly moved to Honduras. There it remained until 1907, when it was forced out of business by federal prosecution of its American agents at home.

But this wasn't the end of Lottery in New Orleans. It seems to have been only the beginning.

There are scores of Lottery shops today, hundreds of vendors, some who walk the streets, have a regular route, regular clients.

Lottery vendors, apparently, do not look upon their profession as lacking in respectability.

'Anything you do ought to be made respectable,' argued one of them. 'You know some people can make any job look respectable; and others would make the same job look just opposite. It's all the way you see life. Me? I make about five dollars a day. Some of the fellows make as much as eight.'

In a certain section of New Orleans the average family income is less than fifty dollars a month. Yet everybody plays Lottery. Somehow they manage to gamble at least five cents a day. They live with Lottery. They live *for* Lottery.

'You got to think about Lottery all the time,' they'll tell you. 'You got to keep the numbers in your mind and nothing else. That's the secret of it. You must think of nothing but numbers and Lottery.'

And that's what they do. They think of nothing but numbers and Lottery. They dream of numbers and Lottery at night. Everything that happens has some bearing on what gigs they pick for their nickels. Every dream has its translation into numbers to be bet on Lottery. And by no means is this passion confined to Negroes. Hundreds of white people make it an inseparable part of their daily lives. They seem to find in the game an escape, an almost glamorous rainbow trail with hope and a pot of gold always ahead. And sometimes they win. Many families seem to supplement their incomes constantly by scrupulous attention to every detail of the art of playing Lottery.

The Pelican Lottery Company is probably the best known and the most prosperous in the Negro section. A great believer in advertising, this company uses handbills, and even sound trucks. In 1937, when the Washwoman's Gig almost broke the Pelican, the manager was astute enough to capitalize on his losses by having sound trucks blast the news from one end of New Orleans to the other about how the Pelican paid off. He gives away free chickens, turkeys and groceries to stimulate attendance at drawings.

There are about sixty persons employed by the Pelican. All the inside workers are Negroes, and the vendors are white or black according to what neighborhood they work. Drawings are held three times a week, on Monday, Wednesday and Friday, and many white people mingle with the colored at these affairs.

Another well-known policy establishment is on the edge of what was once New Orleans's notorious Storyville, now replaced by a Federal Housing Project. Here business starts early in the morning. One of the first clients is a well-dressed young Negro, who keeps walking in and out of the shop, seeming unable to make up his mind what to play.

'That's his system,' the vendor explained. This particular vendor is dignified and soft-spoken, the scion of a once distinguished Creole family. 'He likes to watch what the others are playing. He's a college student. Frequently he wins, though not as often as those fool niggers who play their dreams and all sorts of crazy hunches. On Lincoln's Birthday one of them played a hunch and won thirty-six dollars. The night before he had dreamed he was a slave and was freed at the time all the others were. That was in 1863, so he placed his money on two, twelve, eighteen and sixty-three. Do you know, every one of those numbers came in!'

As the morning wore on, the shop crowded with both black and white customers. A favorite number seemed to be fifty-nine. This was one popular with the Creoles in the old days when open Lottery flourished. A nurse from Charity Hospital came in to collect yesterday's winnings. The night before she had been playing Keno at one of the big gambling-houses in Jefferson Parish, and had missed three times on twenty-one. A man sitting next to her had advised her to keep playing it, that she couldn't miss. So she had played it on Lottery and it had headed the list. The vendor said this young lady played all her hunches and seldom lost.

A white man grumbled: 'My wife sends me here every day to play numbers, and do I get bawled out if they don't hit! She gets the damnedest ideas. Day before yesterday I brought home some lemons and there turned out to be only eleven in the bag instead of the dozen I had paid for.

'Right away she starts hollering, "Go back and get that lemon, you dumb ox!" Then she says, "Wait a minute!" And I knew what was coming. "Go play eleven, first station," she says.

'Well, of course *twelve* came in yesterday. Did I catch hell! She said if I had brought home that other lemon she would have played twelve. She chinned about it all night long. And she wouldn't have done that at all. She would have played some other fool hunch.

'Know what I'm playing today? Six, twelve and twenty-four, and you wouldn't guess why in a million years. It happens the washerwoman is going to have a baby, and last night my wife dreamed it would be twins and that each twin would have six toes on each foot. Can you beat that one? She decided that the babies would probably have two feet apiece, so she multiplied the toes by two and by four. God help me if they don't all come out! I'll bet that woman ain't going to have but one baby with five toes on each foot. Maybe she ain't going to have a baby at all. How the hell do I know?'

Over one thousand persons are employed in this business, as clerks, callers, bookkeepers and vendors, all but the latter receiving a straight salary of $2.50 a day, the vendor being paid a commission on collections.

Many persons attend the drawings, believing it better to be there, and frequently the companies encourage this as good advertising, often giving additional prizes of groceries, radios and articles of furniture to the holders of the winning tickets for being present at the drawings.

The caller, standing on a platform, places seventy-two numbers in the wheel, then selects someone from the audience and blindfolds him. When the wheel is spun, this selected drawer shoves in his hand and picks one of the little wooden balls. The number on the ball is then loudly announced by the caller. This is done twelve consecutive times. These numbers are then stamped on a vendor's list, and copies of this list are distributed by the vendors to everyone who played in this particular drawing. To have won, your numbers must, of course, appear on this list.

There are innumerable ways of playing Lottery. If your nickel gig wins — all three numbers appearing on the vendor's list — you receive nine dollars. If it was saddled, you win a dollar, twenty-five cents more. If saddled and only two numbers appeared, you'll get forty cents. Play your nickel on a number for capital position and if it shows in the first three stations, five dollars is yours. Or you may play one number to·appear anywhere on the list and the nickel might earn two dollars and fifty cents.

Negro tenements are favorite places for Lottery vendors to set up business. Here in dingy rooms, under green-shaded drop lights, they write numbers and accept gigs. Inside vendors are never permitted to work outside. Most of the tenement vendors are white and they are careful to treat their clients with every courtesy. Walls are decorated with the numbers of popular gigs, also with numbers that coincide with dreams, many of them invented by the vendors themselves. They can always supply a gig on any dream, idea or hunch a customer may have. A prospective customer never gets away. That different vendors will undoubtedly supply entirely different numbers for the same dream, or even that the same vendor might do this on different days, is nobody's business but the vendor's. The important thing is that the customer is always satisfied. 'Everybody has a right to a mind of his own,' says Beulah Howard, a regular customer. 'If you see diff'runt numbers in your brain than somebody else does, that ain't nothin'. You gotta play what's in your head.'

When a player gets the blues about his Lottery, especially when his numbers 'ain't runnin' right,' he always blames his bad luck on something. Often it's his love life. He'll sing:

> It's a funny thing them numbers ain't treatin' me right,
> It's a funny thing them numbers ain't treatin' me right,
> Maybe some black nigger's with my old lady tonight.
>
> When a man's under your bed in the fall,
> I say when a man's under your bed in the fall,
> You just don't have no luck atall.
>
> Ain't no foolin' with Lottery, no indeed,
> No need to fool with Lottery, no indeed,
> 'Cause you'll never git the money you need,
> Not if a man's sneakin' under your house in the fall.

Dreams, hunches, automobile licenses, all are played in these establishments and with the street vendors. Of particular importance is the 'Lawd,' many people calling on Him to 'bring their numbers home,' and for protection, should it be suspected that someone 'has done rubbed their pants pockets with some devil stuff.' Preachers are seldom asked for help with Lottery, but spiritualist 'mothers' do a heavy business in this direction, often receiving a cut in the winnings. 'Sometimes it takes powders and stuff to bring them numbers 'round,' is the common opinion. But the preachers have no objections to their flock playing Lottery. They usually profit from it. Many gamblers are superstitious about leaving the church out of their winnings. Anyway, the preachers couldn't stop them.

'Why does Negroes play Lottery?' muses Willie Jones, who is a philosopher as well as a gambler. ''Cause they dreams so much. You see, Lottery is dreamin' and dreamin' is Lottery. That's the truth. Ain't no cause and ain't no effect unless you dreams in Lottery, is there? I always say find the cause and you'll find the effect, and the cause of cullud peoples playin' Lottery is dreamin'. We is just natural dreamers 'cause we eats too much. So eatin' is the cause, and the effects is dreamin' and Lottery. Take me. All I got to do to dream is just eat four or five bananas before I goes to bed. That sure do make me dream! Then next day I makes me a gig and wins nine dollars. That's plenty of money, 'specially for a nickel.

'Every now and then the Lawd pussonally shows me numbers. The Lawd took me out of sin, you know, and put me in the land of the religious. And when the Lawd shows me numbers I is bound to win. How does I know? I reckon the Lawd 'tends to take care of Willie Jones.

'I eats my bananas, goes to sleep, then I sees the Lawd. He stands right smack before me like a natural man. He points one finger at me. I says, "One." He points two fingers. I says, "Two." Then He raises His whole hand. The Lawd done told me to play one, two and five. I is filled with joy straight from the Lawd. "Hallelujah!" I cries. My crazy wife wakes up and yells: "Look at that nigger! Just look at that man! That damn fool!" Then I reaches over and busts her one in the mout'. That shuts her up for a while.

'Let me tell you somethin', brother. I got a strong 'preciation of the Lawd. You is lookin' at a man what's been shot five times by a woman. I told the Lawd if He'd let me live, I'd never do another wrong. That's why I married me a Christian woman. Then I joined the Baptist Church. Went straight from sinner-man to board member to deacon to head deacon. That's what I is now, head deacon.

'No, indeed! Lottery ain't no sin, Lottery is just dreams. Cullud people got to gamble cheap and all of 'em plays Lottery. Does they win? Sometimes they does. And, man, when a cullud man wins Lottery it's worser than a fat woman gittin' religion. They just jumps up and down and hollers.'

Willie looked very wise for a second. ''Course you knows who them big shots is what really makes money out of that game,' he said. 'Man, one of 'em has a big mansion down in Gentilly. It's like a king's palace or somethin'.

'Guess you heard 'bout the time this big shot went to the bank with so many sacks of money the cashier's eyes was poppin' out his head. "What you got there?" that cashier asked. You know what that Lottery King done told him? He said, "Nigger dreams." That might sound funny, but it was the truth. That's all it was. Just nigger dreams.'

Chapter 8

The Creoles

LIKE THE GREEKS, THE CREOLES HAD A WORD
for everything. For themselves they even did better than that.
Every Creole was *sorti de la cuisse de Jupiter* — a piece from the
thigh of Jupiter; and privately each one considered himself a
slice of deity of no mean proportions. That was not all. They
were *crème de la crème*; and if a Creole family was not exactly
de la fine fleur des pois — literally, not of the most select blooms
of the sweet pea blossom — it was certainly one of *les bonnes
familles*. And woe to the *gens du commun* — the common people
— ambitious enough or foolish enough to attempt to enter
Olympus! The gates were closed. It has been said that the Low-
ells spoke only to the Cabots and the Cabots spoke only to God,
but it is fairly safe to say that in the very early Creole era both
families would have been snubbed by the Creoles of New
Orleans.

The French founders of Louisiana arrived in the last year of the
seventeenth century and by 1765, when Spain took possession,
French culture was so entrenched that the appointment of the
Spanish governor caused an insurrection that cost many lives.
But the Spanish had come to stay, and marriage and interbreed-

ing were inevitable. It was even the newcomers who gave the Creoles their name. *Criollo*, eventually corrupted to *Criado*, was the Spanish name for children born in the colonies. Adopting this, the French speedily changed it to Creole.

In 1803 Louisiana passed back to France, but the joy of reunion with the mother country was short-lived. Napoleon, conquering Europe and in need of cash, quickly sold the territory to the United States. There were protests from the Creoles, but no uprisings this time. They watched the changing of the flags fluttering above the *Place d'Armes* with heavy hearts, but quietly, solemnly. Already the determination to live within themselves must have been engendering in their minds. These Americans might come to New Orleans, but never would they enter its inner circles. They would always remain foreigners. The impregnable barriers went up. The bitter struggle against Americanization had begun.

Creoles were predominantly French, though much Spanish blood had been absorbed. Some German and Irish settlers also intermarried in the early days, but all the national characteristics of these peoples seem to have completely vanished. They became 'so Frenchified,' says Gayarré, 'that they appear to be of Gallic parentage.' German family names were, in many instances, literally translated; Zweig, for instance, became La Branche. An Irish family of O'Briens pronounced their name Obreeong!

All Creole children received a French education. Often the boys were sent to Paris, and the girls were instructed in local convents guided by French nuns. French thought, literature and art impregnated them so deeply that they existed in a completely French culture, their ideas and manners as much imported as their household furnishings, wines, books, clothes and pictures.

No true Creole ever had colored blood. This erroneous belief, still common among Americans in other sections of the country, is probably due to the Creoles' own habit of calling their slaves 'Creole slaves' and often simply 'Creoles.' Too, there are proud light-colored families in New Orleans today who are known as 'Creoles' among themselves. But Creoles were always pure white. Any trace of *café au lait* in a family was reason for complete ostracism.

Among themselves Creoles divided into various castes or strata, both socially and financially, though no one seems ever to have agreed as to the category in which his family belonged. There were Creoles, Chacks, Chacas, Catchoupines, Chacalatas, Bambaras and Bitacaux. The term 'Chacalata,' for instance, indicated much the same thing as does 'Hoosier' or 'countrified'; 'Bambaras' (untidiness) perhaps hinted at uncleanliness. 'Cachumas' were those whose ancestors had acquired a strain of *café noir*, and even today in the Barataria section this term is sometimes heard.

Everything they used or possessed received, like their slaves, the Creole appellation: their cooking, horses, chickens, vegetables and axe-handles. To become acclimated was to be 'Creolized.'

They were seven to one in the city in 1803, three to one in 1812, only two to one by 1830. But between 1812 and the Civil War they were wealthiest and their influence most dominant.

And this was not entirely confined to New Orleans. Many of the plantations lining both sides of the Mississippi River belonged to them. Far out in western Louisiana, in the land of the Attacapan Indians and the Cajuns, they founded a little town then known as Petit Paris. Here French noblemen, refugees from the Revolution and 'Madame Guillotine,' tried to recreate the courtly days just past, and Petit Paris was soon a tiny Versailles, the residence of such as Le Baron du Cloyal, Le Chevalier Louis de Blanc and Le Comte Louis de la Houssaye. Later Petit Paris became St. Martinville.

In New Orleans the Creoles were resentful and contemptuous of the American strangers, even considered them wicked. 'They do not even attach importance to the Commandment of honoring their fathers and mothers,' wrote one shocked Creole lady. 'The sons marry to please themselves, and even the daughters do not ask their parents' permission!' For the Creole boy or girl who married one of these 'foreigners' there was no forgiveness; they had stepped beyond the pale.

The Creoles refused to speak English. The Americans refused to speak French. Creole boys ran behind Americans in the streets singing this taunting song:

'Méricain coquin	'Merican rogues
Billé en naquin	Dressed in nankeen
Voleur di pain	Stole loaves of bread
Chez Miche D'Aquin!	From Mr. D'Aquin!

Monsieur D'Aquin was a well-known baker in the Vieux Carré.

Americans reacted by disliking the Creoles with equal enthusiasm. One wrote home to New England, 'Smiles and bows are abundant and cheap and in these they are profuse and liberal, but there is little sterling, honest friendship in existence; and exhibition, outward show and pretensions are the ruling passions!'

Gradually New Orleans became not one city but two, Canal Street splitting them apart, dividing the old Creole city from the 'uptown' section, where the Americans were rapidly settling. To cross Canal Street in either direction was to enter another world. Even today these differences are noticeable.

Among themselves, Creoles were warm, affectionate, extremely loyal. *La famille* was the very core of their life, and, like the humbler Cajuns, this extended to the utmost limits of relationship. Cable wrote: 'One thing I never knew a Creole to do; he will not utterly go back on the ties of blood, no matter what sort of knots those ties may **be**. For one reason he is ashamed of his or his father's sins; for another he will tell you he is *all heart*.'

Creole gentlemen could only enter certain professions and occupations. Most of them were planters, bankers, brokers in rice, sugar or cotton, occasionally clerks in establishments of these types. Sometimes they ventured into politics. They were barred from entering trade or working in a store or shop. Because of these rigid limitations in their caste system, ambition was often stunted, opportunity ignored. No Creole could do anything that would cause him to work with his hands or to remove his coat. A gentleman never appeared in public without coat, cravat and gloves.

Most family heads had a few *fainéants* — loafers — in their homes who could not — or would not — work. These relatives or old friends must be supported, and usually without complaint. Occasionally a male *fainéant* might be jokingly accused of having *les côtes en long* — vertical ribs; this was the extent of the criticism. Of course there was no way in which any Creole woman could earn money, so spinster *tantes* — aunts — and *cousines* must be 'carried on.' Many of these more than earned their maintenance, however, in helping to raise the children. Aged relatives and orphans could never be placed in an institution. No Creole was ever guilty of such a thought.

Within the Creole world the father was absolute head of his household and his word was final in all matters. Merely to upset any of his convictions required tremendous skill and subtlety on the part of his wife, combined with every *tante* and *cousine* in *la famille*. But this Creole father was always generous, devoted, kind to a fault, unless some member of his household transgressed one of the rules set down to keep the family free of *scandale*; then his wrath was terrible, sometimes without forgiveness; otherwise he would lavish all he possessed or could earn on his numerous children and perhaps a half-dozen *fainéants*.

The Creole mother, though she might have been a beauty in her day, was nearly always of generous proportions. Creole ladies did not diet, and meals were always sumptuous. She was an excellent housekeeper — economical, hospitable and a devoted mother. Usually she possessed an equal number of social assets, was a skilled dancer, a charming conversationalist, a perfect hostess, and accomplished in all the graces and manners of her world. Deeply religious, she prodded her men toward the Church and saw that the children were trained in all its teachings. She was loyal to her husband until death. Even if she knew he maintained a beautiful quadroon in a separate establishment, no word of the matter ever passed her lips. At her husband's death she invariably manifested great grief, rarely remarried, and always observed strictest mourning in dress and deportment for the required period of several years.

Many widowers remarried, however. It was considered that the children should have a mother and frequently a match was arranged for the man, often to his deceased mate's sister, should there be one unmarried. Thus many a Creole spinster was saved from an — in her day — ignominious rôle in life by her sister's death.

Early travelers through Louisiana wrote of the Mississippi River water and its marvelous effect on the fecundity of the Creole woman. Ten or more children was the average for any family, and the father's respect for the mother increased with each additional birth. There was once a prominent Creole judge who, with true Creole values of courtliness, paid his wife a formal call each time she bore him a child, which was practically every year. A few hours after the birth he would don his most formal attire, including tall silk hat, long cape and cane, step into her bedchamber, remove his hat with a sweeping bow, and present her with a bouquet and his congratulations.

From the lips of the Creole mother sprang many of the proverbs which have become famous: *Ta finesse est cousue de fil blanc* — Your shrewdness is sewed with white thread; *Chacun sait ce qui bouille dans se chaudière* — Each one knows what boils in his own pot (in the close-knit Creole society everyone else knew as well!); *On lave son linge sal en famille* — Wash your dirty clothes in your own family; *Dans le pays des aveugles, les borgnes sont rois* — In the country of the blind the nearsighted are kings; *Elle joue à la chandelle* — She plays the candle (applied to the mother of a girl who would not go to bed until the girl's *beaux* went home); and *C'est la fée Carabos* — literally, She is the fairy Carabos (meaning an ugly, quarrelsome woman).

Among its slaves every Creole family had a Negress as nurse for the young children. The importance of Mammy in the household and the extent of her influence over her young charges can scarcely be overestimated. Through all her life she shared the children's affection with the parents. When Mammy grew old, she was retired, the family supporting her to the end of her days. At her death the now adult people she had raised, often several generations, grieved deeply.

Years after her passing, a Creole woman wrote of her nurse:

'Her devotion was so great she would make any sacrifice for us; her money was our money; all she had was for her dear children. In sickness she would spend sleepless nights watching over us while our parents slept. She would come into our rooms during the night to see that we were properly covered. When we grew older and began to go out at night to balls or to the the-

ater, Mammy sat up by the downstairs fire and awaited our return, anxious to hear the details of the party, to give us a bite to
eat and to tuck us into bed.

'But Mammy could be stern and she would not hesitate to
punish us if we needed it. When we were small Mammy had a
terrible time on Saturday nights. When we saw her carrying in
the tub of warm water, the soap and washrag, there was a battle
royal, but Mammy always won.

'The greatest treat of all was to awaken every morning to
Mammy's words, "*Alà vous café*," and see her standing beside
your bed, her round black face broken with a white smile, her
tignon neatly tied about her head and pushed high with a comb
worn underneath, her spotless apron stiff with starch, a tray in
her hands on which was piping-hot drip coffee, ground and
roasted at home.

'Mammy was really the boss of the house, was consulted on all
subjects. Father and Mother often went to her for advice and her
judgment was always wise and sound.

'Her death plunged us deeply into grief. She had been in the
family for sixty years. Her funeral was most dignified, my
father and uncles serving as pallbearers; and she was laid to rest
in the family tomb in old St. Louis Cemetery No. 2. I remember
wearing mourning for months and refusing to go to any place of
amusement. The mammies of that era should have a monument
raised to their memories, for their lives were filled with devotion
and self-sacrifice for their white families.'

Mammy invariably spoke Creole, the soft patois Negroes developed from their attempts to speak French and which, like
everything else the Creoles used, received their name, though the
Anglo-Saxon element in the city referred to the dialect as
'Gombo.' This tongue, really far more expressive and beautiful
to the ear than a mere dialect, was moreover, sentimental, slyly
humorous, often filled with sharp aspersions against the whites,
bitter and merciless in its indictment of those colored people who
imitated their white masters. 'Toucoutou' is an example of the
latter in song — 'there is no soap white enough to wash your
skin.' (See 'Songs,' page 428.)

Mammy had her male prototype, too. Many an old 'Uncle'

was as well loved within the family circle. A present-day Creole described Prosper Ernest Fournier, famous in Creole New Orleans as the perfect male servant, saying: 'Prosper was a Negro with the instincts and culture of a white gentleman. He was one of the most polished individuals with whom I have ever had the pleasure of shaking hands.'

Prosper, no part-caste Negro, but full-blooded African, was a great cook, an authority on the opera and operatic voices and a student of the French and English classics. He was only employed by two families in his life. A member of one of the families for whom he worked remembered:

'He remained aloof from the other servants, both black and white, but was scrupulously polite in his relations with the family. The only place that was taboo was his kitchen. We respected that and rarely entered that room without an invitation. Like many other slave cooks he had, in his youth, been apprenticed to a great chef in Paris, and after a number of years had returned, stating that he wished to prove that his master's trust had borne fruit, and his cooking was an exquisite art. He insisted on writing a menu each day and this was placed before my father at the sacred dinner hour, to be passed to the rest of the family after his perusal. Prosper was very strict about the dinner hour. Seven P.M. was seven P.M.; he always reminded us that a delay of five minutes ruined a dish.

'Prosper never left the house except to go to market, to church, and each Saturday night (the fashionable night) to the French Opera. On the latter occasions he rode in the family carriage with us, then went upstairs to the top balcony reserved for colored people. Here he had always the same seat, in the front row, center. Whenever any white person he knew entered one of the dress circle boxes he would rise and offer them a Chesterfieldian bow, which they always returned. Then, the cynosure of all the other Negroes' eyes, he devoted himself to the performance. I have heard many well-known music lovers ask his opinion of the leading voices of a troupe, and he would always state his views respectfully but frankly, and his judgment was always accepted. When a famous diva gave a farewell performance in New Orleans, an authority on the opera asked Prosper his opinion. "She should never have been permitted to sing in this city again," was the answer, "for her once incomparable voice is now forever gone." The man was stupefied. "I thought so, too," he admitted, "but I did not dare express myself. I am glad, though, that you have indicated my own musical sense."

'Prosper was a connoisseur of fine wines, and insisted that to cook without wine was an absolute impossibility. However, he imbibed only a *demi-bouteille* of claret while having his dinner — in solitary state. He held the keys to the cellar and never asked permission to do this. Each day when he drew the claret, Madeira, sherry and sauterne for the various dishes, he added his "due" irrespective of who was present. He would discuss freely with my father as to its qualities and bouquet as compared to the other vintages on the shelves.

'He took good care of the boys in the house. If any of us were sick he insisted on sitting up by our beds all night, and no nurse could have given us better care than this tall, dignified black man. If any of us came home very late after a rather intemperate evening, he would sneak us into the house without Father hearing us. Once my brother was particularly noisy and Prosper had to hold him tight and put a firm hand over his mouth to keep him from singing and shouting. Father awoke and came part of the way down the stairs, demanding to know what was going on. Prosper lied like a gentleman, saying that he had been unable to sleep and had been walking in the garden. Father told him he was crazy, then returned to his room, and Prosper managed to get that young man to bed without his ever knowing the truth.

'Prosper came to a sad end. There was an old mulattress who did some of the family washing, and who was held in great awe by all the Negroes as a witch and a seeress. Once she kept some of our curtains too long and Prosper offered to go and get them. The other servants advised him not to, but he laughed at their fears. Returning, he told his brother, who was our gardener and general utility man, "Guess what Clémentine told me? She said you will be dead within a week and that I shall be in the insane asylum!" He thought this was a great joke, since he was too well educated to be at all superstitious.

'But within a week his brother was run over by a cotton float and instantly killed. A few days later Prosper, returning from market, went stark mad, throwing his marketing and money all over the street and yelling like a Comanche Indian. He had to be placed in a mental-disease hospital. When he emerged he was a shrunken, stooped old man. He did not live much longer. Before he died he made a last request. No colored man must touch his coffin. This wish was granted and some of the most prominent business men in New Orleans bore Prosper Ernest Fournier's casket to the grave.'

The importance of these servants — the Mammies and the 'Prospers' — cannot be overestimated in their influence on Creole family life. Mammy's influence was so great and so much of her time was spent with her children that most young Creoles grew up speaking the language. Gradually it became the custom to speak Creole even in the drawing-rooms at times, for it was far more native to Louisiana than French could ever be, and more flexible, being capable of turns and twists impossible in French.

As a whole, Creole children were very spoiled, but their restrictions were many. They were seldom allowed to speak at the table, except at dessert, when the whole family would sing.

Coco Robichaux must have been a little sister of the modern 'little man who wasn't there,' though she was very much alive in the mind of every Creole child. No one ever knew who she was or where she lived or what she looked like, but poor Coco Robichaux received the blame for everything. Every time a naughty little girl did something she shouldn't, she was told, 'You didn't do that. That was the Coco Robichaux!' or, 'A nice little girl like you wouldn't do that. Only Coco Robichaux could be so naughty.' The only thing really known about this Coco Robichaux was that she was very, very bad. She had all the faults any child between two and ten could possibly possess.

Children loved to help clarify the drinking water. In all houses there were several large jars, called *ollas*, which were kept filled with Mississippi water. A lump of alum was dropped in, and the children would stir for hours, until the water was purified.

School started at eight or nine years of age. The primary

training was usually received in the private establishment in the home of some spinster in financial straits. After First Communion, at the age of twelve, the boys were sent to study with the Jesuit Fathers, while the girls entered convents.

When she finished at the convent, the young Creole lady made her initial appearance at the French Opera House, was given a reception and thus considered launched in society. There were no débutantes; a girl was usually as popular her third season out as during her first. This initial appearance at the Opera House was the only event similar to the modern début. For the occasion she wore a gorgeous gown imported from Paris, carried a bouquet with long ribbon streamers and a fine lace fan.

Accompanied by her parents, the girl would receive callers in the box rented for the performance. Between the acts the young men would drop in to pay compliments and their respects to the chaperons. And, behind their fluttering fans, the gossips would watch each box closely, keeping careful count of the number of male visitors each received, for by this was a girl's popularity gauged.

The Creole girl was schooled in self-effacement. Her picture must never appear in the newspapers nor must a single line ever be written about her. When a young man wished to call, it was necessary that he have a friend act as intermediary and ask the permission of the girl's father.

But the young couple were never allowed to be alone. If the youth were guilty of any wishful thinking, it was soon dispelled, and completely. His fate usually was to spend the evening playing a riotous game of dominoes with the girl's father, while the mother and *tantes* questioned him regarding family background, financial and social assets.

No great importance was attached to this first visit. However, should he continue to call, and not mention his intentions, the parents would demand that he do so, without hesitation. There was no respect or time to be wasted on a young man with *le cœur comme un artichaud* — a heart like an artichoke (that is, a leaf for everyone). Creole girls had no time to waste on flirts. Marriage was the entire aim of their lives. And if unmarried at twenty-five hope was forsaken; they 'might as well throw their corsets on the *armoire*.' An unmarried girl was never permitted to wear a velvet dress, though she might have one in her hope chest. After the fatal twenty-five, if unmarried, she was supposed to adopt the hooded bonnet with ribbons that tied under her chin.

Should a young man fall in love and wish to marry the girl he had been visiting, his friend was called into service again in the capacity of a John Alden, only her father must be approached again and asked for his daughter's hand. The young lady had nothing to do with it. The whole exciting situation created an occasion that demanded the utmost caution, tact and diplomacy. Accepted, the prospective groom and his father called on the girl's father and every obstacle was cleared away. Each family carefully scrutinized the family tree of the other. Material wealth meant little, *la famille* was everything. Did they come from a good family? Were they even faintly of the *gens du commun*? Even that really unmentionable consideration must be investigated; was there any possible trace of *café au lait*? All the skeletons were dragged forth for inspection.

Only when both parties had passed this rigid examination did material considerations enter. But they were by no means neglected. A formal marriage contract was drawn up, listing the boy's and the girl's financial assets; properties, furniture, number, names, worth and capacity of slaves, and cash — all were included. The girl's dowry, usually ranging from one to forty thousand dollars, was submitted to the examination of the young man and his father. Despite all this, husbands were valuable for their own sakes, and should the youth be unable to support a wife, this was no bar to the marriage. Often the bride's father would find or create a place for him in his business, if his background were satisfactory.

Creole women always enjoyed a reputation for great beauty. Some of the Americans coming to their city were tactless enough to remark that they were a bit plump, but others, perhaps liking the well-fed appearance, penned ecstatic praise home to New England.

One, evidently completely enchanted by the New Orleans girls, wrote: 'In entering a sanctuary the soul bows down. The pen feels moved when it touches upon a sacred subject. The

flower and woman are two treasures; the flower must have its
perfume and woman her soul, a perfume that is more fragrant
and less ephemeral. One finds in the traits of the Creole a distinction perfect in harmony and form. Pure profiles, patrician
lines, oval and delicate chiseling, lacking in vigor perhaps — a
little aerial — the ethereal dominating the material, the ideal
combating reality.'

Luxuriant hair was the pride of every Creole lady. Washing
it was a rite. When it began to gray, she secretly darkened it
with coffee. Creoles denied using rouge and makeup, admitting
only that occasionally a girl might rub her cheeks with crushed
rose petals, but the Americans accused them of much elaborate
artificial embellishment, though they admitted that it was done
with great art. And they always took extreme good care of their
complexions, wearing veils when out-of-doors at all times. Sun
tan, instead of being valued as now, was considered disgraceful,
indeed it might start ghastly rumors of *café au lait!*

They loved fine clothes. No woman would ever leave her home
unless completely attired, including gloves and veil. For evening
wear most of their gowns were imported from Paris, and their
beauty was accentuated with many jewels.

The Creole girl was never left alone with her young man, even
after the engagement was announced. Often the entire family
remained in the parlor throughout the evening. And when they
went out, the future husband must expect plenty of company. It
was perfectly proper that as many members of the family accompany them as felt so inclined.

After the formal announcement of the betrothal there was the
déjeuner de fiançailles — engagement breakfast — which all members of both families attended. The ring, presented to the girl at
this event, was not the usual solitaire of today, but a large ruby
surrounded by diamonds, in a flat, yellow gold setting.

As the wedding day approached, the future groom presented
his bride-to-be with the *corbeille de noce* — wedding basket. This
contained several articles of lace — a handkerchief, veil and fan
— a Cashmere shawl, gloves and bits of jewelry. None of the
jewelry was ever worn before the wedding day, nor could she
leave home for three days before the marriage.

Old Creole Ladies Dream of the Opulent Past

Spiders Dwell in Haunted Houses

The Loup-Garou Holds his Convention on Bayou Goula

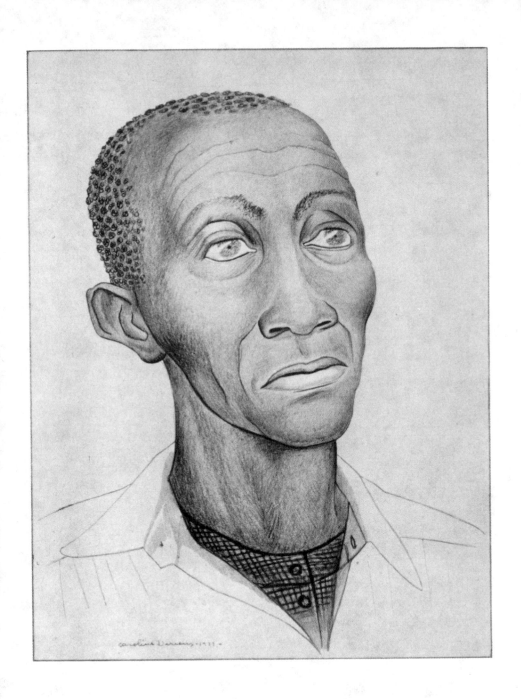

He Believes Everything

Monday and Tuesday were fashionable days for weddings, Saturday and Sunday being considered 'common' and Friday 'Hangman's Day.' The latter was the day for all local executions.

For many years the old Saint Louis Cathedral had a detail of Swiss Guards, who met all wedding and funeral processions and preceded them up the aisle. Behind them, at the wedding, would walk the bride, accompanied by her father. Then came the groom, escorting the bride's mother. Next would be the groom's mother and father, the best man escorting a sister or some other relative of the bride, followed by every brother, sister, aunt, uncle and cousin either of the pair possessed.

The bride's gown was usually of tulle or silk muslin, trimmed with pearls and lace handed down through generations in *la famille*. She wore a short veil, orange blossoms in her hair, carried a bouquet. There were no ring bearers, no matron or maid of honor, nor any floral decorations in the church. The ceremony was always in the evening, as Creoles would have considered it embarrassing to have the couple around all day after a morning marriage. Thus, as the Catholic Church does not permit the celebration of Mass after noon, Creoles were never married at Nuptial Mass. Not until 1910, when the Archbishop issued a decree forbidding Catholics to marry in church after twelve o'clock noon, did marriages at Mass become popular in New Orleans.

The wedding ring, called the alliance ring, was a double ring of gold, which when opened became two interlocking bands revealing the initials of the bride and groom and the date of the wedding. Both parties wore alliance rings. These can still be purchased in New Orleans.

After the ceremony all the relatives signed the register, sometimes as many as fifty. Rice was never thrown, nor did the bride toss her bouquet; it was sent to the church, the cemetery or to the convent where she had been educated.

A great reception always followed. Champagne and a supper were served. The bride and groom mingled for an hour or so, then it was considered decent that they retire. The bride cut her cake, every girl present receiving a piece. This was placed under the pillow at night along with the names of three eligible young men of her acquaintance. The one she dreamed of would be her husband — and she always retired determined to dream.

The Creole newlyweds went on no honeymoon. Usually they remained in the bride's home. After the hour at the reception, the bride was escorted to her room by her mother. Here she was assisted in disrobing and carefully dressed in the hand-embroidered nightgown and négligée made for this great occasion. Her flowing hair was tied back with a ribbon or perhaps adorned with an elaborate boudoir cap. Then she was propped against the pillows in the heavy four-posted bed and left to await her new husband. The Creole bride, often sixteen years old, and unbelievably sheltered until now, must lie there, trembling and frightened at the unknown, gazing up at the pale blue bridal tester above her until the groom appeared. Apparently young Creole grooms were not without their own qualms. One cautiously carried an immense umbrella into the bridal chamber and undressed behind it!

These bridal testers, at least the most elaborate ones, were the creations of a certain Monsieur Dufau, a merchant at 37 Rue Chartres. But poor M. Dufau was the victim of an unfortunate occurrence that all but wrecked his career and business.

This gentleman's shop was noted for its *objets d'art*, bric-à-brac, and fine paintings. But the most famous articles of merchandise were the artistically fashioned *ciel-de-lits* or testers. These were very popular, even the ordinary ones being tastefully made of calico or sateen. But most of M. Dufau's art was expended on *ciel-de-lits* for brides. These were always of pale blue silk, gathered in the middle by gilt ornaments. Across the pale blue heaven chubby cupids would chase each other with bows and arrows, pink ribbons modestly draping these tiny love gods. A wide cream-colored *dentelle valencienne*, the finest lace obtainable, trimmed the edge. It all combined to create an atmosphere symbolizing eternal love, blue horizons and rosy dreams.

Then ruin descended upon M. Dufau. A member of a club called Le Comité des Bon Amis, the time came for him to entertain his good friends. And it seemed that an extraordinarily good piece of luck occurred at about the same time. A sailor offered M. Dufau a keg of rum at a ridiculously low price. Seizing this opportunity, the merchant bought the liquor with no loss of time and invited his friends over to enjoy it. When the first round of drinks was passed everyone remarked on its peculiar flavor. The second drink was so bad that no one could finish it.

There was great consternation and curiosity. An axe was brought and M. Dufau himself split the keg open. What met the eyes of his guests was enough to stand their hair on end. Inside the keg, sitting upright, in a perfect state of preservation, was a little old man with long whiskers!

Poor M. Dufau, though technically cleared of any connection with the corpse in the rum, was immediately banished from his club, and he received no more orders for his masterfully fashioned bridal *ciel-de-lits*.

The bride and groom could not leave their room for at least five days! Their meals were brought in and a special servant assigned to their needs. The bride could not appear on the streets for at least two weeks. If they were spending their ' honeymoon' at the groom's house or in a home of their own, she could not even visit her mother. If she were so daring as to do this, she could be sure that while she would be received courteously, her mother would not fail to get in a little remark about the shame and indecency of being seen on the streets after having so recently married. And no one — not even the parents — called on the young couple during these two weeks. After that the families were practically one. A Frenchman who married a Creole girl of that era said that a man marrying one of them married not only the girl but also her five hundred relatives!

Charivaris were given widows and widowers who remarried. Tin pans were beaten, cowbells rung and as much noise as possible made. The newlyweds were supposed to treat the celebrants to a supper. If they failed to do this, the charivari might continue night after night.

The most notable charivari ever given in New Orleans was that rendered the widow of Don Andres Almonester, the great benefactor of New Orleans. In 1798, when middle-aged, she bestowed her hand on a young man in his twenties, Monsieur Castillon, the French Consul to New Orleans. This young man was most unpopular and generally conceded to be a fortune-hunter; and the widow was considered to be vain and selfish.

The charivari that followed their marriage lasted three days and nights. The house in which the couple sought shelter was surrounded by hundreds, many on horseback, some disguised and wearing masks. Try as they would, the newly wedded pair could not escape their tormentors. Fleeing the house, they were followed from end to end of the city, across the Mississippi River and back. Some of the crowd carried along a coffin on a cart, which contained an effigy of Madame Almonester's first husband, while she was represented by a living person sitting beside it. Finally, the newly wedded couple had to give three thousand dollars in coin for the poor. Almost immediately afterward they left for France.

Long after charivaris were banned in the city, they continued in the country. And even today in New Orleans many a married couple is driven about the city, followed by a dozen other cars, all blowing horns and generally making as much noise as possible.

Weddings on Creole plantations, outside the city, were even more elaborate affairs. Everything was ordered from New Orleans and shipped by boat. Wedding cakes and nougat pieces, fragile as they were, would arrive undamaged. Even hairdressers would be summoned to arrange the coiffures of the bride and the other ladies. Five hundred guests at a wedding was not unusual. Often the bride's father chartered a steamboat to bring the guests out to the plantation.

The Creole's home was always his pride. Especially the first parlor. Whatever wealth or pretensions a Creole possessed went into this room, and many of its furnishings were imported from France. Never was this salon open to casual intrusion, but always kept tightly closed against the sun and air so that the rugs and furniture would not fade. This room was only for very special company, weddings, funerals and celebrations. Woe to the child caught entering this room.

Most prominent feature in the room was the fireplace, always of marble except in the poorer homes, where it was usually brick. The mantelpiece was always elaborately draped and a huge mirror, framed in gold-leaf or gilt, was hung above it. Before the fireplace gleamed the screen and andirons, always in a bright gold finish. The furniture was apt to be rosewood, richly carved, and upholstered in expensive silk or tapestry. Along the walls were oil paintings of ancestors. There were always an *étagère* — whatnot — in one corner, holding china and bric-à-brac, porcelain vases of varied design and an ornate crystal chandelier hanging from the center of the ceiling.

The second parlor, separated from the first by a *porte à coulisse*, so that when these folding doors were thrown open the two rooms would form a grand salon for very formal occasions, was neither so carefully nor so expensively furnished as the first. In this room the family gathered evenings to talk and enjoy their music and their books. Portraits of humbler ancestors than those in the first parlor were hung here. There were usually ornamental wax fruit, wreaths and flowers of human hair — all under glass — statuettes of ivory and bronze, antimacassars on sofas and chairs and *éventails lataniers* — palmetto fans — in sand-filled vases.

Every bedroom in the house contained an altar, for of course all Creoles were staunchly Catholic, usually a small table covered with blue sateen and a lace cloth with a wide valance and holding candles, votive lights, statues of favorite saints and holy water. There were four-posted beds with testers, tremendous *armoires* with full-length mirrors, washstands holding bowl and pitcher of gaily flowered china accompanied by numerous matching receptacles.

In summer the floors of every room were covered with matting. This was not removed when old and faded, but simply covered with another piece. In winter the rugs were laid over the matting.

During the warmest months of the year, the Creole practically lived in his courtyard. Here was an outdoor living-room, walled with tropical greens. Vines entwined the white pillars of the piazza, and climbed up the tinted walls toward the green shutters of the windows that gazed downward like numerous sleepy eyes. Banana trees waved their huge leaves with every breeze. Large urns held plants of every sort. Usually a fountain bubbled and sang in the center. Along the gravel walks among the flower beds benches and old-fashioned rockers were set out. Here were escape from the heat and perfect quiet and peace for reading or for conversation. Creole houses often faced these patios, were built with their backs on the street, their salons opening here. There were always balconies above — still known as 'galleries' in New Orleans.

The Creoles were gay and festive. The ball, the theater, private soirées and receptions were of prime importance. Americans moving into the city thought the Creoles pleasure-mad. It was nothing for a Creole girl, amazingly frail for all other purposes, to dance at balls for four nights in succession without showing the least sign of fatigue.

When they could afford it their parties were tremendously elaborate and expensive. After one of General Beauregard's victories, the Creoles of New Orleans gave him a party during which a fountain of champagne flowed all evening. This was set up in the center of the salon and guests had only to hold their glasses under the golden flow to refill them.

The soirée, a party less formal than a ball, was held in a private home. These were simple but delightful affairs, where young couples danced far into the night, though always, of course, under the watchful eyes of parents, *tantes* and all the rest of *la famille*.

But the opera was really the center of all Creole social life. Here, in the old French Opera House, the music and performances were unrivaled anywhere in America. Attendance was always plentiful, there even being *loges grillées* — screened boxes where men escorting women of questionable reputation, people in mourning and pregnant ladies might enjoy the opera or play without being seen. Often, after a performance, some patron gave a ball in the Opera House; at other times the entire building was rented for the evening and an immense reception given. Between performances punch was sold in the foyer and here young men might escort young women and the chaperons. In front of the Opera House lounged aged Negro crones selling steaming bowls of gumbo.

Passionately fond of the opera, the Creoles viewed it with an enthusiasm unknown today. Someone wrote: 'At the end of a performance the Creoles stand up, wildly waving their hands and filling the air with loud bravos. Much has been written in prose and in verse on the power of music, but I have never read anything recorded so vividly and expressed so eloquently as in the face of a Creole girl when the spell of one of these French operas is upon her. The nervous twitch of the hand that grasps the railing in front of her box, the glow in her eye, the heightened color of her cheeks, the rapid change of expression, responsive to the change from joy to sorrow in the hero, gladness to lamentation in the music — all show that she is carried away far beyond the bounds of herself into a world created within her by the power of a Meyerbeer or a Gounod.' Once a Creole woman sold the last piece of furniture in her home to purchase a ticket to the French opera.

Invitations to social affairs were brought by a servant, never mailed. And on her way to and from a party a girl would carry her party shoes in a little silk bag, wearing more practical street shoes to brave the then muddy and unpaved streets of New Orleans, changing at her destination, and again to return home.

Sunday was anything but an unworldly day, a fact which shocked Protestant travelers from the North. Weyth wrote: 'New Orleans is a dreadful place in the eyes of a New England man. They keep Sunday as we in Boston keep the Fourth of July.' And until now no 'blue' Sunday laws have ever been successfully imposed on New Orleans.

Creoles attended Mass faithfully each Sunday morning, but once that duty was performed they turned the rest of the day into one of pleasure. Guests came for breakfast and remained until past midnight. In the afternoon attendance at a performance of light opera was customary. In the evening, after a huge dinner, the Creoles danced and flirted at numerous planned and impromptu soirées until late.

Sunday mornings at the French Market must have given as typical a picture of Creole New Orleans as was possible to obtain anywhere. There was not only the unique variety of characters, but a contagious spirit of festivity, as if everyone were on holiday instead of merely shopping for the traditionally large Sunday dinner. There was such chattering among the housewives, as they met among the stalls and stands, that even today the expression 'It sounds like the French Market!' is common in New Orleans any time a roomful of people seem all to be talking at once.

At early dawn the women would appear, huge baskets on their arms, peering into the butchers' stocks, smelling, touching and examining the fruit and vegetables, wrangling over prices. Itinerant vendors would line the edges of the market, offering for sale parrots, monkeys, mockingbirds, canaries, alligators, mousetraps, rat poison, toothache cures, crockery and all sorts of notions and knick-knacks. These merchants would often shout their wares:

'Only a picayune!'

The parrots would scream, the monkeys jabber, the fowls cluck and gobble. Indian squaws, wrapped in gaudy blankets, some with papooses on their backs, would offer baskets, pottery and bright beads. Half-naked bucks would stalk here and there among the milling throng, some of them staggering a little, their eyes glassy with firewater.

A huge woman, the numerous keys dangling from her belt revealing her profession as keeper of a boarding-house, attended by a lank, cadaverous black slave, might appear, driving hard, sharp bargains, much more concerned with price than with quality. Graceful ladies, wives and daughters of Creole gentlemen, followed by several servants, would shop with more care, fastidiously selecting only the best.

There would probably be one of the city's lovely quadroons in sight, trailed by a single servant. She would walk like a queen, her chin high, her jet brows disdainful, her handsome silk gown lifted just the proper inch or two from the cobblestones. She would be as proud as any Creole lady in the city. And why not? Her father might be one of its most fashionable residents. Her lover, to whom she is absolutely true, another. She would be the mistress of a fine house, with slaves, a carriage and horses at her disposal. She is well educated, can receive guests with elegance and grace, and preside over the largest dinner with dignity.

But what caused most excitement at the French Market during

that period was the dentist, who, perched on a platform, aided by an assistant and a brass band, pulled teeth in full view of the crowd. A victim would advance timidly, but before he changed his mind the assistant would push him into the chair and give a signal to the band. Immediately those gentlemen would strike up a loud piece, completely drowning the yells of the patient as the tooth was yanked out — of course without anesthetic. This was always very amusing to everyone but the patient.

Young Creole men, though also bound by the restrictions of caste, lived in a much broader world than their sisters. Theirs was the privilege of attending the famous quadroon balls, to dance and flirt with beautiful young women, so lightly touched with *café au lait* that a stranger would never have suspected their mixed blood, and eventually to select one as a mistress.

In 1790, New Orleans, a city of eight thousand, had fifteen hundred unmarried women of color. The fairest of these were trained and educated by their mothers and presented each year at the quadroon balls.

These balls were always conducted with great dignity and elegance, and attendance there risked no social stigma. The affairs were gay and lavish, but never vulgar, the young women being quite as well trained and as ladylike as the white belles of the era. Many of them were so fair that they boasted blonde hair and blue eyes.

When a young Creole took a fancy to a particular girl, he approached her mother, gave satisfactory proof of his ability to support her, and a small home was established in the quadroon section of the Vieux Carré. Many a father willingly footed his son's bills for the upkeep of his mistress, for the custom was practically universal. The arrangement usually terminated at the young man's marriage, a financial settlement being made, the girl afterward marrying another quadroon or going into the rooming-house business. Some, however, seem to have continued for life, a genuine attachment having arisen between the Creole and his quadroon sweetheart. Children born of these unions were well cared for, often splendidly educated. The girls often followed in their mothers' footsteps.

Quadroon men were less fortunate than their sisters. They

could not attend the balls, were often scorned by the women of
their own color. Usually they were compelled to marry mulatto
or Negro women, unless they married a discarded mistress in
later life.

The women, however, were ostracized by white ladies. They
were not supposed to ride in carriages within the city limits, nor
to remain seated in the presence of a white woman. A white
woman could have a quadroon girl flogged like a slave at any
time.

The balls were advertised in the newspapers of the period.
One in the *Daily Delta*, January 1, 1857, reads:

> Louisiana Ball Room, corner of Esplanade and Victory Streets.
> Grand Fancy Dress Masquerade Quadroon Ball every THURS-
> DAY EVENING, and Fancy Dress Ball EVERY EVENING.
>
> Admission Fifty Cents. Doors open at seven o'clock. Ball to
> commence at eight.

Dueling prevailed in New Orleans to an extent unknown even
in France. Creole society was an aristocratic and feudal organization based upon slavery, and Creoles lived like princes, de-
veloping a tremendous pride. Too, Latin passions tropicalized
under the Louisiana sun seemed to assume a violence surpassing
anything in calmer France. Young men fought over the slightest
affront, for such absurd reasons as the honor of the Mississippi
River, more than often for the sheer ferocious pleasure of it.

At least half of these duels were caused by arguments at public
balls and soirées. To tread on a Creole's foot, to brush against
him, to gaze at him with certain expressions, accidentally to
carry off the lady he had chosen to dance with, any of these were
ample grounds.

Everything was arranged very quietly. The young man who
had suffered the crushed corn dropped his lady partner with her
chaperon, had a few minutes' conversation with one or two of
his friends and slipped outdoors, followed by a group of men, all
wearing pleasant, indifferent smiles. Just back of the Saint
Louis Cathedral, in Saint Anthony's Garden, the men would
gather, concealed from the streets by tall growths of evergreens.
The first blood drawn usually appeased Creole wrath. The unin-

jured participant would replace his coat and return to the dance as if nothing had occurred; the other would go home, and be seen wearing a bandage for the next few days.

These events became so frequent that there were often three or four a day in New Orleans. This rear garden of the Cathedral and the oaks in City Park were usually the scenes of the encounters. Though swords were most popular, pistols were sometimes used, and though honor was usually satisfied by the first sight of blood, it is certain that many duels terminated only with the death of one or other of the participants. Fencing schools were numerous and every Creole gentleman was skilled in the art.

And, according to the *New Orleans Weekly Picayune* of June 6, 1844, all duels might not have been confined to the male sex. This newspaper reported:

> Two girls of the town, with their seconds, who were also girls, were arrested by the police when about to fight a duel with pistols and bowie knives near Bayou St. John. Finding they would not be allowed to endanger each other's lives according to approved and fashionable rules, the belligerents had a small fight 'au naturel' — or in other words, set to and tore each other's faces and hair in dog and cat style. They are all in the calaboose.

Cockfights were popular among these young men. Often as many as six birds would be set to battling in a single pit. Betting was the most important part of the sport, and it is possible that as much money changed hands over the scrappy roosters as is won and lost on the New Orleans racetrack today.

Baptisms, name days, birthdays, anniversaries, holy days, all were affairs of ceremony in the Creole household, each the occasion for a reception or perhaps an elaborate meal of the sort known as *un repas de Lucullus* — a feast of Lucullus.

Even the daily dinner was an occasion. Extra places were always set at the table, for no one knew how many guests Father might bring home. Every self-respecting household owned dinner service for twenty-four. Some had sets for a thousand, with silver and glassware to match! Should the salons not be large enough for a planned soirée, the Creoles would convert their courtyards into ballrooms. Walls were set up, a canvas ceiling stretched, flooring laid and the whole of it decorated and painted so that it resembled a part of the house itself. For all social affairs every member of the family, every relative, no matter how distant, must receive an invitation. To forget one was a gross insult and grounds for a terrible *scandale*.

Should there be a bachelor in the family, he would take dinner with a different member every week. It was customary for him always to bring the dessert, the favorite, in later years, being a Sarah Bernhardt cake — a cake with wine poured over it and spread with rich jelly. Other contributions might be *tête de fromage* — hogshead cheese — or birds' tongues. One Creole had a noted delicatessen proprietor save snipes' tongues for him all week, and on Sunday when he went visiting he brought a gift of *vol-au-vent* — pattie shell — containing the tongues. Every dining table of any pretensions at all had always a center piece called a *pièce montée*, which was a mounted figure of nougat, moulded while still hot into the form of a church, a pyramid or similar shape. Many were very elaborate, often two feet in height, the leading confectioners in the city competing with each other in originality of designs and decorations. There might be a *café brûlot*, a festive brew of coffee, citrus peel and burning brandy.

A bachelor was a valuable addition to any family. Once well past middle age, he was considered a real asset as an escort for young ladies. The girls always did a lot of whispering about why he had never married, always romanticizing his past and suspecting some tragic love affair. Usually of charming manners and a good dancer, he played an important rôle in the Creole family.

Baptisms took place when a child was about a month old. The *parrain* — godfather — and the *marraine* — godmother — were always relatives, usually one from each side of the family. Those chosen considered it a great honor, and the child would be raised to be most attentive to his godparents. The *marraine* would always give the infant a baptismal gift of a gold cross and chain, while the *parrain* would invariably give either a silver cup or silver knife and fork. Besides this he must pay the priest his fee, often from twenty to one hundred dollars, presented to him in the bottom of a cone of *dragées* — sugar-coated almonds. He also gave the *marraine* a gift and an elaborate cornet of *dragées* and contributed something to the huge repast that followed, frequently the *pièce montée*. The honor of being chosen *parrain* was considerable but expensive.

Name days, the feast days of the saints for whom they were named, were always celebrated among Creoles. A child born on Saint Joseph's Day or Saint Louis' Day or Saint Theophile's Day was given the name of that saint and always honored him as his personal patron. The most important of all the feast days was that of Saint Marie.

There were so many Maries that girls were called Marie Josephine, Marie Anne, Marie Marguerite, and by such nicknames as Mariette, Mamie, Mamaille, Minette, Mimi, Maille, Mane, Mamoutte and many others.

There were Cousine Maries and Tante Maries in every family, and no one dared forget one of them on Saint Marie's Day, August 15. A special cake was always made for the occasion, a *massepain*, much like the modern sponge cake, but with a sugar icing on which was written in pink '*Bonne Fête*' (Happy Feast Day) — or the words '*Sainte Marie.*' To conceal the hole in the center of the *massepain* a pink or red rose was used, held in place by four outspread silver leaves. Of all the gifts brought the honored Marie, the cake was the most important one.

Even the servants were not forgotten on this day. All these were given bright *tignons*, wide cotton aprons, round hoop earrings, brooches and checked calico 'josies.'

At a party for Tante Marie, the children would always gather in a circle after the gifts had been presented and sing the special 'teasing' song of the day.

> Oh, Miss Mary, set your cap,
> Oh, Miss Mary, set your cap,
> Oh, Miss Mary, set your cap,
> Miss Mary has a beau.
> > Wow!

> Aie — set your cap,
> Aie — set your cap.

Aie — set your cap,
How she loves her beau!
Wow!

At the mention of a beau, Tante Marie would let fall a tear
and her face would turn crimson. Was it because of some romance in her past? Perhaps the smile of someone killed in a duel
rushing back into her memory. Like the bachelors, all old maids
were supposed to have had secret and tragic romances.

First Communion was another excuse for a reception and a big
meal. After the Communion Mass there was a tremendous
breakfast and in the afternoon a reception for the family and
friends. The child, attired in snowy white, proudly displayed a
large collection of medals and holy pictures. The more medals
the greater the pride.

Christmas was strictly a religious festival. Papa Noël came
down the chimney to fill stockings, but left only inexpensive
gifts and trinkets. There were family dinners, but turkey was
not served.

Midnight Mass on Christmas Eve was an occasion for everyone to attend church. To help pass the hours before midnight,
and knowing the walk to the Cathedral would be long and cold,
hot eggnog was served, the preparations being long and elaborate. There must be just the right amount of whiskey, exactly
enough sweetening, a precise temperature. Father performed the
ritual of the eggnog. Midnight Masses are still the custom in
New Orleans on the night before Christmas.

New Year's Day was more exciting. Then were the children
given their better gifts. This was done very early in the morning,
for on this day every child must visit his *marraine* and *parrain*, all
his *tantes*, his grandparents and numerous other relatives. New
clothes were always made for the day, and children spoke of
ma robe de jour de l'an and *mon chapeau de jour de l'an* all through
the coming year. Before receiving his presents each child presented his parents with a carefully prepared *compliment de jour de
l'an* in a large pale pink envelope. This was a sheet of pink
paper trimmed with tinsel and pictures of fat cherubs ringing
silver bells. Painstakingly written with a pencil, in French,
would be the verse:

> My dear Papa, my dear Mama,
> I wish you a Happy and Prosperous New Year.
> I will be a good little boy.
> I will not tease my little sister any more.
> I love you with all my heart.

Immediately after breakfast the visits would begin, first to Mémère's, for Grandmother should come first. There was seldom far to go. All Creoles lived in the downtown section, the *faubourg d'en bas*.

When Mémère received the children — in the first parlor, opened for this occasion — they would recite some verses before she gave them the presents awaiting them.

> These four little verses tell you good morning,
> These four little verses give you my love,
> These four little verses give you my gift,
> These four little verses ask you for mine.

Then off — to the *tantes*, the *marraines*, the *parrains* and other relatives, to receive gifts at every stop, until small arms ached under the weight of them.

In the last half of the nineteenth century, *reveillons* became popular on Christmas Eve and New Year's Eve. These were all night parties that terminated only at dawn. Modern counterparts of these affairs are still popular in New Orleans on these nights. Fireworks were always beloved on these nights until recently when banned by law.

The *saison de visites* — season of visits — opened with the French opera in November and ran until Easter. One day each week the Creole family was 'at home,' and friends were informally entertained. Liqueurs and coffee were always served. Everyone left cards when visiting. If the hostess were not 'at home,' the cards were left anyway. Later in the evening the men made their rounds and at nine o'clock a supper was served to a few intimate friends. A group in the same neighborhood would always have the same day, since travel about the city was considered quite arduous and every Creole lady was the personification of frailty — no matter what her weight.

Teas were unknown in New Orleans until about forty years

ago, when a Mrs. Slocomb introduced the custom. Returning home from many years abroad, she purchased a large house in Esplanade, decided to meet all her old friends at a tea. She forgot to consider some might have died during her absence, but invited them all. From then on it was said, 'Mrs. Slocomb was so polite that she even invited the dead to her tea party.'

March fourth was 'Firemen's Day,' and always a gala event on the Creole calendar. The firemen would parade, the streets were decorated, and friends tossed them bouquets of flowers in which cigars were concealed.

Saint Barbé's Day was dedicated to the soldiers. At nine in the morning they all attended Mass at the Cathedral, and, after the parade, enjoyed a feast at the armory.

The Mardi Gras gradually became the most important event in the year, as it is today. Street masking and balls were popular in the earliest years of the nineteenth century. Young Creole blades would march on foot through the Vieux Carré in costume on Fat Tuesday, while young ladies on the galleries would shower them with flowers, all in imitation of the centuries-old festival in Europe.

Creole girls were not, of course, permitted to mask, but received the young men on their galleries, where there was much flirting and exchanging of compliments, sparkling wit and delight in guessing which of their friends it was disguised as a Spanish cavalier, or as Satan, or a fierce pirate. Once in a while a playful *tante* defied convention and masked, but those wishing to risk a *scandale* were few.

Carnival balls were much rarer than now, and the invitation committee extremely strict, scrupulously examining every name, to make certain only the *crème de la crème* were admitted. Money was no consideration, family all. A very few such exclusive organizations still exist.

Discontinued during the Civil War, Mardi Gras returned in vigorous new birth and gradually grew to the magnificent spectacle the whole country comes to view today.

Of the religious feast days, those of Saint John the Baptist, Saint Médard, Saint Joseph and Saint Martin were all ones for particular observance. On Saint Blaise's Day faithful Roman

Catholics went to the Cathedral to have their throats blessed. They still do so.

Holy Week was closely observed by the Creoles. Holy Thursday was always spent in visiting various churches to see the repositories. Children were told that the ringing of the church bells in the city Holy Thursday meant that they were flying to Rome to see the Pope. On Holy Saturday they were told the ringing of the bells meant that they were flying back to the belfry.

On Good Friday Creoles visited nine churches on foot and in silence, this bringing good fortune. The Way of the Cross was also performed on that day at the Cathedral, where a *Stabat Mater* was sung by a noted singer.

There were many quaint customs and superstitions connected with Holy Week. Holy Thursday morning the housewives, on hearing the ringing of the church bells, would take the pots from the stoves and place them on the floor, making the sign of the cross as they did so. For good luck nine varieties of greens were cooked in every home — a concoction known as *gumbo zhèbes*. Eggs laid on that day were believed never to spoil, only to dry up.

All kinds of superstitions were rife among the Creoles. On the first Friday of a month a girl must place her right foot on the footboard of the bed and say, 'Today, the first Friday of the month, I place my foot on the footboard and I pray the great Saint Nicholas to make me meet the one I am to marry.' Then she must jump into the bed without touching the floor, lie on the right side, her hand over her heart, and fall asleep, without talking, without laughing, without moving.

If a housewife dropped a fork, a lady caller was coming; if she dropped a knife, it would be a man. No one seems ever to have figured out what a spoon indicated.

Burning the berries of the juniper bush in the house was supposed to purify the air and kill all germs. It did work havoc among the mosquitoes.

The howling of a dog and the chirping of a cricket were both thought to foretell the death of someone. If you slept with the moonlight in your face, you went crazy. And should you be so unfortunate as to develop a spell of hiccoughing, everyone around was positive you had stolen something and would have no relief until you returned the article.

Even voodooism found — at least secret — adherents among some of the Creoles. It was whispered that many an elegant gentleman and lady took part in Marie Laveau's orgies along the Bayou St. John. Medical men found it impossible to combat the million petty superstitions in which some of these people had implicit faith. Roger Baudier wrote in *Catholic Action* regarding this:

'The list of things that one should not do for fear of evoking misfortune was, among the old Creoles, as lengthy as the tresses that hung from *Tante Coco's* head. You couldn't turn around or breathe without running into some superstition and get a gasp or a little cry of dismay over something dreadful you had done. *Nonc' Étienne*, him, he had studied in Paris and when he came back, well, he gave *Mémère* and *Cousine Doudouce* and all the rest of the women in the house chills and goose pimples, the way he flouted the most venerable superstitions. *Doudouce* said it was tempting God, what he was doing, but Étienne mortified her when he told her that she made a mockery of God with her voodoo *gris-gris*. Said he thought himself *le grand monsieur* because he had studied in Paris. *Cédonie*, her, she was very religious, and she wouldn't believe all that nonsense, though she wasn't any too brave about certain things, and it was always a struggle to follow out what they had taught her at the Ursulines and to suppress the little *frissons* — chills — that she got at the sound of a cricket in the house or a dog howling at night. However, she lost all patience when *Doudouce* jumped all over her one day, because she was standing in front of the mirror with *Lala's* baby and allowing the child to catch itself in the looking glass. *Doudouce* gasped, "Ma chere!" What had she done? Now the child would have endless trouble teething, since she had looked at herself in the glass! *Nonc' Adéodate* had the terrible habit of keeping his hat on in the house. That always put *Doudouce* on pins and she always asked "Dada," as they called him for short, for his hat, but he always refused and said he was afraid her brother might get away with it, he was such *un pauvre diable* — a poor devil. Whenever the children were lying down, *Doudouce* would never allow anyone to cross over them, without making him or her cross back, because crossing over a young person stunted growth. She was always fussing also at *Cédonie* for putting her umbrella on the bed, and she almost fainted one day when she found *Étienne's* umbrella open in his room. That was nothing to the *bougonnement* — fussing and grumbling — she had with *Bibi*, the cook, when she found her sweeping the kitchen after the Angelus had rung at the Cathedral at least an hour. Still, *Doudouce* told you, *grand comme le bras*, that she wasn't a bit superstitious.'

Apparently, all Creoles would tell you '*grand comme le bras*' — as big as your arm — that they were not superstitious, but hardly one of them would ever have dared flout a single belief handed down from generation to generation among them. And there is more respect paid many of these beliefs today than might be realized at first thought. It is said white ladies may still be seen knocking at the door of the tomb of Marie Laveau, performing the prescribed ritual to receive the grant of a wish. Love potions and *gris-gris* are still sold in New Orleans.

During one of the fever epidemics Creole gentlemen fired a cannon into the air — to kill the germs. Perhaps this was indicative of Creole tempestuousness rather than anything else.

'Night air' was the deadliest thing in all the world and every window was shut tight at night. However, all Creole bedrooms were equipped with fireplaces, through which some degree of ventilation occurred.

Fantastic concoctions brewed at home were believed capable of curing all sorts of ailments. Moss, sassafras, orange leaves, camomile, potato leaves and bitter roots were a few of the ingredients used.

If a child were very ill, the Catholic Creoles vowed him to the Virgin Mary, which meant the wearing of white-and-blue garments or else a white-and-blue cord around the waist for a certain length of time. Some children wore their cords until grown.

Tisanne de feuilles de lauriers, a tea made from laurel leaves, was used for cramps and stomachache. For fever the sufferer wore a pair of boots made of yellow paper covered with tallow, snuff and mustard. Small squares of yellow paper smeared with tallow and stuck to the temples would break up a head cold.

If a person had a cut or abrasion, someone would rush under the house or into some dark and dusty place and procure some cobwebs, which would be applied to the wound to stop the flow of blood.

Sarsaparilla tea was imbibed each spring to purify the blood. Crushed crab and crayfish eyes were used in the treatment of certain diseases. Water in which rusty nails had been soaked overnight was imbibed for anemia. Leeches were placed on the nape of the neck to draw blood. These can still be bought in New Orleans.

Boils and inflammation were relieved by a poultice of the leaves of the wild potato plant. Snake bite was cured with balsam apples soaked in whiskey. To loosen a chest cold Creoles swallowed tallow.

Bags containing camphor were worn suspended from a string about the neck during epidemics. These were used as lately as the influenza outbreak following the first World War.

Appendicitis was known among the Creoles as *colique misérere* and was treated with a poultice of flaxseed or potato leaves. Copal moss was used for pains following confinement, being soaked in hot water with a little whiskey, and the strained liquid drunk while very hot.

Plantain leaves were applied to sores, banana leaves to the forehead for headaches. Emetics were the first thing given any sick person. Plantain leaves were used also to perfume household linens and keep insects out.

Other things used for cure and prevention of illness included hair plant, button tree, fever bush, oil tree, bite of the devil, angel's balm and mouse's eyes.

When gas mains filled with water and were pumped out, this water was eagerly sought by the Creoles, who doused it on their dogs and cats. It was supposed to cure and prevent mange.

Creoles loved to spend an evening walking on the levee, the girls with their ever-present chaperons, the young men in pairs and trios. Flirtations were extremely mild, but none the less exciting. With great tact, with many compliments extended the chaperon, a gallant might even exchange a word or two with a belle!

As late as the early 1900's, just before what is still known as 'the exodus of the best people from Esplanade Avenue,' the front steps of many homes along that thoroughfare were scenes of no little calling, courting and romancing. On warm spring and summer evenings the young Creole girls would sit out on these steps to receive young blades who sauntered in groups from one house to another. The steps here were often built in a recess, assuring a quasi-privacy and allowing greater than usual seating capacity. Here 'sweet crackers,' Grenadine, lemonade and *bière Creole* would be served the callers, and delightful chats and very mild flirtations were possible.

The young men took great care to be impartial in their visits, stopping at one house one evening and another the next. Should any youth become a very assiduous visitor he immediately became a source of interesting speculation throughout the whole neighborhood. Mothers boasted of the calls of a suitor on their daughter and discussed frankly his morals, manners, breeding, background and financial condition. When he started making engagements for the balls or cotillions, it was considered that romance had bloomed, and woe betide the insincere young man not thoroughly aware of the delicate implications attached to showing a Creole girl such attention without the proper and expected intention.

To this day Orleanians are fond of sitting out of doors on summer evenings. There are probably few other cities in America where people will place rocking chairs out on the sidewalk before their homes, sit rocking and fanning, perhaps drinking lemonade or beer, forcing pedestrians to walk around them, while they chat and gossip, including whispered remarks about everyone passing.

Creoles were fond of quiet evenings at home. There was always music offered by some members of *la famille*, or perhaps someone would read aloud, while the ladies would busy themselves with sewing and embroidering.

Many exquisite arts, some now lost, were known to the

Creole woman. The making of *macrémé* was one at which all
girls were skilled. This was a type of weaving in which heavy
string was woven into lace curtains and portières. Flower-
making was popular. These were made of wax, tinted appropriate colors and put under bell glass to decorate the salons.

Cooking was the highest of the Creole home arts. Though
kitchen equipment was meager, the Creole woman and her
servants created one of the finest schools of epicureanism in the
world. Their recipes were a blend of French and Spanish dishes,
with typical Negro skill at making a fine dish out of a little
added.

For years all cooking was done in a wide, open fireplace, or on
a clay furnace. An iron pot — often handed down from mother
to daughter — was highly prized by Creole women. Before a
new one could be used it must be 'broken in.' First the pot was
washed thoroughly, then red brick-dust rubbed in. After another washing, the inside was smeared thickly with pork fat
and the pot placed on the fire to 'season.' Then the pot was
ready for the cooking of the red beans and the black-eyed peas.
These were always cooked with a thick slice of ham or salt pork.

Even at family dinners tables literally groaned under the
weight of the spread of food. At every large meal fish, fowl
and flesh were all served. Occupying the center of the table
might be a *cochon de lait* — a milk-fed suckling pig — roasted a
golden brown. There would be a large *vol-au-vent* — a baked
shell filled with delicious oyster stew, a tremendous roast of
beef and a turtle shell stuffed with turtle meat and richly seasoned. Sea food was often present, the meal frequently starting
with a crab *gumbo*. Wines were always served. Some families
drank it at all three meals, the children receiving theirs diluted
with water. Root beer, induced to ferment by the addition of
rice, corn and sugar, was also popular. *Bière douce*, unknown
now, was made of pineapple peelings, brown sugar, cloves and
rice. Coffee was always ground, roasted and entirely prepared at
home. Chicory was added, to the degree to please each family's
taste. Pepper was also bought whole and ground at home.

Elderly Creole ladies were fond of gathering at each other's
houses to spend the day. All the gossip would be exchanged,

family histories combed through, the actions of this person or that discussed. Greatest pleasure was derived from guessing who would be heir to a certain fortune, who married who and why, and what family, though they of course denied it, was undoubtedly touched with *café au lait*. Dreading exposure to the 'night air,' the ladies would scurry home just before dusk, well supplied with gossip for a long time to come. Some of them were living encyclopedias of genealogy and could, on occasion, render family histories for generations, with a thorough knowledge of both the lateral and horizontal branches of the family trees. Such a gathering of women was known, scornfully, as a *gumbo ya-ya*.

Nicknames were as popular among Creoles as they were among their poorer *cousines*, the Cajuns. Roger Baudier says of this in *Catholic Action*:

> One still finds among the descendants of the Creoles the familiar *petits noms* which were used so generally in former decades, in conversation in the family and among intimates. The custom of giving these short, phonetic names based on a person's baptismal name, however, has all but passed away, but Creoles still recall grandfathers, grandmothers, aunts, uncles and cousins by these short names, in many cases being unable to recall them by any other designation. *Tante Fefé* and *Cousine Titine* are just that — they are never known by any other names. It is difficult to explain some of these cognomens, as they were derived not only from some syllable of a name, but also from some characteristic, peculiarity, pet expression or some such source. *Bébé, Boy, Mimi*, and *Bouboutse, Chérie, Tounoute, Nounouse, Doudouce* and *Piton* are examples of short names that almost defy tracing back.

Petits noms like *Loulou* might come from Louis and Ludovic. A girl named Clementine or Armentine would be called *Titine* or *Tine, Julo* was substituted for Jules, *Zèbe* for Eusèbe or Zebulon, *Zime* for the queer name of Onésime. Girls named Eliza and Elizabeth would each answer to the appellation of *Zaza*; Adèle and Adélaïde either to *Dédèle* or *Dédée*.

Every family included these nicknames, often, because of the size of Creole families, several members with the same one.

There were scores of others, many of them fantastic and impossible to trace to any derivation.

Lagniappe was always given customers in the stores during the Creole era, giving special pleasure to children and servants. No matter how small the purchase, the merchant always added a bit of candy, a cake or some other small item as *lagniappe*, meaning something extra, something for nothing.

Webster claims that *lagniappe* is derived from a Spanish word, but there is no country where Spanish is spoken that uses such a term. M. Bussière Rouen, a noted French scholar, advanced the theory that four or five centuries ago, in Normandy and in Brittany, grain like oats, wheat and barley, when sold, was spread on a woven cloth known in French as a *nappe*. When the seller delivered or emptied the contents of the cloth into the buyer's receptacle, there were always quite a few grains clinging to the cloth. To compensate the buyer, the seller would take one or two handfuls from his stock and give it to the buyer, saying this was for *la nappe* (the cloth). When the Bretons and Normans settled in Canada and then were driven out by the English, eventually to find homes in Louisiana and become known as Acadians, they kept the custom of giving a little something for nothing when purchases were made, saying, '*Pour la gnaippe*' instead of '*Pour la nappe*,' and from them the curious custom was passed on to the Creoles of New Orleans.

Despite lack of ventilation, meal-time gorging and the most curious remedies conceivable when ill, Creoles seem often to have lived to incredible ages. They said of themselves, '*Creoles pas mourri, li desseché*' — 'Creoles don't die, they dry up.'

But on the other hand, death seems to have always been in evidence by the amount of mourning worn. Regarding this, it was said, *Si un chat mourrait dans la famille, tout le monde portrait de deuil* — If a cat should die in the family, everyone would be in mourning. Every *tante* and *cousine* was an excuse for *la famille* to drape themselves in black.

M. Raoul Bonnot was the popular *Croque-Mort* — undertaker — of the Creoles for years. M. Bonnot was quite a figure in the Vieux Carré, always appearing in formal gray striped trousers, Prince Albert, high-heeled shoes and tall silk hat. His toupee was center-parted and combed in bangs over his forehead. His expression was always so gloomy that the Creoles said of him, sympathetically, '*Il a une figure de circonstance.*' There must, however, have been a certain amount of secret frivolity under M. Bonnot's glum exterior. It was asserted by those who knew that he wore ribbons on his underwear.

When a death occurred, each post in the Creole section was adorned with a black-bordered poster, informing of who had died, the time and place of the funeral. Invitations to the events were issued as for social functions. All services were from the home.

Until the Civil War Creole ladies never attended funerals, but always paid a visit of condolence within nine days of the death. But during the War women were compelled to take charge of these affairs. The first funeral attended by women in New Orleans was that of Mrs. P. G. T. Beauregard, first wife of General Beauregard. The ladies marched in rows which extended the whole width of Esplanade Avenue.

The Civil War marked the beginning of the end for this Creole world. Very slowly the structure of their culture crumbled.

From the beginning of the coming of the Americans the Creoles were doomed. These Anglo-Saxons were too aggressive, too practical. Everywhere they rose to ascendancy, in politics, in business and in trade. Every year the leading places in commerce, banking, planting and the professions were taken over by the newcomers. Unlike the Creoles, they were not ashamed to soil their hands. They did not have the Creole's secret contempt for hard work. They almost made a fetish of it.

Even the French language began to lose popularity. For a long time generations were bilingual, speaking one tongue at home, another outside. In the new public schools Creole children were Americanized, eventually refused even to speak French because the others taunted them with the appellation of 'Kiskee-dee!' when they did so.

Through the years Creole jealousy of the Americans continued to be bitter. They held themselves aloof, refusing to mix with the strangers. But as the American city grew larger, swiftly passed the old town in size, it became very evident that these 'foreigners' were faring quite well without their aid. They saw it was a choice between acquiescence or complete commercial domination. In one matter, however, the Creoles remained the masters for many years; they set the standard for and exercised control over everything related to social life.

As long ago as 1892 a certain Creole gentleman, famous for his impeccable attire, his erect carriage, his monocle, his evening strolls along Esplanade Avenue, bemoaned the passing of the old ways of life. Each sunset he would appear on the Esplanade, bowing to ladies of his acquaintance with a lordly flourish, tipping his top hat to men. He constantly regaled friends with nostalgic tales of the *bon vieux temps*, as compared to what he considered the vulgar and *parvenu* customs and manners of this later period. He told of days when a gentleman never crossed his legs in a drawing-room; when a lady had no legs at all, but floated mysteriously on the hems of her skirts, wore steel corsets and a daring décolleté; when a gentleman did not ask a lady's permission to smoke — no lady could refuse, and the odor of tobacco was obnoxious to all females! — and would have died before he did so in her presence; when cocktails were unknown; when gentlemen supported their dancing partners with the lightest touch of the back of their white-gloved hands at their waists; when to appear at a social affair in an intoxicated condition meant certain and permanent ostracism, and when the telling of a risqué joke in the presence of a woman was equivalent to inviting one's self to a duel. He particularly deplored the passing of dueling, which custom, he averred firmly, 'held down murders, preserved good manners, upheld the sanctity of woman and safeguarded the sacredness of the home!'

But little by little the majority of the Creoles became poorer. Their fine homes had to go. Family records were lost or destroyed, heirlooms, precious and treasured for generations, were sold as desperation drove these gentle people, scarcely capable of earning their livelihoods, to antique dealers and the Americans. The past began to be a thin memory in the minds of very old people.

Striving to maintain their independent culture, the Creoles organized a Creole Association as late as 1886. Bitterly attacked by outsiders as an exclusive organization, Charles A. Villeré, himself of a distinguished Creole family, vigorously denied this, saying their aim was to aid the state as a whole, to assist in the spread of education and the growth of the culture of all its peoples. In his speech at the first meeting of the Association he said, in part, 'We are battling for our rights; we are scoffed at, ridiculed, blackened, tortured, deformed, caricatured.... This is our soil.'

But the life of the Creole Association was short. Internal differences ensued, and it quickly passed out of existence.

Most of the old ways are gone now, though tangible evidences of the splendid past are not difficult to find. There are the old houses in the Vieux Carré, with balconies of wrought iron like fine lace and winding stairs and tinkling crystal chandeliers and dreamy patios. There still remains the Saint Louis Cathedral where Creoles knelt in prayer, with its rear garden where rapiers flashed in moonlight and in sunlight, until the flow of Creole blood appeased the tempestuous heat of Creole anger. And the convent in Orleans Street, where the warm laughter and gay music of the past has been displaced by the mystic silence of the *religieuse*. These things remain.

There are names, some still of great social prestige, others long buried under poverty, their aristocratic origins almost forgotten by their bearers. There are words like *gumbo* and *banquette*, still common on Orleanians' tongues. There are Creole cabbages, Creole lilies and Creole horses. And a thousand other little things, little inbred habits, superstitions, proverbs, all with derivations springing from that past that belonged to the Creoles.

In the show windows of a Royal Street antique dealer may rest a silken fan, yellowed now, frayed a bit, but once it accentuated the coquetry of a dark-eyed flirt; bits of bric-à-brac, stalwart shepherds and plump dairy maids with dirty china faces, old jewelry created to adorn Creole beauty, music boxes that still respond to your touch to play half-forgotten tunes, snuff boxes of silver and gold that once flattered the vanity of gallants. Inside the shop may be immense mirrors with fat cupids chasing each other about the gilded frames, a huge bed of solid mahogany with four massive posts and a *ciel-de-lit* — perhaps the creation of Monsieur Dufau before his ill-fated rum party? — of pale blue silk, stained and faded now, but once the bridal canopy of some trembling Creole bride.

It is even possible to find a gentle lady or two of great age, who doesn't speak English and rarely ever journeys to Canal Street, less than a dozen city blocks away, who wears black alpaca dresses to the tips of her shiny patent leather shoes, a cameo brooch at her throat and her thin white hair in a forgotten fashion.

To this patrician race New Orleans owes a debt of immeasurable proportions; the Mardi Gras, the world-famous cuisine, the gaiety, the whole intricate fabric of the charm that distinguishes the city from any other in America.

Chapter 9

The Cajuns

I am a true man, me. I got credit at Fisher's Store; I got a share in
my boat; and I make fourteen children for my wife!
Overheard from Cajuns' conversation

'IT IS LIKE THIS' — THÉOPHILE POLITE NARROWS
dark eyes that glitter hotly in the Louisiana sun — 'we Cajun
are damn fool, us. Most of the time we are poor, then we catch
lots of muskrat, sell the skin, and we are rich. Some Cajun make
plenty money now, stay rich, but most time is not like that, no.
We spend all our money quick. Boom! Like the big storm she
hit the little boat, everything is gone from us. My family live
always since two hundred years on this bayou, and always we is
poor.'

Théophile's bronzed forehead wrinkled angrily. 'One time a
mans comes and wants me to work for him, that fool! *Paillasse!*
That is insult for me, hein? We Cajun stand always on our own
two feets. Any mans works for 'nother mans he is low. Me, I do
all right. I trap them big rats. I fish for the shrimps and the oysters. Marie, she has eleven childrens, all living, nine boys. We
are still *amoureux comme deux colombes*, us. If a mans got him

shrimps and oysters for his *gumbo*, and his wife and him still is loving each other like two little sweetheart doves, what more he want I ask you, hein?'

Marie waddles out of the small house, takes a seat on a log close to where her husband stoops over his crab net. She sighs. She is quite fat, especially her stomach, which stretches her white cotton dress until the material seems about to split. It is evident the Polite children will soon number an even dozen. But her features are good, the nose slightly arched, but thin, the lips, cheekbones and jawline strongly modeled. Her short hair, black as ink, frames a face strangely patrician for her peasant's body. Many Cajun women are like that. Her hands are small, her naked feet, the toes digging into the dust, delicately shaped.

'She is worried for Ovide,' Théophile explains her silence. 'He is the oldest boy we have from us. All the childrens we name with O, 'cause Polite she is named with P, and O she comes from before P, hein? We call them Ovide, Oristes, Olive, Onesia, Otheo, Odalia, Octave, Olite, Oristide, Odelée and Odeson.' He flipped a black-nailed thumb at Marie's middle. 'He is gon' be called by Odeo or Odea, if she's boy or girl.'

He rose, brushed his hands on his pants. 'Me, I forget myself. Wait, I get you some coffee.'

Marie had taken some peach seeds out of a paper bag and was pounding them to bits on a rock, using another rock as a hammer. They were to 'settle the water.' If bayou water must be used for drinking, Cajuns put crushed peach seeds on the bottom of a pail of it and all dirt is drawn to the bottom, leaving the top clean and purified.

'Ovide gives us help, him.' Marie looked up, her dark eyes distressed. 'He make two, three dollar for his crabs. Sometime he get a hot head and drink up all his money, but most time he give it all to me. He use good way to catch them crab. Is real Cajun way to do them, yes. He go out on bayou with big line what has little lines tied on it, maybe every two feets. He tie one end of that big line to a tree, then he row his pirogue down the bayou and tie up other end to 'nother tree, good. All the little lines is hanging down and the crabs they bite them. Then my Ovide he pull big line up from water and he catch them.

That is fine way, hein? He's got good brains in his head. But now he catched himself the woman sickness and is gone to the city to get cured.'

She sighed, rolling her fine eyes around, and went on to another of her troubles. 'My daughter, she is Onesia, is married twice as old as herself to a man. I don't like that, no. He is named Ulysse Boudreaux, is thirty-two years old. Onesia, she is sixteen. She is one fine cook. Can make better *gumbo* than me, her.'

She raised her brows proudly. 'When Théophile and me get ourselves married to each other, he is eighteen and me, I am fifteen. That is right, hein? This Ulysse Boudreaux is almost old mans as me; I am thirty-five. All the time I tell him he is better for me, if there is no Théophile, Holy Mother, may such a thing never be!, than for Onesia. But when I ask the priest at time he marry them, the priest he say hokay, so I guess is hokay. That Ulysse have four children and two twins from his first wife — was Céleste Thibodeaux before they was married with each other. She died two years ago like from last Christmas. Ulysse is fine trapper, though.'

Marie's Cajun humor came to the fore at last. She winked one limpid eye, revealed two flashy gold teeth in a wide smile.

'I just don't believe it's no fun being married twice as old as yourself to a mans,' she said.

These are Acadians of today, but they might be Longfellow's famed lovers, Evangeline and her Gabriel. There has been little change these two centuries. If the course of true love had run smoothly, that tragic pair might have lived out their lives together much as Théophile and Marie Polite.

There are contemporary counterparts of the expulsion of these people from Nova Scotia by the British. Refugees still flee from intolerance, are still banished from their homelands because it is expedient to their rulers that they be so treated. But there is no recent case more tragic than the brutal uprooting of these Acadians, none more filled with misery than the long wanderings of these homeless fifty thousand. Today travel is swift. Liners can carry the expatriated to new continents in a few days. The Acadians straggled southward, on foot, in small boats, for three decades.

Yet here in what Longfellow calls 'the Eden of Louisiana,' along the picturesque, winding bayous, they found a new home. And here they remain, four hundred thousand of them, for they are extremely prolific and twenty children in a single family is not unusual. One old lady counted eight hundred lineal descendants, all blood relatives.

Many still live in rude shacks, weave their own cloth, continue to cling to a chronic aversion to wearing shoes. Until recently many of them had never journeyed twenty miles from their homes, many of the women had never traveled five. Today some have automobiles of a sort.

But automobiles have not entirely supplanted the buggy in southwestern Louisiana. Many of these antique vehicles are still in use, and they are not all of ancient vintage, either. Many are brand new and glossy black. For buggies are still manufactured for these bayou folk, and more are in use in Louisiana than in any other locality in the United States of today. Every Sunday morning it is possible to see many of them filled with families, all dressed up in starched white apparel, bare feet scrubbed clean, on the way to Mass.

These bayou Cajuns are usually poor, though some are making money today. As fishermen they are eminently successful; the heritage of their Norman and Breton ancestry is not wasted. The great shrimping, crabbing and oyster-fishing industries of Louisiana are entirely in their hands. They are the world's finest trappers.

Their language, entirely spoken — few can read or write in French — has been held in contempt by many people as a crude patois, though some authorities insist it is pure seventeenth-century French. Until the first World War relatively few spoke English at all. And those who speak it today have a humorous, if expressive, jargon of their own. In many ways this is not really a dialect, but a literal translation from French, such as, 'He live in that house which is white, him.' The last pronoun being repeated to impress you with who it is living in 'that house which is white.' Sentences frequently terminate with an interrogative 'Yes?' or 'No?' or 'Hein?' as if desiring your assurance that the speaker is correct in his opinion and that you agree.

A Cajun oysterman of Barataria with his oyster tongs
Courtesy of Jefferson Parish Review

A Cajun fisherman's family in their bayou home
Courtesy of Lee, Farm Security Administration

Cajun girls of the Bayou Country
Courtesy of Shahn, Farm Security Administration

An old Cajun woman hangs garlic from the rafters
Courtesy of Lee, Farm Security Administration

Shrimp Fleet waiting to be blessed, Little Bayou Caillou

The Archbishop on the way to bless the Shrimp Fleet
Courtesy of New Orleans Times-Picayune

Pronouns are scattered here and there, liberally. Usually in the wrong places. The Cajun's hands, shoulders and eyes, which are all put into play when he launches into a conversation, are really almost as much organs of speech as his tongue. And when he cannot remember an English word or phrase he shoves in a French one, lapses right back into English and goes on from there, always speaking rapidly, betraying his impatient and nervous nature.

Listen to Placide discouraging Papite's ambition to travel to Chicago. Papite had heard about this Chicago somewhere, and though he knew nothing of geography, had probably never seen a map, his desire to view the wonders of that metropolis was the constant topic of his conversation. Placide, tiring of this and really afraid he might lose his good friend Papite, put it this way.

'Papite, for why hell **you** want to go to She-cow-go, you? Look at the sun. See how she shine on the bayou, hein? If you was in She-cow-go you would not see sun like those, no. In She-cow-go when the sun come up, the smoke from Pittsburgh he pass all over She-cow-go and keep the sun from shining on all those poor peoples. Now, Papite, you don't want to go no place where there ain't no sun, no?'

Education is seeping into even the most remote bayou settlements now, and Cajun children attend school — at least for a few years. But for the most part this alters life but little. Cajun boys learn to fish and hunt and trap almost from infancy; it is only the rare individual who for a moment dreams of entering any other profession. They marry young, often before they are twenty, and are at that age quite as adept at earning a living in these occupations as their fathers. Their brides are usually dark-eyed children of fourteen or fifteen, but already equally as skilled at the tasks necessary to a good cook and housekeeper. The tiny houses in which they live, in many instances two-room shacks, are clean and orderly, the floors scrubbed white, the kitchen utensils polished. And Cajun cooking, especially in the preparation of sea foods, may rival that of any famous city chef. Marriages last for life, and morals, as a whole, are relatively good among them.

A Cajun woman's life is of course a failure should she not capture a mate, and this dreadful prospect causes her much worry. The Cajun old maid is so rare as to be the object of both scorn and pity. From the time she is about fourteen her family begin to nag her about getting herself a husband. Each night many Cajun girls examine their heels for any tinge of yellow, for such a sign is a certain portent of spinsterhood. Tante Thérèse — herself a horrible example — will remember mournfully that at the age of seventeen the fatal yellow tinge appeared on her own heels, and here she is, well into her thirties, and of course without hope, since no man along the bayous wants such an old woman. Tante Thérèse reports that eighteen is just about the latest a girl may have hope of marrying.

But, says Tante Thérèse, there are many ways of rendering a man susceptible, though they didn't work in her case. Powder made from a green lizard dried in the sun, when thrown upon the object of a girl's desire, makes him her victim. Or she might ask him to dinner and put the scrapings from the four corners of the dinner table into his coffee. She may also put parings from her fingernails into his pockets, or write him a letter in her own blood. For an immediate proposal, she should tie a rooster under her porch, seat the man in a rocking chair right over the fowl, sit beside him, and wait. He can't help but fall in love with her then.

However, even should all this fail, there is still *poudre de Perlainpainpain*. This takes time and patience, but is worth it. The young girl must catch seventeen floating seeds blown from a thistle on a windy day. The down is removed from the seeds, then the seeds are rubbed over the honey sac of a bee, caught on a clover blossom leaning in a northerly direction. This must be carefully mixed with three white beans buried for three days previously under a mound of table salt, then added to a portion of salt — measured in a black thimble. Now she really has something. *Poudre de Perlainpainpain* rubbed into any article of the clothing of her lover makes him hers forever and all time.

Charivaris are still popular at Cajun marriages, especially at that of widows to single men, or widowers to single women. The marriage of Ulysse Boudreaux to Onesia Polite might have been celebrated in this manner, if they were well liked in their community, for a charivari is an expression of affection and approval. A Cajun described the custom this way.

'Charivari? Sure, M'sieu. I been to plenty, me. It's given a womans what's been married and her husband is dead, or to a mans when he marries for the second time. These is only given to peoples you like and you have respect for. You go with pots and pans and make noises all day long and maybe all night long on the outside from their door. They got to come out and promise you something, yes, like icecream and cake or wine. If they don't do this you never stop making noise, no. Or you decide they ain't no good to bother with, and they get no more charivari if they get themselves married five or seven times! That's right, hein?'

Cajun weddings are sometimes grand affairs. Mrs. Joe Giffault described her first one in all its glamorous detail, as soon as Mr. Giffault, her second husband, left the room.

I didn't want to talk about my first wedding before him,' she explained. 'I don't think that's right, me. But I sure had some wedding the first time, God, it was beautiful! Me, I got myself married young; I was not made sixteen, no. We was two pairs getting married together, and each of us girls had seven friends with us and each of the mans had seven. There was fourteen peoples on each side, fourteen pairs of them. We got us married in church and everybody was there except my mamma. And she had a good reason. You see, my mamma always wore a sunbonnet and didn't never have herself no hat. I tell her to get herself a hat, but she say she ain't gon' buy no hat just for that one occasion, so she stay home. She didn't believe in nothing like that, no.

'After the wedding there was a big barge waiting on the bayou. Everybody danced on the barge all the way back to the house, and when they got to the house they danced all night. It was fine. Me, I had the best time I ever knowed. I always likes to promenade myself like that, me. And food! We had everything anybody wanted, us. One of my aunts made that cake. I ain't never seen a wedding like that, me. We dressed ourselves just like brides, yes. And we carried paper flowers what a Cajun lady made for us. They was red and blue and yellow and purple. They sure was pretty. The party and the eating and the dancing lasted all night and all the next day. That's for true!

'No, we didn't go on no trip.' Mrs. Giffault laughed at that idea. 'How could we do that, hein? I had me plenty work the morning after the wedding. My husband had him a fine chicken yard, and I had all them eggs to pick up and a cow to milk and I had to cook him his breakfast.'

At the reappearance of Mr. Giffault his wife ceased talking.

'Clementine is my second wife,' he said. 'My wife that die is mother for my first twelve childrens. Clementine is got four childrens from her first husband and we got us three more together.'

'My name ain't Clementine,' interrupted Mrs. Giffault. 'It is Armentine.'

'Hokay! Hokay!' said Mr. Giffault impatiently. 'If you want to be called by that it's all right with me.'

'Non!' said Mrs. Giffault emphatically. 'My name she is Armentine! That is what my mamma called me by and that is my name.'

'Well, that's the first time I ever know that,' said Mr. Giffault. And in explanation: 'Me, I don't worry what her name is. I never call her nothing. Everybody call her Miz Joe since she married with me, anyway.'

'Before that,' said Mrs. Giffault, 'they call me Miz Alex, 'cause my first husband he was named Mr. Alex Thibodeaux. Lots of peoples calls married womans by their husband's first names. They got plenty Cajun lady called Miz Joe, Miz Papite, or Miz Henri. Me, most times I calls myself Miz Joe. Nobody ever calls me Miz Giffault, no.'

Still in use along the bayous, relics of the days when everyone spoke French, are various picturesque expressions. Common are ones used to describe a person of great age.

Any resident of the Bayou LaFourche section will understand you immediately if you say a man is *vieux comme les chemins*, for a man as old as the highways would indeed be old.

In Golden Meadow there is a term which has become almost a local proverb: *Vieux comme le billet a M'sieu Étienne. M'sieu*

Étienne is seventy-five-year-old Étienne St. Pierre, and his *billet* is a piece of paper money, once worth twenty-five cents, though long out of currency, that has been in his possession for sixty years. It is the first money he ever earned, and he has always kept it. That's why folk in Golden Meadow have coined the saying: as old as Mr. Étienne's bill.

Rosalee Barrosse remembered her Tante Bébé well.

'We is all live for be good old age in our family,' Rosalee boasted. 'Tante Bébé live for be one hundred and seex; that is long time for this world, hein? She was real French, was opera singer in Paris, but she come live with us when she get old and just sing for us keeds. She all time sing and laugh till time she die. She use make us keeds laugh funny way she speak English after live in Paris so long. Sure was funny way she had, her. When we laugh she don't get mad, though. She just say, "You laugh for way I say thing in English, hein? Well, I can't do no different and if that make you happy, you laugh." You know when she want for say English word she gonna say it even if she bust, her. *Oui, Monsieur*, she get raid in face sometime trying to say one English word. All the time she make up funny song. You know when they take them sheeps to the slaughterhouse how sad it is? Them poor little sheeps they got tears in their little eyes and they cry "Baa — Baa!" all the way. Sure, they know where they go, them. Well Tante Bébé she make up song like this:

> *Mouton, Mouton — est ou tou vas?*
> *À la Abbatoire.*
> *Quand tu reviens?*
> *Jamais — Baa!*

In English that mean:

> Sheep, sheep — where are you going?
> To the slaughterhouse.
> When will you return?
> Never — Baa!

'Once we had little cousin we call Tee Sharle, that mean Lil' Charles. He was kind of sickly. Tante Bébé she gave him a little raid wagon, and he crazy 'bout it, play weeth it all time. Then

Tee Sharle die in convulsion. Poor Tee Sharle was put in little
white coffin and taken away to graveyard. Poor Tante Bébé she
stand on her front porch when the funeral pass and after it is gone
by her house she cry hard and she say over and over again,
"*Pauvre Tee Sharle! Jamais* I see him again! *Jamais* I see his little
raid wagon!" Then she take one hand down from before her
eyes and she wave, all time crying, "*Adieu! Adieu! Adieu, pauvre
Tee Sharle!*" But all the time she wave in wrong direction. I say
to her, "Tante Bébé, the funeral go other way.' She is go other
way you wave your hand." She stop sudden-like and she say,
"Hein?" I tell her again, "The funeral go in other way." "O
mais oui!" she say. Then she turn 'round and wave her hand in
right way and start say all over again, "*Pauvre Tee Sharle!
Jamais* I see him again! *Jamais* I see his little raid wagon!
Jamais! Jamais!*" '

Curious names are popular along the bayous. Some that graced
heroic characters of Greece are hereditary among the Cajuns.
Hundreds of males titled Achille, Ulysse, Alcide and Télémaque
now row pirogues through the Louisiana waterways. There is a
penchant for nicknames. Even animals have them. Every cat is
'Minou,' and every child is given some diminutive of his name.
It is perfectly safe to say that no group of Cajuns ever assembled
without a Doucette, a Bébé, a Bootsy or a Tooti among them.
At one school a family of seven children, named Thérèse, Marie,
Odette, Lionel, Sebastian, Raoul, and Laurie, were known even
to their teachers as Ti-ti, Rie, Dette, Tank, Bos, Mannie and
La-la. It is said every Cajun family has a member known as
'Coon.' Other families, like the Polites, give their offspring
names that all start with the same letter. An 'E' family might
be, respectively, Ernest, Eugénie, Euphémie, Enzie, Earl, Elfert,
Eulalie and Eupholyte.

However, there are comparatively few family names. There
are literally thousands of Landrys, Broussards, Leblancs, Bour-
geoises and Breauxs, these being the largest families of Acadian
descent in the state.

The Cajun has great reverence and affection for family ties, and
this extends to the utmost limits of relationship. Among no
people is respect for their elders more sincere, and *nanaine* (god·

mother), *parrain* (godfather) and numerous *tantes* (aunts) and *cousines* are held in high regard, to be upheld against outsiders at all times, to be taken into the family and supported for life if the need arise. Distant connections still reside in Nova Scotia, and more prosperous groups of Cajuns make pilgrimages there, and Nova Scotians journey to Louisiana to visit the Evangeline Oak at St. Martinville and to kneel at the grave of Emmaline Labiche, original of the heroine of Longfellow's poem, where a light is kept burning.

Death receives even more than usual respect among these people. Widows drape themselves in black veils for a year, wear black without the veil for another, and black and white the next year or two. Men wear crêpe arm bands, and children are often put into mourning at tender ages. So large are some Cajun families that there seems always to be evidence of death among them.

Cajun widows sometimes soon recover from their grief, however. A stranger paying a visit of condolence to one was informed by the bereaved's sister-in-law, 'Oh, you ought to see her already! She is all *frisée* and *rougie*. Every time she see a man she roll her eyes, *toute gougou!*'

Of first importance in their lives is religion. They are, almost without exception, Roman Catholic, and the parish priest is an important personage. Catholicism is responsible for some of the most colorful customs.

Perhaps the best known of these is the annual blessing of the shrimp fleet. For this ceremony, which takes place each August, the Archbishop from New Orleans goes into the bayou country to bless the boats and trawlers for the opening of the shrimp season. Rites are held at Bayou Petit Caillou, Bayou Grand Caillou, Bayou Barataria and Golden Meadow. These pious people would not begin the season without having their boats blessed.

Fifteen hundred Cajuns gathered at Mass and Holy Communion at Bayou Petit Caillou in 1939, the morning the blessing was to take place. Immediately after Mass, the procession, headed by three altar boys, then the Archbishop, gorgeous in a rich golden cope flowing from his shoulders almost to the ground, in towering golden miter and golden crozier, followed by visiting bishops and at least twenty-five priests, walked to the platform over the bayou where the ceremonies were to take place. His Eminence first blessed the boats collectively, the choir singing lustily as, one by one, the boats were unloosened. Some boats carried as many as ten people, men, women and children, all attired in their best Sunday clothes, and every boat was freshly painted and gaily bedecked with brilliantly colored flags and pennants.

Atop the cabin of one boat perched a two-hundred-pound woman, breathlessly fanning herself with a palmetto fan and looking acutely uncomfortable. In all probability this was the first time she had worn a corset since last year. The corset and her pink Mother Hubbard were her only concessions to the occasion, however. One of the spectators pointed at her and called out, '*Regarde* Naomie in her bare feets!'

As the boats approached the Archbishop everyone knelt and made the sign of the cross. Someone became worried that the Archbishop would not have enough holy water, and cried, 'There ain't enough holy water in that thing to bless all them boats, no.'

These boats go out as far as forty miles in the Gulf and return about every fifteen days to refuel. The freight and ice boats make daily rounds to pick up the catch and bring it to the factories. Approximately fifty thousand of these Cajuns are employed in the Louisiana shrimp industry.

Another impressive Catholic rite takes place on All Saints' Day, November 1. Priests gather at dusk in the cemeteries of the Cajun parishes to offer Masses for the souls of the dead, hundreds of blessed candles being lighted on graves, filling the advancing darkness with weird flickering lights and eerie shadows.

Cajuns celebrate not only the American Christmas, but *Le Bonhomme Janvier* on New Year's Eve, at which time the children receive candy, fruit and fireworks, and *nanaines, parrains, tantes* and other relatives visit branches of the family, exchanging gifts and greetings. Besides, there are many religious holidays in the Cajuns' calendar, each with its peculiar customs.

Intermingled with this passionate Catholicity is much superstition of an entirely primitive type. There are even werewolves in Louisiana! Here they are known as *loup-garous*, and are the most dreaded and feared of all the haunts of the bayouland. Accounts of lycanthropy are rare in America, but Cajun children are constantly warned, 'The *loup-garous* will get you, yes! You better be good.' And many of the children's elders believe emphatically in the existence of these horrible wolf-things.

There are many *loup-garous*, some, people under a spell, and others enjoying self-imposed enchantment. A Cajun will explain: '*Loup-garous* is them people what wants to do bad work, and changes themselves into wolves. They got plenty of them, yes. And you sure know them when you see them. They got big red eyes, pointed noses and everything just like a wolf has, even hair all over, and long pointed nails. They rub themselves with some voodoo grease and come out just like wolves is. You keep away you see any of them things, hein? They make you one of them, yes, quick like hell. They hold balls on Bayou Goula all the time, mens and womens, both together. They dance and carry on just like animals, them. If you see one, you just get yourself one nice frog and throw him at them things. They sure gon' run then. They scared of frogs. That's the only way to chase a *loup-garou* away from you. Bullets go right through him.'

Loup-garous have bats as big as airplanes to carry them where they want to go. They make these bats drop them down your chimney, and they stand by your bed and say, 'I got you now, me!' Then they bite you and suck your blood and that makes you a *loup-garou*, and soon you find yourself dancing at their balls at Bayou Goula and carrying on just as they do. You're a lost soul.

'Is a good idea to hang a new sifter outside from your house, yes. Then they got to stop and count every hole in that sifter, and you catch them and sprinkle them with salt. That sets them on fire and they step out of them shaggy old skins and runs away. But, me, I don't fool 'round with no *loup-garous!*'

Some *loup-garous* change themselves into mules and work their own land, a power which must have certain and definite economic advantages.

The *letiche* is the soul of an unbaptized infant who haunts small children in their beds at night, a wandering, restless young spirit for whom there is no peace. Down in Terrebonne Parish the children talk as familiarly of mermaids as if they were their daily companions. And the age-old tale of the sirens, whose sweet music attracts men and costs them their souls, is as alive among the Cajun fishermen today as ever it was in Ancient Greece.

Belief in the Evil One is very strong. Woe to him who is so unfortunate as to be caught in his snares. And the Devil uses many a subtle wile in securing his victims. Even the most innocent appearing or beautiful things may be traps set by His Satanic Majesty.

'You be careful, Noonie!' will warn a mother as her daughter departs for school. 'You keep your feets on the road, yes. Don't you go wandering off after a flower or nothing. I know you, me. You is *bête comme un chou*, but plenty a foolish cabbage been caught by that Evil One. You walk straight to your school-house and don't pay no mind to nothing else, hein?'

And Noonie will walk very fast down the road winding with the bayou, looking neither to right nor left, her bare feet kicking up the dust. Hasn't she heard that story about the Cajun lady who almost got herself caught by the Evil One just because she went into the woods to pick a flower?

This lady was in a strange and fearful condition for a Cajun lady. She had been married for years and as yet she had never had a baby! Her husband was disgusted, too. All he did was talk about what a fine son he would have, how much he would fight and drink and have all the women chasing him, because he would be one fine lover like his father. He would always say, too, 'My son, when he grow up would be best damn hunter in whole bayou country and Unite' States, him!' And this poor woman would brood about it all the time. 'Every day she watch herself close and sometimes she say, "Now I'm gon' have this *bébé* for Alcide!" But always she is fooled herself. Nothing ever happen.' She lived in church all day, praying to the Virgin Mary, but nothing occurred.

Then one day she was walking along a road and she spied a beautiful flower. She picked it. Then she saw another and another. She began to gather a bouquet of them and each one led her deeper into the woods. Suddenly she spied something white under a tree, and instantly she dropped her flowers and ran toward it. It was a handsome little baby boy, and when she reached and lifted him in her arms he laughed and gurgled in a way that went straight to her heart. 'His cruel mother has left him here to die,' she told herself. 'Maybe the Virgin has answered my prayers and sent me to find him. I will take him home, yes, he will be a son for Alcide.'

Then, the child in her arms, she hastened out of the woods, but as she neared the road she remembered she had not thanked the Virgin for this son. So, spreading her shawl for the baby to lie on, she knelt to pray. But when she did this the baby began to yell and he shrieked louder and louder, almost as if he didn't like her prayers. 'So she told the Virgin she got to wait until she gets home, her. Then she'll pray some more.'

Then she started to pick the baby up... 'and when she seen him her heart she turned like ice inside her, yes. 'Cause that baby wasn't no pink-and-white baby like before, no, but a thing what was all black and shiny and ugly. And that black thing began to grow and get bigger and bigger every minute. That womans got so scared she almost died, her! All she could think to do was to make the sign of the cross quick. And she done found herself the right thing, too, 'cause the Devil he didn't like that; when he seen that sign of the cross, he let loose a yell like somebody hit him and he run off into them woods and that Cajun lady don't see him no more, never!'

That's why Noonie isn't picking any flowers. She wouldn't even look at them, her.

After the birth of a child the backbone of a shark must be secured and kept in readiness for his teething period. The dog shark is noted for the large number of its sharp, strong teeth, and it is believed that to string eight of the fish's vertebrae for the child to wear about its throat will result in a transfer of the quality of the dog shark's teeth to the infant.

From a small child's breast there is often a sticky exudation called witches' milk by the Cajuns. Children who become cross and fretful are believed victims of an evil witch, who comes nightly to suckle at their breasts. A broom placed across the threshold of the door will prevent this. No witch will step over a broom.

Until very recently doctors were almost unknown among the Cajuns. Only good roads and the extensive use of automobiles brought them. Besides, the general poverty of the Cajuns had offered no inducement for medical men to settle among them. In all communities certain people, usually old women, came to be looked on as their equivalents. Many strange remedies became popular and these cures are by no means extinct today. In some places doctors are still viewed with suspicion, and their prescriptions if used at all are secretly accompanied by the ones of the past eras.

'I know some of them old things, me,' Marie Polite would probably tell you, despite the fact that her Ovide had to go to the city to obtain treatment for his 'woman sickness.' 'Them old things is the best, you bet. *Si t'as des douleurs ou des mals*, take pepper grass and bathe yourself all over with it. All your pains and aches gon' go away then. Fill yourself a tub with hot, hot water, put in a handful of that grass and soak good. It sure makes your bones feel nice. You ought to take a prickly pear and peel him like a potato and soak him in water and drink that. That good for you all over your inside, yes. When your blood is hot it sure make him cool for you. You know the flower what the elderberry tree makes is good for measles, hein? And you take the first bark off the elderberry tree, then scrape the second bark good and make yourself some tea with that. There ain't nothing better than that elderberry tea, no.'

Babies are fed tea made of earth from a mud dauber's nest to strengthen them; children are made to sleep on mattresses of moss gathered from the cypress tree. The strength of that tree goes into the moss and right into them, making them very strong.

Rheumatism is treated with fly blister, an ointment made by mashing lightning bugs which have been soaked in alcohol. The thick leaves of the prickly pear, boiled down with plenty of sugar, are the best cure in the Cajun world for whooping cough. Sunstroke is treated with a brew made by boiling the sticky young branches of willow trees. Those suffering with kidney disorders receive tea made from the swamp lily. Athlete's foot is bathed with a liquid of boiled pecan leaves with a pinch of cooking soda.

A person tormented with asthma should wear a muskrat skin over his lungs. If a snake bites you race him to the water. If you beat him there and dip in the wound, he will die instead of you. Soap mixed with the yellow of an egg and sugar will cure a boil, as will an ointment of lard and charcoal. For chills and fever go toward the bed as if to get into it, but get *under* it instead.

Most Cajuns sleep with their houses tightly sealed, no matter how hot the night. This is not only for fear of the *loup-garous*, but also because the 'night air' is deadly and filled with germs.

You can always tell whether a woman's labor pains will be severe or not from the way in which the steam rises from her kettle the day she is to give birth to her child. An expectant mother must not let anyone comb her hair or sweep under the bed during the time she is confined, else she will have trouble having her baby.

Common bayou belief holds that mothers must not comb their infants' hair until they are nine days old. It is darkly hinted that all bald men owe their bare pates to ignorance of this fact. No child should have his hair cut until he has passed his first year. Even then the operation must be performed during a full moon; if done while the moon is fading to a thin sliver the baby's crop will fade accordingly. Neither must fingernails be cut until *le jeune enfant* is past that first year, violation of this taboo being considered very serious, though no one knows exactly what might happen. Mirrors must be kept away from the infant; it would not do for him to develop vanity when so young! He must never be allowed to see anyone who is extremely ugly; he must always wear white; and he must never be taken to a funeral or to a cemetery. Raising a babe on the bayous presents even more problems than in other places.

Once there was a man and a woman who were just married. The man had a Bible, and the woman said, 'I'd rather have the Devil in my house than any Bible.' Before long she had a child and it had horns on its head. And, of course, if the mother is frightened by an animal while carrying the child, the infant will certainly be marked in some way, maybe resembling the animal when born.

There are many superstitions besides the medical ones. Marie

Polite can tell you about them. 'When you find out you forgot
something and got to go back to the house, before you go back
there, you be sure to make a cross mark right on the spot where
you turned around, yes. And when you come back you rub that
cross mark out, or bad luck she gon' sure follow you, her. If you
go out on picnic and she is rain hard, go out in yard and make
cross with two sticks and put some salt on top that cross. That
sure stop rain! That what us Cajuns call *gris-gris*.

'Be sure on New Year's Day you cook some cabbage, even if
nobody she don't eat him. You won't have to worry about food
all the next year, no. M'sieu, that is *for true!* Me, I don't believe if black cat walk front from you that be bad luck. I think
is good luck. But plenty Cajuns believe other ways. If you see
spider in room, don't you kill him, no. That very bad for your
luck. But if you hear cricket sing by your house — ah! — that
she is fine for you. You gon' have best luck all year, yes. Turn
up your collar when you is under the full moon and you is get
yourself all the fine clothes you want for the whole year. 'Course
you know about open embrella in your house is very worse thing
you can do; and that bride on her wedding day must have something old, something new and something she borrows from a
good neighbor and something blue. Those not Cajun only, no.
Everybody in the whole Unite' State' believe in them, hein?'

You must spit on your bait before you throw it in the water if
you hope for a good catch. If you burn your finger striking a
match, put the burnt match behind your ear, as the heat of the
match will draw the pain from your finger. Always leave one
end of a loaf of bread until last. If you eat both ends before the
middle, then you'll have trouble making ends meet in your life.
And if a neighbor asks you to sell him a pig, or cow or any other
animal, you had better do it, because if you don't the animal will
die.

'One thing you must not do,' said Marie, 'is to take down curtains from your doors and windows to wash in month of August.
That is very bad thing, yes. For sure as you hang curtain back in
month of August, so sure is you gon' hang crêpe on your door.
And I tell you something else bad, me. You must never lay your
bread on table on his backside. Always lay bread on his belly

side. Don't never kill no spider. That is bad luck for long time. Is worse than breakin' lookin' glass, that. If you just bust up spider web, that means is gon' rain before day is through. If you put your drawers on wrong side out by mistake like, you is got to spit on them before you change. If you spit like that you have good luck all day long.'

If an alligator crawls under your house it is a portent of death. If a woman is *infidèle* to her husband just before doing her baking, the bread will not rise. This evidence has caused many a husband to beat his wife when her bread failed. If a designing woman can sew hair combings of the man she desires in her mattress, the rest is easy.

Old Monsieur Rigaud, a descendant of one of Lafitte's lieutenants, for whom Bayou Rigaud was named, offered the details of a sure-fire *gris-gris*, absolutely guaranteed to evict an unwanted neighbor. You take a piece of red flannel, twelve inches by twenty-four inches, and at each corner sew the foot of a baby duckling. On the right end sew a dried lizard and on the left sew a dried frog. Place this on your neighbor's doorstep, sprinkle sulphur in the center in the shape of a cross. When the man sees that, you can bet he'll move. The only antidote he can use is to throw the *gris-gris* into the closest stream and let the current carry the bad luck where it will. Dried frogs are always especially bad; one placed on your doorstep will bring tragedy to the home, particularly if it has been put in a black coffin.

The Cajun is usually healthy, lusty and red-blooded. He likes a good time better than anything in the world and always has a bit more enthusiasm for his play than for work. Balls and dances, usually given on a Saturday night, are beloved and never fail to attract everyone who can get there.

Typical is the all-night dance known as a *fais-do-do*, the name being a corruption of *fête de Dieu* or Festival of God. All the family attend a *fais-do-do*, the old, the young, *nanaines*, *parrains* and old maid *tantes*. There is even a room set aside, known as the *parc aux petits*, wherein you can actually 'park' the babies. But the *fais-do-do* is extremely exclusive so far as the outside world is concerned, the exclusiveness often being enforced with the point of a knife, or with a gun.

Married women seldom dance at a *fais-do-do*, no matter how young they may be. Most Cajun men believe it improper for their women to dance, and these wives, sometimes fifteen or sixteen years old, must sit on benches lining the walls, gazing wistfully at their husbands and the single girls and men enjoying themselves.

King and Queen dances, a type of modernized cotillion, are still immensely popular. A boy and girl must be chosen who are 'King' and 'Queen' for the evening, and riots often result because of these chosen two.

An inhabitant of one village described another type of dance. 'You ought to see them Yankee dances. Some people call them Variety dances. They is the same things. A crowd gets together and forms sets with a leading couple in the middle from the floor. Then they dance by commandment, like. They call what dance is to be danced and you dance that dance until they change. They do the polka, mazurka and two-step dances, all the real popular dances what is danced in North Unite' State', yes!'

The Mardi Gras, so elaborately celebrated in New Orleans, has festive echoes in the bayou country. Those who have automobiles decorate their cars and nearly all don costumes of one sort or another.

Peculiarly Cajun is the Mardi Gras custom of begging for small coins and for chickens to make gumbo on that day. A group of gay maskers will approach a house, mount to the front porch, and be invited in by Madame, who serves the traditional refreshments of *tac-tac* (popcorn), *beignets* (doughnuts) and *gâteaus* (tea cakes). They chat for a while, then, with a 'Bien merci' and one more chicken added to their sack, depart.

The women make their gumbo outdoors, fry some of the chickens and cook rice. There is much chatter and gossip. Julie Bourgeois' trousseau is enough to make your eyes pop out like M'sieu Frog's, hein? The priest is to read her bans in church Sunday. Madame Joubert's rheumatism is worse. That crazy doctor from the city wanted her to have all her teeth pulled out, that *paillasse!* How can pains in her legs have anything to do with her teeth? What a flirt is that Louis Thibodeaux, yes! And him engaged to Clothilde LeBlanc over a year now. Poor Clothilde! That harelip is sad.

Mardi Gras Night there is the ball. Everybody attends. The babies, maybe fifty of them, are all in the *parc aux petits*. It'll be a hard job finding your own baby when the ball is over. As a matter of fact, some mothers take home the wrong baby and the next day they must be redistributed. When a child turns out a disappointment to his parents, many Cajun mothers and fathers have been heard to exclaim that they must have taken home the wrong infant from a Mardi Gras Ball. Surely their own offspring could not be so wicked, no!

Sports occupy much of the Cajun's time. The annual pirogue race on Bayou Barataria is immensely popular. It attracts throngs, not only from the Cajun country, but also from New Orleans and neighboring towns. Each year hundreds of people line the marshes along the three-and-one-quarter-mile course to watch the stirring contest.

A pirogue is a frail shell of a boat, hewn out of a single log, averaging thirteen feet in length and twenty-two inches in width. They are indispensable in the swamps and along the bayous and coastal marshes, being the only practical means of transportation. While their frailty makes them difficult to handle, these Cajuns skim over the water at amazing speeds, the boats often loaded with shrimp and crabs. Children often use them in traveling to and from school.

So great is Cajun skill that the races are thrilling sights. In 1940 Adam Billiot won the race for the fourth consecutive year, establishing a new record of thirty-five minutes and twenty seconds for the four-mile course. Billiot was only a youth of twenty at the time, but for years the highest praise anyone of the bayou folk can give another has been, 'That man, he paddle like a Billiot, yes!' In 1940 a 'Nawthun Yankee' entered the pirogue race for the first time. This caused much consternation. If this 'Nawthuner' won, the humiliation of the Cajuns would be without precedent. They managed very well, however. The 'Nawthuner' came in *last*. Pirogues are for Cajuns.

Papegai shooting offers the winners the portions of a calf or ox that correspond with the particular part of the wooden animal they manage to hit. This large animal is attached to the top of a long pole and those taking part must pay a fee. Lubin Laurent, in his *History of St. John the Baptist Parish*, tells an amusing story in connection with this. It involves one Telesphore Cynporien, who had shot off the head of the wooden animal and as a consequence must be the one to lasso the ox in the pasture. To make sure he could hold the ox once he caught him, Telesphore tied one end of the rope about his waist — and proudly walked into the pasture, leaving the gate wide open. All at once spectators saw the ox running at a terrific speed toward the open gate, dragging Telesphore behind him, and as the ox went through the gate someone yelled, 'Where are you going, Telesphore?' Telesphore yelled back, 'How I know, me; for why don't you ask the ox?'

All Cajuns love frog legs, so hunting the frog is a favorite pastime. Even children take part. In the spring frogs come out of the mud where they spend the winter and begin to croak. It is said that the entire population of a settlement can be depended upon to take part in a frog hunt.

Children take part in the important crawfish industry, too. So popular is this that they even have a little song about it, a taunting jingle flung at the Cajun youngsters by Negro children.

> Poor crawfish ain't got no show,
> Frenchmen catch 'em and make *gumbo*.
>
> Go all 'round the Frenchmen's beds,
> Don't find nothin' but crawfish heads.

Here is another version of the same teasing song:

> Frenchman! Frenchman! Nine days old!
> Wrung his hands off in a crayfish hole.
>
> Frenchman! Frenchman! Nine days old,
> Got his hand broke off in a crayfish hole.

'Creeping the goose' is the Cajun's method of hunting geese. They believe geese always leave a member of a flock posted as a sentinel, and that this sentinel is alert for only one thing, the appearance of any watching human eyes. So the Cajuns, when they have spotted geese feeding in a pond or bay, begin to creep toward them, snaking through the sawgrass and holding their heads down so that their eyes cannot be seen by the sentinel bird. When they are near the geese, one of the Cajuns, who has been previously selected, claps his hands, and at this signal all the hunters spring up and fire.

In the Attacapan country the people are mostly herdsmen, for cattle thrive on the marshland. There they have become skillful and daring riders. Their horses are small Creole ponies, descendants of the mustangs which once ran wild on the prairies. These the young men train as courting horses, teaching them to prance, curvet, rear and dance, so as to impress the young ladies whose favors they hope to win.

The Cajun has little opportunity to enjoy the theater, but he makes the most of what he has. Occasional tent shows reach the Cajun communities, and when this happens the whole village turns out. Paul English operated one of these repertoire companies for years, and many amusing incidents occurred when his troupe performed for Cajun audiences. He was very popular and was known as 'M'sieu Paul' to everybody along the bayous.

On one occasion while playing the murder mystery 'The Gorilla,' English used the same uniform for the gorilla character as was used in the New York production, a very realistic and terror-provoking costume. At the end of the play the gorilla leaps from the stage and runs down the aisle of the theater, most of the other characters in the play behind him. In the most cultivated communities this sensational bit always evoked screams from the women and much amusement from anyone who had never seen the production before. In the bayou country the response was overwhelming. Many a Cajun fled, or joined in the chase.

While playing one small town, English received a call from three Cajuns carrying bulky bundles on their backs. After being greeted by English, one, acting as spokesman, revealed:

'M'sieu Paul, we is all gon' come see your show tonight, and we want to promise you all this trouble she been having is gon' stop, yes. We is all your good friend, M'sieu Paul, so we is take care of all that for you.'

Puzzled, English asked, 'What do you mean, boys?'

'Well,' said the spokesman, 'we understand that in the last go 'round (last act) is a beeg animal that she bust up your show every night. That ain't gon' happen no more, no. Me, Léon and Tee Jacques, we is gon' put all these things we got here in them aisles, and you bet your life that's the end for that monkies!'

They had all brought their animal traps!

Movies are popular all over the Cajun country, cowboy and other types of action pictures being first choice. 'Quiet, please!' signs are wasted in Cajun cinemas, for no Cajun ever stops talking except when he's asleep, much less when Gene Autry is chasing rustlers across the screen. At such tense moments, leaning forward in their seats, Cajuns will yell: 'Come on, Gene! Get him, you! I would not let him get away with that, no. Not me!' And with anxious sighs, '*Sacré bleu!* That Gene Autry is sure dead now. There ain't never gon' be no more pictures from him. That's for true!'

Baseball has its devotees as elsewhere. Nearly every town has its home team. They are exceptionally good teams, too. The Empire Louisiana nine, made up of brothers and first cousins, won every Sunday game they played for three consecutive years. Some of these boys found their ways into minor leagues, but none can be traced as having joined the majors, possibly because a Cajun gets homesick very quickly and has an absolute horror of cold weather, which is anything under fifty degrees. Auguste Breaux explained: 'Even this water down here don't like cold weather, no. You see how as soon as she gets a little cold she turns herself into ice?'

Food, its preparation and consumption, must be classified as a Cajun pleasure. Cooking is an art. Eating, one of life's genuine delights. At community gatherings, at church fairs, in the home, great skill and infinite patience go into the creation of their dishes.

Favorites are oysters, which can be served in at least thirty-five different ways, crawfish bisque, courtbouillon, crabs, soft-shelled and hard, spaghetti and bouchettes, the latter a kind of meatball made with chopped onion and sweet pepper, fried chicken — and no one can fry chicken like a Cajun! — fish in a hundred and one different ways. Always there is gumbo, made with crabs, shrimp and ham, sometimes with chicken, beef or sausage, and thickened with *filé*, the powdered leaves of the sassafras plant, or with okra. Various *jambalayas* are favorites, combining rice, tomatoes and seasoning with oysters, shrimp, ham, sausage or other meat or sea food. *Grillades* are popular; these are veal rounds cut into squares and cooked in a *roux*, a highly seasoned brown gravy nearly always present on Cajun tables. Rice is always there, too, white and dry, each grain separate. *Bouillabaisse*, a stew of several kinds of fish, usually redfish and red snapper with crabs, shrimp, oysters and crayfish, all highly seasoned, with tomatoes and shallots in the gravy, is common. *Café noir* — strong black coffee — pours down Cajun throats all day long, and the coffee-pot is always on the stove, hot and ready.

Like many Cajuns, Alastair Foucheaux deplores the development of the oil industry in southern Louisiana.

'Me, I'm afraid we don't get no more oyster soon,' he groaned. 'Why? Them oil business she kill all the oyster in the bayous. You know them machines what look like steeples on a church? Derreeck? I don't call them things nothing good, me. They spill oil all over the bayous and kill everything, them. M'sieu, they is crazy! What happen we have no more oyster, hein? Then maybe we have no more shrimps and no more crab, how we gon' make *gumbo* or *jambalaya*? And if we don't have no more *gumbo* and no more *jambalaya*, what hell Cajun gon' eat that's any good, hein? Oh, M'sieu, *ça c'est* awful!'

It has been said that Cajun Heaven is 'gumbo, go-go and do-do!'

Occasionally a Cajun will go on 'one beeg Bambache,' a drinking spree. 'Mine friend,' said Paul Dada, 'it just happen, that's all. We get in our boats and all of a sudden, us, we find ourselves thinking life ain't nothing to a mans without womens and wine. We sit and think a while, then one of us, he say "This boat, she ain't actin' right, Paul. I think maybe she need a new spark plug." They everybody say he think so too. Before you can say "boo" we is going back up that old river to the town, us.

'We stay in town maybe Friday, maybe Saturday, maybe Sunday. Those *bambache* is bad. Me, I always have head like one big barrel.'

Cajuns, in their own way, make good husbands, so long as their wives behave. A visitor in a Cajun home where a young couple lived with the husband's parents was astonished to hear blows and screams from a room into which the young couple had just entered. The door flew open and the young wife ran out of the house with a great bump on her forehead. The boy's mother turned to her husband and complained: 'Charles Alex is bad, yes. He should not hit Lulu like that. You would not do that to me, you.'

The older man took his pipe out of his mouth and said quietly: 'I never had no reason for to hit you. But if Charles Alex did not beat hell out of that womans he's got once in a while there would be nothing he could do with her.'

Then the mother turned to the visitor and explained gently, 'Outside of these little things them two children love themselves plenty and get along fine.'

The Cajun is shrewd and often clever at outwitting the 'foreigners' trespassing in his bayou land. Apparently his motives are mixed, on one hand the fun of proving himself smarter than the city stranger, on the other the opportunity of financial gain.

Two New Orleans men drove through a Louisiana storm toward Vacherie, Louisiana. Lightning flashed, thunder roared, rain came down in glittering sheets. Suddenly the automobile groaned and sank axle-deep in a mudhole. To make matters worse, the storm abated within a few minutes, the clouds vanished and a mockingly cheery sun beamed down on the wet world. Just at that time a team of animals appeared, a horse and a mule, harnessed for pulling. And on the back of the mule rode a Negro, and on the back of the horse straddled a Cajun.

The white man dismounted and approached the driver of the car. 'Hello!' he said brightly. 'I am Paul Auzot (pronounced O-zoo). Me, I live on farm up way a little bit. This here is Étienne.' The Negro grinned. Paul Auzot examined the wheels of the car. 'Uh huh,' he mumbled. 'Uh huh. You is stuck good, yes. If you had sense to pull over 'bout two inches you would not be in here. But there is worse hole farther on, so maybe it is just as good you get in this one. 'Course you is city fellow and you don't know damn thing anyway.'

'Listen, Mr. O-zoo,' said the city fellow, 'how about letting up on the sermon and pulling us out of here?'

'Mr. O-zoo' looked at Étienne. 'Leesten him,' he chuckled. 'He don't like to talk, no. M'sieu, if you was talk a little 'fore you come out here you would not be in there, and you would have save five dollars she gon' cost you to get out, hein? If you was talk a little and first ask about this road you would be smart, yes.'

The driver tried to be hard-boiled. 'Look here,' he said. 'That's enough. All I want you to do is to get me out of this mudhole. And, by the way,' he added suspiciously, 'there's something very peculiar about the way you and your friend there came along here all harnessed up.'

Auzot laughed. 'Is nothing funny, m'sieu. Is business, yes. And it cost you five dollar.'

'That's too much,' the driver snorted.

'Five dollar is what I charge,' said the Cajun. 'You want me and Étienne take a little ride? Is another car stuck farther down this same road.'

'No. No,' groaned the victim. 'Get to work. Just shut up!'

'Hokay! Hokay!' The Cajun turned to Étienne. 'Now, Étienne, first we hitch car and pull her to bridge, hein? Then we is turn on bridge 'til nose she points to Vacherie.'

An elaborate procedure followed. Auzot mounted the horse, and Étienne, to its occupants' amazement, straddled the hood of the automobile, holding fast to the harness. With much wheezing and chugging, the car pulled out of the mudhole and slowly began to approach the bridge. Suddenly, there was a loud 'Ouch!' from Étienne and he seemed unable to keep his seat.

Paul turned and laughed at him. 'Well, of all damn fools you is wors' *borique* in whole world!' he chuckled. 'If you ain't got no more sense than to sit your gogo on hot engine you ought to get burned good, yes.'

Étienne jumped off and walked the rest of the way.

At the bridge, Paul accepted the five dollars from the driver.

'I do good job, hein?' he asked proudly. 'You see, me, I got one horse and one mule for team. I keep mule to pull and horse for his brains. *Adieu, monsieur.* We see you again sometime, hein?'

'Look here,' asked the driver, 'is that your land there?'

'Yes, monsieur, on that side of bridge,' Paul admitted.

'Is that road yours?'

'Yes, monsieur,' Paul again admitted. But by this time both he and Étienne were mounted on their steeds.

'And this road I'm going to use,' asked the motorist with a final sigh, 'does it belong to you too?'

'Oh, no, monsieur,' answered Paul cheerfully. 'That road she belong to Joe Serpas. And you don't need to worry about nothin' like holes in his road. That Joe Serpas he ain't got sense enough to see that his roads got holes. He ain't smart like me, no. *Adieu, monsieur!*'

A Cajun is proud of his race, his family, his strength, his prowess as a hunter, fisherman, fighter or lover, and he boasts of any or all of these with a childish lack of restraint. A Cajun told a friend: 'I am a true man, me. I got credit at Fisher Store; I got a share in my boat; and I make fourteen children for my wife.'

Tell a Cajun woman that she is beautiful and she will shrug her shoulders and say, with a roll of her dark eyes,

'You is tell me something what I is already know!'

Chapter 10

The Temple of Innocent Blood

ON THE OUTSKIRTS OF NEW ORLEANS, NEAR COF-
fin Avenue, is the jumble of decaying frame buildings which
comprised the foundation of Mother Catherine Seals. Pigs wal-
low in the 'baptismal pool' and snuffle about the huge misshapen
feet of her 'Jehovah God,' chickens are busy in her 'Temple.'
'Saint Michael, the Archangel,' surveys the fowl with a look of
studious appreciation as a dropping is gaily deposited on the
slain serpent at his feet.

Although the spirits appointed Mother Rita to be Mother
Catherine's successor in the Temple of Innocent Blood, they have
practically abandoned her. Or perhaps she has simply forgotten
how to summon them — for she is old and confused, and the
spirits like a priestess with some get-up. No use trying to ani-
mate the shriveled body of Mother Rita. So the services are now
little more than a memorial. A handful gathers to survey the
relics and to brood on the greatness of the departed leader, there
is a little singing and praying, but no one lingers long amid the
dust and clutter. It is a relief to get back to the streets and the
reassuring clamor of life.

Mother Catherine originally planned the building known as

the Temple of Innocent Blood as a hospital and refuge for pregnant unmarried women. It had been her object to prevent abor-
tions — 'the shedding of innocent blood' — to give the needy
mothers care, and to place the infants in institutions. However,
she was unable to complete the structure, so it was converted
into a temple after the church burned down. A layer of shells
serves as a floor, and tattered canvas hanging from the beams
indicates that blinds once protected the interior.

The cylindrical object above the altar, Mother Rita explains,
is the 'Key of the World.' Mother Catherine made it shortly before she died, and no one knows what it means, but it is a holy
symbol formed according to the instructions of the spirits. All
that Mother Rita remembers is that soil, salt and herbs were
mixed in the composition. Most of the inscriptions on the brown
reptilian body of the Key have been effaced, but still discernible
are the words 'Rice, sugar, salt,' 'My Jehovia' and other expressions. The four voodoo faces at the ring, or top end of the
Key, would seem to offer a sufficient explanation of its inspiration. The four faces gaze indifferently over the dusty heads of the
'saints' busy with their exhortations, blessings and devotions;
their reptilian body rears positively above the cobwebbed nega-
tions teetering uncertainly on the shells below.

Most of the Catholic images, vessels, etc. were gifts from those
Mother Catherine is supposed to have healed. Among the jumble is a large statue of Saint Benedict d'Amour. This was given
by a white man, who, because his name was unfamiliar to the
colored congregation, was known by the name of the statue he
donated. One is startled by seeing valuable reproductions in
bronze and among the life-sized statues are several similar to
those seen in cathedrals. Remnants of sacred vestments hang
carelessly from poles nailed to cross beams, while more molder in
drawers and cupboards. Galvanized tubs which were used to
hold food during feast times are lettered in red with the following inscription: 'The blessing of Sweet Jesus, and Sacred Heart
(represented by heart-shaped device). The Blessing Jehova
handed down to Mother Seal.'

There is a stair leading to a balcony, or choir loft. Two or
three hundred kerosene lamps stand about the floor. The large

blanket-covered objects are band instruments. On a table is an enormous brass trumpet; on the floor are the drums: a tom-tom, bass and kettle drums. An automatic piano stands in the center, accompanied by a rack of rolls. The throb and beat of the Congo, the blare of Harlem, the torchlit ceremonies of Haiti, flash by as one touches the brooding alien head of the tom-tom and the cold impassive brass of the great horn.

Down there among the dust-laden pews lie the forgotten figures of a crèche — little Jesus and his mother and a few decrepit ovines. It is a wonder that they have survived so long, but perhaps Mother Rita's grandchildren do not find them very interesting. Mother Rita has half a dozen grandchildren living in the ramshackle abode adjacent to the 'Temple.' They are friendly, happy young ones, and reasonably may be supposed to have little fear of retribution from 'Jehovah God,' for he has been standing at their front door for a long time. Mother Catherine made him in April, 1927. It took her only fourteen days: the inscription on the base says, 'Started April 16th 1927, finished April 30th 1927.' There must be few statues more hideous than Mother Catherine's 'Jehovah God' as he stands there in monstrous decrepitude in the pig yard.

Mother Catherine founded her cult, the forerunner of many 'spiritualist' churches among the Negroes in New Orleans, in 1922. She had suffered a paralytic stroke, and a white 'healer' whose services she had solicited had refused to cure her because of her color. Right then she resolved to pray herself into a state of grace and good health. A spirit told her that her prayers would be answered and suggested that she found a religion of her own as soon as she was able.

Mother Catherine set about her task without money and without followers. She chose a tract out by the Industrial Canal, and in some way was able to secure the services of the builders who erected her first temple and residence.

She became known as a healer. Soon she had many followers, and gifts from grateful devotees made possible the furnishing of her church. Flags of the Sacred Heart, Jehovah and the Innocent Blood flew from atop her building, and the interior became crowded with holy pictures, statues and altars; five hundred oil lamps burned constantly. She cured by 'layin' on ob hands an' anointin' dere innards' with a full tumbler of warm castor oil, followed by a quarter of a lemon to kill the taste. 'You gotta do as I says if you wants to be healed an' blessed,' she told those who objected.

Mother Catherine always entered the church through a hole in the roof of a side room, intimating that she was sent down from Heaven to preach the gospel. She had no particular uniform. The Lord told her what to wear. Often it was an ample white robe and nun-like headdress. About her waist she always wore the blue cord of power and purity, and from it dangled a large key. Members were permitted to kneel at her feet and make wishes as they kissed this key. She wore no shoes on her grotesquely large feet, saying that 'de Lawd went widout shoes.'

Because of her illiteracy the High Priestess did not bother with the Bible. She told her congregation that she read her Bible all the time, and remembered everything in it. 'Ah's gonna gib ya facts,' she would say.

After her sermon there would be singing, and then healing. If the candidate for healing did not respond to her treatment, someone would say, 'Sumpin's wrong wid him. Boy, clean yo' soul 'fo' de debbil gits ya too much.' The lame were sometimes whipped with a wet towel, and told to run out of the church. The blind were treated with rainwater, or in stubborn cases Mother Catherine 'called lightnin' right down from Hebben' to clear the clouded visions of her patients.

Mother Rita's memories of the great teacher and healer are growing shadowy, but she will relate what she can remember willingly enough. Mother Catherine, she says, was born near Lexington, Kentucky. She never went to school, and first married at the age of seventeen. The two children born of this union died when quite small, and no children resulted from her two subsequent marriages. As she was unable to read, her teachings were not based on the Bible; all her inspiration came from the 'Holy Spirit.'

Two weeks before her death she was confined to bed by illness. Her plan was to go to Niagara Falls for her health as soon as she recovered sufficiently. But, according to Mother Rita, the Good Spirit told her that she had only a very short while to live. So Mother Catherine left her bed and traveled to her birthplace in Kentucky, where she died August 9, 1930, two days after her arrival. She believed that she would be resurrected. 'Ah's gonna sleep while, not die. De great God Jehovia, He's callin' me to come an' rest awhile. But on de third day Ah's comin' back; Ah's gonna rise again. Ah's gonna continue ma good wuk.'

Thousands attended the funeral. The congregation first intended that its High Priestess should be buried in the Temple, then planned a tomb near the building. But the city health officials objected and Mother Catherine was buried in the Saint Vincent de Paul Cemetery, vault number 144, 4th tier. . . .

On warm days Mother Rita sits beside the 'Temple' in the sun like some small bronze god, hands upturned passively in her lap. At night she sleeps amid the monumental clutter of Mother Catherine's old room at the rear of the 'Temple.' Mother Catherine prays and sings with her every night, she says, but never talks about the church, for 'Mother Catherine's wuk is done. She's restin'.'

Chapter 11

The Plantations

TALES OF DEVASTATION WROUGHT BY THE FED-
eral troops on their march into the South have, with the passing of time, been blended into a composite picture with details familiar to all. The traditional pattern of events preceding
the arrival of the Northerners is equally familiar, as are also the
heroic and resourceful attitudes of the women and slaves who
faced the invaders. Admirable attitudes, however, rarely prevailed against the needs of hungry and threadbare troops, and
after the storm had passed those remaining in its wake usually
found themselves bereft of every movable possession except those
which had been too well hidden for a hasty search to reveal.
Sometimes, it is said, failure to produce some desired valuable,
or too haughty a manner toward the conquerors, provoked the
burning of a mansion, but whether or not this occurred, the old
life of the home departed with the last whisper of marching feet
— Plenty had made her exit from the scene, and Want took her
place.

It is of the Utopia of Before the War that old Southerners
speak. It was here and it is gone. The best of all possible worlds
existed in the South and it was destroyed. And, truly, if merely

a part of this remembered grandeur once existed in reality, Louisiana plantation life must have been almost paradisiacal.

The old home places were not built in a few months nor even, in some cases, in a few years. John Hampden Randolph, builder and original owner of NOTTAWAY (thirty-one miles south of Baton Rouge), spent four years in selecting, cutting and seasoning the timbers for the mansion and in building the limekiln for the brickwork. Completed, Nottaway was a fortress calculated to defy the attacks of time and shelter a dozen generations of Southern gentility yet unborn. The way of life in what we term the Old South was expected by those who lived it to last forever, and two generations might be spent erecting and furnishing a home which was destined to be destroyed in a few hours by the fire of war.

Another such mansion was that of Charles Duralde, a legend now, even to his descendants in St. Martinville, where settled many exiled patricians in the early decades of the past century. Nothing could have seemed more permanent than the life of the Duralde family at PINE ALLEY. The Duralde acres numbered in the tens of thousands, with a corresponding number of slaves, and the Duralde progeny an even two dozen — twelve children from each of his two wives.

Rarely equaled in pure fantasy is the story of preparations for the first Duralde wedding, a double ceremony at which two of the daughters became the brides of prominent members of St. Martinville society. While such stories have doubtless gained with retelling through the years, they yet seem to have an indigenous quality quite in keeping with the spirit of the times in which the events recorded are supposed to have taken place.

It is told that for the occasion of his daughters' wedding Charles Duralde prepared far in advance, bringing from China the strangest shipment ever to leave the shores of Cathay: a cargo of spiders, which he had freed in Pine Alley to spin a cloud of webs among the branches. Then slaves sprinkled the webs with gold and silver dust, and through this blazing corridor, over imported carpeting, the wedding procession wended its way to the magnificent altar which had been erected in front of the mansion. Food and wine were provided for two thousand guests, and the wedding festivities lasted for days.

It is said that the rooms of the mansion were sprayed each morning with costly perfume; that he and his family bathed in cologne and that his carriages were decorated with silver and upholstered with cloth of gold. Yet Charles Duralde lived to behold the ruin of all that he held dear. He served with his sons and grandsons in the War Between the States, and returned to witness the dispersal of his slaves, the raiding of his mansion and the utter destruction of his personal world. Dying a few years later, he hinted that a large part of his fortune was somewhere buried or hidden away in a foreign bank, but never revealed its location.

The slaves never returned to the Duralde plantation; the sugar mill has long since crumbled to ruin, and the mansion, decayed and abandoned, was demolished some years ago. His family scattered far and wide, nothing remained of the dynasty of Charles Duralde save a few fine portraits by an unknown artist, and these were lost in the flood of 1927.

Of greater prestige and wealth even than Duralde was Gabriel (Valcour) Aime, known as the 'Louis XIV of Louisiana.' Romanticists may stress that he was the owner of 'Le Petit Versailles' — so called because the elaborate formal gardens of THE REFINERY, only completed after twenty years, were the product of the genius who had arranged the Garden of Versailles — but historians are more apt to note that Valcour Aime was the first (1834) to refine sugar in Louisiana.

The Refinery, about twenty miles south of the present town of Donaldsonville, was really a vast agricultural experiment station developed to the fullest state of self-sufficiency. At one time Valcour Aime was dining with a friend in New Orleans. Both were epicures, and as they fell to comparing their personal chefs, then to speaking of the distant markets from which costly delicacies were obtained, Aime said to his friend:

'If you will be my guest at my home in St. James, I will promise you a dinner that you yourself will admit is perfect, every item of which will come from my own plantation.'

'Impossible,' said the New Orleans epicure. 'I do not doubt, my friend, that you can supply most of a dinner from your land, but a perfect dinner from your own plantation, that is impossible.'

'Do you care to wager that it is impossible,' asked Aime, 'and you yourself, on your word of honor, to be the judge?'

'Ten thousand dollars,' said the New Orleans man.

'It is a bet,' said Valcour Aime.

The dinner was eaten in the great dining-hall in St. James. There had been terrapin, shrimp and crabs, snipe and quail, breasts of wild duck, vegetables, salads, fruits, coffee and cigars, wines and a liqueur at the end.

'What say you, my friend?' questioned Valcour Aime.

'The dinner is perfect. But I think you lose,' answered the epicure, 'for no man can supply me with bananas, coffee and tobacco grown in St. James, Valcour Aime.'

'Ah, my friend, wait a moment,' smiled Aime. He ordered horses, slaves with lanterns. They mounted and rode out on the plantation, where the planter displayed a conservatory covering plots of coffee and tobacco, bananas and pineapples.

The master of 'Le Petit Versailles' was noted for his princely hospitality and lavish gestures. When the future king of France, Louis Philippe, was entertained at The Refinery, it is said that the plates and platters of gold from which His Highness had eaten were thrown into the Mississippi.

The mansion, built in 1799, appeared to be in traditional Louisiana style, with eight massive columns supporting the front galleries, but wings extending backward enclosed a Spanish-style patio. The floors and stairways were of marble, and secret stairs were built into the thick walls.

Though the mansion burned in the second decade of the present century, the remains of the fort from which cannon boomed a welcome to visitors and where children played at battle with oranges can still be seen, and the channel of the 'river' is there, with its decaying bridges over which the wild vines creep.

Lafcadio Hearn, after visiting the site of 'Le Petit Versailles' — once the classic abode of white gazelles, peafowl, and kangaroos — described it as:

A garden once filled with every known variety of exotic trees, with all species of fantastic shrubs, with the rarest floral products of both hemispheres but left utterly uncared for during a generation, so that the groves have been made weird

with hanging moss and the vines have degenerated into para-
sites, and richly cultivated oleanders have returned to their
primitive form. . . .

One of the earliest plantations of which we have record,
MONTPLAISIR, established by the Chevalier de Pradel in 1750 on
the west bank of the Mississippi opposite the Place d'Armes, is
described by George C. H. Kernion in the *Louisiana Quarterly*.
He writes:

> The Chevalier had reached the zenith of his power. From a
> country gentleman he had become a '*grand Seigneur*.' Wealth,
> slaves, a plantation in the country, a home in town (in whose
> romantic garden shaded by venerable trees, the revolutionists
> La Frenière, Foucault, Villeré, Noyan, Mazan, Milhet and
> others were to secretly gather in 1759 and after his death, to
> hatch their revolutionary plot), fine clothes, jewels, social
> position — all now were his. But one thing was lacking to
> make his happiness complete. It was a château, yes, a French
> château like those he had known in his beloved Limousin,
> built in Louisiana, near New Orleans, where he could spend
> the last years of his life in peace and semi-regal magnificence!
> The act of sale was passed in France during the year 1750,
> and in 1751, the erection of the fairy palace, which was not to
> be completed before 1754, was started. The plans provided for
> a main building one hundred and six feet long by forty-eight
> feet wide, with wide galleries whose flooring was covered
> with cloth, running about its four sides. It had a gabled roof
> and wide attic, and contained a large dining-room, parlor,
> numerous bedrooms, study, laundry, and a room provided
> with large kettles known as the wax room, where the fruit of
> the '*ciriers*' or wax trees that grew on the place was to be
> heated in order to extract therefrom wax with which the
> Chevalier was to manufacture the candles which he later ex-
> ported to France or sold in the colony. The main house, whose
> every window was glassed, was elevated from the ground, and
> leading to the main entrance was an imposing flight of steps
> which gave the edifice an imposing appearance. Montplaisir
> must have been truly a marvel for its day, not only on account
> of its architecture but also on account of its interior decora-
> tions and the beauty of the furniture that embellished it. In

the letters that he wrote to France about his new home, the Chevalier was always most enthusiastic. Everything used in its construction and furnishing, with the exception of brick and lumber, had been imported from France, and the numerous invoices which still exist show that he was unsparing in making it the finest home in the colony....

Montplaisir, with its stately mansion and the wonderful gardens that surrounded it, where '*parterres*' laid out in the most approved French style were resplendent with blooming flowers, gladdened the now aging Chevalier's heart, and its wide expanse dotted with indigo, rice, corn and vegetables, with productive orchards, with innumerable '*ciriers*,' and with a sawmill and a brick yard, contributed materially in defraying his enormous expenses.

The Chevalier died at his beloved Montplaisir, March 28, 1764.

AFTON VILLA, in West Feliciana Parish, is a forty-room mansion built by David Barrow in 1849, and said to have been modeled after a villa near Tours, France. It was so named because Mary Barrow, daughter of the owner by his first wife, was locally famous for her singing of 'Flow Gently, Sweet Afton.' At the present time it is open to the public.

At the time of the Northern invasion the Union Army passed that way, and the officer in charge, noticing the grandeur of the gateway, ordered his men to enter and take quarters in the house. The men, noticing the design of the gate and being unable to see any trace of the house hidden far back in the trees, refused to go in, declaring that such an entrance led only to a cemetery. So Afton Villa, as it is now called, escaped pillage.

The house has cathedral-like Gothic windows with stained glasses, battlemented towers with cannon, Moorish galleries; but while it is of hybrid style the general effect is pleasing. A moat was once contemplated, but fear of breeding mosquitoes saved the mansion from having a portcullis and drawbridge.

HARVEY'S CASTLE at Harvey, near New Orleans, built by Captain Harvey for his bride, was a home of quite another type. Though it was constructed in ninety days on a wager, and the work was all done by free Negroes, yet when it was demolished it was found to be almost as solid as when first built. Planned by Harvey and his contractor without other assistance, this house displayed the current influence of the time, the writings of Sir Walter Scott, and externally was much like the old State Capitol in Baton Rouge built three years later.

Each of its three stories contained ten rooms, and the ceilings on all floors were eighteen feet high. Its two turrets afforded an unobstructed view of the river, and for years served as a landmark for river pilots. Expensive furnishings, velvet hangings and oil paintings imported from abroad embellished the interior, and in its time it was one of the show places of the New Orleans area. Then the home was sold, to become an amusement resort, then a cheap tenement, and finally an abandoned pile which was demolished in 1924.

Deserving of more than passing mention is GREENWOOD, near St. Francisville, whose lands were originally granted by the Spanish Government to Oliver Pollock, the merchant who, with the assistance of young Governor Galvez, financed the colonies to the amount of three hundred thousand dollars during the American Revolution and saved the Mississippi Valley from British troops advancing from the north. Pollock sold the plantation to the Barrow family, and the plantation house, one hundred feet square, with Doric columns, was built by William Ruffin Barrow in 1830. The paneled cypress doors have silver doorknobs and hinges.

KENILWORTH, about twelve miles southeast of New Orleans, was originally built, in 1759, as a blockhouse or fort, and remodeled in 1800. It was in this mansion during the Bienvenue tenure that General Beauregard was presented with a golden dress sword, commemorating his brilliant Mexican campaign. Kenilworth has its ghosts — a headless man and a lady in white whose footprints are said to be visible on the stairway the morning after the full moon.

Mention should also be made of the SOLIS PLANTATION, which is not far from Kenilworth, for it was here that for the first time in America sugar was granulated. Solis, a refugee from Santo Domingo, had brought with him a small wooden sugar mill with which he made unsuccessful attempts to make sugar. In

1791 his holdings were bought by Antonio Mendez, who, with the aid of a sugar-maker from Cuba named Morin, was at last successful in inducing granulation. In the following year Étienne de Boré, having procured cane from Mendez, hired Morin, and in 1795 produced sugar for the first time on a commercial scale.

PARLANGE, south of New Roads, is now a national monument to the Old South, selected by Secretary of the Interior Harold A. Ickes as a mansion typifying the taste and tradition of the days before the Civil War.

The house was built in 1750 on a land grant to the Marquis Vincent de Ternant, and the plantation has descended in direct line to the present owners. On either side of the driveway are octagonal brick *pigeonniers*, and the house, approached through a grove of live-oaks and pecans, is a white, green-shuttered, one-and-a-half-story raised cottage of cypress, mud and moss construction. The furnishings of Parlange include rarities in silver, glass and porcelain, and many fine pieces of old furniture. The slave-made implements with which the house was built have been preserved.

During the War Between the States the cash assets of the Ternant estate, amounting to three hundred thousand dollars, were placed in metal chests and buried, and not one of these has ever been found. Parlange served as headquarters for both General Banks, U.S.A., and General Dick Taylor, C.S.A., during the Red River Campaign.

Another plantation home which is still in much the same condition as it was a century ago is THE SHADOWS, home of Weeks Hall, in New Iberia, where five generations have lived. It was built in 1830 by David Weeks, is of brick fired by slave labor, and the woodwork is Louisiana cypress. The blinds are the original ones, unchanged after more than a century of use.

This structure is one of the most photographed homes in Louisiana. Eight masonry columns of the Doric order adorn the front, and above are three attic dormer windows. All the interior woodwork and plaster detail is the original. The gardens are famous for the number, size and beauty of their camellias and azaleas. In the east garden is a clump of camellia trees planted when the house was built. Nowhere in the state do camellias flourish better than in New Iberia, to which these natives of China were brought from France.

An article appearing in the *Times-Picayune* for January 12, 1930, describing the house and grounds, concludes:

> Aspidistra fringes both sides of the curved paths to the street, and on either hand azaleas and camellias crowd in well-arranged shrubbery groups with oleanders glowing at one corner of the house against young bamboo lances; yellow butterfly lilies dappling shrubbery with gold and here and there the pink filaments of tassel-like flowers lifting ... mistily over albizzia mimosa trees.
>
> Many rare plants appear among those which fill the side gardens and encircle the ends of the house.... It is like entering Eden from a village street.

OAK ALLEY, near Donaldsonville, built in 1836 for I. T. Roman, brother of André Bienvenu Roman, Governor of Louisiana (1831–35; 1839–43), is one of the most magnificent old plantation houses now to be seen in Louisiana. It is of plastered brick, seventy feet square, girdled by twenty-eight Doric columns each eight feet in circumference. On this plantation, it is said, the first successful pecan grafting was performed by a slave gardener.

Adjoining Oak Alley are Saint Joseph and Felicity Plantations, wedding presents of Valcour Aime to two of his daughters. Next is the site of the famous 'Little Versailles.'

Among the often visited homes of Louisiana, some are noted because of having been the homes of famous people, others because of some historical event with which they are connected, others for their lassic or bizarre architecture, and others for some single feature.

CARPENTER HOUSE, near Delhi, is visited because Jesse James once shared its hospitality, and the owner proudly exhibits a bedspread under which the famous bandit is said to have slept. OAKLAWN MANOR has a bathtub carved from a single block of white marble, in which it is said that Henry Clay used to refresh himself. The walls of the great hall of LINWOOD, and other rooms, were originally painted to represent jungle scenes. Eliza

Ripley, in her *Social Life of Old New Orleans*, wrote her impressions thus:

> A great tiger jumped out of dense thickets toward savages who were fleeing in terror. Tall trees reached to the ceiling, with gaudily striped boa constrictors wound about their trunks; hissing snakes peered out of the jungle; birds of gay plumage, paroquets, parrots, peacocks everywhere, some way up, almost out of sight in the greenery; monkeys swung from limb to limb; orang-outangs and lots of almost naked dark-skinned natives wandered about. To cap the climax, right close to the steps one had to mount to the floor above was a lair of ferocious lions.

Though good taste frequently gave way to whimsicality, it would, in general, be difficult to exaggerate the magnificence of these establishments, which in their time were unrivaled in the New World. Northern visitors often experienced sympathetic pangs after viewing the remains of some ransacked and vandalized abode. Said one, in the *New Orleans Democrat* of June 19, 1877:

> My principles now lead me to abhor slavery, rejoice in its abolition, yet sometimes in the heat and toil of the struggle for existence, the thought involuntarily steals over me that we have seen better days. I think of the wild rides after the deer; of the lolling, the book; the delicious nap on the gallery, in the summer house; of the long sittings at meals, and the after-dinner cigar of the polished groups in the easy but vivacious conversation in the parlor; of the chivalric devotion to beautiful women, of the clownish antics of pickaninnies when you tossed them a nickel, how they screamed for the rinds after you had eaten your watermelon on the piazza in the afternoon, and 'as fond recollection presents them to view' I feel the intrusive swelling of the tear of regret....

The food and the social life of the days 'Before the War' were indeed something to recollect. Whole families often went visiting and stayed a week or a month, and to entertain and feed fifty guests was not unusual. A midnight snack before going to bed might consist of a dozen items, such as gumbo, hot meats, cold meats, salads, galantines, fruit, cakes, charlotte russes, whipped cream garnished with red cherries, caramel, sorbet and ice cream. A real dinner might terminate with a dozen desserts.

For really important occasions famous chefs were brought out to the plantations from New Orleans, perhaps several at one time; one famed for his sauces, for instance, and another whose pastries were reputed to be the finest in the State. At WALNUT GROVE a miniature railroad ran from the kitchen to the dining-room, bringing food in piping hot, and also testifying to the amount of edibles served. Over these groaning tables waved the punkas, operated by small black slaves, in exact imitation of the lordly customs of the Far East.

The plantation bells, used to summon slaves from the fields and for other similar purposes, are subjects of numerous legends. It is said that Bernard de Marigny tossed one thousand Mexican dollars into the cauldron when the bell for his estate was in preparation. The completed bell, we are told, possessed the purest and most delightful of tones. But like 'grandfather's clock' it refused to function when its special duty was at an end; on the day of freedom its fastenings gave way, it fell to the ground and was cracked beyond repair. Judah P. Benjamin had six hundred dollars melted into the bell at BELLECHASSE. The ZACHARY TAYLOR HOUSE is famous for the same reason, the President having brought back many dollars from the Mexican War for the express purpose of creating a bell for his plantation with as sweet a tone as possible.

Every plantation had a name, most of them simple and chosen for fairly obvious reasons. A glance at an old map reveals the existence of MAGNOLIA, HOME PLACE, OAKLAND, HARD TIMES, REVELRY, EXPERIMENT, LAKESIDE, WHITE HALL, SUGAR LAND, NORTH BEND, CRESCENT, RIVER LAND, LOCUST GROVE, OAK GROVE, MYRTLE GROVE, WILLOW GROVE, SOUTHERN RIGHTS, FORLORN HOPE, HARD SCRAPPLE, SPENDTHRIFT and FIFTH WHEEL, and many others.

Local gossip testifies that SPENDTHRIFT was so named because the original owner of the estate lost it to another man during a poker game, but HARD TIMES, FORLORN HOPE and FIFTH WHEEL remain mystifying with their pessimistic implications.

Such names as MAGNOLIA, LOCUST GROVE, MYRTLE GROVE and

WILLOW GROVE are, of course, the result of the existence of a particular kind of tree which might be numerous on the plantation. The many 'oak' names, such as THREE OAKS, TWIN OAKS, OAKDALE, THE OAKS, OAK ALLEY, LIVE-OAKS, are evidence of the profusion of oak trees in Louisiana.

Sir Walter Scott's works were extremely popular throughout the State, probably because he pictured a society whose mood was much the same as that of the South during the period, and many a plantation was christened with such a name as WOODSTOCK, ROB ROY, MELROSE, IVANHOE and KENILWORTH.

Nostalgia for the land of their forefathers may have prompted others to call their homes VERSAILLES, CHÂTEAU DE CLÉRY, KENT, FONTAINEBLEAU and such names. AUSTERLITZ PLANTATION was, of course, so called in honor of Napoleon's victory at that place.

Some of these remain; many are gone. All suffered change, and bad fortune has, at one time or another, laid its depressing hand on every one. Evidences which verify the old tales of indignities to Southern homes and properties may be seen to this day. Treasure is found by some heir three or four generations removed from the harassed forebear who had hastily hidden it. Happily, among all the stories of wanton depredations are others, difficult for the Southerner to understand, but readily and frankly admitted by him — such as the one told by the master of CRESCENT PLANTATION HOUSE. He said that when he had advised the Union soldiers of the illness of his wife, they not only refrained from burning the mansion or disturbing the premises in any way, but the officer in charge bowed sweepingly, and said: 'Sir, we do not murder women. I bid you good day!'

Chapter 12

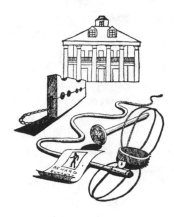

The Slaves

ONE OF THE LAST SLAVE SALES WAS ADVERTISED in *The Bee*, a New Orleans newspaper, on April 12, 1862, in this manner:

COOK, WASHER and IRONER at AUCTION
by N. Virgie, Auctioneer

Saturday, April 12, 1862, at 12 o'clock M., will be at the Merchants and Auctioneers Exchange, Royal Street.

Elizabeth, a Mulatto girl, aged about 22 years — cook, washer, ironer and house servant — fully guaranteed. Terms cash.

She might almost have been Cecile White, who, nearly a century old in 1941, remembered being sold on the auction block in just such a way.

'I was borned back in the old country,' said Cecile, 'in South Carolina. My Marse died, and me and my ma was shipped down the river to this heathen land. I was sold right at the French Market in New Orleans.'

The first black slaves were brought to Louisiana from Martinique, Guadeloupe and San Domingo, five hundred being imported in 1716 and three thousand during the year following. But the West Indian Negro was found to be steeped in Voodooism and of a rebellious, troublesome type, and soon nearly all slaves were being brought from Africa. Under the rule of Don Alexander O'Reilly admittance of slaves from the Indies was rigidly forbidden, and after the American acquisition in 1804 a law was passed prohibiting entry of such merchandise from any country; only those brought into the United States prior to 1798 were to be admitted to Louisiana. But shiploads of contraband Negroes continued to arrive, and free Negroes in the eastern and northern states were frequently kidnapped and carried down to New Orleans to be sold into slavery. Too, slaves bred rapidly and soon there were two distinct types on the market, those from the jungles and the Creole Negroes, those born in Louisiana or in the West Indies.

Slave sales were advertised almost daily in the newspapers of the era, the Blacks being classified by the occupations for which they were best suited, such as field hands, washers, or cooks, and later, as miscegenation became widespread, according to approximate degree of Negro blood, as mulatto, griffe or quadroon. Attractive, near-white wenches brought the highest prices of all, frequently being purchased by wealthy men as mistresses. The *Daily Picayune*, in 1837, gave an account of a girl 'remarkable for her beauty and intelligence who sold at $7000 in New Orleans'; and the *New York Sun*, the same year, describing another auction in New Orleans, said, 'the beautiful Martha was struck off at $4500.'

The slave mart at the old St. Louis Hotel in New Orleans was probably the most famous on the continent. A typical notice of a sale here, appearing in *The Bee*, January 18, 1842, was as follows:

AUCTION SALE BY COURT ORDER

At the St. Louis Exchange, between Chartres and Royal Sts. — at noon.

> Riley — about 28 years old.
> Dick — about 34 years old.
> Cook — about 30 years old.
> Oliver — about 26 years old.
> Marie, negress — about 35 years old.
> Marie Anne — about 35 years old.

This syndicate is not responsible for the characters nor vices of the slaves.

Slaves increased in value to a certain age, then rapidly decreased. A Negro who sold at twenty-nine years of age for $750 brought $1000 at forty, but probably not more than $400 at sixty.

By 1850 there were 245,000 slaves in Louisiana. In 1860 there were at least twenty-five slave marts within a few squares of each other in New Orleans. The fruitfulness of the Louisiana soil and the proximity of the port of New Orleans made it profitable to turn all cash into slaves for the purpose of cultivating that land, with the result that slave property alone ran into millions of dollars. The year 1856 was an exceptionally good one for slave traders. High prices were being paid and there was considerable money in circulation, and there seems to have been little vision of the rapidly approaching end of the South's feudal aristocracy. On July 31, 1856, the *Daily Picayune* stated:

> There has been a greater demand for slaves in this city during the months of May, June and July than ever before, and they have commanded better prices during that time. This latter is an unusual thing, as the summer months are generally the dullest in the year for that description of property. Prime field hands (women) will now bring $1000 to $1100, and men from $1250 to $1500. Not long since a likely negro girl sold in this city at private sale for $1700. A large number of negroes are bought on speculation, and probably there is not less than $2,000,000 in town now seeking investment in such property.

One of the features that helped make New Orleans unique among the great slave markets of the country was the custom of dressing up the slaves to be sold, it being said that 'nowhere else in the South did the promenade attain such glory as in New Orleans. Some of the traders kept a big, good-natured buck to lead the parade (of the slaves to be sold) and uniforms for both men and women, so that the high hats, the riot of white, pink, red and blue would attract the attention of prospective buyers. . . .'

The following notice of the sale of a slave, quoted here from the *Louisiana Historical Quarterly* (Volume 10), reaches the height of callousness:

January 21, 1741 — Petition to sell syphilitic slave.

Sale of | Attorney D'Ausseville reports that the negro
Diseased Slave | Hypolite belonging to Constilhas Estate has
At close of | been disabled for past eight months by vene-
High Mass | real disease now in its final phase. It would
On Sunday | cost a round sum to treat, feed and lodge him. Better discount his remnant value to heirs concerned by selling next Sunday at exit of High Mass rather than incur total loss of him by death.

Judge Salmon assents and he is bought by Francois Seguier for 1080 livres.

There is a friendly, come-browse-around-no-obligations-to-buy air to the following advertisement which appeared November 18, 1859, in the *Daily Delta:*

NEGROES FOR SALE

Just arrived with a large lot of Virginia and Maryland Negroes, which I offer cheap at my old stand, corner of Esplanade and Chartres Streets, and will be receiving fresh lots every month during the season. Call and see me before you purchase elsewhere.

JOSEPH BRUIN

The *Louisiana Gazette*, March 3, 1820, offered:

TO BARTER

For Sugar, Whiskey or Groceries of any description, several likely Negroes of all descriptions. For particulars inquire at the American Coffee House of

JOHN M. EDNEY

Slaves were essential to the plantations, and as planters grew wealthier the numbers of their slaves increased accordingly. John McDonogh owned three hundred slaves, Julien Poydras nearly five hundred, and many others owned even more. Plantations such as Chatsworth, with fifty rooms, and Belle Grove, with seventy-five, gave occupations to numerous house servants. while their vast acreages required small armies of field hands.

Business corporations were large slave holders. The early railroad and gas companies in Louisiana maintained crews of Negroes for the laying of tracks, mains and for other sorts of labor. The first gas plant in New Orleans, built in 1834–35 by Caldwell, on the square bounded by Perdido, Gravier, Magnolia, and Robertson Streets (the latter two then called St. Marc and St. Marie), possessed a brick wall, one section of which enclosed living quarters for the slaves, wherein they were shut when not working. When business took a slump, the management of the New Orleans & Central Railroad stepped from under by leasing its slaves to Harper and Merrick, along with the balance of its assets. Two slaves with notable names, 'America' and 'John Bull,' were sold at the board's order. A Doctor Carter of Carrollton was given free transportation in 1842 on the railroad's cars 'for services to the slaves of the company.'

Pending their disposal, slaves were held in barracoons, especially assigned quarters, not peculiar to Louisiana, since they existed even in Washington. Many persons carried on a business of training Negroes, then selling them, even renting them to people who could not afford to buy. In the service of caterers, blacksmiths, carpenters and tradesmen of various sorts, slaves became proficient in many lines of work, thus selling — or renting — at better prices than as unskilled labor or as field hands. There were frequent advertisements such as this, from the *Louisiana Gazette*, December 10, 1805:

WANTED TO HIRE

A *Steady* active Negro Woman, for the purpose of cooking and washing, for *Three Steady Bachelors!!!* — Enquire of the Editor.

And if that one has a mysteriously humorous implication, it was surpassed by a paragraph in *The Bee*, June 24, 1835, which stated simply:

The mayor has been singularly censured for refusing to allot 6 negresses to each of the 8 commissaries of police; although not more than 6 are at his disposal. Our worthy mayor cannot increase and multiply negro wenches for the Alderman to dispose of *ad libilum*.

The *Courrier*, July 16, 1830, suggested another means of disposing of slaves, with:

NOTICE

The Lottery of a Negress, made by Mr. Joseph Santo Domingo, will be drawn To-Morrow at 6 o'clock, P.M. at the office of Judge Preval. Persons who have not paid for their tickets, are requested to do so, either in cash or in bonds, as the tickets which shall not be paid, shall be disposed of.

Though slavery in the South is usually interpreted as meaning white persons owning Negroes, the United States Census of 1838 showed that 3777 free Negroes owned slaves throughout the nation. In Louisiana many prosperous free people of color purchased Negroes to serve as house servants or field hands. Occasionally, it is said, a free woman of color bought a slave out of pity for the creature's plight and out of racial sympathy, but in general the Negro master of other Negroes is reputed to have been the sternest of all slave owners.

Much of the existing information regarding slave life on the plantations is stored in the aging minds of those few still living ex-slaves. Martha Jackson, who celebrated her one hundredth birthday in 1936, told this story of life 'before the wah':

'We lived good,' Martha said. 'Don't never think we didn't. My white folkses was never mean or crabbish, and our boss man never did 'low nobody to mess wit' his slabes. He never did whop us. He called us "his niggers," and the slabes on the plantation next door used to call us Mr. Cook's "free niggers." They was jest jealous, 'cause they got whopped and they didn't have nothin' like we did.

'Our boss man let us have our church and our 'sociation. Twice a year he give us new clothes, at Christmas time and in July. Us used to sing when we worked and nobody said nothing. Us raised our own chickens and us had our vegetable patches, and 'sides the boss man give us sugar, flour, eggs, salt pork and stuff like that. When a woman had a baby she got lots of cotton to make quilts. And when the white folkses up at the Big House had a big dinner or a ball, they sent down all the food lef' over and 'vided it 'mong us niggers. If a slabe got married like on

Saturday, the boss man get everybody together and we have a big feast and a dance.'

Bongy Jackson, eighty-five in 1939, remembered his childhood as a slave, and recalled, 'We got milk and bread for breakfast, bread, greens, pot licker and peas for dinner, and bread, milk and 'lasses for supper. We had clean beds with plenty of fresh sheets and pillowcases. My old Marse was so kindhearted he wouldn't hardly whip the niggers hisself. He used to call in the overseer from the plantation next door to do it.'

'Marster and Mistress even nursed us when we was sick,' Jim Booker declared. 'We had good food and our own patch where we could raise things for ourselves. Some of them niggers even raised cotton for themselves. I knew one what raised enough working in the moonlight at night to make a whole bale. He sold it and Marster even let him keep the money. Sometimes I thunk I wanted to be free, but I got more to eat then than I do now.'

Slaves had various ways of addressing their owners. Creole slaves, speaking a French *patois*, called their master *Maître* or *M'sieu Jean* — or whatever his first name happened to be. The mistress was *Maîtress*, *Madame* or *Mam'zelle*, or one of those titles and a first name. In families where there were several married sons, the wives would be addressed with one of those titles and their husbands' given names, such as *Madame Jean* or *Madame Jules*. English-speaking slaves used such terms as Massa, Marster or Marse when addressing their owner. The mistress up at the Big House was usually Ole Miss or Missy. If there were two ladies, a mother and a daughter, for instance, they were Ole Miss and Young Miss, but it was always Ole Miss if there were but one, regardless of her age. And, if two, Young Miss remained Young Miss until she was old and whitehaired, so long as Ole Miss were still alive. The slaves frequently assumed the surname of their first owner, and retained it when sold and resold to other planters.

Each plantation had its own laws and work regulations. On a few places the slaves were set to shucking corn, or some other light chore on Saturdays and Sundays, but on most estates the two days were holidays for the Negroes. On the Sabbath, they would garb themselves in their most prized finery and go to church. Many planters insisted on their human property attending to its religious duties.

'Our master better not catch us missin' church,' said ex-slave Catherine Cornelius. 'Saturday was the day we did our own washin', sewin', and cleaned up our cabins. If we was finished our tasks ahead of time we was free for the rest of the day. At Christmas time we got a week's holiday, but all slaves didn't get what we did. Doctor Lyle was good to us. At Christmas he always gived us presents and money.'

Francis Doby remembered New Year's Day on the plantation where she spent her childhood.

'On Christmas each little nigger hung his stockin' on the mantel in the Big House and he got a piece of peppermint, two candy hearts wit' writin' on 'em and a blueback spellin' book; but New Year's Day was the day we liked.

'On the mornin' of that day the Massa, he stand on his gallery and wit' a big trumpet he make noise like, "Ta ratata, ta ratata," and all us little coons come runnin'. Then he give us picayunes. 'Course we don't know nothin' 'bout picayunes, and there ain't no place to spend money on the plantation. All we do is turn it 'round in our hands and say, "Look what Massa give me. A picayune." Like that. Wasn't no candy or nothin' to buy. Sometime the banana man or the dago man sellin' little cakes pass on the road, so we save it. I spent mine for bananas one time. Then after I et 'em I started to cry. My ma say, "What you cryin' for, honey?" I say, "I done spent my picayune, and I et my bananas. Now I ain't got nothin'." She say, "You is the craziest chile I ever knowed in my life!" '

Francis returned to Christmas.

'We greeted everybody in the Big House wit' our yells,' she said. 'We'd yell "Christmas gif'! Christmas gif'!" and we were all happy. Befo' dinner Massa give each of us a big glass of eggnog, and we sing, "Christmas comes but once a year an' everyone mus' have good cheer." Mos' the time all the colored peoples have turkeys and chickens, a real Christmas dinner.'

Slaves were valuable property and the owner of any intelligence provided adequately for their physical welfare. The larger estates operated hospitals for those who were ill. Trinity Plantation, for example, maintained two white physicians on its payroll, Doctors Stone and Baillot, whose duties were to attend the slaves when ill. Often, on smaller plantations, the mistress personally cared for sick Negroes. Nurseries were often provided for small children and were cared for by the older Negresses, so that the mothers of the youngsters might work in the fields. Women in childbirth received careful attention in most cases, for each new child increased the planter's wealth.

Small slaves were sometimes assigned jobs like those of shelling peas and beans in the kitchen garden, or assisting in the kitchen. At times boys in their teens, especially if intelligent or light-colored, were indented out to tradesmen. The *Orleans Daily Delta*, August 12, 1852, offered 'One Cent Reward' for Francis or Franklin Allen, a runaway apprentice, 'a good bartender, about fourteen, fair and blue-eyed.' Perhaps the absurdly small reward indicated a secret hope on someone's part that he had made good his escape?

Newborn children of planters were assigned slaves at their birth, a woman for a girl, a colored youth for a boy. Often the attachments endured through life, the Negress remaining the girl's 'Mammy' for the balance of her days, the Negro serving his young master as valet, and aging into one of the beloved 'Uncles' of which so much has been written. Many of the latter even followed their masters into the firing lines of the War Between the States. Slaves presented as wedding gifts to brides were usually proud of the honor, boasted of raising 'the chillun' resulting from the marriage.

Treatment accorded slaves varied in proportion to the personal disposition of their owners, but slaves were financial investments and aside from any particular virtue, planters were business men and cared neither to destroy their property nor to hamper the operation of the estates. Flogging, usually administered by an overseer or driver, was common, but it must be considered that all punishment of this period was more severe than it is supposed to be now; white people were harsher to their own race, prisons, asylums, even mental institutions, being rife with brutality. Unfortunately, though, there are a great many tales of sadistic cruelty inflicted on slaves by their masters.

George Blisset, reared a slave, remembered, 'On our plantation the overseer used to line up all the young nigger men every Monday morning and give 'em a few lashes over their backs. He said niggers wasn't no good on Mondays 'less they had a little taste of the whip. They had too much of an easy time on Sunday, he said. He wanted to get 'em started with a 'termination to work.'

'Lots of folks was real mean,' said Francis Doby. 'Like I said, they was always good to us at my place, but other places I knows it was jest whippin', whippin', whippin' all the time. My ma once belonged to Massa De Gruy and he was sure a hard man. My ma was hardheaded and sassy, and she'd talk right back to anybody, Massa or nobody. Lots of times she got a bull-whip on her nekkid back.'

Charity Parker, about twelve or fourteen when freedom came, swears she never saw a slave whipped in her life, but she heard of many such instances. 'Maybe I gettin' old,' she said, 'but I know this, I sho' never did see any nigger whipped, but I knows, too, lots of 'em was.'

'My ma died when I was about eleven years old,' said Janie Smith. 'Old Marse was mean to her. Whip her all the time. Made her work on the fields the very day she had a baby, and she borned the baby right out in the cotton patch and died. Old Marse couldn't stand for his slaves gettin' educated, either. If he so much as caught one with a paper or pencil, trying to learn how to write, he'd beat him half to death. People didn't want niggers to learn nothin' in them days.'

John McDonald told a similar story, saying, 'My boss man catch any nigger with a book or a pencil it was twenty-five lashes.'

Slaves were punished for lying, laziness, insolence, stealing, being late for work, and for various moral infringements. Planters usually punished Negresses for associating with low-caste white men. Nothing much has been said about their association with high-caste white men.

Elizabeth Ross Hite remembered seeing Negroes put into stocks, though the time slaves spent in these contraptions has undoubtedly been exaggerated in her memory.

'They put in their hands and feets and buckle 'em so they couldn't move and they'd stay there for months and months. I never did see no massa hang his niggers like some peoples say, but maybe they did. Most of the mean massas would just have a driver tie a nigger up to a tree, nekkid, and beat him to death with a whip. I seen 'em do that.'

It was always the driver or overseer's job to flog the slaves. Sometimes a driver did not like to lash Negroes, so he would tie them up, pop his whip a few times, and instruct the victim to yell, so the planter, who might be within hearing distance, would think his instructions were being followed.

'That nigger would holler jest like he was being beat bad,' said Bongy Jackson. 'I recollect one time a Massa come out the house and told the driver to stop. He thought that coon was gittin' whipped to death, and that nigger ain't never been touched.'

Sometimes resourcefulness was required to administer punishment. When a pregnant woman was to be whipped it was the custom to dig a hole in the ground, then spread-eagle her, face downward, so that her abdomen would fit into the hole. Then the whip was applied.

'I seen that lots of times,' said Odee Jackson, aged ninety-three. 'They'd dig a hole for that poor soul's belly 'cause they didn't want her child to get hurted. It worth money. Then they would beat her 'til her back was a mass of blood. After that they'd rub salt into it, or throw a bucket of salt and water over her. Sure they done that. I seen 'em.'

The lashes given a slave during a flogging might be ten or fifty or two hundred — or at least there is evidence to that effect. Of course two hundred blows usually meant a death sentence if administered at one time, so such a sentence was nearly always meted out twenty-five or fifty blows on different dates.

It is said that a certain Mr. Reau used to hang incorrigible slaves in the woods near his plantation. There is a legend that Reau died in a most peculiar fashion. One morning he began to jump up and down in his bed, was at last suspended in midair, eyes and tongue protruding. He had every appearance of having been hanged.

Perhaps the cruelest master in Louisiana was M. Valsin Mermillion. One of his punishments was to place a slave in a coffin-like box, stood on end, in which nails were placed in such a way that the creature was unable to move. He was powerless even to chase flies and ants crawling on some portions of his body. Mermillion prided himself on possessing only slaves with fine physiques. It is said that once he purchased an extraordinarily splendid young Black, and immediately ordered him hitched to the plow. When the boy refused to perform such an order, never having done such work, Mermillion had him dig his own grave, stood him in the hole and shot him with his own hand.

The Black Code was sometimes invoked in cases of unnecessary cruelty, though it is highly probable that ascertainment of guilt was difficult. The *Weekly Picayune*, July 29, 1844, contained a protest against one such case, however, in the following article:

CRUELTY

The most revolting spectacle we have ever looked upon was the case of two slaves belonging to a free man of color, named Etienne Fortin, who lives on Melpomene Street; the one a boy of fourteen, the other a girl of eighteen years of age. They had been beaten and lacerated in a most brutal manner, by their master. A gentleman who happened to be passing Fortin's house, yesterday evening discovered the slaves in the yard chained to a log, and suffering the most excruciating torture. . . .

Bienville established the Black Code in 1724, and it contained fifty-three specific regulations regarding the care, treatment, instruction and general conduct of slaves and freed Negroes, following the first provision, which called for expulsion of Jews from the Colony. Another law specified that all Negroes held in slavery must be baptized in the faith of the Roman Catholic Church. Aside from these examples of intolerance and bigotry most of the other laws were designed for the betterment of the relationship between slave and master. Provision was made for aged slaves and hospitalization for those in any way incapacitated. No work was allowed on Sundays and holidays Mass meetings and fraternization among slaves on different plantations was outlawed. Rigid rulings were set up forbidding miscegenation, amalgamation, forced marriages or breeding, and marriages between slaves of different masters. Excessive cruelty by slave owners was condemned, slave purchases were restricted and slaves' use of firearms sternly prohibited. The separation of families, especially the parting of children under fourteen years of age from their mothers, was discouraged. And although a slave's testimony was of no value in court, a trial was assured such persons except where infidelity to a master was involved.

Penalties for violations of the Black Code were extremely brutal according to our standards. First offenders had their ears cut off and were branded on one shoulder with a *fleur-de-lis;* second offenders were hamstrung and their one shoulder branded. Third offenders were executed.

Carlyle Stewart, ex-slave, said, 'My Missus and Marse was both cruel. Every nigger on the place had whip scars on his back. My Grandma run away and when they brung her back she got whipped and ol' Marse had her shoulder branded with a redhot iron. I seen him put a woman's eye out with a fork, just because she talked back to him. He'd take men and hitch 'em to plows like mules. The drivers would come through the quarters at night and check on who was missin'. God help them what was! They'd git one hundred and fifty to two hundred licks with a whip.'

The *Louisiana Gazette* carried a notice on June 23, 1810:

> Yesterday afternoon a negro man was executed in the rear of the city. He was found guilty of assaulting his master with an intent to kill, and is the first example in this parish under the Black Code.

The following notice from *The Weekly Delta*, March 30, 1846, was probably intended to be a cynical comment on public executions:

> Today the citizens of New Orleans may have the opportunity of enjoying themselves in witnessing the public strangulation of a black woman.
>
> As this exhibition is one of great interest and of rare occur-

rence, we presume that it will draw together a large crowd of spectators — men, women and children; black, white and yellow — who will attend for the sole purpose of strengthening their moral principles, increasing their detestation of crime, and enabling them hereafter more firmly to resist the temptations of sin.

One of the best known stories of cruelty to slaves is the famous case of Madame LaLaurie in New Orleans' Vieux Carré. Few visitors to that section have not heard the sensational tale. One day Madame's house caught fire, and those who entered to extinguish the flames found seven slaves, variously mutilated, chained to the wall in an upper room. One woman had been kept on her knees so long she could no longer stand. Another, a man, had a horrible gaping wound in his head and 'his body was covered with scars filled with worms.' So infuriated was the citizenry of New Orleans that a mob quickly gathered outside the mansion, threatening violence and bodily harm to the lovely and socially prominent Delphine LaLaurie. Suddenly, says the story, the gates swung wide and a swaying carriage drawn by plunging horses dashed through the crowd, escaping out the Bayou Road and vanishing. Other versions of the tale picture Madame as a much maligned and entirely innocent victim of spite and gossip, and brand the whole story as the falsification of an envious relative and neighbor.

Occasionally it seems a slave reversed the conditions, and meted out brutality to the master or mistress. Perhaps the most startling case of this sort recorded was brought out in the court trial of a slave known as Pauline in New Orleans. Pauline is described as having been a statuesque quadroon beauty with flashing black eyes and pale golden skin, with whom her master had become violently infatuated. The mistress of the house and her three children were found one day, by police officers, in a cabinet in the home, naked and starving, and covered with scars of beatings and burnings. The wife related a story of how her husband had forced her to watch his lovemaking with the Negress, who had entirely usurped her place in the home; then how, while the husband was away, Pauline had imprisoned her and the children and tortured them with live coals, a white-hot poker and a whip, refusing them any food and scarcely any water. Pauline was tried under the Black Code and subsequently hanged, five thousand persons witnessing her end.

The clothes worn by the plantation slaves were simple. Men usually wore loose blouses and pantaloons, and sometimes kerchiefs about their heads and necks. The present-day Negro's habit of wearing an old stocking on his head may have come down from this custom, though now it is usually done for purposes of 'hair-straightening.' Women wore full gathered skirts and tight bodices, sometimes adding spotless white neckerchiefs, aprons and *tignons*. This headgear is said to have been brought to Louisiana from Martinique and San Domingo, and evidence of this is borne out by the old family portraits of beautiful women with Madras handkerchiefs bound about their heads. White women discontinued wearing the *tignon* in 1786, when a legal manifesto was issued, designating this headdress as the only one that might be worn by free women of color. These women, many of them beautiful and perfectly white in appearance, had caused so much disturbance in the Colony by attracting the attention of white men, that the law was issued, barring them from wearing hats or plumes or jewels, and designed to render them less attractive. It is said, however, that the *tignons* increased their beauty and made them more appealing than ever!

Slave footwear was usually made on the plantations. Catherine Cornelius remembered, somewhat vaguely, that, 'the slaves' shoes was heavy worked shoes.' Trinity Plantation had a shoemaker's shop and a cobbler, a free man of color, who tanned the leather and made the shoes. Pierre Landreaux, one of the wealthiest of Louisiana planters, imported the shoes from France. Charity Parker boasted, 'One thing I gotta hand my marse. He sure done give us good shoes for our feets.'

'Possum hunting was one of the chief causes for slaves violating plantation regulations. Negroes could not resist the urge to go on these nocturnal expeditions. Drivers and the night patrols were constantly on the alert to prevent this, but without much success. When the animal was being cooked, the Negroes would close all openings in the cabin where the feast was being prepared 'to keep the smell from leakin' out.' If the drivers caught a whiff of roasting 'possum, it was bad for the offenders. A general whipping would probably be administered.

''Possums?' said West Chapman, ex-slave. 'Sure, we ate plenty of 'em. We'd clean 'em and wash 'em, parboil 'em, then roast them fellows on hot coals 'long side sweet potatoes. You could dry 'em, too, by smokin' 'em like hams.

'We made persimmon beer, too,' continued West. 'Jest stuck our persimmons in a keg with two or three gallons of water and sweet potato peelings and some hunks of corn bread and left it there until it began to work. It sure is good to drink 'long with cracklin' bread and potatoes.'

Slave weddings were usually held on Saturday nights and celebrated with a feast and a dance. There was no fixed procedure regarding the marriage of slaves. Sometimes they were joined merely by the consent of the master. Jordan Wingate said, 'My woman and me just made an agreement.' Elizabeth Ross Hite said, 'My master would say to two peoples what wanted to get married, "Come on, darky, jump over this here broom and call yourself man and wife."'' So many went to the master, Elizabeth said, that she has always believed it was because they received presents. Sometimes there was a preacher and a real marriage. 'It was jest like peoples today,' she declared. 'The bride wore all the trimmin's, a veil and a wreath, and carried a bouquet and all.' Bongy Jackson attended her parents' wedding and can't understand that this amazes people. 'During slavery,' said Bongy, 'us niggers jest jumped the broom wit' the master's consent. After the Cibil War, soon's they got a little ole piece of money they got a preacher and had a real weddin'. My ma dressed like a bride an' all, an' she done already had nine children by my pa. All us kids was there an' we sure had us a fine time.'

Preacher or no preacher, marriage among slaves frequently lasted through life, and if an occasion presented itself there seems to have always existed a willingness to have the relationship legalized. Any occasion such as a marriage called for a big celebration with feasting and dancing that lasted all through the night.

'We had plenty of good times,' said Catherine Cornelius.

'Don't you think we didn't. We had singin', dancin' and vistin' 'mong ourselves on the plantation. Every big plantation was like a little ole nigger town, there was so many of us. The slaves had lots of fun in their quarters, I don't care what peoples say. They played guitar and used a barrel with a skin over it for a drum. They sure talked about the master's business in the quarters, too.'

The slaves were often summoned to the Big House to sing and dance the buck and wing for guests. Here they were given drinks and food.

'Them smart-alec niggers'd make the white folks yell wit' laughin' at their crazy antics,' said ex-slave Dan Barton. 'You know a nigger is jest a born show-offer. They'd dance the buck and wing and another step nobody does any more. It went two steps to the right, two steps to the left. The womens shake their skirts and the mens dance 'round them. Let me tell you, niggers was all right on the plantations. I never seen no whippin'. Half that stuff you hear ain't true at all.'

But George Blisset said, 'Our marster couldn't stand noise. Us slaves used get together in one of the houses in the quarter and take a big iron pot with three laigs — the kind you use for killin' hawgs — and dance and sing around that, and there wouldn't be no noise could be heard, 'cause all the noise go right into the pot. Us held balls by candlelight, though they was strickly against orders. If they catched us we got whipped. We couldn't look tired next day, either. First thing ole driver's say was that we was up late the night before, and he sure lay that bullwhip on our nekkid skin.'

The fact that punishment was risked on some plantations might have inspired the singing of:

> Whip or whop, whip or whop, you-ee,
> We gonna sing and dance and sing,
> Whip or whop, whip or whop, you-ee!
> Singin', singin' and dancin', you-ee,
> Dancin', singin' and dancin', you-ee,
> Whip or whop, whip or whop, you-ee!

Charity Parker said, 'Saturday was our day. Sunday we had

to go to church. When I was young I didn't care 'bout no church, but I could sure beat them feets on the floor. We had no music, but we beat, "Boum! Boum! Doum! Doum! Doum!" One day a old man we called Antoine say, "I'm gonna make you-all a drum what'll beat, 'Boum! Boum! Boum!' Wait 'til Massa kill a cow." You see, they only keep that old man 'round to play with the children, 'cause he was too old to do any work.

'Well, he get that hide and he make us a drum. He straddle that drum and beat on it, and fust thing you know we was all a-dancing and a-beating the floor with our feets. Chile, we dance 'til midnight. To finish the ball we say, "*Balancez Calinda!*", and then we twist and turn, and holler again, "*Balancez Calinda!*", and turn 'round again. Then the ball was over.'

Slave balls seem to have grown in number, and though operated with a certain amount of secrecy, at last aroused the ire of the white population. On May 22, 1860, *Le Vigilant*, a newspaper, published the following angry letter, given here in part:

> For the last two or three months, the balls for white persons have given place to balls and parties for negroes. When a new house is built, following an old custom, it is christened by our slaves having a grand ball at night in the building. Twice, to my knowledge, this 'privileged' class has given a ball so close to our Donaldsonville Ballroom that I nearly walked right into their place, and was only stopped by hearing the discordant notes of the violin, which I knew could hardly come from our own orchestra.
>
> Besides the Balls, our slaves have musicals at night, mixed with games and round dances, etc. . . .
>
> Mr. Editor how can this state of things go on, in the face of an Act of Legislature and ordinances of the Police Jury, and the laws of Donaldsonville, prohibiting negro assemblies at night? . . .

Watermelon feasts and fish fries were of course popular among slaves, as they still are with Negroes, though today they are usually used as a means toward raising funds for church or personal use.

The slave was forced, in most cases, to adopt the religious be-

liefs of his master, and did — superficially. Under French and
Spanish owners the Blacks were baptized Roman Catholic in
practically every instance, while under American masters, usually Protestant, they were christened whatever denomination
their particular owner professed. But under the thin veneer of
Christianity African fetish worship and voodooism continued
to flourish for a long time, until there came about the queer
blending of Christianity and voodooism still common among
some Negroes today.

Catherine Cornelius said, 'We was all christened in the church.
We wasn't never dipped in no river like some peoples was. The
church we belonged to was the 'Piscopalian Church.'

Elizabeth Ross Hite added her bit on this subject, declaring,
'We was all supposed to be Catholics on our place, but lots didn't
like that 'ligion. We used to hide behind some bricks and hold
church ourselves. You see, the Catholic preachers from France
wouldn't let us shout, and the Lawd done said you gotta shout
if you want to be saved. That's in the Bible.'

Elizabeth continued, 'Sometimes we held church all night
long, 'til way in the mornin'. We burned some grease in a can
for the preacher to see the Bible by, and one time the preacher
caught fire. That sure caused some commotion. Bible started
burnin', and the preacher's coat caught. That was ole Mingo.
And ole Mingo's favorite text was "Pure gold tried by fire." I
always say that Mingo must've had to be tried hisself, else
the Lawd wouldn't made him be catched on fire quick like
that.

'Next day everybody was late to work, and everybody who
was got whipped by the drivers. See, our master didn't like us
to have too much 'ligion, said it made us lag in our work. He
jest wanted us to be Catholicses on Sundays and go to mass and
not study 'bout nothin' like that on week days. He didn't want
us shoutin' and moanin' all day 'long, but you gotta shout and
you gotta moan if you wants to be saved.

'We used to have baptisms in a pond by the sugar house.
Everybody was anxious to get baptized and be saved. The
preacher would yell, "Hallelujah! Hallelujah!", and the niggers would sing,

> I baptize you in the ribber Jordan,
> I baptize you in the ribber Jordan,
> Hallelujah! Hallelujah! Hallelujah, Lord!
> Children, come a-runnin',
> Children, come a-runnin',
> I baptize you in the ribber Jordan. . . .

'One old sister wanted to be saved one time and the preacher told her he was willing to save her, but first she's gotta prove to the Lawd that she was in a position to be saved. You know, when they checked on that old gal, they done found out she was the biggest rascal and worstest witch on the plantation. She was so bad even the mens didn't want her, and that is somethin'. When no man don't want you, you is really nothin'.

'It was too late to save her. She was really a lost soul, heavy wit' sin and bound for Hell. It used to make us all so sad. You know, when we saved a sister there was glory in our hearts. When she was baptized, the crowd would shout, "Thank Gawd! There goes Sister Amy! I been prayin' for this night on to two years now! Bless Gawd! She is saved at last. Her sins are washed away!"'

There was another factor beside the white folks' religion which did much to weaken the hold of fetishism and voodooism on the Negro. This was the belief in good-luck and bad-luck amulets and charms, and the traveling fortune teller and peddler who preyed upon those who held belief in these things. One of these peddlers, mentioned in the *Daily True Delta*, May 29, 1852, tried to induce slaves — females — to steal from their masters and run away with him. The *Delta* said:

> The slave William belonging to the estate of Creswell was yesterday committed in the Fourth District . . . on a charge of having tried to induce two colored women to run away from their master. The girls were brought up to testify, and the development made was of a rather novel character. One was a young and fine looking wench, who stirred up the hot blood of the accused. He gave her a 'brass copper,' which she was to put in a little bag and wear it around her body. She was also told to bruise some garlic and wear it in her shoes. This was

to give good luck in general, and the copper was to insure the kindness of the whites. . . .

She was also to throw whatever she could find in the house in the shape of money, plate, clothing, etc., outside the fence where he could find them. Of this a fund was to be raised wherewith to procure free papers from a Frenchman residing in New Orleans. With these they were to wend their way to Washington, thence to Liverpool, after which they were to visit the court of Louis Napoleon. . . .

William received fifty lashes and was sentenced to wear an iron collar for one year.

Death during slavery times was of the same importance to the Louisiana Negro as it is today, and funerals possessed many of the same festive aspects. Most of the larger plantations had a special coffinmaker.

'I can still recollect my ma's funeral,' said Catherine Cornelius. 'They sure give her a nice one. The preacher on the place, Brother Aaron, was a cane cutter, and when anybody died, they done let him off from the fields to preach the funeral. We had our own buryin' grounds a good piece in the back of the plantation. We didn't have no headstones, but we used to plant willow trees to know the place where one of our relatives was buried. All the coffins was made on the place, and they was plain wooden boxes, but nicely made. The bodies was carried off in the carts and the others walked. When anybody died all the slaves were let off from work to go to the funeral. Sometimes the people come down from the Big House, and if it was some nigger they like, they cry, too.'

The *New Orleans Weekly Delta*, September 16, 1853, gives the following description of the burial of a devoted slave who was burned to death:

A more solemn and affecting sight than the funeral procession which followed this poor slave to his everlasting home, we have never witnessed. The coffin was placed in a magnificent hearse; there were twenty-four pall-bearers, and then followed about four hundred slaves, all dressed with the utmost neatness. . . . This poor slave was well cared for, even to the last. His body was thrown into no common trench with indecent haste, but was quietly placed in a brick tomb, which would have satisfied the affections of the most fastidious mourning friend that any token of regard and respect had been paid. . . .

Elizabeth Ross Hite says that at Trinity Plantation there was a preacher, the Reverend Jacob Nelson, a slave who spoke five languages. He was 'educated jest like white folks,' explained Elizabeth, 'and went around growlin', cryin', talkin' in them languages what nobody can understand. People didn't know what he was a-sayin', but the crowd went wild. It was jest like a picnic when the Reverend Nelson preach a funeral; some people fainted.'

But there's another side to the story, too.

'Mind, what I tell you,' Cecile George said. 'I tell you what I seen wit' my own two eyes. The people on the plantation they take sick and they die. Ain't no coffin for them. They take planks and nail them together like a chicken coop. You could see through it. And it's too short, the neck's too long. So a man stand up on the coffin, jump on the corpse, break his neck and his head fall on his chest. Then they nail the top and one nail go through the brain. You think I make that up or dream it? I seen that wit' mine own eyes.

'Then they put them in a wagon — the one they haul the manure in, nobody wit' them. The people have to go right on to work. Make no difference it your own father, you gotta go out in the fields that day. I seen that wit' my own eyes. It was wicked! Wicked! Wicked! Wicked! And I seen it wit' my own eyes.'

Yet, despite the tales of inhumanity of masters to the slaves, there is every reason to believe there were few actual cases of excessive and extreme cruelty. Without a doubt, the affection directed toward his owner by many a slave was a deep and imperishable thing. The loyalty and fidelity of the household servant, in particular, were often unquestionable. The mammies, for instance, practically ruled the Big Houses. Mammy was always a more than competent cook, and a second mother to the planter's children. Indeed, in many cases, she was probably closer to the youngsters than their own mother. Mammy was so integrally a part of the family that she was lifted far above the other servants.

During the war Mammy Marianne baked cookies each week and trudged overland through the woods to an army camp on the Mississippi River to deliver them to her 'boy,' one of the Confederate officers. Mammy Nancy lived all her life with no other religion than the innate goodness in her own big heart, yet, at their request, she received Holy Communion in the Roman Catholic Church, kneeling beside three generations of her 'babies.' Old Mammy July, when photographed at 119 years of age, maintained her dignity, even though only four feet tall and entirely bald, by wearing five hats telescoped together and tied on with a scarf, saying, 'I ain't no Mardy Graw, white folks!' At 120, probably the oldest living woman in the United States, Mammy July trudged from New Roads, Louisiana to Baton Rouge, to visit her 'chillun,' members of the Lorio family there. But there are few living mammies of the old type left now, and soon there will be no more of these grand persons on whose capacious bosoms the South at one time found peace and comfort and security.

There were remarkable instances of slaves rising in the world, despite their seemingly insurmountable handicaps.

William Cooper, owned by Alonzo Roberts, near Cheneyville, while hired out to J. A. McCormick, earned not only his own freedom but that of his bride also. His employer allowed him to work overtime in order to earn the money. After being free he continued the work at wages because he had been attracted by a girl on a neighboring plantation. He saved one thousand dollars, borrowed five hundred dollars, bought her and married her. Later he purchased the freedom of his brother and was saving money to free the rest of his family when the Civil War emancipated them. When Cooper and his wife died they owned considerable property, and they willed their estate to members of the family which had formerly owned them.

The intelligence and determination of James Derham, a slave, made him one of the outstanding physicians of his day. Born in Philadelphia in 1762, he quickly learned to read and write, and, while helping his master, a doctor, compound medicines, absorbed much of the profession. He was sold to Doctor George West, a surgeon in the Sixteenth British Regiment during the

Mother Catherine's grave and statue

Statue of Jehovah made by Mother Catherine

Mother Maude Shannon, leader of a popular cult of today

When the "Mother" of a cult dies she is often buried with a crown on her head
Courtesy of Michael Kirk

Revolutionary War, who aided him in furthering his medical studies. Then, at the close of that war, he was sold to Doctor Robert Love of New Orleans, who encouraged his studies and eventually freed him on very liberal terms. As a doctor in New Orleans he became so proficient that he enjoyed an income of several thousand dollars a year, amazing for a man reared as a slave. Of a modest and engaging personality, Derham spoke French fluently and possessed some knowledge of Spanish.

The slave often resorted to superstition and queer homemade remedies for the treatment of his own ills. Warts were rubbed with wedding rings, mud and tobacco juice piled on bee-stings. Fresh mint was eaten to 'sweeten the stomach,' bay-leaf tea administered for cramps, and a cow's tooth was suspended from a string around the baby's neck to aid teething.

'When we had rheumatism, we took an Irish potato, cut it up in pieces, and tied it 'round the pain,' recalled West Chapman. 'It always cured, too. Potatoes was also tied 'round the waist for the same purpose.' Rubbing with lotions made of alligator fat, buzzard grease, or rattlesnake oil, wearing a brass ring or a hatband or belt made of snakeskin were also effective for treatment of rheumatism, according to West. He added that 'hog-hoof, parched and ground into dust, dissolved in water, moved pain.' Jimson weed was given children for worms. 'It was cooked down like 'lasses and it was good tasting like candy.' West concluded, 'But nobody uses things like that no more. Everything has to come out a drugstore. I can't understand it.'

'I used to know a ole Democrat what didn't like colored people,' said Cecile George. 'He wouldn't look at us when he spoke. Said a nigger, a dog, and a alligator was the same to him. His name was Mr. Jerry and his wife's name was Mrs. Jerry.

'Yellow fever was ragin' and Mrs. Jerry took wit' it. She was really a good woman, 'cept she had married Mr. Jerry. He called in Doctor Levere, then the doctor, he took wit' it, too. Mrs. Jerry, she call me and I went to her bed. She say, "Oh, Cecile, I'm sick. Make me some of that tea of yours." But I was scared of Mr. Jerry, and I wouldn't do it 'cause I know how that man didn't like niggers or nigger medicine. But I prayed and somethin' told me, "Trust God, and make that poor woman some tea." So I went out and got me some grass what I use, got some Indian root, boiled it all down, and made me that tea. I give it to Mrs. Jerry, but at first she won't sweat, then I cover her up some more and she start. You know she sweat that fever all out right there? And wit' God's help I pulled her through, and got her on her feets. She lived a long time. Doctor Levere, he went crazy, died in a 'sylum. Mr. Jerry, he died and went to Hell. His spirit used to come back in the daytime in the shapes of bulldogs. Haunted everybody for a long time.'

Slaves made black pepper tea for smallpox. 'It'd pull all the bumps in and not leave no scars or nothing like that,' vowed Emily White. Cornshucks, boiled down into a tea, were also used for that once prevalent disease. Lizzie Chandler, ex-slave, recalled this, also that 'when a person couldn't stop hiccoughing, all you had to do was to make him smell sneezeweed. He sure start sneezing then and not hiccough no more.' Red pepper tea was administered for chills and fever, as was peach-tree leaf tea. 'Bird-eye vine is good for croup,' said Lizzie, 'dry it an' give it to a baby in his milk.' Swamp lilies were dried and strung around a baby's neck for teething.

Of course charms against voodoo and witchcraft were worn, as they are today. 'Little bags wit' somethin' made out of red flannel,' were recalled by George Sanders, who added that they contained bones of a black cat and similar items.

The slave never knew when a voodoo woman or a witch doctor was on his trail. Victims suffered from shooting pains caused by needles, wads of hair, knives, pebbles, and such evil *gris-gris* concealed somewhere about their homes. Even their deaths might be brought about this way. A voodoo woman could put a snake in your leg and that reptile would probably remain there for the rest of your life.

'I've had a ole snake in my laig all my life,' swore Clara Barton. 'It's been better these last years, but at fust it like to drove me crazy. I can still feel that thing, though. Had a bad woman come after my man back on the plantation. One night she snuck in my room and stuck that snake in my laig. I felt it and I screamed, but it was too late. The room was dark and I couldn't see her, but I heard her paddin' over the floor, going through the door. She left that door creakin' and swingin'. When my ma woke up and run in the room I was jest layin' on the floor yellin' in the dark, and that door was still creakin' and swingin', creakin' and swingin'.'

'I don't believe in no hoodoo at all,' declared Bongy Jackson. 'One time one of my nephews got into police trouble, and a woman come to my house and say if I pay her she could help me with hoodoo. I give that woman some of my money and the best ham we have in the smokehouse, and she give me a paper with some writing on it and some kind of powder in it and somethin' what looked like a root dried up. She told me to send 'em to that boy and tell him to chew the root in the courtroom durin' his trial, and to hold the piece of paper in his hand, and to spit on it now and then when the judge wasn't lookin'. I did all that and he did all that, and that boy go to jail just the same. No, I don't believe in no hoodoo.'

Good and bad luck played prominent parts in the common, everyday life of the plantation. Slaves planted sweet basil on either side of the cabin door. The screech of an owl was a death sign, while for a spider or a butterfly to light on a person was a good omen. Cowpeas and hog jowl served on New Year's Day would guarantee plenty to eat all during the ensuing year. Keeping a 'frizzly' chicken around the house alleviated all bad luck.

'We called sweet basil by another name,' explained Francis Doby. 'We called it *basilique*, and it sure was good to have 'round the house. They is got two kinds of *basilique*, you know, the papa plant what's got them long thin leaves, and the mamma plant, what's got fat round leaves. You got to put 'em both in the ground at the same time so they'll get together and grow. And when you got them in your yard you sure is got good luck for yourself all the year 'round.'

'Pickin' up tracks' caused great consternation among slaves. If anyone was seen picking up the dust of footprints in a handkerchief, it meant that 'a stumblin' block is sure gwine be put in somebody's way.'

Of course many slaves believed implicitly in witches. 'A witch,' said Elizabeth Ross Hite, 'is like a big turkey wit' no eyes. Sometimes, they looks like the Devil, wit' horns and everything.'

Even the faithful mammy was not above resorting to witch-craft to gain her wishes. According to the *Times-Democrat* of August 5, 1888, the attention of a household was one day at-tracted to the antics of old Aunt Dolores. The woman, during a thunderstorm, was seen anxiously searching the house for some-thing, then to run out into the yard, still hunting. 'Hither and thither she ran,' stated the article, 'in rapid quest, until at last she stumbled upon the object of her search, no less a thing than an axe for chopping wood . . . a bright expression of joy irradi-ated her face.' Snatching up the axe, Aunt Dolores sped into a corner of the yard, and raising it above her head, 'she made pass after pass in the very face of the rushing current, as if chopping some invisible thing quickly in twain.' When a sudden abating of the wind's violence was noticed, the woman marched back into the house, wearing a defiant look of triumph on her rugged dark face. She had defied the evil spirit of the storm; it dared not advance against her sharp-edged axe. *Tante* Dolores con-tended that it never failed if she 'jest got there in time enough.'

'I never seen a witch,' admitted Rebecca Fletcher, 'but my Grandma knew lots of 'em, and she done tol' me plenty times what they looks like. My Grandma told me about a witch what went into a good woman's house when that woman was in bed. That woman knowed she was a witch, so she told her to go into the other room. Ole witch went out and lef' her skin layin' on the floor, and the woman jumped out of bed and sprinkled it wit' salt and pepper. Ole witch come back put on her skin. She start hollerin' and jumpin' up and down like she was crazy. She yelled and yelled. She yelled, "I can't stand it! I can't stand it! Something's bitin' me!" Ole witch hollered, "Skin, don't you know me?" She said this three times, but the salt and pepper keep bitin'. The woman took a broomstick and shooed that ole witch right out, and she disappeared in the air.'

Rebecca isn't afraid of witches, though, because she knows how to handle them. 'They ain't never gonna hurt you if you knows how to handle them and how to talk to them. When you pass a place and feels creepy and scared, you feels a ghost or a witch. If you say, "Holy Father, don't let this thing bother me," He ain't gonna let it hurt you. Spirits come in sometimes and drinks liquor spilled on the floor, but they don't make no trouble. They gets drunk and passes you like steam goin' by.'

Discontented slaves were always seeking greener pastures. Accounts of runaways and their return, notices of vanished slaves and of those found or captured, appeared almost daily in the newspapers of the pre-emancipation period. Professional slave-catchers, equipped with packs of bloodhounds, chains, guns, and whips did a lucrative business returning runaways either to their masters, if they could be located, or to the jails in the various parishes, where they were held for a certain period and finally, if not claimed, auctioned.

Brief and to the point is the following advertisement in *The Bee*, February 26, 1828:

FIFTEEN DOLLARS REWARD

The above reward is offered for the arrest of the Negro Wench Nancy, who absconded about fifteen days since, she had the habit of selling cakes, she has a very black skin, a large breast, a fearful look. She had on a blue cottonade gown with squares, she is generally at the port, toward Mr. Morney's — about 25 dollars equally offered to the person who can discover where she is harbored.

A. La Coutere

This one, from the *Louisiana Gazette*, October 16, 1817, did not offer much inducement to the finders:

ONE CENT REWARD

Ranaway from the subscriber about the 1st instant, a Mulatto Apprentice to the Harness making business, named Charles Roche, about 18 years of age. 5 feet 3 or 4 inches high, sallow complexion, and a lazy indolent walk. Had on when he went off a cottonade coatee and pants.

. Captains of vessels and all others, are warned against harboring or carrying off said apprentice.

H. Beebe

The next one is typical of the 'found' advertisements, and appeared in the *Louisiana Gazette*, January 4, 1816:

RUNAWAY SLAVES KEPT IN JAIL

Michael, a mullato aged about 38 years; five feet two inches high; speaks English and very little French; of middle size. Said mullato says he belongs to Mr. Robert Lackey, postmaster of Woodville, from whence he has absented himself since two months.

The negro Clark, of the Congo nation, having some marks of his country on his forehead, aged about 20 years; a round face, four feet nine inches, American measure, high, speaking very bad English and in the habit of answering in Congo the question put to him. Said negro says he belongs to Mr. William or Frank, whose residence he is not able to indicate.

JACQUES LAMOTHE, Jailor

This jailor, advertising in the *Daily Picayune* on April 4, 1840, seemed anxious to get rid of his charge:

Was brought to the Police Prison of the Second Municipality the following slave, viz:

A negro woman named Sally, about 26 years of age; says she belongs to Mr. Kerr.

The owner of said property will please call at the Police Prison in Baronne Street, prove property and take her away.

H. S. HARPER
Captain of the Watch

Rather pathetic is this notice, run in *L'Ami Des Lois Et Journal Du Commerce* on August 8, 1821:

KEPT IN GAOL AT THE PARISH OF ST. JOHN BAPTIST

A Negress named Rosalie, between 50 and 60 years of age, having an iron collar with three branches. She does not remember her master's name, but he lives in Faubourg Lacourse. The owner will please claim the said negress and pay the costs.

N. TREPAGNIER, Sheriff

The Iron Collar was a heavy instrument fitting tightly about the throat, about an inch wide and having three branches curving up around the face, one behind the head and one on each side. Sometimes these branches were surmounted with brass bells which tinkled with every movement. Slaves were sentenced to wear the collar for various infringements and for a certain length of time. Sometimes it might not be removed for years, occasionally had to be worn for life. After a first attempt at escape a common sentence was a given number of lashes and six months or a year wearing the Iron Collar.

The most famous of all runaways in Louisiana history was a gigantic mulatto renowned as the greatest Bamboula dancer ever to shake the earth of the Congo Square in New Orleans, and whose stentorian shouts of 'Bamboula! Bamboula! Bamboula!' thundered through the bloodstreams of the voodooists assembled in the Square.

His name is said to have been Squire — or Squier — and it is believed he was the personal slave of General William de Buys, though the only newspaper account of his ownership mentions him as the property of a John Berry West, living somewhere between Plaquimine and Baton Rouge. However, it is generally accepted that he was the property of de Buys, and that he was accorded the most lenient of treatment, accompanying the General on hunting expeditions, was even allowed to carry arms and go on hunts alone. Despite this, Squier ran away again and again. After one such escapade he was shot and suffered the amputation of an arm. Almost immediately he received the appellation of *Bras Coupé*, by which his notoriety spread throughout the balance of his long and hectic career. He quickly became a legendary figure among both the white and colored races and his reputation for daring and infamy spread. Little children were for years frightened into instant silence and obedience at the mere mention of the name of *Bras Coupé*.

The day after the amputation of his arm hospital attendants found his bed empty. He had vanished into the near-by cypress swamps, where, it is said, he gathered a band of renegade slaves and led them in nocturnal raids on the plantations in the neighborhood. Becoming known as the 'Brigand of the Swamp,' tales of his prowess and immunity to death grew. Terrified hunters returned to tell of having shot him, having seen their bullets go through his body, without apparent harm. No plantation was safe from the nocturnal raids of *Bras Coupé* and his henchmen. Female slaves were sometimes carried off, and it is reported that at least one white woman fell into his hands.

On April 6, 1837, a New Orleans city guard brought in a report of having killed the Negro. He said he had met *Bras Coupé*, shot and wounded him seriously. Then, after being certain he was seriously wounded and helpless, he had beat him to death with the butt of his rifle. When returning officers located the spot where the incident had occurred, however, there was no body, only a perfectly perceptible trail of blood where the 'dead man' had escaped into the swamp.

But an attack on a white man finally cost *Bras Coupé* his life. This occurred on July 7, 1837, and *The Bee* of July 20, the same year, published the details of his end, in a story headed *Death of Squier*, telling how a fisherman, leaving his boat, had turned at the detonation of a gun, and had seen a giant Negro fitting another cap into his weapon. The fisherman had then rushed the brigand and killed him with a kind of crowbar, having to bring it down on his skull three times.

The body of *Bras Coupé* was then brought to New Orleans and exposed for inspection on the public square. The marks of the wounds given by one of the city guards who had left the brigand for dead, were very visible and completely corroborated the story told by him, against which some discredit had been thrown.'

Slave uprisings were surprisingly rare. Le Page du Pratz, friend of Bienville, and one of the first of Louisiana settlers, told the story of the first slave uprising. A French soldier struck a Negress for disobedience, and she told him that no white man had a right to strike a Negro. For this impertinence the governor sent her to prison, and suspecting some rebellion in her attitude, he began an investigation. Finally, some slaves were overheard conversing in a shack, scheming an attack on their white masters. Eight were captured and shackled separately. 'The day after,' reports du Pratz, 'they were put to the torture of the burning matches, which, though several times repeated, could not bring them to any confession. One of the leaders of the proposed insurrection, a slave named Samba, was threatened with further torture if he did not identify his confederates. He finally did this and the eight Negroes were sentenced to be broken alive on the wheel and the woman to be hanged before their eyes; this was accordingly done.'

The first slaves in Louisiana were captured Indians. But they proved to be more troublesome than useful when held in bondage. Various shrewd bargainings were tried, one being an agreement with agents in Martinique and St. Lucia by which three red men were exchanged for three black ones. This failed, however; the West Indian planters refused to have them at any price. At last all Indians were freed and were finally emancipated by order of the United States Government. This resulted in a Negro uprising near New Orleans, which was put down with considerable loss of life. During this revolt, which occurred in 1811, five hundred Negroes on the German Coast marched along the levee with flags and drums, defying the Whites, and declaring themselves free. The insurrectionists were at last rounded up by forces led by General Hampton. The leaders were executed in New Orleans and their heads exhibited on posts along the levee road.

Behind many a slave uprising was the Abolitionist from the North, especially after the American acquisition. As early as 1839 there was evidence that such persons were fomenting discontent among the Negroes and actually promoting disorders. In the Forties Negroes inspired by them were found to be meeting in secret assembly in many parts of the State. In June, 1853, New Orleans newspapers carried the astounding story of a plotted uprising. This insurrection had been inspired by James Dyson, an Englishman, who, keeping a school for colored boys, was teaching other things than the three R's. Women members of the group of two thousand who were to arise against the Whites, were discovered in a camp in the suburbs of New Orleans engaging at making cartridges and preparing other ammunition. Within a few days the entire city would have been in the hands of slaves, the Whites probably massacred.

Slave assemblies in the rural parishes were discouraged by the *Vigilantes*, a citizens' organization, dedicated to the maintenance of white supremacy, keeping a watchful eye on all gatherings of Negroes, since what appeared to be a perfectly innocent dance frequently turned out to be a revolutionary meeting.

In 1860 a nine o'clock curfew was rigidly imposed in New Orleans. At that hour a huge bell was rung nine times to warn Negroes to be in their quarters. In October, the same year, police closed all churches in the city where Negroes, free or bonded, assembled, together with all dance halls and other places where they might gather, unless a special permit was issued by the mayor of the city.

Living ex-slaves remember the day when freedom came with conflicting emotions. Most slaves were confused and like lost children, many exhibited strange reactions to emancipation.

'The day we was set free,' said Silas Shotfore, 'us did not know what to do. Our Missus said we could stay on the place, but my Pa didn't want to. We hung around a few days then Pa went to work so we could get something to eat. You see, we didn't have a thing and peoples was so ignorant they didn't have no sense like they got now. I seen my Ma work plenty weeks just for a peck of meal.'

Henry Reed told how he felt when freedom came.

'I was about nine years old,' Henry figured, 'and I can remember when the steamboat came up the river and a man hollered, "You're free! You're free!" Everybody yelled and cut up so. I was scared 'cause I didn't understand what it was all about. You know after the war was over lots of families split. Husbands go one way, wifes the other. Lots of colored women left their childrens. I remembers some throwed their babies in the river and in the bayous.'

Rebecca Fletcher recalled, 'After freedom come we was on our own and we sure had a hard time. We made our own soap by saving bones and stuff like that.'

On most plantations there were Negroes, particularly house servants, who were faithful to their former owners and remained, often working exactly as if nothing had occurred, without wages and without wanting them. Mammies could not be pried loose from their 'chillun,' and many of the old 'Uncles' displayed the same affection for the white folk who had kept them all these years. In many cases some of the field hands stayed on their jobs, but now that the transition had occurred the 'Marse' sometimes worked side by side with them, and the 'Missus' fed the chickens and performed other chores. Often the family was impoverished and every member of the group had to do his share so that there would be sufficient food for them all.

But, in general, the plight of the slaves was pathetic. Most fled in the first wave of elation at this new 'freedom,' and found themselves completely unable to earn a livelihood. Little Negroes were put into asylums, except for a few very light ones who were adopted by white families.

The *Daily Picayune*, August 3, 1867, tells of the long line of anxious Negresses who flanked the Poydras Market in New Orleans day after day, looking for work, of their tramping the streets, going from door to door pleading for odd jobs so they could buy food, a few of them even women who had enjoyed the best of meals as house servants on the great plantations, who might have been pets of the families that had owned them. Negroes became beggars, squatters on the levees, criminals.

Matilda Jones, ex-slave, talked of wars and marriage.

'You see I've seen a lot of misery in my time 'sides wars. I done had six husbands. I seen two of them in their coffins and the rest just went away. They was all the most triflin' niggers I ever knowed. If I'd done tried I couldn't have picked worser ones. I always been careful, though, and I ain't never had two or more husbands at the same exact time. I been mighty particular about that. I don't believe in havin' your husbands in bunches. I is a member of the church and I can't stand for no 'sinuations 'bout my conduct. I never married one husband 'til the last one was dead or out of the parish.'

Matilda sighed. 'The poor old husband I got now, he's starvin' to death before my eyes. You can count his ribs.'

'Sometimes,' said Annie Flowers, 'we still sets and talks of plantation days, and cuttin' the cane in the field; and we sings,

> Rains come wit' me,
> Sun come dry me.
> Stay back, boss man,
> Don't come nigh me.

'Sometimes I thinks them days was happier, sometimes these. But so much trouble done gone over this old haid I ain't sure of nothin' no more. I jest don't know.'

Chapter 13

Buried Treasure

'THERE SURE IS PLENTY OF TREASURE BURIED IN Louisiana, but you gotta be careful of them spirits. They do some funny things. I knew one real well what would come to my house all the time. He would get behind a door and milk a towel, and all the cows in the neighborhood would go dry.'

That is the warning of Gaston la Cocq, who has spent years searching for buried wealth. But Gaston knows how to handle these guardian phantoms.

'You have to take a spirit controller with you,' he says. 'And you have to be a mixed crowd; some white and some colored. You see, when your controller talks to the ghost that thing's gonna say if white or colored men should dig, and it means one or the other has to do all the work. That's the way it goes.

'All buried treasure has got spirits watching over it. Like Lafitte. You know how he used to do? He would take five or six men along to hide his stuff, and he would tell them all but one who he was gonna have kilt. The one he picked was the one what would be the spirit to watch his treasure forever. After they buried all the gold and silver and jools, Lafitte would say very quiet, "Now, who's gonna guard my stuff?" and the man

who didn't know no better would want to shine with his boss
and he'd say, "I will." Then he would get kilt. Of course,
Lafitte didn't shoot him, himself. He was the general and he
always stayed in the back. You know how generals don't never
get near to where the shooting is at.'

Gaston's spirit controller is named Tom Pimpton, and he's a
colored man. He has been hunting for treasure for years, too, and
is one of the best controllers in the State. Practically all his
knowledge, you see, has come from the *Book of Hoyle*, the *Book of
Moses*, *Little Albert* and the *Long-Lost Friend*. He purchased these
mystic volumes from a Sears Roebuck catalogue, and he considers them priceless, for you can hardly buy them nowadays. Tom
devotes himself exclusively to the supernatural angle of the
treasure-hunting business.

'I just masters them spirits,' he says. 'I don't dig; anybody
can do that. I just fights the spirits. There ain't none of 'em can
mess with me.

'There's land spirits and there's water spirits, and you gotta
know how to talk to both kinds. The land spirits is bad and the
water spirits is good. They got seven kinds of land spirits; that's
part of the trouble. There is bulls, lions, dogs, babies, snakes,
persons and pearls. When you see a cat, that's a bad one and if
you ain't careful your hole's gonna lap up water right as you dig.

'You gotta be careful and you gotta be clean. You gotta suffer, too. The man's gotta suffer and the woman's gotta suffer.
You sure can't touch no woman, not even your wife, for four
days 'fore you start out.

'If something is wrong you knows it right away. You can't
ever fool a spirit. Your treasure is sure to start sinking and slipping, and once it sinks it ain't coming up again for seven years.
Last time I was out you know a fool man done gone and forgot
and left his Buzz tobacco in his pocket? You can't be careless
like that and 'spect to find treasure.

'Sometimes when your treasure slips you can tie it up, but you
gotta use white silk thread. Ain't nothing else gonna hold it.

'When you go out you use your divining rod or a finding-
machine until you knows where the treasure is at. Then you
drives sticks in the ground in a circle and stretches a clothesline

around it. Never use no wire! Your ring's gotta be thirteen feets to the east, thirteen feets to the south, thirteen feets to the west and thirteen feets to the north. You leaves a gate in the east side for your men to come through, then you closes it up. Once your mens get inside that ring, nobody can't talk, nobody can't sweat, nobody can't spit. And don't let nobody throw dirt outside that ring, 'cause that brings bad spirits.

'Soon as I gets my mens in the ring I 'noints them on the forehead with Special Delivery Oil. That oil's expensive; it costs me five dollars an ounce. You see, I won't mess with none of them cheap oils what has been 'dulterated.

'After everybody been 'nointed I reads the Twenty-Third Psalm with them all joining hands and repeating the words after me. Then I reads the Ninety-First Psalm to myself. Next I gotta read page 87 and page 53 from the *Book of Moses*. Page 53 has got the Master's Seal on it and you gotta know that by heart.

'Sometimes I takes liquor along when I go out. Some spirits likes liquor. They is call the drunken spirits.

'I done dug up plenty of treasure in my time. I just made up my budget the other day and I needs $40,000. I'll get it easy. Shucks, that ain't no money. Me and a friend of mine dug up $65,000 apiece over in Gretna one day. Had a big snake standing straight up in the air over it; he was tall as me and big enough around to hug. I just walked up and talked to it like it was a baby, and it crawled away. Underneath we found a great big mess of gold.

'The best treasure I ever found was a diamond the size of a brick out of the *banquette*. It was wrapped in kidskin and had Lafitte's name carved in it. It was worth about $1,500,000, and it was setting in a kettle of $5,000,000 worth of gold coins. I spent all that on my wife when she was sick and I just saved enough out of it to marry this here wife I got now.

'It's an easy way to get money, but you sure gotta be careful. When you is digging funny things happen. Trees begin to fall, and fences come tumbling down and the whole earth shakes and makes a loud rumbling sound. Spirits don't never like to give up their treasure.'

Louisianians have been dreaming of finding buried wealth for years, and practically everybody believes there is much to be found. The first white settlers found Indian tribes wearing massive ornaments of gold and silver. When they began to murder the Indians for their trinkets, the valuables promptly vanished. Pirates operated for years in the Gulf of Mexico and through the maze of Louisiana bayous, supposedly burying loot on every island and in every swamp. Rich wagon trains are reported to have been lost in the swamps, too. Along the coasts gold-laden ships were wrecked. Plantation-owners, fleeing Union troops during the War Between the States, committed family wealth to the comparative safety of the earth. Everybody in the State has a great-grandmother who sunk the silver plate in the well and buried caskets of jewels in the backyard. It is all wonderful and appeals to the getting-something-for-nothing desire in human nature. All these things await the treasure-hunter, if he can perform the tasks. Many try. Some just go out and dig. Others employ systems as elaborate and as detailed as Tom Pimpton's.

Leaving it to luck seems actually to be the most profitable method. At Shell Beach on Lake Borgne, children playing near the water's edge found Spanish coins mingled with the shells. At Thompson's Creek near McManus, doubloons coined during the reign of Charles IV were found in a gravel pit. A farmer near Ruston shattered his plow blade on an old iron chest which showered forth more than 1000 coins. Another farmer, in Avoyelles Parish, uncovered an iron pot filled with 3000 gold pieces. A fisherman on Barataria Island, removing flagstones from the fireplace of a deserted house, discovered a tin box beneath in which were doubloons, jewelry and a silver image of the Virgin. Cutting down trees in Opelousas, a citizen turned up 485 gold pieces of Spanish origin. There was an epidemic of digging on Pecan Island in 1925, after someone bragged of finding coins there, and searchers even uprooted giant oak trees. One man searched on Kelso's Island for more than twenty years, firmly believing Jean Lafitte had buried immense wealth there.

Pierre Rameau and his *Chats-Huants* (Screech Owls), a notorious band of buccaneers, had their base of operations at Honey Island. Wounded while fighting in the battle of New Orleans, both arms rendered useless, Rameau escaped to a plantation home owned by friends. Here, however, he met a man named Vasseur, once an associate, but now his mortal enemy. Vasseur sprang at him with a knife, crying, 'Die, Pierre Rameau! Die! Die!'

Rameau kicked out and sent Vasseur spinning across the room. Then, crashing through the door, he fled to a near-by swamp. Days later his body was recovered.

Of course, it is believed much treasure was buried on Honey Island by the Screech Owls, and once two hunters stumbled over an iron chest filled with Mexican money dating from 1827, and worth about $1000. These coins must have been cached on the island long after Rameau's demise, yet there was an immediate and feverish rush to the spot. Nothing else was ever found.

John Patorno of New Orleans is probably the most scientific treasure-seeker in the State, and the most practical. Patorno has invented a mechanism to locate treasure, a radio device with an affinity for non-magnetic metals, and this he rents, together with his services, for twenty-five dollars a day. He has done a thriving business.

When an Algiers ferry pilot, named Clarke, found a map showing the location of buried Lafitte loot on Coca Island, he went to Patorno for assistance. An investigation seemed to give credence to the existence of the treasure.

More than a century ago, said legend, two of Lafitte's henchmen deposited several chests of silver on the island, then staged a drunken brawl. When it was over one of the buccaneers was dead and the other not far from it. A fisherman nursed the injured man back to health and in gratitude the pirate gave him the map showing where the chests were buried. This the fisherman passed down to his descendants, and it was from one of these that Clarke had obtained it.

Clarke, Patorno and a group of assistants set out for Coca Island at once. This island is not easily reached, and even after landing, it was days before they found the spot. Then the Patorno diviner began to buzz. Excavations were begun, but the soft and sandy soil presented a formidable problem, often filling with slimy water as soon as dug. Tom Pimpton would have said there was a ghost-cat or something of the sort about.

On the third day the whole side of a pit gave way and two of the men, caught in an avalanche of mud and sand, narrowly escaped being killed. Rather than risk lives, Patorno refused to continue the search after that. So, if legend and the map told the truth, treasure still lies buried on Coca Island.

More of Jean Lafitte's loot is supposed to be hidden in the Mississippi bluffs near Baton Rouge. A farmer digging there enjoyed a golden moment of elation when his spade struck what appeared to be an old chest. It turned out to be an old coffin, with nothing inside but a skeleton. Grand Isle, where this most famed Louisiana buccaneer had headquarters, has, naturally, innumerable myths of buried gold. But Niblett's Bluff, near Lake Charles, tops them all with the display of a huge sign reading:

LAFITTE BURIED HIS TREASURE
BENEATH FORTY GUM TREES HERE!

Tales of hidden Lafitte treasure increase from year to year, yet, on the other hand, authorities agree that Lafitte was without funds when he departed the Louisiana scene, and that it is decidedly unlikely that he would have left such immense wealth behind.

Residents of Calcasieu Parish have tried many times to find the Lost Mine of Wyndham Creek, subject of one of the best-known stories of the De Quincey section. Early pioneers told yarns of an Indian-owned gold mine somewhere along Wyndham Creek. Many persons have searched in vain. There are no more redmen in the section, and their secret, if any, died with them. At the turn of the twentieth century three men hunting for the mine were found brutally murdered. Even now a woman living at Lunita claims to have wandered into a gold mine one day, while lost in the woods. She has never been able to retrace her steps, though she has tried many times.

In 1924 scores of individuals dug in Lakeside Park at Shreveport, after a rumor spread of pirate gold to be found there. A Negro claimed to have seen a man carry off twenty thousand dollars' worth of coins. When the city decided to create a park on the site their principal job was filling holes left by the searchers.

The *New Orleans Daily Picayune* of April 1, 1869, told an amazing story of a treasure-trove in New Orleans's Jackson Square. The newspaper said that the evening before two citizens were conversing near the equestrian statue of General Jackson when one noticed what appeared to be a small iron pin in the seam of one of the granite blocks. Putting his cane against it a wooden door, painted to blend with the marble, swung open and within was a vault about five feet square, literally crammed with gold and silver coins, even nuggets. Scattered about were watches, jewelry and unset gems. An open casket overflowed with diamonds, emeralds and other precious stones. The newspaper asked, was this the hiding place of a gang of thieves? It is worth noting that the story appeared April 1. April Fool's Day.

However, most treasure-hunting in Louisiana is a serious matter and not to be approached in any haphazard manner, but is brimful of rules and superstitions. When you note the strange and harrowing occurrences which have taken place, you can't blame experts like Tom Pimpton for not taking chances by using a wrong procedure.

'A bunch of us gathered to dig in a certain place just after midnight,' said one New Orleans man. 'Suddenly chickens started coming out of the hole we had made. First come a rooster, crowing to beat hell. Then he vanished in a puff of smoke. Then the chickens come, one by one, every one of them vanishing just like the rooster. Last of all, a horse come trotting right out of the ground. He was breathing smoke and had fire coming out of his eyes and ears. We left after that. That treasure can stay put for all I care.'

'When I got married I wore a fork-tailed coat,' said Wilkinson Jones, native of McDonoughville. 'Me and my wife had a real nice wedding. Her name was Emma. But I tell you, the spirits had been bothering me all my life, and after I got married they seemed to be worse. Still I think you need them when you go treasure-hunting. If you let spirits tell you where the treasure is at and that it's okay to dig it up, you ain't facing much trouble. But if you just head out without asking 'em, you making things bad for yourself. There ain't no treasure anywhere what ain't got its spirit watching it. One time I was digging for

Lafitte's treasure in that old shell pile down by Lake Salvadore, and I had an evil-hearted man with me. I should have known better'n to take him along, but you know how it is. Anyway, we dug until we hit one of them oldtime iron chests. Right then the spirits started coming running out of that hole, whooping and hollering. We never is went back there. Any time you dig for treasure you are bound to meet spirits. If you never seen one before you gonna then.'

A story prevalent around Hubbardville tells of a planter's burying much money and silver plate before departing for the War Between the States. When he did not return, the abandoned slaves who had buried the wealth for their master decided to dig it up. They went to the spot and one jabbed his shovel into the earth. Great flames shot heavenward. The Negroes fled and, if the story is true, the wealth still lies beneath the plantation soil.

Legends of pirates wandering up the Pontchatoula River have brought searchers to that section. Once a white man and two Negroes dug a deep hole in a certain place. Suddenly a hoarse voice began to scream and curse, emanating from the chasm, and the men departed the scene in haste. In this section of the State 'Jack o'Lanterns,' the elusive phosphorescent swamp lights, are common and are here believed to lead to buried pirate gold.

The superstitions connected with this business of treasure-hunting are numerous. The following are the ones most religiously believed and followed:

The best day to find treasure is the second day of the full moon.
The best time to dig for treasure is during a full moon.
The best time of the day to dig is between 9 A.M. and 4 P.M.
If you talk, spit, curse or sweat while digging you will find none.
A sleepwalker will eventually lead you to buried treasure.
Lights bobbing up and down in the swamps will lead you to treasure.
Lights bobbing up and down in the swamps will just get you lost.
A dream of a light over a spot means treasure is there.
Lights are liable to appear wherever there is treasure.
If treasure is buried with a rooster's head, the rooster will crow when the rightful heir to the wealth approaches the spot.
No one who has ever shed blood can hope to find treasure.

A certain Mr. Bald of Bogalusa gave warning against over-
looking that last rule.

'Well, when you go out looking for treasure,' said Mr. Bald,
'you got to take a sounding rod, someone who can talk to spirits
and a Bible. Don't never go with a murderer. Me and five other
fellows went into an old house near here once that was haunted
and so bound to have money hidden somewhere in it. We found
a trapdoor in the dining-room floor. There was steps going
down, and, after the man who knew spirits knocked to see if any
was around, we started down those steps. We got just about
halfway when the place began to fill with water. I don't know
where it came from. It got so high we had to turn back. Just
then we seen a big rat run across the top of the water. The man
who knew spirits said that rat was a spirit, and that someone
among us must be a murderer. We all looked at each other hard,
but, of course, nobody would admit he was the one, so we all had
to leave.'

Divining rods of various types are used as aids in locating
treasure, and mechanical devices of all kinds are invented for the
same purpose. Many persons advertise their particular mechanism for sale or for rent. For instance, the *New Orleans Times-
Picayune* ran the following in its Personal Column on March 12,
1930:

TREASURE HUNTERS

Buried treasure accurately located by radio device. Reasonably priced. Portable and simple to operate. Free demonstra-
tion.

R. D. Burchard
816 American Bank Bldg.
Phone Ma. 6688

There is some disagreement as to the virtues of types of divining rods. Tom Pimpton says: 'The best divining rod is a piece of
steel about a yard long and as thick as a broomstick. It's sort of
like a magnet and when it is placed in the ground where the
treasure is at, it bends itself over like. You sure got treasure
then.'

Eugene Mumford, colored worker at the New Orleans French
Market, says: 'A branch from a witch-hazel tree with a fork at

the end is what I always use. It makes a better divining rod 'n steel, and you can use it to find either treasure or water. Go right along with it in your hand, and as you go stick it in the ground and sound the earth. If that branch weaves to and fro, there's water or treasure there.'

But probably the most remarkable of all is the one used in Saint John the Baptist Parish. A colored resident explained: 'A real divinin' rod is a piece of iron just like a rod in an iron bed, 'cept it's got little pieces of iron stickin' out on one end. You just set it up in the ground in front of you and it starts hoppin' along and all you got to do is follow it. When it gets to a place where treasure is, it's gonna start jumpin' up and down over that one spot. Then you can start your diggin'.'

Each one is positive his divining rod is the best and the others practically no good at all.

As Tom Pimpton always says, 'Hell, some of them divining rods ain't good for nothing but finding old toilets!'

TABLE OF BURIED TREASURE IN LOUISIANA

Locale	History
Ruins of old fort at Barataria, 1841	L. Counobo, a fisherman, needing bricks for a furnace on which to boil kettles of pitch, removed a flagstone from an old fireplace and found a box containing Spanish doubloons, gold earrings and a silver image of the Virgin.
Coillon Island, 1851	Rumors spread that $20,000 in gold was found here that year.
Bayou Chicot, near Opelousas, September, 1851	Fritz Lertz, cutting down trees, found coins of German mintage, mostly dated 1823. There were about 300 of them, each worth $4.85.
Breaux Bridge	Death keeps the secret of the lost treasure here. In the early nineteenth century slaves murdered their master, Narcisse Thibodeaux, and fled with his gold. Captured by irate white men of the section, the nine Negroes were forced to dig a deep trench, and were shot and buried therein. It was not until some time afterward that, checking the gold, it was discovered that one whole sack was missing, and its whereabouts now hidden forever.

Corner of Orleans and Bourbon Streets, New Orleans, 1859	An impoverished charcoal peddler, repairing the flooring in his home, found a box containing 1500 doubloons, dating from the Lafitte era.
Highway between Convent and Lutcher	Along here is an Indian mound fifty feet high. Silverware and other valuables from near-by plantations were buried here during the War Between the States, it is said. Yet men once dug more than forty feet and found only bones and palmetto leaves.
Grand Écore, near Natchitoches	Much wealth is believed to have been buried in this vicinity during the occupation of Union forces.
Western Isle of the Chandeleur group, 1871	A man was drowned here that year trying to find three chests of Spanish doubloons and some rough diamonds. For three generations his family had unceasingly sought this supposedly pirate loot, claiming to have positive proof of its existence.
Isle de Gombi	It has been long believed that buccaneers buried great wealth here.
Linceum	A party of men carrying a vast amount of gold through the Louisiana wilderness in the early days were here set upon by Indians. To travel faster and so escape the gold was hastily buried. But before the end of the journey the men quarreled and fought among themselves and all were killed. The gold is yet to be found.
Banks of the Tensas River	A Colonel Frisbee was building a mansion here when the War Between the States broke out. He ordered a wagonload of gold buried near the half-completed house. It has never been recovered, and folk in the neighborhood believe it to be guarded by the phantom of a giant black panther!
Grand Isle	Jean Lafitte's headquarters, and so presumed to conceal many caches of treasure. Nothing has ever been found.
Marksville, Avoyelles Parish	Valuables are believed to be buried on the site of an Indian village. One man spent years constructing an elaborate mechanism to locate the treasure, but had no success. Also, near here, a farmer uncovered an iron pot in his field which contained 3000 pieces of silver.

Parlange Plantation, Pointe Coupée Parish	A planter buried $300,000 worth of silver here during the War Between the States, a part of which has never been recovered.
Honey Island, St. Tammany Parish, 1907	Two hunters found chest containing Mexican coins worth $1000.
Fairfield Plantation, Jefferson Parish	As Admiral Farragut came up the river during the War Between the States a planter buried his valuables in the *battures* near-by. In 1928 a mysterious dark lady with a tattered map staged a search, but with no success.
Adam Dufresne's Village, Bayou Pirogue, Jefferson Parish	Twin oaks with roots pointing south are supposed to mark the location of pirate gold. Folk of the vicinity are always digging, and hoping.
Kelso's Island, between Cameron and Calcasieu Parishes	It is whispered that the pirate loot buried here is enormous, more than a million dollars in gold, but no one knows where it is.
Wyndham Creek, Beauregard Parish	The famous 'Lost Mine of Wyndham Creek.'
Mississippi bluffs at Baton Rouge	A farmer digging here, where Lafitte is said to have buried treasure, hit what at first appeared to be an old chest, but turned out to be only an old coffin with a skeleton in it.
Berthoud Cemetery, Barataria	Very old, it is supposedly built over an Indian mound. Many people have dug here, but, so far as is known, have found nothing.
Houma, Terrebonne Parish	Men dug near here one day, returned the next to find the holes mysteriously filled. The same thing happened four or five days in succession and the men became frightened and gave up.
Old bed of the Red River near Dixie, 1914	Jake Shelton of Hosston, digging in the mud for fishing bait, struck the trade boat *Monterey*, long buried there. He hoped for gold, but found only cowbells, dog chains and a barrel that had once held pickled pork.
Ruston, 1916	John Skinner, farmer, found a chest in his field holding 1000 old coins of German, Mexican and Spanish mintage, some dating back to 1777.
Milneburg, 1917	Louis Morgan, a fisherman, found a ragged five-dollar bill on the beach. Joined by other searchers $500, all in old bills, was picked up. It looked as though someone had thrown away his old money.

Jefferson Island, 1923	An unknown number of silver coins were found here by a Negro.
Pecan Island, 1925	After a report of treasure found here, searchers practically dug up the entire place. Even huge oak trees were ripped out of the ground.
Abbeville, 1925	A Negro boy, hypnotized by a white man, uncovered a treasure-trove of silverware in the earth near here.
Bogalusa, Washington Parish	A certain man consulted Carrie Mae King, a fortuneteller, regarding a peculiar mark on the ground, and was told that treasure was buried there. But she also said he would have bad luck if he tried to dig it up. The man would not attempt to find it and refused to divulge its location to any less superstitious person.
Calcasieu Parish, 1929	Coins said to amount to at least $75,000 were found in the dry bed of the Calcasieu River. They were believed to have been hidden there by a planter of the War Between the States period.
Louisiana and Arkansas Railroad tracks, near Baton Rouge, 1929	Twenty-one Spanish doubloons were found in a load of gravel. Negro section hands shot craps for the coins.
Shell Beach, Lake Borgne, 1931	Children playing on the beach picked up coins dated 1800. The money was believed lost when U.S. war vessels were sunk by the British as General Pakenham advanced on New Orleans.
Naval Station, Algiers, 1935	John Patorno's divining machine located two caches of coins, one worth $500, the other $800.

Chapter 14

Ghosts

OF COURSE EVERY OLD PLANTATION HOME IN Louisiana has at least one ghost. Any that did not would sink into the earth in sheer shame the moment such a fact became known, for a spook is as necessary to a plantation as a legend of family silver buried in the ground by faithful slaves the day the damyankees came.

As a matter of fact, a plantation with but one lone haunt does not brag about it particularly. Ingleside Plantation, for instance, has a whole colony of invisible phantoms who offer as complete and as varied a program as anyone could wish for, except that they are invisible. On certain nights chains bang and clang in the attic, bones rattle, and the traditional moaning and groaning may be heard. Sometimes the chains and bones perform on the stairs and in the hallway. Out in the fields the old bells toll dismally, though no human hand is anywhere about. And, if this grows monotonous, a venerable spirit, known as Uncle Naplander Richardson, renders lovely old-fashioned tunes on the parlor piano.

At The Cottage, the Conrad plantation, near Baton Rouge, a group of slaves give impromptu musicales on the wide front gallery on certain evenings, playing and singing all the old songs they knew in the days they worked the surrounding fields. When the musicians tune their fiddles and banjos, there are also the sounds of dancing feet, of light social chatter and gay laughter. The original master of the house used to invite his friends over on summer nights for small balls on the galleries. Now all return. Occupants of The Cottage testify that the music is so distinct it could probably be transcribed by a trained musician, though the conversations that go on cannot be understood.

But 'Mr. Holt' is the most famous ghost at The Cottage. The original of this apparition was secretary to Frederick E. Conrad, who built the house about 1830. Both men were imprisoned during the military occupation of the Union forces, and Conrad died soon after his release. Holt, however, lived on at The Cottage for about twenty years. It is said that he was never the same after his imprisonment, and that he developed abnormal notions of impending poverty. Bit by bit he stored away old clothing; he filled trunks with stale biscuits; he wandered from room to room during the night, in his white nightshirt and flowing beard. After death he seems to have continued his nocturnal wanderings, and has been seen by a number of people. In recent years *Elks Magazine* published a photograph of The Cottage, and in one window a man's face could be plainly seen. Of course, everyone knew it was 'Mr. Holt.'

At Lacey Branch, near Natchitoches, there is a headless horseman who rides about the road, frightening motorists and late pedestrians. The story of his origin seems to be unknown, which makes him all the more awesome, since to understand what some of these phantoms are about partially alleviates the terror of the person who meets them. Also at Natchitoches is the Simmons house, an old two-story dwelling, with the usual or plain ghost type, who raps on walls and rattles chains.

There is a haunted wood near Marksville on the Red River. Near-by residents will not enter the dim interior after sundown or at night. Many witnesses swear to have seen headless men marching among the trees. It is said that these are soldiers who once fought a battle in this wood. After the battle a long trench was dug and the killed were buried without religious service.

Now the ghosts of these soldiers cannot rest and must march all night.

Ponchatoula has a haunted gum tree, which was the scene of a young woman's suicide. At certain times, it is said, the tree weeps pearls which are, of course, her tears. Another tree, which formerly stood near the heart of the town, was known among certain white inhabitants as 'The Christmas Tree,' because once four Negroes hung there during a lynching. The colored folk of the town always avoided the tree, claiming a hanged Negro will invariably haunt the spot near where he is hanged.

Kenilworth Plantation, just below New Orleans, boasts a pair of lovers, a man and woman who walk the stairs and halls at night, affectionately clasping hands, garbed in ante-bellum costumes. The sweethearts are marred, however, by the fact that neither has a head.

A headless man stalks the grounds surrounding the Skolfield House, not far from Baton Rouge. He seems to be perfectly harmless, and wanders rather aimlessly, perhaps in search of his missing skull. There used to be a more destructive ghost there. She was a female, and created dreadful disturbances, sending pots and pans crashing to the floor, and generally raising an awful racket. It was said that this kitchen-haunter was the spirit of the first wife of a former occupant of the house who resented her husband's remarriage. After the man's death she vanished, apparently having got hold of him again.

Limerick Plantation, which stood formerly on the site of the Sherrouse House, near Monroe, possessed a whimsical and mischievous ghost, who every night sent the stair spindles rolling down the rear staircase, one spindle at a time, with such noise and clatter as to arouse the entire household. This exhibitionist continued his playful pastime until the house was razed.

Myrtle Grove Plantation has a lovable specter in the person of a little old French lady in a faded green bonnet, who tiptoes through the rooms at night, evidently searching for someone. Tirelessly, she journeys from bedchamber to bedchamber, raising mosquito *baires* and peering hopefully into the face of each sleeper. They say she is always disappointed, for the face is never the one she seeks.

On the other hand, the ghost who appeared on the old Mercier Plantation in St. Bernard Parish was far less gentle. One warm summer evening an aged Negress stepped out of her kitchen to the back porch to get a breath of air, and ran right into a white man.

'Hello, Sarah,' the white man said. 'I want you to meet me behind the milk house at eleven o'clock. I have something for you.'

Sarah didn't even answer him. Sarah just opened her mouth and began to scream. She shrieked so loudly that all the other house servants ran out. Then Sarah told them she had met no one but the spirit of her former master, Mr. Mercier.

'It sure was him,' Sarah vowed between yells and sobs of terror. 'I'd of knowed him anywhere. He done told me to meet him at eleven o'clock. Just before he vanished, he said he got gold buried behind that milk house. But I don't want no dead man's gold. I don't want to even see no dead man.'

Gold! The other Negroes pumped her dry. In a day or two it had spread all through the neighborhood. *Gold!* Even the group's preacher became excited, and finally it was he who led them on a treasure hunt.

They met behind the milk house one night and the preacher took a shovel and began to dig. All of a sudden, as the 'reverend' worked away with his shovel he began to yell. He dropped the instrument and sprawled face downward on the earth, crying out louder and louder, screaming the Devil had him, that he was dying. The bystanders could hear the sound of a whip lashing through the air, could see the preacher's back begin to cover with thick welts, his shirt darken with his blood.

Sarah came running up, fought her way through the paralyzed throng. She shrieked: 'Mr. Mercier is whippin' the preacher! I can see him! He's mad 'cause you all went after his gold, and he's whippin' the reverend.' No one else could see the wielder of the whip, but they could all see the man, now moaning and writhing in the mud. A few days later he died from the effects of the beating.

Louisiana has a haunted river. From a certain spot in Pearl River the sweetest music may be heard at night, issuing from its dark depths. There are various legends. Some say Indians were drowned there a long time ago and it is their spirits who play and sing; others that a group of early Spanish settlers marched into the river and committed mass suicide to avoid capture and death by torture at the hands of marauding redmen, marched in playing drum and fife and flute.

At Raccourci Cut-Off, there is an even stranger phenomenon. Here is the ghost of an old paddle-wheeler. The night the Mississippi River changed its course, the boat was trapped in the cutoff, and the pilot, screaming curses, bellowed that he hoped they never got out of the place. He received his wish. Now, especially on very foggy nights, the old boat can be heard chugging back and forth, its signal bell jangling, and, above it all, the roaring of the pilot, cursing the Mississippi, the boat, his passengers and himself.

Of course ghosts of pirates are common. According to tradition, they always, when burying treasure, murdered a member of their band, and left him to guard the hidden loot, in spirit form. The ghost of Jean Lafitte appears so often and in so many places that it is unlikely he finds time for anything else in the world beyond this one. In one old house, Jean appeared nightly, pointed a bony finger at the tiled flooring. When news of this spread, treasure-hunters dug up the entire lower floor of the house, tile by tile.

The Pirate Ghost of L'Isle de Gombi is one of the most famous of this type of apparition. Gombi Island lies just off the gulf coast near the mouth of Bayou Caillou. Cajuns in the vicinity have every belief in the pirates' ghosts who reside here. One brave young man, known as Louis, scorned the idea of spooks, and decided to make his fortune by uncovering the treasure of L'Isle de Gombi.

Louis climbed into his *pirogue* and set out for the tiny island. Landing, he began to dig. All of a sudden he heard a noise and turning saw his boat floating away, though he had pushed it well up onto the land. He ran after it, dragged it back to the shore and tied it to a tree. Then he returned to his digging.

Suddenly he looked up and there were three pirates. Each had a long knife with blood dripping from it. Then, said Louis, later, 'I sure thought I was digging my grave, me, instead of for treasure!'

But Louis was a brave man and a good Catholic, so instead of running, he fell on his knees and asked the Blessed Virgin to help him, vowing never to look for treasure if he emerged from this situation alive. The moon was very bright and as the pirates came closer, Louis could see that they had come from the water; seaweed dripped from their clothing and shrimp clung to their hair and fierce mustaches. Then, as he prayed, the specters vanished, and he ran for his *pirogue*. But his misery was not ended.

'There,' said Louis, 'I seen a big fat pirate sitting right in my *pirogue*, me! I knew he was the captain because he had him a big wide belt over his coat like, and long earrings what shined in the moonlight like balls of fire. Him, he had blood dripping down his mustaches and shrimps crawling all over his face.'

That ghost pirate looked at Louis and Louis looked at him. Louis rowed, because that ghost pirate told him to row. Louis said: 'When he say that to me my teeths start to knock together in my mouth. Me, I row like hell. I knew he wasn't kidding, see? In one big hairy hand he had a big pistol like a cannon, almost.'

Poor Louis rowed and rowed. At last they were far from that island. Then, 'That pirate, he slid over the side of the boat and was gone. Me, I knew for true he was a ghost then, 'cause when he sinked there wasn't no bubbles come after him.'

Louis went straight home, and when he walked into his wife's room without knocking she almost killed him, because she didn't recognize him. His hair was snow white. Strangely, he didn't go crazy. His friends could not understand that. 'But,' ends the story triumphantly, 'soon after that he die.'

A certain young man in Napoleonville, like Louis, boasted loudly that he was not afraid of ghosts. And one night, when passing a graveyard with some friends, he was challenged to spend the night there alone. He accepted, went inside and sat down on a grave. Friends watched him from a hidden place. Attempting to rise, the boy's coat was caught on a forked stick shoved down into the earth. Uttering loud shrieks that a spirit had him, he ripped his coat to shreds getting loose, and ran yelling out into the road. His friends didn't catch him until the following morning. He was a raving maniac. There are many versions of this story.

Shreveport has had its share of visiting folk from the spirit world. One attracted much attention from newspapers all over the State a few years ago. The figure of a ten-year-old girl appeared on the porch of a private home every night for weeks. Lights in the vicinity were removed or rearranged, and still the small phantom returned. There was a story of a little girl's being electrocuted on that porch some years before. After a while, but in her own good time and of her own volition, the young ghost ceased to appear.

Mrs. Rosie Altrano of Lafayette stated that she frequently sees ghosts walking casually around the streets, even in broad daylight. They don't bother her at all now, but she admits she was frightened the first time she met a spook.

'I was in bed all by myself,' says Mrs. Altrano, 'and wasn't worried or didn't have nothing to scare me, or nothing. A big man ghost come up to the side of my bed, looked at me and said, "Rosie, I'm in your room." I began to shake all over. He said, "Rosie, I'm by your bed." I shook even worse. "Rosie," he said, "I'm in your bed." And he sure was, right there next to me. I was like ice. Then he said, "Rosie, I'm under your quilt." By that time I was almost dead. "Rosie," he said. "I got you!" He had me, too. All of a sudden I got my wind and I screamed loud as I could. Then he vanished.'

A man named Taylor in Vermillion, like Mrs. Altrano, has grown quite accustomed to seeing spirits. They're everywhere, declares he, in every street, in every house; sometimes they ride on people's shoulders. Lots of times, Mr. Taylor says, friends come to visit him with a ghost sitting on their shoulder. He says he never tells them this, however, because it might make them nervous. Most of them look just like people, though occasionally they'll assume other shapes. 'One thing,' he says, 'I've always noticed is that almost all the women ghosts are beautiful. I guess that's because all women want to be beautiful and after death they get their dearest wish.'

Genuinely macabre is the legend of 'The Singing Bones,' which took place out in the bayou country.

A man, father of twenty-five children and unemployed, grew more and more morose. No matter how he tried he could not find work, and most nights his brood went to bed crying with hunger.

One day, after his usual exhaustive search for work, the father was amazed, as he dragged his lagging feet up on the porch of his home, to have the tantalizing aroma of roasting meat strike his nostrils. The family had had no meat for months. Rushing back to the kitchen he found his wife tending a large roast in the oven.

Immediately he demanded to know where the meat had come from, but his wife begged him not to ask questions, but to sit down and eat. Too tired and hungry to care anyway, he obeyed her like a child.

The next night and the next there was meat on the table, always the same delicious boneless pork-like meat, and the father and the children ate in unquestioning silence. Strangely, the mother never joined them, saying always that she had already eaten.

Soon after this he looked for a certain one of his children and couldn't find him. Asking his wife about him, she replied simply that she had sent several of the youngsters to her sisters for a few days.

But a week later he missed his favorite son.

'He's gone to my sister's, too,' the wife said.

But weeks passed, then months, winter grew into spring, and one day, counting carefully, the father discovered that more than half of his offspring were missing. He was strangely saddened and depressed, but hesitated about questioning his wife, for she had developed a very bad temper lately and if any of the children were mentioned flew into a violent rage. Yet he knew something was wrong.

One afternoon, sitting out on his back steps to brood, he heard a faint humming sound from beneath the steps. The hum grew louder and louder. First he thought it was mosquitoes, but then, with horror, he knew what he heard was the voices of children They seemed to sing right into his ear:

> Our mother kills us,
> Our father eats us,

A haunted summer house at "The Shadows" in New Iberia
Courtesy of Fritz Henle: from Black Star

The strange old LePrete house has many ghostly legends
Courtesy of United States Housing Authority, Photo by Sekaer

Ruins of Fort Livingstone and lighthouse on Grande Terre. In the background is
Grande Isle, once the haunt of LaFitte's Pirates
Courtesy of Jefferson Parish Review

Madame Perrin is a volume of folklore. "Napoleon? LaFitte? John Paul Jones?"
She has buried them all in a single grave!
Courtesy of Jefferson Parish Review

We have no coffins,
We are not in holy ground.

Leaping to his feet, the man stooped and lifted the concrete slabs that served as steps. Beneath lay a pile of tiny human bones. Now he knew the ghastly truth behind the meat they had been eating, of what had become of his children.

He rushed into the house, strangled his wife, and beat her head to a pulp with an axe. Then he fetched a priest and had the bones of his murdered children properly buried. It is said that he was never able to eat meat again.

Not many years ago a woman named Matilde lived on a farm near Killona. A neighbor used to pasture his horse on her land, but eventually she had all her land planted out and she forbade the horse to set a hoof on her property. The horse ignored this, invaded her grounds, so Matilde threw a stone, struck him on the nose, and killed him.

Evidently the horse's owner put a curse on her after that, as he was reputed to be in communion with the spirit world. She could hardly remain in the house after that, for instead of just a horse, she was invaded by ghosts. Furniture moved from place to place; voices taunted her, saying: 'Our master told us to move in here. You get out, Matilde.' Sometimes unseen hands would beat her black and blue, and she would flee the house screaming. Then they would follow her into the fields, cursing and tormenting her. At last the ghosts told her, since she was stubborn and refused to obey their orders to move, she would be dead by Christmas. She was. One morning neighbors found her cold and stiff in her bed.

Nobody could live in that house after that, though several families tried. Once a spiritualist meeting was held there, and the irate spooks chased the group out of the place, ripping their Bible to pieces, turning over benches and causing the people to run for their lives. Witnesses testify to the absolute truth of this occurrence.

New Orleans has more ghosts than there are wrought-iron balconies in the Vieux Carré. Of course, it isn't very strange that such an old city with such a past should have a spook stored away in every nook and cranny, an apparition inhabiting many rooftops and nearly every one of the aforementioned balconies.

Once, not inappropriately, the Devil lived in New Orleans. He had at the time taken a French mistress and set her up in a stately mansion in St. Charles Avenue.

The Devil was very fond of his girl friend, and very jealous. Nevertheless, while he was away six days of the week, attending to other duties, the coquette took another lover, a dashing young Creole of the city. Satan returned one night and, leaning against a post outside, waited for the youth to emerge from the house. When he encountered him, Satan told him frankly that he was the lover of the Frenchwoman, but said that now he did not want her any more, and that the boy was to take her and a million pounds of gold and go away. There was one condition, however; they must always be known as Monsieur and Madame L.

The youth agreed, and next night told his sweetheart about the condition at dinner. The French girl was both terrified and furious, for she realized that the 'L' stood for Lucifer. In a rage she rushed at her lover with a napkin, whipped it around his throat and strangled him to death. At that moment the Devil appeared, killed her and carried both the bodies to the roof, where he devoured them, all but the skins. These he gave to cats wandering on the housetop.

From that time on the Devil's head was fixed in the gable of that roof, bound there by the sticky flesh of the mortals he had eaten. For years afterward Orleanians used to pass and stop to stare up at the living head of Lucifer set right there in the front of the house. You see, he had forgotten, in his jealous anger, that he must not work in the full of the moon, and was thus punished for his folly.

But the drama in the dining-room continued. Night after night, the great dining table and the magnificent crystal chandeliers materialized. Always a young man and a girl sat down to eat. Then the girl would rise, her face contorted with fury, and strangle her companion with a napkin. Then the girl would find her hands drenched with blood, and try frantically to wipe them clean, but of course she never could. Weeping and wailing, she would gradually fade from view. Night after night the whole sordid crime was re-enacted, again and again.

Many families tried to live in the Devil's Mansion, but no one could endure the nightly drama. Only one family stayed for any length of time, that of Charles B. Larendon, husband of the daughter of General P. G. T. Beauregard. Mrs. Larendon died with the birth of a child, but her husband stayed on in the house until his death. Later, a Mrs. Jacques moved in, but she reported that she could not bear the ghastly manifestations which took place in the dining-room. Her family had to cease using the room entirely and at last moved.

For a number of years the Devil's Mansion remained unoccupied. In 1930 it was demolished. No one would live in a residence where the shades of Lucifer's mistress and her lover returned, and where the living head of the Devil was set in the gable above the roof.

The *New Orleans Times-Picayune* of September 17, 1933, told the horrible story of a haunted house in Fourth Street. Because of the constant tales of weird happenings the building was at last turned over to a group of Negroes who could not pay rent. They huddled in a small outer building, avoiding the main dwelling for terror of the supernatural happenings there. They reported many eerie things. Ghostly faces appeared at the windows. When the moon was full, the kitchen door would creak open to reveal horrible misty *things* crawling about the floor on their hands and knees.

At one time two elderly spinsters moved into the front portion of the house. They said the ghosts came creeping in like an army of gray rats, their hair covered with blood; one pulled his leg off and threw it at the new tenants. Another dug out his liver and tossed it at a lamp. A third gouged out his own tongue and stuffed it into the teakettle. One vomited into the ladies' Sunday shoes; one clawed out his eyes and ate them; and one emptied a sack of live green worms into the tenants' bed. They smashed dishes, tore up clothing, smeared the parlor sofa with filth, put feathers into the pot of *gumbo*, and sifted ashes into the butter. After that the maiden ladies moved.

Finally the owner of the house had the floor of the house torn up and replaced, and after that the ghosts failed to appear. It was never verified, but the Negroes vowed a number of ancient skeletons were found under the flooring, and it was not until they were decently buried that the haunting ceased.

In April, 1874, the Treme Street Bridge, crossing the Old Basin in New Orleans, was haunted by the wraith of a woman. Usually she was, as all female ghosts should be, pale and beautiful and young, but often she took other forms. Sometimes she would be older and have a child clasped in her misty arms. Again, she would appear as a haggard old creature, her body rotted and obscene, her toothless mouth drooling, her scanty white hair dripping with slime, her draperies green with filth; worms would crawl about her throat and often she carried a lighted candle. Always at midnight she would appear, and great crowds gathered to view the scene, many vowing they saw her standing there, shivering with terror. New Orleans newspapers of the period made much of these manifestations.

Legend had it that this phantom was the ghost of a woman who, discarded by her lover, became a prostitute, bore a child, and, in premature old age, drowned herself in the waters near the Treme Street Bridge. That, it was said, was why she appeared in three forms: as the young girl, trusting and happy in her love for the man, as the older woman with the child, and as the broken derelict she was at the time of her death. The man, it was stated, had adopted the child, not knowing it was hers. The baby died and, blaming himself for it all, he had committed suicide in the same spot where the girl had taken her life. Later, when the apparition ceased to appear, it was reasoned that the lovers had been reunited at last beneath the surface of the water.

At 1447 Constance Street stands a mansion built about 1820. It is said that here two white-faced soldiers in blue uniforms stare out of the upper windows, waving their arms and babbling in a muddled jargon. Sometimes they clasp hands and parade up and down the halls, singing the 'Battle Hymn of the Republic,' famous song of the Union Army during the War Between the States.

This house eventually became a lamp factory. One night, a Negro stayed late to clean up. He was alone on the second floor when the door swung open; in marched a pair of heavy boots, or at least he could hear, though he could see nothing; a moment later there was the sound of a second pair. Then he heard laughter and the whistling of that song. The colored boy stood it just one minute, then he fled down the steps and out of the house.

Another morning the two proprietors had arrived early. No one else was there. Suddenly a huge block of cement came hurtling down the steps, barely missed the two men. No one had ever seen the block before. How had such a definitely huge and solid thing got into the house?

At one time a widow took a portion of the dwelling as an apartment. Sitting sewing one afternoon a drop of blood fell from the ceiling on her arm. Another. She stared upward. Blood dripped from a spot in the ceiling, one drop at a time. Then she heard someone singing:

> John Brown's body lies a-moulding in his grave,
> John Brown's body lies...

The next day, when the widow moved, two young men in the blue uniforms of the Union Army appeared at an upstairs window, looked down and smiled.

Patrolman William Fleming remembered visiting the house as a small boy, taking two other boys and a pair of dogs. The floor had been ripped up in an upper chamber and the youngsters walked the joists. Suddenly a door swung open slowly, and an icy draft blew in. One of the dogs fell through the floor and was instantly killed. The other cried and carried on strangely. The boys made a hasty departure. Behind them came the song in a deep baritone:

> John Brown's body lies a-moulding in his grave,
> John Brown's body lies a-moulding in his grave,
> John Brown's body lies a-moulding in his grave,
> But his soul keeps marching on.
>
> Oh, we'll hang Jeff Davis to a sour-apple tree,
> Oh, we'll hang Jeff Davis to...

The story is that two Federal officers in New Orleans during the occupation of General Ben Butler stole army funds, and when accused of the crime, hid themselves in this house. Then, one night, they lay side by side on the bed, and each placing his revolver over the other's heart, they pulled the triggers. There were two shots, as one. Then no sound but the drip, drip, drip of their mingling blood. This happened more than three quarters of a century ago, yet still they walk, singing their old Yankee song.

The backyard of a house in Saratoga Street is still haunted by the ghost of an old miser who once lived there. This old man worked hard, denied himself everything, and hoarded his money in pieces of gold. Night after night he would sit by the dim oil lamp that was his only light, counting and caressing his gold. 'My beautiful children!' he would say to the coins. 'My beautiful, beautiful children!'

Before he died he buried all his 'beautiful children' in a deep hole in the backyard. Now he returns almost every night to search frantically for his gold. This isn't very difficult for him, you see, because he was buried in a cemetery just across the street from his former residence. Sometimes he brings other shades to help him claw at the hard earth, one in particular a hideous wraith of an old woman, whose flesh hangs in decomposed tatters from her bleached bones and who has no face, but just burning eyes set in a skull. They hobble about muttering and whining, the man begging his 'beautiful children' to show themselves. Frequently neighbors watch the scene, hoping to be shown where the gold is buried. Many people have dug in the yard, but nothing is ever found.

The Seamen's Bethel in St. Thomas Street, New Orleans, was once haunted by the ghosts of two young sailors, who would appear each night, weeping and sobbing, and frightening the wits out of the transient lodgers. At last one courageous sailor asked them what they wanted. The answer was, 'Mother!'

The tale was finally pieced together. A century before the boys had lived in the house with their parents when it had been a private residence. Both had been drowned while at sea. Returning as spirits, they had appeared to their mother several times, but she had always been too frightened to answer their cries. They never showed themselves again after the sailor answered them. But — a few nights later that same sailor was found strangled to death in his bed.

Cherokee Street was once the scene of a ghost war. The 200 block was literally showered with bricks and stones one night. The next night it happened again. This went on for days. Police were summoned, circled the block, searched feverishly, but nothing or no one was ever found. Neighbors remembered an old man and a little girl who had lived in the block, and who had hated each other violently. Strangely, the two had died within the same week and had been buried in adjoining tombs in the cemetery. It was said that now the two spirits were warring against each other. The child's parents had her body removed to another tomb and the shower of bricks and stones ceased immediately.

Miss Rica Hoffman, a New Orleans resident, remembered the case of 'The Ghost Who Walked the Sausage Factory,' a fantastic crime and supernatural aftermath which occurred in the city some years ago.

'A long time ago, right before I was born, my mother met Hans Muller,' Mrs. Hoffman said. 'My parents and the Mullers had both just come from Germany, so naturally they were friendly. Hans Muller was a hard-working young man, but he was in love with another girl and tired of his wife, who, working very hard in the sausage factory they owned, grew old and wrinkled before her time. One night Hans pushed his wife into the big meat grinder in the factory. Nothing of her was left. But a few days later customers began to complain of bits of bone and cloth in their sausages. Even his girl, hearing the gossip, grew cold toward him and would not see him any more.

'One night, soon after, he heard a "thump! thump! thump!" around his boiler vat. Then he saw the bloody ghost of his wife, with her head crushed to a pulp, coming toward him. Shrieking, he fled from the place. Neighbors, hearing his screams, questioned him, but he said he had suffered a bad dream. He had told everyone Mrs. Muller was out of town.

'Then a customer found a bit of a gold wedding ring in a sausage. She called the police, but they found Hans Muller in his factory screaming and crying, a raving maniac. He kept saying his wife was coming out of the sausage grinder and would get him. He spent the rest of his life in an insane asylum.

'A man bought the factory, but the ghost continued to appear. Nobody could stop it. At last Muller committed suicide in the asylum, and the phantom never appeared again. My mother ate some of the sausages Mrs. Muller was made into.'

New Orleans taxicabs still avoid one of the St. Louis cemeteries whenever possible. At least they never stop to pick up a young woman dressed in white who might hail them from the entrance. One driver answered her signal late one night and drove her to the address she gave him. There, she asked him to go up on a gallery, ring the bell and inquire for a man who lived there. The man came out, but when the driver told him of the girl waiting in the cab, he asked for her description. And when this was given, he said that was his wife, but she had been dead and buried for some time, that she had been interred in her bridal dress. Then the taxi driver realized that it had been a wedding gown the girl was wearing. The men raced down to the cab and jerked open the door. The phantom was gone. Husband and driver fainted. From then on the bride at the entrance of that cemetery hails taxis in vain.

Cemeteries are, of course, ideal places for specters, since here lie the remains of their earthly bodies. No haunted house ever received more attention and publicity, for instance, than the 'glowing tomb' of Josie Arlington, famed Storyville lady.

Then there is the young woman who spent a night in an old cemetery on a bet, and told a remarkable tale next morning. She said that as soon as the moon left the sky, and it became pitch black, a bluish light filled the place, and from the graves stepped a company of ghosts, weaving back and forth like wisps of fog. Then a second group rose from the ground, these looking much older than the others. Presently a third lot appeared, these quite elderly. There followed a fourth set, so bent and feeble with age that they had to lean against the others for support. When a fifth group appeared they could not stand at all, but crawled and writhed on the ground like reptiles. Finally, a downpour of rain descended upon the seething mass and they all vanished underground. The girl did not wait to win her bet.

Next day, however, she returned to investigate and discovered that this cemetery was in reality five graveyards, one built over the other; there had been an Indian burial ground, an old Spanish graveyard, the family cemetery of a Creole, an ancient potter's field. As she had no previous knowledge of this, the girl was convinced she had seen into the spirit world.

A New Orleans woman who had lost her sweetheart in the first World War, recovering from her grief, decided to marry another man. Something made her hesitate, however, and she went to the grave of her first lover to ask his spirit's guidance. All night she sat beside the tomb, talking to the marble slab. At last she heard a noise and glancing upward saw an old owl circling overhead. Each time the owl circled it dropped a beautiful rose into her lap, until she held fourteen scarlet blooms and fifteen white ones. Then she realized that the corresponding letters of the alphabet were N and O. As soon as she awakened to this fact the roses withered and died. Later she learned that the man she had nearly married was a criminal and had swindled numerous women by pretending to marry them.

A widow of the city used to visit her husband's tomb in Saint Louis Cemetery Number I almost daily, where she would grieve deeply. She grew more and more morose, even contemplated suicide. One day she fell asleep in the cemetery and when she awoke it was dark. Then she saw a pale form emerge from the tomb, and she recognized her husband. She was overjoyed, and began to question him. Suddenly she became conscious of the fact that she could see *through* all the tombs in the graveyard. All about her were happy, laughing, chatting people of all ages. Turning, she looked through the cemetery walls and there she saw hordes of ghastly skeletons, scrambling and plunging by, hurrying and falling and crushing each other in what appeared to be a stupid, insane race to get somewhere first. Laughing at her horror, her husband said: 'That is the way your world looks to us. You see, it is they who are dead. We are alive.' From then on she grieved no more, but became a happy and successful personality, knowing that her husband was alive and happy.

One of the most fearful of all the legends is that of the ghosts who haunted the old Carrollton Jail. So many witnesses, among them hard-boiled and exceedingly realistic officers of the law, testified to the eerie happenings that it is almost impossible to doubt that strange things did occur in that establishment.

Originally the old Jefferson Parish Prison, when the Carrollton section was a part of that parish, the building later became the Ninth Precinct Station, though colloquially it seems to have always been known as the 'Carrollton Jail.'

One evening, in the summer of 1899, two men and a woman stepped in to chat with Sergeant William Clifton, police commander of the District. The lady leaned against a wall in the office, and immediately was spun out into the room as if someone had pushed her violently. This happened three times, when she continued to lean against the wall as a test. Terrified, she screamed that there was *something* in that wall. The men then leaned against it in turn, and to each one's amazement, he was sent whirling into the middle of the room.

Several nights later, an Officer Dell, driver of the patrol wagon, lay down to nap on a sofa which stood against the same wall. The couch began to roll, carried the policeman out into the center of the room and back again. The next night, another policeman, boasting of his disbelief in the supernatural, lay down on the couch in the presence of a number of his fellow officers. Suddenly the sofa tilted and bounced the brave officer to the floor. From then on no one touched that wall. There was a story of a man who had killed his wife and boiled her body in lye. Arrested, the wrathful police had beaten the man to death against the wall. Before he died he had screamed he would return, and evidently he had.

One night in October, the same year, Mounted Officer Jules Aucoin saw a portrait of Admiral Dewey, hero of the day, revolving like a wheel on the wall of the office. Yet, when closely examined, it was found to be fastened tightly and perfectly normal in appearance. On other nights a portrait of General P. G. T. Beauregard and a mirror crashed to the floor. Both were hung with strong cord from stout nails, and on each occasion the cord was unbroken, the nail still firmly fixed in the wall.

Corporal Harry Hyatt vowed that he heard heavy footsteps in the corridors, one foot dragging. Everyone remembered a murderer who was lame and who had been imprisoned there. The night Corporal Hyatt heard the footsteps, the murderer, who had escaped, was found dead — in Pennsylvania. Other nights iron paperweights were raised from desks and flung violently at policemen.

On one floor, several condemned cells had been remodeled into a courtroom. Footsteps were often heard up there. At three o'clock one morning great hands grasped the throat of Sergeant Clifton and almost strangled him to death. There was no one about.

One hot July day about noon two quadroon girls appeared in the Sergeant's office. Suddenly they vanished right before his astonished eyes. It was believed they were the wraiths of two wenches who had carved out their lovers' livers. On another occasion an Officer Foster saw Sergeant Shoemaker, who had been dead more than a year, standing beside his desk. The ghost walked over to the sofa and vanished.

Requests for transfers to other precincts became frequent among officers stationed at the Carrollton Jail.

Whenever prisoners were placed for the night in cell number three they were found terribly beaten the next morning. Each victim, removed bloody and half-dead, told the same story, of three ghosts who came through the walls and battled each other all night, half-killing the mortal occupant. Once three murderers had been locked together in this cell and had fought each other all night, one night, each man for himself. In the morning two were dead and the third lived only a few hours.

In 1937 the old prison was razed. Workmen, pulling down the gallows in the central courtyard, declared that even then human shapes writhed in the clouds of dust, grinning and grimacing, as though every murderer who had ever died on those gallows returned to revel in the destruction of the scene. Through all its long life the jail had been a grim and perfect setting for ghostly manifestations.

The old Parish Prison at Tulane and Saratoga had its share of ghosts, too. The *New Orleans Daily Picayune*, January 23, 1882, reported that there had been fourteen attempted suicides in cell number seventeen, and most of them succeeded. The survivors jibbered of a red-haired woman who came down the corridor, entered the cell with a smile and sadistically tortured them until they sought relief in death. Suicides became so prevalent that the cell was not used for years. Then the beautiful apparition haunted another cell on the same floor. Here six women killed themselves within three months. Police, too, vowed to have seen the woman often, gave her the title of 'The Redheaded Countess,' because of her fiery tresses and regal manner. Once a Captain Bachemin passed her on the stairs. She touched his coat, and her fingers seared through the material, leaving a hole in his clothing and scorching his flesh. Or so he claimed.

An entire crew of malevolent spirits tormented a Mrs. Lee and her daughter, who resided at Coliseum and Ninth Streets. The father had been murdered by thugs and returned often to beg his daughter to play the piano for him. Yet when she did so evil spirits accompanying the father would beat her black and blue. Every time she played the poor girl emerged from the ordeal feeling and looking as though she had been tossed into the center of a free-for-all fight. The most gruesome angle of the affair was that Mr. Lee had no head, and that he was always begging his daughter to find his head.

One Sunday a minister, preaching a doleful sermon on sin, exhibited a skull on his pulpit as an example of the end of mortal man. A woman in the congregation learned that the skull was Lee's, that it had been turned over to him by a doctor, who had obtained it from the coroner. Having read the ghost story in the newspapers, she begged the skull from the minister and brought it to the widow and daughter. After it was buried beside the balance of his remains the ghosts never returned.

A headless phantom paraded about a Derbigny Street house for years. No one could live there, and literally a dozen people swore to the existence of the apparition. A male specter with a slashed, blood-dripping throat used to stroll about the Old Shell Road, terrorizing numerous persons. Just a few years ago uptown Baronne Street was cast into excitement by a ghost who walked about the house where he had resided in life, seeking and begging for a drink of water. Sometimes he found a faucet in the bathroom or kitchen and then he always left the tap open. Mornings the people living in the place would find a faucet running full blast. This ghost had been a grocer and had maintained his business in the first room of the house, living in the rear. Rumor spread that he had accumulated great wealth and had hidden it in the walls of the place, and that this explained his return from the grave. Nothing was ever found, however.

A few years ago there was a shower of bricks at 1813 St. Anthony Street. For days a single brick crashed into the yard every few minutes at regular intervals. No matter how many persons viewed the phenomenon the bricks continued to come. Windows were smashed, at least one woman was struck and injured. Police came and went and wrung their hands. No cause was ever discovered.

A Frenchwoman who operated a boarding-house in New Orleans suffered a streak of bad luck back in 1925. Then one of her roomers became ill and complained to the doctor that he felt as if he had been eating great quantities of raw turnips. He died, leaving all he possessed to Madame. A few days later a second roomer fell ill and died, also leaving Madame the proceeds of a substantial life-insurance policy. When a third boarder passed away the next week, again leaving Madame insurance money, the balance of the inmates of the establishment began to whisper unkind things, and when a fourth boarder fell ill, his brother moved him from the house, saying the place was cursed. This last man recovered.

It was now recalled that every ill person had complained just as the first one had — of a sensation of having eaten a large amount of raw turnips. But nothing came of it; each death had, according to summoned physicians, been from natural causes. Madame, embarrassed by gossip, sold her business and moved to a nice cottage in the suburbs, where she was able to live very comfortably on the various insurances left her by the deceased boarders. Years afterward she revealed an amazing story to a close friend.

Just before the first death, she said, she had been so desperate for money that she had not known where she would find sufficient funds to buy provisions for her table. Sitting in the dining-room that afternoon she had been at her wit's end; there was nothing in the kitchen to eat and the dinner hour was drawing closer and closer. Suddenly, in the middle of the dining-room, there appeared a large bed and in it lay a man with snow-white hair. He smiled and asked her to tell him her troubles.

When she had finished, his advice was simple. Why not feed the boarders on raw turnips? Oh, no, Madame protested. Who could live on raw turnips? What would her boarders say? That was too ridiculous, and she had always enjoyed such a reputation for a fine table and Creole cooking of the best. Certainly, they would all leave. But the man begged her to try it.

'But who are you?' cried Madame, in amazement.

'Mark Twain,' said the ghost, and promptly vanished, bed included.

So Madame went to market, without any thought of wrong, and spent the little money she had on turnips. When she returned she sliced them, diced them, pared them and served them whole, filling every dish on the table with turnips in all shapes, sizes and conditions. The boarders sat down, ate heartily, and complimented her on the excellent beef, the superb vegetables, the delicious dessert. Yet all they had eaten was raw turnips.

This went on for some time, Mark Twain appearing every day to chuckle over his joke. Madame began to make money. But, unfortunately, either she overdid it or the boarders overate. The deaths worried Madame a great deal. The cases attracted attention all over the city. As recently as January 19, 1930, the *New Orleans Item Tribune* carried an account of this amazing instance of spectral assistance in making a financial success of a boarding-house.

Another Frenchwoman, this one living in the Vieux Carré in about 1930, claimed to have been in constant communication with the spirit world. One day a couple moved in the house next door to hers and she learned that they had lost their five little daughters — that all had been kidnapped and never found. Soon afterward she saw five beautiful bubbles, large glittering spheres of silver and gold, floating over the house. Immediately she told the family next door that the bubbles were their lost children. The mother could see the bubbles, too, and on one occasion she heard childish laughter as the globes were wafted over the back-yard. The clairvoyant told the parents that the children had been murdered and that their bones were in a box, and the box buried near a certain bayou. The couple and witnesses journeyed there and the box and bones were found exactly where the woman had predicted they would be found.

Of course New Orleans's Vieux Carré is haunted by scores of ghosts. Practically every house has its phantom.

The famous 'Haunted House' of Madame La Laurie, undoubtedly the best known of those in this oldest section of the city, has been so much publicized that there is no use repeating here its controversial tale of slave-torture, flight and envy.

The quadroon slave girl who walks *sans* clothing on the roof of a house in the 700 block of Royal Street is almost as well known. This girl was the mistress of a young, aristocratic Creole. Ambitious, she demanded marriage, and her lover promised to give her his name if she would prove her love by spending a night on the rooftop naked. It was December and bitter cold, but the girl, determined to take her place as his wife, mounted to the roof and removed her clothes. Within a few hours she collapsed from the cold and died. Now this young and beautiful shade still does her phantasmal strip-tease on December nights. Or so say the neighbors.

The *New Orleans Daily News* of July 4, 1907, reported a phantom in St. Ann Street near Royal. This apparition attracted widespread attention and became known as the 'Witch of the French Opera.' Beginning a nightly pilgrimage from the old French Opera House, this terrible wraith, a woman with snow-white hair and a bony, ashen face, lit with fiery red eyes, would, after descending the steps of the opera house, walk to St. Ann Street and Royal, and there vanish into a certain rooming-house. Many persons saw her, especially tenants of the rooming-house, who met her in the hall and on the stairs. Next day they always moved.

Legend reported that a woman in the vicinity, growing old, had taken a young lover. After discovering his infidelity with a young girl, she wrote a letter to the police, saying she would return, and then committed suicide. The next night her spirit entered the room where the young lovers slept, turned on the gas and asphyxiated them.

For the next decade her ghost haunted that neighborhood,

always making the journey from the opera house to the room where she had killed the youth and his mistress. Then one day a new tenant discovered a yellowed love letter between the mantel-shelf and the chimney. When she tossed it into the fire the ghost appeared and tried to snatch it from the flames. Failing, she uttered a furious shriek and vanished. After that the phantom was never seen again.

Père Dagobert, once pastor of the Saint Louis Cathedral, still appears, it is said, walking up and down the aisles of the Cathedral, singing the same hymns he loved to chant during his life.

It seems Père Dagobert exhibited many earthy characteristics for a priest. He is reputed to have had a passion for good food and fine wines. Furthermore, instead of always appearing in the somber garb of his profession, he often wore the most magnificent silks and laces, long silk hose and shoes with buckles, as was the fashion among the dandies of his era. He was an extremely handsome man with a superb baritone voice, and his appearance and singing used to thrill the feminine portion of his congregation. But he was genuinely beloved, and not one of his parishioners ever doubted his spirituality, though once a bishop accused him of gluttony, drunkenness and a fondness for brown women. The bishop failed to prove any of his charges. Now Père Dagobert haunts his cathedral, occasionally can be seen dressed in his satin breeches and coat and flowing lace cuffs, his hair modishly dressed and curled, dipping from his jeweled snuff box. Of course you have to have 'the sight' to see him.

A certain apartment at 714 St. Peter Street, in the very heart of the Vieux Carré, is still usually unoccupied because of the ghastly wraiths who appear to torment anyone who tries to reside therein.

In the eighteen-fifties a Doctor Deschamps, a dentist, hypnotized a young girl for the purpose of using her as a medium to locate buried treasure. When his scheme failed time after time, he began to beat and abuse her. The girl finally died after long weeks of abuse and, directly, from an overdose of chloroform. Arrested and charged with murder, Deschamps was hanged.

Now his ghost and that of his victim return to the scene of his crime to enact and re-enact the tragic drama. They always appear together, the tenants will tell you, a burly, muscular man with hairy, apelike arms and the cringing girl. A most amusing touch has been added to this story by the introduction of Oliver La Farge, the well known author, who once lived in this house. Nowadays when the story is told, it is said that Mr. La Farge was driven out by the ghosts.

One young man occupying the apartment was taking a bath when suddenly in midair above his head appeared the leering and monstrous apparition of Doctor Deschamps. Terrified, the youth bounded from the tub and raced naked and soapy into St. Peter Street, up Royal. A policeman gave chase and halted him with startled yells and an overcoat. The young man refused ever to set foot in the apartment again, even to collect his belongings. Friends had to perform the task for him.

A house at the corner of Burgundy and Barracks Streets is said to have been erected about 1760 to house fifteen hundred Spanish soldiers. It is told that double files of soldiers march up and down the old galleries, their sabers clanking, amidst horrible groaning and cursing.

In early days soldiers of two Spanish kings were quartered there, and there occurred a scandal which did not leak out for many generations. In the 1860's a young business man, descended from one of the participants in the affair, told the story.

During the Spanish régime, when the gold in the Colony was stored in these barracks, it was spirited away from the strong room in which it was kept and hidden somewhere within the walls of the house. When troops were dispatched to the Floridas, a company of men was left in the building and they conceived a bold scheme to steal the gold. Some, however, dissented and they were put in irons. One night these men were taken into a certain part of the house along one of the galleries and hung by their bare backs on heavy hooks set into the wall, like quarters of beef. Their feet were then spiked to the wall, and a live rat was tied to each man's naked abdomen. Then the walls were plastered up, all but a small portion where their faces were, so that they might not die the comparatively easy death of suffocation, and also so that the rest of the men could enjoy their agony as the rats ate their way into the living bodies.

After they had died the faces were plastered over. The gold was divided, after which each of the men became a fine dignified gentleman and the founder of a great family.

To this day, along that thick wall, a row of hideous faces appears in the moonlight. Mammoth rats come out of the walls, to play and roll about like kittens on the floor and in the courtyard. Many persons have tried to feed these rats, but they never eat; their ghost bodies survive forever on that feast of human vitals. One young man, in 1932, allowed a rat to step on his hand and crawl up his arm. The arm was immediately crushed and had to be placed in splints for weeks.

Every night a light glows on the winding staircase. A man's head and shoulders can be plainly seen, sitting at a small table beside a window, counting gold coins. There is no table here, no window. Only the stair and a wide corridor. People have even dared to walk up to the place where the man is seated at night, but they see nothing then. In the garret the thick walls are a mass of inner tunnels. Legend guesses that the man on the staircase was the keeper of the gold, in a narrow room between the walls, and that he, too, died within the stiffening cement. The fact that this house was not standing in Spanish times is ignored by those who tell the story.

Another old New Orleans house was visited by a newspaper reporter a number of years ago. The house, built in 1770, had been a magnificent mansion, but by this time had fallen into a disreputable state, though still the home of a descendant of the original family. The reporter was grudgingly admitted by an ancient mulatto servant, who made him swear at the door that he would not let any ghosts in. Then he was ushered upstairs and into the presence of 'The Señorita,' a revolting old hag, loaded with priceless jewelry and wearing a blazing tiara on her almost hairless scalp. Bunched in a featherbed in a huge armchair, she looked about to fall apart right before the young man's eyes. Even her rings were tied to her fingers with pieces of twine, the ends of which had been soaked in perfumery, and these she sucked noisily all the time.

'The Señorita' was ninety-five years old, and her father had been dead more than seventy years, but she fancied herself a young girl and had no memory of the Don's death, imagining him on a trip to Spain. She chatted with grotesque gaiety of her young beaux, always wealthy young Spaniards who came to the Casa Rosa to sue for her hand. She talked much of her own beauty and desirability, of the balls her father, the Don, would give in her honor upon his return. She admitted, though, that her callers never left the house once they called. They didn't want to, said she. One even poisoned his mother to give her the woman's jewels. The Don always stole the valuables, but 'The Señorita' invariably stole back whatever she wanted. She spoke whimsically of the rose garden, and implied it was extremely 'useful.'

During the interview she constantly gave orders to the mulatto servant for a great dinner that night, hinting at promises of torture for any slave guilty of the slightest clumsiness. At last, quite suddenly, she fell asleep and began to snore.

Then the reporter sneaked off and began to explore the moldy house. In the hall he encountered the phantom of a wobbling young man in a costume over a century old. This ghost dragged him up some slimy stairs and into the presence of half a hundred other spirits, all of young men. The place was a mass of writhing phantoms and oozing filth, thick with the stench of rotting human flesh. Somehow the reporter got away, fleeing down those stairs. At the street gate a ghost swung the gate wide, then fell in two, as though he had been sawed in half.

When 'The Señorita' died, a year later, new tenants, renovating the house, tore down the wall north of the rose garden. Under it lay buried about fifty skeletons, all male and young, undoubtedly the unfortunate beaux of the beauty of the Casa Rosa.

One of the most unusual apparitions recorded is the lady ghost who, instead of rapping on tables or slamming doors or frightening folk with icy hands, appeared as a fountain in the center of a room in a certain downtown home. Suddenly and without warning, the tenant of the room saw this fountain manifested, a leaping, bubbling thing, throwing jets of water to the ceiling. And the water didn't wet anything. Investigation uncovered the fact that a young woman had died in the room after a blighted love affair. It was then decided that the fountain represented the tears she had shed.

The lady on one or two occasions appeared as herself, young and, of course, beautiful. Then she started to spout. This ghost finally refused to confine herself to the one room of the house, however, but began appearing in all the rooms, separately and simultaneously. In the following years four or five families viewed the phenomenon.

Gertrude Apple, New Orleans Negress, intends to be a ghost when she dies, and she is going to haunt the white woman for whom she works.

'You better leave Gertrude alone,' the husband of her mistress told his wife, according to Gertrude. 'That dark gal's sure gonna haunt you when she dies.'

'And I sure is gonna haunt her,' Gertrude admits. 'I'm gonna haunt her very soul. She's nice in her way, but she pays cheap.'

One night a ghost came into Gertrude's room. He wore a flashy checked suit, carried a walking cane and he was black as ink.

'He come up to my bed,' Gertrude said, 'and dropped that cane on the floor, and it didn't make no noise at all. Then he throwed one of his legs over me. I yelled, "Get away from me, you!" And he wented.

'Another time,' said she, 'a rooster done appeared in my room. That thing changed into a man, then into a cow. Then it disappeared — jest evapulated. Was I glad. Whew! Sometimes I'm sorry I can see spirits, they scare me so. Spirits is bad if you ain't a Christian, but if you is and you is borned with a veil over your face you ain't got nothin' to worry about.

'I seen plenty of witches, too. Them things ride you at night. They done tried to ride me, but I hollers, "In the name of my religion, help me, good spirits!" And the witches run. Witches don't mess with spirits. I think lots of white peoples is witches. Others is just plain bitches.

'I sure cried when Huey P. Long died. He was gonna give me money from them rich peoples. He was gonna strictly share the wealth. I sure cried when he was 'sassquanated. I been tryin' to see his spirit, but I ain't had no luck with him. But my grandma came back from Heaven and she tell me he is fine — lookin' better and feelin' better than he ever did. He's got money, too. That I knows!'

Aunt Jessie Collins, an authority on supernatural manifestations, explained it all this way,

'Ghosts is liable to look like anything,' said she. 'Some comes back just like they was when they died, but others turns into animals and balls of fire or things with long teeths and hairy arms. You can just walk around all your life lookin' at things and you don't never know when you is lookin' at a ghost. My grandpa seen one once and it sure did him a lot of good.

'You see, my grandpa was a drinkin' man, and you know how mens sees things when they is in their cups. Still, my grandpa didn't drink quite that much. We was livin' way out in the country then, and he had to walk to town and back to get hisself his gin. Well, one night he come home, walkin' down that dark country road, not studyin' about nothin', or nothin', and he heared somethin' walkin' behind him. My grandpa turned aroun', and seen it wasn't nothin' but a little ole white dog. "Hello, little ole dog," my grandpa said. "Where you goin' at?" Outside of that he didn't pay it no mind. Jest kept walkin'. That little old dog followed him clean to his door.

'Now, when my grandpa reached his front door, he heard that dog paddin' up on the porch back of him, and he heared my grandma breathin' mad-like right inside, jest waitin' for him. He turned around, and say, "Go 'way, little ole dog. You don't want to mess in this business."

'He went to say more, but the words jest stuck in his throat, 'cause he seen now that that dog wasn't no dog at all, but a big white ghost fifteen feets tall with two heads and 'bout twelve arms. My grandpa jest fell right smack down on that porch and lay. My grandma run out when she heared the noise and drug him inside. She didn't hit him or nothing, 'cause he had done plumb fainted. He was in bed nearly a week. No, my grandma didn't see no ghost. I always figured that ghost knowed my grandma and he run when he heared her comin' out. But you know after that my grandpa didn't touch no liquor for more than a month?'

Chapter 15

Crazah and the Glory Road

'GOT A FUNERAL? GOT A WAKE?' CRAZAH blinked his eyes, passed a hand over his black forehead, rubbing his brow gently, as if in hope of coaxing his brain to function with more speed.

'His nose done smelled a wake and his ears done heared Gabriel's trumpet,' commented an old woman, gazing down on the little man in the much-too-large tuxedo. 'Ain't never been a funeral in town Crazah couldn't find.'

He ignored her completely, moving to the coffin at the other end of the undertaking parlors. He bowed before the corpse several times, his lips grinning sardonically, but his eyes, as always, perfectly blank.

'Hello, Louie!' Another woman touched his elbow. 'Come sit by me,' she invited, and led him gently to a chair far in the rear of the room.

But he couldn't sit quietly. He moved up and down, clapped his hands, stared at the ceiling, squirmed restlessly. When the singing started he contributed rhythmic clapping of his hands and stomping of his feet. When the praying started, he prayed loud and with all the energy he could muster. Only when the preacher began to preach did Louie retreat to a seat, to sit there with his bulging eyes glued to the preacher's mouth, as if he were soaking up every word.

Time came to eat; ham and crackers and coffee were passed among the mourners, and he helped himself at least three times. Then, slouching down in his chair, eyes closed, mouth open, he went to sleep.

Every Negro in New Orleans knows Louie Williams, called, variously, Crazah, The Dead and Alive Man, The Goofy Man or just THAT Man. Whenever and wherever there is a funeral, Louis will be there as surely as is Death itself.

Perhaps this Crazah is only a personified exaggeration of colored people's love for 'buryin's'; for if Negroes don't greet the actual act of dying with joy, they certainly make the most of the rites that follow it. And the more important the person, the more elaborate are those ceremonies certain to be. Negroes prepare for dying all their lives. As one of them put it, 'Moses died, Elijah died. All the strong men die and all the weak men die. There is no two ways about it, we all must die. So why not be ready for it, brother?' They save money carefully for this inevitable day, join numerous lodges and funeral societies.

'A woman's got to belong to at least seven secret societies if she 'spects to get buried with any style,' revealed Luella Johnson. 'And the more lodges you belongs to, the more music you gits when you goes to meet your Maker. I belongs to enough now to have shoes on my feets. I knows right now what I'm gonna have at my wake. I already done checked off chicken salad and coffee.

'I'm sure lookin' forward to my wake. They is wakin' me for four nights and I is gonna have the biggest funeral the church ever had. That's why everything I makes goes to the church and them societies. I wants a pink casket and I'm gonna be wearin' a pink evenin' dress, with pink satin shoes on my feets and a pink hat on my haid so they won't look too hard at my wig.

'Geddes and Moss is the funeral parlor where they has the real 'ristocratic buryin's. They serves them cocktails and little sandwiches and big society suppers. Sometimes they gits so many peoples at wakes they gotta feed 'em in shifts. But most people like chicken and spaghetti or weiner sandwiches. The mens always brings liquor and then you really hears some shoutin' and weepin'. Does they put it on! They always has a light in the coffin, shinin' right smack in the dead person's face, and a clock to show the sad hour they was took. A girl corpse is turned on one side and her right hand hangs out the casket with a big dinner ring on one finger. Man, it sure looks pretty! 'Course they takes it off before they close the coffin, 'cause they uses it all the time. In their other hand girl corpses always carries long white gloves. All the mens is laid away in them stylish full dress suits, and is kind of raised up high so you can see 'em good.

'When my husband died I give him a fine funeral. I went in deep mourning and wore me a long widow's veil. Every day I'd go to the cemetery and cry all day by his grave. But his spirit started to haunt me somethin' terrible. I had chickens and every night he'd come back wearin' a white apron and shoo my chickens. Every mornin' some of 'em would be dead. We had a horse and that haunt done drove me and him both crazy. Then I got mad and I quit goin' to the cemetery, and I took off that widow's veil. I put black pepper 'round the sills of all my doors. That stopped him; that always chases ghostses. You know I wouldn't go near no graveyard on All Saints' Day for nothin'. No, sir! Them evil spirits just whizzes by you like the wind and knocks you flat on the ground.'

The big ''ristocratic' funerals are the ones Crazah likes best. They're more exciting than the humbler affairs and there's more to eat and drink and more music. And next to death, food and music are Crazah's passions. He never leaves any wake until the eating is over, though he is very tolerant regarding what is served. If the family is well fixed, they'll be chicken and whiskey, and he'll help himself freely to the chicken, but will pass up the whiskey, as he doesn't drink or smoke. If the family is poor, he is perfectly satisfied to feast on cheese sandwiches and coffee. After eating he usually makes his departure, unless there is only the one wake in town. In that case, he'll curl up and nap until breakfast is served. He particularly likes home funerals, for there is often more to eat at these than at the affairs in the undertaking establishments.

Joe Geddes, of Geddes and Moss, said, 'Louie has a grand time at funerals and wakes. And don't think he's as crazy as people imagine he is. Oh, I admit he's a little cracked, but aren't we all? He sure knows how to get by without working. He does all his eating at wakes and most of his sleeping. He always dresses in clothes people give him, and they're always too large because Louie's so small, hardly five feet. Sometimes he'll show up in a frayed tuxedo, other times in overalls. But we like to have him around. Everybody knows him.

'The boys played a joke on him one time. We weren't so busy that night and one of the fellows dressed up in a sheet and stood beside an open casket. We told Louie there was a spirit in the back and he ought to go see it. Louie went on back and just stood there staring at the fellow in the white outfit. It was okay until that "ghost" moved. Then Louie let out one yell and ran right out of the building. Afterwards he explained, "Me not scared of dead man, but scared of man that moves."'

In his befuddled mind Louie considers himself a preacher. Sometimes he attempts to preach a full sermon at funerals, but no one can understand very much that he says. At church he's always testifying and leading the singing. But he'll never preach a word unless somebody gives him money. 'Preachers don't work for nothin',' he says. And neither will he do any other sort of work. 'Preachers don't work at nothin' but preachin'!' is another of his strong beliefs.

Sunshine Money is his favorite preacher. Sunshine Money is known all over the state as a hard praying soul-saver, and also as 'the man who changes automobiles every year,' the latter indicative of his financial success.

Crazah loves to imitate Sunshine Money at funerals. He stoops over and waves his hands and carries on just like Sunshine Money does. Johnny Jackson related this story at Geddes and Moss:

'Louie went to a funeral Sunshine Money was conducting. The body was brought into the church at one o'clock, and Sunshine preached that soul into Heaven from then until five-thirty, and was still going strong. Louie hadn't been to the wake, had arrived at the funeral late, and hadn't eaten a thing, so he wasn't having a very good time. He kept squirming around on his bench until the woman next to him asked him what was wrong. Louie said, "Late. Let's go to graveyard." Then he went to work on Sunshine Money. That ole preacher was still going to town preaching that man into Heaven. Louie stood up, pointed a finger toward the ceiling, and said, "That's him. That's him. He's almost there!" Sunshine Money frowned, looked at Louie, at the ceiling, then at his big gold watch. Finally he said, "I guess I got to stop now. He ain't quite in Heaven, but he's close. Louie done showed him to me. I guess that nigger can go the rest of the way by hisself." And with that the funeral left for the cemetery. You think that Crazah's dumb?'

When Mother Clara James Hyde passed to her reward, Louie had a wake to attend that was definitely in the A-1 class. Mother Hyde's body rested in a casket of orchid plush. She wore a gown of royal purple, trimmed generously with ruffles on the bosom upon which so many had poured forth tears of woe. On her head she wore a crown of brilliant rhinestones, and inside the casket was a pink bedlight; over all, cascading frothily to the floor was a filmy veil of brightest red. The followers of the famous healer and prophesier had placed her in a setting of which they could be proud. Tall palms arched above the coffin and at each end was a standing basket holding a lavish bouquet of flowers, and by each of these, in constant vigil, sat one of Mother Hyde's co-workers, silent and lachrymose, except for occasional emotional outbursts, when one would howl: 'Lord Jesus, bless Thy Name!' or 'Mother ain't daid. She's just sleepin'!'

As the church she had conducted for so many years — St. James Temple No. 2 — filled, the speakers' platform crowded with the pastors of other churches. The service opened with the singing of 'What a Friend We Have in Jesus,' accompanied by the feeble notes of a loose-stringed piano. Suddenly all heads turned. Mother Kemper, resplendent in white velvet, was swaying up the aisle, undulating slowly and voluptuously to the music. A voice shouted, 'Now we is gonna hear some real preachin'!' But it was not to be. Mother Kemper struck a very effective pose before the casket for a few minutes, then modestly retired to a seat with the other church leaders.

Now the competition began in earnest. One preacher after another rose to extoll the virtues of Mother Hyde. One of the reverends was heard to remark, as the competition grew fiercer, 'This is gettin' to be a cutthroat business!' Every speaker talked for at least an hour. And between sermons solos were rendered, mourners clapping their hands and stomping their feet to the music, shouting 'Amen! Amen!' at the end of every line. The first 'passing out' occurred. A woman fell flat on her face before the casket.

Mother Kemper at last contributed her bit. Standing majestically in the center of the platform, her eyes raised and her white velvet clad arms outstretched, she intoned, 'I can see the Angel Gabriel lookin' through the periscope of glory down the long road of time and he sees a weary traveler. That's Mother Hyde carryin' her burden of good deeds to the Golden Gate.'

Members of the congregation shouted:

'Very nice!'

'Sure feels good.'

'Tell it to me!'

'Mother don't want to come back to this world. Sleep on, Mother!'

'Amen, sister! Amen!'

'Lawd, you knows our names and the numbers of our pages! You calls us like you pleases and if you pleases!'

It continued until midnight. Then one of the guards sprang to her feet, her emotions at a boiling point, and screamed, 'Jesus God! Bless Thy Name! Bless Thy Name!' Her head lolling around on her thin neck and her eyeballs protruding, she proceeded to collapse. This seemed to bring on a recess, which was spent by everyone making numerous trips to the basement for ham sandwiches and coffee.

This over, the body was viewed by all present, tears streaming down dusky cheeks, big black bucks crying like children as they gazed down on the crowned head of Mother Hyde. Then the speeches started again.

A preacher ventured to say that Mother Hyde had had a fault.

This was answered by catcalls and cries of, 'Sit down! 'Tain't so, brother!' Then he explained her fault had been in too much goodness of heart, in trusting people too far. Now they shouted, 'Say on, brother! Ain't it the truth!'

A quartet rose and sang, jazzing their hymn, patting their feet and swaying. When they finished the crowd was swaying and shaking with them. There was no avoiding an encore. Some-one cried, 'We is gonna sing, we is gonna shout, we is gonna preach until everybody is gone.'

And it went on all night long. A wake to warm the cockles of Louis Williams's heart.

Marching to the cemetery is a mournful and sad affair, but it's an important kind of mournfulness and an impressive kind of sadness. The Young and True Friends Benevolent Association of Carrollton, 7th Division, turned out in full force not long ago, when a member went to glory. To the poignant strains of 'Massa's in the Cold, Cold Ground,' attired in black suits, white shirts, black derbies and white gloves, with arm ribbons of black and silver, and led by the gorgeously attired, six-foot, coal-black Grand Marshal, who wore a jet velvet cordon trimmed with silver braid and stars, they marched with solem-nity, with dignity, and gusto, their brand new, shiny-black shoes keeping perfect time with the music. The organization banner was red lined in silver and bore the words 'Young and True Friends' in huge letters of gold. In the center were two hands clasped across a turbulent sea, a white dove and a pair of closely cuddled and burning hearts. One member carried a gavel wrapped in black crepe, another an American flag, and still an-other a Blue Jack, with silver stars on a blue background.

The ceremonies at the grave were short and simple, but every-one stayed until the last clod of dirt was put on the casket. A sister of the deceased waited until everyone else reached the grave before she began a slow march forward, the crowd parting to let her through; she was supported on each side by a woman, in a condition of semi-prostration, and moaned over and over again, 'I cain't stand it! I cain't stand it! Jesus have mercy on me! I cain't stand it!' As she reached the hole in the ground, her knees buckled under her and she collapsed completely.

But when the procession was half a block from the cemetery, enroute home, the band burst into 'Just Stay a Little While,' and all the True Friends performed individual and various dances, and the sister, but lately unconscious with grief, was soon trucking with the rest of them.

'I said Sister Cordelia might outlive me, but she's sure gonna die.' That's what one of Cordelia Johnson's friends admitted was her conviction the last time she had seen Sister Cordelia alive.

'She died an unexpected death due to bad symptoms,' another revealed.

On the raised cover of Sister Johnson's gray casket was a small hammered tin clock with the words 'The Sad Hour' painted under it in black, and the clock's hands pointing to the hour of death, this being a favorite addition to coffins among Negroes. Similarly, all clocks in the house were stopped at the time Sister Johnson died.

The wake was anything but dull. One of the sisters described it, 'We had solos and duets and hymn-singin' all night long. The womens was passin' out right and left. A doctor was kept busy and the smellin' salts was more popular than the food.'

The husband and two daughters made a most spectacular entrance at the funeral, coming up the stairs and into the room, screaming and moaning, alternately. The daughter who hadn't seen her mother for nine years made the most noise.

'What'll I do! What'll I do!' she wailed. 'I ain't got no mother to consulate me. Poor me!' Facing the mourners, her eyes squeezed tight, but her mouth wide open, she shrieked, 'Mother! Mother! I'm goin' to join you. Yes, I am! Yes, I am! It's a horrible hole. That's all it is, a horrible black hole. I ain't got no mother! Ooh, Jesus!'

She fell to her knees, rocked back and forth, tearing at her hair with her hands, her black face swollen and twisted.

'I ain't got no mother to consulate me!' she screamed. 'Jesus Gawd!' Then she fell forward and was carried out.

The church service was just as eventful. After the preaching and the praying and the psalm-singing, members of the various societies circled the casket. Some of them would shout and

scream hysterically, finally fainting and having to be carried out
One huge woman taxed the strength of five men. Other sisters
just kept walking up and down, releasing screams periodically.
This is called the 'walkin' spirits.' One immense sister almost
tore down the church when she had a sudden attack of the
'runnin' spirits.' Some of the women trucked, others shook all
over, one kept knocking off as many hats as she could possibly
reach.

Even Crazah, a connoisseur in such matters, had to admit Cordelia Johnson's wake and funeral were events to remember.

Crazah is probably the only Negro in New Orleans who does
not belong to at least one burial society. Joe Geddes has promised to bury him free of charge and in befitting fashion. Besides
Geddes says, 'He brings me business. You know, no one under-
stands how Louie locates all the deaths. Some people say he
finds sick people and prays that they die, but I don't believe that.
Often he'll tell me about a death of which I didn't know, so I
can go and bid for the job. I won't forget those favors.'

There are literally hundreds of Negro lodges, burial societies
and similar organizations in New Orleans. For a small weekly
fee these benevolent and mutual aid associations furnish a doctor
when a member is ill and a funeral of a specified type and price —
most often a hundred-dollar affair. Every detail is included in
the contract, though it is of course true that the more societies
belonged to, the grander is the funeral. The following are only
a few of the better known organizations:

> Ladies Independence B. M. A. A.
> Juvenile Co-operators Fraternal Society
> Ladies Morality B. M. A. A.
> Harmony B. M. A. A.
> Young Friends of Hope B. M. A. A.
> The New Ladies of Magnolia B. M. A. A.
> Hall of the Ladies, Friends of Louisiana
> Young Men's Provident B. M. A. A.
> Ladies and Young Ladies St. Celena B. M. A. A.
> Artisan's B. A.
> Young Men of St. Michael B. M. A. A.
> Ladies Kind Deeds B. M. A. A.
> Ladies Protective B. M. A. A.
> Young Friends of Order B. M. A. A.

And in a fashion suitable to Louisiana, many have French names, such as:

Societe de Bienfasance Mutuelle
Les Jeumis Amis
Societe Des Francs Amis
New Ladies *Dieu Nous Protege*
Nouvelle Societe Des Amis Sinceres
Societe Des Amis Inseparable

Because the Negro is tremendously impressed by ceremony and especially by uniforms of all kinds, these organizations have been extremely successful. Every funeral worth anything calls for at least one band of music, street marching, and uniforms. Solemn dirges are always rendered on the way to the cemetery; the hottest swing numbers when homeward bound. Uniforms usually include hats with plumes, brass buttons and medals, golden epaulets. The ones that require the carrying of a sword are particularly favored. There isn't anything that lends dignity and importance to a mourner like a big shiny sword.

A typical hundred-dollar funeral is offered by the Crescent Burial Society. Premiums are twenty-five cents a week and the deceased must have been a member six months to receive full benefits. These consist of a casket — peach-colored for young people, gray or lavender for old ones — a harmonizing shroud, two automobiles, a floor rug, candles, and wakes for two nights. The family must supply the food, however, and other associations the music, if any.

There are many details attached to this job of putting away the dead which must be observed. They must always be buried facing the east and the rising sun, if you want them to go to Heaven, for if they are buried facing the west, they will surely go to Hell; thus might advantage be taken of a relative of whom one was not overfond. And everyone should be buried wearing a new pair of shoes on their feet; these are of course essential for that long journey ahead. When it rains on a corpse it is a sign he regretted dying. If a person dies on a Sunday and is buried on a Sunday, he is certain to become an angel.

Watch out if you sneeze while eating! It's not from using

black pepper too lavishly; it's a sign of death. And should you dream of pork meat or a wedding or a proposal of marriage, you're going to hear of a death soon. You can smile if a hearse passes you on the street because that's a sign of a happy day ahead for you. If you'll hold the hand of a small child when passing a graveyard, the ghosts won't bother you. Some member of the family should always throw a small piece of red brick into the grave or tomb before it is closed, as a last good-bye.

When a woman dies in confinement she must be buried in white stockings and black shoes. The feet of the corpse must always be borne out of the house first because the feet always enter and leave the house first; when laid out the feet of the deceased must point always to a window or door. One way of laying out the dead is to pin geranium or ivy leaves all over a white pillow, but these must be removed before the coffin is closed and, after the funeral, carefully burned, the ashes and pins thrown into a toilet. No one pin must be dropped, for it would be the worst sort of luck for anyone to pick it up.

Mattie Ford contributed a homemade way of embalming.

'If a person dies and you don't have no money to have 'em embalmed to keep the body right you buy yourself a nickel's worth of charcoal, two packs of King Bee Tobacco and some whiskey. You beats the charcoal up fine as dust and mixes it with the tobacco. When you wash the corpse you takes half of an old sheet and puts the tobacco and charcoal in that sheet and puts it on the body like you does a diaper on a baby. Then you holds that dead man up and pours a bottle of whiskey down his mout'. You can keep a body as long as you wants if you does that.'

'If somebody treats you bad and are mean to you,' says Luella Johnson, 'git yourself some black candles and go to St. Roch's Cemetery. Light one candle before each of nine tombs, any tombs will do. When you gits to the last one, turn your back to it and hit it hard as you can and say, "Oh, Lawd! Remove this stumbin' block from my path." In nine days that man gonna die or leave you alone.

'When a man or woman is bad and won't do no good and no harm comes to them they makes a novena to the Devil and sells

South Rampart Street Sports

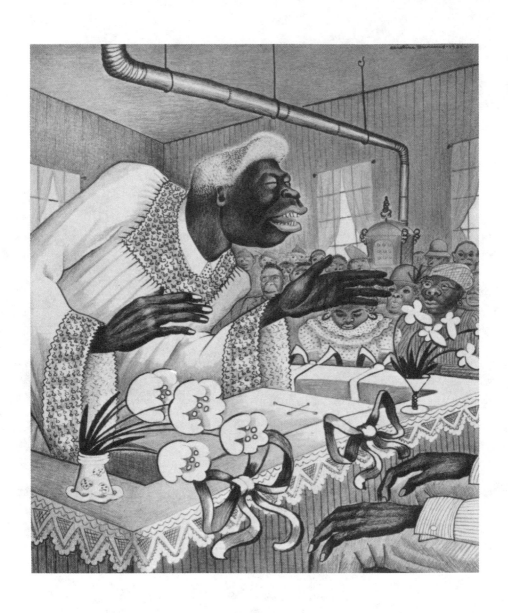

A Cult Leader Exhorts his Flock to Obedience

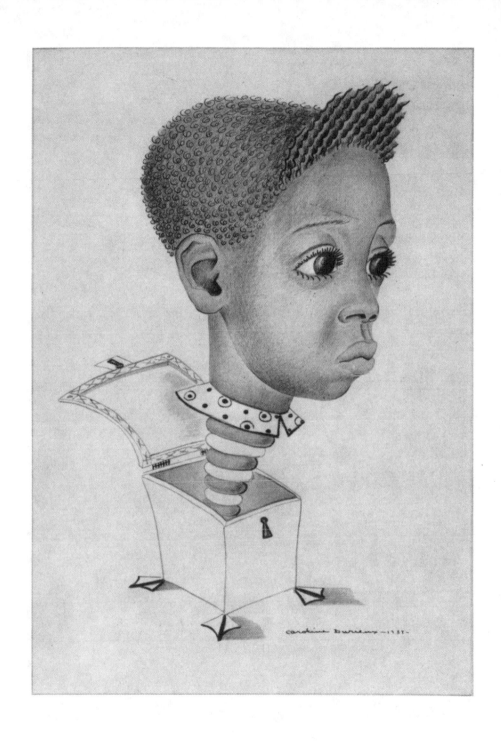

'A Child Is a Jack-in-the-Box'

Hands of the Dead Reach Out for the Living

themself to him for seven years. He sure do take care of them, too.'

By far the most elaborate Negro funeral ever held in New Orleans was awarded the late Major J. Osey, member of twenty-odd different lodges, several of which he had organized and many in which he had served as high dignitary at one time or another. The death notice in the newspapers, one of the longest on record, read as follows:

OSEY — At his residence, 2311 Upperline Street, Tuesday, July 20, 1937, at 11:55 o'clock p.m., Major ADOLPHE J. OSEY, a native of Bellalliance, Louisiana, and a resident of this city for many years. Beloved husband of Henrietta Webb Osey, grandfather of Oscar J. Osey, uncle of Emanuel, Jr., Edgar Porter, Eddie and Joseph Howard, Manuella Porter McCleanton, Henrietta Webb Gumbs, Ethel Howard McTurner, great-uncle of Nellie Porter Walker, James and Juanita Porter, brother-in-law of John Webb and Emanuel B. Porter, and a host of other relatives.

Grand Staff Patriot, 13th Regiment of G. U. of O. of America, Louisiana Creole Lodge, G. U. O. of O. F. 1918, Past Grand Masters Council No. 30, Orleans Patriotic and Auxiliary, No. 7, Queen Esther H. H. of Ruth No. 3964, Cyprus Lodge, A. A. & F. M. No. 43, Capitol Lodge of Elks No. 595, Progressive Friends Ben. Ass., Young Men's Perpetual Help. Ben. Ass. Live Wire Circle of 5th Baptist Church, Star Light Circle of Tulane Baptist Church, Pastor, officers and friends of Trinity M. E. Church are respectfully invited to attend the funeral, which will take place from the late residence, Sunday, July 25, 1937, at 11:30 o'clock a.m.

Religious services 5th Baptist Church, Sixth and South Robertson Streets.

Reverend W. B. McClelland officiating.
Interment St. Louis Cemetery No. 2.

The Major was waked for five days and nights, lay in state at his residence with both public and private wakes by the numerous lodges to which he belonged, and all during these five days, the small four room cottage was crowded with 'brothers' and 'sisters.' The front door was heavily draped with a dark canopy of velvet edged with silver fringe, bearing the inscription 'Louisiana Creole Lodge, 1918, C. U. of O.'

Laid out in the front room, in a casket of purple plush, with a lining of heavily shirred white silk, a bedlight attached to the coffin's lid poured down on the Major's black face, with the mouth fixed in a wide and snowy smile that revealed every tooth. The toothsome expression — and the teeth were real! — symbolized the fact that he had gone to Heaven 'with a contract in his hand.'

He was dressed in the uniform of the Odd Fellows, jet black with shining brass buttons and epaulets of gold braid and fringe. One white-gloved hand held the purple fez of the Elks; around his waist was a white lambskin apron of the Supreme Council of the Masons and on his breast was pinned a medal of the Past Grand Council Encampment of the Past Patriarch, signifying, according to one of the mourners, 'that the Major was in the groove.' Beside him rested the hat of the Odd Fellows, a black continental with a white and purple plume. On top of the closed end of the casket was a Bible, an Elk's sphere, small brass buttons from the Progressive Friends, a rosette from the Odd Fellows, and a small artificial wreath representing the laurel wreath of the Masons.

The procession was led by the six-foot three-inch, black and burly Grand Marshal of the Odd Fellows, trailed by his clan. His every move was kept in perfect time to the slow but 'stomp swingin' ' music of the thirteen-piece band. Only the Odd Fellows marched on foot, all of them resplendent in their black and gold uniforms, with braid and epaulets and other gew-gaws, hats with plumes and either white or bright yellow gloves. Members of other lodges rode in big and shiny black limousines. Many of the mourners marched, however, and among them was Crazah, swaying and swinging his dwarfish little body with the rest of them, his face wreathed in a smile of delight at such a grand and glorious affair. From the house to the cemetery was a five-mile hike, but he never faltered.

Behind the dark Odd Fellows came the Patriarchs and the Household of Ruth, the women's auxiliaries, the Patriarchs in white flannel costumes much like the men's, the Household of

Ruth in blue, all carrying swords. The last three Odd Fellows carried a gilded but rather seedy looking lion, a lamb, and a bow and arrow, the significance of these being a lodge secret. A statue of Father Time rode in the first limousine behind the marchers.

An even larger crowd waited at the church than had been present at the house. The coffin was removed from the hearse one block away and carried inside by the pall bearers. On the church steps there was shouting and weeping, as most of the mourners fought to get close enough to touch the coffin. A woman screamed, 'There is a good man gone from here!' and promptly fainted. In less than a minute four others followed suit.

The Fifth Baptist Church was packed. The crowd filled it to the doors. They did everything but climb up the bright red beams to perch on the bright red rafters under the sky-blue ceiling.

Before the pulpit, at the head of the coffin and in full view of the congregation, was placed Father Time, a statue wearing scarlet pants, immense gold wings and a self-satisfied grimace on his bewhiskered countenance; and carrying an hour glass and a scythe. The entire church was decorated for the occasion. Black and white crepe draped the entrance door and pulpit. Above the door to the men's room, on one side, was a large picture of the Virgin — right over the word 'MEN'; and above the word 'WOMEN,' on the other side, was a picture of the Sacred Heart. The mixed choir wore black robes and appropriate funereal expressions. At the entrance one of the bands struck up 'I Am Coming to You.'

The Masons opened the service by filing past the casket and each dropping in a rose, the last one tossing in a crown of evergreens. Then the Reverend W. C. McClelland offered a prayer. Programs, distributed throughout the church, read as follows:

1. Devotional
2. Remarks from the Deacons' Board — Bro. H. Walker
3. Remarks from the Stewardess' Board — Sister Walker
4. Solo — Miss Irene Williams, Greater Tulane Baptist Church
5. Remarks — Sister Louise Walker
6. Solo — Brother Joseph Young

7. Solo — Brother O. W. Owens
8. Solo — Past Grand Exalted Ruler
      J. C. Hensley of Order of Elks No. 595
9. Solo — Past Grand Ruler
      Dr. B. Thompson of Order of Elks No. 595

ODD FELLOWS

10. Condolence — Auxiliary No. 7
11. Remarks — D. M. Patterson — His life as an Odd Fellow
12. Remarks — Reverend G. C. Amos — an Odd Fellow
13. Condolence — From Queen Esther H. H. No. 3964
14. Past Most Noble Governors — Agnes Johnson
15. Remarks — Grand Master of District Grand Lodge No. 21
16. Grand United Order of Odd Fellows — Honorable William Kelso
17. Remarks — Endowment Secretary and Treasurer Dr. J. H. Lowery
18. Remarks — Reverend J. R. Poe, St. James A. M. E. Church
19. Remarks — Reverend T. R. Albert, Trinity A. M. E. Church
20. Duet — Sisters R. Knight and F. Garrison

---

21. Sermon — Reverend W. B. McClelland

Unfortunately, the funeral had been so late in starting that the program had to be considerably shortened, much to the disappointment of many brothers and sisters, who expressed themselves on the subject in loud and far from dulcet tones. When anyone spoke too long, the Reverend McClelland pulled him by the coat and made him sit down. Some of the remarks were:

'He was a Gawd-sent man!'

'He was too true to falsify!'

'We wants heavy prayin', and mournin' what's its deepest.'

'His relatives were many, but his faults few!'

Odd Fellows crossed swords over the door, as the body was borne from the church.

Major Osey was interred in an upper vault — an 'oven' — in Saint Louis Cemetery No. 2. Lieutenant-Colonel Naomi Patterson, of the Women's Auxiliary of the Odd Fellows, read a burial dialogue, particularly praising the late Major's tongue, cheeks, eyes and nose, and ending this by placing a bouquet of evergreens within the vault, just as taps were blown on a bugle by her daughter, Mrs. James LaFourche. Following that Mrs. Patterson rendered a solo, 'The Will of God Is Accomplished,' while mourners paid their last respects by throwing handfuls of ashes into the tomb. Just as the coffin slid into the vault, rain came, a hard shower, which everybody considered an unfortunate omen for Major Osey on his long journey up the glory road.

But, nevertheless, as the mourners left the cemetery gates behind, the entire aspect of the procession changed. The bands changed their tune and the marchers began trucking, and all the way back to Major Osey's house gaiety was complete and contagious.

So ended one of the most colorful funerals Negro New Orleans has ever seen. Even that funeral expert, that Crazah, that Louie Williams, had never seen its like before. His eyes bulged and his mouth hung agape at the splendor and magnificence of the whole affair. He even forgot to eat a toasted ham sandwich, which he carried, gripped tightly in one fist, all day long.

Chapter 16

Cemeteries

A CREOLE LADY KNOWN AS TANTE ADELINE WAS famous in old New Orleans because of an inordinate fondness for funerals. So copious were the tears she shed on these occasions that she earned the name of *Saule Pleurer* — Weeping Willow. In some rural sections of Louisiana it is still customary for everyone to attend any and all funerals within a radius of ten miles. In other sections announcements like the following, which appeared in the *Colfax Chronicle* May 24, 1935, are obeyed with complete seriousness:

> There will be a working of the Fairfield graveyard on Saturday, June 8th. Everybody invited to come and bring tools to work with and a basket of dinner.

The whole community turns out, to cut grass and weed, to clean and sweep graves and walks. In some cases great pains are taken to keep the grave free of grass; graves are sometimes even covered with sand. Other people prefer the grass and frequently plant rosebushes and other flowers.

There is nothing macabre about the day. Spirits are as high as if the workers were on a picnic; laughter echoes among the tombs. Children play along the shaded walks and chase each other over graves. Food is consumed with usual Louisiana gusto while the eaters sit on copings and tomb steps. And before departing homeward mutual compliments and other remarks garnish the day's achievements:

'Your place sure looks nice, Miz Joe. If Mr. Joe come out of his coffin he sure would be proud.'

'Grandma don't get so many flowers for the children she's got, but she don't do bad.'

Children are admonished:

'Honey, don't you touch them flowers!'

'Goddammit, I'm gonna whip you good. Ain't you ashamed?'

'Charlie, look at the seat of your pants. My God!'

As the homes of the living are regularly cleaned and decorated, so are the homes of the dead. And in Louisiana graveyards the decorating is unrestrained. Ground plots are covered with vari-colored shells or bright bits of broken glass. Oyster shells or pop bottles, the latter shoved neck-downward into the earth, are popular as finishing effects to border graves and walks, and are thought to be both neat and fancy — in an appropriate sort of way. Conch shells, painted pastel shades, perhaps gilded, silvered, even painted a doleful black, add a not ineffective touch, as do china dogs, pig banks, hand-colored serving trays, pin trays, and vases of every conceivable kind, size, shape and color.

Artificial flowers are common, are often made at home — of paper, wax, silk, beads or silver foil. 'Fish bouquets,' flowers and wreaths made of garfish scales used to be favorites, but are seldom seen now. In sections where Catholicism is widespread graves and tombs are profusely adorned with holy statues, holy pictures, rosaries draped over stone or iron crosses, and crucifixes, sometimes enclosed in glass cases to protect them from the elements.

Each Louisiana cemetery has its individualities, its interesting graves and tombs. At Monroe, in the Old City Cemetery, is the tomb of Sidney W. Saunders, which is surmounted by a life-sized statue of a man holding a scroll in one hand, which, when closely examined, proves to be a stone replica of a marriage license, reading:

This is to certify that Sidney W. Saunders and Anne Livingston of Monroe, in the State of Louisiana, were by me joined together in holy matrimony, March 25, 1875.
Witnesses:

John W. Rice	John W. Young
Frank Gregory	Justice of the Peace
	City of St. Louis

The local explanation is that there had been some doubt in the minds of the residents of Monroe as to the legality of the Saunderses marriage, and that Mrs. Saunders had the monument erected as a rebuke to the gossips. It is said that she also had her husband's desk and chair placed within the large tomb, and there she would sit for hours, giving unrestrained vent to her grief.

Berthoud Cemetery, some twenty miles from New Orleans, is the source of the most fantastic legend in the entire State. Here, it is said, the remains of Jean Lafitte, John Paul Jones and Napoleon Bonaparte lie in three adjoining graves. Lafitte is supposed to have rescued Bonaparte from St. Helena, leaving a double in his place, and the Emperor to have died while being carried to Louisiana; then he was buried here beside the Bayou Barataria. John Paul Jones, according to the legend, joined the Lafitte band, was killed in action, and buried in another of the graves. Then, when Lafitte died, his pirates buried him in a grave between the other two. The fact that Jones died in 1792, when Lafitte was about twelve years old, doesn't seem to bother anyone.

There are no headstones, no inscriptions. The owner of the graveyard, Madame Toinette Perrin, says simply: 'I tell you like my mamma and my *gran'mère* tell me. Lafitte is buried dere. Other mans? Napoleon? *Mais, oui!* Zat is his name. Me, I'm old, and don't remember like I used to, but I know dis: every year some woman comes to zat grave on All Saints' Day, and light candle and pray. She say she come from far away and he is her kin. And she give me plenty money to keep his grave nice. Where she live? I don't remember, me. But she come from far off place once every year, on All Saints' Day. Zat is all I know, me.' On certain occasions the trio of ghosts appear. (See 'Ghosts,' pages 271–300.)

On the grave of Adelate Trosclairée, who departed this world March 1, 1909, there is a wreath of pink and white paper flowers tied with purple ribbon, a vase, a vinegar cruet, a whiskey jigger turned upside down, an old-fashioned cocktail glass and a striped water glass, turned down. On another grave, a half-filled bottle of medicine (filled at the Gretna Pharmacy, December 21, 1938), a deep saucer filled with oil, a purse mirror and a tiny white elephant served as adornments.

Whether Napoleon rests on Bayou Barataria is, of course, doubtful, but there is no doubt as to the numbers of his admirers in Louisiana. When he died, the citizens of New Orleans held a funeral for him. The *Louisiana Gazette* of December 20, 1821, described the services.

SERVICE FOR NAPOLEON BONAPARTE

The adherents of the late Napoleon Bonaparte who reside in this city, having caused a splendid bier or catafalco to be erected in the Catholic Church, which was hung in black for the occasion, they yesterday walked there in procession, and a funeral service was performed by the priests. Mr. Canouge delivered an oration to the crowd who attended the church; and the singers of the French Company of players sang several pieces during the celebration of Grand Mass.

A collection was also made in the church, which produced a very handsome sum for the poor.

There was once in Washington Parish, as there is in most places, a man named McGee. This one kept a stable, and is said to have been cruel to his horses. When anyone remonstrated with him, he would laugh and say, 'If I'm as bad as that, I guess I'll be a mule when I die.' McGee donated a cemetery plot to the poor of his parish and when he passed on was buried there, a handsome headstone marking his grave. Soon afterward the outline of a mule's head appeared on three sides of this stone and, despite washing, scraping, even a coat of paint, may still be clearly seen.

Graveland Cemetery, in Orange Grove, has a pair of unusual tombs, in each of which is buried a young boy. Over each one is a monument that is a replica of a straw hat, a pair of shoes and a pair of stockings. In a cemetery in Baton Rouge a bereaved father built a doll house on top of the tomb of his small daughter.

McDonoghville Cemetery, at Gretna, was once a part of the plantation of John McDonogh, famous Louisiana philanthropist. The body of McDonogh rested here for ten years, was then moved to Baltimore, his place of birth. This is probably the most democratic cemetery in the South, for Protestant and Catholic lie side by side, instead of being separated by fences as is customary in the State; and scattered among the graves of 'respectable' citizens are those of more adventurous spirits, including a few hanged murderers. The sexton explained: 'They is got all kinds buried here, people killed, people murdered; anybody can come here. Everybody is welcome to McDonoghville Cemetery!' The sole exception to this is the division of Whites and Negroes by a neat picket fence.

Negroes of the section idolized McDonogh, and two of them, Fanny Thornton and her son Edward, took it upon themselves lovingly to tend his burial place, even after the remains had been removed. When Fanny died in 1887, Edward had her laid to rest in the abandoned tomb, and not until 1890, when administrators of the estate took steps to build a monument over the tomb, did they find what had once been Fanny. These remains were promptly removed to the other side of the picket fence.

At Grace Church Cemetery in St. Francisville is the grave of a United States naval officer whose death 'stopped a war' so that he could be buried. The *New Orleans Times-Picayune* of October 24, 1937, recounted the story in detail. In 1863, after New Orleans had fallen to Farragut's fleet and Butler's army, Federal gunboats, among them the U.S.S. *Albatross*, ranged up and down the Mississippi River, the latter under the temporary command of Lieutenant Commander J. E. Hart. Captain Hart became stricken with fever and, while delirious in his cabin, shot himself. All this occurred while St. Francisville was being shelled, the town reported to be a 'perfect hotbed of secession,' and the 'constant resort of the Confederates... where they were continuously urged on to commit acts of plunder and abuse...,' according to Navy Department files in Washington.

While the battle raged a boat was put out from the *Albatross*, a white flag of truce at its bow, and bearing the body of Hart. Upon landing, the officer in charge requested that they be allowed to bury Hart with Masonic honors, as he had requested before he died, and Captain W. W. Leake, himself a Mason, agreed that the fighting should be suspended while this ritual was performed. The battle stopped and a strange funeral cortège of Federals and Confederates was organized and proceeded to the cemetery. Then, after it was over, the boat was allowed to return to the *Albatross* and the battle was resumed. Even now, it is said, relatives and descendants of the Confederate officer, Captain Leake, keep the grave of the Yankee officer in perfect order.

While in some parts of Louisiana the ground is solid enough to permit the digging of graves, in others, especially around New Orleans, water is so close to the surface that early French settlers referred to it as *flottant* — floating land. Until very recently, when modern drainage and engineering skill minimized this condition, practically all interments were in tombs or vaults of some sort, many being of magnificent proportions and designs, belonging to wealthy and prominent families. For the poor, crypts were erected, vaults built tier upon tier, usually into the cemetery wall, looking not unlike ovens in some gigantic bakery, and therefore becoming known locally as ' ovens.'

Strangers are always amazed — or amused — at these queer vaults. The *New Orleans Weekly Delta* of July 19, 1847, carried an article containing a portion of a letter written home by an English tourist, who said:

> Frequently while in Louisiana I heard of men gouging out eyes and biting off ears and noses. I do know that *they bake their dead in ovens as we do our brown Johns for breakfast!*

Ovens may be bought or they may be rented. If the latter, it is usually for a year and a day, and if no further payment is forthcoming, the remains are removed and burned. A single oven may be used again and again, for most are provided with a depository at the bottom where the bones may be pushed to make way for the new coffin. The remnants of old caskets are burned.

One New Orleans cemetery offers ' three-day burials,' which means you can rent the vault for three days, have a nice funeral to impress your friends, and see the coffin placed in an oven. After three days all is removed.

One of the oldest and most fascinating cemeteries in the State is Saint Louis Number 1 in New Orleans. Only one block square, enclosed by high brick walls, partially composed of ovens, if Gabriel blew that horn tomorrow many of the most famous characters of New Orleans's history would step out of the white-washed brick, granite and marble tombs and vaults.

Entering the gate on Basin Street, the first sight is a pyramidal tomb bearing the notice 'St. Louis Cemetery No. 1 — 1720.' But that date does not seem to mean what it suggests. The old-est inscription to be found is dated 1800, though records at the Louisiana State Museum Library list a burial as early as 'Jeanne Durand, slave of André ——, aged 33 years, died May 17, 1772.'

Little is known of burial in New Orleans during colonial days, as interments were beneath the earth and no slabs or monuments remain. Old documents reveal that during an auction sale of lots in Rampart Street, remains of some dead were removed from that area and transferred to the square now bounded by Bienville, Chartres, Conti and Royal Streets, and that in 1743 the cemetery was removed to a site opposite the Charity Hospital of that day, in a square bounded by Toulouse, St. Peter, Burgundy and Ram-part Streets. In 1788 it was transferred once more, this time beyond the ramparts of the old city and one block south. Doctor Erasmus Fenner in his *Southern Medical Reports*, published in 1850, stated, 'In the earliest days of the city the cemetery was situated in rear of the Cathedral, near the *Place d'Armes.*'

When Basin Street was cut through, the cemetery, now outside the original city, lost all the ground from Basin to Rampart Street. Bones dug up in that vicinity as late as 1900 seem to sup-port this fact, and the belief that the present day Saint Louis Number 1 is actually only a portion of the old burying ground. Coffins and bones discovered under Canal Street in 1903 were be-lieved to be the remains of early French and Spanish colonists.

Saint Louis Number 1 is, as is not unusual in Louisiana, divided into Catholic and Protestant sections by a fence, though the Catholic portion is many times larger than the small space filled with deceased Protestants. In the latter section the most pretentious tomb is inscribed to the memory of Eliza W. Claiborne, 'wife of W. C. C. Claiborne, Governor-General of Louisiana, who died at New Orleans on the 27th of September, 1804, in the twenty-first year of her life,' and of Cornelia Tennessee Claiborne, her only child, who died on the same day, aged three years. Also buried here is Micajah Green Lewis, 'brother of Eliza W. Claiborne, who fell in a duel Feb. 14, 1805, in the twenty-fifth year of his age.' It is said that Lewis, Claiborne's secretary, died in defense of the Governor's honor. Just beyond the fence, in the Catholic section, stands another Claiborne tomb, this one inscribed, 'In memory of Clarice Duralde Claiborne, youngest daughter of Martin Duralde of Attakapas, and wife of Wm. C. C. Claiborne, Governor of the Territory of Orleans, who died at New Orleans on the 29th of November, 1809, in the twenty-first year of her age.' On both the tombs of Claiborne's young wives, both dying at twenty-one, is the same epitaph: 'For the virtuous there is a happier and better world.' Claiborne was buried in this second tomb, but was later moved to Metairie Cemetery.

Only a few steps from the Basin Street entrance is the 'Widow Paris' tomb, a three-tiered, whitewashed structure with queer green flowerpots extending on both sides of each tier. On one slab may be read:

FAMILLE VVE. PARIS
née Laveau

Ci-Gît
MARIE PHILOMEN GLAPION

decédée le 11 Juin 1897
agée de soixante-deux ans
Elle fut bonne mère, bonne amie et
regrettée par tous ceux qui l'ont connue
Passants priez pour elle

Here lie the remains of the Widow Paris, the 'first' Marie Laveau, mother of the 'second' voodoo queen bearing the same name, though the epitaph above is probably that of another of the Widow Paris's daughters.

Other interesting tombs include the curious low brick vault of

Étienne de Boré, first mayor of New Orleans, and his grandson, Charles Gayarré, famed historian, and of Paul Morphy, the chess king. The tombs of François Xavier Martin, Claude Treme, Alexander Milne and Oscar Dunn — the mulatto lieutenant-governor under Henry Clay Warmouth — may also be found here, as well as those of members of the Marigny, Fortier and many other prominent New Orleans families of the Creole era. Such epitaphs as '*Mort sur le champ d'honneur*,' '*Victime de son honneur*,' and '*Pour garder intact le nom de famille*' mark the burying places of hot-headed and hot-blooded young Creoles who died for their 'honor' or for their family name.

Saint Louis Number 1 is a close-packed city of the dead, with few trees or shrubs; there is even little grass to be found in the Catholic section. Tombs stand so close together that sometimes it is necessary to squeeze between them in order to get to certain ones, and instead of being laid out in regular squares the place is a haphazard maze without plan or design. Almost all the tombs are white, either of stone or whitewashed bricks, and the effect, especially under a bright sun, is dazzling. Many of the bottom ovens are sunk into the earth, showing only an inch or two, with the inscriptions entirely or partially vanished from view; there is a possibility that in some places an entire 'story' may have been swallowed by the earth. Above, along the tops of the tombs, is cross after cross, sometimes of stone, often of iron, punctuated here and there by an occasional angel or the figure of a lady drooping with grief.

Tragedy of Shakespearean proportions once occurred in Saint Louis Number 1, when a man entombed himself with the remains of his daughter. For a long period this father, suffering under pathological grief, would visit the tomb of his only daughter and unscrew the slab. Then he would gaze for hours at the crumbling casket. One day he entered the cemetery, crawled inside the tomb, fastened the slab as best he could from the inside, and swallowed a vial of laudanum. Late that evening his wife, searching for him, and knowing of his habit of spending hours in the cemetery, went there, noticed the slab not as usual, and found the body, already in its grave.

Among the larger tombs are the Mausoleum of the Orleans

Battalion Artillery and the Mausoleo de la Campania de Voluntaries, the latter bearing an 1848 date. The tomb of the Italian Mutual Benefit Society, a handsome structure, has been called the 'Hex Tomb,' because of the fact that those who planned and built it were the first to be buried therein. I. T. Barelli conceived the idea of the mausoleum and brought Piero Gualdi, a noted sculptor of the period, from Italy for the express purpose of designing the tomb. Gualdi was the first man to be buried there. Barelli was the second.

Myra Clark Gaines is buried in the Catholic section of Saint Louis Number 1, and Daniel Clark, American Consul to Louisiana during the Spanish possession, who she claimed was her father in the famous lawsuit.

The Protestant portion is in bad order; grass and weeds grow high. Many burial places have completely vanished, practically all the headstones lie flat, most are broken. One of the very few tombs displays what is apparently a discrepancy in dates, stating:

Sacred
to the memory of

Miss Margaret H.

daughter of
Mr. Robert Layton

Born May 15, 1821
Died November 14, 1812

Not overly scrupulous guides sometimes point out this tomb and unless carefully examined those appear to be the actual dates. But on close inspection the '1812' proves to be actually '1842,' a portion of the 4 having become almost indistinguishable.

Many of the names on the flat, broken headstones are of heroes of the War of 1812; others are of yellow-fever victims of the epidemic of 1817–18. One reads:

Sacred to the memory of William P. Cauly, midshipman of the U.S. Navy, born Norfolk, Va., Aug. 30, 1796, who fell in the unequal contest between the U.S. gunboat squadron and the British flotilla on Lake Borgne, near New Orleans, Dec. 14, 1811.

Another:

> Erected to the memory of Oliver Parmlee,
> a native of New Orleans, who was killed
> in the defense of the city of New Orleans
> in the battle with the British army Dec. 23, 1814.

The epitaph of a young officer who died of the fever reads
(here and there a word cannot be deciphered):

> By his only remaining brother, William, of
> the United States Navy, this stone is placed,
> sacred to the memory of Capt. Robert Sinclair,
> who in the morning of his days and in the
> bloom of youth fell a victim to yellow fever
> at New Orleans, Aug. 24, 1818.
>
> Lamented youth, beneath this sculptured stone,
> The mortal . . . of his fled spirit lies,
> To wait the call to see a happier home,
> Joined to its shade of glory in the skies.
>
> The high-rolling waves and the loud-rolling
> tempest I have left to the living, for here
> I am anchored in peace, awaiting the return
> of the . . . eat Tide of Life.

Most of the names in this section are decidedly Anglo-Saxon,
in sharp contrast to the Creole ones in the Catholic portion,
many of the young soldiers and fever victims having journeyed
to New Orleans from New England. It is said today that many
New Englanders visit New Orleans in attempts to trace members
of the family tree of whose fate they have no records.

Saint Louis Number 2, not so old and not quite so crowded, as
it covers three city squares, possesses much the same atmosphere
as Number 1, and there are many of the same queer things to be
seen. Here the ovens lining many of the walls are frequently in
a dilapidated state, and the sexton claims have sunk two or three
deep beneath the surface, though this is doubtful. A sign on the
cemetery office gives information not only for this graveyard but
for Number 1 and Number 3 as well. Badly printed and with the
word 'funeral' misspelled, it reads:

St. Louis Cemeteries
No. 1, 2, and 3
Furnerals And Removals

Babies up to one year	$5.00
Children up to five years	6.00
Adults	8.00
Overtime after 5 P.M. per hour	1.00

F. X. Lefebore, Pastor

Some of the ovens are adorned with small balconies of wrought iron, equipped with gates on hinges, sometimes with small iron shelters above, which look as though they might be waiting for ghostly Romeos and Juliets. Many slabs are broken or have vanished; around the office, oven slabs, still bearing names, dates and epitaphs, have been used to form a walk to the tool shed, to the men's rest room, to the office entrance.

Many ovens are empty and ferns and grass grow within. Others are choked with giant spiderwebs. On top of all grass grows and, in the spring, very pretty buttercups and other wild flowers. Some ovens have wooden 'balconies' instead of iron ones. Several have glass cases holding statues of the Virgin and Saint Joseph, as well as fresh or artificial flowers. Many have a crucifix before them, usually set in a stone block in which a single word such as 'Baby' or 'Mama' or 'Annie' is chiseled.

Tombs are embellished with iron wreaths — one has an iron 'crown of thorns' — lead lambs, crosses, crucifixes, conch shells — gilded, silvered or painted — and stone images. One has a pair of beer glasses cemented to it, evidently to be used as flower receptables. Another has a flower-holder which is a long tin, marked 'Roth's Spiced Meats.'

On many tombs are small bas-reliefs depicting graves with willow trees drooping over them, angels flying above headstones, lonely graves on hilltops, backed by the setting sun, angels blowing trumpets, widows and children weeping beside a grave, and sheep 'going home.'

In the rear of Saint Louis Number 2 is the 'Wishing Vault,' an oven distinguished from the others by literally hundreds of red cross marks made with brick, a small piece of which is always resting on the shelf before the vault. Of course it is said that Beautiful Young Ladies steal into the cemetery, make a wish and add their cross mark to the collection, dropping money through a crack in the slab. But at present there is no crack in the slab. Many Negroes believe that the 'second' Marie Laveau is buried here, though others deny this, saying she is buried in the 'Widow Paris' tomb in Saint Louis Number 1, or in Saint Louis Number 3, in Saint Vincent de Paul Cemetery, in St. Roch's Cemetery, in Girod Street Cemetery, etc., etc. Practically every New Orleans graveyard except the Hebrew's Rest has claimed her. From other sources comes the information that the 'Wishing Vault' holds the remains of Marie Contesse, a voodoo priestess of an earlier date than the Laveaus. However, at least one other 'authority,' an employee in the cemetery, stated: 'That oven don't contain nothing but some old bones. Nobody knows who they belonged to; maybe they was yellow-fever victims. I don't know how all this "Wishing Vault" thing started. It's true, though, that people come here and make wishes. I seen lots of 'em. Some of 'em white, some of 'em colored.'

As in Saint Louis Number 1 there are many handsome tombs, some being encircled with iron fences and having iron benches in front. One particularly fine tomb is that of Amable Charbonnet, 'Born December 10, 1790 — Died November 4, 1832.' It is an exquisite example of marblework, there being a floral design, delicately chiseled, a child's head at each corner, and a Masonic emblem at the top front center, all hand carved. The craftsman's signature is chiseled into the base:

DUVEY	MARBRIER
RUE ST. ANDRÉ	POPINCOURT NO. 2
PARIS	

Though imported from Paris more than a century ago, the tomb is nearly as perfect as the day it was built, while others around it, erected much later, are already crumbling.

The tomb of Dominique You, Lafitte's lieutenant, is in Saint Louis Number 2, and is a low structure bearing a Masonic emblem and the epitaph:

Intrépide guerrier sur la terre et
sur l'onde
Il sut dans cent combats signaler
sa valeur
Et ce noveau Bavara sans reproche
et sans peur
Aurait pu sans trembler voir s'écrouler
le monde.

Saint Louis Number 2 was built in 1822, and Saint Louis Number 3, last of the trio of New Orleans graveyards bearing that name, was established about 1833. This one is similar to the others, though it covers more ground and contains more graves and more trees and shrubbery. Saint Louis Number 3 was built on the site of what was once known as Lepers' Land, because Galvez (1777–1785) banished the city's lepers to that neighborhood and his successor, Governor Miro, built a house for them there. At first Saint Louis Number 3 was known as the Bayou Cemetery.

Señor Pépé Lulla sleeps in his own Saint Vincent de Paul Cemetery, though many wonder how peaceful is his slumber. When it was known as the Louisa Street Cemetery, Pépé Lulla owned all the ground for a time, and rumor has it that the Señor helped to fill the graves. The most skilled duelist of his day, there are so many stories concerning Pépé's artistry with swords and pistols that undoubtedly many of them are romantic fables. It is said he mastered every weapon, was the South's greatest expert with the saber, was invulnerable when armed with the rapier or small sword. He could balance an egg on his small son's head and crack the shell at thirty paces with a bullet. He could hit a coin tossed into the air twenty-five times in succession without missing once, using a rifle. He was a positive genius with a bowie knife. If he didn't fill a graveyard singlehanded, says the legend, he at least furnished one with a beginning to be proud of, and one of his less serious diversions was to wander the aisles of his cemetery and knock the pipes from between the teeth of Negro workmen with rifle shots. Only occasionally, however, did he ever receive a new client for his cemetery in this particular fashion; he was too capable a marksman.

Now he lies in Saint Vincent de Paul himself, in a modest tomb, simply inscribed:

Joseph Lulla, Sr.
Native of Mahon, Spain
Died March 6, 1888
Aged 73 years.

Saint Vincent de Paul (Louisa Street) Cemetery was, however, built by a priest in 1832 and acquired by Señor Lulla about two years before the War Between the States. In general it is much in the tradition of the Saint Louis cemeteries. There are ovens in many of the walls, tombs, often of fine design, and few ground burials.

Cards reading as follows may be seen on many of the ovens:

IMPORTANT NOTICE
Anyone interested in the remains of person
or persons interred in this vault

CALL AT CEMETERY OFFICE TODAY

This indicates that the rent is unpaid and that the remains are about to be removed. A charred pile of coffin handles and other refuse in one portion of the grounds shows that remains *have* been removed.

Epitaphs offer some variety. Occasionally a word is mis spelled:

THE FAMBILY
of
Jake Hendrick
and
George Ticker

A headstone of a plot expressed appreciation for the departed:

Sacred
to the memory of

Margaret Keym

16th Sept. 1826
30th Oct. 1850

This stone was erected by her husband
that knew her worth.

The following, on an oven slab, is mystifying because of the additional notation.

Louise J. Stuart
wife of
Claude J. Barrilleaux
Died Sept. 19, 1934

Beneath, in pencil, is: 'C. J. COME SEE F. G.,' as if someone had used this means of communicating with the husband of the deceased.

Saint Vincent de Paul's is famed as the last resting place of a noted gypsy queen. On November 9, 1916, word spread through lower New Orleans that an unusual funeral procession was in progress. Men, women and children lined the streets near the graveyard to watch the long line of carriages and the mourners marching on foot, all garbed in their vivid gypsy costumes, munching grapes as they walked and drinking wine from huge cups. Marie, daughter of Bosche, King of the Tinker Gypsies, was being borne to her grave.

The body was placed in a large, specially constructed tomb, and after it was sealed all members of the tribe made indentations in the soft cement with coins of many nations. The ceremony proceeded with dances and singing by many of the gypsies. Finally each man and woman of the tribe approached the tomb and sprinkled wine over it, then drank the remainder from his or her bottle. After this, all departed silently.

But the next day they returned, spread long tables before the tomb and held a feast. After masons had applied a second coat of cement, certain members of the tribe, apparently 'royalty,' made impressions in the new cement with their rings. After the marble slab was set in place, grapes were thrown against the tomb. Then, after lighting a candle in a black receptacle on the tomb, the tribe departed.

Every time a Tinker Gypsy comes to New Orleans his presence may be noted by a candle burning on the grave, and frequently grapes are seen about the tomb. In 1937 a man came to the sexton and demanded that the marble slab be removed. This was done, and as soon as the stranger saw the impressions of the rings beneath, he asked that the slab be replaced, apparently satisfied that the royal remains had not been disturbed. He then drew wine and grapes from his pocket and performed the usual rites, lighted a fresh candle. Then he made a queer request. Would the sexton do this for him each year? Each year two bottles of wine and some grapes would be sent, and the extra bottle of wine would be in small payment for the trouble. In the event of his own death, the sexton was to pass on the custom to someone else.

'Come on down next year and watch me play Tinker Gypsy,' the sexton invited. 'Every year on November 9th the grapes and wine arrive and I've always done as I promised. You see, before the stranger left, he told me quietly, "I have come over ten thousand miles just for this. Marie, Queen of the Tinker Gypsies, was my mother!" '

There have been reports of 'whizzing noises' from within some of the vaults, but the sexton says it is his belief that the 'whizzing noises' are only bats which sometimes get inside the tombs. When there was an arch over one of the gates, visitors complained of being followed by an unseen presence. They could distinctly hear footsteps, but there was never anyone in sight. Finally the arch was destroyed. The sexton says that this was caused by the echo of the walker's own footsteps and was an acoustical rather than a psychic phenomenon.

Then there is the story of the woman who used to visit the cemetery every evening, light a candle before a vault and kneel to pray. This would, in itself, have caused no excitement, as it is a common sight in New Orleans graveyards. The strange thing was that the flame of the candle never flickered, never went out until it burned down to a black smudge. Rain, wind and storm had no effect upon it. Much speculation began as to the identity of the woman. Was she a witch? A saint? Every description conceivable was broadcast; she was white and beautiful; she was young; she was old; she was an octoroon, a lovely pale tan creature who came to pray at the tomb of her white lover; she was a wrinkled hag as black as jet; she was Creole; she was foreign; she was a voodoo priestess. No one ever decided, though hundreds must have seen her. Only one thing is certain: for over a month she came and lighted her candles and knelt in prayer, and the defiant candles defied all natural law and burned through wind and rain. Then she vanished as quietly as she had come.

Saint Roch's Campo Santo is one of the most unusual cemeteries in New Orleans. Surrounded by high brick walls, in which are the usual ovens, there are chapel-like niches in the four corners and at the middle of each wall, forming a Way of the Cross, all marked with wooden stations and serving as small shrines. Saint Roch's, strangely, has the appearance of being of great age, though it is not nearly so old as it appears.

In the center aisle is a huge cross, holding a life-sized figure of Christ; before it is a sundial and a reclining image of a child. There is a strange belief that the child is not really a statue, but the petrified body of the first child buried in the cemetery. The toes are missing from one foot, and many persons stoop and feel the broken place, mistaking the porous appearance of the interior of the statue for petrified human flesh. But there is no truth to the story. Cemetery officials have positive proof that the statue was imported from Italy, *and is a statue*.

But it is Saint Roch's Chapel that attracts most visitors. Though the slender Gothic building is only a little more than sixty years old, it has the appearance of a medieval structure. Inside, replicas of human limbs and organs hanging against one wall testify to the cures attributed to prayers offered to Saint Roch. Beneath are stacked crutches, braces and artificial limbs. On a wall opposite are scores of little marble plaques, square, circular and heart-shaped, each bearing one word: 'Thanks.' The shrine is famous for 'healing.'

The chapel contains but seven pews, five on one side, two on the other. On the altar is a statue of Saint Roch with his dog; beneath, in a glass-fronted tomb, a life-sized image of Christ removed from the cross.

Besides his efficacy in rendering 'cures,' Saint Roch is popular with New Orleans girls, who go to the chapel to pray for husbands, despite the belief that 'Saint Roch will give you what you want, but he always takes something else away.' Saint Roch is thought to be one of the eccentric saints like Saint Anthony, whom some New Orleans folks say must always be addressed roughly, with a threat such as, 'Look here, Saint Anthony, you'd better grant my wish or I'll kick you in the pants.

Other people turn the saint's statue with its face to the wall and they say he obeys their wish in a hurry.

At the foot of the altar within the shrine is buried Father Peter Leonard Thevis, who alone and with his own hands built the chapel. The inscription — in German — states that Father Thevis was born February 7, 1837, and died August 21, 1895. Two other priests are also buried beneath the marble floor — one, Reverend F. X. Couppens of Saint Theresa's Church, who died in 1897; the other, Reverend J. D. Thevis, former assistant pastor at Holy Trinity Church.

In Saint Roch Number 2, just behind Number 1, the Mausoleum of Michael the Archangel still stands, looking even more ancient than does the Saint Roch Chapel, though it was erected in 1891. There is little else in this square. Three of the walls contain ovens, but many of these are empty or in a disreputable state. There are few graves, even fewer tombs.

The mausoleum looks like something left over from an air raid. The Gothic building is flanked by medieval towers, one containing the former belfry. Beneath and in all the walls are crypts which were formerly occupied by deceased priests and nuns, but are now empty with a sole exception, this one bearing a comparatively new marble slab and a name. Old and rain-beaten notices on all sides of the ruins warn that all remains must be removed by November 1, 1931, and apparently this order was thoroughly obeyed. Ferns, goldenrod and Virginia creeper grow abundantly on the roof and wave from the yawning crypts. All the once handsome stained-glass windows are smashed and most of the murals, executed by Carmelite monks — formerly at Carmel, Louisiana — are defaced, though a few are in remarkably good condition. Once statues of saints occupied pilasters on all sides of the exterior of the structure, but all are gone now except one which has no head. There has been much discussion regarding whether the mausoleum should be demolished or restored. Once some of the crypts were rented out at ten dollars a month and many were let to Chinese, and the sexton remembers seeing fruit and other foods left outside the slabs.

In 1937 a ghost came out of a tomb in Saint Roch Cemetery Number 2 and sat on a grave. She did this every night for weeks.

Louis Haley, the sexton, said he saw her every night and that she was positively a spook; he approached her several times and she always faded right back into her tomb and was nowhere to be seen about. As soon as the story broke in the newspapers, thousands of people crowded about the walls determined to see a real spirit for once in their lives. Gradually the story died a natural death when it was discovered that the ghost-woman was only a peculiar shadow caused by the combination of a white urn and two trees. This sad fact was revealed by the *New Orleans Tribune* on July 10, 1937.

The oldest Protestant cemetery in New Orleans is the Girod Cemetery. This is, without a doubt, the weariest graveyard in the world. The whole place seems to sigh perpetually; even the fig trees which grow within the grounds sag with hopeless acquiescence to time and neglect. Grass and weeds are knee-high, and grow abundantly on tombs and graves and in the walks. Thick wistaria vines twist and coil grotesquely about ovens, as if to squeeze out the bones of the buried. And in many places skulls and bones are bleaching under the sun in dismal symbolization of decay and dissolution. Poe might have found inspiration in this morbid and macabre scene. A family of black cats add their bit to the sinister atmosphere, following visitors and purring and rubbing at their ankles, or sleeping lazily in the sun amid a miscellaneous collection of skulls and femurs.

Yet the tombs and vaults in Girod Cemetery possess epitaphs that are rich with sentiment. Among them is one revealing a great love. J. W. Caldwell, a prominent citizen of the early nineteenth century, fell madly in love with Jane Placide, an actress at the old Saint Charles Theatre in New Orleans. Unable to marry, because his wife refused him a divorce, their clandestine affair was the scandal of the day. And when the beautiful actress died in 1835, Caldwell chose lines from the poetry of Barry Cornwall as an epitaph, which, even more than a century later, proclaims the depth and fervor of their passion:

> There's not an hour
> of day or dreaming night but I am
> with thee;
> There's not a breeze but whispers
> of thy name,

And not a flower that sleeps
beneath the moon
But in its fragrance tells a tale
of thee.

Another tomb is that of John David Fink, who left money for an asylum for Protestant widows, a refuge which does not accept spinsters. Once John David Fink had loved a girl who ridiculed his devotion and told him she would rather be an old maid than his wife, and work out her own destiny. His will, bequeathing the funds for the Fink Home in New Orleans, contained a clause forbidding that any unmarried woman ever be admitted. 'Let every old maid work out her destiny,' said the document with grim irony.

One of the most interesting epitaphs in Girod Cemetery is the briefest; it says, 'After a Painless Death he passed to Paradise.' Another reads:

William Lewis
April 16th, 1870

Also Gone to the Golden City

Mary E. Lewis
May 10, 1882

And — from a wife to her husband:

Robert E. Conway
Died May 8, 1875, aged 61

Dearest, forgive the thought that would wish thee here.

On an oven wherein lie the remains of a young Englishman is this rather pathetic inscription:

Sacred
to the memory of

HENRY KENDALL

born in the county
of Cumberland, England
who died 26, Sept. 1841
aged 29 years.

By foreign hands his dying eyes were closed,
By foreign hands his manly limbs composed,
By foreign hands his humble grave adorned,
By strangers honored, and by strangers mourned.

The Girod Cemetery was at one time troubled with ghoulish thieves, who stole iron and brass from the tombs, and carried off flowers and shrubs. Both sexes seem to have been suspected, for the *Crescent City Weekly*, May 2, 1841, reprimanded them in this fashion:

Lady, forsooth! A lady, Mr. Editor, is a being so refined in her feelings, that she would shun the possibility of inflicting pain on anyone, much less would she commit a moral wrong. ... A lady would intuitively shrink from such an act as this. As to the male of the species, all that need be said of him is that a man who will steal in a graveyard cannot have the slightest pretensions to the character of a gentleman.

Girod Cemetery reflects in a small way what all New Orleans graveyards once were. In early days burials were all in the ground and were terrifying affairs. Caskets were lowered into gurgling pools of water and were sunk into pits of oozing mud. As often as not, the coffin would capsize as the water seeped within. Heavy rains or a storm would cast newly buried, half-decomposed cadavers to the surface. A correspondent for the *Courier* of June 11, 1833, described a walk in the Catholic Burial Ground in this way:

The horrid image of this place is still in my mind. I cannot drive it from my imagination. The tombs are all above ground, and those who can afford it will never be buried under-ground....

This graveyard is all on a dead level and on rainy days inundated with water. It is a morass, a swamp partly rescued from its wilderness. I followed the procession to the grave. The coffin was taken from the hearse.

I now watched the process of interment.... The body was that of a colored person who had died of cholera (which is an epidemic now). They tarried to see the last of their friend.

The grave was not over two feet and a half deep, I measured it for curiosity. The bottom was soft mud into which could be

thrust a stick to almost any depth. The water was within a
foot of the top of the grave. The clods of earth around all
clay, such as earth as would be dug from a bog. The coffin was
put into the grave and it floated so as to be level with the surface.

A negro, a fiend-looking brute, with his pantaloons above
his knees, all covered with clay in which he had been working, without hat, without coat or a whole shirt — but with a
hoe and a spade, mounted the top of the coffin, and tramped it
under the water, and then a brother-looking being threw the
clods on. . . .

I then looked around among the graves. A hole here and
holes there were all ready for the next comers — some six feet
or more long, some three or four feet long. The water was in
all the graves. The ground beneath our feet was like that of a
swamp the surface of which the sun had encrusted. I tumbled
over broken coffins, pieces of which were piled in little heaps,
and pieces of which were placed as stakes to mark the spot of
the last buried.

The very earth gave way under my feet. The vegetation
was that of a swamp. The rank weeds flourished roughly over
many a dead body. Old sticks, old poles, such as our garden-
ers stick peas with, while sides of coffins were put up as grave
stands. What a spectacle!. . . I hurried away, sickening from
the spectacle. For from the earth pestilence seemed to be issuing. In many places the odours were insufferable. . . .

I went to the Protestant, the American burying ground, but
not any were as neat as I saw in the French graveyard. . . .

The Americans here would not tolerate it, if they made this
their abiding place and not the place to alight and make money
in. But no man calculates on dying here. . . . I had heard much
of the trenches or pits in which the cholera victims were buried. Language cannot, if it were proper to array words in the
description, portray the facts as they happened at that alarm-
ing season. A friend tells me the worst accounts, but half
realized the terror of those times. He saw a few bodies without coffins piled in masses around these pits. The dray-men
raced off, full gallop to the yard, so brisk was their business,
and then chuckled at their profits.

Two of these pits were filled with victims; and dirt was
thrown over them. The earth was moist and with a stick I

sounded the ditches. My stick was pushed down with ease.
I know not how far it would have driven. The exhalations
from these ditches were unsufferable. I turned from it to catch
a breath of less contaminated air. . . .

I lost only a breakfast from this stride among the tombs,
gratifying a curiosity which is now quite satiated!

Of course the cholera and yellow-fever epidemics added much
to the horror, and the death rate in New Orleans was appalling.
The *New Orleans City Guide* shows that the rate per thousand from
1800 to 1880 was scandalous, that the lowest was 40.22 from
1860 to 1870, while the highest was 63.55 from 1830 to 1840.

During the great yellow-fever epidemic of 1853 there was even
a serious shortage of gravediggers and men were offered five dollars an hour to perform this task. The streets of New Orleans
rumbled with cart wheels, whose drivers stopped before houses
with the grim invitation, 'Bring out your dead!' And by the
light of flaring torches, shallow graves were dug and the bodies
hurriedly covered. When the rains came, it was not unusual for
these decaying bodies to be washed up. The *New Orleans Bee*,
August 9, 1853, complained:

> Upon inquiry yesterday we ascertained that the festering
> and decaying bodies which had been deposited in the Lafayette
> Cemetery, had at last been consigned to mother earth. The
> eyes will no longer be pained and the nostrils offended by the
> further continuance of the horrible neglect. The Mayor of
> our City, though absolutely destitute of all direct authority,
> upon learning the facts on Sunday, secured the labor of the
> chain gang, and set them immediately to work. After many
> hours of incessant labor, the task was completed yesterday.
>
> A more disgraceful administration of our municipal affairs
> have never been witnessed. It is unworthy of a civilized peo-
> ple. . . .

In his *General Butler in New Orleans*, James Parton stated:

> It is not generally known at the North, that in the worst
> years, the mortality from yellow fever in New Orleans exceeds
> that from any epidemic that has raged in a civilized commu-
> nity. It is worse than the modern cholera, worse than the
> small-pox before inoculation, worse than the ancient plague.

A competent and trustworthy visitor gives the facts of the yellow fever season of 1853, the most fatal year ever known:

'Commencing on the 1st of August, with one hundred and six deaths by yellow fever, one hundred and forty-two by all diseases, the number increased daily, until for the first week, ending on the 7th, they amounted to nine hundred and nine deaths by yellow fever, one thousand one hundred and eighty-six of all diseases. The next week showed a continued increase to one thousand five hundred and twenty-six of all diseases. This was believed to be the maximum. There had been nothing like it in the history of any previous epidemics, and no one believed it could be exceeded. But the next week gave a mournful refutation of these predictions and calculations; for that ever memorable week, the total deaths were one thousand five hundred and seventy-six, of yellow fever one thousand three hundred and forty-six. But the next week commenced more gloomily still. The deaths on the 22d of August were two hundred and eighty-three of all diseases, two hundred and thirty-nine of yellow fever. From this it began slowly to decrease.

... Funeral processions crowded every street. No vehicles could be seen except doctors' cabs and coaches, passing to and from the cemeteries, and hearses, often solitary, taking their way toward those gloomy destinations. The hum of trade was silent. The levee was a desert. The streets, wont to shine with fashion and beauty, were silent. The tombs — the homes of the dead — were the only places where there was life, where crowds assembled, where the incessant rumbling of carriages, the trampling of feet, the murmur of voices, and all the signs of active, stirring life could be heard and seen.

'To realize the fierce horror and virulence of the pestilence, you must go into the crowded localities of the laboring classes, into the miserable shanties which are the disgrace of the city, where the poor immigrant class cluster together in filth, sleeping a half-dozen in one room, without ventilation, and having access to filthy wet yards, which have never been filled up, and when it rains are converted into green puddles — fit abodes for frogs and sources of poisonous malaria. Here you will find scenes of woe, misery and death, which will haunt your memory for all time to come. Here you will see the dead and the dying, the sick and the convalescent, in one and the same bed.

Here you will see the living babe sucking death from the yellow breast of his dead mother. Here father, mother, and children die in one another's arms. Here you will find whole families swept off in a few hours, so that none are left to mourn or procure the rites of burial. Offensive odors frequently drew neighbors to such awful spectacles. Corpses would thus proclaim their existence, and enforce the observances due them. What a terrible disease!...

As many as three hundred persons a day were buried during the 1853 epidemic, an accomplishment that was almost impossible. Sometimes caskets were simply borne to the graveyards, stacked up, and left waiting their turn. Conditions arising from this necessitated extreme measures. One day the *Louisiana Spectator* notified citizens:

Residents will be glad to know that the spreading of lime and the constant burning of tar has removed all traces of odor so concentrated during the last few days.

On March 23, 1835, a funeral road was established in New Orleans, according to the 1835 Scrapbook at the Howard-Tilton Library, when an ordinance was passed to contract with a J. Arrowsmith for a railroad from St. Claude Street toward Bayou St. John, its purpose being to convey funeral parties to the cemeteries. There were detailed terms as to the number of corpses to be carried each trip, separate cars being provided for Whites and for slaves. Branch lines were to run into all the cemeteries. Apparently, however, the project amounted to little.

As late as May 29, 1875, the *New Orleans Bulletin* contained a dreadful accusation against conditions in the Pauper's or Locust Grove Cemetery, located in Sixth Street between Freret and Locust Streets:

... In our other cemeteries, friends and relations in the pangs of bereavement rear, above loved ones, and their last homes, mausoleums of regret which in a great measure, serve to mask the terror of the dark angel, but here death was visible everywhere. Visible in the latch you raised to enter the yard, made from an old coffin, visible in the stained and mouldy winding sheet, rotting in the laughing clover beside the walk. On the left of the central path, it was evident that friends had cared for many of the graves, but on the right the picture was a sad one indeed. Here in a pile some five feet in height were some fifty babies untenanted. After the weary little bodies had wasted away, they were heaped carelessly together like so much old lumber, one upon the other, and the sacrilegious flies seemed to be feasting upon the sickening odor hanging over them. Scattered about lay coffins of all sizes, and the reporter turning over one remarkable for its length, was almost stifled by the stench, to the effects of which was added that a case of small pox had been taken out of it. Coffin lids were used in many places to mend the fences, and so many were the uses they were put to, the whole place breathed of destruction and pestilence.

Charity Hospital in New Orleans once had a wagon to carry the dead to the Pauper's Field, and on at least one occasion a driver seems to have done more than his duty. The *New Orleans Bulletin* of May 29, 1875, related the story under the following 'shocker' headlines:

BURIED ALIVE

SICKENING TALE OF OUR HOSPITAL DEAD

A MAN IN THE CHARITY WAGON REVIVES

HE ATTEMPTS TO GET OUT OF HIS COFFIN

THE DRIVER SMOTHERS HIM

FULL DETAILS AND STATEMENT OF WITNESS

The story accused the driver of killing the 'dead' man as the latter attempted to get out of his coffin. A witness (C. H. Beggs) testified that he saw the incident, stating, according to the newspaper: 'The driver lifted out a coffin and was about to deposit it in the hole prepared for it, when the occupant of the coffin kicked off the lid and cried, "For God's sake, do not bury me alive!" The driver picked up a brick, and crying, "You ——— ———, I have a doctor's certificate that you are dead, and I'm going to bury you." He then struck the man, and stunning him or killing him, proceeded with the burial.' The *Bulletin* remarked that 'The police took the matter very coolly and did not seem to think it worth working up.' It then announced that a reporter was as-

"Skeletons," a painting by Edward Schoenberger, was inspired by the New Orleans cemeteries
Louisiana Art Project

The Devil in a Cemetery, from a painting by John McCrady
Louisiana Art Project

The Mausoleum of Michael the Archangel. Abandoned Gothic chapel in the Campo Santo adjoining St. Roch's Cemetery. Note the empty tombs in the walls

Old tomb, Girod Cemetery

Charity Hospital Cemetery, the Potter's Field

Prices posted for cemetery burial and removal, St. Louis Cemeteries

signed to the case, who was determined to get to the bottom of the affair.

Various witnesses made statements, scarcely two alike. Melinda Smith testified: 'I was close to the wagon. I saw that man move his hand. The driver took a cushion off the seat, put it over the man's face and sat on him until he was smothered. Then he took a hammer and nailed down the lid.' Mary Thompson said: 'I saw a man in that coffin He was alive. The driver picked up a baby's coffin that was also in the wagon and put it on top of him, and sat on it.' Rosa Johnson said: 'I saw the arms of the man raised. I know he was alive. The driver put a pillow over his head and smothered him.' William Harrison said: 'I looked into the coffin. The man was breathing and the driver had dropped a big cobblestone on his chest.' Mrs. Louise Weber said: 'The gravedigger told me the driver was a funny kind of man and he did it all as a joke.'

It was discovered that the deceased was one George Banks, a colored youth of nineteen, who had entered Charity Hospital as a smallpox victim. Authorities there identified the driver as one Jim Connors, saying that 'Naturally Jim's work is suitable to his nature. You can't expect him to be very goodhearted or tender. But he wouldn't commit murder.' Schwartz, sexton of the Pauper's Field, swore: 'The man was dead. I buried him. The coffin had fallen to pieces from the jolting of the wagon over the cobblestone streets. I've known Jim a long time.' Nowhere is it mentioned what Jim Connors had to say. However, he was actually arrested and held, according to the *Bulletin*. That seems to have been the end of it. There is no further mention of the case. Evidently it was never satisfactorily concluded.

Even in days made dark by epidemics and death, Orleanians retained their sense of humor. On August 30, 1840, the *Daily Picayune* said:

> It is necessary again to inform the public that we never insert marriage or obituary notices unless when fully authorized, either by personal knowledge or known endorsement. Vicious persons would have it in their power to create great mischief if this rule were not enforced. An obituary notice came to this office yesterday unauthenticated, and consequently it does not appear.

Years later, on September 13, 1876, the *New Orleans Times* told of fun in jail:

> Directly a new man beams upon the prison yard he is sadly informed that a fellow-being having just departed from life, the funeral ceremonies will be straightway inaugurated, and of course participation is expected. Then joining in a procession which soon forms, he moves to a secluded portion of the yard, where robed in the habiliments of the dead, looking for all the world like a dead man, with lighted candles placed at head and feet, lies a negro — the supposed late lamented.
>
> In accordance with the traditional observance of such occasions, each member of the procession, as he passes, stoops to imprint a last loving kiss upon the brow of the deceased Senegambian, and so in turn the stranger seeks also the kiss, when behold, the corpse, heretofore well behaved, awakens to sudden animation and grasping the stranger about the neck holds firmly in a grip of iron, while the balance of the negroes, already provided with sticks, proceed to belabor that stranger until he howls much after the fashion of the festive dervish and when his tormentors have sufficiently enjoyed his misery, they let up and proceed to console him with the information that thereafter he will be one of the boys, and that moreover he may have the first whack at the next candidate for the sacrifice.

In Lafayette Cemetery Number 1 (perhaps better known as Washington Cemetery, because of its location on Washington Avenue) is the tomb of Henry Watkins Allen, governor of Louisiana during the War Between the States. His epitaph is slightly baffling with its four lines of confused rhetoric. The chiseled words announce dramatically:

> Your friends will be proud to know that Louisiana had a governor who, with an opportunity of securing millions in gold, preferred being honest in a strange land without a cent.

Cypress Grove Cemetery (also known as Firemen's Cemetery because of the mausoleum there for firefighters of another era) contains a burial place wherein many Chinese of the city are temporarily entombed, to await the passing of a year and a day, when they may be shipped home to Cathay, though the apparently endless wars have prevented these shipments during the past few years. Large Chinese characters are inscribed above this mausoleum's entrance, and figures in the same language are scribbled in pencil on many of the vaults within, though often the name and date of death are also written in English. Many slabs are cracked and broken and coffins and remains are at times partially exposed. One slab has a window in its center. Pieces of burnt joss sticks litter the floor and the twin fireplaces at one end, the latter for the purpose of heating for cold-weather funerals. The entire place is in a disreputable state.

'The gravediggers of Carrollton and Saint Mary Cemeteries are on strike for back pay.' Thus read signs carried by pickets who stalked up and down before the Carrollton and Saint Mary Cemeteries one day. Behind the radicals marched a diminutive, grinning colored boy, beating a large tin pan with a stick to attract attention. According to these pickets the sexton owed them eighty dollars' back pay, and there was no reason why they could not go on strike as everybody else was doing these days. So was the labor movement carried to the grave.

Carrollton Cemetery enjoyed a mild sensation in 1933 when the corpse described in the following paragraph, from the *New Orleans States*, May 7, 1933, was discovered:

> The body of a man, apparently petrified, is still attracting persons to the old Catholic cemetery in Carrollton, some of them having come from St. Bernard Parish. Apparently the tomb was broken open by vandals. The iron casket is exposed and, by turning the iron cover over the small round glass window set in the coffin top, one can get a good view of the man. The inscription on the tomb shows that he died in 1879. He has red hair, but is bald on top. He has a mustache. His eyes, which are blue, are open, and his mouth is open. He wore a turned-down collar of the period.

Carrollton Cemetery has a decidedly German atmosphere, names such as Weber, Schaeffer, Muller and Francken appearing on many slabs and headstones. To the rear is the Negro section, which is in a dismal, weed-infested state. Here one may read such epitaphs as 'Alcida Lewis, faithful servant of The Family J. A. Legendre.'

Near Cyprus Grove, already mentioned, at the end of Canal Street, is a cluster of cemeteries, including Saint John's, Greenwood, Saint Patrick Number 1 and Saint Patrick Number 2. In contrast to the older graveyards these are in general in good order and well kept, with the exception of the Saint Patricks, which are usually in a deplorable condition. Here weeds and grass grow knee-high, except at All Saints' time, when there is an annual cleaning and painting program. Irishmen used to be interred free of charge in these graveyards named for their patron saint, but this has long been discontinued. Saint John's Cemetery is the home of Hope Mausoleum, a handsome marble building of generous dimensions and tasteful architecture, the first of its kind built in the South. Still expanding, when completed Hope Mausoleum will be one of the most beautiful of such burial places in the country.

Metairie Cemetery, almost around the corner from these others, is in even sharper contrast to the old graveyards. Of immense acreage and holding tombs of great cost and elaborateness, besides being impressively landscaped, it has become a showplace for visitors to New Orleans. Originally a racetrack, the tremendous grounds were converted to their present use by Charles T. Howard, president of both the New Orleans Racing Association and the Louisiana State Lottery Company at that time. The racecourse became the main drive, other fine roads were laid, artificial lagoons dug, trees, flowers and shrubs planted, the result being the creation of a lovely park fit to hold the elegant tombs of the wealthy people of the city.

The *Daily Picayune* reported on June 6, 1872:

> The task of converting the Metairie Race Course into a cemetery, which will compare favorably with any in the country, is receiving the attention of those gentlemen who conceived the plan. The organization of the Metairie Cemetery Company was perfected at a meeting held on May 24, 1872, when the officers were elected: W. S. Pike, President and W. C. Lipscombe, Secretary.

At the entrance stands the Moriarity Monument, a tall shaft embellished by four life-sized female statues. It is said that

Daniel Moriarity ordered a sculptor to do a group of 'Four Graces' for his wife's monument and when informed there were but Three Graces — Hope, Faith and Charity — he insisted that there be Four Graces on the monument anyway. So, the sculptor obliged, and there they are — Four Graces.

A statue of Stonewall Jackson dominates the marble shaft of the monument to the Army of Virginia, and Albert Sidney Johnson rides his bronze horse atop the mound covering dead heroes of the Army of the Tennessee, which include the remains of General Beauregard. Elsewhere in Metairie are tombs of General Richard Taylor, General Fred N. Ogden and General John B. Hood, all important Confederate leaders. Jefferson Davis was buried here, but was removed.

But perhaps the most interesting tomb is that of a scarlet lady, once reigning queen of New Orleans's Storyville. Known as the Scarlet Grave of Josie Arlington, this tomb has attracted so much attention from a curious public that on several occasions police detachments have had to remain all night on the spot to maintain order. Near-by corpses of respectable females must spin as on spits with envy.

It seems that on certain nights Josie's tomb glows with an eerie, fiery light, that, though appropriate, causes as much commotion as did the lady during her hectic life, as if even Death could not completely extinguish her brilliance. Almost as much of a mystery is the bronze figure of a girl rapping on the door of the tomb. Sometimes, vow folk who live near the cemetery, the Maiden becomes angry and pounds the slab with both metallic fists with a din that may be heard for blocks. Strangers in the city inquiring about the noise are told, 'It's the Maiden trying to get in.' You see, rumor had it that Josie possessed her own code regarding her elaborate Storyville bagnio: she never permitted a virgin to enter her establishment, and when she erected her tomb in 1911, she had the statue placed there to symbolize this principle. Twice the Maiden has taken walks. Once she was found lying in a dump heap in the rear of the cemetery, the other time sprawled on her face in the grass along the Bayou St. John. People say the Maiden tired of knocking and tried to run away. Both incidents occurred on Halloween nights. The conventional-minded blame small boys.

But there is another legend concerning the Maiden. This one states that the statue is of Josie, herself. As a young girl she had stayed out too late, they say, and her father locked her out of her home, and though she pounded the door and pleaded with him, he would never allow her to enter again. So she went away to a career that was so successful as to allow her to build herself a tomb which cost seventeen thousand dollars.

As far as the scarlet light is concerned, police once became tired of the public's curiosity and decided it was the reflection of a traffic light on the pink marble, and this is what they told everyone who asked. But there is not a traffic light anywhere near it.

At the entrance to Holt Cemetery, where only Negroes are buried, is a sign reading:

NOTICE

ALL PERSONS WHO HAVE BOXES
IN THIS CEMETERY MUST KEEP
SAME CLEAN, OTHERWISE THEY
WILL BE USED FOR OTHERS.
BUY A HEADBOARD WITH YOUR BOX
and HAVE IT LETTERED HERE price 2.50, 3.00 and up.

On the other side of the entrance is another notice, with these instructions:

HEADQUARTERS
PAINTED
& RE-LETTERED 1.50 up
By a Headboard with your Box
& have it Lettered here
BOXES FOR SALE
SINGLE $9.00 Double $11.00 with Filling

These 'boxes' are ground plots surrounded by plain twelve-inch boards, about six feet long and four feet wide, each and every board painted a 'battleship gray.' The purpose of the board is to provide inexpensive coping, so as to keep the dirt from washing from the grave. Headboards are also of wood with epitaphs painted thereon, usually crudely, and with black paint. There are a very few marble or granite headstones.

The white sexton at Holt is well acquainted with the superstitions prevalent among the Negroes who bury their dead there. 'Sometimes when we dig open a grave we find all kinds of things,' he said. 'I've seen potatoes scooped out and filled with salt, and the top placed back on, and I've seen the people take some of the dirt from the grave home to sprinkle around their house. That's all voodoo stuff, you know. Some of 'em throw packages of needles or papers of pins on top the grave.' He smiled. 'And you ought to hear how they yell when they have a funeral!'

Negroes say, 'Trample on the dust of the dead lightly,' and though it has a subtler meaning, Negroes don't walk on graves without experiencing some qualms. Perhaps the best-known belief has to do with lizards. Hundreds of these small green reptiles may be seen darting through shrubbery or in and out the crevices of tombs. And, say those who believe such things, he who kills or maims one in a graveyard will undoubtedly die within a year.

> Kill ole lizard on the grave,
> Ain't no charm your life can save.

But it is extremely good luck should one cross your hand. On sunny days, when the chameleons are certain to appear in great numbers, many people may be seen in the graveyards resting their hands against tombs and waiting, sometimes for hours, for one of the little green lizards to crawl voluntarily over them.

Funerals are not what they used to be. Nowadays we strive to lift as much of the gloomy atmosphere surrounding them as is possible under the circumstances; in other days every effort seems to have been made to create one as grim and mournful as possible.

'I remembers lots of stuff about funerals in them olden times,' admitted Eddie Ybos, retired hearse driver. 'It makes me mad the way they have funerals now. I see them with all the new-fangled doo-dads — the way they put the coffin on top the grave on a artificial grass carpet and don't dump it in the hole until the family has gone home. They even have a little iron cart to wheel that coffin to the hearse from the house, and from the hearse to the grave It makes me think of the days when they really had funerals.'

In many sections of the State, an announcement of the death, the hour of dying, the place and hour of the funeral and other details were tacked up in prominent spots, usually on posts and trees. The notices were black-bordered, usually handwritten, though later they were sometimes typed or printed. Creoles of New Orleans had a 'Death Notice Blackboard' at the old Saint Louis Cathedral, and practically every Catholic Church in the State possessed the same convenience. These notices may still be seen in the Cajun portions of the State.

'Now you just look in the papers to see who is dead,' said Eddie Ybos, 'and then you call your friends up on the telephone and tell 'em. But in my time we had to tack the notices on posts or sheds, or anywhere we could. Most of the ones I seen were handwritten. You had to get so much stuff on 'em. You know, who the dead man was — husband of so and so, cousin of so and so, uncle of so and so; you know how New Orleans people have relatives. Grocery stores would let us put the notices up on their sides. Poles and fences and stores used to have tons of tacks in 'em, from people ripping old notices down and not bothering to take out the tacks. Usually notices were just put up in the neighborhood where the dead person lived, but if they had money they'd spread 'em all over town. High-faluting people, I mean.'

Before the advent of the automobile the horses pulling the hearse were draped with black and decorated with black plumes on their heads, if the person were old or even middle-aged; white was used for children and very young adults. The horses were often well trained, marching with impressive dignity, taking a single step with each note of the music, if there were a band. Old people were buried in black coffins and the door of the home was adorned with a black crêpe. For middle-aged persons and married individuals of any age, lavender or gray was used; white was always for children.

At the hour of death all clocks were stopped in the home and if some family heirloom refused to stop it was broken, if necessary. Mirrors were covered, and the crêpe hung on the front door. Many families had special coffee-pots, which would hold perhaps a full gallon, which they reserved only for wakes. One family in New Orleans retained the same pot for twenty years, and it was often borrowed for wakes by friends and neighbors. Some of these customs still exist.

Hearse drivers wore special regalia, including high black hats known as beavers and black suits with frock tail coats. The hearses themselves were very black and very shiny, elaborately carved, and usually contained a window on each side of polished beveled glass through which the flower-bedecked coffin could be seen. People always glanced at the flowers and speculated on whether or not the deceased had received his due. Carriages were provided for the family and friends, usually in greater numbers than are the limousines of today, and practically all the women attending wore black clothing and mournful — if possible, tear-streaked — faces.

Mourning raiment could, if necessary, be bought second hand, as in the following advertisement from the *New Orleans Times*, September 21, 1867:

MOURNING GOODS

Black, Double and Single Dalaine, Double and Single Alpacas, Tamise and every description of Mourning Goods for sale for the present and coming season. Two hundred slightly damaged Delaine Shawls at $2 worth $5; 100 in good order from $2.50 to $4. Fine Delaine Shawls 50¢, worth 75¢. $10s and $20s at par.

S. G. Kreeger
No. 607 Magazine street

Mourning was so widely, and so frequently, worn — since it was adopted for every relative, no matter how distant — that the business must have been a profitable one.

Before the days of the funeral parlor, when everyone was buried from home, people of less than moderate means were often ashamed of their poorly furnished houses. Undertakers remedied this by redecorating the place before the funeral. Carpets were laid, fancy lace curtains hung at the windows, appropriate touches of black crêpe draped here and there, and chairs provided for the visitors at wake and funeral. This service may still be secured, though in New Orleans, an increasing number of families use the mortuary parlors. One old man said: 'Nowadays people are born in hospitals, get married in hotels, buried from the undertaker's. All they use their homes for is a place to change clothes.'

The *New Orleans Courier* carried the following announcements on July 18, 1810:

LOUIS HOUDON

No. 25, St. Louis Street

Has the honor to inform the public that he has formed a society with MR. FERNANDEZ, Cabinet-maker, St. Ann Street, for the decorating of Coffins and mourning hangings only. They will neglect nothing to satisfy those persons who may favor them with their custom, by giving 4 hours notice.

MOURNING HANGINGS & CATAFALQUE

will be hired on moderate terms and at various prices. They will also undertake to hang in black the front of the church as well as to provide coffin furniture at reasonable prices.

Mr. Houdon continues to keep his store in St. Louis Street, where he makes every species of the most fashionable ornaments for beds, curtains, etc. Hangs bells in chambers, having lately received everything necessary for the purpose — Paints in imitation of marble or wood. Makes and sells feather beds, mattresses, pillows, bolsters and the necessary furniture.

In those other days, the days of thick and trailing veils for widows and mournful black for children as young as three years of age, it was considered no less than indecent for grief to be restrained. Lamentations like this one, from the *Times-Democrat* of a half century ago, were considered beautiful.

No! 'Tis not true that we shall never more see his face, and hear of his unselfish and charitable deeds! Oh, no, no, no! It cannot be that ever more will we be robbed of his unselfish devotion to all who needed his assistance. Oh, Lazare, Lazare! Why were you so good to all but yourself! Why, oh, why did you so wrap yourself 'round the heart of all with whom you came in contact, only to be ruthlessly torn away from them, laid low by the assassin's bullet? It had been better had you not been so good and so unselfish; then the blow would not be so hard to bear. Oh, 'tis too much, 'tis grief unbearable! Flow on, thou tears; he deserves them all. But, oh! 'tis hard to have to choke them down, for the doctor says I must not, must not weep; oh, to be forbidden to even weep for you, good, good, oh, good Lazare! 'Tis too hard; 'tis too much wringing of the heartstrings! Oh, the tears; oh, the wails of the broken hearts around your bier; but flow, flow thou on, dear tears; he was worthy of them all, the tears of the sisters and brothers and widows and orphans, all, all, he deserves them all! How we shall miss you, miss you, Lazare! Only thirty-seven years old, and to be laid away forever! Nevermore to see your kind, laughing blue eyes, no, nevermore! Oh, Lazare!

A sister

Morris Hoy recalled a strange incident which occurred in New Orleans some years ago, when a woman 'died' three times in a day.

'I'm only telling you what I seen with my own eyes,' Morris said. 'It was either in 1904 or 1905, and this woman was about sixty or seventy at the time. She did some sewing for a family named Heyl that lived next door to us. One day Ira Heyl and me went to her for his mother — we was just kids then — and we walked in and seen this old lady sitting at her machine with her head down, looking awfully funny. We called to her and when she didn't answer, we got scared, but Ira was a tough kid and he lifted her head and said, cool as you please, "Morris, the old lady's croaked!"

'We called the neighbors and a lot of people come in, including O'Toole, a cop in the neighborhood, so plenty people saw that old lady besides Ira and me. The women got to work and got the corpse dressed and laid out on the bed and I swear she was as dead as a doornail. Then everybody went outside to wait for the undertaker and all of them went home except Ira and me. We were standing there and all of a sudden we heard something. Ira said, "What's that I hear?" I listened and then I sure was skeered, 'cause it was the old lady's sewing machine. And nobody in that house but her!

'Ira had to do a lot of talking, but at last we walked on in — and do you know that dead woman was setting there sewing? "Oh, hello, Ira," she said. "I'll have your mother's things ready in a few minutes." We didn't say nothing. We just dived out the door and started running. We ran right smack into a neighbor, Mrs. Schroeder — and her heading into the house. Ira and me got O'Toole, the cop, and come back, and just as we got there here come Mrs. Schroeder, tearing out of the house and screaming, "*Gott in Himmel! Gott in Himmel!*" She grabbed hold of O'Toole and kept saying, "Mrs. King's come back from the dead. *Ach, Gott in Himmel!*" O'Toole went inside and come out white as a ghost. "Glory Be!" he cried. "If it ain't the truth. The old girl's risen from the dead!"

'Then all the neighbors that had come to see her dead went in to see her alive again.

'Well, about an hour afterwards Ira's mother asked us to go see Mrs. King again about her sewing. We were still skeered so we got O'Toole and all three of us walked into the house again. All the sewing was finished and piled up neatly on a trunk, and there lay the old lady on the bed — dead as a doornail again. O'Toole shook her, then he stuck pins in her. "Well," he said, "she's dead again!" We got Mrs. Schroeder and Ira's mother, Mrs. Heyl, and then what do you think we noticed? The old lady had changed clothes. Remember she had been dressed in her burying clothes the first time she died. Now she had on her old clothes. Now, five of us saw that, don't forget it! That ain't all. We waited around outside for the undertaker, and O'Toole went back inside for a few minutes. In less time than it takes to tell about it, he come beating it back out white as a ghost again. "Guess what?" says he. "The old girl has changed her clothes again. Now she's dressed like she was laid out before!" The five of us run in and, sure enough, that old lady had changed her clothes again. I'm telling you the truth. That old lady died three times in about two hours. This last time she was croaked for good. They buried her.'

Eddie Ybos remembered a funeral of a certain man during a rainstorm about 1895.

'This day it teemed,' he said, 'and the funeral kept waiting for the storm to stop. People didn't embalm much then and the body was getting very bad. You could hardly stand it in the parlor. We knew something had to be done. Some of the men took off their shoes and socks, rolled up their pants, and carried the coffin out to the hearse. The next thing was to get the people into their carriages.

'The widow of that dead man was a very fat lady; must have weighed over two hundred and fifty pounds. You know in them days women didn't diet. Well, I was driving the family carriage and I pulled up in front of the house slowly and made a runway of planks from the front steps to my carriage. The widow was crying and shrieking and she got on those planks with the men all straining to hold her up. This was her big moment now, you gotta realize that! She was all dressed up in her widow's weeds and a heavy black veil, and she was bawling to beat the band. She made that plank fine. It swayed and wobbled, but everything was all right.

'Then it happened. As she went to get into the carriage, and had one foot on the step, her weight was too much for the thing. It tilted over and all the water that had collected on top come down on her like Niagara Falls. She let out a yell like a wild Indian, forgot all about her husband, and began shrieking her beautiful veil was ruined. It sure was, too. It was rolled up right on top of her head like a wet ball.

'Yeah, finally we got her into the carriage, but that ain't all. Her sister, who was much fatter than she was, and a couple of other women, was right behind her, and when the carriage tilted, kerplunk! they all went down into the flood. The sister landed flat on her bottom and sat there with water almost up to her neck howling like a hurt dog. "Oh, my leg is broke! It's busted! Get a doctor!" It sure was funny. Everybody started laughing.

'We finally got to the graveyard. Then we had to use a flat-bottom boat to get the coffin to the tomb. Everybody just walked through the water. The widow was already wet and had her veil off, so she decided she couldn't get any wetter. Years afterwards they would laugh and say, "Remember when Charles died?" And the grandchildren would say, "Remember when Grandpa was buried, and Grandma ruined her beautiful veil?" '

ALL SAINTS' DAY

'It sure is dead around here,' remarked Mr. Saint Pé, standing in the center of Saint Roch Cemetery Number 2. 'The men ain't even started whitewashing the fences, or nothing. How the hell they expect to have things ready for All Saints' Day, me, I don't know. I ain't never seen a year slow like this in my whole entire life.'

Mr. Saint Pé referred, of course, to the annual clean-up campaign which takes place in all Louisiana cemeteries, starting a week or two before All Saints' Day. He offered the information that he was 'just passing through the graveyard like,' and apparently he does that quite often.

Pointing to the ruins of the Mausoleum of Saint Michael the Archangel, he said: 'That ain't used hardly any more. They started to demolish it down, but they found out they can sometimes rent a vault for somebody with a baby to bury in it.' Then he pointed to a tomb. 'That's old Freddie Dudenhopfer in there,' he stated. 'He was the man who owned the brewery's son. He run off with a girl dancing in a show, you see, and stole a lot of money from the City Hall where he was working at. Then he come back, got married and lived thirty years. Ended up with another job at the City Hall. Now his wife — the poor thing! — comes out and puts flowers on his tomb.'

Mr. Saint Pé rolled his eyes expressively. 'I just hope All Saints' ain't slipping,' he said, rather sadly. 'People shouldn't let nothing beautiful like that slip, huh?' He added softly, in an extremely confidential tone, 'I love flowers, me!'

It seemed the cleaning and beautification of the cemeteries was actually a bit slow getting started in 1941, but of course it did. They came slowly at first, but day by day their numbers increased, until by the afternoon of October 31 — Halloween afternoon, the day before All Saints' Day — men, women and children, carrying buckets of whitewash, scrubbing brushes and yellow soap, paint and gilt, shears, rakes, trowels and spades, crowded the more than thirty graveyards of New Orleans, scrubbing and whitewashing tombs and plot copings, blackening or silvering ironwork, gilding epitaphs and battling vigorously against grass and weeds. Louisianians are as a whole great cemetery-goers all year round, but even most of those who don't attend all year appear for this occasion. They would as soon allow the family place to appear in a neglected state on All Saints' Day as would a Creole dowager attend a Mardi Gras ball wearing her third-best wrapper and in her bare feet.

The cemeteries do some cleaning themselves, whitewashing the high brick walls that surround many, cutting grass and weeds, cleaning walls, attending to those burial places which have purchased 'perpetual care,' the latter a sort of insurance some of them offer. Every provision is usually made for this All Saints' Day, which is probably to the dead what the New Orleans Mardi Gras is to the living of that city. Holt Cemetery, a Negro graveyard, for instance, had six new graves dug — 'just in case we have some funerals,' explained the sexton. 'Nobody wants to stop to dig graves on All Saints' Day.'

Every part of Louisiana honors the day. In the rural sections to the south — 'the Cajun country' — nocturnal Mass is said in the cemeteries Halloween night. Blessed candles are lighted on the graves, and priests perform the ancient rites of the Roman Catholic Church for the souls of the departed. Some families spend the entire night beside the family tomb, praying, lighting fresh candles as the old ones burn out — all with a faith marvelous to behold. Once candles were burned on graves in New Orleans, but this practice has been discontinued.

But the preparations for the day continue. Mamma and the children will spend at least one morning or one afternoon at the work. Shoes and stockings are frequently removed, and the walk before the burial place is 'scrubbed' with a broom and a bucket of water, then the tomb or vault is cleaned. Should the vault be one of the 'ovens' high in the wall, ladders are brought along — or borrowed from the sexton. Later Papa will probably appear with whitewash and a brush and set to work. Epitaphs are blackened or gilded. Lately color seems to be coming into its own in New Orleans cemeteries. While there was always a pink tomb to be seen here and there, lavender, bright, bright green, sky blue, orange-yellow and silver ones were seen on All Saints' Day, 1941, promising endless, though rather startling, possibilities for the future.

Young white boys and Negroes haunt the cemetery gates for a week or two before All Saints', stopping everyone entering to offer their services in cleaning the graves, or selling buckets of sand, which is frequently used to cover plots. 'Clean up for you, Mister?' they offer. 'Wantcha tomb washed, Lady? I got sand, Lady.' Hired, they go to work, washing, weeding, whitewashing, their trousers rolled above their knees, their feet bare.

The women meet in the graveyard and gossip.

'Did you hear about Willie Metz? He's dead, you know. Had a pain in his back and dropped in his tracks. It was women done it. *You* knew Willie.'

'Remember poor Mrs. Grandjean? Yes, my Gawd! she's been dead over a month. She was in bed almost a year, poor soul, and her daughter didn't go near her. I tell you, children don't do you much good. They always find out too late how they need you. When a mother's dead, children ain't got nuttin'. Wish you'd have heard the way that daughter yelled at the funeral. I gotta go make my stations now.'

'Stations?'

'That's just what I call it. You see, I got my daughter-in-law in Saint Louis Number 1, and I got a husband and a daughter in Number 2, and my grandson's in Number 3, and my second husband's in Saint Roch's. You see, I gotta fix 'em all up for All Saints', so I call it making the stations. The husband I got now wants to be buried in that Hope Mausoleum, but I tell him, "My Gawd, if you die before me, and I have to go to your place, too, I'll be a wreck!" '

A young woman with dark hair and a pretty face was silvering a fence around a tomb in Saint Vincent de Paul's. Her small son, playing in the walk, called out, 'Mamma, what time does it start?'

'He loves All Saints',' she explained. 'He sees all the candy and icecream men, and he thinks it's a party.'

A fat woman rested on a coping, while her daughter covered a wooden slab in a vault with white enamel. Popping her gum loudly, she encouraged the girl with, 'That looks swell, kid. You're doing a swell job! You know that's the same enamel I'm gonna use in my kitchen. You can see how nice it's gonna look. Gee, that looks swell.'

Suddenly there was a gust of wind and two vases filled with filthy water toppled from the shelf of the vault above, streaming down the freshly painted slab and into the girl's hair. The mother jumped to her feet.

'Oh, God! Oh, God!' she screamed. 'Look at that! Here, use this rag. Get it off the slab quick. Don't worry about that hair of yourn. You can wash that when you get home. Oh, God! Look at that beautiful enamel. That's them Duprés up there. If they kept their place decent and emptied their vases sometimes that wouldn't happen. Oh, I hope you can get it off. Them Duprés! I used to know some of 'em. I always say people must keep their houses just like they keep their graves, me!'

Another woman came quickly down the walk, placed three chrysanthemums in a vase, then slapped her hands together briskly. 'There!' she said. 'Now they can tell I been here. They always talking I don't come. Well, I ain't much for graveyards. I say, everyone to his taste! Now, I know one woman and cemeteries is her hobby, I tell you the truth. When her husband died she had to build a great big expensive tomb and all, and she's always there with flowers and all. I say, there's always remorse when you see things like that. That poor man couldn't hardly never go out at night or play a game of cards. She really nagged him to death, I believe. Sometimes he'd drink a little bit, and would she almost kill him! Too bad she couldn't have been as good to him when he was alive as when he's dead. But now the cemetery is her hobby. It's all she lives for. They got lots of people like that.' She sighed. 'I had an awful thing to do once. They was digging up my Uncle Henry to move him, and some member of the family had to be there as a witness. Of course, they picked on me! I was scared to death. They pulled him out and I had to look at him. Do you know that man looked just like the day he had died, his mustache, shroud and all. His flesh was solid. Of course, I could easily understand how he got petrified. He drank so much he got pickled from the inside out!'

The flowers usually start arriving about noon of Halloween, continue until well after dark. Most of the New Orleans grave-yards are kept open until about 9 P.M. on Halloween, and some-times people bring their floral offerings on their way to parties. Many cemeteries keep watchmen there that night to ensure against theft or vandalism. Children dressed in their 'ghost' costumes, carrying pumpkin lanterns, accompany their parents 'to put out the flowers.'

All Saints' Day begins early. Soon after dawn the streetcars and buses are packed with people carrying chrysanthemums wrapped in green tissue paper. Everyone wants to get their flowers out as early as possible, if they have neglected to place them Halloween, for if anyone sees their tomb or grave sans floral adornment it will cause 'talk.' Many Orleanians actually shudder with horror at the sight of an undecorated burial place that day, and will almost feel called upon to ostracize the 'heart-less' relatives of whoever is buried therein.

While in other sections of the country graves are decorated on Memorial Day and All Souls' Day, there is actually no counter-part of this day elsewhere in the United States. Here there is rivalry, a bit of envy, much gossip. Woe to the person who places a cheap bouquet in a vase for All Saints' Day, when every-one knows he can afford better! Chrysanthemums — often as large as cabbages — are the 'All Saints' flower,' often costing a dollar or more apiece. Some families place out a basket contain-ing a dozen or more of these. Orleanians will go hungry to buy flowers for this occasion. While not a general holiday, State and City offices and banks close, and many other business places allow employees time off to 'go to the cemeteries.' It is an ac-cepted fact that all Orleanians 'go to the cemeteries' on All Saints' Day.

As the day proceeds toward noon, cemetery neighborhoods are thickly crowded. Automobiles and streetcars block and jam around the Metairie section, where more than a score of traffic police are on special duty. Pedestrians, bearing their flowers, cross streets at great peril, run, skip and leap for their lives. In such large cemeteries as Metairie and Greenwood there are other policemen, one directing traffic at every turn and interesection. Vendors line the street curbings, selling peanuts, popcorn, icecream, hotdogs, balloons and toys. 'Fresh parched peanuts!' they cry. 'I got peanuts. Five cents a bag! I got chewing gum anda candy!' Negro women hawk pecan and coconut pralines, calling, 'Pyrines! Pyrine candy!' Men peddle cold drinks from wooden tubs filled with ice.

The morning of the 1941 All Saints' Day there were many out — a large white pushcart with red wheels, green awnings, and with an American flag waving gaily from the top sold pralines, pecan rolls, nougat and other candy, besides peanuts. A Mexican sold hot tamales from another pushcart. Across the street from Greenwood Cemetery the 'Ritzy Dot Café' offered on its signboard:

TODAY'S SPECIAL! BLACK 👁 PEAS AND RICE. 15¢

ALL KINDS OF SANDWICHES 10¢ and 15¢.

Other peanut wagons passed, most of them decorated with colored crêpe paper and peanuts strung into garlands. At cemetery gates sandwiches and small pies were sold from pasteboard cartons. Icecream men were everywhere, with such signs as 'Try a WHALE! The big 5¢ frozen goodie.' Other vendors approached automobiles at stop signs to offer 'Carmel Crisp Popcorn.'

There was a small crowd around a notice posted at the entrance to Saint Patrick's Cemetery Number 1, which read, in part:

> Dear Lot Owners:
> In line with our plans for improving these cemeteries, on and after Nov. 1st. 1941, all grass mounds that have not received attention and were overgrown with weeds during the past year will be removed. All open spaces will be leveled to grade in order to control grass growth next year.
> The St. Patrick cemeteries are now in a position to offer you first class grave cleaning service at a rate of 50¢ a month, or $5.00 a year.

The notice was signed, 'Rev. Carl J. Schutten.' There were many complaints in the crowd, protests of 'I can't read. I didn't bring my glasses.' A young nun, who had been kneeling before a grave, rose and walking quietly over to the notice began to read it aloud. Sitting on the coping of a plot within the cemetery, a red-faced, very stout Irishwoman wept profusely and at the same time drank beer from a carton of six bottles.

By noon every *banquette* was crowded, some still arriving with flowers, but most strolling from one graveyard to another, since many folk 'make' as many cemeteries as possible on All Saints' Day. In fact, some bring or buy lunch and stay from dawn until dusk. And there is nothing sad about it all. Rather there is, in general, the atmosphere of a fiesta.

Downtown, on Louisa Street, Saint Vincent de Paul's has more than its share of this spirit. No other cemetery has so many peddlers and vendors, none is more crowded, and none clings more firmly to the old ways. At least until 1940 *gumbo* and hot coffee were still sold there, and that year one grave held a chipped white saucer in which reposed a slice of fruitcake! Some curious things decorated the graves and vaults on All Saints' Day, 1941 — elaborate paper flowers, a huge cross of pink and white tissue paper entirely covering one grave, holy statues enclosed in glass, flowers in tins left over from meats, coffee, jam, pickles, peanut butter and pork and beans (and no one ever bothers to remove the labels). At the gates vendors offered icecream, candy, pralines, peanuts, apples on sticks, soft drinks, balloons, toy birds flying gaily from sticks, hot dogs and *toy skeletons*.

Outside one gate, two young colored women sold pralines from a wooden table on the *banquette*. 'My grandma left me this recipe,' explained one. 'Nobody makes 'em quite like us. Grandma was a hundred years old when she died, and she sold 'em here up to the last year. She used to make the best popcorn balls in town, and everybody called her "Popcorn Mary." I didn't make none of them this year; it's been too wet and rainy.'

A customer purchased one of the small skeletons, and when he bounced it up and down from the rubber attached to its head, the head came off. There was some argument, and finally the vendor gave him a new skeleton and he went strolling down an aisle between the high whitewashed tombs bouncing his toy up and down.

A woman came running down another aisle, seized a young girl by the arm. 'Ain't you Teeny?' she gasped excitedly. 'My, I ain't seen you in years! Honey, I knew your mother long before you was born. My God, yes! Come on over and meet my husband, Teeny. Sure, I married again, but he's the sweetest thing. He always comes to Joe's grave wit' me. I know that ain't nuttin', but you know how some men is.'

Other women conversed before another grave. 'Now, what do you think of that!' remarked one. 'I knew right down to my toes there wouldn't be nothing here. Much *she* cares. Got one man right behind the other.'

'She's just a slut,' said her friend casually.

Boys walked about trying to sell vases — 'Thoity cents apiece. Git a brand-new vase for your flowers — thoity cents!' Others sold milk bottles, pickle jars and like containers for five cents, and these brought more buyers.

Many vases were adorned with ribbons of satin or tulle, some bearing golden letters reading, 'Beloved,' or 'To Our Loved One,' or 'Grandmother and Papa from Children and Grandchildren.'

In the midst of it all, two men entered carrying a casket. The visitors cleared a way for them in the walks, then hurried behind to see who was being buried. The men and the coffin journeyed to an 'oven' in the rear wall, where efforts were made to fit the coffin into the vault. It wouldn't fit. Then one of the men said to the other: 'They're just gonna have to buy a smaller one. This'll never make it.' With that they turned around, and carried the casket back down the aisle and out of the cemetery. Apparently the big gray coffin was empty, and they were just ascertaining whether or not it would 'make it' and fit into the 'oven.' Everyone returned to the other businesses of the day. A fat and female cynic plumped herself down on the steps of a tomb, removed her shoes, and groaned: 'My God! My feets! This is just a big show, that's all it is. I don't know why I come.' A mother passed dragging a small boy by one arm. He wore his tall, pointed, bright orange Halloween hat and was engaged in blowing noisily upon a bright orange Halloween horn.

Years ago there were many things to be seen that have now vanished. Nuns used to beg at the gate of each New Orleans cemetery, orphans beside them, who shook coins noisily in a tin pan or rang a cowbell. Negro mammies, resplendent in blue calico, red *tignons* and starched white aprons and *fichues*, sold steaming bowls of *gumbo*, pralines and slices of *pain patate* — the last a now almost forgotten delicacy of sweet potatoes, baked into a sort of cake, highly seasoned with spices and black pepper — fanning their wares with colorful *chasse mouches* — fly whips, made of strips of vari-colored paper.

The observance of the day seems to be as old as the city, brought over, of course, from Latin Europe. Creoles used many elaborately designed wreaths of beads on wire frames, more artificial flowers than now, these often made from fish scales, wax or metal, as well as paper. Royal Street establishments specialized in such adornments, families demanding special and individual 'made to order' designs, not wanting anything similar to their friends' displays. Tombs were frequently draped in black crêpe and velvet, and vigil lights were burned before the slabs, with crowns of jet beads topping all. A few days after All Saints' Day the designs were usually returned to the family so that they might be reused another time.

The dahlia, rather than the chrysanthemum, was formerly the most popular flower. As there were comparatively few florists, most flowers were homegrown. Coxcombs — a coarse red flower resembling a rooster's headdress — once enjoyed a great vogue among poorer Creoles. Some families used so many flowers that a horse and wagon was hired to convey the whole to the cemetery. Often servants were left to spend the day beside the family tomb, to prevent theft or destruction. Rosaries draped the slabs, and may still be seen occasionally. Besides food and refreshment, vendors sold statues of saints from trays, potted plants, wreaths. Many people made their own wreaths, and for days before the great event, the house would be littered with paraphernalia for these creations. A favorite type was of black beads and wire, with a central, glass-enclosed section containing strands of hair from the head of the deceased.

Creoles kept close watch over who visited whose tombs, for

this had all sorts of amazing implications. Should a widower fail to be seen at the resting place of his dead wife, it indicated he was about to remarry; even so, some scorn was felt at his neglect. Old ladies would spend the day seated on the wrought-iron benches then so numerous in the cemeteries, saying their rosaries, but with one eye on the beads and the other on who came and departed. Even tears were almost counted, one by one, and a certain number were expected under certain circumstances.

It was virtually impossible to find a grave without a flower. Should a family die out, some friend or acquaintance would remember to leave at least a single blossom on All Saints' Day. One gradually aging Negress brought one flower every year to the tomb of a white soldier killed in the War Between the States. At the end of more than forty years the flower ceased to appear; then everyone knew she had died. During the last years of the nineteenth century Negresses were often seen placing flowers on the graves of white men, and gossip always had it that they were the former mistresses of the white men they thus honored.

Though some of the things belonging to an earlier era have vanished, there seems little chance of the whole 'slipping,' as Mr. Saint Pé so aptly put it. The cemeteries were as crowded as ever in 1942. In the Roman Catholic ones, priests appeared at three o'clock in the afternoon, and 'blessed' all the graves, walking swiftly up and down the aisles, sprinkling holy water and trailed by swarms of people.

But All Saints' Day is not entirely Catholic. The Protestant and non-sectarian graveyards are as crowded and as flower-bedecked as any of the Catholic ones, for the day has become the day to 'put out flowers' and to 'go to the cemeteries.'

Chapter 17

Riverfront Lore

THERE IS MAGIC IN THE YELLOW WATER OF THE Mississippi River as it flows through Louisiana, especially at New Orleans. A visitor who drinks of it will surely return to that city; if he washes his face in it, his luck is bound to change from bad to good. And because all New Orleans water comes from the river there is no way he can avoid doing either. The river water is beautifying, too; everybody knows all Louisiana women are beautiful. Furthermore, it increases fecundity. Women who cannot bear children in any other part of the world invariably become pregnant within a year after their arrival in Louisiana.

If you are suffering under a voodoo curse, if some potent *gris-gris* has been concocted to do you harm, it is wise to hire a skiff and row across the river. When you get to the other side, you step on land; then you get right back in the skiff and start for the side from which you came. In the middle of the stream stop and throw a coin over your left shoulder. That will break the most powerful curse an enemy can place upon you.

However, you must be careful of the river, too, for there are bad-luck things, as well as good-luck things. You must never throw an animal or fowl into the Mississippi. That is almost the most dangerous thing you could possibly do.

And the riverfront is alive with ghosts, ghosts of murdered seamen and river pirates and stevedores, of great early explorers and of ignominious 'wharf rats,' bad ghosts, good ghosts and just plain ghosts. Jakie Walker met a ghost one day and the ghost did him a lot of good. Jakie was a roustabout and had been working on the river for more than thirty years, knew most of its secrets and all its tricks, so undoubtedly the story is perfectly true.

Jakie had enjoyed a very hectic evening. He was quite drunk. Now that the party was over and his friends had all drifted homeward, worry of the most profound sort began to seep into his somewhat befogged brain. Mostly on account of his wife. Jakie's wife was one of those strong-minded females with an antipathy to drinking husbands. Sometimes she beat Jakie. That was why he decided not to go home until his condition was less obvious. He started walking and before he realized where he had been drifting he found himself on the wharves where he worked.

'I jest drifted around out there,' he explained. 'I seen the watchman, but he knowed me, so he didn't say nothin' but, "Jakie, what you doin' out here lookin' like you sick?" I told him 'bout my woman and he jest laughed and let me alone.

'It felt real good out there, you know, with the wind from the river blowin' in my face and all them nice river smells. I found me a corner and set myself down to rest and try to think what I could tell that woman when I got home. I didn't go to sleep. No, sir. I kept me eyes wide open. Then it happened. Man, I'm tellin' you straight, I can still see that *thing!* It ain't no word of lie, either.

'That *thing* come driftin' right over the top of the river. *It* was shaped jest like a man — only *it* weared a long black gown what dragged behind *it* for a long piece. That *thing* kept comin'. *It* come slowly, too. I wanted to run, but I couldn't. I wanted to holler, but I couldn't. *It* got closer and closer to me. I swear I could feel the heat of that *thing* on my body — that *thing* was burnin' and burnin' right into me. Looked like *it* wanted to crawl through my eyes! And I couldn't do nothin'. I had hell on my hands.

'Then all of a sudden my voice come back. I jest opened my mouth and the words come out.

'"What I got you want?" I yelled, with that *thing* right there blowin' *its* breath in my face. "What I got you want?"

'You know that *thing* didn't say nothin' right away? Jest stood there, lookin' at me; and I set there just lookin' at *it*. Then them long arms opened up like a cross and the waves in the water started hummin'. I thought that *thing* was gonna hug me. "Don't you touch me!" I hollered. "I ain't got nothin' you want." Then *it* spoke to me and *its* voice was deep down and awful.

'"Jakie," that *thing* said, "the waves is callin' me back, but I ain't movin' a step until I talks with you. You remembers me, but I ain't tellin' you who I is. I drownded right here in this river. I is a ghost now, Jakie I is a ghost of the Mississippi River, and I got something to tell you, Jakie. You is gonna leave this here earth soon unless you stops your drinkin'."

'I didn't say nothin'. I jest looked at that *thing* hard. Scared as I was I was thinkin' even a ghost got nerve to come around and try to rectify my drinkin'.

'"Jakie," that *thing* said, "I done been sent to take you away with me. I done been sent to take you to my watery grave. But you is a good man, Jakie, you really is, outside your drinkin'. All you got to do is stop. Tell me right now, boy, what is your determination in this matter?"

'I thought a minute and I studied a minute.

'"Ghost," I said, "drinkin' is the pleasure of my life. I ain't stoppin' for nobody."

'"Jakie," that *thing* said, "you knows that ain't my answer."

'"Does you know my wife?" I asked that *thing*.

'"I does," *it* said, "and I knows how you feel, but, Jakie, you gotta stop drinkin'. Now I'm gonna do some of my stuff so as you'll know I mean what I says."

'Then that *thing* started to do *its* stuff. The waves in the river started rollin' and they started risin'. All of a sudden they makes a noise like I ain't never heared to this day. Then they comes up over that wharf and they was like arms reachin' out for Jakie Walker. Brother, what would you do?

'"I promises you, ghost," I said. "If you will jest go away and take them waves with you, I promises you I ain' never gonna drink again."

'Then everything was all right. That *thing* turned around and went right away and them waves stopped risin' and stopped rollin' and hollerin' for Jakie Walker. I swear I ain't touched a drop of liquor of no kind since that night. Every payday I totes my money home to my woman and we ain't had much trouble since. And this is the funniest part of it. Do you know that when I got home that night my wife was waitin' for me right in the door? I was scared stiff, but you know what she done? She jest throwed her arms 'round my neck and screams, "Jakie, honey, I dreamed you was dead. And I sure is glad to see you!" "Baby," I says, "I was almost dead, but I is a new man now."

'Some people says she done the whole thing, that she done had me hoodooed. Maybe so. I don't know. I jest knows I ain't drinkin' no more.'

The longshoreman takes himself very seriously and he takes the river very seriously, with all its ghosts, its legends and its customs. Every once in a while one of them meets a ghost personally and shines for a long time in his own particular spotlight, for the yarn is never forgotten, but repeated again and again. They never, for instance, forget the fellow who met the Sprinkle Man.

'One day I was walkin' out here,' testifies this black laborer, 'on my way to work in broad daylight, mindin' strictly to my own affairs. I just happened to turn around and lo and behold! I seen a man sprinklin' dollar bills all over the *banquette*. I know there's no man in his right mind gonna do a thing like that. I called out and asked him why he was doin' that. I begun to think maybe no man in his right mind was gonna see a thing like that. That Sprinkle Man wouldn't answer; he kept right on throwin' them bills around. Then I knew either he was crazy to be doin' that or I was crazy not to do somethin' about it. So I jumped. Man, I jumped right at them bills all over the *banquette*. I jumped and I grabbed. And what do you think I

jumped at and what do you think I grabbed at? Leaves. That's
what. Nothin' in the world but leaves. All them dollar bills
turned into leaves before I could touch 'em. Then that Sprinkle
Man stood there and laughed at me. "See?" he said. "That's
what's the matter with all you people. You puts money first
before everything else." That's how come I know I ain't never
gonna be rich. The Sprinkle Man told me so.'

Amy Guidry, seventy-six-year-old Negress, who dwells in a
willow grove along the river *battures*, is familiar with many of
the ghosts. 'I'se can see ghosts every night,' Amy declares.
'I'se always sees 'em on All Saints' Night. There's two mens
walk around here wearin' dark pants and white shirts. The peculiar thing about them is that they ain't got no heads. There
used to be a wolf what would run right out of the water and then
run back in. Mens come out and try to shoot him. I told 'em
they was wastin' their time, but they kept on tryin' for a long
time. 'Course that wasn't no real wolf at all, but the spirit of a
bad person what changed hisself into a wild beast. The riverfront is full of ghostses. You can see them all the time out here.'

Longshoremen still sing as they work, black man's blues and
chants.

Got the riverfront blues, baby, and I'm blue as I can be,
Got the riverfront blues, baby, and I'm blue as I can be,
That ole Mississippi sure is makin' a fool out of me.

My baby is there when the man gives me my check,
Oh, my baby is there when the man gives me my check,
When I looks at the river I feel like cuttin' my neck.

That river, that river, ole man riverfront blues.
Oh, the riverfront blues, talk about havin' them riverfront blues....

That's the *Riverfront Blues* as Buddy Hackett sings it. 'I ain't
worryin' 'bout nothin' at all,' says Buddy. 'I jest sings 'bout it
all. Wimmen and the river and hard work, they is all the same.
Trouble. Listen here:

Say, I'm gonna give you my lovin' and my money, too,
Mamma, I'm gonna give you my lovin' and my money, too.
Tell me, baby, what else can I do?

On the riverfront every mornin', when the clock strikes five.
Baby, I'm on the riverfront every mornin' when the clock strikes five.
And I don't even know if I'm comin' back alive.

I got a gal in Texas and a gal in Tennessee.
Mamma, I got a gal in Texas and a gal in Tennessee.
All I got to do is write and she'll come runnin' to me.

So, keep goin', black woman, my day will come.
Keep goin', black woman, my day will come.
That's the day, you rider, I'm gonna have you on a hum.

With recreation promised, Buddy looks forward to 'knockin' off' with

> Let's truck this here cotton, unload this ship,
> Boys, let's truck this cotton, unload this ship.
> 'Cause when we finish I'm gonna look for my wench.

You have to carry on, Buddy says, just as you are told to do in the *Riverfront Toasts*:

> When you tumble from the top,
> Keep agoin'.
> If the weather kills yo' crop,
> Keep agoin'.
> It's no need to sit and whine,
> If them fish ain't on yo' line,
> Bend yo' hook and keep atryin',
> But keep agoin'.

'Pushfoot' Wiley offered this one:

> A hook on a cistern is boun' to rust,
> Lots of N'Awlins wimmen is hard to trust.
> If we two was like we three,
> We'd all git together an' then agree.
>
> A nickel is a nickel,
> An' a dime is a dime,
> The best work is on the riverfront,
> All the time.

Negro longshoremen are always boasting of their women,

especially how much money they can get from them. This song
typifies that particular spirit:

> You boys got wimmen, but mine is a honey,
> The rich white mens they give her money.
> And jest like that she give it to me,
> That's why I'm sailin' like a ship on the blue sea.
> I got a pinch-back coat comin',
> Gonna walk down Rampart Street hummin',
> And I want it very plain to see,
> Don't want you black bastards talkin' to me.
> I'm gonna put on airs,
> Like that woman who makes her money hustlin' upstairs.

Negro longshoremen say you have to be fast and alert to operate on the riverfront, even in this era, though it isn't what it
used to be. Yet, even today, it is a world of its own, with a
language all its own. 'That talk you hear on the riverfront is
junk talk that nobody but us can understand,' they'll tell you.
'Where it come from I don't know.'

Longshoremen either like a *wag* — a sailor — very much or
they hate him. The types of ships docking at New Orleans have
various names. A ship that crosses the sea is a *deep-water ship*, a
coastwise vessel, a *shallow-water ship*. A *don't-and-do ship* sailing
in *Suicide Alley* is the worst sort of ship to be on because that is a
merchantman sailing in a war zone. *Streamin'* means a boat is
going upriver. *Notches* are miles. A rich shipper is always *Mr.
Rockefeller*. *Slicin' time* is saving time. *To lay out* is to take a few
days off. *You're out* means you're finished for the day and you
move on or go *down the line*.

A *drift* is a beggar along the riverfront. To *ride the tide* is to
take advantage of someone. A *rabbit* is a fellow who won't pay
his bills, and to pay a bill is to *lay it on the line*. *Hopped up* refers
both to drunks and to drug addicts. *Hip the jive* means to be careful of unnecessary talk. When a longshoreman wants to start
an argument, he is told to go out to Perdido and Saratoga Streets
where 'they talks that barroom talk.' Two longshoremen angry
with each other are at *organheads together*. The women who sell
hot lunches, sandwiches, pies and doughnuts along the wharves
are *bucket women* or *pan ladies*, because their wares are usually sold

from buckets, huge flat pans or baskets. The food has fantastic names, too. Meat is *bullneck*, bread pudding is *heavy devil*, jelly doughnuts are *elephant ears*, *stage planks* are flat ginger cakes, and a *nigger's lunch* is a *stage plank* and a dipperful of river water. Any restaurant or saloon is a *barrel house*.

A young man will gibe at an older one, saying, 'Old man, you is like a linen suit, out of season.' When a man says another man is 'like the stars' he means he stays out all night.

If a woman passes along the wharves one longshoremen will say to another, 'Blow that twiff!' or 'Man, gun that broad!' or 'Pipe that business, boy!', all meaning the same thing — 'Look at that woman's shape!'

Carolina Slim is a poet, a wandering black minstrel, who sings of his own prowess constantly, as longshoreman, fighter and lover. Slim has a favorite composition, though; this one is about his girl, Agnes, he vows, but Agnes is not mentioned throughout the song, only *The Titanic Ship*, the title of the epic. This song he sings most tenderly, most passionately.

'It's a long story,' Carolina says. 'When the *Titanic* sunk me and my baby was fightin'. When word come that the ship was down, she told me she didn't want me no more. Then after she gone and left me, I thunk up *The Titanic Ship*. It goes like this:

I always did hear that the fif' of May was a wonderful day,
You believe me, everybody had somethin' to say,
Telephones and telegraphs to all parts of town,
That the great *Titanic* ship was a-goin' down.

The captain and the mate was standin' on deck havin' a few words,
'Fore they know it, the *Titanic* had done hit a big iceberg.
Had a colored guy on there call Shine, who come down from below,
And hollered, 'Water is comin' in the fireroom do'!'

Shine jumped off that ship and begun to swim,
Thousands of white folks watchin' him.
Shine say, 'Fish in the ocean and fish in the sea,
This is one time you white folks ain't gonna fool me!'

There is lots more. Carolina Slim can sing a dozen or two verses. The hero, Shine, reaches land, and

There was thousands of people waitin' to shake his hand.
Shine said, 'Push back, stand there and hear my pedigree.
I don't want nobody messin' with me.

'My pillow was an alligator and a boa-constrictor was in my den.
I lived on the water and I didn't have to pay no rent.
And I don't owe nobody a damn red cent.
When the great *Titanic* in the river sank.'

Carolina Slim calls himself a 'roamin' longshoreman,' but he is more a hobo than a worker. He boasts that he has the strength of three men, can do the work of three men. Most of the time he gets his money from women and he always invests it quickly — in crap games. The women don't really mean anything to him, because he's always thinking about Agnes. He says he 'jest cain't stay put for long,' so he is a wandering minstrel. He sings:

The boys in Wisconsin they take their time,
They go to work to make eight and a dime.
The boys in Chicago they gits a draf',
They go to work to make eight and a half.
The boys in Noo Yawk they oughta be rich,
They go to work to make eight, six bits.
The boys in Noo 'Leans they oughta be dead,
They go to work for fish and bread.

They'll work for the rich and they'll work for the poor,
Will work for a man jest day long so.
They'll work for Saint Peter and they'll work for Saint Paul,
They'll be in Noo 'Leans workin' when the roll is called.
And I ain't bluffin',
I ain't gonna work for nothin'.

And that's Carolina Slim's philosophy.

Rooster Jim is well known on the riverfront. His foreman testifies that Rooster, who is only five feet seven inches tall and weighs but a hundred and fifty pounds, never tires. Rooster will often work sixty hours on a stretch without stopping, and he keeps in good humor all the time, singing, shouting and laughing as he labors, remaining at the end of the day as fresh and as strong as the hour he had started. And when Rooster is paid off, he doesn't trudge home to sink into exhausted sleep. Not then. Not with all his money. He receives as much as ninety cents an hour, with time and a half wages for overtime, and that's plenty of money in Rooster Jim's world.

Rooster doesn't have any one home. While he works he sings about his woman, but he doesn't have any one woman, either; he has many women and any place there is one of these women, that is Rooster Jim's home. But even the women don't come first. As soon as he gets paid, he makes the rounds of the half-dozen bars he patronizes and at each he leaves five or ten dollars with the bartender. Then, with what is left he heads for a certain hangout around the Basin Canal. There he works up a crap game.

The dice roll until some woman who knows him comes along and coaxes him out of the game. He goes home with her, but only for a little love-making. As soon as this chore is over, Rooster is back at the dice game. Comes a second woman and the routine is repeated. About now, Rooster will probably decide to do a little drinking, so he'll drift around to the various bars where he has distributed money. Women punctuate the drinking, but they are of less importance.

Bar after bar, woman after woman, it goes on, until at last he falls asleep in the arms of one of his women. Then he'll sleep for days. This is the lucky girl. If Rooster hasn't visited too many saloons, she's hit the jackpot. When he awakens she escorts him from bar to bar and collects the remaining cash. Next morning Rooster Jim is back on the wharf waiting for a ship to unload, and a job.

To this day many Negro longshoremen cannot read and a 'flag system' for sorting is often used. Each man passes the sorter who taps the sack he 'totes' with a long stick. One tap means the sorter cannot see the mark; two taps that the bag must be tipped downward so the mark can be seen; three that the bag must be lifted higher. The rest of the code is just as simple. Instead of the firm's name being called, his flag is called: blue diamond, black heart, white ace, red cross, etc. The sack is then carried to the pile beneath that flag.

Often longshoremen are out of work for long periods; then

when a ship comes in there is an eager cry of 'Come git hot! Money's to be made!' *Gimme a head* means to ask for aid in lifting a heavy load. *Gimme a bumper* means a lift onto a wagon.

Oldtimers say that the Negro longshoremen and all life on the riverfront are not what they used to be. It's gone soft now, say they. In other days men were really men, yet the toughest of them all was a woman.

Her name was Annie Christmas. She was six feet, eight inches tall and she weighed more than two hundred and fifty pounds. She wore a neat mustache and had a voice as loud and as deep as a foghorn on the river. The tough keelboatmen, terrors of the river in other days, stood in awe of her, and there wasn't a hulking giant of a stevedore who didn't jump when Annie snapped her black fingers. She could lick a dozen of them with one arm tied behind her back, and they knew it.

Most of the time Annie dressed like a man and worked as a man. Often she worked as a longshoreman, pulled a sweep or hauled a cordelle. She would carry a barrel of flour under each arm and another balanced on her head. Once she towed a keelboat from New Orleans to Natchez on a dead run, and never got out of breath.

Annie could outdrink any man in the South. She would put down a barrel of beer and chase it with ten quarts of whiskey, without stopping. Men used to buy her whiskey just to see her drink. Sometimes she got mad in a barroom, beat up every man in the place and wrecked the joint. Sometimes she did it for fun.

Then, every once in a while, Annie would get into a feminine mood. When this happened she was really all of two hundred fifty pounds of coal-black female, really seductive and enticing in a super sort of way. At these times Annie would rent a barge, fill it with the best fancy women in New Orleans and operate a floating brothel up and down the Mississippi, catering to keelboatmen and stevedores, river pirates and longshoremen. She would always stage contests, and offer a hundred dollars cash to the woman entertaining the most men satisfactorily in a given period of time. Of course, Annie was as magnificent amorously as she was as a fighter and drinker and she always won her own first prize.

She would really dress up for these occasions, wearing red satin gowns and scarlet plumes in her woolly hair. She always wore a commemorative necklace containing beads for all the eyes, ears and noses she had gouged from men, a bead for each one. The necklace was only thirty feet long, but then she only counted white men; there would not have been enough beads in New Orleans if she had counted Negroes.

Annie had twelve coal-black sons, each seven feet tall, all born at the same time. She had plenty of other babies, too, but these were her favorites. Whenever she got ready to have a baby, she drank a quart of whiskey and lay down somewhere. Afterward she had another quart and went straight back to work.

Finally Annie met a man who could lick her and then she fell in love for the first time in her life. But the man didn't want her, so Annie bedecked herself in all her finery and her famous necklace and committed suicide.

Her funeral was appropriately elaborate. Her body was placed in a coal-black coffin and driven to the wharf in a coal-black hearse, drawn by six coal-black horses. Six on each side, marched her coal-black sons, dressed in coal-black suits. At the riverfront the coffin was placed on a coal-black barge, and that coal-black night, with no moon shining, her dozen coal-black sons floated on it with the coal-black coffin out to sea and vanished forever.

A century or more ago, seamen and keelboatmen, roustabouts and other wharf laborers had to be tough. The New Orleans riverfront was infested with saloons, gambling places and brothels of fabulously bad character. Bill Sedley, who staged many a history-making brawl, was typical of the period. Sedley was a six-foot-two keelboatman and as formidable a foe in a fight as he was skillful with a sweep.

One night in 1822, Bill stomped out of the back room of the Sure Enuf Hotel, a saloon, gambling place and hotel run by two Mexican brothers, Rafe and Juan Contreas, with blood in his eyes.

'I be danged,' Bill shouted, 'whether it's the whiskey or I seen right, but I'm a yellow bantam pullet if Rafe Contreas didn't deal a card from his sleeve.'

'I'm a child of the snappin' turtle and was raised with pan-thers!' said Bill. 'I'm a child of the snapping turtle, I am!'

He flung himself into the larger gaming room, shouting, 'I am a man, I am! I am a horse! I am a team! I am an alligator, half-man, half-horse. I can whip any man on the Mississippi, I can!'

Bill was well known. His temper was famous. His brawling ability was celebrated. The crowd in the Sure Enuf Hotel began to dwindle. In a few seconds Bill, Juan and Rafe were alone. One of the Mexicans bolted the doors. Outside the crowd pressed against them, listened at the windows. Furniture was heard crashing to the floor, there was the sound of smashing glass, and over it all Bill Sedley's boasting, 'I am a man, I am! I am a child of the snapping turtle, I am!'

In a few minutes the doors swung wide, and Bill Sedley, hacked and bloody, but chest extended and head high, swaggered forth.

'Gentlemen,' he invited, 'walk in. The drinks are on the house! The American Eagle has lit on the Alleghenies again.'

On the floor the two Mexicans lay dead.

The 'broadhorns,' as the keelboats and flatboats were called, were the first to follow the explorers and missionaries down the broad waters of the Mississippi River, and their crews were rough giants who defined trouble as fun and fighting as recreation. They had a fantastic way of boasting of their prowess, always likening themselves to wild animals. In *Remembrances of the Mississippi*, an article in *Harper's* in December, 1855, the following example of this strange braggadocio is given:

> I'm from the Lightning Forks of Roaring River. I'm *all man*, save what is wild cat and extra lightning. I'm as hard to run against as a cypress snag. I never back water. Look at me — a small specimen — harmless as an angleworm — a remote circumstance — a mere yearling. Cockle-doodle-doo! I did hold down a buffalo bull, and tar off his scalp with my teeth, but I can't do it now — I'm too powerful weak, *I am*, I'm the man that, single-handed, towed a broadhorn over a sandbar, and if anyone denies it, let him make his will and pay the expenses of a funeral. I'm the genuine article, tough as bullhide,

keen as a rifle. I can out-swim, out-jump, out-drink, and keep soberer than any man at Catfish Bend. I'm painfully ferocious — I'm spilin' for someone to whip me — if there's a creeter in this diggin' that wants to be disappointed in tryin' to do it, let him yell — whoop-hurra!

James Girty, famous riverman, was reputed to have had a solid bone covering over his chest that knives and bullets could not penetrate, amazing strength and courage, and never to have been licked.

Then came the era of luxurious steamboats, gambling boats and pleasure boats, lavishly furnished and adorned, combining tons of gilt with elaborately carved wood and mother-of-pearl. Carpets were thick and rich, chandeliers always massive and of crystal, huge mirrors always framed in gilt or gold leaf. Only the brothels of this era outdid the steamboats in unrestrained decorativeness. And many of the people traveling on the steamboats suited their surroundings.

Mrs. Boland Leathers, captain of the fifth *Natchez*, and the only woman ever to be a Mississippi River captain, described the most notorious of all river gamblers, George Devol.

'I knew him personally,' said Mrs. Leathers, 'the most notorious of them all. George Devol was a stout, florid-complexioned man, who though he was not exceedingly tall, created quite an impression. He was very talkative and was considered at the time a gentleman. He was dressed well, but toward the flashy side, and wore loud checked suits, fancy vests, loud cravats, and was actually a gentleman gambler. I was crazy about George Devol, in a purely platonic way, of course. One of the main reasons I went with him was that he used to buy me the most delicious chocolates. . . .

'I guess he did cheat at times, but I should like to see the river gambler who didn't. I can remember him saying so plainly, in his soft, cultured voice, "Come on, Blanche, let's start a game and give them a ride." You see, I would start the game off, which was usually roulette, and this would attract other people, and when enough had gathered around and were playing I would slide out unnoticed.

'I remember one time when he was going up on our boat. At

the same time there were a large number of Texas families on the boat who were going to Mississippi and the northern portion of Louisiana. He had just skinned one man in a game and naturally words followed and the man threatened to kill him. Before he could pull out his gun, Devol ran to the side of the ship. This particular *Natchez* was a side-wheeler, and I can remember well we were just passing Port Adams. He jumped overboard just behind the wheels, shots flying fast and furious. They shot at the water but Devol remained under water and how he did it I never shall know, considering the current formed by the big side wheel. But he stayed under long enough until he was out of gunfire and finally swam ashore.'

George Devol wrote his own story in *Forty Years a Gambler on the Mississippi*, a series of racy anecdotes detailing fights, swindles and escapes from those seeking vengeance. His head was extremely hard and he could take a terrific amount of punishment, so, his favorite dodge was to let his opponent hit his head until his hands became so swollen and sore they were useless. Then he would finish the fight by butting!

Negro roustabouts had to take plenty of punishment in the old days. The captains and mates on the boats were a hard-boiled lot and of the conviction that the only way to make a Negro work was to be tough. 'Clubbing' was common, being done with a stout hickory stick or a barrel stave. When a longshoreman moved too slowly he was given a hard whack on his back. The laborers were fed rough food in tin pans and forced to eat with their fingers, it being considered unnecessary to provide them with knives and forks.

Captain Fred Ketchum, nostalgic for these days, said: 'I'm here to tell you we had a better bunch of niggers working then than we have now. Sure we used to club them. We always used a thick hickory stick. Of course, some fellows used a barrel stave, but I always thought they were too thin and weak to hit a nigger with. Clubbing was usually done when a nigger got smart or worked too slow. You know, they're quick to take advantage. I never did fool with them, and they were scared to death of me. There were a few who tried to get smart, but I put them in their places. I killed five niggers. But don't get me wrong. I didn't kill them because I enjoyed it. It was absolutely necessary. They came after me with knives. There is only one way to treat a nigger and that is to be positive with him. In other words, if you are right, you are right, and if you are wrong, you are still right.'

The story of the 'fricasseed nigger' is still told along the riverfront though the incident occurred more than a century ago. An old Tennessee packet, according to this yarn, refused to budge from a wharf owing to the rusty condition of the machinery, and as was the custom the engineer sent a Negro down into the flywheel to give it a start. Next morning the passengers were at breakfast when suddenly there was a terrific noise, a convulsive motion of the boat and the breakfast table crashed to the floor. Then into the midst of the horrified travelers was projected the naked body of a Negro done to a crisp! The ladies fainted, the gentlemen rushed from the dining-salon.

'What nigger is this?' bawled the furious captain at the top of his lungs.

'Oh, that's only Jim!' cried the engineer, rushing in. 'That rascal must have gone to sleep in the flywheel. I plumb forgot he was there.'

'Thank God it's Jim!' sighed the captain, mopping his brow with a handkerchief. 'I had him insured before I left Nashville. Here, boys, lend a hand and take him aft. I must see after the ladies.'

Negro roustabouts of other days had many queer superstitions. If gulls flew excitedly and in circles it was because they knew bad weather was coming; bad weather was also predicted if horses were seen running or jumping about on the levees. If the moon and stars reflected clearly in the water of the river, it foretold the coming of fog. If all the stars came out at night, or if the sun showed a dark streak across it, rain was in the offing. Whenever a cloud appeared from the southwest, the roustabouts cried, 'Morgan's gonna take the lid off the well. Bat down the hatches!' Despite rain clouds all over the sky, one from the southwest came from Morgan's direction and it alone meant rain. The sex of a drowned person, it was believed, could easily be told at first observation. A man's body always floated face downward, a woman's face upward.

The old roustabout would suffer a terrific amount of clubbing before he would work on a 'hoodoo' ship, which was any ship that had suffered some disaster. And if they did work on such a vessel it was only with the protection of the strongest *gris-gris* — like lucky beans and rabbit's feet and horseshoes.

In the steamboat days there were many strange remedies for illnesses and injuries suffered while working. If hooked by a catfish fin while fishing for their favorite sea food, they would smear the wound with what they called 'black oil,' which was the dirty oil from the engine room. The dirtier and blacker the oil the more potent it was considered to be. A tea was brewed from weeds growing along the river and was a 'cure-all' known as 'fever-tea.' This was consumed practically all the time, whether they suffered any fever or not.

Early roustabouts were famed for their songs and their 'coonjines.' The 'coonjine' was a rhythmic shuffle affected to expedite loading and unloading; the songs were usually doleful, yet served to lighten their labors, often queer little songs like

> Markey Faye,
> Down the bay,
> What you say?

This was sung by the 'screwmen.' Cotton bales were loaded by means of a boom, block and tackle and a 'heisting horse.' Once on the skid on its way to the hold of a ship the bale was taken in charge by these screwmen. In the small holds of old sailing vessels, every inch of space was valuable and as much cotton as possible had to be packed in. This was done by a process known as 'screwing in cotton' and was much like raising a house with a jack. The screwmen would sing their little song as they screwed, and at the words *Faye*, *bay*, and *say*, all turned the screw together.

Edward Ashley remembered this old song:

> I looked up river as far as I could see,
> No boat blowin' but the *Cherokee*.
> She roun' the bend loaded with men,
> She loaded with cotton,
> She want to get to town,
> To run the *Robert E. Lee* down.

'I saw the *Robert E. Lee* and the *Natchez* when they made their big race,' Ashley says. 'I was down at Canal Street and saw the start. The riverfront was lined with people way back to Jackson Square, and as far as you could see. They throwed wood and about two thousand boxes of salt meat in the fire to make steam. Everybody was excited and bettin' and nobody even pretended to work. It was like Mardi Gras. It sure was a great race.'

The riverfront has always been home to many people. For practically all of New Orleans's history there have been the folk who live under the wharves, usually termed 'wharf rats' by the police, who wage unceasing war upon them.

As early as 1853 these under-the-wharf dwellings were already established. The first wharves were flimsy affairs, and no sooner were they built than the first wharf rat appeared. The *Daily Delta* of New Orleans on December 21, 1853, reported the discovery of such a home. The article entitled 'O Home!' states: 'An Italian woman who is quite young, and who had with her a most beautiful child, was yesterday found by some of the police officers under a wharf in this district. The woman had supplied herself by the thousand of those little appliances of knives, forks, provisions and clothing. The place was perfectly dry, the wharf above being heaped up with sacks of corn and covered with tarpaulins. Who shall say the Italian woman was not more content in her wharf-roofed home than many of the proud daughters of the land who dwell in marble halls!'

Many of the people who established temporary homes beneath the wharves seem to have been thieves, pilfering from merchandise lying along the riverfront. Through the wide-spread wharf planks the thieves would slit sacks and drain the contents from below. For years the police broke up the homes regularly and systematically, but with little effect.

As late as 1938 families were found beneath a section of the Mandeville Street wharf at New Orleans, evidently some of them Depression victims. Taciturn, they would speak to no one and nursed a bitter hatred of the 'damn police.'

Back in 1877 'Frank the Barber' set up a shop under the wharf at Nuns' Street. His chair was made of driftwood and the shop was decorated with the most diverting illustrations from the old

Police Gazette. Frank bragged of the coolest shop in town and charged regular prices.

'I guess they'd call me a wharf rat,' confessed Bud Schroeder. 'I've eaten, lived and slept on this riverfront ever since I was knee-high to a duck. It's different now, though, with all these new modern docks and wharves. Not like the good old days when the levees were like pretty green hills. I've earned my livin' all my life catchin' driftwood and sellin' it. There's no better way to make a livin' easy. The wood just kinda floats in to you. Sometimes I get as much as two dollars a load for firewood. I just go on the same way, year to year. Conditions and politics and wars don't bother me at all. And I don't have no expenses livin' on the river at all. No rent or lights or nothin'.'

Outside of New Orleans, where the lights of skyscrapers are like tall candles against the sky, are Depressionvilles and *batture* settlements. Baton Rouge and other Louisiana river towns have similar colonies. Hovels, shacks, houseboats and tattered tents cluster in strange villages. Occasionally there is a neat cottage, with a flower garden. The people are a queer conglomeration, derelicts, tramps and beggars, petty thieves, sometimes an artist, always a fortuneteller. Many derive a livelihood from the river, fishing, catching driftwood to sell, rowing out in boats to collect bananas and such merchandise thrown from the ships. Others sometimes work in the nearest town. After a while they seem to grow to love the river. Some will not, if given the opportunity, leave their makeshift homes. They never fear the river.

'It never comes up to the houses,' they'll tell you. 'Besides, if it does, we can always move to the other side of the levee until it goes down again.' And they will. If the temperamental Mississippi threatens to flood them, they'll move — temporarily. When the danger is past, they return.

'Ole Mississippi can be mean,' they'll tell you, 'and tease you, but he won't do you any real harm, if you handle him right.'

Chapter 18

Pailet Lane

ALMOST IN THE VERY HEART OF NEW ORLEANS, skirting along the edge of the Bayou St. John and extending back toward the rim of Lake Pontchartrain, lies Pailet Lane. You cross the railroad tracks at St. Bernard Circle, walk out Paris Avenue. The weeds are as high as your head and the sidewalk is only occasionally paved, sometimes bricked, but mostly just hard-packed earth. The houses here are small, but many of them are quite neat, some are even new, for this is the most prepossessing thoroughfare in all of Pailet Lane.

A very stout, amazingly black Negress comes padding along, her bare feet slapping hard on the earth *banquette*, a gay pink-and-pea-green parasol held over her head.

'Pailet Lane?' She frowns, moves the parasol a bit to shade her face better. 'Pailet Lane? No, sir, I ain't never heared of that.' Then, 'Say! You doesn't mean Pellet Land? Lawd, sure! You is right in the middle of it.'

An Italian grocer is equally as confused regarding the name of the section in which he lives.

'Pailet Lane? Pellet Land? Mister, you must be trying to say like Pailetaville, eh? Sure, that is the name I call it, and that is

its name. I live here all my life, see? Is all the time call like
Pailetaville. Where is the dump? Hell, they got lots of dumps
back here. What you gonna do in a dump, eh?'

Leaving Paris Avenue, there are no longer any paved or brick
sidewalks, no longer any new little cottages, no longer any white
faces. Walking toward the Bayou, unpainted shacks, widely
scattered, are the rule rather than the exception. Consisting in
most cases of two or three rooms, these are usually constructed
of scrap wood, pieces of tin, discarded advertising signboards, on
many of which the copywriters' messages to the public are still
perfectly readable. There have been but halfhearted attempts at
beautification, flowers bordering a few of the walks leading to
the stoops before the houses. Too, a rare few have been provi-
dent enough to attempt small truck gardens. But nothing seems
completed or properly maintained. Laziness and weeds have
defeated all such ambitions. One house, however, boasts a particularly homey touch. On each side of the entrance is a wooden
pig; on one pig's's body the name 'Ellen' is scrawled, on the
other 'Steve.' Evidently they are the couple residing within.

The populace of Pailet Lane is everywhere. Black bucks, most
of them in overalls and blue jumpers, sprawl on the rude porches,
many of them asleep. The women gossip comfortably in the
shade of an occasional tree or over sudsy tubs of wash in neighboring backyards. Scarcely anyone wears shoes. Children run
naked.

Not all Pailet Lane is settled. Walk a few blocks in any direction and you'll run into vacant lots and fields. Here and there a
cow or two graze; chickens forage through the weeds, run hap-
hazardly all over the neighborhood. Grocery stores, a pool
room or two, an occasional corner barroom, before which barefooted black males loaf, about comprise the business of the
neighborhood. But perhaps the enterprises most typical of
Pailet Lane are the dump piles and junk yards.

Tall, black Blanche Jackson admits she is tough. Blanche is
about twenty-five, usually wears a bright kerchief about her
head, large hoop earrings, dirty print dresses and red shoes. She
and her husband Joe are the proud owners of their own junk pile,
in the center of which is a shack of their own creation. Before it

a fire burns in a large tar barrel covered with an iron grill, on which rests a bubbling pot of coffee. Blanche was busy this morning, arguing with a truck driver to prevent him from dumping a load of trash in her yard.

'Hey, you!' Blanche yelled. 'Git that damn stuff in the back! Don't you dare try to unload in this road. Man, I'll bust your haid! Mr. Henry'll take care of you. Hey, Mr. Henry! Honest to Gawd! They drives up here and just stays put in the road and don't give a damn if nobody gits in or not.'

Mr. Henry, a lean white man, appeared, directed the truck to the rear of the property.

'That there is really a fine man,' Blanche explained. 'He can read and write and everything. Just down on his luck. He been sleepin' in that shack and watches at night. No, me and Joe ain't livin' here no more. We got us a house down past the school. Sure we been here a long time; ever since I married Joe. Poor Joe! He sure had a hard time with me when we was first hooked. Every day I would cook him rice and potatoes and hard-boiled eggs. Couldn't and wouldn't cook nothin' else. Joe got tired of eatin' that stuff. He say, "Woman, I can't live on no bird food like this." Then I learned to cook real good. But Joe is always had a time. I sure is mean.'

Blanche pulled a sweat-dampened package of cigarettes out of her bosom and lighted one.

'Yes,' she went on, 'I is a mean woman. Mean and tough. I gets it from my pa's peoples; they was all mean as hell. I done been in the House of Good Shepherd for cuttin' a womans. I was only twelve years old then, too. See my sister had her a big fight with another gal and I was takin' up for her when a big black wench by the name of Octavia come buttin' in and say, "I gonna knock hell outta you," to me! I told her she better not mess with me or she sure gonna git cut. Well, the next day I run right into her in front of a dago grocery near my house.

'"What you gonna do?" she said.

'"Bitch," I said, "you gonna leave me alone."

'"Don't you call me no bitch," she said.

'"That's 'xactly what you is," I said.

'"Jump in the gutter, nigger gal," she said. "We is gonna fight."

'I look and she picked up a rock. I done felt the breeze of that rock pass my ear. Je-sus! I seen red. I whipped out my razor and she start runnin'. Right behind her was me. I done cut her down. She screamed like hell and jumped into that dago grocery store and slammed the door plumb in my face. But I was satisfied. I had done cut her seven times. Then the horse riders come and brung me to the House of Good Shepherd. I didn't care none. I had me a good time there.

'I was only seventeen years old when Joe married me. He had done been married before, but his wife kicked him out for messin' round with the womens. I done told him when he married me he better not fool me that way. I just dared him to try it. I say, "I ain't gonna kick you out, me. I is gonna cut you up." He ain't never tried nothin' neither, 'cause he knows the first time I catches him he is a daid nigger. Hell, I'm mean and I knows my wifely rights.

'There is only one thing in the world I is scared of and that is voodoo peoples. No, sir, I don't monkey with no voodoo peoples. There got one woman named Lala lives on Governor Nicholls Street. She'd scare you just to look at her. I remembers when I was a little girl there was a woman I knowed called Aunt Laura. She was real old and one day she took sick in her laig and went and seen that Marie Laveau. This Laveau woman boiled up a lot of snakes and made her a powder and put that there powder all over Aunt Laura's laig. Do you know that after that you could see the snake crawl from her foot up to her belly under the skin? Then the poor soul started to vomit snails. A sore come on her laig and it got so bad them maggots was just droppin' off it on the floor. When she died they didn't embalm her and when she was layin' in her coffin you could hear a frog croakin' in her throat. Ever since then I been scared of voodoo peoples.' Blanche spit on the ground, crossed her fingers.

A few minutes later Blanche was singing, her high, sweet voice chanting the words of a spiritual — 'The Shepherd' — her face lifted toward the bright blue sky, eyes closed. Her small sister, a slight, black eleven-year-old named Rosalie, joined her in the song.

'I sings in the choir at my church,' Blanche admitted. 'The preacher thinks he knows music, and he says I can really sing. He wanted to raise money from the congregation to send me up to Major Bowls, that radio man, but I wouldn't let him. I'd just giggle like a fool and be scared. I likes to sing here around my dump pile when I is busy, though. Sometimes you can hear me for miles. Even if it ain't good singin', it sure is loud. They got some fine peoples out here, 'specially Saint Ann Johnson and Mother Duffy. Them is really fine peoples what has the spirit. Sure, Rosalie knows where they lives at.'

En route to Saint Ann Johnson's house, Rosalie contributed a brief history of Pailet Lane.

'Yeah,' she said, 'all this is Pailet Lane. 'Course, I ain't sure of nothin' much, but my aunt says it was named for a man called Pailet. He daid now, but they say he owned all this land with another man named Smith and a womans named Miller. My Aunt Sallie moved out here in 1914, and there wasn't no houses but four shacks. Then Mr. Pailet built some places and people started movin' in. I done heared he got as much as six hundred dollars for some of his places.

'Be careful! You'll slip in that mud and be a mess. You know the Government is buildin' some slums down here. Yes, sir. They builds good-lookin' slums, too. And the City is puttin' in sewerage. It sure gonna all be fine when they gits done foolin' around. I been told them Government slums is gonna hold seven hundred and thirty-eight families. My Aunt Sallie knows everything about everything in Pailet Lane. See, she done lived here longer than anybody what's here now. She helped build the first church and she put up the first dollar for buildin' the Saint John Baptist Church Number 5. Now there is the Fairview Baptist Church and the Azure Baptist Church Number 1 and the Azure Baptist Church Number 2 and one Catholic Church called Saint Raymond's. All them churches just in Pailet Lane. It sure is nice.'

Saint Ann Johnson is about seventy-five years old. Her eyes are bad, but she says her 'remember' is still very good. Her small kitchen is neat, clean and warm.

'I was borned right here in Pailet Lane,' Saint Ann said, 'but

I left when I was a little girl. My ma reared me on the plantation where she went to work. They sure was good to us, too.
I don't like city life for nothin'. No, I cain't remember the Civil
War. 'Course Pa used to tell us stuff. There was good folks and
bad folks same as now. I guess it's always been like that. Some
peoples was mean to their niggers. Sure. They would take a
pregnant woman and lay her on the ground with a hole dug
underneath her to hold her belly. Then they'd lift her dress and
beat her with a whip on her nekkid skin.

'Then I remembers Elizabeth Stokes. She didn't have no
teeth, and Pa told me she used to have the prettiest white teeth
of anybody he ever seen, and her face was so black they'd shine
like pearls. Well, Pa didn't know why, but every day at 'xactly
twelve o'clock her master would take her to the blacksmith's
shop, put her haid down on an anvil and knock out one of her
teeths — just one. He done that every day until they was all
gone.

'Pa had two wives, you know. They didn't make him take
'em. He just done it 'cause he liked 'em. No, I don't believe in
that neither.

'I tell you what I does believe in — singin'. I sure does like
singin'! Sometimes I sings until I gits to cryin', and that's the
truth. And sure as I does I hears somebody is daid. I tell you
when they gits to singin' at a baptizin' — sure I'se a Baptist — I
just plain loves it. I was baptized when I was a little girl. The
old preacher had to tote me out in the water, and all the peoples
was standin' on the bank singin' their hearts out with

> On the rough, rocky road,
> I'se most done travelin',
> On the rough, rocky road,
> To my Lawd;
> On the rough, rocky road,
> I'se most done travelin',
> Got to carry my soul
> To my home.

'Then they all joined hands and singed together and stepped
around kind of fancy while they singin',

My sister, in the Lawd,
I'se most done travelin',
On the rough, rocky road,
To my Lawd;
My sister, in the Lawd,
I'se most done travelin',
I'se had to carry my soul,
To my Lawd.

'After that the preacher said some prayers. Then he said, "I baptize you in the name of Jesus." I come up out of the water hollering, "Look at the gold! Look at the gold!" The sky above me was just like gold. I seen it! One woman got so excited she walked right plumb out on the water and her feets didn't even sink. She strutted around on top of that water, shoutin' all the time, "Look at Jesus! Look at Jesus!"

'You know you gotta have faith. Just singin' for you has made me feel better.

Who die in Jesus' arms,
Honor the Lamb,
Who die in Jesus' arms,
Honor the Lamb.

'No, I don't believe much in spirits and all them things. They still talk about that Marie Laveau. Once when I was a little girl I went to her house with my sister. She had boxes sittin' all around the place with chicken wire over the tops of 'em. Honest to the Lawd, them things was full of snakes. I keeps away from peoples like that. There is too many bad spirits around to go lookin' for more.

'Sure, there's good luck things and bad luck things. That's different. Only I don't believe in them all. One time I walked into a lady's house and walked out the back way. She says, "You can't do that to me, Saint Ann. That's bad luck." And she was always mad at me after that. Lots of peoples around here won't clean their houses or change their curtains during August 'cause they thinks that's bad luck. One time a man comes around here with a Bible. He put a key in it and says to me, "Make a wish and if this here Bible turns over when you turn

that key you sure gonna git your wish." Well, he takes one end
of the key and I takes the other. He was sure tryin' to make
that Bible turn over, but I held it so tight he couldn't do it. I
knows I don't believe in nothin' like that. What I likes is
singin'.

> Shake hands and good-bye,
> I'se bound to follow my Jesus,
> Shake hands and good-bye,
> I'se goin' home.'

Which might have been construed as an invitation to leave.

Mother Duffy was sitting in the sunshine before her house.
She was a large woman with snowy hair edging from under her
red and white *tignon* and white whiskers on her round black face.

'You sure catched me on a bad day, yes!' Mother Duffy, like
many Louisiana Negroes, speaks with a slight 'Gombo' accent.
'I tell you that. I had me a smotherin' spell this mornin' and I
don't feel no good yet. I don't know how old I is. They never
did teach us nothin' about that. They just teached us to work.
Yes, Gawd! I done remembers when the Yankees come. All my
folkses .was slaves on the Camille Plantation. Sure, they was
good to us. One of them Yankee soldiers says to me, "Little
girl, ain't you glad to leave here?" I says, "No, I ain't. I don't
never want to leave here, me." He look at me like I was crazy.

'Yes, I chews tobacco. Don't be 'fraid. I won't spit on you.
I can spit clean across the *banquette*, me.

'I lives here with my boy Andrew and his wife. He works in
the City Park for that W.P.A. He's a real good boy, him. This
mornin' when I had that smotherin' spell, he git up and lit me a
fire and made me my hot sweet water. He wouldn't go to work
until I told him I felt all right. If I go I pray the good Lawd to
look after my boy. I worry about this cold weather. If he die
first I sure won't be long behind. I'm gonna make him git me
some hog's hoofs and make some tea. That's the best thing for
pneumonia. And if you ever gits the earache, don't put on no
oil, no. You just split a pod of garlic and wrap it up in cotton so
it won't burn you none and stick it in your ear. It sure is good.'

Albertine Taylor operates a beauty parlor in Pailet Lane.
Albertine is herself a walking advertisement for her own skill;

her fingernails are long and scarlet, her hair straightened and gleaming with brilliantine, and her extremely stout body is always clothed in the most colorful garments. But today she was in bed, being nursed through an indisposition by her mother, Sister Lydia Lee.

'Albertine has her hairdressing business,' Sister Lydia said, 'and she's doing real good, but she was borned to be a missionary. She got her call, but she just ain't followed it yet.'

'Seven years ago when I was real sick,' Albertine explained, 'I had been in bed a long time and on this morning I had terrible pains. My mother was in the kitchen making coffee and my husband was sleeping in the bed. I got up and stood by the window for a while and a voice said right in my ear, "Albertine, if you want to come home, come. But if you want to stay and do my work, you can stay." Just like that.

'I looked at my husband. It couldn't be his talking I had heard; he was asleep. Right then I started to weep, 'cause I knowed who it was. It wasn't nobody but the Holy Ghost Himself! The Holy Ghost had revealed Himself to me! I started praying. I wanted to shout that good news. Then two ladies come in. I told them I would live to do Jesus' work.

'A few days after that I said to myself, "When I get through what I'm doing, I'm going to eat my cabbage and drink my beer." I always loved my beer. But when I is in the kitchen and I starts to open a bottle of beer, a voice pops in and says, "Albertine, how're you going to do My work and drink beer? You forgot your promise." Then I stood up on my feet, and I cried, "No, I ain't, Lord! No, I ain't! I'm sorry, Lord. I'll never touch no beer again." And I ain't, neither. That was more 'n seven years ago, and there was plenty whiskey here Christmas time, but I didn't touch a drop of the stuff. I don't even want to look at it.'

Someone knocked at the door. Sister Lydia called out, 'Papa! Hey, Papa! Go open that door, please.'

Papa emerged from another room, crossed to the door. He was a boy of fourteen, one of Albertine's children, whom everyone called by that nickname. He opened the door, two women entered.

'Get chairs from the other room, Papa,' Sister Lydia instructed the boy. 'How you all feeling? Albertine's much better today. Yes, indeed. See how she's watching the clock? We has prayers here every day at this time, you know. Papa, get some newspapers for the ladies to kneel on. Wait a minute, Mildred, honey. You'll dirty your dress. Papa, get your Book.'

Papa returned with a worn and shabby Bible. Everyone knelt.

'The Lord is my Shepherd, I shall not want...' In a still childish treble, Papa read the whole of the Twenty-Third Psalm. Then he said the Lord's Prayer.

After that they all prayed, Sister Lydia, Albertine and the two visitors, Sister Laura and Mildred. Mildred prayed loudest and she would punctuate the others' prayers with 'Hear us! Oh, hear us, Lawd!'

Back at the dump pile, a week later, Blanche was behind a large pile of papers and bottles and broken glass. She had a large rake and was tearing down the pile, sorting out the good bottles to sell, breaking the others into bits. Today she was wearing a faded blue dress, a large sun hat and shoes through which her naked toes showed.

'You sure catched me workin',' she said. 'You know, they is about to ruin me. Ever since they closed that road over there, I been havin' to stand for 'em stoppin' at three other dumps before they gits to me. How the hell I'm gonna make a livin' this way? I hates them Public Service trucks not comin' worse than any of the others. Them is the trucks what brings the dirt swept out of the buses, and I used to always find my carfares in that dirt. Peoples drops change in buses, you know. Now I just gotta put out my own money since Mr. Public Service don't come here no more.

'I tell you the truth, today I is really out of my mind! I gotta move, you know. It's on account of 'em buildin' them new Government slums. If I don't move soon them horse riders is gonna come move me. It ain't really the Government makin' me git out, though. It's the Board of Health. The Health mens don't like the stink and they say my dump'll cause lices. If they'd just give me time I could git all this junk together and make me a little somethin', but they ain't givin' me time to do nothin'

You ought to come back out here on a Sunday. Come see our church. We has a fine time.'

Sunday night in Pailet Lane was dark and quiet. There are no street lights and little electric lighting in the houses. Lamps flickered palely in the windows. Under a bulb suspended before a grocery a group of Negro boys were on their knees. From the group came shouts of 'Come, seven!' 'Little Joe, come to Papa!' 'Baby needs shoes!'

The Fairview Baptist Church is very crude and very small. There is a stove to one side; the long wooden benches are painted a dull gray. On the pulpit were more wooden benches, a piano and a preacher. The Reverend Strudwick is small and lean and black.

'If you plants a seed,' intoned the Reverend, 'what's it gwine do?'

The congregation answered as one, 'Grow!'

''Course it's gwine grow,' agreed the preacher. 'Then what's it gwine do?'

'Bloom!'

''Course it is,' said the little man on the pulpit. 'It's gonna bloom and bear fruit and that's what we wants. If you plants the seed of the Lawd — Christianity — in your hearts, it's bound to grow, too, ain't it? It's gwine bear fruit, too.'

Reverend Strudwick took a breath.

'Now, then,' said he. 'You cain't grow the seed of Christianity without pain. Look at Job. He was a rich man and he denied his Gawd and he losted everythin', even his son. Then he planted the seed of real Christianity in his heart, and still he kept gettin' sick, gettin' blind. The Devil came and tempted him sore, but he say, "No!" His wife say, "Deny Gawd!" He still say, "No!" Then he say, "There's only one thing. I wishes the day I was borned was never on no calendar." You ain't never seen no thirtieth of February, is you? You know you ain't. And that's why.'

The door in the rear of the church opened and Blanche Jackson came up the aisle. She was almost unrecognizable in a polka dot silk dress, bright blue shoes, a flaming red straw hat set jauntily on her head and a bag to match the hat. She smiled widely and every gold tooth gleamed.

Reverend Strudwick announced, 'We is closin' this meetin' now. Sister Blanche Jackson has a guest who has come to hear us sing.'

The pianist struck a few bars and the choir rose and sang,

> Oh, they tell me, yes, they tell me,
> Of an uncloudy day...

Throughout the song, seated on a bench at one side, the Reverend punctuated with such remarks as 'Oh, yes!' and 'Bless us all!' or 'Hallelujah!'

The entire congregation rose and joined in the last chorus. Then Blanche sang a 'ballad,'

> I'll go, yes, I'll go...

Her voice was low and sweet, untrained, of course, but rich with feeling. And as an ending she ad libbed,

> In our midst is a stranger,
> I'll go, yes, I'll go...

Leaving the church and walking back through Pailet Lane, the night was darker than ever. There was no moon and most of the lights in the little houses had been extinguished. Even the boys in front of the grocery store had vanished. Now only insects circled the lonely, still burning electric bulb. Except for a few church-goers straggling homeward, Pailet Lane slept.

Chapter 19

Mother Shannon

MOTHER SHANNON IS CLOSE TO THE LORD AND she knows it. She'll tell you: 'I is married to Jesus. Minor Shannon died one month before my little girl was born, and I ain't looked at anybody since.'

Clad in a robe of brocaded golden satin, with filmy veil to match, or, on other occasions, in virginal white, also with veil to match, Mother Shannon prays and preaches, heals, and prophesies. Like all leaders of the Spiritualist Church of the Southwest, she has been instructed in all four of these difficult arts. And Mother Shannon prays and preaches and heals and prophesies with all the vigor of her huge, three-hundred-pound body. Before you see her in action you may arrive at the erroneous conclusion that she is a rather indolent and phlegmatic person; she is very fat and has the sort of heavy-lidded eyes that might add sultry appeal to a glamour girl, but which, unfortunately, only make Mother Shannon look sleepy. However, this is deceptive, for when she steps before her congregation to conduct her services, she gives her all. When she prays, she prays hard and passionately. When she preaches, it is stirring and thorough and loud. She sways and jerks and shudders, and sometimes, completely overcome with the *spirit*, she bends forward, until her hands almost touch the floor, and lets loose a shriek, and has to be lifted and put back together again.

You never doubt her sincerity. It is apparent in those sleepy brown eyes, in her loosely fitted, thick-lipped mouth, in the tenseness of her clasped hands. And whether you believe in her or not, when you're away from her, you believe while you watch.

Even when others take charge, while she sits on her throne beneath the electrically illuminated cross on the wall at the front of her church, you forget the others and look at Mother Shannon sitting there, sometimes with eyes closed, lips mumbling, head nodding, sometimes glancing shrewdly at the congregation, those heavy-lidded eyes shifting from one face to another.

The St. Anthony's Daniel Helping Hand Divine Chapel, branch of the Spiritualist Church of the Southwest, is at 2139 St. Ann Street in New Orleans. The building is a modest cottage, with most of the lower floor devoted to the chapel; one whole side — with walls torn down between the rooms — is the chapel proper; on the other side is an anteroom from which the church dignitaries may enter, and where they may rest or arrange their regalia. Behind this is a bedroom, which also seems to serve as a dressing room for visiting ' mothers' and others. There is a small kitchen behind the chapel.

The chapel walls are adorned with a multitude of holy pictures; plaster statues of saints are everywhere. The walls are painted white, but are almost hidden by the pictures and by strips of pink and white crepe paper. Crepe paper also is strung across the ceiling, festoon-fashion, gathered here and there in the center, and draping out to the walls. Wooden chairs and benches are lined before the altar, with a single aisle between. In the center of the aisle is an ancient and much-used piano and an old-fashioned revolving stool. The altar stands at front, to one side; and on it are innumerable objects: statues, pictures, candles, votive lights. Facing the congregation are more statues and pictures and candles, the illuminated cross (the gift of a white truck-driver whom Mother Shannon cured of ' nervousness'), Mother Shannon's throne, and a table, covered with white cloth, holding more statues, candles, and votive lights.

Most of these objects and decorations are borrowed from the Roman Catholic Church, such borrowing being a common practice among New Orleans' Negro churches. But Mother Shannon's chapel has some things of mysterious origin. For instance, beside the crucifix on the wall behind her throne hangs the 'Key to Heaven.' This is a large, gilded key, decorated with a bow of ribbon.

Mother Shannon says she has led her church for about eighteen years, though.the chapel has been at its present address for only about three years. But her spiritual life began when she was fourteen years old. 'A vision of a child appeared to me in spirit,' she says. 'I know this child was a spirit because I could tell it come from Heaven. I had a feeling then that I was gifted. Right then I started preaching about Christ off and on, but not steady like now.' She didn't preach 'steady' until her husband died. 'I was given a sign before he passed. He ain't been sick or nothing then, but he was just laying on the bed and I seen a spirit pass over him. I just went out and told people "Minor is dead." And when they looked he was dead.'

Besides healing the sick souls and sick bodies, Mother Shannon's chapel does charitable work among the poor in her neighborhood. 'Don't make no difference what color they is,' she says, 'if they is poor they gets aid. Christmas time we gives away toys and dollars and baskets of food. We has our altar on Saint Joseph's Night just like the 'talian people, and we gives away all our food to everybody what comes.'

Two days before Saint Joseph's Night, sitting in her kitchen, dressed in an ordinary checkered house dress, her head without its usual veil, Mother Shannon stirred at the contents of the large pot in her lap, and talked.

'It been fourteen years now I been having my Saint Joseph Altar. That day I started out with thirty dollars to pay my rent and I met Saint Joseph and he told me to take the money and make a Saint Joseph Altar. I was scared I never would get my rent together again. I'm a poor widow woman and sometimes I gets up and there ain't a cent in the house. Still, I got faith, so I built me the altar.'

Mother Shannon turned to Reverend Clothilde Davis, her assistant, and ordered briskly: 'Sister Davis, you better take a look in the oven at that cake. I can smell it!' Then she resumed her chatter. 'Sure, I've cured lots of peoples in my time. I was real sick myself once, and nobody thought I'd live. So I just went in the bathroom and talked to God. I said: "God, I'm not ready to leave this world. You need me here to do your work. And I'm here, ain't I?" Child, I just love to talk about Jesus. I swear, I get so happy! See how I can beat these eggs now?

'There was a man come here and he was sick. His legs was so stiff when he sat down they stuck out in front of him like they was made of wood 'stead of meat. I prayed for him and he was cured. He say to me, "Thank you, Mother Shannon!" I say, "Don't thank me! Say 'Thank you, Jesus!' Just keep saying, 'Thank you, Jesus!'" Child, look how good I can beat these eggs! I gets so happy when I talks about Jesus!'

Removing the cake from the oven, Sister Davis muttered, 'Amen, Mother!' In the chapel, up on a stepladder, hanging curtains for the Saint Joseph's Night celebration, a young Negro hollered toward the kitchen, 'Listen, Mother! Hallelujah!'

'All my statues and pictures and everything I got,' continued Mother Shannon, 'was donated by people what have received divine help. I got twenty, what I calls really good members, the kind that don't forget to give to their church. You got to give to your church, so the church can give. Do you know we gives away ten baskets of food every month? Last Christmas we gave away a hundred. That's besides all the toys we makes. We makes dolls with pearl buttons for eyes, and doll furniture out of old crates, stuffed animals made of calico, and all sorts of things.' Mother Shannon exhibited a stuffed something which she said was going to be a chicken when it was finished.

'God sure has been good to me,' she said. 'Like about my daughter. When she was little I asked God to give me the power to send her to any school she wanted to go to, and to let her be anything she wanted to be. Now she's going to Loyola in Chicago, studying to be a dietician. You know I lived in Chicago for twenty years.' Mother Shannon beat her eggs. 'Come see my altar on Saint Joseph's Night. We sure have a crowd, and everybody gets a plate.'

The chapel was packed with people Saint Joseph's Night; they poured in and out of every door. Freshly-starched lace curtains hung at the windows, and the small anteroom, usually used for a dressing room, held the Saint Joseph's Altar. Here walls and ceiling were entirely covered with white sheets, and the altar, taking up half the room, was literally concealed under platters and plates and bowls of food, most of it identical with that found on the altars in Italian homes of New Orleans on that occasion. There were the immense loaves of Italian bread — most of them shaped like rings — the Italian salads and seed cakes. There were shrimp and stuffed crabs and a huge lobster, and a hundred other kinds of foods. Missing were the pigolate and the redfish, always associated with Italian altars. In the front center was a cake baked in the form of an open book, covered with white icing and embellished with the following words in pink icing: 'Come thou with us, and we will do thee good; for the Lord hath spoken good concerning Israel.' There were the usual tall candles, decorated with pictures of angels and rosebuds. A big wooden ring above the altar bore the inscription 'Daniel Helping Hand Divine.'

Opposite the altar, on a mantel, were votive lights and smaller candles, and a box to receive offerings. A white man entered, stood before these, said a prayer, and dropped a coin into the box. On the altar, a white bowl also received money. Another contained Saint Joseph's beans, and those dropping coins took a bean or two.

Mother Shannon appeared from the bedroom in the rear, and tonight she wore her golden robe of heavy, brocaded satin, with bright glass buttons down the front, and long full sleeves gathered at the wrist by a tight band. The full skirt touched the floor, and a yellow cord was fastened about her huge waist. Every dignitary of the Spiritualist Church of the Southwest wears this cord. It is the *power*. A veil of yellow crepe was gathered about her head and hung to the middle of her back.

A photographer took Mother Shannon's picture. She was very shy during this procedure, grinning sheepishly and dropping her already droopy lids. Sister Davis, short and stout, with protruding, jagged and yellowed teeth, appeared in a costume of white silk and a white veil, with a big pearl brooch at her neckline.

After the pictures everyone entered and took seats in the chapel, and Johnny Jones, a natty young Negro in a gray tweed suit and a maroon tie and breast pocket handkerchief, took a seat at the ancient piano and struck a few chords. Everyone rose, as a procession of visiting Mothers came slowly up the aisle, headed by Mother Shannon. There were at least nine of these leaders, and each wore a robe and veil of a different color; there was blue, green, white, and black. This over, Mother Shannon took a seat in her armchair — the throne — and bid Sister Davis start the services. Another sister, also in white, had been left as a sort of hostess in the anteroom, and as the congregation began singing 'It's That Old Time Religion,' she could be seen doing little 'trucking' steps. More than once Mother Shannon shot her a reproving glance through the door between the rooms.

After that hymn, Mother Shannon rose and spoke, quietly, but authoritatively: 'If you has come here with Jesus in your hearts,' she said, 'you will receive the help you seek, but if there are doubters among you, you will be cast out.' She then looked silently from face to face in the congregation for a minute, and everybody followed her eyes, but no one was 'cast out.'

Now she turned her back to the congregation, facing the electric cross, and offered the Lord's Prayer, in which everyone joined. Turning again, she said:

'One of our dear brothers has just departed from our midst, Brother Thomas, and it has made us sad indeed. But we know God was ready for him and we all must be ready for the call.' There were 'Amens' and 'Hear it!' and 'That's right, Mother!' from the congregation.

'Tonight,' said Mother Shannon, 'we is greatly honored by having Sister Roxanna Moore with us. Roxanna Moore was with me at my first Saint Joseph's feast, and tonight is our fourteenth feast for him. I am going to turn this meeting over to Sister Davis, like I said before. Sister Davis has been with me eight years. She is a good woman and I know her words will be a blessing to all of us.' Then, with great dignity, Mother Shannon made an exit into the anteroom, where the altar was located.

The Reverend Davis addressed the congregation briefly, then she introduced Sister Roxanna Moore, a short, plump, elderly Negress, who, instead of the robe and veil worn by most of the Mothers, wore a neat black and white street dress and a black hat. Roxanna Moore proved to be an eloquent and impressive speaker. She spoke long and loud and pounded at the air with one black fist until the chapel vibrated with the congregation's 'Amens' and 'Hallelujahs.'

'I was here fourteen years ago when Sister Shannon give her first altar,' she said. 'It wasn't easy for her, and it ain't easy now. I hesitated to come here tonight. I should have done been here two days ago, but the weather was so bad I put it off. And now I is glad and I is happy I done come. I hated to come just in time for the feast, without doing no work, but now I is glad and I is happy.

'Sister Shannon has come far. And it ain't been easy for her. Don't you all get no idea it's been easy for her. I told her years ago she was gonna be a great leader, and she is! Today she is bigger in every way than she was fourteen years ago. Her feast is bigger; her flock is bigger; everything is bigger! And I want Sister Shannon to go on and grow bigger and bigger and lead the way for all you sisters and brothers.

'I loves Jesus. You know,' and here her voice softened and took on an affectionate and tender tone, 'sometimes I goes into my room and I is alone. I shuts my door and turns on the light, and there is Jesus. Jesus comes to me, and He takes me in His arms, and we is alone. He spreads a table and we dines. You all is gonna dine with Jesus some day!' Now Roxanna Moore began to sing 'Come and Dine' and the congregation took it up, until everyone was singing, without accompaniment from Johnny Jones, who still sat at his piano, staring into space. They sang with the infectious rhythm only Negroes can achieve:

> Jesus has a table spread, where the saints of God is fed,
> He invites His chosen people: Come and dine!
> With His manna He doth feed, an' supply every need,
> It's sweet to sup wit' Jesus all the time.

Chorus:

Come an' dine, the Master's callin', come an' dine!
You may feast at Jesus' table all the time.
With His manna he doth feed an' supply every need,
Oh, it's sweet to sup wit' Jesus all the time!

There were at least twenty verses and choruses. When they were finished Roxanna Moore resumed her spirited address. 'Some day we is all gonna feast with the Lord, I say. We all got our robes on, ain't we? Look at me. I'm seventy-five years old, and I'm ready any time. 'Course I hopes to live awhile yet. But I is ready any time. Look at my hair.' She removed her hat, and her hair was gray in places, a change which occurs only in Negroes of great age. 'I is white-headed! I say to Jesus: "Look, Lord, I'm gettin' hoary!" Yes, I is ready when my time comes! I is ready to sit down at His feast any time!'

After Sister Moore resumed her seat, Sister Davis began a song, simply by opening her mouth and emitting the first line, and the room took it up. Then there were prayers, some led by Mother Shannon, when she re-entered the chapel, then more songs, a piano solo by Brother Johnny Jones, more songs. During all this a young Negro entered and took a seat on a chair near Mother Shannon, carefully tying a gray silk cord about his waist — the *power* — and it was passed from ear to ear that he was a 'traveling missionary.' Later he led the congregation in a prayer, then a song. About midnight, all filed into the ante-room, to the Saint Joseph's Altar for food, everyone holding a paper plate and helping themselves to whatever they pleased from the delicacies on the altar. Many persons entered from the street and also ate. Whatever was left would be given away the day following — if there was anything left.

'Come back in July and see my Ordination services,' Mother Shannon invited, with a big smile and a friendly fluttering of her heavy eyelids.

Invitations were sent out for the Ordination, in gold letters. They read:

'AND He said unto them, Go ye into all the world, and preach
the gospel to every creature.' MARK 16:15

The honor of your presence and congregation is
requested at

THE ORDINATION

of

Sister Mary Augustine

and

Sister Lillie Walker

On Sunday, July 20, 1941
At the hour of eight of the clock P.M.

St. Anthony's Daniel Helping Hand Divine
Spiritualist Church of the Southwest
2139 St. Ann Street

REV. MOTHER MAUDE SHANNON, Pastor
REV. CLOTHILDE DAVIS, Asst. Pastor
SISTER MARTHA JACKSON, Secretary
BRO. EDWARD JACKSON, Sr. Deacon-Treas.

This meant that Sister Mary Augustine and Sister Lillie Walker
were about to be graduated in praying and preaching and healing
and prophesying and were to be ordained as 'Mothers' of the
Spiritualist Church of the Southwest.

The chapel was entirely redecorated for the great occasion of
these ordinations. Everything was snowy white, with sheeting
covering every inch of walls and ceiling, and all the chairs
painted white. The altar had been moved from beneath the
mantel to the front of the room. All the colored crepe paper had
been exchanged for white, chains of it stretching across the
ceiling and meeting here and there in big bells of the same material. Mother Shannon explained, when asked: 'White is for
purity, ain't it?'

Candles burned on the altar and to one side of it stood two
huge candles — about five feet high, as yet unlighted. Before
and between them was a white satin pillow. This was for the
candidates' use when they knelt to be ordained.

Mother Shannon wore white, too, with a veil of white crepe

binding her hair and hanging down her back. She and Sister Davis — also in white — were quite busy, rushing about as fast as their weight permitted, greeting this person and that one, and attending to mysterious duties in the rear of the house. The night was insufferably warm and not a breath of air seemed to get into the chapel, until at last three or four electric fans were resurrected and placed here and there. Mother Shannon's daughter, a shapely young black girl in a slack suit and with a modern 'upswept' hairdo, attended to this very efficiently, climbing on chairs to rig up extension cords, and yelling from one end of the rooms to the other. It was noticeable that after performing these tasks, she took no further interest in the services at all, but vanished for the rest of the evening, and with a certain perceptible disdain no doubt suitable to a co-ed from Loyola of Chicago.

Every leader of the various chapels of the Spiritualist Church of the Southwest was present. Three rows of chairs up front were reserved for these dignitaries, who floated in wearing every sort and color of robe and veil conceivable. Queerly out of place was a single white 'mother,' who, wearing a light blue regalia, knelt immediately upon reaching her place, and prayed loudly and dramatically, the prayer sounding like this: 'Oh, my Father, oh, my Father, oh, my Father, oh, my Father, oh, my Father, oh, my Father, oh, my Father, oh, my Father, oh, my Father, oh, my Father! Ohmyfatherohmyfatherohmyfatherohmyfatherohmyfatherohmyfatherohmyfather! Bless the white girls and boys, oh, my Father! Bless the President of the United States, oh, my Father. Bless all the colored people, oh, my Father! Bless all the white and the colored and all the white and the colored and all the white and the colored, ohmyfatherohmyfather. Havemercyhavemercyhavemercyhavemercy. Ohmyfatherohmyfatherohmyfatherohmyfatherohmyfatherohmyfatherohmyfatherohmyfatherohmyfatherohmyfatherohmyfatherohmyfatherohmyfatherohmyfatherohmyfatherohmyfatherohmyfatherohmyfather . . .'

It lasted about twenty minutes, with practically no variation in theme or tempo. No one paid any attention to her at all though she prayed loudly enough to be heard across the street, her eyes shut tight, her thin, pale face set and tense, her hands

Part of the ceremony that precedes All Saints' Day

All Saints' Day in St. Vincent de Paul Cemetery

On All Saints' Day refreshments and souvenirs are sold at the cemetery gates

"Banjo Annie," one of the gayer characters of the Vieux Carre

Chimney Sweeps still do a thriving business in New Orleans

knotted before her. It was learned later that she was Mother Theresa Cordiz, a member of Mother Shannon's Church, and trained under the latter's guidance. The Negro 'mothers' ignored her throughout the entire evening.

The services were very late beginning, but at last the bishop of the Spiritualist Church of the Southwest appeared on the altar, from the anteroom, and raised his dark brown hands in blessing. Bishop Thomas B. Watson, a teacher at Sylvians Williams, Negro school, graduate of Xavier University, began speaking, using precise English, not without some affectations, and with a studied manner that made you wonder if he didn't don his diction with his robes, and speak differently on week days. He reminded the congregation that it was late, that he was a very busy man, a very tired man — though of course he was always glad to do his duty — and that he and they all had to go to work on the morning not so far away. Then he proceeded to speak for forty-five minutes, explaining at great length how hard he worked and that he was a 'professional man of this fair city.' At last he said that there might be time for a little testifying, but that each speaker must be as brief as possible.

A sister rose and began these dearly beloved testimonials. She had, she said, been a wicked sinner for a long time. Then walking down the street one day she had met Jesus, and had been saved. As she mentioned Jesus, she was afflicted with an attack of the 'jerks' and she shuddered and jerked until she had to be assisted back into her chair. Another sister rose immediately, sang a few lines of a hymn, then went into her testifying. She had been a sinner, too, and had been saved. Then she bent forward, leaned back, shuddered, shook, and jerked. From then on it was entirely repetitious. Each testifying sister told approximately the same story, sang a little, suffered the 'jerks.' Each speaker was echoed with 'Amens' and 'Hallelujahs' and such comments.

This over, the pianist, the same Johnny Jones who had accompanied the singers Saint Joseph's Night, gave a solo. Then there were hymns and prayers, and prayers and hymns. Bishop Watson spoke again. Then a lean, very black Negro dressed as a Roman Catholic priest, except for a striped gray shirt and bright orange necktie, showing above the edge of his cassock, who spoke with a definite Cajun accent and ended every single sentence of his talk with 'Amen!', took his turn. 'You know Jesus is your true friend, yes?' he said. 'Amen! You know you ain't got nothing to worry about if you got him for be your friend? Amen! He say go forth and don't sin no more, huh? Amen!' He sweated profusely and was forced to dab at his brow with a handkerchief.

Finally the procession of the candidates to the altar began. First appeared a little girl dressed all in white and carrying flowers. She was light brown and had a thick mass of jet curls which hung to her shoulders and were tied with a white silk ribbon. She came up the aisle slowly, painstakingly, making two even steps, then coming to a complete halt, then two more steps. At last, some ten feet and three minutes behind her, appeared the first candidate — Sister Mary Augustine. Sister Mary Augustine was quite tall and very black. She was dressed in white satin and wore a veil like a bride. Her jet hair was elaborately curled and arranged, and she carried a bouquet of white gladioli. From the very first glimpse it caught, the congregation could tell this was the biggest moment in Sister Mary Augustine's life.

Her ecstasy was so extreme she could scarcely walk at all. At exactly every third step she stopped and gave way to an attack of the 'jerks.' She shook so violently that it seemed she would never retain her balance, but somehow she proceeded up the aisle until she reached the altar. Here she collapsed completely. Bishop Watson and Brother Peterson, a young Negro who had been sitting quietly until now, each seized an arm and replaced Sister Augustine on her feet, assisting her to the white satin pillow before the candles. But here she outdid herself, shaking and jerking, and sucking in her breath as she knelt. As many as half of the sisters in the congregation were affected by this, and they began jerking, too, eyes closed, shoulders twisting and contorting. Even Mother Shannon had an attack. Her whole huge body jerked and shuddered and she fell forward and was caught in the arms of Bishop Watson. Sister Mary Augustine was lifted gently from her kneeling position on the floor and half carried to one of the two chairs awaiting the candidates before the altar.

Now everyone awaited the appearance of Sister Lillie Walker. Little Bessie Lee Jackson, the small girl who had led Sister Augustine, vanished quickly to the rear, holding up her ankle-length white organdy dress, then reappeared in the aisle a moment later, walking with the extreme slow and measured pace she had used before. At last came Sister Lillie Walker, and it was evident she had either watched Sister Augustine from the rear or else was more emotional, for she outdid the first candidate with jerking and shuddering and much sucking in of breath. Tears poured down her cheeks, and it was a temptation not to bet money that she wouldn't make it to the altar. Bishop Watson and Brother Peterson had to almost carry her to the pillow, then to the chair. Even there she collapsed again — for at least the seventh time, fell limply forward and had to be pushed back to a sitting position. At sight of this Mother Shannon was again overcome and had to be aided, and members of the congregation jerked and emitted little strangling cries of ecstasy.

However, most of the emotionalism at last quieted, though occasionally a sister would be seen to drop her head, eyes closed, and shake it violently. Bishop Watson addressed the candidates, stressing the difficulties they would encounter, but the honor that was theirs. After him Mother Shannon spoke, then the visiting mothers. All said about the same thing, amounting to something like: 'You have a hard road ahead of you. You will be called a voodoo! Doors will close in your face. Your best friends will turn against you. They will say you are a voodoo! But wasn't Jesus called a voodoo? Yes, doors will close, but follow Jesus and He will open the doors for you! Put your hands in God's and you will never falter.' Through each little advising address there were, of course, the echoing cries of: 'Amen!' 'That's right!' 'Ain't it the real truth!' 'Yes, Mother!' Then there were songs.

At last it was announced that Mary Lou Green of Chicago would honor with a solo. Mary Lou proved to be a dark brown girl of about fifteen with long curls and a red mouth containing very white teeth and the pinkest tongue ever seen. Without musical accompaniment, but with many gesticulations, she stood before the altar, facing the congregation, and sang 'The

Highway To Heaven.' At each pronouncement of 'Heaven' she would point a rigid arm and finger toward the ceiling, and her mouth would open very wide. She had a curious but fascinating habit of thrusting her pink tongue in and out as she sang.

After this the entire congregation sang 'When the Moon Go Down and Vanish Away,' which begins:

> When the moon go down and vanish away,
> When the sun refuse to shine,
> Oh, when every star in the Heaven give way
> Then I want to take Jesus to be mine.

A Negro from the Algiers church sang, then announced his wife would sing, too. This over, five members of the Algiers choir rose, all white-robed women, and sang. Then one sang alone. At last Bishop Watson asked that Enit Ellis, apparently an often featured soloist at the Daniel Helping Hand Divine, sing 'What a Friend We Have in Jesus.' After that Bishop Watson called on Bishop T. Morris Kelly, who proved to be a large, fleshy, light Negress stylishly dressed in a beige street costume with turban to match and baring a number of beautiful gold teeth when she smiled. A great many diamonds flashed as she emphasized her talk with gestures.

Others were then called upon, including an amazingly long thin Negress in blue velvet, who turned out to be a Mother Clark from Washington, D.C., and Mother Lottie Davis, a missionary.

It was now about one-thirty in the morning. Bishop Watson and the Bishop with the Cajun accent assisted Sister Mary Augustine from her chair to the pillow between the candles. The jerking started immediately, affecting Sister Augustine, Mother Shannon, and members of the congregation. But at last Sister Augustine reached the white satin pillow and was helped to her knees. Bishop Watson held a wreath of orange blossoms above her head and muttered a few words. She shuddered violently and had to be held under the armpits. Then Mother Shannon and Bishop T. Morris Kelly, one on each side, pinned the wreath in place. Then all the mothers gathered around in a ring and held outstretched hands, palms downward, over the head of the new recruit for a moment. It was noticeable that the single white leader, Mother Theresa Cordiz, had a difficult time finding a place, and that she was subject to a particularly violent attack of jerking. Then Bishop Watson snapped his fingers and the ring broke. The candidate — now Mother Augustine — was helped to her feet.

Mother Shannon presented her with a rolled diploma. Bishop Watson handed her a membership card bearing a golden seal, and a 'traveling card,' entitling her to travel anywhere in the United States and represent the Spiritualist Church of the Southwest. She was now graduated in preaching and praying and healing and prophesying. As a final touch, Bishop T. Morris Kelly gave her a Bible — a new one.

Mother Shannon was so overcome with the 'jerks' that she couldn't help Sister Lillie Walker at all, when her time came. After the bishops, with much hard work and perspiring, got her onto the pillow, Bishop Watson remarked: 'Mother Shannon is a wonderful woman. She gave twenty-two dollars to the dedication of our church in Algiers.'

The procedure ordinating Sister Walker was precisely the same as for the first candidate, except that the Bible presented her by Bishop T. Morris Kelly was noticeably old and worn. It was later learned that both Bibles were donated, and evidently it was a case of 'first come, first served' as to who received the better of the two.

Now there appeared a huge imitation cut glass punch bowl, and the candidates, bishops and 'mothers' washed their hands in it. Holy Communion followed, with church dignitaries partaking first of the wine and crackers, then members of the congregation.

This over, Brother Peterson stepped before the congregation with a wooden bowl in his hands. Smiling genially, he announced: 'Now, listen, everybody! I wants nine dollars! Mother Shannon got to have nine dollars, and this bowl's gonna keep comin' back to you till Mother Shannon gets her nine dollars!'

Another brother took the bowl and started down the aisle. Brother Peterson burst into song, rendering 'Just a Closer Walk with Thee.' He sang loud and well, with gestures reminiscent of Al Jolson's 'Mammy.' The bowl went through the audience three times, but unfortunately only $4.85 was collected from all three. Thus did the services come to an end.

It was two-thirty in the morning, but, despite this, church dignitaries and most of the congregation retired to the anteroom for sandwiches and punch. Mother Shannon looked very tired. She could hardly keep her eyelids up at all.

Chapter 20

The Sockserhause Gang

NEW ORLEANS IS, AND HAS ALWAYS BEEN, CON-
sidered Creole and Latin in character. But though the French
and Spanish undoubtedly comprised the major portion of the
population in the early days, other races soon found homes here,
Irish, with fists ever ready for a brawl, and Germans, always
equally as willing to join in any mêlée. No tougher element ever
lived in the city than the old Sockserhause Gang.

A decade or two after the War Between the States, these Germans settled in a section of the lower city, near what was then
known as the Bone Factory, a wild and swampy region, infested
with the nauseous odor of bones drying in the sun. The stench
was fearful and notorious, and on bad days was wafted for miles,
but those who resided in the Sockserhause community seemed im-
pervious to this. The land was cheap, the woods were close, and
the frugal German folk appreciated the advantages of building
homes at extremely low costs. Too, the swamps provided ideal
pasture for raising their hogs — a favorite occupation. Garbage
was gathered from the adjacent vicinities on which the pigs
could be fed. The Sockserhausers were not proud.

Neither were they very clean. In fact, only a rapid succession of miracles occurred during this era or they possessed the most remarkable constitutions ever recorded; otherwise no Sockserhauser would have lived very long. When the epidemics, once so prevalent and so violent in New Orleans, struck, they were nearly always the first to suffer. Smallpox and cholera, malaria and yellow fever raged through the settlement again and again, yet most of them seemed to survive. There is certainly no mystery attached to the frequency of the plagues. All drinking water was derived from cisterns fed by gutter pipes on the roofs of houses. During dry spells, these rooftops collected dust, dirt and bird excrement, all to be swept into the cisterns when the rains came. Dead rats, birds, even an occasional human corpse were discovered in these reservoirs. Drowning in cisterns became a popular method of suicide. There was even a saying, 'If you're over forty, go and jump in the cistern.' Consequently, whenever a member of the settlement vanished everyone took care to examine their cisterns, if they were at all fastidious. Fortunately, the Sockserhausers had a certain contempt for water. They preferred beer for drinking purposes.

When baths were necessary — *when* was entirely relative and completely a matter of individual opinion, though Saturday night was probably the usual occasion — equal disregard of Herr Leeuwenhoek's discovery of the microbe was exhibited. One tub of water would be heated and each member of the family would bathe in turn and in the same water. This was all managed by a system of rotation according to age. For instance, if the eldest child was bathed first this Saturday, next week he would be at the end of the line. Whether the children were boys or girls made no difference. Mothers and fathers always emersed themselves in the — now really delightful — bath last. Sometimes young people swam in mudholes in the neighborhood and this of course eliminated them from the competition on Saturday nights. For drying purposes, after these baths, there was always the family roller towel hanging on the kitchen wall, which was never changed until it was black. The drinking bucket with its tin, usually rusty, dipper, was also in common use, providing means of refreshment for all the family, neighbors and visiting friends.

All this led to certain disadvantages to those Sockserhausers who were not tough enough to withstand them. For instance there was Faldene. He was a shoemaker and, as was necessary in those days, an artist at his craft. He was not the fighting kind. Poor Faldene lost a leg just because someone stepped on his toe during a race at a picnic at Milneburg, favorite resort of the day. Faldene's toe was swollen and he had to go to a doctor. From that worthy soul he received instructions to sit in his backyard all day with his sore toe under the cistern faucet, letting the filthy water drip, drop by drop, upon it. Gangrene set in. Faldene lost his foot. A second and a third operation cost him the rest of his leg. This misfortune did not, fortunately, damage his career. He continued to be a shoemaker and an artist.

Another unfortunate Sockserhauser was Long Nose. His real name was Ernest and he had two children, but after the development of a tremendous growth on his already remarkably large proboscis, even his offspring refused to have anything to do with him. Long Nose became a hermit, shunning mankind as it avoided him. It was perfectly natural that in time Long Nose should become a legend, and soon he was the bogeyman of the neighborhood. Parents frightened children with the warning that 'I'm going to give you to Long Nose if you don't do so and so.' Among themselves the adults whispered of voodoo and the ability of Long Nose to place a 'curse' upon those he disliked. As always, fear and misunderstanding bred hatred for the nonconformist.

Neighborhood children tormented him constantly. They would throw missiles at his shack, leap the fence to pilfer productive orange, fig and peach trees growing on his property, only to flee for their very lives should the hermit appear. There were mysterious and ghastly certainties regarding the fate of any lad captured by the old man. Parents always writhed in horror upon the discovery that their offspring had eaten of Long Nose's fruit. Surely it was cursed! If any ailment followed, it was considered absolute proof. It was reported that sickening odors emanated from Long Nose's chimney, evidence that some evil cauldron boiled within.

He owned a huge dog which howled through most of the

night, and should a death occur in the vicinity while the animal was serenading the moon, there was no idea but that Long Nose's occult powers had played some part in it. Occasionally the dog would be poisoned, but invariably another of identical type would appear. Most of the abuse was borne patiently. Police were never summoned, vengeance never sought. Probably had Long Nose been left alone he would have been happy and quite harmless, exercising the rightful human prerogative of living out his existence in his own peculiar fashion.

But who could be convinced of this? Wasn't it true that his trees bore a wealth of fruit with no attention whatever? When storms struck the neighborhood and giant oak trees were uprooted, were these fragile ones ever harmed? Did the frequent fires in his neighborhood ever touch his wooden shack? How did he live? — where did his food and clothing come from? He never earned any money. Several times during his lifetime the plagues swept through the Sockserhause community; they never touched Long Nose. Floods and other catastrophes would damage or entirely destroy other homes, it was said, but never his. No. Undoubtedly, only voodoo and other evil powers protected him.

But Long Nose outlived all the slander, all the torment, even most of the neighbors who hated him and the urchins who stoned him. He lived to a great age, it is reported to be more than a hundred. No one ever knew who attended to the last details of his interment. Evidently his daughters had kept closer contact with him than was suspected. And a final mystery accompanied him to his grave. It is an established fact that when he died he no longer bore the hideous and disfiguring growth on his nose that had ruined his life. There are two rumors regarding this: one that he attempted to remove the thing himself and that this caused his demise, the other that he at last consented to go under the surgeon's knife, regret for his long, self-imposed exile coming at last, but too late. Poor old Long Nose.

Mary Bartell is eighty-five years old and she remembers the Sockserhause Gang well, particularly an ancient lady named 'Mudder' Hecht, who was old when Mary Bartell was a girl.

'I'm the oldest living member of the Second Methodist

Church,' she said. 'But when I joined it wasn't called that; it was the Craps Methodist Church and nearly all the members were Sockserhausers. When Craps Street became Burgundy Street the name of the church was changed. Yes, I know craps is a dice game, but in them days people never bothered about nothin' like that, 'specially the Sockserhausers.

'I was real pretty when I was young and a good dancer. All the boys liked me plenty. Even that Johnny Gouse used to make love to me, but I wouldn't have nothin' to do with that man. Not me! The best of all the Sockserhausers was "Mudder" Hecht. Do you know when she was young she almost married Long Nose? Well, everybody said she was a little cracked, but that didn't matter. She was the best cook in the world. She could make the best Sviebel Cougan — onion pie, yes, sir — I ever had in my life. No, I don't know how she made it, but you couldn't taste the onions and it was kind of sweet. All Germans love pastry. You should have tasted "Mudder" Hecht's Schoofnoodles! They were little pieces of dough she would roll in her hands; they looked like the Pee Wees the boys used to play a game with — those were little wooden pegs about two inches long that they'd stick in the ground, striking the other end with a broomstick. "Mudder" always dried her Schoofnoodles in the sun, then she'd boil them and brown them in a pan with vegetables and eggs. She made all her own noodles too. She'd cut them into thin strips and put them out in the yard on a piece of newspaper to dry. Unsanitary? My, Mister, we never bothered about things like that.

'She made Kneflers, too, and Dompfernoodles to eat with chicken stew or Hassenpfeffer. But her hams were the best of all. Every Christmas she fixed up a lot of them hams to give as presents. I don't believe anybody cooked them the way she did. She'd take whole big hams and boil them — with a big red brick in the water to take out the salty taste — and then bake them with spices and sugar. After that she would wrap them in a special kind of dough and bake them again. You never tasted anything like that in your life. "Mudder" Hecht might have been a little cuckoo, but it didn't make any difference because she sure could cook. My, I wish I had a piece of her Sviebel Cougan right now!'

Lena Muller and her strange will is famous among the legends of the Sockserhause Gang.

Lena Muller was a buxom fräulein, without real beauty, but with a vibrant, fun-loving personality and a pair of dancing feet that made her extremely popular among the Sockserhause men. Lena loved a joke and she never took a dare. It is said that once her brother put his finger on a chopping block and dared Lena to cut it off, and that the girl calmly swung the hatchet and lopped the finger in two. Working out, as did most of the Sockserhause girls, Lena would cook and wash all day, then spend almost the whole night at a pig raffle or dancing heel-and-toe dances.

One of her favorite stunts was answering advertisements in the newspapers, especially those in the Men's Help Wanted column. If a truck driver were needed, Lena would write a letter answering, giving the address of one of her girl friends, and think it a great joke. She had three intimate friends — Christine, Mary and Emma — on whom she usually played her jokes. One day she answered an advertisement for a young lady to travel and demonstrate a sweet biscuit, giving the address of a fashionable home just across the street from the place where she worked. Then she arranged for her three friends and herself to watch the arrival of the advertiser. At last a tall and exceedingly handsome stranger wearing an elegant Prince Albert appeared, entered the house and emerged with a baffled expression on his countenance. Then Lena announced her intention of crossing the street, apologizing, and applying for the position. Immediately there was consternation.

'He's a dandy!' observed Christine.

'He's no good,' declared Mary. 'Look how well he's dressed.'

'He looks like a villain in a play!' warned Emma.

But Lena could not be dissuaded. She ran across the street, accosted the gentleman, and in few minutes returned to announce that she had the job, was leaving for Texas at once, that the man had a wife to chaperon, and that it was nonsensical to consider every well-dressed stranger a 'wolf in sheep's clothing.'

The day Lena left New Orleans she was serious for the first time in her life. Calling her three friends into a room, she closed the door and began talking.

'Girls,' she said, 'I'm happy about this nice position, but leaving you almost breaks my heart. I'm going to miss you more than anything in the world. Yet I can't turn this down. All my expenses are to be paid and I'm to get ten dollars a week besides. But I'm going to ask you something before I go. I don't want any of you to ever forget me. Now, I haven't any photographs of myself to give you, but I do have fifteen dollars in three five-dollar bills. I've written my name on each of them and taken down the numbers. Now I'm going to give each of you one of the bills and I want you to promise me that you will never spend them, but will keep them always.'

The girls protested but Lena won out as usual, giving each a bill and accepting from each a one-dollar bill in return. A few hours later Lena Muller left New Orleans forever. None of the friends was ever to see her again.

But they received glowing letters; Lena liked her job; everything was fine. Months passed, then years. At last the news came that she was happily married to a Texas farmer, Jim Roberts. Gradually her letters became less frequent, until only Emma heard from her, and then but rarely. Each time she wrote, though, Lena mentioned the five-dollar bills, reiterating her hope that the girls still had them. More years passed. Christine and Mary were married, Emma remained single. Then one day Mary came to Emma. Her husband was ill and she and her two children were in great financial difficulties.

'Emma,' she said, 'I haven't a cent in the world but that five dollars Lena gave me. I'm going to spend it now. I just wanted you to know that I wouldn't if things were not as bad as they are. That five dollars could never do me as much good as it will right now. I know Lena would understand if she knew.'

So Mary spent her five dollars. Shortly afterward, Christine spent hers, too. Of the three, only Emma retained Lena's bill throughout life. A few years afterward, however, Emma died and a nephew found the five dollars in her family Bible, and, unaware of the women's pact, spent it. Thus all the bills passed from their original possessors.

Twenty years after Emma's death, Christine passed on, and one day soon afterward a lawyer came to New Orleans and found

Mary, the lone survivor of the trio, and confronted her with a queer document. It read:

> Dear Emma, Christine and Mary:
>
>   Years have passed since I heard from you. I have lived happy and contented on our farm. I've worked hard and haven't much money, but our farm land is large and ought to be worth something. Jim died. I haven't anyone left, but I've leased the farm and can get along nicely until I, too, pass on. They are striking oil all over Texas, and who knows maybe they might hit it on my land someday. I'm putting this letter among my papers and should I be worth anything when I die, I am leaving it to you and your heirs, providing you still have that five-dollar bill I gave each of you when I left. If you have it yet I know that you always remembered me. I have the three one-dollar bills that you each gave me. If any of you has a bill, you are to receive all. If two of you have bills you receive half each, and if all three have bills, you split three ways. If you haven't the bills, then I am leaving whatever I own when I die to charity here in Galveston, which I name as follows. . . .

Death had come to Lena Muller, too, and it was disclosed that she had accepted an offer of thirty-five thousand dollars cash for her land, and that this was the amount to be distributed under the terms of her will. Under the circumstances, charity received the entire amount.

But even in the case of Mary, the only living member of the odd pact, there was little if any regret, for when Mary had spent that five-dollar bill it had given her family a new lease on life. Her husband had recovered from his illness and found work. Now her two children were grown and working to help them. Her last years were peaceful and very happy. So there remained only the question — was that five dollars worth more to Mary at the time she used it, or if she had saved it?

The Sockserhausers loved to dance, and much rivalry in this respect existed between them and rival neighborhoods in New Orleans, especially if any of the German girls were seen dancing at functions in other parts of the city. And these girls, being female, would often start trouble deliberately by seeking invitations to rival affairs. Many dances would terminate in fights, but these Sockserhausers never stooped to use any weapons but their fists, except for an occasional lead pipe in extreme emergency.

Principal foes and most hated were the Irish Channel gangs, living in the uptown section of the city, near the river. Though nearly five miles separated these 'kingdoms,' when one side craved a brawl with the other they would form and march to the other's neighborhood.

One of the major causes of antagonism between the gangs was the difference in their taste as to liquor. The Sockserhausers always drank beer, the Irishmen straight whiskey without a chaser, it being considered 'sissified' to drink water afterward, with a penalty for so doing of immediate dismissal from the gang, preceded by a thorough 'going over' by former bosom pals as a farewell sentiment.

Often during one of the fights at the dances the fire department would be summoned, which would cheerfully turn loose giant hoses without compunction or regard for household effects. Peace would then ensue until some flaxen-haired fräulein or some dark-eyed colleen again strayed from the fold.

But when death occurred both sides would declare a holiday from fighting and attend the wake of the deceased *en masse*. These wakes were always held for several nights, and food and drink were served abundantly. So whenever an Irishman felt the mood for a little beer drinking he ascertained whether there was a Sockserhause wake that night, and whenever a German felt inclined to imbibe a bit of harder liquor he reversed the procedure and journeyed to grieve beside the remains of some Irish Channel corpse. Decorum at these affairs was always strictly Emily Post, though of course negotiations might be arranged for a later meeting.

Both factions were always boastful of the strong men among their members; and despite poverty and absolute ignorance of hygienic laws, their physical development was remarkable. The Sockserhausers usually made their livings at the hardest of physical labor, at woodcutting and similar trades, while the Irishmen worked on the wharves loading the ships, carrying the cargo on their backs. Undoubtedly it was these occupations that made giants of the men in both gangs, lending much zest and gusto to their frequent battles.

A favorite Sockserhause diversion was picnicking out at Milneburg, a point on Lake Ponchartrain near New Orleans. Along a wharf edging the lake were rough camps of one or two rooms which could be rented by the day. At the Sockserhause picnics there were always such contests as greased-pole climbing, mixed-shoe races, greasy-pig chasing and races consisting of pushing wheelbarrows loaded with heavy sacks. Prizes were always given the winners, and this and the small admission fee of perhaps twenty-five cents, which included all the beer you could drink, caused the events to attract practically the entire Sockserhauser settlement.

Transportation to Milneburg was achieved via a branch line of the L. and N. R. R., on a wheezing vehicle, pulled by an engine known as 'Smoky Mary.' When put to the test, Smoky Mary could, amidst great puffing and blowing and much expulsion of smoke and cinders, attain the remarkable speed of ten miles an hour. Passengers usually emerged with clothes blackened and eyes and throat stuffed with cinders. Johnny Gouse was fireman to Smoky Mary, and his fame is still remembered in New Orleans.

'Uncle Johnny?' reminisced Emile Gouse, a nephew. ' Yes, sir, that was a tough bird. He fired Smoky Mary for years and that was a job that took a real man. Uncle Johnny used to fill that old boiler to the busting point and that hunk of iron would puff along just about as fast as a horse can trot.'

Johnny was even more famous as a fighter and a lover than as Smoky Mary's fireman. His strength was such that he licked all comers, including the mighty Irish, and when two of these bruisers slugged it out, it was with bare fists, and both were so strong and tough that the fight would continue for hours, until both were bloody and bored and badly in need of a drink. Even then they often arranged to renew the fight at another date.

This Johnny Gouse could tear a deck of cards in half with his hands, let men break rocks on his chest with a sledgehammer He could strike a match on the naked sole of his foot.

Then there was his prowess as a lover. He had a terrific yen for the girls, but those girls who were in the know avoided him. Even some of the prostitutes would refuse to do business with Johnny, no matter how large his bankroll. Suffice it to say that Johnny was a big man in every way.

Yet when Johnny got licked it was women who were blamed for his downfall. Despite anatomical unusualness, he finally married, and managed to keep several other women on the side. This, it is said, gradually undermined his strength, and a growing addiction to alcohol finished the job. One time when he met the Irish Channel champion wails of woe rang out through Sockserhause-land. Johnny Gouse was beaten. There were those cynics, of course, who averred that the mighty Johnny had 'laid down' to please his wife, who was always after him to stop fighting, but most of his friends preferred to blame it on the women.

A tradition shattered, a legend dying while its hero still lived, Johnny Gouse moved to Texas. It is rumored that there he built a whole street of shacks in some small town, christened it Gouse's Lane. And here in Texas Johnny came to a sudden and suitably violent end. His family had always fought fiendishly among themselves, and one day a stepson blew his head off with a shotgun, and, gripped in one hand of Johnny's headless carcass, was found a villainous-looking butcher knife, with which he had been chasing the stepson. Friends in New Orleans sighed rapturously at the beautiful compatibility of the life and death of Johnny Gouse.

Back in the eighties and nineties, when gambling flourished throughout the city, the Sockserhausers gave vent to their own gambling instinct by means of raffles. Churches would give plays lasting about an hour and the rest of the evening would be devoted to the raffling. Pin wheels and paddles were the devices used, the paddles bearing three numbers in different combinations, and the numbers on the wheels usually running from one to ninety. Members of the sponsoring committee would walk through the crowd selling the paddles while the play was in progress, completely ignoring it by yelling the praises of the prizes offered at the tops of their lungs. These prizes were always donated by parishioners and were usually homemade, various women in the neighborhood being particularly noted for certain creations. For instance, if a Mrs. Muller were famous for her cakes, when the peddler cried out the prize was one of Mrs. Muller's cakes he would sell out in a very few minutes.

Besides cakes, prizes were usually legs of pork, candy, geese, ducks or young and squealing pigs. All receipts for the raffles and the admissions — never more than twenty cents a person — went to the society sponsoring the show, and whether the auditorium used seated five hundred or five thousand persons it was always overcrowded. Many people attended all these shows, sometimes walking miles, and, if lucky, walking home again with a struggling live goose, turkey or pig under one arm. The next day it would be promulgated throughout the neighborhood that Mrs. So-and-So had won a pig at Saint Peter and Paul's raffle and Mrs. So-and-So would be the subject of envy for days, there existing always the characteristic gambler's disregard of the amount spent for the paddles, often enough to have bought several geese or turkeys or pigs.

A Mrs. Schindler and a Mrs. Farley were particularly well known for their Saturday night 'shindigs,' the affairs always including free beer, dancing and the raffling of pigs, chickens and other prizes, all handled in much the same manner as the church affairs. Keen rivalry existed between the two women and each constantly worked to outdo the other.

Mrs. Schindler excelled with her pig raffles. Daily she collected the garbage of friends and neighbors — always called 'slops' — and fed her pigs until they grew to be enormous sows. Then she would announce a dance and pig raffle to be held at her house on a certain date. These announcements were handwritten, and were tacked on lamp-posts throughout the Sockserhause community and neighboring sections. Admissions were twenty-five cents for men and forty cents for couples, this including the dancing, beer and audience at the hog-killing and raffling.

Before the dance began all attending would congregate in Mrs. Schindler's backyard to watch the butchers — always dressed in snow-white uniforms — slaughter the pigs. After this came the drinking and the dancing, and while this ensued the butchers would be preparing the various cuts of pork which were to be raffled.

The entire crowd would collect for the raffling. One number would win a leg, another a loin, until most of the meat was gone. Then dancing and beer drinking would continue until the butchers made sausage of the pork remaining. This, of which liver and blood sausage were the favorites, would be given free to the friends who had kept Mrs. Schindler supplied with slops. Bets were often made on the butchers' abilities, on which man would be the first to kill, skin and dress his hog.

Dancing would last all night. Marathons were unknown, but some couples would dance continuously. Heel-and-toe experts would give exhibitions, dancing on heels and toes within a chalked circle. Judges would eliminate anyone who moved a heel or a toe beyond the chalk mark. A certain Charley Joseph and a Mary Gause were known as the heel-and-toe couple who could 'swing on a silver dollar.'

From Carl Sellers, seventy-nine-year-old Orleanian, came the story of the origin of the Sockserhause name.

'I was only a youngster at the time,' said Mr. Sellers, 'but I remember the Sockserhausers well. The name? Oh, it came from a beer garden run by an old German named Schrieber. He called it the *Saxon Hause*. You see, Saxony was famous for its pretty girls, and they used to sing a song about it — "Where do all the pretty girls come from? From Saxony! From Saxony!" I can't remember all the words. Mr. Schrieber used to say the girls who came to his beer garden were just as pretty as the ones in Saxony and that that was why he called it the *Saxon Hause*. We used to have fine times there, singing and dancing to all the fine German music. That was, of course, when Germany was a country of good music and culture.

'There were no radios then or those things you stick a nickel in. All the music at the Saxon Hause came from a real band. There were two cornets, a trombone, a clarionet, a fiddle and a oompah. You know what an oompah is? I used to have a friend, when I was a boy, named Rudy Schmidt. One day our school-teacher asked Rudy what his father did for a living, and Rudy replied that he played the oompah in the Saxon Hause band.

You know how that tuba sounds — OOOM — PAH — PAH! OOOM — PAH — PAH! But that band could play good dance music. We used to dance those heel-and-toe dances to all the Viennese waltzes. We'd sing the *Schnitzenbank* — *Die Lorelei* — all those oldtime German songs. *Ach!* Those were the good old days. You could take a girl, stay all evening and never spend more than a dollar — a large glass of beer for a nickel, pretzels, cheese, crackers and all kinds of sandwiches on your table free of charge. Sometimes those Irishmen would come down and try to steal our girls. It was good fun. Maybe plenty of fist fights, but no one was ever hurt seriously. *Ja, das Saxon Hause!* I'll never forget it.'

And now the Sockserhause Gang lives only in the memories of men like Carl Sellers. The years passed and the city grew, and the Sockserhause community passed as a separate section of New Orleans. Education, civic pride and the modern trend toward uniformity worked together to banish forever most of the individualities of customs and characteristics that set apart certain races to certain parts of the city; with time all were absorbed and mingled and molded in the turbulent melting pot of a great American city.

Chapter 21

Songs

BECAUSE THE FIRST MUSIC WAS VOCAL AND BE-
cause not only music but all literature had beginnings in the
folk songs of early peoples, much of their history and racial
psychology is revealed in their songs. To the American folk
song the states of the South have perhaps contributed more than
any other section of the nation, and though the songs of all may
possess certain basic resemblances, each state also reveals definite
and unique individualities.

The ballads popular among white folk in the rural communities of Louisiana display their local origins in many instances,
though some are sung, and may have been born, in other states.
The children's songs also demonstrate frequent state, even sec-
tional differences and customs.

Negro songs of all these states, similarly, are akin, yet each
also demonstrates profound differences. In Louisiana this is particularly true of those songs of Blue and Spiritual characters. To
the huge Negro population and to the black man's primitive and
innate propensity for expressing himself by singing, all the
Southern States are indebted for their folk music.

The Creole songs — since the Creole inhabited no other part of the continental United States — are perhaps the most typical of all, exhibiting peculiarly exotic departures from the Anglo-Saxonism of practically all other American folk music.

Creole songs are romantic or morose. Motifs range from the most sensuous dances to sheer nonsense rhymes. Some, improvised by servants and slaves as sly thrusts at their white masters and mistresses, are taunting and insinuating, others point contemptuously at the attempts of colored people to pass as white. Many approach purest fantasy.

One of the best known of all Creole songs is *Toucoutou*, which has been published before, but is repeated here because of the incongruity of omitting it from any fairly representative Creole collection. There are dozens of versions, but this one is probably most famous.

TOUCOUTOU

Ah! Toucoutou, ye conin vous,
Vous té in Morico.
Na pas savon qui tacé blanc
Pou blanchi vous la peau.

Ah! Toucoutou, we all know you,
You are a blackamoor.
There is no soap strong enough
To whiten your dark skin.

Endans théâtre, quan va prenne loge
Comme tout blanc comme y fot
Yé va fé vous jist délogé,
Na pa passé tantot.

In the theater, when you take a box
Like all the nice white folks,
They will just put you out,
You will never stay inside.

Quan blanc léyés va donin bal
Vous pli capab'aller.
Comment va fé, vaillante diabale,
Vous qui l'aimin danser?

When the white folks go to a ball
You will never be able to go.
What will you do, you pretty devil,
You who like to dance?

Mo proche fini mo ti chanson
Pasqué mo envie dormi,
Mais mo pensé que la leçon
Longtemps li va servi.

I'm almost through my little song
Because I am so sleepy,
But I do believe that this lesson
Will serve its purpose for a long while.

The following is one of the many songs written around the *Dansé Calinda*; it concerns a Negress's boast of superiority in beauty and wits over her Creole mistress.

DANSÉ CALINDA

Mo té ain négresse,	I was a Negress,
Pli belle que Métresse.	More beautiful than my mistress.
Mo té volé belle-belle	I used to steal pretty things
Dans l'armoire Mamzelle.	From Mamzelle's armoir.
Dansé Calinda, Bou-doum Bou-doum,	Dansé Calinda, Bou-doum Bou-doum,
Dansé Calinda, Bou-doum Bou-doum!	Dansé Calinda, Bou-doum Bou-doum!

The Calinda was a voodoo dance brought to Louisiana from San Domingo and the Antilles by Negro slaves. Considered indecent by the respectable portion of the population, it was officially banned throughout the State in 1843, but continued to be performed for many years afterward. An early version of the Calinda was danced only by men, stripped to the waist and brandishing sticks in a mock fight while at the same time balancing upon their heads bottles of water. As soon as a dancer spilled a drop of his water he was banished from the field. Later the Calinda degenerated into a thoroughly lascivious performance.

Bou-doum Bou-doum was a sound meaning to fall down. When a Creole child took a tumble his mammy would say, 'He make *bou-doum bou-doum* on the floor.' They would amuse a child when bathing him by jumping him up and down in the water, saying, 'Ooh, the water is fine! You make *bou-doum* in the tub.' The child would shout with glee and Mammy would clap her hands and keep time with her feet, singing, '*Dansé Calinda! Bou-doum Bou-doum!*'

Belle-belle referred to any pretty article in a woman's wardrobe: dresses, ribbons or trinkets, any particularly feminine thing a slave girl might covet.

Among the *Dansé Calinda* songs were those on the absurd side, such as *Jump, Bullfrog, Your Tail Will Burn.*

JUMP, BULLFROG, YOUR TAIL WILL BURN

Sauté crapeau, to chieu va bruler,	Jump, bullfrog, your tail will burn,
Prend courage, li va repousser.	Take courage it will grow again.
Dansé Calinda,	Dansé Calinda,
Bou-doum! Bou-doum!	Bou-doum! Bou-doum!

Dans Nous Cabane was a song referring to clandestine love and eating:

DANS NOUS CABANE

Dans nous cabane,	In our shack
Nous va manger bainyan,	We will eat fritters,
Mo cher bébé, to conin mo laimin toi,	My dear baby, you know I love you,
To chanté comme zoiseaux dans bois,	You sing like the birds in the woods.
Pou to la beauté, mo eré connin	For your beauty, I would
Marcher divan Canon;	Walk in front of a cannon;
Pou to la beauté, mo eré conin	For your beauty, I would
Marcher divan Canon.	Walk in front of a cannon.
Dans nous cabane	In our shack
Nous va manger bainyan,	We will eat fritters,
Mo cher bébé, to conin mo laimin toi;	My dear baby, you know I love you;
Bien souvent to dit moin to la peine —	So often you have confided your sorrows to me —
Queque fois mo dit toi non,	Sometimes I said no,
Queque fois mo dit toi oui,	Sometimes I said yes,
Alors ca fé moin la peine	Then I felt so sorry
Mo dit toi, vini dans nou cabane	That I asked you to come in my shack
Pou manger bainyan, pou manger bainyan.	To eat fritters, to eat fritters.

This one moralized, pessimistically. Apparently there is no title.

Négue pas capab marché sans maïs dans poche,	Negro cannot walk without corn in his pocket,
Ce pou volé poule —	It is to steal chickens —
Milatte pas capab marché sans corde dans poche,	Mulatto cannot walk without rope in his pocket,
Ce pou volé choual —	It is to steal horses —
Blanc pas capab marché sans l'arzan dans poche,	White man cannot walk without money in his pocket,
Ce pou volé fille.	It is to steal girls.

The next little song had a double meaning. The last line really means 'not to cheat on me when I am not there.'

UN PETIT BONHOMME PAS PLUS GROS QU'UN RAT

Un petit bonhomme pas plus gros qu'un rat

A little man not bigger than a rat

Qui battait sa femme comme un scélérat

Who like a rascal beat his wife,

En disant: Madame, ça vous apprendra,

Saying: Madame, this will teach you

À voler mes pommes quand je n'y suis pas.

Not to steal my apples when I am not there.

The following song was still popular in New Orleans at the turn of the century.

Mo pas connin queque quichause,
Qu'appé tourmenter moin la,
Mo pas connin qui la cause
Mo coeur apé brulé moin comme ca.
Ah Dieu! Qui tourmen, qui peine,
C'est in souffrance passé la chaine,
Plutôt mo mouri sin fois.

I do not know what it is that torments me,
I do not know the cause,
That makes my heart burn so much.
Ah God, what torment, what pain,
It is suffering worse than fetters,
Better that I die five times
Than suffer like this.

To connin belle rigole là,

You remember that beautiful little brook,

Qui couler dans bananiers,
Ou té fé la folle,
Quan to té couri baignéla
Dolo la pas coulé encore;
Des fois li rété tout court,
Li sembe regretter toujours
Que li pas baigne toi encore.

That ran through the banana trees,
Where you played the fool,
When you used to bathe over there.
The water has ceased to run,
Sometimes it stops real short,
It seems always to regret
That it no longer bathes you.

Here is a curious song which is considerably more than a century old. 'As old as d'Artaguette' was a Creole proverb to express extreme age.

Di tams Missieu d' Artaguette,
Hé Hó — Hé Hó!
C'était, c'était bon temps —
Ye té menin moune à la baguette,
Hé Hó — Hé Hó!

In the days of d'Artaguette,
Hé Hó — Hé Hó!
It was the good old times —
You ruled the world with a switch,
Hé Hó — Hé Hó!

Pas négues, pas ribans,	No Negroes, no ribbons,
Pas diamans	No diamonds
Pou cochons.	For pigs.
Hé Hó — Hé Hó!	Hé Hó — Hé Hó!

Mo Ché Cousin, Mo Ché Cousin was one of the most popular of all the Creole songs. It is said that more than one hundred verses were written to the same tune, all dealing with cooking and mulattoes striving to pass for Whites.

MO CHÉ COUSIN, MO CHÉ COUSIN

Mo ché cousin, mo ché cousin,	My dear cousin, my dear cousin,
Mo laimin la kisine,	I love to do the cooking,
Mo manzé bien, mo boi divin,	I eat well, I drink wine,
Ca pas couté moin a rien,	It does not cost me a thing.
Tou to milatresses layé,	All you mulattresses there
Apé passé pou blanc,	Are passing for white,
Avec to blancs layés	With your white men
Yé allé dans l'Opera Français	You go to the French Opera
Mais yé fout yé déyer.	But they throw you out.

Fizi Anglais depicts in song the misery and resignation of a slave, who ran away, but returned to the lesser of two evils.

FIZI ANGLAIS

Fizi Anglais, yé fé Bim-bim,	The English guns, they make Bim-bim,
Carabine Kaintock, yé fé Zim-zim,	The Kentuckian's rifle makes Zim-zim,
Mo di moin: Sauvé to la peau.	I say to myself: Save your skin.
Mo sauté jusqu'à bord dolo —	I ran away to the water's edge,
Quan mo rivé li ti fé clair,	When I returned it was daylight,
Madame, li pren in coup colère,	Madame flew into a fit of rage,
Li fé donne moin quate piquets	She had me given four lashes
Pasqué mo pas servi Missieu.	Because I had not served Master.
Mais moin, mo vaut mieux quate piquets	But me, I much prefer four lashes
Passé in coup fizi anglais.	Than a shot from the English guns.

There were many, many Creole lullabies, to which mammies sang their young charges to sleep. One of the favorites was *Fais Dodo Minette*.

FAIS DODO MINETTE

Fé dodo Minette,	Go to sleep, Minette,
Trois piti cochons du laite,	Three little suckling pigs,
Fé dodo mo piti bébé,	Go to sleep, my little baby,
Jiske lage de quinse ans —	Until the age of fifteen years —
Quan quinze ans aura passé	When fifteen years shall have passed
Minette va se marier.	Minette will then marry.

Crab Dans Calalou was another song to which many children were put to sleep.

CRAB DANS CALALOU

Fé dodo, mo fils, crab dans calalou,	Go to sleep, my son, crab is in the shell,
Fé dodo, mo fils, crab dans calalou.	Go to sleep, my son, crab is in the shell.
Papa, li couri la rivière,	Papa has gone to the river,
Maman, li couri péché crab.	Mamma has gone to catch crab.
Fé dodo, mo fils, crab dans calalou.	Go to sleep, my son, crab is in the shell.
Fé dodo, mo fils, crab dans calalou.	Go to sleep, my son, crab is in the shell.
Mo papa li couri la rivière,	My papa has gone to the river,
Mo maman li couri peché crab.	My mamma has gone to catch crab.
Dodo, mo fille, crab dans calalou.	Sleep, my daughter, crab is in the shell.
Dodo, mo fille, crab dans calalou.	Sleep, my daughter, crab is in the shell.

Mo Gagnin in Piti Cousine is interesting, very old. Marriage among cousins was common to the Creoles. Their world was small and clannish.

MO GAGNIN IN PITI COUSINE

Mo gagnin in piti cousine	I have a little cousin
Qui donne moin coeur à li —	Who gave me all her heart —
Li gagnin si doux laimine;	She looks so sweet,
Nouzotte yé marié sordi,	We will be married today,
Nouzotte marié sordi, hi-hi-hi,	We will be married today, hey-hey-hey,
Nouzotte yé marié sordi.	We will be married today.

Li gagnin si doux la mine
Mo bo li beau matin,
Pou entrer so crinoline
Mo té cassé in vié baril.

She looks so sweet
I kissed her this morning,
To hold her crinoline
I broke an old barrel.

Mo gagnin in piti cousine
Qui don moin coeur à li —
Li gagnin si doux laimine,
Nouzotte marié zordi,
Nouzotte marié zordi, hi-hi-hi,

Nouzotte yé marié zordi.

I have a little cousin
Who gave me all her heart —
She looks so sweet,
We will be married today,
We will be married today, hey-hey-
hey,
We will be married today.

The *tignon* was a headdress of brilliant colors worn by Negresses and mulatto women. *Madame Caba*, an early Negro dancing song, refers to the expression that the wearer of the *tignon* had followed her own inclinations in matters of love regardless of conventions and morals by singing 'your headdress fell,' thus symbolizing Madame Caba's fall from virtue.

In this song the word *tignon* takes the Creole form of *tiyon*.

MADAME CABA

Madame Caba, tiyon vous tombé,

Madame Caba, your headdress fell
down,

Madame Caba, en sortant dibal,
Michie Zizi, cet in vaillan nomme.
Michie Zizi, cet in vaillan nomme.

Madame Caba, as you left the ball.
Mister Zizi, he's a handsome man.
Mister Zizi, he's a handsome man.

Wa-ya, ya-ya-ya, tiyon vous tombé!
Wo-wo, wo-wo, tiyon vous tombé!
Wa-wa, wa-wa, tiyon vous tombé!
Wo-wo, wo-wo, tiyon vous tombé!
Wa-ya, wa-ya-ya-ya, tiyon vous tombé!
Wo-wo-wo-wo-wo-wo, tiyon vous tombé!

... your headdress fell down!
... your headdress fell down!
etc., etc.

Repetition played an important part in the effectiveness of songs of this type. The same lines were sung again and again, sometimes for hours, until the taunting words took on the monotonous rhythm of drum beats.

Here is a very old version of something fairly close to the 'Knock-knock, who's there?' craze of the early 1930's.

CAP, CAP, CAP!

Cap, Cap, Cap!	Cap, Cap, Cap!
Qui ca qui la?	Who is there?
Cé Dédé.	It is Dédé.
Qui Dédé?	Who is Dédé?
Dédé Coq.	Dédé Rooster.
Qui Coq?	Who is Rooster?
Coq Boyau.	Bayou Rooster.
Qui Boyau?	Who is Bayou?
Boyau Cochon.	Bayou Pig.
Qui Cochon?	Who is Pig?
Cochon toi-même.	You, yourself, are a pig.

Dame Tartina tells the remarkable story of a 'lady made like a sandwich,' her equally remarkable home and family, and their tragic fate.

DAME TARTINA

Il était une Dame Tartina	There was a lady made like a sandwich
Dans un palais de buerre frais,	Living in a palace of fresh butter.
La muraille était de farine,	The wall was made of flour,
Le parquet était de croquet,	The floor was made of crisp biscuit,
La chambre à coucher de crême et de lait,	The bedroom was of milk and cream,
Les lits de biscuits,	The beds of cookies,
Les rideaux d'anis.	The curtains of anise.
Elle épousa Monsieur Gimblette	She married Monsieur Gimblette,
Coiffé d'un beau fromage blanc,	Who wore a hat of fine white cheese,
Son habit était de gâlette,	His suit of buttered roll,
Et sa veste de vol-au-vent,	His vest of puff pie,
Calotte en nougat,	His cap made of nougat,
Gilet de chocolat,	His vest of chocolate,
Bas de caramel,	Stockings of caramel,
Et souliers de miel.	Shoes of honey.
Leur fille, la belle Charlotte	Their daughter Charlotte
Avaiet un nez de massepain,	Had a nose made of sponge cake,
De belles dents de compotes,	Her fine teeth of jam,
Des oreilles en crequelin,	Her ears of cracknel,
Je la vois garnir	I see her trim
Sa robe de plaisir	Her party dress
Avec un rouleau,	With a roll
De pâte d'abricots.	Of apricot paste.

Le grand prince Limonade,	The great Prince Lemonade,
Bien frisé vient faire sa cour	His hair well curled, comes to court her;
Son habit de marmelade	His suit was of marmalade
Orné de pommes cuites au four.	Trimmed with baked apples.
On frémit en voyant sa garde	Everyone shuddered on seeing his guard
De capres et de cornichons	Made up of capers and pickles
Armés de fusils de moutarde	Armed with guns of mustard
Et de sabres en pelures d'oignons.	And with swords of onion skins.
Sur un trône de brioches	On a throne of brioches
Charlotte et le roi vont s'asseoir.	Charlotte and the King are going to sit.
Les bonbons sortaient de leurs poches	The candies were dropping from their pockets
Depuis le matin jusqu'au soir.	From early morning to night.
Mais voilà que la fée Carabosse,	But here comes the fairy Hunchback,
Jalouse et de mauvaise humeur —	Jealous and in bad humor —
Renversa d'un coup de sa brosse	She upset with a sweep of her brush
Le palais sucré de bonheur.	The palace sweetened with happiness.
Pour le rebâtir	To construct it again
Donnez à loisir	Give indulgently,
Donnez bons parents,	Give, dear parents,
Du sucre aux enfants.	Plenty of sugar to the children.

There are many versions of *Mamzelle Zizi*. In the one below *Mamzelle Zizi* is grieving for her lost lover and shows jealousy of her rival, who wears pretty clothes, which at that time consisted of a brilliant madras *tignon*, imported from the Indies, a gaily embroidered petticoat and earrings.

MAMZELLE ZIZI

Pov' piti Mamzelle Zizi!	Poor lil' Mamzelle Zizi!
Li gagnin bobo dans coeur!	She has a pain in her heart!
Pov' piti Mamzelle Zizi,	Poor lil' Mamzelle Zizi,
Li gaignin tristesse dans coeur!	She has sadness in her heart!
Calalou porté madras,	Calalou wears madras,
Li gagnin jupon brodé,	She has an embroidered petticoat,
Li gagnin des belles allures,	She has fine manners,
Boucle d'oreilles en or tout pure.	Earrings made of pure gold.

Pov' piti Mamzelle Zizi,
Li gagnin bobo dans coeur!
Pov' piti Mamzelle,
Li gaignin tristesse dans coeur!

Poor lil' Mamzelle Zizi,
She has a pain in her heart!
Poor lil' Mamzelle Zizi,
She has sadness in her heart!

If I Die or *Si Je Meurs* speaks for itself.

SI JE MEURS

Si je meurs, je veux que l'on m'enterre
Dans la cave, où il y a du vin,
Les deux pied contre la muraille
Et la tête sous le robinet.

If I die, I wish to be buried
In the cellar, where there is wine,
Both feet against the wall
And the head under the faucet.

Si il tombe quelques gouttes
Ce sera pour me rafraichir,
Si le tonneau se défonce
Que j'en boive à ma fantaisie.

If a few drops happen to fall
It will be to refresh me,
If the barrel opens up
I will drink all I want.

In the next one Creole practicality is demonstrated.

Je voudrais bien me marier
Mais je crains trop la pauvreté.
Tout garçon qui n'a pas d'argent,
L'amour lui passe et la faim lui vient.
Je voudrais bien me marier
Mais je crains trop la pauvreté.
Toute jeune fille qui n'a pas d'argent,
Va s'enfermer dans un vieux couvent.

I would like to get married
But I dread poverty.
Any young man without money,
Love leaves him and hunger comes.
I would like to get married
But I dread poverty.
Any young girl without money,
Goes to enter an old convent.

Delaide, My Queen and *Every New Year's Day* are two odd little Creole songs which were favorites of Bernard Marigny de Mandeville, during the years the famous Creole lived in splendor. It is said he often had them sung in his home for the amusement of his guests, among whom perhaps was Louis Philippe, who visited him at his father's home in 1798.

DELAIDE, MY QUEEN

Delaïde, mo la Reine,
Chimin-là trop longque pou aller,
Chimin-là monté dans les hauts;
Tout piti que mo yé
M'allé monté là-haut dans courant.

Delaide, my little Queen,
This road is too long to travel,
This road climbs into the heights;
As small as I am
I will get there, by the stream.

C'est moin, Liron, qui rivé   It is I, Liron, who am going
M'alle di yé   To tell you
Bonsoir, mo la Reine —   Good night, my Queen —
C'est moin Liron qui rivé.   It is I, Liron, who am coming.

EVERY NEW YEAR'S DAY

Tous les jours de l'an,   Every New Year's Day,
Tous les jours de l'an,   Every New Year's Day,
Tous les jours de l'an,   Every New Year's Day
Vous pas vini ouare moin.   You never came to see me.
Mo té couché malade dans litte;   I was sick in my bed;
Mo voey nouvelles apprès mo la   I asked for news about my Queen —
  Reine —
Vous pas soulement vini ouare moin You did not even come to see me,
A présent, que mo gaillard,   So, now that I am well,
Cher ami, mo pas besoin ouare vous. Dear friend, I do not need to see you.

When Marigny was old and penniless, living in a small house in Frenchman Street in New Orleans, he spent his days walking through the streets of the Vieux Carré, visiting with Creole friends living in that section.

He always carried an old black umbrella, with a crooked handle hooked over his left arm, a palmetto fan in his right hand. He was always hatless.

Marigny loved to entertain friends with the old Creole songs, especially the risqué ones, and when young ladies were present, he would make them cover their ears with both hands. If the hands came down, perhaps to slap a mosquito, he would stop instantly, resuming his song only when the hands were firmly pressed over both ears again. He would accompany his songs by picking his palmetto fan as if it were a guitar, keeping time by beating the floor with his right foot.

It is said that while most of the young ladies were modest and obedient, there were always some who cheated by raising one hand a little, anxious to hear the words of Marigny's naughty songs.

Aie! Souzette is a song of love, in which the gallant lover threatens even to 'carry cane' — i.e., go to work — certainly the epitome of devotion.

AIE! SOUZETTE

Aie! Souzette, Souzette belle fome,	Ah! Souzette, Souzette, beautiful woman,
Souzette, belle fome, mo cher ami,	Souzette, beautiful woman, my dear friend,
Prie bon Dieu pou moin.	Pray to God for me.
Ma palé attende li mo cher zami,	I will wait for her, my dear friend,
Ma porté di canne, mo cher zami,	I will carry cane, my dear friend,
Su coin mo l'épaule.	On top of my shoulder.

FOLK BALLADS

These are songs popular in northern Louisiana where the French and Creole penetration has been insignificant and where the folk more closely resemble the inhabitants of neighboring states than do southern Louisianians. Most of these ballads are sung to the accompaniment of guitars and banjos when the day's work is done and rural groups gather in the evenings. In these epics the women are always chaste, heroes extremely heroic and bad men very, very bad. In *The Jealous Lover*, for instance, there is a superabundance of jealousy.

THE JEALOUS LOVER

Way down in love's green valley, where the roses bloom and fade,
There lived a jealous lover, in love with a beautiful maid.
One night the moon shone brightly, the stars were shining, too;
Into this maiden's cottage, this jealous lover drew.
Come, love, and we will wander, down where the woods are gay,
While strolling we will ponder upon our wedding day.
So arm and arm they wander, the night birds sang above,
And the jealous lover grew angry with the beautiful girl he loved.
The night grew dark and dreary, said she, I'm afraid to stay,
I am so tired and weary I must retrace my way.
Retrace your way, no never, for you have met your doom,
So bid farewell forever to parents, friends and home.
Oh, Willie, won't you tell me, I know there's something wrong,
You must not harm me, Willie, for we've been friends too long.
Down on her knees before him, she pleaded for her life,
But deep into her bosom he plunged that fatal knife.

Oh, Willie, my poor darling, why have you taken my life?
You know I always loved you, and I wanted to be your wife.
I never have deceived you, and with my dying breath,
I forgive you, Willie, and she closed her eyes in death.

Roses and moonlight are always appropriate settings for 'true love.' Many a tear drops from the girls' eyes when the singer pops the guitar strings and renders the heart-throbbing *Little Sweetheart*.

LITTLE SWEETHEART

Little sweetheart, we have parted,
From each other we soon must go,
Many a mile will separate us
In this world of sin and woe.

Will you cherish every promise
That you made me in the lane?
And remember, I will meet you
When the roses bloom again.

How this parting gives me sorrow
None but me will ever know;
When I leave you on tomorrow
My heart stays while I must go.

Will you give me all your heart, dear?
Will you love me all the same?
And remember, I will meet you
When the roses bloom again.

Sentimentality and melodrama are unrestrained. Love is often blighted by jealousy. The lovers suffered for naught in *Nell and I*.

NELL AND I

Nell and I were quarreling,
Just as two lovers do.
I was mostly jealous,
I thought Nell was untrue.
Nell received a letter, 'twas from an old sweetheart,
'Twas then I told her, we had better part.

Dearest, I am sorry that I have caused you pain;
Come and kiss me, Nellie, let us be friends again.
I shall always love you, as long as life shall last.
Darling, forgive me, let's forget the past.

Nellie said, I'll tell you
Since we are to part,
All about the letter
From an old sweetheart.
It was from a sister, who had gone astray
Oh, the tears are bitter, oh, I cannot say...

Just a short while after,
Poor Nellie passed away;
Softly within her bosom,
Two tear-stained letters lay.
One was a fatal message, that had caused much woe,
The other she had written to me long ago.

The Broken Vow is even more heartrending.

THE BROKEN VOW

'Twould have been better for us both had we never
In this wicked wide world to have met,
For the pleasures we've both seen together
It is I who can never forget.

Oh, you said that you always would love me,
And no other should ever come in between,
It has been long ago since you spoke them,
But your words in my memory are green.

Oh, how fondly my heart grows toward you,
Though the distance has thrown us apart.
Do you love me as last when you held me,
On your bosom so close to your heart?

Oh, you said that you always would love me,
Oh, but why do I speak of it now?
Have I not long ago felt the danger
Of a heart broken through a lost vow?

Fare thee well, since all hope has departed;
I will struggle through life until death.
Since you have left me broken-hearted,
Your words shall employ my last breath.

When the cold, cold grave shall enclose me,
Won't you come, love, and shed a single tear?
And say to the people around you
That a heart you have broken lies here.

There is evidence that this next one originated at Spring Creek, just south of Alexandria, Louisiana. This hero was not in the preferred 'true-blue' tradition, but he was a dashing rascal, who must have made all the feminine hearts flutter.

I'll eat when I'm hungry, I'll drink when I'm dry,
And if women don't kill me, I'll live till I die.
My mother was a sweeper, she wore her blue jeans,
My father was a gambler, and he died in Noo'r'leeens.
Up in my saddle, my quirt in my hands,
I'll think about you, Mollie, in some distant land.
Your parents don't like me, they say I'm too poor,
They say I'm unworthy to darken your door.
I'm a reevin', I'm a rovin', I'm a rarin' young blade,
I've clem up Pike's Peak and I've set in the shade.
Jack o' Diamonds, Jack o' Diamonds, I knows you of old,
You robbed my pockets of silver and gold.
Oh, the cuckoo is a purty bird, and she brings us good cheer,
But the cuckoo never sings till the spring of the year.
If the ocean was whiskey and I was a duck,
I'd dive to the bottom, and take one sweet suck.
Pick, buzzard, pick, buzzard, pick a hole in my head,
My sweetheart don't love me and I wish I was dead.

In the same Spring Creek community the memory of John Hollin will never fade. He was a desperado extraordinary.

JOHN HOLLIN

John Hollin was a desperate man, he wore his gun every day;
He killed him a man in the West Virginia lands,
And you orta seen Hollin get away, Lord God, you oughta seen Hollin
    get away.

John Hollin was a-standing by the barroom door, not a-thinking of a
    doggone thing;
Along come a woman with a one-dollar bill,
Says I'll lead poor Hollin in the game, Lord God; says I'll lead poor
    Hollin in the game.

John Hollin took this one-dollar bill, he quickly drew his gun,
And shot John Paddy right through the heart,
I'll never tell a lie to my gun, Lord God, I'll never tell a lie to my gun.

John Hollin went to the big stock gate, he did not go for to stay,
Along come a man and took him by the hand,
Saying, Hollin, won't you step this way, Lord God, saying, Hollin,
    won't you step this way.

I've been to the east and I've been to the west, I've been this wide world
    over.
I've been to the river and I've been baptized,
But now I'm on my hanging ground, Lord God, but now I'm on my
    hanging ground.

If you see anybody wants to know my name, just send them up to Num-
    ber 9.
There you'll see two charming maids,
That brown-eyed woman, she's mine, Lord God, that brown-eyed
    woman, she's mine.

With a silver spade go dig my grave, with a golden chain let me down,
And the last words that I heard him say,
Tell Mamma not to weep for me, Lord God, tell Mamma not to weep
    for me.

In this one a bad man wins a heart and saves his neck. The
maiden arrived on the scene just in the nick of time.

THE HIGHWAY MAN

I went down to the town depot
To see that train roll by,
I thought I saw my dear old girl
Hang her head and cry.

Hang her head and cry, old girl, hang her head and cry,
I thought I saw my dear old girl hang her head and cry.

The night was dark and stormy,
It sure did look like rain.
Not a friend in this whole wide world,
No one knew my name.

No one knew my name, poor boy, no one knew my name.
Not a friend in this whole wide world, no one knew my name.

Wait, Mr. Judge, won't you wait, Mr. Judge,
Wait a little while?
I think I see my dear old girl,
She's walked for miles and miles.

Dear girl, have you brought me silver?
Dear girl, have you brought me gold?
Dear girl, have you walked these long, long miles,
To see me hanging on a hangman's pole?

Dear boy, I brought you silver,
Dear boy, I brought you gold,
But I have not walked these long, long miles
To see you hanging on a hangman's pole.

She took me from a scaffold,
She untied my hands,
With tears rolling down that poor girl's cheeks,
Said, 'I love that highway man.'

The next one was heard in Ponchatoula. It offers financial advice.

Sez the first old geezer
To the second old geezer,
'Have you got any terbaccy
In your terbaccy box?'

Sez the second old geezer
To the first old geezer,
'Save up your rocks
And you'll always have terbaccy
In your old terbaccy box.'

PLAY AND NURSERY SONGS

Louisiana is rich in a store of children's songs, many showing Creole and Negro influence. Some are local versions of well-known songs, parodies of Mother Goose rhymes, etc.; others are original both in words and music.

The following version of *Humpty Dumpty* from New Orleans bares a frank mark of adult sex consciousness.

Mumty Dumty sat on a wall,
Mumty Dumty had an awful fall.
The lady was passing by
And her dress was rather high —
And for her not knowing
The wind was blowing —
Oh, the lady kept going.
She stooped down to buckle her shoe —
That was all I saw.
Folks, that's what made Ole Mumty
Run home and tell your paw.

These next are counting rhymes, used when playing Fate.

Inny ke nicky nacky noe
Rivaly divaly dommy noe
Ex a blow, soffa, low, tissue.

And:

Ooka dooka soda cracker,
Does your father chew tobacco?
Yes, my father chews tobacco,
Ooka dooka soda cracker.

Children form a ring and go around and around with one in the middle and sing this one:

> Way down yonder
> Soup to soup!
> Where dem white folks
> Soup to soup!
> Tryin' to make man
> Soup to soup!
> Biscuits hot
> Soup to soup!
> Corn bread cold
> Soup to soup!
> Thank God Almighty
> Soup to soup!
> Just give me a little mo'
> Soup to soup.

In another game played in a circle, the leader shouts the first lines and the others answer in unison.

> Leader: Did you go to the hen house?
> Chorus: Yes, mam!
> Did you get any eggs?
>   Yes, mam!
> Did you put 'em in the bread?
>   Yes, mam!
> Did you bake it brown?
>   Yes, mam!
> Did you hand it over?
>   Yes, mam!
> Good old egg bread,
>   Shake 'em, shake 'em!
> Good old egg bread,
>   Shake 'em, shake 'em!
> Did you go to the lynchin'?
>   Yes, mam!
> Did they lynch that man?
>   Yes, mam!
> Did that man cry?
>   Yes, mam!

How did he cry?
Baa, baa!
How did he cry?
Baa, baa!

Freedom among early slaves often meant spiritual salvation, freedom from sin. Later, of course, the idea of emancipation grew, and the Negro began to hate his master in many cases. In the following game song bitterness against a mistress is expressed and a gruesome hope mentioned. The person contributing the song remembered only that in the game the ring was handed from one player to another.

My old mistress promised me
Before she died she would set me free.
Take your lover in the ring,
  I don't care,
Take your lover in the ring,
  I don't care.
Now she's dead and gone to hell,
I hope that devil will burn her well.
Take your lover in the ring,
  I don't care,
It's a golden ring,
  I don't care.
It's a silver ring,
  I don't care.

The next comes from New Orleans. To sing it two children joined hands and two others joined hands across those of the first two. They sway back and forth, singing,

Drawin' a bucket of water
For my oldest daughter.
Give me the racket and
  the silver spoon
And let my pillar come over,
  come over.

At this point the first two put their right arms over the heads of the other two, letting the arms slide along until they reach the waistline. Then they shout,

> Bunch o' rags!
> Bunch o' rags!
> Bunch o' rags!
> Bunch o' rags!

The Rooster and the Chicken is a favorite. *Gumbo* is, of course, the favorite soup of Louisianians.

THE ROOSTER AND THE CHICKEN

> The rooster and the chicken had a fight,
> The chicken knocked the rooster out of sight,
> The rooster told the chicken, That's all right,
> I'll meet you in the gumbo tomorrow night.

The following little mocking songs are popular among Louisiana children.

> Mary, Mary, with a tin can,
> Waiting for the milkman, bah?
> Mary, rust tin can,
> Where is the milk man, rah?

> Straw caty, number eighty
> Put me in mind of a dago lady.

> Cream cheese, cream cheese
> Floating in the air,
> That bald-head man
> Ain't got no hair.

> Once upon a time, the rooster drank wine,
> The monkey played a fiddle on a streetcar line,
> The streetcar broke, the monkey choke,
> Trying to get to heaven on a green goat.

> You dirty mistreater,
> You robber and cheater,

> I'll put you in the dozen,
> Your mammy and your cousin,
> You pappy do the lordy lord.

> Big fat maw
> And skinny paw
> Went downtown
> To catch the 'lektricar;
> The 'lektricar
> Jumped the track,
> Big fat maw said,
> 'Gimme my money back.'

This folk verse of German-American origin has been taken over. The third line was originally 'And I'm the little wiener wurst.' In New Orleans 'weiner wurst' has become 'winny wish' among children.

> My papa is a butcher,
> My mamma cuts der meat,
> And I'm the lil' winny wish
> Dat runs around der street.

WORK SONGS

Practically all Negro songs are expressions of the elementary desires for survival, for spiritual and sexual outlets. Work songs all have the escapist quality. Through all the years since his importation to the New World the Southern Negro has made his burden more tolerable by lifting his voice and his spirit in song.

Plantation-owners soon discovered song was a far more effective means of increasing the slaves' output than the whip. The slaves sang in the cane and cotton fields, and the railroads running through the Southern States were built to the accompaniment of their voices. Along the Mississippi, the roustabouts sang as they worked, as if their music borrowed strength from their souls. The Negro often borrowed his melodies, improvising words to fit his moods. The songs sometimes reflected resentment against the white master, as in this one, apparently originating in La Fourche Parish.

THE CANE CUTTERS

White folks want de niggers to work and sweat,
Wants dem to cut de cane till dey is wringin' wet.
We poor niggers gits nothin' atall,
White boss cusses and gits it all.

Cut high, cut low,
Swing fast, swing slow.

Bend yo' back, tote it to the lift,
White boss hollers if yo' ain't swift.
De Lawd take keer of us when we is dead,
But in de canefield de white boss cracks yo' on de head.

Cut high, cut low,
Swing fast, swing slow

The 'Cap'n' in the following is the Negro's boss. This one, too, shows resentment, but also childish pride in his own cunning thievery.

Cap'n, don't yo' know me, don't yo' know my name?
I'se de same old rascal stole yo' watch and chain.

Cap'n, oh, Cap'n, now can't yo' see
Dis hard work about to kill po' me?

In the next the Negro looks upward for rescue from his daily toil, hopeful of rest and 'glory' in the next world.

I wonder if I'll ever get to Heaven,
I wonder if I'll ever fly away
To my new home, Heaven.
I wander up and I wander down,
I wonder if I'll ever get my crown.

Working on the railroads, the black man has replaced many of the old field songs with such ones as this:

Oh, French fried potatoes
And a good line of beans

I wouldn't mind eating
But the cook ain't clean.
Let's move —
Big boy, we're rollin'!
Big boy, we're rollin'!

What did the hen duck
Tell the drake?
No more crawfish in this lake.
Let's move —
Big boy, we're rollin'!
Big boy, we're rollin'!

This is the way
We line this track:
Put the tungs in the rails
And snatch 'em back.
Let's move —
Big boy, we're rollin'!
Big boy, we're rollin'!

I'm a poor railroad man
Ain't got no home,
Today I'm here, tomorrow I'm gone.
Let's move.
Big boy, we're rollin'!
Big boy, we're rollin'!

Here, too, is the boss — the 'Cap'n.'

Oh, captain, captain, what makes yo' head so red?
Had a fight with the Devil and he scorched my head.

Big boy, can't line 'em,
Can't you line those rails?

The captain called the water boy and the water boy frowned.
The captain made water boy put the water bucket down.

Big boy can't line 'em,
Can't you line those rails?

'Ridin' the rails' or 'workin' on the line,' the railroad plays a great part during the day's singing. The 'cannon ball' is a train. References to the 'cannon ball' appear in several songs.

> How long, tell me, how long will dat evenin' train ride?
> De bumps in dis railroad is beginnin' to hurt my side.

> Up wit' you, son, 'taint no time to stall,
> Dis train you is loadin' belongs to de cannon ball.

Bogalusa, some thirty miles north of New Orleans, was at one time an important sawmill town. The following two lines are sung without any particular reason or provocation.

> New Orleans is a city, Bogalusa is a sawmill town;
> I rang up Cleveland and dere was de capitol justa burnin' down.

Adam and Eve are popular subjects for the songs the workers sing. There are many favorites like the following.

> Adam and Eve they went out to play,
> When Eve saw the apple then she gave 'way.
> Adam said, 'Hold on, fool,
> Dat's the forbidden fruit
> 'Cause you knows God's rule
> And you know it's the trut'.'
> Just about then the Devil appeared,
> He looked at Eve and said, 'Come over here,
> Don't be nobody's fool, 'cause dere ain't
> No such thing as God's rule.
> I command you go, Eve, and take a bite,
> And lo! and behold you'll find the light' —
> So Eve done as she was told.

Here's another one, with a title.

GOD CALLED ADAM

Adam was in the garden,
He didn't have nothin' to worry 'bout,
Eve made Adam sin and that's when the trouble begin to start.
God called Adam, Adam refused to answer.
God called Adam, Adam refused to answer.
Adam said here am I, Lord,
I'm most done waggin' with my crosses.

When the Depression started in 1929, the Negro met hard times with characteristic good humor, and composed songs about the débâcle.

> It's only depression in old New Orleans,
> The jobs are so scanty you can hardly buy red beans.
>
> It's a tumble-down town, where only tramps hang around,
> The parks are so crowded, they sleep on the ground.
>
> I gave up my room 'cause I couldn't pay rent,
> I went to the Welfare, they wouldn't give me a cent.
>
> You can all plainly see
> It's the poorhouse for me.
> In a tumble-down town in New Orleans.

Real privation and hunger are displayed in this one — to the tune of *Stormy Weather*.

> Don't know why Mammy don't make no apple pie —
> Starvation —
> Since Pa lost his occupation —
> Keep hungry all the time.
>
> Since Pa went away
> The blues walked in and got us,
> If Pa stay away it will be in charge of the undertaker.
> Can't go wrong, things in life is always dull,
> Starvation.
> Since Pa lost his occupation —
> Keep hungry all the time.
> If Pa stay the landlord will run us away.
> Don't know why Mammy don't bake no banana and lemon pie.
> Starvation —
> Pa didn't have to take no vacation —
> Keep hungry all the time.

Even the W.P.A. has obtained a place in the Negroes' songs, as in the following.

> My pa is dead and gone to glory;
> My sister still drinks gin;
> She's got a W.P.A. man,
> And he won't take her in.

BLUE SONGS

> Love is a funny thing shaped like a lizard,
> Run down your heart strings and tickle your gizzard.
> You can fall from a mountain,
> You can fall from above,
> But the great fall
> Is when you fall in love.

Blues started in New Orleans, but they've swept around the world. To Negroes the Blues are love songs. They wail over the infidelities, warn against 'messin' around,' threaten 'sweet mama' or 'my man' or 'babe.' Frank references to sex make many of them unprintable, for the Negro's vocal expression of lust as it exists for thousands of them seems degraded to white sensibilities. In the Blues there are no lofty conceptions of love. Rather they express the superlative of the obscene and extoll unrestrained sexual relations. Blues belong to city Negroes, and every ten-year-old child in the Negro slums knows the songs.

But today sophisticated versions of the Blues have risen from this level. From New Orleans, birthplace of jazz, these Negro chants of unfaithful lovers and torrid love lives, the Blues, have gone out to form part of the fabric of the music to which the whole world dances. Yet the Negro retains a preference for such Blues as given here. A few of this type have been recorded, but most survive almost solely by being passed from one singer to another.

Among Negroes of this element your man or woman is yours only as long as you both are amused. A better lover may walk in the back door at any moment. There is always another woman waiting; maybe nineteen.

> My big woman quit me and my lil woman did me wrong,
> When my other woman quit me it is time to leave home.

> I'se got nineteen women, I need one mo';
> When I git that one I'se gonna let the others go.

> I woke up one mornin' just about the break of day,
> Found that my friend had took my gal away.

I look up my gal's address, don't know where she went to,
Now she's gone and I don't know where she went to.

I woke up this mornin' wit' the blues all 'round my head,
Had a dream that I was dead.

Say, I'se goin' to the W.P.A. to work and save
And I'se gonna find my gal if I gotta find her in my grave.

Sometimes when they walk out indifference may be expressed in a song like this:

I DON'T CARE IF YOU NEVER COME BACK

I don't care if you never come back,
Get a move on, you nigger duke,
There's a lot of coons in this here town,
So I won't grieve after you.
There's lots of coons, I can boss 'em 'round;
But none with their hair so black.
So trot along, my honey, you haven't got no money,
So I don't care if you never come back.

The Negro's sex life is always getting him into trouble. Fights, shootings and stabbings are frequent, but loud boasting and threats are even more so, the idea being that the more completely is valor indicated the more chance there is of averting an actual test. To 'bug' is to fight.

Winchester Fanny told Automatic Sue,
'Keep foolin' around wit' me tell you what I'm gonna do.
I'm gonna git Shot Gun Sammy and his whole dern crew,
Gonna git Bucket Leg Pete we gon' bug wit' you.'

Old Sue turned 'round and begin to say;
'Listen, black woman, you know I'll bug wit' you any old day.
I'm now send you git up paw, black woman,
Tell him bring his wife,
We gonna battle here for our doggone life.

'I'm gon' send you git Shot Gun Sammy and his whole dern crew,
I'm gon' send you git Bucket Leg Pete I'm gon' bug wit' you.
I'm gon' saddle you, black woman, for that's what I crave,
Wit' my black-handle razor I'm gon' send you to your doggone grave.'

Sometimes there are mild threats to the trifler.

Now Joe de Coo Joe, now Joe de Coo Joe,
You better change your ways,
If you keep on foolin' wit' a ninny horn ninny
You gonna have trouble all your days.

Keep on Going sings of an undying passion.

KEEP ON GOING

I beg you, baby, to treat me right,
You didn't do nothin' but fuss and fight.
Now you keep on goin', honey,
'Til I change my mind.

Bring me back to the one I love
And take the one I hate away,
Must I go bare and he go free,
Lovin' someone who don't love me?

Some say it's a sin to love,
I never ask the reason why,
If it's a sin my lovin' you,
I'll sin and sin until I die.

Nine long years I been waitin',
You know nine long years is a mighty long time;
Nine long years I'll be waitin',
Tryin' to git him off my mind.

Occasionally there may be melodramatic threats of suicide.

Git me a thirty-two pistol,
Let me pay up the debts I owe,
My woman done quit me,
Says she don't want me no mo'.

These two lines express grief:

> Ever since my woman been dead in her grave
> Rocks been my pillow and cross ties my bed.

Familiar is the boasting of the ebon Casanova in the following.

> I ain't no jockey,
> And I ain't no jockey's son,
> But, baby, I can ride you
> Till your jockey comes.
>
> I feel like a Ford V–8, baby,
> Now don't you hesitate,
> I'm good and ready for you
> To put that thing on me.
>
> Coming to your house tomorrow,
> Tell me where's your best man
> Is gonna be,
> Oho, black horror, put that thing on me.
>
> I'm deep, deep down in sorrow,
> Layin' sick in my bed,
> Can't make no connections
> And it went up to my head.
>
> Now early in the mornin'
> When I used to lay by my baby's side,
> She say, turn over, Little Joe,
> And git your mornin' ride.

When a woman leaves a man he may feel blue — at least for a little while. The 'M. N. & O.' is, of course, a railroad line.

> My baby's gone
> And she won't be back no more,
> She left me this mornin'
> Callin' for that M. N. & O.
>
> She bought a ticket
> Just as long as she was tall,
> She said if I can't have my baby
> I don't want no baby at all.

When she was leavin'
She didn't even shake my hand,
She said, I'm leavin' you, baby,
But you just won't understand.

I got two lovin' babies
And you can't tell them apart,
One is my lover
And the other is my heart.

Now my lover she loves me,
And my heart won't let me be,
So you see, kind mamma,
There ain't no room for three.

Sometimes a lover becomes surfeited and his 'mama' becomes a nuisance.

I woke up this mornin' when I heard my backbone crack;
I woke up this mornin' when I heard my backbone crack;
It was my baby with her leg throwed across my back.
I turned over and caught her in her side;
I turned over and caught her in her side;
I said, 'Push over, Mama, 'fore I tan your hide.'

And there are too many women to die for love!

Tell me, tell me, pretty baby,
Tell me what more can I do?
You must want me to lay down, baby, and die for you.
I may, I may lay down, baby,
But dyin' I ain't gonna do;
'Cause there's too many womens who can take the place of you.
Gimme pork chops when I'm hungry;
Gimme whiskey when I'm dry;
Gimme a brown-skin woman when I'm lonesome;
Gimme Heaven when I die.
I'm gonna ring, ring up Heaven
And see if my baby's there;
If she ain't in Heaven,
She must be in Hell somewhere.

A determined, perhaps masochistic lady is represented in these two lines.

> You can cut me, papa, and push me down a hill;
> When I'se done, sweet daddy, I'm gonna be your mamma still.

The Romeo singing the next one is evidently losing his patience, and temper. And he means what he says, he says.

> Say, I mean it, buddy, right from my heart,
> Buddy, I mean it, right from my heart,
> If that gal quit me, I'se gonna tear this town apart.

Right in the same class with pork chops and chitlings and watermelon are red beans and rice, as far as food-loves are concerned, so this one is extremely complimentary.

> I love you once,
> I love you twice,
> I love you next to beans and rice.

The next two sing of profound admiration. Rampart Street is, of course, the 'main drag' for New Orleans Negroes.

> A brown-skin gal went walkin' down Rampart Street,
> She look mighty good, but she had very bad feet.
> That gal will make you think she was some good.
> They tell me she's the worst thing in any neighborhood.
> She is a long mistreatin' rider
> Got devilment in her eyes,
> That walk she got make you think
> She's got devilment in her thighs.

Here is real love.

> I was gonna pawn my pistol,
> I was gonna pawn my watch and chain,
> I was gonna pawn my brown,
> But she left a note saying I'm goin' insane.

> I got a gal lives up the bayou
> Where the water goes 'round and 'round,
> If that gal ever quits me,
> I'll jump overboard and drown.

Here is a favorite, about a gal named Jane.

> I got a gal, her name is Jane,
> And the way she shakes is
> A doggone shame.
> She shakes it to the East;
> She shakes it to the West;
> And she shakes it to me
> 'Cause she loves me best.

To hold a man a woman has to treat him right. If she doesn't he might wake up one morning with this kind of Blues.

> You ever wake up in the mornin' your mind made up two different
>   ways?
> You ever wake up in the mornin' your mind made up two different
>   ways,
> One mind to leave your baby and one mind to stay?
> Just tell me, baby, what can I do to make you change your mind?
> Just tell me, baby, what can I do to make you change your mind?
> I have a mind to love you, baby, if you only treat me nice and kind.
> Now tell me, baby, what more can I do?
> Now tell me, baby, what more can I do?
> I tried so hard, baby, to get along with you.
> I'm lonesome, baby, just as blue as I can be.
> I'm lonesome, baby, just as blue as I can be.
> Wondering why, baby, that you mistreat poor me.
> Ooh, baby, what have I done wrong?
> Ooh, baby, baby, what have I done wrong?
> Lord, I wonder, baby, why you want me gone.

Of course family fights are frequent. And after the smoke has cleared away and the combatants crawl from the débris, someone is liable to receive his 'walking papers.'

And here is one not so complimentary to Louisiana belles of sultry complexions, apparently popular with railroad men.

> Jack Johnson runs the engine and Jefferson throw the switch,
> Louisiana women got no hair, but they git them wigs that fit.

This one might be labeled *A Husband's Complaint*.

Now some of you married women I can't understand,
I say some of you married women I can't understand.
You have beans for your husband and chicken for the back-door man.

JUNKERMEN BLUES

The use of marijuana has spread among Negroes, and here again the fantastic life of the addicts is often expressed in song.

In New Orleans smokers of the drug are called 'junkermen.' Cigarettes made of the narcotic (derived from the Indian hemp plant, an older name being hashish) are called 'reefers' or 'mootahs.' The junkerman is usually supported by a woman who is always known as 'Alberta.' It is supposed the original Alberta was a well-known prostitute who tended her profession diligently, smoked her mootahs contentedly and kept plenty of money in her man's pockets. That her name should be passed on in this fashion is only just, nor do these women object to it, for, as is the opinion, 'Them dames is all crazy anyhow.' Junkermen are reputed to be kind and considerate so long as there is no lack of their mootahs. 'There is some what will give you their hearts, but, man, you take away their junk, and you is gonna git a knife.'

Junkermen occasionally work if the work is not too hard. They despise confinement or any task involving the taking of a great many orders, so many of them are fruit and vegetable peddlers. In an unfortunately large number of cases they are burglars, petty thieves, shoplifters of rare ability or receivers of stolen goods. Their cunning and daring when 'high' and their close cooperation with each other make police work constant and difficult.

Few junkermen smoke an entire cigarette at one time. They will usually tear off a small portion, light up, holding the stub under their upper lips, dragging in the potent smoke with a sucking, hissing noise, hands cupped over mouths.

When the junkerman steps into the 'needle' class, he is usually finished. Death comes quickly because of the inferior grade of the drug he can afford, sometimes because of carelessness in using the needle.

His songs are Blues, often more debased than the others in this class, calling for his junk, his Alberta, or just telling how high he is, 'hittin' the sky,' how smart a fellow he is.

> Alberta, Alberta, come to my weary bed,
> Alberta, Alberta, come to my weary bed,
> Give me my junk 'fore I lose my head;
> Alberta, Alberta, 'fore I lose my head.
>
> If I ain't back at half past fo',
> You know I done gone to the corner sto',
> To git my junk, to satisfy my mind,
> I just got to satisfy my mind.
>
> I can do without coffee, I can do without tea,
> I can do without coffee, I can do without tea,
> But I sure can't do without my weed,
> I sure can't do without my weed.
>
> If you see me comin' down the street full of smiles
> That means I done been over half a mile,
> To git my junk, to git my junk,
> And let my mind go high.

The junkerman has his own conception of Heaven.

> Gimme angel liquor when I'm thirsty
> Gimme reefers when I'm dry
> And gimme Heaven when I die.
> If I had a million dollars I'd buy me a mootah farm
> And blow my mootahs all day long.

The *Reefer Blues* is sung to the tune of *I'm Going to Sit Right Down and Write Myself a Letter*.

REEFER BLUES

I'm gonna set right down and roll myself a reefer,
I'm gonna make believe it came from Mose.
I'm gonna roll it careful and sweet,
It's gonna knock me off my feet.
A lot of inhaling from the bottom,
I'll be glad I got 'em.

I'll attempt to smile and say,
I know I'm high and better
With Chinese eyes the way the Shanghais do.
If the narcotic agent run down on me with that reefer,
I'm gonna make believe, make believe, it came from you.

This one apparently includes unrelated stanzas.

Sheelin' and rockin'
Spinnin' like a wheel
If you ever been a junker
You know just how I feel.

Never loved nobody
But the gal and she's my wife,
I wouldn't quit that girlie
Save no caser's life.

Comin' to your house tomorrow,
Where will your best man be?
Ain't none of your business,
Please connive with me.

Would not been a caser
She made her mammy shame,
Would not been a caser
Took her mammy's man.

Never loved but one man,
His name was Jack the Bear.
He was a good ole peddler
But his mug wasn't fair.

The Junker's Blues following is the usual incomprehensible mixture.

THE JUNKER'S BLUES

Deep down in trouble, trouble to my head,
Deep down in trouble gonna carry me to my grave.
Have me, have me, Alberta, just like poor Percy had the twelve
All in all in an uproar by his lonely black self.

Don't want no black woman to fry no meat for me,
She is low down and dirty and she'll try to kill poor me.
If I had a holler like a mountain jack
I would climb on top the mountain and call Alberta back.

My baby woke me this mornin' just about the count of fo',
She said, roll over and look at me, baby, you might not see me no mo',
Goin' up to the country ain't comin' back no mo',
I'm goin', pretty mamma, where women like you can't go.

I ain't got no more to tell you, ain't got no more to say,
Goin' to see you good folks some old rainy day.

SPIRITUALS

There would seem to be a vast difference between the Negro's
Blues sung to and about his women and his dope and his vocal
outletting of his spiritual craving, but essentially the expressions
are closely akin, and the whole patterns of the melodies not so
dissimilar. Listen to a Negro humming, singing no words, and
it is difficult to tell whether he hums a Blue song or a Spiritual.

Of course in the early days Protestant missionaries were very
active among slaves and white and colored people often sang the
same songs. For the uneducated Negroes the songs were 'lined
out' — a leader reciting a line or two until the song was memo-
rized. Many of the Spirituals sung today still have verses of
rhymed couplets, relics of 'lining out.' Most Methodist and
Baptist hymnals had a section of Spirituals in the back of the
book. From these the Negro Spirituals were born. They still
cry for freedom, not from slavery now, but from worry and
trouble and the struggle for existence. There is always that
longing to start the 'heavenly pilgrimage' up the 'glory road.'

Repetition plays a great part in all Negro songs; having a few
singable words, he is often disinclined to bother with further
elaboration, preferring to devote his energies to the music. As in
the following, the lines are repeated again and again.

My chariot jubilee,
My chariot jubilee,
My golden chariot jubilee,
My chariot jubilee.
My golden chariot jubilee.

This is demonstrated again in *Jesus Is My Captain*, still sung when services begin at the Progressive Baptist Church in New Orleans.

JESUS IS MY CAPTAIN

I shall not be moved, I shall not be moved,
I shall not be moved, I shall not be moved.
Just like a tree planted by the wayside,
I shall not be moved.

Jesus is my Captain,
I shall not be moved.
Jesus is my Captain,
I shall not be moved.
Just like a tree planted by the wayside,
I shall not be moved.

God's Gonna Set Dis World On Fire uses this repetitive method also, and is an excellent example of old-fashioned religious warning to 'sinners.'

GOD'S GONNA SET DIS WORLD ON FIRE

God's gonna set dis world on fire,
God's gonna set dis world on fire,
Some o' dese days. God knows it!
God's gonna set dis world on fire,
Some o' dese days.

I'm gonna drink that healin' water,
I'm gonna drink that healin' water,
Some o' dese days... God knows it!
I'm gonna drink that healin' water
Some o' dese days.

I'm gonna drink and never git thirsty,
I'm gonna drink and never git thirsty,
Some o' dese days... God knows it!
I'm gonna drink and never git thirsty
Some o' dese days.

> I'm gonna walk on de streets of glory,
> I'm gonna walk on de streets of glory,
> Some o' dese days ... God knows it!
> I'm gonna walk on de streets of glory
> Some o' dese days.

To be 'washed of sin' is the desire of the religious Negro, and this washing symbol is one of the most often used.

> Wash me, yes, wash me,
> Whiter than the snow;
> Cleanse me, cleanse me,
> 'Til I sin no more.

In *Now My Soul Want to Go Home to Glory* 'a reelin' and a rockin' ' describes aptly a certain part of all Negro church services. The Spirituals are sung to the accompaniment of hand clapping, and as the fervor mounts, the singers sway from side to side, jump to their feet, arms jerking, shoulders twitching, often stomping and shouting until they become hysterical.

NOW MY SOUL WANT TO GO HOME TO GLORY

Tell me, sister Mary, tell me now, where you been so long gone?
I been a reelin' and a rockin' at de ol' church do'.
Now my soul want to go home to glory.
Reelin' and rockin' at de ol' church do',
Reelin' and rockin' at de ol' church do'.
Now my soul want to go home to glory.

Tell me, sister Mary, tell me now, where you been so long gone?
I been swimmin' in de river eatin' catfish liver.
Now my soul want to go home to glory.
Swimmin' in de river eatin' catfish liver,
Swimmin' in de river eatin' catfish liver.
Now my soul want to go home to glory.

Tell me, sister Mary, tell me now, where you been so long gone?
I been jumpin' them ditches and a-cuttin' them switches.
Now my soul want to go home to glory.

Here's a vocal tale of Samson and Delilah titled *Ef I Had My Way I'd Tear This Building Down*. Delilah becomes 'Della,' Samson — 'Samsen.'

EF I HAD MY WAY I'D TEAR THIS BUILDING DOWN

Della was a woman, Lord, bright and fair;
She had pleasant looks and coal-black hair,
Now the jint Samsen saw battlin' one day
And tole his maid go bring this woman to me.

Chorus:
Now ef I had my way,
Now ef I had my way,
Now ef I had my way,
I'd tear this buildin' down.
I said ef I had my way,
Now ef I had my way,
Now ef I had my way,
I'd tear this buildin' down.

Now when this woman was brought to him,
How she did grin,
Fo' she knowed what she had to do.

Now Samsen was so enthosed until he turned a perfect fool.
Now Della took Samsen upon her knee and said,
I know you are a mighty man,
But tell where your strength lieth if you please.
He told her, Jus' shave my head as clean as your hand
And strength will come like a natchal man.

Della done as she was told,
Now wasn't that mighty bold?
Now poor Samsen set there like a fool,
His eyes lookin' jest like two black pools,
Then he cried out,

My God, ef I had my way,
My God, ef I had my way,
My God, ef I had my way,
I'd tear this buildin' down.

The 'Rock' is a popular symbol in Spirituals, the well-known *Rock of Ages* probably being responsible for its frequent use. *Stand on the Rock a Little Longer*, a favorite, follows.

STAND ON THE ROCK A LITTLE LONGER

Stand on the rock,
Stand on the rock,
Stand on the rock a little longer.
Stand on the rock,
Stand on the rock,
Stand on the rock a little longer.

Just like you see me going along so,
Stand on the rock a little longer.

I have my troubles as I go,
Stand on the rock a little longer.
Stand on the rock,
Stand on the rock,
Stand on the rock a little longer,
Stand on the rock,
Stand on the rock.

Lucy Wells, who contributed *This Earth Is Not My Home*, said that at one time it was the only song used in one of the Baptist churches in New Orleans. The line 'Mattah where I may roam' is probably plagiarized from *Home, Sweet Home*. 'Continue pressin'' your claim' and 'He went my bond one day' are interesting bits reminiscent of the Negro's legal and financial difficulties.

THIS EARTH IS NOT MY HOME

I'm layin' treasures there and it's way beyond the sky,
And no moths or robbers can go nigh.
I've got loved ones watchin' there;
I dearly love them and adore, this earth is not my home.

It's on the other shore, this earth is not my home,
Mattah where I may roam.

To love Jesus sometime you walk alone,
For I'm just passin' through this land,
Tryin' to do the best I can.
This earth is not my home, it's on the other shore.

Over in that glory fair, there will be no dyin' there,
Saints are sure I'll enter there when the toil of life is ovah,
For this earth is not my home.

If I fail and leave you heah, jest continue pressin' your claim,
While in this world jest lift up Jesus' name for me.
He went my bond one day, a great long time ago.
This earth is not my home.

If to judgment we be called, jest before agin we meet,
Pray we walk the golden streets, my name is written there.
I know on the pages white as snow and there I must go,
For this earth is not my home.

I have a mother there on that golden shore,
Father dear went there a long time ago,
Brother already gone, sister waitin' on that shore.
This earth is not my home.

Now if you don't want to see me no more,
Come on that golden shore.
I don't want to live in this world no more,
For it is not my home.

Jonah and the Whale refers to the Bible story of God sending
Jonah to preach at Nineveh. Jonah's disobedience brought down
the wrath of God. 'Neviah Lan' ' is, of course, Nineveh.

JONAH AND THE WHALE

God sent Jonah to de Neviah Lan',
To preach de gospel to de wicked man,
Jonah git angry, didn't want to go,
He hail a ship and git on board.

God rode in a windstorm,
God rode in a windstorm,

God rode in a windstorm an'
And trouble everybody's min'.

Jonah stay in de whale three days and nights,
He obeyed God's will all right.
They searched de ship down in de deep,
Fin' ole Jonah fas' asleep.

Weary of traveling, Jesus rested at the curb of Jacob's Well. A Samaritan woman approached, drew water, and Jesus asked her for a drink. She was astonished at the Jew's addressing her, as the two races did not fraternize. Jesus commanded her to call her husband, and she lied, saying she was unmarried. Then Jesus told her she had been married five times and was now living with a man to whom she was not married. The woman returned to the town crying that Christ was a prophet.

OH LIS'EN, DON'T YOU HEAR WHAT HE SAY?

Jesus met a woman at the well,
She went runnin' home,
She said I met a man settin' on the well,
And he told me everything I've done.

Chorus:
Oh lis'en, don't you hear what he say,
Oh lis'en, don't you hear what he say,
Oh lis'en, don't you hear what he say?
He say the truth is the light and I am the way.

When the people of that city
Came and saw Jesus settin' at the well,
He say I can give water free
That'll save you from a burnin' hell.

Frances Lewis, born a slave in Georgia eighty-six years ago, contributed the next group of songs. 'I remembers lots of old religious hymns, but they don't sing 'em any mo'. They'd think you was crazy if you did. I'll sing you some of 'em.' These are the ones Frances remembered:

O Sister Mary, who's on the Lord's side?
Mary wept an' Martha mourned,
Who's on the Lord's side?
I let you know befo' I go
Who's on the Lord's side.

ALMOST THERE

I'm almost over an' I'll soon be there,
I'm climbin' up Zion's hill,
I'm almost there.
I'm goin' up Calvary an' soon will be there,
I'm climbin' up Zion's hill.

If you git there befo' I do,
Tell Jesus I'll soon be there,
An' tell Him that I'm comin' too,
I'm climbin' up Zion's hill.

One day when I was walkin' 'round,
I heard a reason from on high,
It spoke an' it made me happy an' cry,
It said my sins are forgiven an' my soul set free.

Jesus is my Cap'n an' He gone on befo',
An' he give me His orders,
An' He tol' me not to fear,
I'm on my journey an' I'll soon be there.

There are many versions of *Roll, Jordan, Roll*, but Frances's differed from the better known ones.

ROLL, JORDAN, ROLL

Roll, Jordan, roll;
Wish I had been there to hear sweet Jordan roll.
Look over yonder, see what I see,
A band of angels comin' after me.

Roll, Jordan, roll, you oughta been there,
To see sweet Jordan roll.
Roll, Jordan, roll, you ought been sittin' in the kingdom,
To hear sweet Jordan roll.

The aged slave woman also offered the following miscellaneous collection of unrelated verses.

> Jesus, I'm troubled 'bout my soul,
> Ride on, Jesus, come this way, I troubled 'bout my soul.
> Old Satan is mad an' I am glad,
> He missed one soul that he thought he had.

> I met old Satan the other day,
> An' what you reckon he say?
> 'Jesus is dead an' God's gone away!'
> I made him out a liar an' I kep' on my way.

> I tell you, sister, what's a nat'ral fac',
> Hit's a mighty bad thing to ever look back.

> I wish I was in heaven,
> To see my mother when she entered,
> To see her try on her long white robe an' starry crown,
> I wish I was in heaven to see my mother,
> In her long white robe an' starry crown.

> A sister on the road she mos' done travelin',
> Hit's a rough an' rocky way,
> But I most done travelin'.
> Heaven is so high an' I is so low,
> I'll fear I never git there.

'If people would worship the Lord more the world would be better,' Frances observed. 'Lots of 'em, white folks, too, don' even say grace but jest gobble their food. Why, on New Year's Eve even the horses an' cows an' sheeps an' all animals ben' their knees an' lie down in reverence to the Lord. Look how horses and chickens lif's up their heads in gratitude when they drinks water!' Then came some more verses of forgotten songs.

> John saw the number in the middle of the air,
> The number counted 144,000 an' then it couldn't be counted.

> Who built the Ark?
> Norah built the Ark.

He built it on a sandy lan',
Norah built the Ark.
Some call Norah a foolish man,
To build the Ark on sandy lan'.

Don't you hear the angel call?
Yes, I hear the angel call,
I got the witness in my heart,
An' the glory in my soul.

'I remembers another one,' Frances said. 'When a sinner got converted she'd sing like this:

You may hold my hat,
You may hold my shawl,
But don't you tech
My waterfall! [1]

'You see when I was young nigger girls wore what was called a "waterfall." It was made of real hair and fixed on a thin wire. They was 'spensive, too, and that's why they was so keerful wit' them. When they got religion they'd faint and swoon and all, but they was keerful not to hurt that waterfall.'

There are innumerable stanzas to *Git Ready*. This fragment was found in New Orleans. The refrain *Git ready, git ready* is repeated over and over until it assumes the effect and intensity of a drum beat.

GIT READY

Git ready, git ready,
Tall angel at de bar,
Git ready, git ready,
Tall angel at de bar.

Canaan, here corrupted to 'canian,' the promised land west of the Jordan, is the end of every pious pilgrimage.

SWEET CANIAN

Sweet Canian, sweet Canian,
Oh, Canian is my home.

[1] Webster defines 'waterfall': 'A chignon likened to a waterfall.'

Sweet Canian, oh, Canian,
Is my happy home.
I'm boun' for de Canian land.

One Good Thing My Mother Done expresses childlike faith in prayer.

ONE GOOD THING MY MOTHER DONE

One good thing my mother done,
Taught me to pray when I was young,
She had me bow down on my knees
Gettin' me ready for the Judgment Day.

Chorus:

This ole world ain't gonna stan' up long,
Reelin' and rockin' soon one morn',
Gettin' ready for the Judgment Day.
The Bible told me so.

Fish'man Peter was on the sea,
Christ came down from Galilee;
He said drop your net and follow me,
I'll get you ready for the Judgment Day.
Because —

Here's one soul that's not afraid to die
For I know my record is gone on high.
Step in, doctor, put your grip aside.
Because I got something to tell you
I'm not ashamed to tell;
I bought my ticket at the gate of hell.
Because —

Soon one mornin' 'bout four o'clock,
This ole world is gonna reel and rock,
This ole world is not my home,
I got business aroun' the throne.
Because —

> God told Hezekiel that he had to die,
> He turned his face to the wall and begun to cry;
> He said save me, Lawd, O Lawdy, save me now,
> Let me stay here 'til I change my mind.
> Because —

I Got Shoes is based on a hymn from *The Revivalist*, published in 1868.

> I'se got religion way up de street,
> Oh, I'se even got religion in my feet.
> Oh, I'se got religion, yes, I'se got religion.
> When I'se git to hebben I'se gonna put on my shoes,
> I ain't gonna be no fool,
> I got religion.
> I'se got religion even in my feet.
> Look out, brother, here I'se comin',
> My heart is full like a shotgun,
> 'Cause I'se got religion, yes, I got religion,
> I'se got religion, oh, I'se got religion.

Symbols of death and burial are favorite themes. Gabriel's trumpet, tolling bells, glad shouts of welcome where flows 'Jordan's glory fair.' To hear the trumpet blowing is the hope of the devout. Death is a release and there is joy in the assurance that he is 'saved.'

> I'se hear a horn, guess it's de horn fo' me,
> Oh Lawdy, I hears a horn.
> Oh Lawdy, I hears a horn.
> Can it be de horn fo' me?
> Can it be de horn fo' me?
> I'se hear a bell, it's de bell fo' me.
> Oh Lawdy, I hears a bell.
> Oh Lawdy, I hears a bell.
> Can it be de bell fo' me?

Old Daniel Saw de Stone, a perfect example of the repetitive treatment, is very old, very well known.

OLD DANIEL SAW DE STONE

Old Daniel saw de stone dat was hewed out de mountain,
Old Daniel saw de stone dat was rolled down through Babylon,
Old Daniel saw de stone dat was hewed out de mountain,
Tarryin' down de kingdom of de world.

I'm lookin' for de stone dat was hewed outta de mountain,
I'm lookin' for de stone dat was rolled down through Babylon,
I'm lookin' for de stone dat was rolled down through de mountain,
Tarryin' down de kingdom of de world.

Jesus Christ is de stone dat rolled down through Babylon,
Jesus Christ is de stone dat rolled down de mountain,
Jesus Christ is de stone dat rolled down through Babylon,
Tarryin' down de kingdom of de world.

Don't you want dat stone dat was hewed out de mountain?
Don't you want dat stone dat was rolled down through Babylon?
Don't you want dat stone dat was hewed out de mountain?
Tarryin' down de kingdom of de world.

Frequently natural catastrophies are worked into Spirituals.
A storm in Terrebonne Parish in 1909 was responsible for this
song:

> In the last day of September
> In the year 1909
> God Almighty rose in the weather
> And that troubled everybody's mind.
>
> The storm began on a Sunday
> And it got in awful rage.
> Not a mortal soul
> In the globe that day
> Didn't have any mind to pray.
> And God was in the wind storm,
> And troubled everybody's mind.
>
> God Almighty and his ministers
> They rode up and down the land;

All God Almighty did that day
Was to raise the wind and dust.

God he is in the wind storm and rain
And everybody ought to mind.

In 1915 New Orleans suffered one of the worst storms in its history, and the Reverend A. C. W. Shelton composed *Wasn't It a Storming Time?*

WASN'T IT A STORMING TIME?

'Twas on the 29th day of September
  In the year 1915
Many Lost Souls that went and Slept
  Just because of that raging Storm.

Chorus:
  Wasn't that a raging and a storming time?
  Wasn't that a raging and a storming time?
  Wasn't that a raging and a storming time?
  People had to run and Pray and Cry.

The Storm held People Day and Night
  And God was Playing just the same.
Wasn't it a Pity and a Shame,
  Seems that God was calling
Everybody's Name.

Business was very quiet all Night and Day,
  Glasses were broken down to the ground.
God playing in New Orleans, just the same,
  People knows that he was God anyhow.

The hurricane making eighty miles an hour,
  So we learn to know.
People of New Orleans they did Run,
God broke the Power and Cars couldn't run.

The weight of the Gale everybody felt,
  Gambling Men and Dancing Women,

You want serve God, Men and Women,
   You are wicked and you seldom Pray.

I have warned you by Lighting,
   People mourning, weeping did Pray,
Just keep on with your sinful ways,
   I am able to stop you People's way.

Many souls Lost that floated
   Down the stream to New Orleans,
Yet the People were caught,
   Not a single soul would tell their Name.

Many Telegraph and Telephone Wires
   Leading out the City of New Orleans,
Milneburg had washed away,
   And they rush to the City for Aid.

People had left their happy Homes,
   With all what they Possessed,
Cry, Jesus, will you hear us,
   And help us in our Distress?

A group of Negro boys in the Cane River section of Louisiana contributed this one.

DRY BONES

Dry bones, dry bones,
Well, them bones, dry bones, that are —
Laid in the valley.
Well, them bones, dry bones, that are —
Laid in the valley,
You can hear the word of the Lord.

Or from my toe bone to my —
Foot bone, or from my —
Foot bone to my —
Ankle bone, or from my —
Ankle bone to my —
Leg bone, or from my —

Leg bone to my
Knee bone.
Well, them bones, dry bones, that are —
Laid in the valley,
You can hear the word of the Lord.

Or from my knee bone to my —
Thigh bone, or from my —
Thigh bone to my —
Hip bone, or from my —
Hip bone to my
Rib bone, or from my —
Rib bone, to my —
Back bone.
Well, them bones, dry bones, that are —
Laid in the valley,
Well, them bones, dry bones, that are —
Laid in the valley.
You can hear the word of the Lord.

Or from my back bone to my —
Shoulder bone, or from my —
Shoulder bone to my —
Head bone, or from my —
Head bone to my —
Skull bone, or from my —
Skull bone to my —
Eye bone.
Well, them bones, dry bones, that are —
Laid in the valley,
Well, them bones, dry bones, that are —
Laid in the valley.
You can hear the word of the Lord.

Or from my eye bone to my —
Nose bone, or from my —
Nose bone to my —
Mouth bone, or from my —
Mouth bone to my —
Chin bone, or from my —
Chin bone to my —

Throat bone, or from my —
Throat bone to my —
Well, them bones, dry bones, that are —
Laid in the valley.
Well, them bones, dry bones, that are —
Laid in the valley.
You can hear the word of the Lord.

Or from my throat bone to my —
Breast bone, or from my —
Breast bone to my —
Shoulder bone, or from my —
Shoulder bone to my —
Muscle bone, or from my —
Muscle bone to my —
Elbow bone.
Well, them bones, dry bones, that are —
Laid in the valley.
Well, them bones, dry bones, that are —
Laid in the valley.
Or from my elbow bone to my —
Arm bone, or from my —
Arm bone to my —
Wrist bone, or from my —
Wrist bone to my —
Hand bone, or from my —
Hand bone to my —
Finger bone.
Well, them bones, dry bones, that are —
Laid in the valley.
Well, them bones, dry bones, that are —
Laid in the valley.
You can hear the word of the Lord.

Oh Lord, I'm in Your Care is a typical example of the devout
and childlike faith of the religious Negro.

OH LORD, I'M IN YOUR CARE

Oh Lord, I'm in your care,
Oh Lord, I'm in your care.
Put your lovin' arms around me,

So no evil cannot harm me, 'cause I,
Great God, am in His care.

Whilst I'm in His care,
In my Savior's care.
Oh Lordy, put your lovin' arms
Around me so no evil cannot harm me,
'Cause I, Great God, am in His care.

One day when I was walkin', Lordy,
Down the lonesome road,
The Spirit spoken to me and it filled
My heart with joy, joy, joy,
'Cause I am in His care.

Whilst I'm in His care,
In my Savior's care,
In His care, in His care,
Put your lovin' arms around me,
So no evil cannot harm me,
'Cause I, great God, am in His care.

MISCELLANEOUS NEGRO SONGS

, The Negro's continual good humor is a legend. Sometimes the grin is only a mask for the benefit of the 'white folks.' There is little truth in the widespread theory that 'niggers are the happiest people on earth.' Usually, of course, he has his own peculiar philosophy, probably the rationalization 'Times is tough — make the best of them,' and 'times' is always tough for the Negro of a low economic level. But often, too, a secret and shrewd cynicism exists, as in the song below.

Don't you mind de people talk,
Jest so their talk be wrong,
For de people see all your faults,
But dey never can see their own.

Some people borrow some money from you
And promise you sure to pay,
But when dey see you comin' again,
Dey go another way.

Some people pretend as your bosom friend,
Goin' to be with you to de end,
Dey are goin' to stick to you in all you do,
But when you git in trouble you through.

Now let me tell you how de world is fixed.
De Devil done got it all full of tricks.
You can go from place to place,
And hear a whole lot of people runnin' down their race.

Drinking is as good an outlet as any. Here is a Negro drinking
song about a fake Negro beggar.

Hipple de cripple,
And help de blind,
All you box-ankled hypocrites
Donate me a dime.

I done walked by a river,
I done walked by a brink.
Now all your dimes together
Will buy me a little drink.

He, He, He, you and me,
Little brown flas', how I love thee.
He, He, He, you and me,
My little brown flas', don' never fail me.
My dog and me was sittin' on a log in the river,
The log slipped and I got wet,
But you can bet on my little brown flas'.
He, He, He, you and me,
Little brown flas', how I love thee.

Negroes are sometimes passionate gamblers. Besides Lottery
and Craps, they love the races, making 'two-bit' parleys, if their
financial conditions permit no heavier betting. The following
songs concern Skew Ball, an Irish race horse of broadside fame.
Songs about Skew Ball are sung in the prisons of Louisiana,
Texas, Mississippi and Tennessee. The name is corrupted, variously, to Skewball, Stewball, Stoball and Showball. The following version is the most widely known in the chain-gang of
the South.

Ol' Stewball was a fas' horse, I wish he was mine.
He never drunk water, but always drunk wine,
Drunk wine, man; drunk wine.

Ol' Stewball was a white horse, before they painted him red.
But he winned a great fortune jest before he fell dead,
Fell dead, man; fell dead.

In the next one the race horse is Skewball in the first line, Showball in the second.

Skewball and gray mare was runnin' a race,
Showball beat gray mare a mile in the lane.

Had a gal by the name o' Isabella,
She run off with another colored fella.

In this Louisiana song, Skew Ball becomes Stoball and great faith in him is exhibited.

Bet on Stoball and your money's gonna win,
Your money's gonna win.
Bet on Stoball and your money's gonna win,
Your money's gonna win.
Oh, bet on Stoball and your money's gonna win.

The Negro's cynicism often includes his preacher. That pompous gentleman receives his full share of distrust, suspicion and teasing.

Some People Say is lifted from an ante-bellum minstrel song, the first line of which is 'Some people say a nigger won't steal.'

SOME PEOPLE SAY

Some people say dat preachers don't steal,
I caught three in my corn fiel',
One had a shovel and one had a hoe,
Dey was diggin' dose 'taters by de row.
Says me to my wife, Keep quiet, will you?
I'm gonna turn 'em to de law, ha! Den what'll dey do?
So I went to de river, I couldn't get across,
Jumped on a alligator, took 'im for a horse.

De horse wouldn't holler,
I sold 'im for a dollar.
Dollar wouldn't take,
I threw it in de grass.
De grass wouldn't grow,
I chopped it in two with my hoe.
De hoe wouldn't cut,
Lawd, here comes a yellow gal slidin' on 'er butt.

Here's a similar one:

I wouldn't trust a preacher out o' my sight,
Say, I wouldn't trust a preacher out o' my sight,
'Cause dey believes in doin' too many things far in de night.

Apparently a preacher is supposed to be singing the next one.

Brother, if you want mo' preachin',
Save a little for me.
Glory Hallelujah! Drinking gin ain't against my teachin'!
Treat me with equality.
Now from dat small it is plain to see,
Dat somebody is holdin' out on me.
So, brother, if you want mo' preachin',
Save a little for me.

And here is a thrust at those dignified pillars of the church, the deacons.

Some o' dese deacons is makin' a plot,
To git dere whiskey in a coffee-pot,
They goes to church and be on time,
To pick up a collection to git a dime.

An aged colored man remembered his 'gran'ma' singing this one:

Who bin gittin' an' who bin tryin',
Who bin gittin' an' who bin tryin',
Who bin gittin' that goodies o' mine?
Nobody, my darlin' chile!

Jay bird went to the yaller hammer,
Yaller hammer saw him when he done it.
Jay bird caught yaller hammer by the tail,
An' throwed him on the other side of Jordan.

Old-time Negroes were fond of songs about animals; the 'possum was a favorite, the raccoon another.

> Possum up in de 'simmon-tree,
> Raccoon on de ground;
> Possum say, 'You son-of-a-gun,'
> Better shake dose 'simmons down.

> Raccoon rides a passenger train,
> An' a possum throws de switch,
> An' a rabbit ride no train at all,
> But he gits dere jus' de same.

> My mammy's little, short an' brave,
> Sent for the doctor an' what you reckon he say?
> Feed the people on shortenin' bread.

The following are known as 'river songs,' probably because of their popularity among Negroes working along the Mississippi.

> Meet me down sweet old Montana,
> I call to Katie an' lef' an' did not leave no news.

> I had a girl and her name was sweet Roberta,
> An' now she's gone an' I'll soon be gone myself.
> She's little an' low,
> She's got two dimples in her jaw.

> She's a little angel chile,
> I been lookin' for my angel chile,
> So I went up to the mountain,
> An' axed the Lord to give me
> My little girl back agin.

A very old Negress, who was born a slave, remembered this song. She said, 'Befo' I got religion I went to dances, an' we danced by a fiddle, and the fiddler kep' time, singin'

> Hop light, ladies, the cake's all dough,
> Don' min' the weather, so the wind don't blow.'

It Just Suit Me is derived from a Spiritual, but in the following verses the refrain has been used for a social song. The reference

to corn, meat, meal and cheese marks it as possibly having originated in the French Market neighborhood of New Orleans.

IT JUST SUIT ME

When you come to my house,
You must come through the field;
It just suit me.
When you come to my house,
You must come through the field;
It just suit me.

When you come to my house,
You must come through the field;
If you can't bring corn, bring meat and meal;
Because it just suit me.

When you come to my house,
Come through the field;
If you can't bring flour, bring dago cheese;
Because it just suit me.

The meaning of the next one is rather vague; evidently there is
a grievance against New Orleans — and some connection with
somebody's love life.

New Orleans, Louisiana,
Mistreatin' state,
I was thinkin' of you so much, sweet baby,
I forgot the date.

Here is an old song, reminiscent of the days of the steamboat
races.

For we'll give her a little more rosin,
And open her blower wide,
To show them the way to Natchez,
Runnin' against the tide.
Oh, a little more rosin, do,
A little more pitch and pine!
Throw in a can of glycerine
And a barrel of turpentine.

Negroes have as much trouble with divorce and alimony as movie stars. Alimony trouble is a common ailment, and woe to the ex-husband who slips up in his payments. To court he goes, perhaps to plead before His Honor in this fashion:

> Can't work dis morning, Judge,
> Tired as I can be;
> My woman is gaged and she done
> Mistreated poor me.
> If I don't pay de alimony
> She comes runs and tells you.
> Judge, oh Judge, please change my woman's view.

And in the following song the height of cynicism — regarding women — is reached.

> Now I'm sick and about to die
> None of my friends won't come nigh.
> But when I gits on my feet,
> Watch the womens say, 'Ain't he sweet?'

Chapter 22

Chimney Sweeper's Holiday

THE CHIMNEY SWEEP WAS TAKING A DAY OFF
from work, and he sat on the porch of a dilapidated tenement
house in a street of similar houses all occupied by Negroes. He
was a little drunk and was having an argument with an old
woman, a neighbor. His wife, sad-eyed and skinny, stood
watching as a male crony at the gate urged the chimney sweep to
join him at the corner saloon.

There was a little whiskey left in the sweep's flask, and as he
drank it the old woman began to talk:

'I remembers the day that boy was born,' she said. 'It was on
a Tuesday night in 1894 in Westwego. And there was a big to-do
at John Simms' house 'cause his wife Stella had just birthed her
first and only child. Them niggers was raisin' it up. Yells was
hittin' the ceilin' and whiskey was all over the place. Stella had
shown she could bring a child to the world even if she had done
run around with so many different mens.

'The crowd waited all day to see the thing happen, settin' on
the front steps and in the side yard while the midwife looked on
Stella, hoping she would prove her point. They was sayin',
"Come on, Stella." And Stella was lyin' there gruntin'; her

eyes was movin' around in her head like a top spinnin' on the ground. But Stella came on all right. A little black boy popped out and he commenced hollerin'. I was one of the first ones to smack him on his behine, bam! He jumped! I remember it so well, like it happened yesterday.

'I don't know, but I'm willin' to bet that John Simms, Junior, opened his eyes to a pint of whiskey and some woman doin' a shake-down dance. 'Cause ever since that day he's been drinkin' whiskey and makin' women do shake-down dances. Them is dances where you slide back and pull up your dress; show your linen, you know.

'I drank with John Simms, Junior, befo' he was born, when he was born, and I been drinkin' with John Simms, Junior, ever since. I can't do no shake-down dance but I can have my fun.'

It was Susie Walker talking, a rheumatic brown woman, little taller than a midget. When she is drunk, she is friendly; when she is sober, she is hard to locate. It is necessary to have Susie around when you're talking to John Simms, Junior, because she is the only one who can handle him. She says boastfully, 'Didn't I pick that black bastard up and put him on my knee when he was a baby? If I handled him then, can't I handle him now?'

John Simms, Junior, dressed in shabby blue overalls, drunk and forlorn, was standing next to Susie, and heard her introduction to his life without saying anything. He approved with a shaking head. John is a tall, slender black man with big eyes and white teeth. He walks proudly and talks at random. Susie says, 'He is the best chimney sweeper in the world.'

He is also a problem and a menace, to his light-hearted common-law wife, Emma Brooks, who is never allowed to say what she thinks for fear of his fists.

Emma whispered: 'You talk to him, I can't. He might sweep me away like he sweeps them chimneys.'

John Junior began to talk. 'Me, I'm a chimney sweep from way back — a chimney sweeper havin' a holiday. My pa was a chimney sweeper... my ma was a chimney sweeper. Ask Susie.' He wanted to say more about his mother and father but Emma interrupted him to remind him that his mother wasn't a chimney sweeper, but was a washwoman. 'Shut up,' John Junior said.

'I was born in Westwego. Took after my pa and ma. She born me in whiskey. My pa drank whiskey like the tank that bottles it. He was a laborer in the Round House of the T. P. My ma didn't work at all. She was a good-time woman. But when she married my pa she settled down. She got into an argument with some people and bore me to prove she could have a baby. I'm sho glad of it. No, my ma didn't have to work. She had enough to do takin' care of my pa when he got drunk.'

He moved away from the post and eased himself down on the step. 'I ain't got no education. Went to the third grade. That was enough fo' me. My pa stopped me, made me get a job on a milk truck. I was makin' two dollars a week. What I did with my money? I had a good time, that's what. Sho, school is all right fo' them who wants it, but I figures all you got to know is how to read and write, then nobody can cheat you out of nothin'. Ain't figures enough?

'I believe my pa and ma liked large families, but they tell me — now I don't know — but they tell me my ma had such a time bringin' me she swore she wasn't goin' bring no more. She and pa drank so much they don't even remember how it all started, to tell the truth. Sho, I drank, too. Pa used to make me drunk, half the time. I've always liked whiskey and who don't like the way I do, they know what they can do.

'I quit the milk truck, couldn't have my fun like I wanted to. Had to get up too early. I was only ten years old then. What I didn't like about the milk truck was I couldn't be wid that sweet little gal next door long enough. Then, I got me a job ridin' a bike. Three-fifty a week. I went to work so I could buy the clothes I wanted. My pa and ma wouldn't give me nothin'. I always did like to be dressed up. I like it now but my money ain't right. That's all a po' man can do — dress up, and have a good time.'

Susie reminded John Junior that he spent three hundred dollars of his bonus on clothes for himself and his women.

But John had a defense: 'Ain't we got to look fine when we walk down the street?' Susie reminded him that he pawned most of his clothes for whiskey, which encouraged John Junior to shout back: 'A good bottle of whiskey is worth a suit in pawn any day. Then agin, a man as ugly as me is got to spend money on women. Ain't that right? It ain't no need fo' me to fool myself. I always did spend money on women and I'm goin' to keep on doin' it.

'Sho, I done other jobs besides workin' on a milk truck and ridin' a bike. I worked at the Round House when I was a man. Made twenty-one fifty. Used every bit of it up, that's right. Man, I used to buy mo' fun than a chicken had feathers. They used to call me lil John Junior. A chip off his daddy's block. I was a mess. Had women shakin' down and doin' the Eagle Rock wid dollar bills in their hands. Have fun, live. You don't live but once. When you die square up the Devil. No, indeed! There never was a Christian in my family, we don't believe in that stuff. My pa used to say, "Get me a bucket full of wine I'll join the church." Spare time? Man, I ain't had no spare time. Don't have none now. In my spare time I have my fun!

'I came to this part of town when I was about twenty. Bought so much stuff I had to go back on the other side. The policeman says: "Boy, go back where you b'long. You is got these womens jumpin' naked."

'Well, I tell you. There ain't nothin' wrong with being a chimney sweeper. The work might be dirty but the money is sho clean and long. Yes suh! You get bucks when you clean chimneys! SWEEPER! ROOAP, ROOAP, SWEEPER! CHIMNEY SWEEPER! GET 'UM CLEAN 'FORE YOU SCREAM.... FIRE! ROOAP! ROOAP! SWEEPER! I charge some people two dollars, and some two dollars and a half, mostly two and a half. I charge by the day and by the chimney. Jews make their own prices. You can't jew them up. The only thing I don't like about cleanin' chimneys is when them womens hang around me. They sho can give orders. What they know about cleanin' chimneys won't fill a book, but they hang around you. Sometimes I feel like tellin' um, "Don't cry around me, lady, I'm not the fireman."

'How I started cleanin' chimneys? Let me see. Say, you wants to know everything. Well, I was friendly with a fellow named

Jeff Scott. He's dead. Jeff was makin' plenty money and needed help. So, me and him made up as partners. We used to make as high as twenty dollars a day fo' both of us. Wasn't bad, eh? Them was the days. Ain't no money in it now. Everybody is usin' gas and electric lights. And then again, nobody wants to pay. Can't make but about four or five dollars a day in the season ... that in the winter time. Some say "Let's get a union" but not me. I don't want no union. Fo' what? Fo' a bunch of black bastards to land in jail.

'How we get our jobs? Well, most of 'em is from our customers. They send us to people. And the fire stations send us lots of business too. But, we just go along the street hollerin'. The reason why the fire stations wants to give us work because it saves them from a lot of work. See?

'It feels all right to clean chimneys. It's a job. And a good job. Sho, I'm proud of it. All them people who laughs at us is crazy. I used to make mo' money in a day cleanin' chimneys than some people who laugh at us make in a week. Money was just that good. Then agin, there is a lot of places that feed you. Everybody likes a chimney sweeper. People think we is Mardi Gras. We don't care. We pick up a lot of tips like that.

'This is how we clean a chimney: We take them long corn vines and tie 'um together and sweep the soot down from top. It takes two men to do it. We draw down a small fire in the chimney by throwin' salt up the chimney. Salt is a strong-actin' agent fo' fire. It can't stand salt.

'I don't know why we wears beaver hats and them kind of clothes. I believes them is the uniforms because they don't look dirty. Nobody minds dirty clothes gettin' dirty. Does they? A white man gave me my beaver. The coat and pants is mine. We tie rope around our waist because we have to use it sometimes, to pull ourselves up and down the roof. We use that rope like a ladder. Man, sometimes we almost go down in one of them chimneys. I seen the time when I was in one of 'um like Santa Claus, reachin' down in there like a baby reachin' for candy. We take our pads, rags, salt and stuff and wrap them up in a bundle.

'The trouble with this business is that them bastards cuts the prices all the time. Some of them womens tell you, "The other man said he'd clean my chimney fo' fifty cents.'' All that dust and stuff gets in your eyes. Man, that's dangerous. Suppose you get consumption? Cleanin' chimneys is bad on your lungs. I drink milk and liquor to keep from losin' my lungs. No, I ain't never been sick in my life.

'There ain't no mo' money in cleanin' chimneys, ain't nothin' to it. Everything is modern and streamline. I'm tryin' to be streamline myself.' He laughed and the women laughed with him. 'I was so streamline I fell off a woman's roof one mornin'. The woman had done said, ''What you goin' do way up there?'' I said, ''I'm goin' to examine things.'' She had to examine my head.

'Say man, them chimneys make you so dirty that when you get home you got to take a bath in kerosene. Everything on you gets black. That work makes you nervous. A white man sho could never be no chimney sweeper. He would look like he was carryin' his shadow aroun'.

'Some white folks like to talk with you, especially them from the North. They say they ain't never seen nothin' like us. They wants to know where we live and how we live. One white lady ain't had nothin' fo' us to do, she just called us in and gave us wine and two dollars to talk with us. Man, we ain't told that woman nothin'. I ain't goin' to never let nobody know all my business. 'Specially no white folks. We get cigarettes, clothes and things from people. All in all we do all right. But, we don't take things instead of money. Some of them white folks try to get you to do that, but not me. I tells them to pay me money, sumpin' I can use. I can get bread, clothes, and what I wants with my money. It ain't coneyfit.

'I strictly haves my fun. No, I ain't tendin' bein' no Christian. That's the trouble with niggers now. They pray too damn much. Everytime you look around you see some nigger on his knees and the white man figurin' at his desk. What in the world is they prayin' fo'? Tryin' to get to heaven? They is goin' to get there anyhow. There ain't no other hell but this one down here. Look at me. I'm catchin' hell right now. I'm drunk and I ain't got no money.

'If I had some? Man, don't ask me no question like that.

What else is I'm goin' to do but have my fun. I pay my rent, give my old lady what she takes to pay the insurance, buy food, and get her sumpin' and that's all. What I'm goin' to do? Ain't no need fo' me to save nothin'. I ain't never been able to save nothin' in my life. I don't want to save nothin'. You want me to have troubles?

'I went to war — didn't get killed. Come on back — got my bonus. And then got me a load of womens and threw it away. Ain't that bein' a sucker? When you spend your money you ain't got nothin' to show fo' it. When you spend your money on whiskey you got whiskey to show fo' it.

'My wife is a good woman. She ain't had to work in two years. I took her out the white folks' kitchen. She wasn't makin' but three dollars a week, anyhow. That ain't no money. Sho, she brought the pots and pans home. But what was in 'um? A lot of leftovers. Man, as long as I can make a dollar sweepin' chimneys I ain't goin' to eat nobody's leftovers. I can buy what I want and I'm my own boss. Do you know that I been sweepin' chimneys off and on fo' eighteen years? Before I did that I used to be a common laborer. If I can help it I'll never be a common laborer agin. I likes to be my own boss. Don't want no white folks hollerin' at me.

'I fo'got to tell you that sweepin' chimneys is a hard thing in the winter time, it's mighty cold five o'clock in the mornin'. I'll never fo'get. Man, I went hollerin' under a politician's window one mornin'. ROOAP...ROO...AP...ROOO... OAP: CHIMNEY SWEEPER...RO...ROOAP...REEE... REE...REE...ROOAP...CHIMNEY! Man, the politician poked his head out of his window and told me, "Say, you black bastard, if you don't get the hell away from here I'm comin' out there and rope your damn neck to one of them trees!" His wife stuck her head out the window and just laughed. It was early in the mornin' too. She just laughed, and said, "Darlin', leave him alone. I think he's cute." The man looked at her and looked at me; I was ready to make haste. He started cussin' agin, "You black bastard, if you don't get goin' you'll be cute. You won't have no damn head." Then, he looked at his wife. "Cute hell. You run your damn trap all night and here comes that chimney man runnin' his mouth early in the mornin' and you say he's cute. I'll kill that nigger.'' Man, did I leave from away from there! That's why we don't go out early in the mornin' no mo'.'

The man with the bottle said, 'Come on, John, quit talkin' and let's go to that saloon on Washington Avenue.'

Emma said, 'John.'

He looked at her and said: 'Baby, get my dinner ready. I'll be back.'

But the woman knew that he was off with his friends. Old Susie was angry; she shrugged her shoulders and said, 'Damn fool, there he goes bummin' with rats when he has a nice gent'man to talk with.'

A black man called to John Junior from a passing automobile, 'Where you goin'?'

He flipped his fingers and shouted back, 'I'm goin' make some women shake down and show their linen. Everybody is worrin' about John. Can't a man have a holiday?'

Emma was 'plum disgusted' with John. 'All he knows is work, more work, fun and more fun. That fool has more holidays than the President. He ain't never had nothin' . . . ain't got nothin' and ain't goin' to never have nothin'. He's the best money-circulator in the whole round world.'

Chapter 23

A Good Man Is Hard To Find

CREOLA CLARK SAYS SHE IS A GOOD WOMAN. She attends Zion Travelers Baptist Church regularly, and prays on her knees. You won't find Creola's name on any of the church's executive boards nor will you find it listed in the church clubs, but Creola is an influential member and is a 'hopin' soul.' She is hoping that Zion Travelers' members are praying with her, and she is hoping that her galloping, slue-foot, light-brown, lazy husband, Buster Clark, will soon find a job.

'Creola better hope that Buster quit looking at that brown-skin gal who lives around the corner,' said a neighbor. 'That gal ain't giving Creola any trouble with Buster yet, but she has her mind on it.'

'You could describe me as a chocolate black,' said Creola. 'I'm forty-seven and weigh two-ten. Any man ought to be able to keep his mind on me and on nobody else. I know how to treat a man, everybody says that. What makes me so mad is that even the church says it. And the church says that Buster ain't treatin' me right. That's why he don't go to church no mo', and that's why the church is prayin' fo' me, I hope!'

Creola says she isn't superstitious, but you can't pay her to mention the name of the girl who is offering her competition. 'I reasons that it ain't good to be callin' women's names 'cause that helps mo' than anything else to make 'em take your man,' Creola said. 'I hates to think of her with her arms around Buster's neck. And she must be doin' just that, 'cause there ain't nothin' better that Buster likes than havin' some woman runnin' her hands around his neck. He's sho weak fo' that. Old fool!'

Buster had just left the house when we called. 'If he was here he wouldn't talk. He ain't sociable,' Creola said. 'All he wants to do is bum in the streets. He won't look fo' work fo' nothin'. He must think that work is goin' to come to him.'

Creola is a cook by heart and by profession; she works on St. Charles Avenue for Mrs. Jakes. Creola likes to be seen walking in her madame's palatial door in the early morning and out of it in late evening. 'My madame lets me walk right through her front door in the mornin' and in the evenin',' she says, 'and I'm a proud sumpin'. She likes to see me walk but she don't like to hear me talk. She says I talk too much about my troubles.'

Creola has been working for Mrs. Jakes about ten years; she lives in one of her houses. Her room is very shabby and crowded with furniture. Clothes hang on the wall, and there are several pairs of shoes under the bed. Creola has many excuses for her untidy room.

'It's a hard thing to keep this room clean. Excuse it. There's so much dust in this neighborhood. And there ain't enough room to take care of things. I'm goin' to fix it up as soon as I get a little time. Buster should be cleanin' up but he's in the street somewhere. I'm ashame' of him and I'm ashame' of myself fo' lovin' him. Son, I got troubles with that man. You don't know what it means to have a man on yo' hands who won't work. Do you know that Buster ain't had nobody's job in three years? I calls him my W.P.A. man 'cause the last job he had was on the W.P.A. He come sayin', "Baby, don't call me no W.P.A. man, call me yo' stomp digger." I can't call him that. He ain't diggin' no stomps. Old fool. He's waitin' fo' his W.P.A. card agin. And if you ask me, it ain't comin'. I keep tellin' that fool that, but he won't listen. Old fool! When they laid him off, the man particular told him to find a job 'cause they had to cut the rolls.

Instead of him lookin' fo' a job he went to all them offices and fussed with the people. Everywhere he went they told him to find another job. He makes me mad, 'cause he ain't got nothin' on his mind. · He done even wrote to the President. I was just wishin' the President would of told him he ain't had no time foolin' wid him. But the President wrote him. Was he happy! That fool got that letter in his wallet, and his wallet is empty. I don't talk to him no mo' about work, 'cause when you wants to make Buster real mad just talk to him about work. Never seen a man gets so mad.

'I'm tellin' you I don't know how we make it. After I takes my insurance money out my salary and pay a few bills I ain't got nothin'. Do you think he'll ask questions? Huh! All he wants to do is sit around till I bring them white folks' pots home. Mrs. Jakes done asked me how many mouths I'm feedin'. That Buster is got three, I feel like tellin' her sometimes. But I'm scared she'll get mad and run him plum out of this room. This is her house, you know. And you know how white folks is. They'll run you clean away from 'em when you ain't doin' what's right.

'And people wonder why I pray. Shucks, I got troubles. Just like I say. After a few things come out of my salary it looks like a silver dime. Worse than that even.

'I'm local. I was born right here. Born on Sixth Street. I ain't had no pa. Don't guess my ma had time to keep up wid that. She told me I ain't had no pa. I didn't argue, she ought to know. Not me. I'm here by the hardest. I don't know why but I'm sho glad of it! I betcha that! And I ain't askin' too many questions about it 'cause somebody might find out that I ain't got no business here and send me on back where I come from. I hear 'um talkin' about Senator Bilbo wants all the cullud people to go back to Africa. Africa ain't did me nothin'. I don't see why I got to go back to Africa. I'm doin' all right here. I don't need nothin' in Africa. Who started that, anyhow? Them people can think of some of the wors' stuff. I thought Buster was bad enough, but I reckon some white folks is just as bad.

'My ma raised me all the way. She was cook and wanted me

to be one. My ma could make any dish put on the table. They used to call her "Toot-it Tot" 'cause when she turned loose a pot it was Toot-it Tot. That means it was ready. My ma had me workin' wid her. No, I ain't had much schoolin' but I got good mother-wit. I can read and write. Ain't nobody can beat me out a dollar, I betcha that. I been around the white folks. When I was little I used to run on errands fo' white folks. Used to eat in their kitchen, mind their chillun and things. Facts was, that was the first job I ever done got. School? I went to the third, did all right too. I didn't like school much. If it wasn't fo' 'rithmetic I would of done all right, I reckon. That's what used to whup me. Just couldn't make it go, that's all. I was a bright child fo' everything else. Got my readin', spellin' and stuff. I went to McDonough Number 24. The principal sho could use a strap. That man ain't had no pity on you. He used to fold that strap and slam you across the hine wid it and almost knock you crazy. I 'members one day he caught me in the hall fo' being late, and he came down on me wid that strap. Did that hurt!

'I can 'member that my ma went to work early every mornin'. Her name was Marguerite Wilson. She was a short brownskin lady. She says my pa was brownskin too. I used to ask her why I'm so chocolate and she used to laugh and say, "We plucked you out of a dark cloud that was hangin' low one day." Fo' the longest I believed that. Me and my ma used to live in a room just like this, only hers had a fire grate in it. We used to sit down in front of that grate and make popcorn and eat 'um. Mamma used to tell me about her old days on the farm. She was from Harahan, used to work for some rich white folks when she was younger. Yes indeed, me and my mamma was good friends.

'Yes, mamma went to church. That's where I got the habit from. She took me to church every Sunday, didn't miss a Sunday. Mamma thought all the world in goin' to church. Used to say, "Divinity is the word. Pray fo' what you want and want what you pray fo'." Them was her true words.

'There was nothin' stylish about my ma. She was just a plain woman. She didn't do no runnin' around neither. I ain't never seen my ma wid no man. I tried to grow up and be just like her.

She was a hard-workin' woman, and she brought the pans right home. Then we'd sit down and eat out of the pans, and she'd tell me all about how them white folks like her cookin' and what they said. That's sumpin' me and mamma sho like to do, make them white folks talk about our cookin'. You is cookin' when you can make them white folks come pat you on the shoulders and say, "Creola, that dinner was sho nice, child." That's the way they say it, you know. Sometimes they give you tips and things. My people does that all the time. They is always sayin' sumpin' nice about my cookin'. It makes you feel so good.

'Well, things went well. Then mamma commenced gettin' old. I was hittin' around sixteen years old and gettin' kind of lively. There was heap of fellows comin' around tryin' to get me but I kept my head up and my mind on mamma. 'Cose, you know I was scrapin' around. Gettin' some washin' here and there, makin' a lil sumpin' and puttin' it right in the house. Well, mamma got sick and she put me in her place. I was workin' fo' Miss Graves. It sho was funny. Miss Graves says to me, "Honey child, does you think you can do my cookin'?" I says yes'm. Shucks, in two days I had Miss Graves sayin', "Honey child, I want you to be my regular cook." She give me five dollars a week fo' cookin' and cleanin' up the house. It was some house, a two-story house. The only thing I didn't like about Miss Graves was that she always messed around the kitchen. She was always sayin', "Honey child, is you got enough seasonin' in the food?" I wasn't no sassy thing, you know. I always says yes'm. But I ain't paid her no mind. Just says yes'm. You got to say sumpin', ain't you?

'I worked fo' Miss Graves two years all by myself. Mamma was home sick. We had some scuffle. I took care of my mamma off of five dollars a week. Talkin' about makin' a dollar stretch! 'Cose I nearly go blind lookin' at my lil money, but I been makin' them dollars go fo' a mighty long time, son. I don't know how it would feel to have some big money. Don't guess I could arrange it much. 'Cose, me and my ma didn't wear no stylish clothes, but our clothes was sho good enough to go to church in. I wasn't no high-steppin' gal, 'cause I loved my ma too well and I wasn't rightly fixed. But if I'd known then what I know now I'd been a solid mess. Don't you know that our preacher had his stuff and he used to keep his eyes on me. Used to tell me all the time, "Sister, I got my eyes on you." I didn't say nothin' much, but I did a heap of thinkin'. You see in them times I didn't know them preachers was runnin' around.

'Things went on mighty bad wid me pushin' here and pullin' there fo' a long time. Mamma was gettin' no better. I was gettin' up in years and the boys commenced comin' around. All of 'um wanted me to pull up my dress. That's all I could hear. "Pull up yo' dress. Pull up yo' dress." I commenced wonderin' what would happen if I'd pull up my dress. That's what you get. Some nice boys used to ask me that. And does you know one thing, like a fool, I waited till old Buster came along and then I pulled up my dress. That was the finals. What Buster didn't put on me, Lawd! I told that nigger he'd hafta marry me 'cause I liked it. He did. Both of us loved each other. But a heap of womens loved Buster. My ma used to tell me all the time that Buster wasn't the kind of man fo' me. I know, I used to hear people talkin' all the time, sayin', "Don't let mamma find nothin' out fo' you, find it out fo' yo'self." So, boy, you got to 'scuse my talk, but I got me two or three mens but they ain't satisfied me none. I was right. Old Buster is the man fo' me. That's the only thing my ma was ever wrong about!

'Yeah, Buster did all right then. He used to work down at the cotton warehouse. But I didn't get too much of his money 'cause he had to take care of his mamma and his papa. Then old Buster spent plenty money on his back. He like to look fine, you know. That's what's hurtin' him now.

'We was livin' in a three-room house. The rent was ten dollars a month. I was still workin'. Did Buster eat them pans, like a goat eats paper! That man used to fall in them pans sumpin' awful. Man, pans is good eatin'. Ain't you never ate none? You get all that comes off the table.

'But let me tell you how I got Mrs. Jakes to give me her pans. When I went there I says I slung pans. She says, "What's that, Creola?" I says, "I slung pans, Mrs. Jakes, that's all I knows." She commenced laughin'. Oh, she got a big kick out of that.

Finally, she says, "I don't know what you is talkin' about,
slung pans, but I give my cook all she can eat here, and I don't
allow her to take anything home because I use the food the next
day." I ain't said no mo'. I just stood there. She says, "What's
the matter?" I says nothin'. She ups and asks me if I wanted to
work under them conditions and I says, "Yes'm, I'll work fo'
you under any conditions, Missus Jakes."

'Well, I went to work. Buster and my ma started worryin'
me about the pans. We was in a bad fix then. Lil money comin'
in, mamma sick, and lil food. Went on three months like that.
I don't care if Mrs. Jakes asked me to climb the house I did it.
Just do what them white folks want you to do . . . no matter
what it is, do it. Man, I was doin' everything round that house.
I was only suppose' to cook but I went to washin' and ironin',
took the maid's job. Made my dinner. Sot down and asked
Mrs. Jakes to read to me the new recipes in the book.

'I was nice with Mrs. Jakes but Buster and my ma was givin'
me hell. Buster told me that if I didn't quit that job he was
goin' to quit me. My ma told me I was an old fool to be workin'
fo' people who didn't give their cook the pans and pots. I ain't
said nothin'. You know, son, white folks think niggers is crazy
anyhow. So you got to be crazy sometimes to get what you want
from 'em. Well, I did all this work and mo' besides. So I gets
myself together one day when Mrs. Jakes givin' a big party.
The house was goin' to be flooded with people. She was fixin'
things here and I was fixin' things there. I folds my hands and
I walks up to Mrs. Jakes. I says, "Missus Jakes, I got you a fine
dinner today and I done done all my work." She says, "Yes,
Creola, everything is finished." Then I walks away from her
and I says, "Missus Jakes, I'm quittin', less you let me slung
some pans to my house." She says, "When is you quittin',
Creola? Would you be dirty enough to leave me now?" I says,
"No, ma'm. If I was goin' to be dirty I'd left you b'fo' all this
was done. But is you goin' to make me lose my husband by not
givin' me some food fo' us? The only thing we cullud people can
do is get home and eat a little sumpin' you white folks can't eat.
Has that ever crossed yo' mind, Missus Jakes? Is you humanity?"
I could see the change on her face. She says, "You know damn

well I'm humanity!'' I says, "Then give me them pans and pots.'' She says, "Why, you Creola! I got a mind to fire you.'' But she only had a mind. She wasn't goin' to fire me now. She looked at her watch and then she told me, "Get back to that kitchen, Creola, and never talk to me like that again.'' I says, "No ma'm, Missus Jakes, I'm sorry.'' And I cried 'cause I was sorry. She says, "I'm goin' let you take home my pots and pans, but I want you to come and go out my front door, 'cause I don't mean fo' you to take home my whole kitchen.''

'The party was fine. I heard all them people talkin' about my cookin'. They wanted to see me. Missus Jakes, she likes that, you know. I met them white folks. Was I happy! Well, let me tell you. Boy, it's no word of lie. Buster was packin' his clothes to leave me. Come tellin' me, "I ain't seen a woman yet who couldn't get the pans from her white folks. The trouble is you ain't askin' fo' no pans.'' Don't you know I asked fo' them pans just in time. If Buster would-a left me what was I goin' to do? He did run around but he was some consolation at night. No, Buster ain't had much education, but he's got a heap of sense.

'Then around 1925 my ma died. I bury her. That was the first time I ever missed work. Man, I been workin' fo' Missus Jakes so long I'm on her dead list. I hope she dies befo' me so I can get some of that heiress money. I ain't the only one waitin' fo' that money either. She's got a nephew there who is layin' in the hole fo' that money. She'll leave a heap of thousands. But, that old woman is goin' to outlive all of us and leave that money to Hotel Dieu or some place. That's where them white folks leave that money. They never gives it to po' folks. Lawd, what is Buster goin' to do then! Come askin' me was I sho that Missus Jakes got me in the will. I says, "Yes. What you reckon?'' He says, "I just want to know, that's all.'' She tell me she's goin' to give me some money some day and look at me circulate it. Lawd, she won't see me circulate it, but she'll see Buster circulate it. There's only one thing worryin' me. It's that cool-lookin' brownskin gal. Oh, you got to give it to her now — she's cool. I think she's got Buster. But let the fool go. She's a young gal, she'll wear him down one day. If she don't the Lawd will.

'Buster's people all dead, and mine too. No, we ain't got no chillun. Don't guess we had the right system. Can't have none now 'cause our joints done got too old. Sho, I likes chillun. Wouldn't want but two — boys. Maybe they could help me out of this storm. Be my social security. I thinks people ought to have chillun. But they ought not to have mo' than they can take care of. Now, what would I do wid three or fo' kids? We'd starve fo' true then. I got a W.P.A. man, I tell you. That's the only work he wants to do. He gets in with the foreman and gets one of them easy jobs. But I guess Buster needs an easy job to have an old and young womens. Poor Buster! I don't know where his mind is but it sho ain't on no work. And Buster sho can't be thinkin' he's no pimp or nothin' like that. Talk to him? Man, Buster gets blood mad when I talks to him. I just let him be. He's raggety, ain't got nothin'. I got to mend his pants and sew mo' buttons on his shirts than anything in the world.

'About this education. It's all right but where is the cullud goin' to use it? There ain't no good-payin' jobs in this part of the country fo' us. I say learn a trade or get good porter jobs. Work fo' good white people. They is wantin' intelligent cullud people now. I heard a lady say the other day she wish she knew where she could get a good college cullud girl to nurse her baby, 'cause them other gals is too dumb. Missus Jakes says them college gals is too damn smart. There was one aginst the other.

'People should marry young and belong to church, 'cause when you got a Christian heart you can do no wrong. Missus Jakes says I'm right on that. She always tellin' me, "Creola, you is glad you is black and you is so happy." I says, Yes'm, Missus Jakes, I'm what I am. And I is proud of it. I got what I wants. A lil home, a good job. And to tell the truth, I done got used to a triflin' man. If he'd change now I'd be sorry.

'Me and Buster ain't never been sick in our life. A little cold, yes, but nothin' else. We go to church sometimes. But, son, I spent most of my time foolin' wid Buster. He gets half-drunk, drunk, and re-drunk, and I got to make him sober. Got to feed him and fix him up. You know, I'm goin' get tired of that man and kill him. Might not do it 'cause I love him. Ain't that a shame? What can I do?'

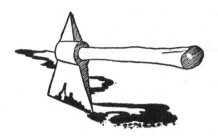

Chapter 24

Who Killa Da Chief?

THE INSULTING PHRASE 'WHO KILLA DA CHIEF?'
is still heard in New Orleans. And to a Sicilian these are fighting
words. The phrase was first used during a mass lynching at the
old Parish Prison on Congo Square in 1893.

Eleven Italians were murdered by the mob: nine shot to death
within the prison, and two others hanged in the Square. Newspaper reporters were on hand, and the news stories offer an excellent account of one of New Orleans' grimmest happenings.

The Chief of Police, David C. Hennessy, had been ambushed
and murdered by assassins of the Mafia. It was at night and the
Chief was going home. When only a few steps from his door the
young Italian boy who had been posted to signal his arrival gave
'a peculiar whistle.' Immediately shots came from the shack
opposite, men sprang from hiding, and the Chief went down
under showers of lead from several directions. Hennessy returned the fire, but fell fatally wounded. The assassins got away,
but suspects were subsequently arrested. Their trial was incredible. The jury was bribed and bullied. The accused were declared not guilty in some cases; in others, a mistrial was announced.

This news so incensed the people of New Orleans that a mass meeting was called and the mob attacked the jail, finally battered in one of its doors. Just before the attack, as the leaders of the mob attempted to parley with prison guards, someone called out, 'Who killa da Chief?' Immediately the cry was taken up by the crowd and, mingled with the 'Italian whistle,' spread through the streets. It is a phrase which New Orleans Italians have never forgotten.

David Hennessy's capture of Esposito, a leader of the Mafia, is generally believed to **have** been the act which first focused the attention of this Sicilian murder society upon him. Hennessy was a boy of twenty at the time. He had spent many years in the police department as a messenger, and had just been appointed special officer with a patrolman's pay. He was already noted for his ability to spot faces previously seen in police lineups or photographs, so was often sent to cruise about the docks and other sections frequented by those in disfavor with the law.

One day as he was passing Saint Louis Cathedral he met a fruit peddler called 'Dago John' who had been a fixture in the French Quarter for some time. The face of the huckster stirred a vague recollection in the mind of the young officer, and as young Dave had so far found such stirrings reliable guides, he requested Dago John to accompany him down to the nearest precinct. The identity of the Sicilian was immediately established by photographs which had been sent to New Orleans by Italian authorities. He was Esposito, wanted for murders and other crimes committed in the Old Country.

Bribes calculated to influence the young detective to change his mind concerning the identity of the prisoner ran as high as fifty thousand dollars, and after this was seen to be of no avail he was threatened with every sort of violence. Esposito was returned to Italy, where he was tried and executed.

Hennessy escaped reprisal at this time, but a poor Italian thought to have informed him of Dago John's identity was set upon in the middle of the night as he slept, and hacked to death in the presence of his family.

His capture of the famous bandit brought young Dave to the attention of Colonel Boylan of the Farrel-Boylan Protective

Police. He later became a partner in this organization; eventually was elected chief of New Orleans' police force.

What was believed by Chief Hennessy's two closest friends and confidents, the famous detective, Robert A. Pinkerton, and George W. Vandervoort, secretary to the Chief, to have been the immediate provocation for the assassination was Hennessy's activity in the Provenzano-Matranga case. Hennessy, it is said, had felt for some time that sooner or later the Black Hand would become active against him for his continued interest in their operations, so had named those whom he felt would be the instigators of any plot against him. Those named by him were Antonio Matranga, whom he said was the chief figure in the Mafia in New Orleans, and three henchmen, James Caruso, Frank Romero and Rocco Geraci. He also suspected rich and urbane Joseph Macheca, though evidence of his connection with the society was hard to obtain.

The Provenzanos were stevedores doing a good business when the Matrangas and Macheca entered the field. The Matrangas cut wages, underbid the Provenzanos. There was shooting, but no complaints were lodged. Chief Hennessy got the factions together, warned them that such an occurrence must not be repeated. They drank together, shook hands, and apparently peace was restored. Macheca, however, insisted to Matranga that the Chief was really on the side of the Provenzanos, who were Americanized and less involved with the Mafia, and that the Provenzanos would certainly take advantage of the Chief's partiality.

Echoes of Macheca's warning reached Hennessy. In a final effort to preserve peace he invited Macheca and the Provenzanos to become members of a club to which he belonged. This only aggravated the situation.

Then to Hennessy's great relief the Matrangas decided to resort to the law. They identified some of the Provenzanos as those who had attacked them. But the Provenzanos, bitter because of the Chief's overtures toward Macheca, engaged as defense Detective Dominick O'Malley, a man who had great reason to both hate and fear Chief Hennessy.

O'Malley had always been a trouble-maker, and to such an

extent that Hennessy had finally sent north for information regarding his past record. These findings the Chief made known to O'Malley, with the result that O'Malley's hitherto partially concealed animosity toward him became well known throughout the force, and among opposing factions.

The Provenzanos were convicted of the attack on the Matrangas. But a number of O'Malley's friends on the police force then swore that the accused were carousing on Royal Street when the shooting occurred. This resulted in the granting of a new trial.

Hennessy then declared himself, saying that he would come forward with documentary evidence secured from Italy revealing the real identity of Macheca and the Matrangas, and would also make public the record of Dominick O'Malley.

Hennessy was then besought with flattery, cajolery, threats and bribery to suppress the evidence, but he could not be moved from his purpose. Two nights before the day set for the new trial Chief Hennessy was murdered.

Detective Pinkerton, during his visit to New Orleans in connection with the trial of the assassins, uncovered that O'Malley had had two hundred and fifty names of persons he had seen beforehand put in the jury box. Later O'Malley and Adams in their suit for slander against the *Daily States* asked for a postponement, although the defendants were willing to have an immediate hearing.

It was on the morning of the 15th of October, 1890, that horrified and incredulous citizens read of the assassination of their beloved superintendent of police. Headings in the *Daily Picayune* were:

SUPERINTENDENT OF POLICE DAVID C. HENNESSY VICTIM OF VENDETTA; AMBUSCADED AT HIS DOORSTEP AND SIX BULLETS SHOT INTO HIS BODY, ONE OF WHICH IS PRONOUNCED FATAL; THE MURDERERS DECLARED TO BE ITALIANS OF THE CRIMINAL CLASS; THE CHIEF REMOVED TO THE CHARITY HOSPITAL IN AN AMBULANCE WHERE HE IS VISITED BY THE MAYOR AND HIS AGED MOTHER; A NUMBER OF SUSPECTS PROMPTLY

PLACED UNDER ARREST; THE WOUNDED CHIEF AT 3
O'CLOCK THIS MORNING WAS RESTING EASILY.

Quoting the *Daily Picayune* of October 16:

The facts of the tragedy are best told in the statement of Captain J. O'Connor of the Boylan Protective Police, and the superintendent's chosen and trusted friend. Captain O'Connor's statement is as follows:

'I went to Superintendent Hennessy's office about ten o'clock tonight (14th) and sat there chatting for about an hour. The Chief was in the best of spirits and said to me, "Wait a few minutes and I will start home."

'We left the central police station about ten or fifteen minutes past 11 o'clock. As we passed out of the door I suggested to the Chief that we should walk up Basin Street, as he lived on Girod Street, between Basin and Franklin. The Chief replied, "No, let us walk up Rampart Street, our usual route, as the sidewalks on Basin Street are very bad."

'We reached Dominick Virget's oyster saloon, corner of Rampart and Poydras Streets, and the Chief invited me to "come in and get some oysters." We eat (*sic*) a half-dozen oysters apiece, and the Chief drank a glass of milk.

'Leaving the saloon, we walked up the woods side of Rampart Street to Girod, where we parted, the Chief saying, "Don't come any further with me now; you go on and look after your business."

'As we parted the Chief started toward Basin Street, taking the downtown side of Girod Street. I took the uptown side and walked out in the direction of the river. On my way I met a city policeman and a Boylan officer.

'I had just reached the corner of Dryades and Girod Streets when I heard a loud report of a shotgun, and turning quickly around and looking toward Basin Street, I saw the flashes and heard two more loud reports. The flashes came from the front of the two-story frame house at the uptown river corner of Girod and Basin Streets.

'Almost simultaneously with the reports of the shotguns, three or four pistol shots, fired in quick succession from the lower side of the street, rang out. These last reports must have been the Chief's return of the murderous fire.

'I at once started on a quick run toward Basin Street, two blocks distant, and on my way overtook Officer M. Colter of the Boylan Protective Police, of whom I inquired, "Which way did they run?"

'He replied, "I believe it was uptown."

'Five or six people were then on the streets in our vicinity.

'I heard the Chief call, "Oh, Billy, Billy!"

'I hurried toward the spot whence came the cry, and found the Chief sitting on the front doorstep of a two-story frame house on Basin, between Girod and Lafayette Streets. As I came up he said to me, "They have given it to me and I gave them back the best I could."

'Almost immediately after my arrival Corporal Hennessy, of the Boylan force, and Doorman Usher, of the city police, came up with a negro whom they had caught running at full speed and who is now held by the police.

'Bending over the Chief, I said to him, "Who gave it to you, Dave?"

'He replied, "Put your ear down here."

'As I bent down, he whispered to me the word "Dagoes."'

(End of Captain O'Connor's statement)

On the lower riverside corner of Girod and Basin Streets was a second-hand store occupied by a Mrs. Ehrwald. Its front doors contained several buckshot deeply imbedded. It was in front of this, about ten feet from the corner, that Chief Hennessy stood searching for his doorkey in the light from the corner lamp when he was shot. His residence was next to the store.

Directly across the street was the shack occupied by the cobbler, Monasterio, which had been rented for him two months previously by Joseph Macheca — as was subsequently brought out during the trial.

The searching party moving toward Franklin was first rewarded with a double-barreled muzzle-loading shotgun, which they fished out of a drain on the corner of Franklin. Sam Petri, a colored boy living in the corner house, said he heard the men running around the corner. One of them slipped in the mud caused by the recent rain and it was right here that the weapon was found.

The searchers went down Franklin Street toward the New

Basin. Traces were soon discovered in the soft mud of the footprints of the pursued men. One of these was about twelve inches long, and with a peculiarly pointed toe; the other was nearly as large, but with a broad round toe.

These prints were traced around the corner to Julia. When they had been traced to the middle of the block, Private John Lornegan, who watched the lumber on the New Basin, was met. He had not heard of the crime, nor was it told to him until after he narrated his face-to-face meeting with the murderers.

'I was walking in on Julia street,' said he, 'when I met three men. That was after I heard the shooting.

'"What was that shooting?" I asked them.

'"Me no know," was the reply by a Dago. The three were Dagoes. I passed on, and right behind the first there were two more men. One of them had a shotgun, which he seemed to be trying to hide under his coat. I had no reason to stop them, and they got past me. Then I turned around and they began running. Three ran out Julia into the lumber, and two of them ran down Liberty. The fellow with the gun was a tall man with a derby hat. I could not see their faces, it was so dark. They had on dark clothes.'

As the police had expected trouble of some sort as the time for the Matranga-Provenzano trial neared, a detail had been set to shadow the Matrangas. On the night of the crime Macheca, the Matrangas and Caruso had supper at Fabacher's. As the party broke up, Macheca was heard to say: 'I did all I could. The only regret I have is that they did not do the bastard up altogether.'

But in the morning the assassins were rewarded, for shortly after nine o'clock Superintendent Hennessy breathed his last. An ominous silence replaced the feverish excitement which had prevailed at police headquarters. Thirty-eight arrests were recorded that day, among them Scaffedi, Bagnetto, Monasterio, Natali and Incardono.

From the *Times-Democrat* of October 17, 1890:

The State witness who saw the shooting going on, and who identified Scaffedi, Bagnetto and Incardono, is Mr. M. L. Peeler, who resides at 272 Girod Street at the corner of Basin. He occupied the second room from Girod, on the second floor, a three-foot gallery runs along the second story of the house on both Girod and Basin Streets, and from his room the gallery is reached by means of a window three feet high, and by a door on Basin Street. He gave the following version of the killing:

'I was in bed asleep at the time of the shooting and jumped up at the first report, which came from the direction of Girod Street.

'Two shots were fired almost simultaneously, and I jumped out on the gallery by way of the window and saw a man in the middle of the street on Basin. He had a gun in his hand, and I helloed to him, "Don't shoot! Stop that! What in the hell are you doing that for?" He fired a shot at the moment and from under the smoke of his gun he looked up at me. He fired another shot, and I yelled at him, "Damn you, if you fire, I'll kill you!" and turning to Mary Peeler, who was in the room, I said, "Give me my shotgun," though I knew there was not a weapon in the house. The man in the street looked up again, and sticking his gun under his coat, he walked to the sidewalk under my gallery and proceeded at a brisk pace toward Julia Street. When he reached the bridge, about two hundred feet from Girod Street, he broke and ran, and I lost sight of him. The man wore an oilcloth coat and his hat was drawn over his eyes.

'After he disappeared I saw two men run out Girod Street and cross to the lower side of the street. The man on the inside carried a double-barreled shotgun with a short barrel. He was dressed in a black cut-away coat and wore a derby hat. The man on the outside was dressed in striped gray clothes and also wore a derby. I did not see anything in his hand. The police then appeared on the scene, but not one of them would go down Basin Street in the direction in which the man in the oil-cloth coat had disappeared. The police found a shotgun about twelve feet from Girod Street on Franklin. The other gun was found on Basin Street, near Julia, where it had been thrown away by the man in the oilcloth coat. I went with the police and was present when an oilcloth coat was found in Scaffedi's house, on Dryades near Girod Street, where it had been hidden behind two empty barrels. The coat was wet when found, and Scaffedi's uncle said that his nephew had left the house at 10:30 at night with the coat. I identified the man as the one who did the shooting from Basin Street, and made an affidavit against him for the crime.'

Another important witness was Rosa Walton, a colored woman, who resided at 270 Girod Street, in the rear of the building (the Monasterio shack) from which the ambushed assassins poured their deadly fire.

The woman went to police headquarters yesterday morning in company with Private Officer McEntee, and voluntarily made this statement:

'I reside in the rear of 270 Girod Street, from which the firing took place. The front room is occupied by the Italian shoemaker, Monasterio, now under arrest. Since last Saturday night I have noticed two strange Italian visitors. They always came at night. They would talk and drink and I went out two or three times to get beer for them at a neighborhood grocery. The men were there last night when I went to bed. A couple of nights ago, on going through the alleyway, into the house, I noticed a small, short gun in the hands of Peter Monasterio, who was sitting in the room with his companions. He was just in the act of bending (folding) the gun when I went through. I had never before seen a gun of that kind.'

Antonio Bagnetto, when arrested by Sergeant Joseph McCabe, said to him: 'If you want to be a friend like a brudder, you keepa his pistol for yourself. You willa make plenty friends with my countrymen, but if you don't want to do it — you know.' Bagnetto was identified by Peeler as the man whom he saw running out Girod Street at the time of the shooting. Bagnetto's room was searched and two loaded revolvers were found in it. Peeler said that Scaffedi had fired all the shots he saw; the other men were running when he saw them.

From the *Daily Picayune* of October 18 comes a record of further arrests: those of Antonio Matranga, Salvador Rocco, Vincent Caruso, Salvador Sunzeri, Charles Traina and John Caruso. The arrest of Joseph Macheca and Frank Romero was also ordered, but they could not be found. Some time later these last surrendered voluntarily, as did also Charles Patorno.

A special session of the city council was called on the 19th, at which Mayor Shakespeare delivered a special message (appearing in the *Times-Democrat* of October 19) which read, in part:

The circumstances of the cowardly deed, the arrests made, and the evidence collected by the police department, show be-

yond a doubt that he was the victim of Sicilian vengeance
wreaked upon him as chief representative of law and order in
this community because he was seeking by the power of our
American law to break up the fierce vendettas that have so
often stained our streets with blood.... We owe it to ourselves and to everything that we hold sacred in this life to see
to it that this blow is the last. We must teach these people a
lesson that they will remember for all time.... It is clear to
me that the wretches who committed this foul deed are the
mere hirelings and instruments of others higher up and more
powerful than they. These instigators are the men we must
find at any cost.... The people look to you to take the ini-
tiative in this matter. Act. Act promptly without fear or
favor.

From the *Daily Picayune* of October 20 it is learned that on this
same day Macheca was identified as the man who had rented the
shack for Monasterio; Traina, as the small man who had run
away from the scene of the crime, and later made himself con-
spicuous by his peculiar actions on the train leaving for Sarpy;
Politz, as the man in the striped suit and pointed-toed shoes.
The clothing was recovered and much evidence given in proof
of the State's contention.

After lengthy questioning Antonio Matranga and Caruso were
released.

From the *Daily Picayune* of the 19th:

The Provenzanos, in prison since April for the wounding of
Salvador Sunzeri, Vincent Caruso and Antonio Matranga,
were eager to talk, and testified to all who would listen that
Matranga's men worked under the fear of death, and that they
were paid $10 or $15 for a murder, and done away with if they
refused. They also stated, thus supporting Superintendent
Hennessy's assertion that Antonio Matranga was the head of
the Mafia in New Orleans, and Rocco Geraci one of his chief
henchmen.

The *Daily Picayune* for February 28, 1891, states that when the
case finally came to trial (in February, 1891), a total of 1150
talesmen were summoned, 780 examined, before a jury would be
secured. There were 557 persons challenged for cause for some

one of the following: (1) conscientious scruples against the infliction of capital punishment, (2) objections to a conviction on circumstantial evidence, (3) having a fixed opinion which would not yield to evidence, (4) extreme prejudice against Sicilians.

When finally assembled the resulting jury presented a picture which caused the heart of every justice-loving Orleanian to fail. Jacob M. Seligman, foreman, and the only mature man of judgment and consequence, headed a group composed of poor young clerks and laborers, evidently only admitted because of their lack of conviction on any subject.

Representing the State in the case were District Attorney Charles A. Lözenburg, W. L. Evans, J. C. Walker and Captain Arthur Dunn. Attorneys for the eighteen accused of either complicity in, or execution of, the murder were D. Henriques, Charles Butler and A. Castinel. Charles Patorno, who at first had a separate defense, later acceded to the persuasion of the rest of the accused and was represented by their lawyers.

The *Times-Picayune* of February 18 describes the nine accused of murder as they appeared in the dock. Charles Matranga, Joseph Macheca and Antonio Scaffedi were conspicuously well dressed and displayed expensive jewelry; Antonio Marchesi, less American in his dress, was clad in poor stuffs, and used a big red bandanna handkerchief; Antonio Bagnetto was plain, dish-faced and sallow; Monasterio, the shoemaker, older than the rest, was sharp and crafty-looking; Manuel Politz, the hysterical fruit and vegetable vendor, was evidently subnormal; Traina, the plantation worker, was also of low mentality; and Bastian Incardono, a poor youth whose connection with the crime was still in doubt, appeared completely bewildered. The boy, Asperi Marchesi, who had whistled the signal to the killers, seemed bright and much interested. In spite of his connection with the crime he appeared to be a favorite with everyone.

Briefly summarizing material appearing in the *Daily Picayune* for March 6, 1891: At the close of the case for the prosecution fifty-seven witnesses had been examined in behalf of the State, the taking of their testimony having lasted four days. As a result of this evidence, Antonio Scaffedi, Antonio Marchesi, Manuel Politz, Pietro Monasterio and Antonio Bagnetto had been identified as the parties who did the shooting and who were seen fleeing from the place of ambush. Bastian Incardono had been identified as being in the vicinity at 8.25 P.M. and at 10.30 P.M. of the night of the shooting. Joseph Macheca had been identified as the party who under an assumed name rented the shack for the shoemaker, Monasterio, in which it was sought to prove the assassins had hidden until the victim appeared. The boy, Asperi Marchesi, had admitted to apprising his father and the others of the Chief's approach by a peculiar whistle.

In the *Daily Picayune* for March 7 considerable space is devoted to Manuel Politz, who all through the trial had been violent and unmanageable, and who finally tried to escape or commit suicide by jumping out of the jail window. Subdued, he mouthed fears of punishment and accusations against the Matrangas and Macheca as moguls of the Mafia, and told that Sunzeri, Geraci and Monasterio were mere tools. He also admitted that he had carried the guns to the rendezvous of the assassins.

On the last day of the trial all proceedings were stopped against Charles Matranga, and against Incardono, who it was said had merely had the misfortune to be in the vicinity of the shooting, and the case then went to the jury.

From the editorial page of the *Daily Picayune* for Friday, March 13, comes this comment:

The testimony presented by the State has been direct, strong and convincing, as far as it went. It shows but few serious defects, as there is scarcely a missing link. The defense has been forced to rely upon testimony to establish alibis. This testimony has not been sufficiently effective to overcome the evidence of the guilt of several of the accused. But they were mostly the miserable tools in the hands of men who had a great personal interest in the removal of Chief of Police Hennessy. There was no effort to show that a few wretched fruit peddlers and a cobbler had any personal desire to take the life of the official.... We know not how the jury will decide the case but we are convinced that the State has established plainly the guilt of some of the accused, particularly of the humble and obscure actors in the terrible scene. But where are the masters, the controllers of these underlings, the arch-conspirators?

On March 13 the jury, 'A Remarkable Body of Men,' says the *Picayune* of March 14, brought in its verdict — mistrial as to three, and all others acquitted.

Said the *Daily Picayune*, 'The murder of Hennessy, after so much exertion and cost to the State, is still unavenged.'

Various writers now expressed fear of violence, and were vociferous in their criticism of official laxity regarding proper reinforcement of the prison personnel, and of the building itself, which had been for long in a state of decay. Their fears were well grounded, for but a few hours later New Orleans arose and went forth to mete out her own justice.

To quote the *Times-Democrat* of March 15:

> Hereafter the fourteenth of March will be almost as memorable an anniversary in the history of New Orleans as the fourteenth of September.... Before noon of March 14 the three men in whose cases a mistrial had been entered, three whom the jury acquitted, and five who had been arrested but had not been brought to trial, eleven in all, had been lynched at the Parish prison. Eight Italians were lying dead on the blood-stained floors of the prison (Rocco Geraci, Pietro Monasterio, Charles Traina, James Caruso, Loretto Comitz, Frank Romero, Joseph Macheca and Antonio Scaffedi), and Antonio Marchesi mortally wounded, and soon to follow his companions.
>
> It was a fair, but terrible day. After days of rain and chilly winds the sun had risen in a clear and cool spring sky that was cloudless but for two or three long streaks of shining silver scales that looked like giant mackerel leaping into the sunshine from out a sunlit sea of deepest azure; the pent-up fragrance of flowers and shrubs that had been dormant for weeks seemed to have suddenly burst forth, and every breeze was laden with it....
>
> A call at the Parish prison shortly after 9 o'clock revealed the fact that the prison authorities were on the alert.... Strict orders had been left at the door to admit no visitors, and workmen were engaged in strengthening the inner grating.
>
> The prisoners spent Friday evening very pleasantly, being naturally elated over the results of the trial, as those who had been acquitted were looking forward to a speedy release. Could they have foreseen the horrible character that release

would assume, they would have had small cause for elation. The morning papers, however, caused some uneasiness to be expressed, although the officials were taking such precautions as were available for the protection of the prisoners. . . .

In the meantime all classes and conditions of people were gravitating toward Clay statue (Canal, Royal and St. Charles Streets). It was a thoroughly mixed gathering, but throughout the vast assemblage the best order and harmony prevailed. Indeed to the casual observer unaware of the real motivation it would seem to be for any other purpose than that of taking the law into their own keeping, and thus enacting the part of judge, jury and executioner.

At ten o'clock precisely the vast throng began to sway, and cheer after cheer went up from the multitude as Messrs. W. S. Parkerson, Walter Denegre, John Wycliffe and others, pushing their way through the dense mass, took their respective positions on the pedestal of the statue. . . .

Mr. Parkerson was the first to address the assembly. His speech was brief, terse, and spirited:

'People of New Orleans — once before I stood before you for public duty. I now appear before you again, actuated by no desire for fame or prominence.

'Affairs have reached such a crisis that men living in an organized and civilized community, finding their laws fruitless and ineffective, are forced to protect themselves; when courts fail, the people must act!

'What protection or assurance of protection is there left us when the very head of our police department, our Chief of Police, is assassinated in our very midst by the Mafia Society, and his assassins again turned loose in the community?

'The time has come for the people of New Orleans to say whether they are going to stand these outrages by organized bands of assassins, for the people to say whether they shall permit it to continue. I ask you to consider this fairly. Are you going to let it continue? (Hundreds of voices: "No! No! Bring on the Dagoes!") Will every man here follow me, and see the murder of D. C. Hennessy vindicated? ("Yes! Yes! on to the Parish!" yelled the crowd.) Are there enough men here to set aside the verdict of that infamous jury, every one of whom is a perjurer and a scoundrel? ("Yes! On to the prison and hang the murderers!" was the cry.)

'There is no more infamous a thing in this community than Dominick C. O'Malley (cries of "Hang him! Shoot him!" from the crowd), and I now pronounce him a suborner of witnesses, a briber of juries and the most infamous being in this community!'

Walter Denegre followed Mr. Parkerson with a few words, but Mr. Wycliffe, owing to the fury of the crowd, was unable to be heard. Soon Royal, Dauphine, Burgundy, Rampart, and all streets branching out from Clay statue were thronged with infuriated people bound for the Parish prison. . . .

When the crowd started for the prison a reporter for the *Times-Democrat*, in order to get there ahead of them, secured a hack. Detectives Lerwin and Pecora, who also wanted to get to the prison, entered the cab. The portion of the crowd near the cab began to shout: 'It's a reporter, he will put them on their guard!' 'No, no,' cried others. 'He's all right; let him alone!'

In a few minutes after the reporter reached the prison, Congo Square was filled with the surging mass of humanity who were rushing pell-mell for the prison. At first they contented themselves with filling the neutral ground. While standing there in a body someone started the 'Italian whistle,' which was taken up by thousands until the air rang with the note. Mingling with the whistling were voices shouting, '*Who killa da Chief?*' When this died out the crowd made a rush for the banquette in front of the prison, and a number of detectives and policemen tried to clear the street, but gave up the attempt almost immediately. A deputy sheriff tried to force a man back, but instantly found a pistol leveled at his head, and with the remark, 'I have done all I can,' gave way to the crowd.

Then the crowd in front of the door began to shout, 'Let us in, or we will break in!' 'Get an axe!' At this point a large squad carrying arms, and headed by Parkerson, Wycliffe and Denegre, was seen marching down Orleans Street. The crowd gave way to let them pass, and in a few minutes they had full possession of the front of the prison.

The next order issued was to throw a guard around the prison, in order that there could be no possible avenue of escape. This done, every part of the prison was examined to discover the best point of attack. . . .

There was a momentary pause, but it was not from irresolution; a glance along the lines of determined men showed the desperate resolve which actuated them. Guns of every description were in their hands. Shotguns were in the majority, with here and there a musket or a Winchester. Some had pistols, while others held their ground ready to do battle with their hands. A rush was made for the front gate, but its sturdy hinges and massive lock resisted the effort to force it open. Then someone whispered, 'The side door!' There was a cheer and a rush for the Treme Street door, a frail barrier leading from the street into the private room of the captain of the prison.

The scene in the prison while the door was being attacked was one which beggars description. As the crowd battered on the outside, those within were wielding hammers and sledges as they drove to the mark spikes and nails to more securely fasten the weak barrier....

To continue, from the *Daily Picayune* of the same date:

Under repeated blows from lengths of cordwood, and a great cobble-stone handled by a burly Negro, the wooden door gave way and the crowd swarmed into the prison.

The prisoners had been mostly on the second floor of the main building, but when Captain Davis heard of the approach of the attacking party, he ordered all the prisoners locked in their cells, and the Italian suspects released so as to find hiding places about the prison. His idea was to divide them up and place them at different points so as to give them a chance for their lives.

The majority of them were taken over to the women's side. The six afterwards shot down in the women's yard, huddled together in a large cell second from the door on the lower floor. Bagnetto was among them. Sunzeri and Prietzo ran along the line of cells until they struck a dark corner under the stairway. Captain Davis had formerly owned a bull terrier, 'Queen,' for which he had built a dog house out of a dry-goods box. The two men crawled into this. Natali, also on the women's side, ran across the yard to the wash-house and crawled under a bench. John Caruso rushed downstairs into the White yard where the other prisoners were just being locked up and slipped into a cell with one of these. He was safe there, and the crowd did not even search for him. Incardono made a short-cut for liberty, running along the gallery on the second floor until he came to a closet at the very end. There he found an old rubbish box, in which he hid. He also, was never found.

Macheca, Scaffedi and the elder Marchesi hurried up to the 'Manchac gallery' on the third floor, but all the cells had been locked and they were trapped, being able neither to evade the fire from the end of the gallery or the yard below. A volley from shotguns, rifles and pistols rang out, Macheca and Scaffedi were killed and Marchesi mortally wounded.... Politz was next found and jerked out unharmed. The proposition to hang him was met with favor, and he was strung up on a lamp-post.

Seven more were found in a cell in the women's yard. When the smoke from the firing cleared away these were identified as Geraci, Monasterio, Traina, James Caruso, Comitz, Romero and Bagnetto. Bagnetto played a daring ruse, but it was unsuccessful. He simulated death and lay motionless until the men with the guns came in. Then he rose and begged for life.

'This one's alive,' said one of the men. 'Complete the work.'

'Who is he?' 'It's Macheca,' was the answer. 'Kill him,' and it seemed as if the man would be shot to death.

'No, you shall not,' said Captain John Wycliffe. 'Find out who he is first. If he is not one of the guilty men he shall not be hurt.'

'It's Bagnetto,' said someone. 'Then we will hang him,' said the crowd. 'Come now! Confess. Who did this thing? Who killed the Chief?'

'I don't know,' answered Bagnetto piteously. It was the Sicilian watchword. He was rushed to the street and hanged to a tree.

The crowd was not satisfied with its work. An armed squad made one more inspection of the cells, but were satisfied that the men they had come there for were dead. Its work accomplished, the improvised army dispersed in an orderly manner, the armed sentries who had been posted to prevent the escape of the prisoners formed in line and marched out Orleans to the main gate....

Toward evening keepers in search of suspects still in hiding reached an old storeroom containing odds and ends of dis-

carded prison furniture. From here they dragged Charles Matranga and Charles Patorno, one of whom had inserted himself
between the mattress and spring of an old bed. Also surviving
the massacre were, besides these two, Salvador Sunzeri, Charles
Prietzo, John Caruso, Bastian Incardono and Pietro Natali.

Dominick O'Malley was never found. It was later discovered
that he had escaped to the plantation of a relative, far in the
country.

Seligman, the juror, after much difficulty, also made good his
escape.

From the *Daily Picayune*:

> Rome, March 15. — The Italian government has instructed
> Baron de Fava, the Italian minister at Washington, to present
> a vehement protest to the U.S. government against the action
> of the mob in New Orleans, and the U.S. government has
> promised to make an investigation.

Later indemnity was asked, and eventually paid by the United
States.

Thus ended the case of the Mafia versus the People of New
Orleans. But Italians were not allowed to forget. Many an
inoffensive citizen was henceforth to burn with shame as small
boys derisively shouted, '*Who killa da Chief?*'

Appendixes

Superstitions

Sickness
(Medicines, Applications, and Charms to Cure and Prevent)

ASTHMA

A charm (or fetish) to cure asthma is made of some of the victim's hair tied up in red flannel, which is then placed in a crack in the floor.

Medicine: Make a tea of the root of the wild plum cut from the sunrise side. Cut and boil two hours in an iron pot. Give two tablespoons three times daily.

Folk practices: Wearing a muskrat skin, fur side in, on the chest. Smoking jimson weed.

BACKACHE

Charm: Make nine knots in a tarred rope and tie it around your waist. — Mrs. A. Antony, 718½ Orleans Street.

Charm: Belt of snakeskin.

BEE STING

Apply seven different kinds of leaves to a bee sting. — Mrs. Josephine Fouchi.

BITES

For insect bites: Soak whole balsam apples in whiskey. Apply apple skin.

Charm for snakebite: If bitten near water, beat him to the water and dip the part bitten. That will remove the poison and the snake will die instead of you. — Mrs. C. Andry, 1947 N. Johnson Street.

Medicine for snakebite: The juice of plantain banana leaves every hour in doses of one teaspoonful, and the mashed leaves applied to the wound. — Raoul.

Charm: Cut open a black hen, and while she is still jumping hold her over the bite. When the chicken has stopped fluttering the poison will be gone. — Mrs. Davis, 2412 Sixth Street.

Charm: Have a snake doctor suck the bite.

Treatment: Burn a reed and let the smoke rise into the bite.

BLADDER
Feed roasted rat to a bed-wetter. — Vance Balthazar, Isle Breville.

Feeding fried rat to a person with a weak bladder will stop bed-wetting. — Mrs. W. Nicholas, 1979 Miro Street.

Feed parched pumpkin seeds with salt for bed-wetting.

BLEEDING
There is a secret verse in the Book of Ezekiel which, if read, will stop bleeding. — Jack Penton, 1508 St. Charles Street.

BLINDNESS
To prevent — Charm: Pierce ears and wear earrings. — Mrs. Truseh.

Medication: Infusion of parsley roots with pinch of alum. — Mrs. S. James, 1951 Johnson Street.

BLOOD (*Poor or Bad*)
Medicine: 'Jack Vine tea is the best blood purify you can get. . . . We allus made tea out of it when we would be in the swamps.' — Verise Brown.

Medicine: For bad blood, a handful of gum moss, thimbleful of anise seed, handful of corn shucks, rain water. Steep and take every morning. — Clorie Turner, 1467 Sere Street.

BOILS
Application: A poultice of catnip leaves for chigger boils, or flea boils. Or, an infusion of equal parts of sumac leaves, sage, and swamp-lily roots boiled down. Add a cup of lard to the strained infusion and boil until the water is out, and use the salve.

Application for ordinary boils: Poultice of mashed jimson weed or mashed elderberry leaves.

Or: Pounded okra blossoms and sugar will bring a boil to a head. — Katherine Hill, 638 Lafayette Street.

To draw a 'rising' to a head, or draw festering splinters out, beat the skin of the tail of a 'possum and put sugar on it, and apply. — Bill Harris, Spring Creek.

BOWLEGS

Treatment (said to cure): Wipe the legs of child with a greasy towel every day. — Theresa Martin, 2318 Jackson Avenue.

BROKEN LIMBS

Treatment: Wrap in clay mud. — Mrs. O. Crowden, 1954 Johnson Street.

BURNS

Cajun treatment: If you burn your finger while lighting a cigarette, stick it quick behind your ear.

Charm for burns: Read the 'fire passages' in the Bible. Those who know these passages never reveal them till death, for to do so would cause them to lose the power. — Bill Harris, Spring Creek.

CHILLS and FEVER

Charm: Squeeze a frog to death in the hand. — Katherine Hill, 638 LaFayette Street, Baton Rouge.

Charm: Go toward the bed as if to get into it, but get under instead.

Medicine: Tea of L'Herbe Cabri (coatgrass).

COLDS, CROUP

Medicine (Cajun): Red wine in which a melted tallow candle has been mixed. — Mrs. Oscar Scott, Natchitoches.

Medicine: Mamou tea made with the beans or the roots. Also crapeau (toadgrass) tea.

Treatment for pleural complications: Mare's milk rubbed on the back of the neck will cure pleurisy. — Vance Balthazar, Isle Breville.

Medicine for croup: Powdered birdeye vine added to milk. — Lizzie Chandler.

Charm to prevent: Wear a dime and some salt in the heel of your shoe.

COLIC (*baby*)

Medicine: Chicken gizzard tea. Or catnip tea.

Charm (fetish): A string with nine knots in it worn around the waist until it rots off.

Ceremony with incantation: Say your prayers and turn the baby head down and heels up three times an hour. — Mrs. S. C. Douglas, 2010 St. Thomas Street.

CONSTIPATION

Medicine: 'Ole missus useter give us Blue Mass Pills when we needed medicine. It sho did make us sick. We had to get sick to get well, ole missus said.' — Rebecca Fletcher.

CORNS

Let a snail crawl across your toes.

CRAMPS (*in legs, in stomach*)

Charm (reptile fetish) for cramps in legs: An eel skin with nine knots tied in it worn around the leg. — Vance Balthazar.

Medicine for cramps in stomach: A tea of snake root. — J. Eccles, 710 Bourbon Street.

CUTS

Incantation to prevent bleeding and infection: Recite a verse from the Bible. — Jack Penton, 1508 St. Charles Street.

Application: Fat meat, garlic, and live cockroaches bound on.

DIABETES

Medicine: Instead of water, drink, for three months, tea made of boiled huckleberry leaves.

DIARRHEA

Medicine: Oakleaf tea.

DROPSY

Medicine: Tablespoon of the juice of elder sprouts three times a day until cured. — Albert Dupont, Houma.

EARACHE

Medication: Pinch the head off a sowbug and drop the drop of blood you will find into the ear. You won't have earache again. — Mrs. Bill Harris, Spring Creek.

Medication: The blood of a live roach, tablespoon of hot water, pod of red pepper, three grains of sugar. Heat and mix with lard. Put on cotton and insert in ear. — Mrs. U. Lipinay, 2522 St. Anthony.

ERYSIPELAS

Application: Poultice of raw cranberries.

Application: Blood from the ear and tail of a horse. If a very bad case, more than one application will be necessary.

FAINTING

Treatment: Let the patient smell his left shoe. Rub his right hand. — E. Blanchard, 1920 Sixth Street.

FEVERS

Chinaberries strung and placed about the baby's neck will absorb and prevent fever. — Mr. and Mrs. J. C. Sanders, Spring Creek.

For a high fever: Obtain a pigeon which has never flown out of the cage, cut him open and lay him on the 'mole' of the patient's head. The fresh blood of the pigeon will draw the fever. — Mrs. W. Nicholas, N. Miro Street.

For fever, wrap the head completely in leaves from the Palma Christi (castor oil plant). — Mrs. A. Barry, 2234 Feliciana Street.

'St. Jacob's quinine grows mos' everywhere, an' that's good for fevers.' — Gracie Stafford.

To exorcise yellow fever: Place about two inches of water in a tub. Stand an axe head on its nose in the water and balance three black horsehairs and a white one on the edge of the axe. Sprinkle a small amount of red pepper on the horsehairs and carefully push the tub under the bed — the contents must not be disturbed. Then scatter a handful of corn meal in the form of a cross in front of the patient's bed and wet this cross thoroughly with rum made from molasses. Then repeat the following incantation (voodoo):

> 'Heru mande, heru mande, heru mande.
> Tigli li papa.
> Do se dan godo
> Ah tingonai ye!'

GOITER

Charm: Touch a dead person, then lay the hand on the goiter.

HAIR

To make it grow, cut off a piece on Good Friday and bury it.

HAY FEVER

Medicine: Tea of goldenrod roots.

HEADACHE

Charm (fetish): A string with nine knots in it hung around the neck will cure. — Mary Rachel, Isle Breville.

Charm: Rattles of a rattlesnake worn in the hatband and *back*. Wear them for twelve months and you will never have another headache. — Mr. and Mrs. Bill Harris, Spring Creek.

Wrap the head in the leaves of the Palm de Christi (castor oil plant).

HEART TROUBLE

Charm (fetish): Two nutmegs worn on a string about the neck until the string breaks and the nutmegs fall off.

HICCOUGHS

Charm: Look directly at the point of a knife blade. This will also cure sneezing. — Rev. E. D. Billoups, 318 Eve Street, Baton Rouge.

INDIGESTION

Eat sand and charcoal.

Make a tea of the inside skin of a chicken gizzard.

KIDNEY TROUBLE

An infusion of swamp-lily root should be used as drinking water. Crush half a cup of the root and steep in a quart of water.

LOCKJAW

'Tea made out of roaches is good for lockjaw. My maw give my brother one spoon and his jaws came unlocked. He ain't never had dat anymore.' — Wilkinson Jones.

Medicine: A strong tea of chicken manure taken while hot. — Miss M. Reiss, 2534 Bourbon Street.

If roach tea does not bring relief to a lockjaw sufferer, mash up live roaches and make him eat them.

MALARIA

Medicine: A tea of blackjack vine.

Charm: Put a piece of nightshade in a pan under the middle of your bed. On the tenth day pick it up, turn your back to the east, and throw it over your right shoulder. Don't look back at it.

MATERNITY

To exorcise after-pains: Cross an axe and a hatchet under the bed and place a jar of water on the dresser.

The red thread attached to egg yolks is fed to young mothers to give them strength.

Turn the child's navel cord to the left to keep it from wetting the bed. — Henrietta Lewis.

Measure an undernourished child from neck to toes with a woolen string. Burn the string and feed the ashes to the child. — Henrietta Lewis.

When a baby has been cross and fretful for several nights, it is a sign that an evil person or a witch has been sucking at its breasts. (The sticky ooze from an infant's breasts is called witch's milk.) To keep the evil person from returning, stand a broom at the front door. — Mrs. A. Antony, 718½ Orleans Street.

MEASLES

Medicine: Shuck tea and sheep pills (dung) are widely employed. — Wilkinson Jones.

Boiled garfish with red pepper.

MUMPS

To exorcise: Make a cross on each side of the throat with lard and retrace with soot from the chimney.

Wrap a snake skin next to the face.

NERVOUSNESS

A piece of valerian root in the pillow will quiet nerves.

NOSEBLEED

To stop it, place a tight coral necklace about the neck. Or a chain of silk.

OVERHEATED BLOOD

Medicine: A strong infusion of cactus leaves in water.

Medicine to prevent babies from having hives: Catnip tea.

PNEUMONIA

Medicine: A strong tea of the roots of wild iris (pneumonia plant).

Application: Boil the hoofs of a pig until of the consistency of molasses and spread on the back and chest.

RASH

Charm: Rub on hair off a black cat's back.

Application: Three crushed oak buds.

Snake skin, raw flesh side next the skin.

RHEUMATISM

Apply: Rattlesnake oil; alligator fat, buzzard grease, worm oil or frog oil.

The Irish potato and buckeye are favorite charms.

Medicine: Fry a toad frog and a handful of red worms and feed to the sick person. — Victoria Boland, Houma.

RICKETS

Treatment: Wash the baby's legs in cow's milk. — Mrs. Regina, 2331 Allen Street.

RINGWORM

Application: The milk from fig trees.

SKIN BLEMISHES

Birthmarks will disappear if the newborn is fed a few drops of whatever caused the mark.

SMALLPOX

Strong black pepper tea. Let the tea stand one night before drinking. — Lizzie Chandler.

SORE THROAT

Tea made of dry dog manure.

Drink rabbit-track tea. One must find the trail and take up the tracks oneself.

Peeled prickly pear in water until the water is slimy. Drink the water. — Miss R. Page, 2510 Annette Street.

SORES

Application: Beat up mullein leaves and apply to old sores.

Years ago when children had sores on their heads the old folks would put tar caps on their heads.

A live frog, split, and applied to a cancerous sore, will effect a cure.

SPASMS

If a person has 'spasms,' pull his clothes off and burn them right away. He will quiet down. — Vance Balthazar.

Strip a child, burn his clothes, and give him two drops of beef gall.

SPRAINS

Favorite treatments are winding with snake skin or applying a piece of mud-dauber's nest mixed with vinegar.

STAMMERING

Make the child eat from the same dish as a little dog.

STIES AND SORE EYES

For sore eyes, take a rose and put it in a water glass and let it stand outside at night where the dew can fall on it. Before the sun rises, wipe your eyes with the dewy rose. Take the rose in and use it three times a day. — Miss I. Prude, 1917 Annette Street.

'When you get a sty, go to the cross-road and say: "Sty, sty, leave my eye, and catch the first one who passes by." It sho will leave.' — Silas Spotfore.

STIFF NECK

Charm: 'A very dirty dishrag stolen from a house unbeknownst to the occupants and wrapped about the afflicted one's neck will cure it.' — Mrs. Blue, 2310 Bourbon Street.

STOMACH CRAMPS

Put a tub of water with stale bread under the bed, or a steel object under the pillow. — Henrietta Lewis.

Medicine: Tea of blackberry roots.

Make a fetish with ashes off the hearth sprinkled with salt and water and put in an old stocking. Place this on the stomach. — Ellen Mollett.

SUN PAIN

In the Delta country there is an affliction called sun pain, which the older people claim is peculiar to that section of the country. Sun pain is a periodic pain located at the back of the head. It grows and wanes with the sun's movements in the sky. To cure this, several remedies have been developed. One old man goes from door to door calling out, 'Cure you sun pain!' He has little bottles of river water in which spiders' eggs have been placed. The user is directed to bathe his forehead with the water. Another cure is to bathe the forehead three times a day in a pan of river water, and when the sun goes down to throw the water toward it. In the most elaborate cure, the affected person must strip and seat himself in a tub of river water, facing toward the setting sun. Then a friend or relative stands behind him and dipping the hands into the water, passes the water first over the seated one's shoulders, then over the head in the form of a cross. When this is done, the pain leaves at sunset and never returns. — Mrs. A. Antony, 718½ Orleans Street.

SUNSTROKE

Treatment: Tie a towel over the top of a glass of water; place glass upside down on patient's head and in a few minutes the water will boil. When it stops boiling, the patient is better.

SWEATS

For night sweats place a pan of water under the bed and the sweating will cease. — Laura Rochon, 2410 Conti Street.

TEETHING (CHARMS AND TEETHERS)

Swamp lily, dried, strung, placed around child's neck. — Lizzie Chandler.

'Take crawfish, rub de chilluns' teeth, will make them cut teeth easy.' — Lindy Joseph, McDonoghville.

If baby is teething hard, let a dog kiss him in the mouth.

Put a hog's eye tooth on a string around the baby's neck (teether).

A necklace of alligator teeth (charm or teether).

To keep a teething baby from being sick, kill a rabbit and rub the child's gums with the warm brains. — Mrs. Bill Harris, Spring Creek.

Negro teether: A cow tooth, or a string of Jacob's Tears (a kind of seed). — Mrs. A. Antony, 718½ Orleans Street.

A necklace of eight vertebrae of the dog shark. (The dog shark is noted for large sharp fine teeth.)

THRASH

A man who has never seen the father of the child may blow his breath in the baby's mouth. A letter written to such a one, giving the name and birth date of child, will be as effective. When the man reads the letter the thrash will be gone.

Rub the liver of a white dog in the child's mouth.

Rub inside of mouth with chicken manure.

Nine live sowbugs worn in a sack about the neck.

TOOTHACHE

Tie a garlic bag around the thumb.

Rub the gums with the bark or seed of a Prickly Ash (known on Pecan Island as the Toothache Tree), or insert some in the cavity.

TUBERCULOSIS

A dime, or copper wire worn around the ankle, will prevent.

Sea gum (a tarry solidified marsh ooze), mixed with grease and taken as well as applied by rubbing, is good for consumption. — Albert Dupont, Houma.

Alligator oil. Give daily. (An old woman, seeing that the dogs fed cracklings of alligator fat left a grease spot, where they slept, knew the oil was good.) — Mrs. A. Antony, 718½ Orleans Street.

An old woman once had a 'vision,' then made a medicine of cow manure and rain water for tuberculosis. It cured the tuberculosis.

TYPHOID

Bathe with a tea of peach leaves.

An aid in convalescence: Teaspoon of chimney soot (not stovepipe soot) steeped in a pint of water. Settle with a beaten egg, drink with sugar and cream three times daily.

'UNDERGROWTH' (*puniness*)

To make a stunted child grow, wipe the soles of his feet every day with an old dishrag.

To make him walk: Set him in the doorway and sweep his legs with a new broom.

VOMITING

Crush and steep peach tree leaves. Drink water slowly.

WARTS

Pass the affected part over a dead person. — Katherine Hill, 638 Lafayette Street, Baton Rouge.

Haydel and Reynold, wart curers of Old New Orleans, examined the growths, then told patient, if a man, to return with a rooster; if a woman, to bring a hen. When this was done, the wart disappeared.

WHOOPING COUGH

Urine and salt taken three times a day for three days. — Isaac Mahoney, Houma.

A Negro charm is to make the patient cough in the face of a catfish.

Have a blown horse breathe into the child's nostrils. — August Coxen, Schriever.

WORMS

Candy made from jimson weed and sugar.

Garlic mashed and put in milk, taken on a dark moon, will stop worms in kids. — Lindy Joseph, McDonoghville.

Tie garlic around neck to prevent.

WOUNDS AND POISONING

A tea of mashed roaches. Tablespoon every two hours. — Laura Jenkins, Hubbardville.

Smoke a wound made by a rusty nail with the fumes of burning woolen cloth or sugar.

MISCELLANEOUS CHARMS TO CURE OR PREVENT:

To prevent poison ivy, wear metal on neck, arm, or leg. To stop nosebleed, let the blood drop on a cross made of two matches. To cure sore throat, swallow a gold-colored bead. To prevent poisoning from snakebite, carry the tooth of the kind of snake to whose bite you may be exposed. Garlic and asafoetida placed around the neck in times of epidemic will make it immune. A remedy, if it is to do the most good, must be given without being asked for, and the recipient must not thank the giver.

Witchcraft: Black and White Art
(*'Good Luck' charms to bring good luck and ward off bad luck*)

WHITE ART

Present the newborn with a silver dime. A hole should be bored in a dime and placed about the left ankle.

Suspend a bit of slippery elm bark about the child's neck to give it a persuasive tongue.

To bring luck to a house, put guinea-pepper leaves in the scrubbing water and plant a guinea-pepper tree in the yard.

Always burn the onion peels and you will always have money.

A picture of Saint Peter hung over the door of the house you have just moved into will bring you good luck, because Saint Peter holds the key to everything and opens all doors.

A wishing fetish is made as follows: Cut a round piece of leather and make a bag of it. In this place 13 pennies, 9 cotton seeds, and a bit of hair from a black hog. Rub the bag when you want a wish to come true.

Eat Creole cabbage on New Year's Day, for good luck all the year.

The inhabitants of Ponchatoula often placed the horseshoe under the front doorstep, rather than overhead. To step over it rather than under was said to bring luck quicker.

To ward off 'hurt' or spells, secure the bristles from a pig slaughtered at a voodoo feast, tie them together with a piece of string, and carry them on the person.

'If you get an egg which a black hen has laid within the hour and eat it, it will remove a hoodoo spell off'n you.'

Keep a frizzly chicken around you at all times. If someone hoodoos you, the chicken will dig it up.

If a black cat crosses your path, make the sign of the cross on the ground with your feet.

BLACK ART

FETISHES OF BLACK MAGIC CEREMONIES

To free a criminal, secure a strand from the rope to be used to hang him and have a 'Conjurer Doctor' say a prayer over it. Slip it to the condemned and he will go free.

To hurt an enemy, put his name in a dead bird's mouth and let the bird dry up. This will bring him bad luck.

A fetish to cause death by sickness: Hair from a horse's tail, a snake's tooth, and gunpowder. Wrap in a rag and bury under your enemy's doorstep.

To drive a woman crazy, sprinkle nutmeg in her left shoe every night at midnight.

To get revenge on a woman, keep a bit of her hair and all her hair will fall out.

To make her drown herself, get a piece of her underwear, turn it inside out and bury it at midnight, and put a brick on the 'grave.'

To get rid of a rival in love, put his name in some ashes and let the chickens pick in the ashes.

To cause a woman to go blind, put powder made out of a dried snake in a powder box. She will put it on her face thinking it is face powder.

To cause to go crazy, write the person's name backwards on an egg from a black hen and throw the egg over his house or bury it under his doorstep.

To cause suffering, light a black candle at the bottom, write the person's name on a piece of paper, and wrap around the burning candle. Stick needles into it while it is burning and let it burn out.

Bury something belonging to the person you dislike and his liver will rot.

If someone has bitten you, put some chicken manure on the wound and all your enemy's teeth will fall out.

To keep your neighbor in a constant state of disappointment, take a piece of earth from a graveyard and throw it in his yard.

To harm a person in any way you may wish, write his name three times on a piece of paper and burn a black candle on it on Thursday, Friday, and Saturday. Whatever you wish will happen to him.

To kill by voodoo, the conjurer has a photograph of the victim which he buries face downward while burning a black candle. The victim will die a horrible death as the picture fades.

To kill by voodoo, mix in a bottle, bad vinegar, beef gall, gumbo filé, and red pepper. Write the names of the victim across each other (superimposed) and place in bottle. Shake the bottle for nine mornings and tell it what to do; then bury it breast deep upside down and the victim will die.

TABOOS

Do not raise your foot higher than your head.

Don't let any kind of greens go to seed in the garden.

Don't walk on salt, peanut shells, or onion peels.

Never sweep a porch after sundown.

Never break a broom handle or kill a black cat.

Don't set your bed 'cross ways o' the world' — set it east and west.

Never entirely remove an old house if building a new one on the same site.

APPREHENDING A MURDERER

Put a cassava stick in one hand of the victim, and a knife and fork in the other. The spirit of the victim will first drive the murderer insane, then kill him with great violence.

Bury a murdered man face down and the murderer will confess.

A murderer can be made to confess by placing a saucer containing a little salt on his chest when he is asleep. Soon he will talk and reveal the name of the man he murdered.

TO WIN A CASE IN COURT

Write the names of the lawyer, the judge, and the person against you, put the names in a beef tongue, and freeze the tongue until the case comes up.

Or, go to the courtroom with a luck bead under your tongue. This will deaden the tongues of your opponents.

Or, rub yourself well with luck powder. This will charm the accusers.

BLACK ART USED TO INFLUENCE PEOPLE

TO WIN LOVE (*fetishes and charms used by men*)

Take some of the desired one's hair and sleep with it under the pillow.

Rub love oil into the palm of your right hand.

Carry a piece of weed called 'John the Conqueror' in your pocket.

(*Charms used by women*)

Write the man's name and yours on separate pieces of paper. Pin them together in the form of a cross with yours on top. Put them in a glass of water containing sugar and orange-flower water and burn a red candle before this glass for nine days.

Place the man's picture behind a mirror.

Wrap a thimble in a small piece of silk and carry this in your pocket for three days. Every time you enter or leave the house, make a wish regarding your sweetheart. Your wish will come true in three months.

TO MAKE A LOVE POWDER

Gut live hummingbirds. Dry the heart and powder it. Sprinkle the powder on the person you desire.

A LOVE FETISH

Put a live frog in an ant's nest. When the bones are clean, you will find one flat, heart-shaped, and one with a hook. Secretly hook this into the garment of your beloved, and keep the heart-shaped one. If you should lose the heart-shaped bone, he will hate you as much as he loved you before.

TO KEEP A LOVER FAITHFUL

Write his name on a piece of paper and put it up the chimney. Pray to it three times a day.

TO WIN BACK A HUSBAND

Put a little rain water in a clean glass. Drop in three lumps of sugar, saying, 'Father, Son, Holy Spirit.' Then three more lumps, saying, 'Jesus, Mary, Joseph.' Drop in three more lumps while making your request. Put the glass in a dark room (never before a mirror), and place a spoon on the top of the glass. Next morning stir the contents toward you, then, with back toward the street, throw the contents against the house or fence, saying, 'Father, Son, Holy Spirit, Jesus, Mary, Joseph, please grant my favor.' Water must not be spilled, for it must not be walked on.

GRIS–GRIS (*for a successful marriage*)

Join the hands of two dolls with a ribbon. Take some sand and pile it up in a mound. On top of this place nine wax candles, sprinkle the whole with champagne, saying: 'Saint Joseph, make this marriage and I'll pay.' When the marriage takes place, put a plate of macaroni sprinkled with parsley near a tree in Congo Square in payment.

SUPERSTITION CONCERNING SAINT ROCH'S

If a young unmarried couple see their reflections together in the chapel, they will be married within the year.

TO SECURE A HUSBAND

Carry an image of Saint Joseph in the purse for six months.

PROSTITUTE'S LURE

Essences of vanilla, verbena, Jack honeysuckle, wintergreen, rosebud, and 'follow-me-boy' water. Scrub place and sprinkle mixture from front to back. Mix thyme seed, popcorn, and brown sugar in a jar, place three lighted candles over it, then fling the last mixture in the four corners of the room. (Marie Contesse method.)

TO GET RID OF A MAN

Pick a rooster naked, give him a spoonful of whiskey, then put in his beak a piece of paper on which is written nine times the name of the person to be gotten rid of. The rooster is then turned loose in Saint Roch's cemetery. Within three days the man dies.

TO BREAK UP A LOVE AFFAIR

Take nine needles, break each needle in three pieces. Write each person's name three times on paper. Write one name backward and one forward, then lay the broken needles on the paper. Take five black candles, four red ones, and three green ones. Hang one of the candles upside down from a string in a doorway, placing a tin pan containing the names and needles underneath where it will catch the drip. Light the candle. Do this every twenty-four hours until the candles are gone. Go into the street and get some dung from a black-and-white dog. A dog only drops his dung in the street when he is running and barking and whoever you curse will run and bark too. Put the dung in a bag with the paper, needles, drippings, and candle stubs, throw the whole into running water and one of the parties will leave town.

TO GET RID OF PEOPLE

In New Orleans it is said that a collector or salesman will never return if you sprinkle salt after him.

Dry three pepper pods in an open oven, then place them in a bottle, fill with water, and place under your doorstep for three days. Then sprinkle the water around your house, saying, '*Delonge toi de la*' (remove yourself from here), and the person will never return.

TO GET RID OF A NEIGHBOR

Kill a black chicken and throw it over his house.

TO MAKE SOMEONE MOVE

Take the hair off a dead black cat, fill its mouth with lemons that have been painted with melted red wax crayon. Wrap animal in silver paper, repeat your desire over it, and place it under the house of the person.

BLACK ART USED TO INFLUENCE ANIMALS

TO MAKE THE CAT STAY HOME

Put some sugar in his mouth at nine o'clock on a Friday morning.

Rub grease on his paws, or make him look in a mirror.

TO MAKE THE CHICKEN STAY HOME

Spit in its throat and throw it up the chimney.

Put a mirror and a piece of codfish in the pigeon cote, and others will come.

TO MAKE THE DOG STAY HOME

Cut hair from his tail and bury it under the front step. If he gets lost, he will find his way home.

TO STEAL A DOG

If you wish to steal a dog, leave two strips of fat from shoulder meat in your shoe for nine days. On the ninth day call the dog to you and he will not return to his master.

TO QUIET AN ANIMAL

Fill your hands with your own sweat and rub on its nostrils and fur.

TO SILENCE AN OWL

Place a shovel in the fireplace. Squeeze your wrist tightly, or turn your pocket wrong side out. Don't mock an owl.

TO KEEP SNAKES AWAY

Plant gourd vines around the house.

HOWLING DOG

Take a left shoe and place it upside down under the bed.

MISCELLANEOUS CHARMS

LUCK BALLS

Contain wool, perfume, and colored brick or lodestone.

A CONJURE BALL

One kind is made of a snake tooth, a piece of human flesh, and a lock of human hair. (These must be obtained from a professional conjurer.)

EASY LIFE CHARM

Have a jet-black girl rub your head every morning at eight for eight days.

RABBIT'S FOOT

The left hind foot of a rabbit that has been killed on a dark night in a cemetery.

CONGO SNAKE POWDER

Ashes of a water moccasin. A conjurer will treat it for whatever luck or misfortune you want it for.

OTHER CONJURE PARAPHERNALIA

Essence of Van Van, Oil of Lemon grass, in alcohol (ten per cent). This is the most popular conjure drug in Louisiana.

The Bible. Many hold that the Bible is the great Conjure Book, and Moses the greatest conjurer that ever lived.

Some of the roots and herbs (used under various names): Big John the Conqueror; Little John the Conqueror (used to win); World Wonder Root, used in treasure hunts, and also to hide in the four corners of your house to keep things in your favor. Ruler Root (used as above); Rattlesnake Root; Dragon's Blood (red root fibres crushed), used for many purposes. Valerian Root, to quiet nerves; Adam and Eve Roots, worn in a bag for protection. Five-Fingered Grass, used to uncross. Make tea, strain, and bathe in it nine times. Waste Away Tea, same as preceding. French Lilac, for vampires.

Stories and Beliefs Concerning the Supernatural

Spirits sometimes make their appearance in the form of a cat or a rabbit. You can tell spirit-cats and spirit-rabbits from ordinary cats and rabbits by the fact that the former can disappear at will. (Negro.)

Sometimes, when a wind is blowing, or there is a small whirlwind, horses in a pasture will break and run. They do so because they have seen a spirit, presumably in the wind. (Negro.)

Jack o' lanterns (swamp lights) are said to lead searchers to buried treasure. (Negro.) They are very mischievous and delight to harass animals, particularly horses, whom they cause to shy, or to resist the rider's directions. They also follow hunting parties, misleading the dogs. They are usually unseen by humans.

Once a party consisting of two Negroes and a white man were digging for treasure thought to have been buried by pirates on the bank of Ponchatoula River. They had dug a deep hole at the designated spot when an unearthly scream, seeming to come from the hole, frightened them so badly that they fled and never returned. (Negro.)

Negroes say that if haunts are seen about a house, it means that money is hidden there. You can never recover such treasure unless you have the permission of the guardian spirits, and there are some people who can communicate with them and gain this permission. Nobody who has ever shed blood can hope to find treasure, and if one talks while digging, the treasure will move away.

Just below Plaquemine, on the other side of the Mississippi from Baton Rouge, and just before you reach a place known as 'Kedoville,' there is a well-known haunted house from which many tenants, and later, passers-by, have been driven by the sound of dragging chains, rolling wagon wheels, thunder, and large objects falling. (Negro.)

The old Fluker place, in East Feliciana, just across Carr's Creek, is haunted by spirits which always take the form of cats. At the close of day these enter in a file, each one larger than the preceding one, and gather silently about the fire. Needless to say, tenants do not stay long. Another haunted house is the Willie West place in West Feliciana, about nine miles from St. Francisville. (Negro.)

Some distance out on the Plank Road, on Cypress Bayou, near Baton Rouge, is the old Puckett place, where one day a party of Negro men went rabbit-hunting. They walked up to the house and met a woman at the door who asked them if they wanted to know where there was a fine rabbit they could hunt. She directed them to a patch of brush, and when they neared it a very large rabbit leaped out. All fired at the animal, but it showed no sign of having been harmed, and the dogs fled from it. It then made its way leisurely into the woods, and was never seen again. (Negro.)

The spirits of people who were associated in life are to be found together, and all keep their original characteristics. Sometimes lying spirits amuse themselves by giving false clues to buried treasure. Spirits haunt the places they frequented in life, and when they are not in the form of a cat or rabbit, they may be seen as a vaporous form resembling their former body. If such a vapor strikes a solid object, it disappears like a burst bubble. Usually spirits do no harm, but merely gather in their former home at night where they may be seen talking until dawn. Sometimes they will appear to a former friend and direct him to some long-lost possession, though often the recipient of the message is so disturbed that the message must be repeated on successive occasions. One man was sitting on his porch when a woman in a car stopped at his gate and directed him to go with her to a place several miles out of Baton Rouge. On reaching an old place, the woman directed him to dig under a peach tree in the yard, saying, 'See that tree? There's something under it for you.' She then got into her car and drove away. The man walked home, and when he came to himself he was sitting on his own front porch. Returning to the place pointed out to him by the mysterious woman, he found that the people who lived in the house were not the owners, and as he did not want to dig without the owner's consent he never discovered what was under the peach tree. (A personal experience narrated by a Negro preacher.)

Vindictive spirits are usually those of murdered men. These never cease to plague and question their murderers. A man who was in the habit of visiting relatives who lived about six miles from his home, and frequently returned through the woods at midnight, met a dumb man wandering through the woods, and, becoming frightened, killed him with a pistol. When the body was found, the murderer confessed, but was released. Thereafter the murdered one's spirit followed the murderer's mules in the field, constantly frightening them. The man could be heard cursing and talking to the dummy's ghost, whom nobody could see but the haunted man himself. (Story told to Forgotson by a Negro preacher.)

Not so long ago on almost every plantation there was someone who was witch-ridden. Such a one would have terrible spasms, screaming and grabbing about him. The only way to give the sufferer relief was to take hold of him, but this was only temporary, for as soon as he again fell asleep the witches would return. (Told to Forgotson by a Negro preacher.)

There is a haunted woods near Springfield which Negro children are always warned to avoid.

The 'Christmas Tree' which formerly stood near the heart of Ponchatoula was so called because it was at one time decorated by four lynched Negroes. Negroes avoided the spot as a hanged Negro is said to invariably haunt the spot near which he was hung. — Jack Penton and family, 1508 St. Charles Street.

Somewhere on the road between Bogalusa and Ponchatoula there is said to be a beautiful tomb. Directly after the body was buried in it, the head of a mule appeared distinctly on the fore part of the tomb. Printing this head out did no good. Each time it would reappear clearly through the print. The stone was finally removed. — Jack Penton.

Negroes about Ponchatoula will never cut or mar a dogwood tree in any manner, for they say that a spirit lives in the trees, and when the tree is hurt, the spirit screams in agony. They are even afraid to tie their horses to a dogwood tree. — Jack Penton.

CANDLES

Candles are used with set meanings for the different colors. They are often very large, one candle costing as much as six dollars.

White: For peace and to 'uncross.' Also for weddings.
Red: For victory.
Pink: For love (some say for drawing success).
Green: To drive off (some say for success).
Blue: For success and protection (for causing death also).
Yellow: For money.
Brown: For drawing money and people.
Lavender: To cause harm (to bring triumph also).
Black: Always for evil or death.

PICTURES OF SAINTS

Saint Michael the Archangel: To conquer.
Saint Expedite: For quick work.
Saint Mary: For cure in sickness.
Saint Joseph with Infant Jesus: To get job.
Saint Peter without the Key: For success.
Saint Peter with the Key: For great and speedy success.
Saint Anthony of Padua: For luck.
Saint Mary Magdalene: For luck in love (for women).
Sacred Heart of Jesus: For organic diseases.

PERFUMES TO BRING LUCK TO GAMBLERS

Carnation: Three Jacks and a King. Narcisse (mild); 'Has-no-harra' (jasmine lotion).

SCRUBBING PREPARATION

Red Fast Luck: Oil of cinnamon and oil of vanilla, with wintergreen. Used in scrubbing water to bring luck. There are many scrubbing mixtures.

Divination

DREAMS

If a person fears or dreams of a death in his family, that person should get up in the morning before sunrise, throw over his left shoulder a glass of water that has been standing overnight, say: 'God the Father, God the Son, and God the Holy Ghost,' and afterward ask the Lord to avert that death. — Father Joseph, Jerusalem Temple, Baptist Church, Fourth and Johnson Streets.

To dream of fresh pork and fish is a sign of death.

If you dream of meat with blood, it means death; if cooked, a disappointment.

A dream of fat meat or of pulling a tooth means death is coming.

Dreaming of trees, particularly apple trees, according to miscellaneous sources, always presages joy and profit.

Dreams of horses are always good.

To dream of a church, a priest, and clear water is a good dream. If you play lottery, play 2-19-33 for the church, 4-11-14 for the priest, and 1-2-3 for the clear water.

If you dream of a baked chicken, play lottery and select 1122-66. I did it. It cost me 25 cents and I won $45.

If you get a love letter from·your boy friend, lay it open and then fold the letter in nine different ways and pin it on your clothes, right over your heart. Let it stay there until you go to bed. Then put the letter in your left glove, placing the glove under your head. If your lover is true to you, you will dream of gold or diamonds, but if you dream you see washing or graves, you will either lose him by death or go through poverty for a long time.

A generally accepted belief in the South concerns snakes. If one dreams of killing a snake, one will triumph, but if one dreams that the snake escapes, one has enemies who are seeking to destroy one.

There are no particular signs given in dreams. The Lord, however, can, in dreams, tell you where to go and where not to go, and through dreams one often learns the best numbers to play in lottery.

DIVINING RODS

With the discovery of oil in North Louisiana, divining rods of all sorts made their appearance. Some are of metal and others merely branches from trees. A divining rod which is capable of finding underground oil deposits is generally known as a 'doodle bug.' This term is likewise used for the true appliances used by geologists. Here, in Louisiana, water-finding rods are either willow wands or forked sticks of peach, black haw, walnut, or witch-hazel.

TREASURE LIGHTS

If you are walking alone in the country on a dark night and you suddenly see lights bobbing up and down trying to attract your attention, do not follow them, for they are treasure lights and very dangerous things. If you follow them, you will not be able to stop until daylight, and they will take you through such a maze that you will be lost.

If you dream that a bright light appears before you as if coming to you, it is a sign that there is treasure for you in that particular spot.

TO FIND TREASURE

When a person walks in his sleep, let him go where he pleases; sometimes he will walk to the spot where there is a hidden treasure.

Nobody who has ever shed blood can hope to find buried treasure.

No one must speak while digging for treasure or the treasure will go away.

Look for treasure on the second day of a new moon, or in the full of the moon.

If burying treasure which you hope your heirs will find, bury a rooster's head with it. When they approach the rooster will crow.

TO DISCOVER FUTURE HUSBAND

During leap year the girl who counts all the gray (some say white and that a gray mule counts for five horses) horses she sees, until she gets up to a hundred, will be married within the year to the first gentleman with whom she shakes hands after counting the hundredth horse. (Some say she will marry the first man she sees who is wearing a red tie.)

On Good Friday one should arise at midnight and look into the mirror in the dark. If you see a face, it is that of your future husband, but if you see a coffin instead, it means you will die soon.

Omens

RAIN

When the rain is coming the bullfrogs sing, or, as the Cajun says it: 'Laplie tombe' ouaouaron chante.'

Three frosts will be followed by rain.

If you kill a cat or reptile, it will rain.

DEATH, ILL HEALTH

(There are 140 omens concerning death and ill health in the files.)

If, when you are walking along the street or sitting quietly in the house, you hear a voice calling, don't answer, because that is a sign of death calling.

The transplanting of a weeping willow will bring about violent death.

If you plant a cedar tree, you will die when the shadow cast by the tree at high noon becomes large enough to cover your grave.

If you are hurt by falling out of a fig tree, you will never get well.

A death in a family is often preceded by a 'little white dog' who suddenly appears in the house and then disappears. He will just 'pass into the wall.' — Mrs. Henry Prudhomme, Natchitoches.

Kill de lizard on de grave, dey ain't no charm yo' life can save.

When 'Chouette' (screech owl) or 'Gimme Bird' sings around a house, it means there will be a death in the house.

A swallow in the bedroom is a sign of death.

A baby whose cradle is rocked while it is empty will die without fail.

WEDDINGS

Rain or tears at a wedding are bad luck.

BAD LUCK

(There are about 150 bad luck omens in the files.)

PLANTS THAT BRING BAD LUCK

It is bad luck to have Spanish daggers growing near the house.

Spanish moss brings bad luck.

Flowers out of season bring bad luck.

Don't let love apples grow in your yard; this brings bad luck.

Arbor vitae brings bad luck.

Night-blooming cereus brings bad luck.

Everything that masters of slaves did not want Negroes to do was presented to them as bad luck.

CAT

If you move a cat, put an ear of corn in the sack to break the spell.

HANDS ON OR ABOVE HEAD

Sleeping with arms over head, the sleeper is calling trouble. Resting the head on the hands, the Devil is hanging on your back.

GOOD-LUCK PLANTS

Sweet basil planted on either side of the doorstep brings good luck.

A pepper bush in the yard brings good luck.

CAT

If a cat follows you home, or if you befriend a cat, it is good luck.

SHOOTING STARS

To see a shooting star is usually said to indicate a death.

CREOLE BELIEFS

In the days of Creole chivalry (only a hundred years ago), the spilling of wine foretold the spilling of blood; and if a sword fell from the wall, it presaged the coming of an enemy.

PIGEONS

Gathering about the house they bring good luck.

HUNTING

If the trail is straight, the animal will return over the same trail.

A hunter who eats the brains of the animal he kills will be able to out-think the next one he chases.

ANIMAL NOISES

If the dog howls with his nose to the ground, there will be a fire; with his head raised, there will be a death.

If the rooster crows at the back door, it means death; at the front door, visitors; if he comes to the step and crows three times, he is saying, '4-11-44,' and if you like to play lottery, play this gig and win.

If the animals of woods, swamps, and barnyard are unusually vocal, it is a sign of rain.

MONEY LUCK

When passing a lavender bush, known to the Negroes as the 'money tree,' pluck a sprig of leaves, count the leaves, and repeat the Commandment of the number counted. This brings luck. Nine leaves on a sprig brings money.

To cook Creole cabbage on New Year's Day is lucky. You will have green money the entire year.

SALT

'Don't loan no salt on Monday 'cause it will take all de seasonin' outen your home for a week.' — Roxanna Moore.

NEW YEAR LUCK

Eat cow peas and hog jowl on New Year's Day and you will have plenty to eat the rest of the year.

LOTTERY

If you play lottery in August, you will lose, because 'It was on the 1st of August dat God put de Devil out of heaven, and dat's why we has a hell, an' since dat happen, de Devil crosses everything we does in August.'

SNEEZING

According to II Kings 4:35, when Elisha raised the child from the dead, the child sneezed seven times. 'Ever since dat day, when anybody sneeze seven times, it's a sign a ha'nt is riz up f'om de dead.'

SPITTING

If you spit at someone, you will die like a dog.

Never spit in the fire. It will draw your lungs up.

A hungry person's saliva looks like cotton.

WHISTLING

Is always bad luck to a woman.

SINGING

Is usually bad luck. Don't sing before breakfast, on Friday or Saturday till past noon, nor while eating, nor in bed, nor when going to bed. 'You mustn't never sing befo' breakfus'. In ol' times, my Pa said, "Look at de pore mockin' bird, he so happy when he opens his eyes that he jes' lets out an' sings — befo' night he's killed — and de slave, if he sang, he wuz whipped." '

SLEEPING

If a little baby cries and jumps in his sleep, an evil spirit is bothering him.

You should never sleep with the moon in your face. It will draw your mouth over and make it crooked.

CUTTING FINGERNAILS

Cutting a baby's nails before he is a year old makes a thief of him. Bite them off.

Cutting a child's nails under a fig tree (or a rosebush) will make him a singer.

Old darkies do not cut their nails, for they say their strength is in them.

HAIR

A red-headed Negro is a witch or wizard.

If birds weave some of your hair into their nests, you will go crazy.

A widely prevailing superstition among some groups in the Delta country concerns the curl and nail paring in a bottle. An enemy will try to secure one or the other, or both. These he will place in a bottle and hide it near the one he wishes to harm. Sickness immediately follows. One woman in the country makes her living by going to the homes of the sick to 'discover the bottle,' while another healer, when called in, places a bottle of charmed wine and a loaf of bread under the bed of the sick. This is supposed to neutralize the effects of the evil charm.

SWEEPING

It is bad luck to sweep after sundown. Don't sweep under a sick bed or the patient will die. Don't sweep under a girl's feet or she will never marry. Don't sweep under a chair. Don't sweep when someone else is sweeping. A broom can be moved into a new house if the spell is removed from it by passing it through the window of the new house.

ASHES

Never take up ashes at night. Never spill any ashes. Never take up ashes until thirty days after the birth of a child, for if you do either mother or child will die. Don't take ashes out of the room of anyone ill.

MIRRORS

If you should break a mirror, you can wash away the seven years' bad luck by throwing the pieces in running water.

Creole mirror superstition: When three men look into a mirror at once, the youngest is to die; but if three girls look into a mirror at once, the eldest will marry within the year.

BROOM SUPERSTITIONS FROM ISLE BREVILLE

A young couple must not bring an old broom with them into the new house unless it is thrown in, handle first.

An old couple moving into a new house must bring an old broom. If they don't, one of them will have bad luck.

August is a bad month in which to buy a broom, and housecleaning should never be done in August.

DAYS OF THE WEEK

It is good luck for a buzzard to light on your house on Monday.

If a red-headed woman comes to your house on Monday, there will be confusion all week.

Never let a woman come into your house on Monday or Friday until a man has first crossed the threshold.

If a person dies on Saturday, the Blessed Virgin will have that person out of purgatory by the following Saturday.

STEPPING OVER A CHILD

There is a widely prevailing superstition that to step over a child will stunt him.

A child's growth will be arrested if he leaves the house by the window.

CAJUN BELIEFS CONCERNING CHILDREN

Playing with keys makes children hard-headed. Looking into a mirror makes children's teething difficult.

TEETH

If a pig gets the baby tooth, a tusk will grow in the child's mouth; if a dog gets it, the child will have a fang.

If the child desists from placing the tongue in the place of the missing tooth, he will get a gold one.

BREAD

If the loaf is upside down on the table, it means the Devil is around.

FUEL

Never use any kind of fruit or nut tree, or one struck by lightning, for if you do, your house will burn down before the year is out.

CLOCKS

It is bad luck to have two clocks going in the house at the same time.

Husbandry

WEATHER

The last six days of the old year and the first six days of the new indicate the weather for the twelve months ahead.

A period of good weather is ahead in the summer time when the weather clears off warm, never when it clears off cool.

In the early spring if a bull bat swoops down and says 'broke,' it is a sign that winter is over.

A whirlwind is a sign of dry weather.

Heavy dew is a sign of fair weather.

A red sunset in autumn is a sign of cold weather.

When sounds like muffled footsteps are heard in a wood fire, there will be snow. As the Negroes say, 'The fire is stomping snow.'

PLANTING

Anything that matures under the ground should be planted in the dark of the moon, and those which mature on top in the full moon.

Vegetable and melon seeds should be planted by a growing child, as they will grow as the child grows.

Always plant four seeds if you expect one to come up. One for the blackbird, one for the crow, one for the cutworm, and one for to grow.

Plant corn when the dogwood is in full bloom.

Some Negroes place rice on the graves to keep the dead from catching their hoes or spoiling their rice crop.

Sometimes rice husks are put in a fish trap and hung high so that the rice may be tall.

When shelling butterbeans (limas) for planting, throw the hulls in the road. If they are burned, your crop will be poor; if fed to the cows, the stock will eat your vines; if thrown in the trash, not only will your crop be poor, but your stock will not reproduce and your wife will not bear children.

FRUIT TREES

Don't put your hand on a young tree that is bearing its first fruit or the fruit will always fall off.

If a tree bears wormy fruit, chop a piece from the trunk and tie a bottle of water somewhere around the tree. Next year you will have solid fruit.

To make a tree bear, bore a hole in the trunk and drop some Epsom salts in it. This purges the tree.

SEEDS

Mix ashes with turnip or mustard seed before you plant and they will 'make' better.

Planting a grain of corn with seeds or cuttings will make them grow.

Plant beans in the scorpion or twin days (by the almanac) and they will bear well. Never plant vegetables on bloom days or you will have nothing but bloom. — Bill Harris, Spring Creek.

Plant cabbage when the signs are in the head.

Plant potatoes on dark nights.

Never plant peas until you hear the whippoorwill. His call is the signal that the season is at hand.

Plant English peas during the 'Old Twelve Days' — the last and first six days before and after Christmas — and the peas will have a better flavor.

Never plant a crop while a woman near-by is holding a flower in her hand.

Cajuns say that sweet potatoes should always be planted when the moon is full because if planted when the moon is in any other shape the potatoes will be like the moon.

Plant pepper when you are mad, or let a red-headed person plant it.

Never plant okra while standing. Always stoop and the plant will bear while still low.

People who are able to plant everything with unfailing success are said to have a green thumb. But children should always plant the vegetable and melon seeds.

PLOWING

If you plow on Good Friday, lightning will strike your field and the ground will bleed.

EGGS AND CHICKENS

To protect one's chickens from predatory hawks, keep a horseshoe in the fireplace and it will cause the hawk's claws to become so soft that they will be unable to do any damage.

To keep eggs from spoiling, place nails in the form of a cross in the nest.

When it thunders, the eggs won't spoil.

If you wish to have more pullets from a hatching of eggs, place the eggs into the nest with your left hand. Using your right will increase the number of roosters.

Chickens which are set to hatch in May will be crippled or crazy.

FENCING
Fence in the dark of the moon if you do not want your fence to settle.

BUILDING
Never start building a house on Friday. If this is done inadvertently, build a piece of green bough into the peak of the house to avert the bad luck. Best days for shingling are from the thirteenth to the twenty-second of the month. Best days for painting are the sixth, seventh, eighth, sixteenth, and seventeenth.

CATTLE
Brand and castrate on the decrease of the moon; slaughter on the increase.

If you stir milk with a fork, the cow will have sore tits; if it is stirred with a knife, the flow will be cut down.

Killing a 'toad-frog' will make your cows dry up.

MORE WEATHER SIGNS
Three frosts or three fogs on successive nights bring rain.

There is always a storm after the death of an old woman.

There is a frog whose call is like a mallard duck. To hear his cry at night foretells a high river.

'If the oak is out before the ash, it will be a summer of wet and splash. If the ash is out before the oak, it will be a summer of fire and smoke.'

FISHING
A silver hook used to be used during full moon, as it was thought that the fishes' mouths were then too tender to bite on any other kind.

Best time to start going fishing is when the dogwood blooms.

Eat onions before you go fishing and you will have good luck.

Fish bite quicker on Good Friday than on any other day in the year.

Fish bite well when the country road is full of fiddlers.

When there is little bait, the fish bite.

If you are having no luck, put a bit of asafoetida on the bait and the fish will come.

If there is no bait, beat the ground with a switch, and the worms will think it is raining and come up.

HUNTING

When a Northwester blows it brings in high tide. This is the time of good hunting.

Don't go hunting on Friday night. It is bad luck. The dogs will bark as if they had treed something, but 'dey won't be nothin' there.'

A trapper must never take a broom or a cat with him when he breaks camp.

If a stick breaks when you are passing through the woods, there are two ghosts arguing over you, saying they know you.

If you hunt on Friday, you will see no jaybirds, for on that day every jay carries a grain of sand to hell where it will be heated to make things hot for you when you get there.

If you get lost in the swamp, you can find north and south by feeling the bark of the trees. Smooth bark is on the south side, rough on the north. — Jack Penton and family.

Don't hunt on Sunday.

MISCELLANEOUS BELIEFS

THUNDER

Some say that when it thunders, Le Bon Dieu is rolling his stones. Others, that the Devil is driving his two black horses and chariot across the sky.

PRAYERS

Said in the dark are said to the Devil.

Every year on Palm Sunday have magnolia leaves blessed and place them in your house to calm storms. During a storm hold a leaf in your hand to shift the wind.

If you are drowning and accidentally cross your hands, you will come to the surface and float. You are saved by the sign of the cross.

Make the sign of the cross over your bread so that you will always have some; over your fire so it will burn, etc.

HEART OF A BLACK CAT
Eat one and no bullet or knife can harm you.

STABBING
Blood spilled will kill the grass, and every time it rains the blood of the slain will appear fresher.

BANANA
Cutting a banana is the same as cutting the cross of Christ.

MIRRORS
Cover the mirrors in the room occupied by a corpse or the image of the dead will remain, and, if seen, will cause the death of the beholder. Others say that the part of the corpse reflected in the mirror is a part of the Devil's body.

SEX CHANGE
If a girl kisses her toe, she will become a boy.
Kiss your elbow and you will change your sex.

CURING
One who has never seen his mother will be able to cure.

Colloquialisms

Personalities

FIRST PERSON SINGULAR

I feel so feelsy. I love I. I'm going wild crazy. I feel like a stowaway. I wouldn't give a pinch of snuff for my life. Big I and little you.

SECOND PERSON SINGULAR (*repartee*)

You gotta it. Somebody hit you on the head real hard. You need a doseta Salapatekie. You're a hickory-nut cracker. You're just slap happy. You're tellin' me. What you got your neck poked out for? Wish you would make up your feeble mind. Come see, Chere. If I'm lyin' I'm dyin'. If I'm jokin' I'm chokin'.

EXCLAMATIONS

Blow me down! Fan my brow! Hush my mouth! I'll be jinks swing! If that don't take the rag off! Sho nuff! Shut my mouth wide open! You're telling I!

EXPLANATORY AND DESCRIPTIVE

Feel like a million dollars that's done been spent. Now I know how a bug feels when he's been stepped on. Cuttin' up just like a little man. Somebody sold some gaged water. Cream-puff sissy. Whopper-jawed (lop-sided). Oh, he's been drinkin' hydraulic brake fluid. He's pushin' fire (making trouble). He won't purge (foam at the mouth) when he dies. (Means he speaks his mind.) He's havin' a blood rush (getting angry).

SAYINGS

Hog dead; no water on. (Country saying meaning that something very unexpected has happened.) There will be a big coffee-drink there soon. (A wake.) God don't like ugly. Answer to stupid question: Digging a file, my boy. Query: Who dug in at the dug-out?

ADMONITIONS

Don't be horsey. Keep your bill out. If you ain't seed nothin', don't say nothin'.

GREETINGS

How you comin'? (Ans.) Nicely. Right smart. How you feelin'? (Ans.) Poly, thank Gawd.

APPELLATIONS

Woman chaser: 'High Flier.' Tall man: 'High pockets.' Singer: 'Songster.' Coal-black Negro: 'Eight Ball.' Minister: 'Rev'und.' Small woman: 'Little Bit.' Seamstress: 'Seamster.'

Peculiar Pronunciations and Grammatical Construction

Bawge, for barge. Tow out the cotton — bring out the cotton. Gyarden sass — okra, turnips, cabbage, onions, garlic, snap beans, lettuce. She birds — female birds. Sŭlo — silo. Palmētto — palmetto. Turckle — turtle. Whop — whip. Wast — wasp. Cameera — camera. Spēcimens — specimens. Cathin' — catching. Difforance — difference. Ha'nt — haunt. Sopin' — something. Jaint — joint. *Sarvey* — survey. Furce — fuss. Retched — reached. Nair — none. Yore'un — yours. Grieved up — filled with sorrow. Drudged — dredged. Keep us hoped up — keep us encouraged. Might stunter you — might stunt you. Aw no — not really. Whatcha gonna say, boy? — how is everything? Passed around — to walk or ride around the same place.

Terms Used in the Home, in Agriculture and in Industry

GENERAL

Mud-daubing: mud and moss used for chinking and chimney-making.

Puncheons: split logs, adzed, then planed, then used for flooring and furniture.

Floor map: a rug.

Sad iron: old-fashioned irons for smoothing clothes.

Ash hopper: a container for ashes used in making lye for home-made soap.

Music-maker: a musical instrument, usually a fiddle.

Chamber lye: urine.

Horse: a wooden stand over which hides were draped while in the process of being scraped clean of hair. Shoe and saddle-making was often done at home.

Lapstone: used in shoemaking.

Carabee: used in making horsehair into ropes and bridle reins.

Des cheveaux Choctaw: in southern Louisiana, a small horse. (The Choctaws were short.)

Leaders: the leading team of oxen.

Old wheelers: oxen broken to the yoke.

Pole whip: a whip attached to a long pole used when several pairs of oxen comprised the team.

Swing: part of the yoke used in hitching oxen to a cart.

Sheep tatling: sheep dung. (Negro.)

Catproof: a term used to describe a pen built to protect pigs from the invasion of wildcats.

BRICKS

Brick mill: used by old settlers for making their own bricks.

Field: yard where bricks were dried after being molded.

Glossy bricks: those bricks in which there was a portion of unmixed sand which melted into glass and made those bricks unfit for use in masonry work.

COTTON

Bowed: an old-time method of fluffing cotton by using a bow held across the cotton with the left hand while the string was snapped with the right hand.

Burrs: the remainder of the boll on the stalk after the cotton has been removed.

Breaking land: the first plowing.

Hand-gin bench: used in front of the hand-gin in ginning cotton for home use.

Drilling: seeding in open furrows.

Pulling staple: pulling the cotton fiber to determine its length.

Sacking it up: putting cotton in sacks.

Steady cropping: repeatedly planting the same land.

Step-dropping: dropping a seed, or seeds, with each step.

FIELD

Clay root: the exposed roots of a tree which has been blown out in such a way that a large hole is left where the tree was standing.

Coups: water drains across ridges.

Courees: same as coup.

Smoke pot: employed in obtaining wax from wild bees' nests.

Goobers: peanuts.

Water chinquapins: seeds of the yellow lotus. (Also called duck acorns.)

HUNTING

Flatboat: a boat designed for use in shallow water.

Flesh fork: used in hunting.

Jumped: said of animals as 'flushed' is said of birds.

'Gators: alligators.

Pole hooks: used in hunting alligators.

To pole: to shove through water too shallow for oars.

Fire-hunting: hunting at night with the aid of a wood fire in a frying pan attached to a long handle.

Still-hunting: waiting beside an animal trail.

Gather up: get up and follow the dogs.

Give tongue: bark.

Tree: put up a tree and remain until the hunter comes (said of dogs).

Sea gum: tar-like ooze which solidifies on surface of marshes in some places.

LUMBERING

Black gum top: black gum tree.

Cant: to turn over with a hook.

Dogging: pulling the log into position for the skidder to lift.

Log rolling: hauling logs from one place to another (?).

Light-wood: small bits of cypress or pine.

Skidder: small derrick on flat car used to lift logs onto the car. Also the man who operates same. (Negroes will not touch live oaks or dogwoods.)

RICE

Baton pill: the stick used with rice pill for pounding hulls from rice. (Creole.)

Rice pill (spelling not certain — pronounced **peel**): the hollowed block on which rice is husked. (Creole.)

Van: shallow tray of cane reed used for separating chaff from rice.

SUGAR

Bagasse: the pulp of the ground stalk of cane.

Brake cane: wild cane.

Piggin: container for liquids.

Skim: the trash and silt from boiling juice.

Stripping: taking the flags from the cane stalks in preparation for grinding.

Similes

Poor as a snake. Deep as a loon. Naked as a jay bird in the whistling time. Nervy as a gnat. Flat as a chinch. Higher than a cat's back (expensive). Crazy as a Bessie bug.

Adages

A patch by patch is friendly, but a patch on patch is 'bomination. — Mary Harris.

He who is able to talk and never talks is a wise man.

Too much sit-down break trousers. (If you are lazy, you won't have any clothes to wear, as they wear out just the same.)

Married got teeth. (Marriage isn't all bliss.)

Hard head bi'd (bird) don't make good soup. (Disobedient children don't turn out well.)

When man drunk, him stagger; when woman drunk, him lay down. (Women go to extremes.)

Take keer, Marster! is better than 'O Lord, Marster!'

Some mans does dead befo' dem time. (They make trouble for themselves.)

Riddles

A boy was standing on the corner with his father's pants on. What two corners was he standing on? (Toulouse and Broad.)

What's the name of a bird without wings? (Jailbird.)

Long slick black fellow, pull his tail and make him bellow. (Shotgun.)

Dere wuz a man who rode through town, Greengraveler wuz his name; his bridle and saddle wuz dipped wid gol'; three times I've tol' his name. (Mr. Was.)

What has patches on top of patches, but no hole? (Cabbage.)

Creole Colloquialisms

'Une aune' — still used by those who weave.

'La banquette' — the sidewalk.

'Casser la paille' — instead of 'rompre la paille.'

'Des pentures' — used rather than 'gonds' or 'charnierès.'

'Le blue grass' — Bermuda grass (said to have been brought from Texas by Rosamond Breaux).

'Des couronnes de chêne' — mistletoe clusters.

'Le cresson' — peppergrass. Also applied to chickweed.

'Le gazon' — carpet grass (*axonopus compressus*).

'Les printanieres' — bluets, *Houstonia* (springers, bluebottles).

'L'Herbe à la Puce' — poison ivy. People used to think that the trumpet creeper was poisonous. Many knew nothing of poison ivy.

'Le cenellier' — the winterberry.

'Une binette' — a face. (Now rarely heard.)

'Des dormeuses' — pendant earrings set with solitaire diamonds.

'Un rabougri' — a very small man.

'Un tonnerre à la voile' — an unruly person.

'Piqué' — adj., drunk.

'Menterie' — lie or story.

'Un tour de Jarnac' — instead of 'un coup de Jarnac' (a brick of Jarnac, instead of a thrust of Jarnac).

'Un carcan' — a small yoke for pigs.

'Le balai de ciel' — the north wind, not the northeast.

'Le train train' — the chores, the little things regularly done.

'Les quatres paroisses' — the whole world (the original four parishes).

'Rester à Lafayette' — for 'demeuer à.' (To stay in instead of to live in.)

'Cotoyer' (sailing coastwise), for skirting the edge of a swamp.

'C'est un charrette à trois roues' or 'c'est une girouette rouillée' — said of anything that is very inefficient, ineffectual.

'C'est bon comme la vie' — said of a person (or thing) who is very good.

'Frou-frou' — giddy.

'La ripopée' — slops, low class.

'Une cargaison' — not a cargo, but a load.

'Une paillasse' — not a straw mattress, but a shuck one.

'Un en-tout-cas' — not necessarily an umbrella, but anything that might serve in an emergency.

'La famille de rikiki' (une plaisanterie) — said of any large family.

'C'est un p'tit homme, mais il a le coeur bien placé, allez!' (Quite a compliment.)

'Cheval donné, on ne regarde pas à la bride' — don't look a gift horse in the mouth.

'Cela ne vaut pas les quartes fers d'un cheval mort' — used instead of 'Cela ne vaut pas les quatres fers d'un chien.'

'La pauvrété n'est pas un déshonneur, mais c'est une fichue misère.' (Poverty is not a sin, but a mighty inconvenience.)

'Se débattre comme un diable dans un bénitier' — to writhe like a demon in a holy-water basin.

'Bon chien tien de race' — instead of 'bon chine chasse de race.'

'Marchand d'oignons connait les ciboules' — instead of 'marchand d'oignons se connait en ciboules.' (Onion merchant knows his chives, instead of Onion merchant is conversant on chives.)

'Il cache son argent dans des cornes à boeufs' — he lives a simple life (does not do business with banks). Not often heard now.

'Ca date du temps d'Artaguette' or 'Ca date de l'an quarante' — of anything very out of date.

'Homme de paille, pistolet de bois' — a man who is a bluff.

'Il a peur de se noyer dans son crachat' — he is afraid to undertake anything.

'Ca marche comme un papier de musique' — there is no trouble, everything is going on smoothly.

'Ficelé à sur quartres épingles' — all dressed up.

'Ca m'enquiquine!' (tsk, tsk!) — it makes me boil.

'Je vais lui foutre un galop' — I'll get after him.

'Se mettre un trente-six' — to do one's utmost.

Cajun Colloquialisms

'Ca grimace' — it's raining (drizzling).

'Un naufroge' — (a shipwreck) for an auto or buggy wreck.

'Je vais naviguer' — I am going to navigate, for, I am going out.

'Grouille ton casaquin' — hurry up.

'A la voirie' — in plain view (illiterate).

'C'est mon chaudin qui fait mal' — my stomach aches (illiterate).

'Ah! gougre non' — certainly not.

'La chanterelle va casser' — that will be the last straw.

'Une zireté' — (something hideous).

'Cognier un bon somme' — to enjoy a good nap.

'Un carabosse' — an ugly, clumsy hat.

'Aller à la passée' — to hunt snipe and woodcocks.

'De la fraicheur' — fresh pork (illiterate).

'Le rhodaire' — a prairie near Lafayette.

'Un warraron' or 'wawaron' — a bullfrog.

The French of rural Louisiana is composed of French, Spanish, and Indian. In French, 'Smoked Meat' is 'Viande Fumé,' but this would not
be understood in the country. One must ask for 'Viande Boucanée,' the
last word being the Choctaw, and the one commonly used.

Locally the Spanish word 'Vamose' (Get out) becomes 'Bamose.'

A familiar term of endearment is 'Mon petite chou' (My little cabbage
head) which has become 'Mon 'te chou.'

Gumbo (Negro) French

'Larguer' — to tire out.

'Braliner' — to bleach clothes in the sun.

'Tiyer la mousse' — to clean moss.

'Faire shingo' — to doze, especially in front of the fire.

'Beurdacer' — to kill time.

'Charrer' — to chat.

'Cthamander' — to beg or ask for things.

'Partir la guinguette' — to go on a frolic, or gad about.

'Les prairies molles' — swamps, trapping grounds.

'Un îlet' — a small island. Also used to designate a square.

'Le large' — the prairie north and west of Lafayette.

'Des cthoucoulouques' — dollars.

'Câille' — black and white, said of cloth.

'Ta cagouette' — your head.

'Un souci d'oreiller' — a pillowcase.

'Un facthin' — about the same thing as *bajoe* (jowl).

'Un baire' — mosquito bar.

'Un bajoe' — an uncultured man (pigface?).

'Une couette' — mattress covering (ticking).

'Un nioque' — a nest egg.

'Un soutadaire' — a saddle blanket.

'Les Zerbes Lapin' — *oxalis europaea.*

'Des jines herbes' — pot herbs.

'P'tit Pâques' — Palm Sunday.

'Ôte ca dans to coloquinte' — get that notion out of your head.

'Mo t'ape jongler' — I was thinking and dreaming, or, I was thinking that (jongler ça).

'Mo coeur tacher dans to chaine comme boskoyo dans cypière' — my heart is linked in your chain like 'boskoyo' in a cypress.

'Ça dépend de la position des gonflots' — maybe, with quite a bit of doubt.

'Lever un lapin' — get a beau.

'Ce fil est assiz long pour pendre un âne' — long enough to hang a donkey (sewing thread).

'Chacta' — mean, contrary (said of persons).

Negro Sayings

To say of a man that 'He is wearing the horns' means his wife is untrue to him.

A person with big feet is called 'Foots.'

'Hugging Molly': a half-wit who wound himself in a sheet and accosted women on the street, frightening them by hugging them. He was never punished, but was greatly feared by the Negroes, as his costume was similar to that of the Ku Klux Klan.

Unidentified Terms

'Le sent bon' — false onion (bivalve).

'Des crocros' — heavy, ill-fitting shoes.

'Des yeux gouères' — very pale-colored eyes.

Customs

Negro Customs

MARRIAGE, DEATH, ETC.

At Ponchatoula, unofficial marriages, with only the ceremony of jumping over the broomstick, were often practiced. (This custom was formerly widespread.) — Mrs. Antony.

Plantations (such as the Esterbrook at Ponchatoula) had their own churches. Because of the young men's habits of using the church for a place to meet their girls, the minister would have all the doors and windows firmly bolted during services so that the young couples could not slip out. — Mrs. Antony.

A Negro mother with child is highly respected. Friends and relatives will tramp for miles around to beg, borrow or steal any special food she desires, because it is said that if a pregnant woman has a desire for any special food, it is because the unborn child is crying for it. — Mrs. Antony.

It is a custom in some communities for whole families to rush to a home to see an ill person, whether or no the disease is contagious.

The Negroes in Louisiana hold wakes for the dead, as do many white families in rural and small urban communities.

Some years ago, when Negro shacks had no windows, and shutters were the only form of ventilation, there was always a very serious problem to be considered when a member of the household died. It was, of course, necessary that the house should be thoroughly aired at once, but it was also true that if the shutters were left open, the corpse would be exposed to dire peril. As soon as death occurs, the cats all over the world are immediately notified and at once assemble in order to try to gain access to the corpse, and if they were able to accomplish this, would eat it up entirely. To prevent this dreadful procedure, relatives and friends kept constant guard over the corpse until it was buried, and this custom came to be known as the Death Watch.

In the case of Negro burials, the corpse is usually kept until all members of the family arrive, regardless of the distance some of them may live. Funeral sermons, usually two or three, are preached at the burial, though sometimes months later.

'Society' members, the term relating to fraternal organizations, are required to attend the funerals of their departed brethren, and are penalized by a stiff fine if they do not do so.

Negroes who have been hanged are not permitted to be buried from the church, which is called 'Christian burial,' unless they have repented and joined the church before execution.

ON THE FARM AND IN THE HOME

FOOD

During the winter Negroes gather any type of edible greens, even grass, to cook, because they say that since the dog and cat must have greens, so must the human. In spring, pokeberry leaves are used. — Mrs. Antony.

A Negro family seldom eats indoors at table, preferring to take the plate of food to the porch or yard. — Mrs. Antony.

Old Negro women always said: 'If a pusson could leave off eating red meat and white flour, they wouldn't never die.' — Jack Penton and family, 1508 St. Charles Street.

Beds were commonly 'pallets.' (Quilts on the floor.)

CHILD LABOR

Currently children are in favor as pickers in the berry fields. They have always been employed for this work.

OLD-TIME AMUSEMENTS

Negroes formerly copied many of their amusements from their white masters. Corn-shucking with singing and dancing, and cock-fighting are still popular.

At Christmas time the Negroes used to go to all the homes where they had worked during the year. If they could sneak up on the white family and say 'Christmas gift' before the white, they were entitled to a present. — Mrs. Antony.

OLE MISS

On the river plantations in North Louisiana, the mistress of the household, regardless of age, is called 'Ole Miss.'

OLD-TIME TOYS
Best remembered are the mammy-dolls and bean-bags.

NAMES USED IN DERISION
Julia la fol (Julia the crazy): She was an old Negro woman of Vermillion Parish who loved to pin scraps of colored material to her blouse, with the idea that they enhanced her appearance. Her shoes were always shoddy and unclean. When anyone appears dressed up, but wearing shabby shoes, the natives say, 'Look at Julia la fol.'

Ginnie: She was a half-witted colored woman who stayed on with her mistress after the slaves were free. On giving her mistress money wherewith to buy cotton for a dress, she could not understand why she should not have the money back again after the storekeeper had seen it. A 'Ginnie' is consequently anyone who cannot understand what is explained to her.

Two-bit Suze: She was an old Negro woman who always wore a variety of clashing colors. Anyone in Saint Martin's Parish who is cheaply and gaudily dressed is called 'Two-bit Suze.'

Pastimes of Old Louisiana

THE MYSTERY LUNCH (*box social*)
Girls prepare lunches and pack them in elaboratedly decorated boxes. At the gathering the young men bid for these boxes, being able to identify their sweetheart's box by some peculiar article used in trimming. — Jack Penton and family, 1508 St. Charles Street.

GREASED PIG (*picnics*)
Pig was shaved and greased. Object was to catch and hold the animal. (Sand on hands disqualified a player.) — Penton.

GANDER-PULLING
Head of gander was plucked and greased. Horsemen tried to pull head off.

GREASED POLE
The one who climbed the highest won the prize.

SILVER-DOLLAR PITCHING
Winner was the one coming closest to the mark or line.

GEORGE WALKING
Stilt-walking. George Walkers was a local name for stilts.

JOUSTING
Catching rings on spears from the back of a running horse.

COCK-FIGHTING

HORSE-RACING
Many plantations had courses. Sometimes races were held on the public roads.

'INFARES'
Soirée, or small party.

Old-Time Customs

CHRISTMAS
Custom: use of fireworks (as in France) and that of 'Christmas Gift.' Toys: bean-bags, mammy-dolls.

LOG-ROLLING
Trees girdled the previous spring, either for building purposes, or to clear the land, were removed and piled in community gatherings, similar to the 'bees' of the north.

MISCELLANEOUS
The custom of calling a married woman by her husband's given name, as 'Mrs. Felix,' is a compromise between the formal 'Mrs. (Felix) Smith' and the very informal 'Louise' (Smith).

It was customary to go to the road to bid newly-weds farewell as they drove by. 'Yoyo tou seul' was the reply of an old Negro whose fiancée failed to meet him at the church. Since that time the old Negroes' reply has been the customary one denoting that one has been left in the lurch, 'stood up,' etc.

Spaniards marrying into French families always spoke French thereafter.

'Mourning' and 'half-mourning' are still worn by families of French descent, and by Negresses.

Face-powder used to be made by scraping young corn and placing it in water until the starch had settled.

Custard pie was eaten on Good Friday; lamb, on Easter Sunday. Egg-fighting was a custom.

The stiffly starched collars worn by men were smoothed out on a piece of tin and baked in the sun.

MISCELLANEOUS BELIEFS

No man is ever exactly six feet tall, for that was the height of Christ.

The ear is the only part of the body that does not stop growing till death.

Wax is supposed to lubricate the brain, and too much thinking will cause this wax to get too hot and cause insanity.

If you live in the swamp, you will become web-footed.

A left-handed person owes the Devil a day's work.

Index